"Information through Innovation"

DATA COMMUNICATIONS FOR BUSINESS

Third Edition

Gerald A. Silver
Los Angeles City College

Myrna L. Silver

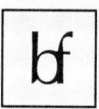

bf

boyd & fraser publishing company

Senior Acquisitions Editor: James H. Edwards
Production Coordinator: Patty Stephan
Marketing Manager: Eileen Pfeffer
Manufacturing Coordinator: Tracy Megison
Interior Design: Rebecca Evans & Associates
Cover Design: Mike Fender Design
Cover Photo: Andy Zito, The Image Bank
Production Management: Mary Douglas/Rogue Valley Publications
Composition: Octal Publishing, Inc.
Interior Artwork: Octal Publishing, Inc.

© 1994 by boyd & fraser publishing company
A Division of South-Western Publishing Co.
1 Corporate Place • Ferncroft Village
Danvers, Massachusetts 01923

International Thomson Publishing
boyd & fraser publishing company is an ITP company.
The ITP trademark is used under license.

All rights reserved. No part of this work may be reproduced or used in any form or by any means—graphic, electronic, or mechanical, including photocopying, recording, taping, or information and retrieval system—without written permission from the publisher.

Names of all products mentioned herein are for identification purposes only and may be trademarks and/or registered trademarks of their respective owners. South-Western Publishing Co. and boyd & fraser publishing company disclaim any affiliation, association, or connection with, or sponsorship or endorsement by such owners.

Manufactured in the United States of America

Library of Congress Cataloging-in-Publication Data
Silver, Gerald A.
    Data communications for business / by Gerald A. Silver and Myrna
L. Silver. —3rd ed.
      p. cm.
    Includes index.
    ISBN 0-87709-142-0
    1. Business—Data processing. 2. Business—Communication systems.
3. Computer networks—Planning. 4. Office practice—Automation.
I. Silver, Myrna. II. Title
HF5548.2.S44895   1994
650'.028'546—dc20
                                94-13400
                                    CIP

2 3 4 5 6 7 8 9 D 7 6 5 4

CONTENTS

Preface   xix

PART I — INTRODUCTION TO COMMUNICATIONS   xxiii

Chapter 1   Overview of Communications   1
Chapter 2   Fundamentals of Communications   27

PART II — HARDWARE, MEDIA, AND SOFTWARE   51

Chapter 3   Communications Hardware   53
Chapter 4   Fundamentals of Communications Channels   81
Chapter 5   Modulators/Demodulators (Modems)   109
Chapter 6   Communications Media   137
Chapter 7   Business Communications Services   165
Chapter 8   Data Transmission Codes and Protocols   189
Chapter 9   Communications Software Packages   213

PART III — INTRODUCTION TO COMMUNICATIONS NETWORKS   241

Chapter 10   Introduction to Networks   243
Chapter 11   Local Area Networks (LANs)   265
Chapter 12   Wide Area Networks (WANs)   295
Chapter 13   Value-Added Networks (VANs)   319

PART IV — PLANNING AND DESIGNING COMMUNICATIONS NETWORKS   345

Chapter 14   Planning and Analyzing Communications Networks   347
Chapter 15   Designing Communications Networks   369
Chapter 16   Implementing Communications Networks   395

PART V — THE FUTURE OF COMMUNICATIONS   421

Chapter 17   Trends and Issues   423
Chapter 18   Applied Case Problem: Fairway Department Stores   437

Glossary   450

Index   465

CONTENTS

PART I   **INTRODUCTION TO COMMUNICATIONS**

Chapter 1   **OVERVIEW OF COMMUNICATIONS**   1

    CASE PROBLEM—Personal Computers with Communications Systems   2
    Increasing Usage of Communications   3
    The Domains of Telecommunications   4
    Some Important Definitions   5
    Need for Communications   7
        Need for Speed   7
        Need for Greater Accuracy   7
        Cost Considerations   7
        Real-Time Processing   7
        Increased Use of Computers   7
    Typical Communications Applications   8
        Electronic Banking   8
        Word Processing   8
        Electronic Mail   10
        Electronic Shopping   10
        Teletext   10
        Teleconferencing   11
        Multimedia   11
        Metering and Monitoring   12
    Evolution of Communications   12
    Enter Electronics   12
    Enter Radio Transmissions   16
    Industry Regulation   16
    The Growth of the Telecommunications Industry   18
    The Era of Deregulation   20
    The Impact of Personal Computers   22
    Summary   23
    Exercises   24
    Hands-On Projects   25
    Case Solution   25

Chapter 2   **FUNDAMENTALS OF COMMUNICATIONS**   27

    CASE PROBLEM—Digital Branch Exchange   28
    The Basic Communications Model   29

Analog and Digital Signals 30
    Analog Signals 30
    Digital Signals 33
    Phase Shift 35
Transmission Rates 36
Communications Channels 36
The Basic Telephone System 37
    Switching 38
    Post-Divestiture Switching 41
Private Branch Exchanges 42
The Digital Telephone System 44
Integrated Services Digital Network 44
    System Features 44
    System Design 46
    Price Structure 47
Summary 48
Hands-On Project 48
Exercises 49
Solution 49

PART II — HARDWARE, MEDIA, AND SOFTWARE

Chapter 3 — COMMUNICATIONS HARDWARE 53

CASE PROBLEM—Facsimile Transmission System 54
Voice Transmission Equipment 55
    Telephone Instruments 55
    Digital Key Telephone System 58
    Local Switching Equipment 59
Data Transmission Equipment 61
    Terminals 62
    Special-Purpose Terminals 64
Emulators 69
    VT100 Emulator 69
    IBM 3270 Emulator 69
Facsimile Devices 70
    Fax Cards 71
Computers and Communications 71
Computer Systems 71
Mainframe Computers 72
    Central Processing Unit 73
    Input System 73
    Output System 73
    Secondary Storage 74
Minicomputer Systems 74
    Front-End Processors 74
Microcomputer Systems 75

Summary 76
Exercises 77
Hands-On Projects 78
Case Solution 78

Chapter 4 FUNDAMENTALS OF COMMUNICATIONS CHANNELS 81

CASE PROBLEM—Electronic Banking System 82
The Frequency Spectrum 83
Evaluating Transmission Channels 86
    Simplex Operation 87
    Half-Duplex Operation 88
    Full-Duplex Operation 88
Hybrid Circuits 88
Serial and Parallel Transmission of Data 90
    Serial Transmission 91
    Parallel Transmission 91
Transmission Modes 92
    Asynchronous Transmission 92
    Synchronous Transmission 92
Data Encoding 93
Modulation 95
    Amplitude Modulation 95
    Modems 97
    Frequency Modulation 97
    Phase Modulation 98
Multiplexing Principles 99
    Multiplexers 100
    Frequency Division Multiplexing 101
    Time Division Multiplexing 102
    Statistical Time Division Multiplexing 103
Data Concentrators 104
Summary 105
Exercises 105
Hands-On Projects 106
Case Solution 106

Chapter 5 MODULATORS/DEMODULATORS (MODEMS) 109

CASE PROBLEM—Electronic Mail System 110
Modems 111
Types of Telephone Circuits 111
Universal Asynchronous Receiver/Transmitter 113
Industry-Standard Modem Designations 115
Modem Features and Design 116
    Microprocessor-Controlled Modems 117
    Transmission Speeds and Formats 118

    Modes 118
    Dialing Features 119
  Microcom Network Protocol 119
  Attention Command Set 120
  Modem Hardware 120
  CCITT Modem Standards 123
    CCITT V.21—300 bps Modems 123
    CCITT V.22—1,200 bps Modems 123
    CCITT V.22 bis—2,400 bps Modems 124
    CCITT V.23—1,200 bps Modems 124
    CCITT V.26—2,400 bps Modems 125
    CCITT V.27—4,800 bps Modems 126
    CCITT V.29—9,600 bps Modems 126
    CCITT V.32—9,600 bps Modems 126
    CCITT V.17 Fax Modems 127
  Bell-Type Modems 127
    Bell-Type 103 Modems 127
    Bell-Type 201 Modems 127
    Bell-Type 202 Modems 128
    Bell-Type 208 Modems 128
    Bell-Type 209 Modems 128
    Bell-Type 212A Modems 128
  Modem Connections 128
  The Modem/Computer Interface 130
  Summary 132
  Exercises 133
  Hands-On Projects 134
  Case Solution 134

Chapter 6 **COMMUNICATIONS MEDIA 137**
  CASE PROBLEM—Teleconferencing Network 138
  The Communications Link 139
    Hard-Wire Circuits 141
    Unloaded Circuits 142
    The 20-Mil Current Loop 142
    Coaxial Cable 143
  Radio Circuits 145
    Medium-Frequency AM Radio 146
    High-Frequency Radio 147
    FM Radio 147
    Wireless Message Center 148
    Multiplexed Radio 150
    Cellular Radio Telephones 150
    Cellular Fax Machines 152
    Videotex and Teletext 152

Microwave Relay Systems 153
Satellite Transmissions 154
Fiber-Optic Transmission 157
    Laser Beams 159
Summary 160
Exercises 161
Hands-On Projects 162
Case Solution 162

Chapter 7 BUSINESS COMMUNICATIONS SERVICES 165
CASE PROBLEM—Integrated Services Digital Network 166
Overview of Services 167
Integrated Services Digital Network 168
Outbound Services 168
Inbound Services 170
Information Services 171
Digital Services 172
    Accessing the Network 173
    ACCUNET Switched Digital Services 174
Unified Network Management Architecture 175
Satellite Services 175
    System Components 176
    Satellite Operations 177
Video Services 178
Teleconferencing Services 178
International Services 180
    AT&T Business International Long Distance Service 181
    Other AT&T International Services 181
Voice Messaging Services 182
    AT&T Voice Mail 182
    AT&T Message Service 183
Consumer Communications Services 183
    AT&T Language Line Services 184
    Find America Directory Service 184
Summary 184
Exercises 185
Hands-On Projects 186
Case Solution 186

Chapter 8 DATA TRANSMISSION CODES AND PROTOCOLS 189
CASE PROBLEM—Integrated Voice and Data Network 190
Data Codes 192
    Baudot Code 192
    Binary Coded Decimal Code 193
    American Standard Code for Information Interchange 194

CONTENTS xi

                Extended ASCII 195
                Extended Binary Coded Decimal Interchange Code 197
        Error-Detection Schemes 199
                Vertical Parity 199
                Longitudinal Parity 199
                X-ON/X-OFF Flow Control 200
                XMODEM Error Checking 200
                XMODEM-IK 202
                YMODEM 202
                ZMODEM 203
                Cyclic Redundancy Check 203
                KERMIT Error Checking 203
                The X.25 Standard 203
        Data Compression Schemes 204
        Interface Standards 204
                The EIA-232-D Standard
                25-Pin Connector 206
                The RS-449 Standard 206
        Protocols and Handshakes 207
        Summary 208
        Exercises 209
        Hands-On Projects 210
        Case Solution 210

Chapter 9   **COMMUNICATIONS SOFTWARE PACKAGES 213**
        CASE PROBLEM—Electronic Bulletin Board 214
        Mainframe Software 215
        Front-End Processors 216
        Front-End Software 218
        Systems Network Architecture 219
        Customer Information Control System 220
        Microcomputer-to-Host Software 220
                PC-to-IBM Host 221
                Macintosh-to-IBM Host 221
                PC-to-DEC Host 221
        Microcomputer Communications Packages 222
        Windows Terminal 224
                Software Operation 224
        Procomm Plus 2.0 226
                Software Operation 226
        Smartcom III 229
                Software Operation 229
        Crosstalk XVI 231
                Software Operation 231

Other Microcomputer Communications Packages 232
    PC-Talk 232
    QMODEM 232
Electronic Bulletin Boards 232
    Types of Bulletin Boards 233
    Bulletin Board Networks 233
    Using a Bulletin Board 234
Public Domain Software 235
Computer Viruses 236
Summary 236
Exercises 237
Hands-On Projects 238
Case Solution 238

PART III INTRODUCTION TO COMMUNICATIONS NETWORKS

Chapter 10 INTRODUCTION TO NETWORKS 243

CASE PROBLEM—Distributed Data Processing Network 244
Basic Network Concepts 245
Distributed Data Processing 245
Introduction to Local Area Networks 248
    Baseband Coaxial LANs 248
    Broadband Coaxial LANs 248
Introduction to Wide Area Networks 249
Network Topology 250
    The Star 250
    The Ring 250
    The Mesh 251
    The Tree 251
    The Bus 251
The Open Systems Interconnection Model 251
    Layers of the OSI 252
    Layer 1 (The Physical Link) 252
    Layer 2 (The Data Link Layer) 253
    Layer 3 (The Network Layer) 256
    Layer 4 (The Transport Layer) 260
    Layer 5 (The Session Layer) 261
    Layer 6 (The Presentation Layer) 261
    Layer 7 (The Application Layer) 261
Benefits of the OSI Model 261
Summary 262
Exercises 263
Hands-On Projects 263
Case Solution 264

Chapter 11   **LOCAL AREA NETWORKS (LANs) 265**
CASE PROBLEM—Local Area Network 266
The LAN Environment 267
LAN Advantages 268
An Example of a LAN Application 269
Other Applications 270
    Educational Uses 270
    Business Offices 270
    Design Applications 270
    Computer-Aided Manufacturing 271
Basic Components of a Local Area Network 272
    The File Server 272
    Workstations 272
    The Print Server 274
    The Communications Server 274
    Interface Cards 274
    Cabling System 275
    Network Hub 275
    Network Software 275
Cabling System 276
    Unshielded Twisted Pair 276
    Shielded Twisted Pair 276
    Coaxial Cables 277
    Fiber-Optic Cables 278
Cabling System Bandwidth 279
    Baseband Systems 279
    Broadband Systems 279
Wireless LANs 279
An Example of a LAN Configuration 281
Other System Configurations 281
Network Software and Security 282
    Novell NetWare 284
    Other Software Vendors 284
    Licensing Considerations 284
    Network Security 285
Network Standards 285
Access Protocols 285
Carrier Sense Multiple Access/Collision Detection 287
Token-Passing Access 287
Gateways 288
Bridges 289
Acquiring a LAN 289

Summary 290
Exercises 291
Hands-On Projects 292
Case Solution 292

Chapter 12 WIDE AREA NETWORKS (WANs) 295

CASE PROBLEM—Distributed Data Processing System 296
Wide Area Network Overview 297
    Point-to-Point Communications System 297
    Multipoint Communications System 298
    Multiprocessor Network 298
Wide Area Network Architecture 299
    IBM's System Network Architecture 299
    Digital Equipment Corporation's Digital Network Architecture 301
    UNIX Transmission Control Protocol/Internet Protocol 302
    CCITT X.400 E-Mail Protocol 304
Networks of Microcomputers 304
Public Networks 306
    Western Union Network 306
    MCI Mail 307
    SprintMail 307
    AT&T EasyLink Services 307
AT&T WAN Facilities 308
    ACCUNET T1.5 Service 308
    ACCUNET Reserved 1.5 Service 308
    ACCUNET Packet Service 309
    Dataphone Digital Service 309
    ACCUNET Switched 56 Service 309
    SKYNET Satellite Service 309
Frame Relay WANs 309
Fast Packet-Switching WANs 311
Private Networks 312
    ARPANET 313
    SABRE 313
    Boeing Network 313
    Bank of America Network 314
Global Virtual Private Networks 315
Summary 315
Exercises 316
Hands-On Projects 316
Case Solution 317

Chapter 13 VALUE-ADDED NETWORKS 319

CASE PROBLEM—Value-Added Network 320
The Changing Network Environment 321

Industry Deregulation 322
Networks Defined 323
Major VANs 325
    SprintNet 325
    Tymnet 330
    Uninet 332
    Other Networks 333
Information Services 335
    CompuServe 335
    Delphi 340
    Dialog 340
    Dow Jones News/Retrieval 340
    GEnie 341
    Official Airline Guide/Electronic Edition 341
Summary 341
Exercises 342
Hands-On Projects 343
Case Solution 343

PART IV PLANNING AND DESIGNING COMMUNICATIONS NETWORKS

Chapter 14 PLANNING AND ANALYZING COMMUNICATIONS NETWORKS 347

CASE PROBLEM—*Global Virtual Private Network* 348
Need for Planning 349
The Telecommunications Department 350
Overview of Systems Analysis 351
Preliminary Study and Planning 352
Communications Feasibility Study 353
    Preliminary Study 354
    Investigative Study 354
    Final Report 355
Analyzing Communications Networks 355
Systems Analysis 355
    The Scientific Method 356
    Interviews 356
    Analysis of Systems Documentation 357
    Questionnaires 358
    Audits 358
    Analysis of Costs 358
    Traffic Analysis 359
    Equipment and Hardware Inventory 363
    Personnel Requirements 363

Distortions in Analyzing a Network 363
    The Hawthorne Effect 364
    The Learning Curve 364
    The Turnpike Effect 365
Summary 366
Exercises 366
Hands-On Projects 367
Case Solution 367

Chapter 15   DESIGNING COMMUNICATIONS NETWORKS 369

CASE PROBLEM—*System Access Control* 370
Designing the System 370
Network Design Software 372
Use of Consultants 373
    Network Management 373
Steps in a New Design 373
    Communications Hardware 374
    Communications Software 374
    Communications Circuits 374
    Personnel Requirements 374
    Systems Accounting 375
    Systems Costs 375
    Benchmark Tests 375
Allocation of Resources 376
    Linear Programming 377
    Queuing, Waiting Line Theory 379
Quality Control Techniques 382
    Forecasting 383
    Simulation and Modeling 384
    Program Evaluation and Review Technique 385
Data Security and Systems Integrity 386
    Access vs. Security 386
    Software Controls 388
    Port Protection Devices 390
    Encrypting Data 390
Network Documentation 391
Summary 391
Exercises 392
Hands-On Project 393
Case Solution 393

Chapter 16   IMPLEMENTING COMMUNICATIONS NETWORKS 395

CASE PROBLEM—*System Changeover* 396
Electronic Data Interchange 397
    Using EDI Standards 397

ASC X12 Standards 398
EDI Benefits 398
Order Processing Systems 400
Inquiry Systems 403
Word Processing Systems 406
Management Information Systems 406
Hardware and Software Selection 408
Vendor Selection 409
Lease Versus Buy Decision 411
The Prototype Installation 411
Overseeing the Installation of the New System 412
    Lead Time Schedules 412
    System Changeover 413
    Training and Orientation 415
Evaluation and Follow-up 415
    Benchmark Testing 416
    Systems Optimization 416
Preparation of Final Documentation 417
Network Management and Control 417
Summary 418
Exercises 418
Hands-On Projects 419
Case Solution 419

PART V THE FUTURE OF COMMUNICATIONS

Chapter 17 TRENDS AND ISSUES 423

CASE PROBLEM—*Telecommuting System 424*
Issues to Watch 425
    The Changing Workforce 425
    Changing Cities 425
    Worldwide System Integration 426
    The Automated Office 427
    Integration of Voice and Data 428
    Growth of LANs 429
    Growth of Information Services 430
    Growth of Information Exchange Gateways 430
    Growth in Microcomputer Usage 431
    Fiber-Optic and Digital Transmissions 431
    Frame Relay Switching 431
    Industry Deregulation 432
    Speech Recognition 432
    Bypass 432

Summary 433
Exercises 434
Hands-On Projects 434
Case Solution 435

Chapter 18 APPLIED CASE PROBLEM: FAIRWAY DEPARTMENT STORES 437

Fairway's Corporate Communications Needs 444
Problem 1—Catalog Sales Desk 444
Problem 2—Purchasing Department 444
Problem 3—Gift Registry Department 445
Problem 4—Retail Sales Department 445
Problem 5—Complaint and Information Desk 446
Problem 6—Advertising and Promotion Department 446
Problem 7—Data Processing Departments 447
Problem 8—Corporate Management 447
Problem 9—Distribution Division 448
Problem 10—Maintenance Department 448

GLOSSARY 450

INDEX 465

PREFACE

TECHNOLOGY is rapidly changing the face of data communications. Today, over half of all personal computers are connected to some form of network, either through a modem or as a workstation on a LAN.

The decade ahead will see an expanded reliance on personal computers, LANs, data and video transmissions, and systems integration. Deregulation continues to bring new vendors into the marketplace and change old communications patterns. The growth of MCI, U.S. Sprint, and other communications carriers has had a great impact on communications costs and alternatives. Today hundreds of firms market communications hardware and software, computer terminals, local area network facilities, modems, and computerized telephones and switchboards.

Communications is now a basic course in many educational institutions. Employees who understand the fundamentals of communications, data transmission hardware and software, LANs, and networks are in greater demand in today's marketplace than those without this knowledge and skill. Organizations ranging from large banks and business establishments to small firms seek to employ people who understand how electronic mail, teleconferencing, electronic banking, and information retrieval networks operate.

ABOUT THIS BOOK

This third edition of *Data Communications for Business* emphasizes the concepts that modern business people must understand in an information age. The selection of topics has been expanded to include state-of-the-art communications technology. The sequence of material in these pages is designed to present students with a foundation in technical terms and vocabulary that will enable them to move rapidly ahead to attain their career goals.

Data Communications for Business explains the fundamental principles of communications in a clear and understandable manner. It presents basic concepts without excessive detail or overly technical discussions. Key terms are incorporated in a summary at the end of each chapter, and concise definitions are given, not only when the term is first introduced in the chapter, but in an expanded glossary at the end of this text.

CHAPTER PEDAGOGY

The pedagogical features make this book useful to students, educators, business people, and others interested in communications.

- Each chapter begins with a statement of learning objectives.
- Key terms are printed in boldface.
- Each chapter begins with a case problem, "Communications in Action," that explores the concepts presented in the chapter. The solution to the case is presented at the end of each chapter.
- Each chapter incorporates a variety of useful end-of-chapter material, including a summary of key terms, exercises, and hands-on communications projects.
- A glossary at the end of the book explains key terms clearly.

ORGANIZATION OF THIS BOOK

This book contains 18 chapters; they are organized as follows:

Introduction

Part I presents key terms and definitions. It sets the stage for many of the concepts that will be explored in greater detail in later chapters. This section reviews the evolution of communications from its earliest beginnings to the latest high-tech satellite communications techniques.

Hardware, Media, and Software

Part II provides a foundation in communications hardware. It explains the fundamentals of communications channels, modulator/demodulators (modems), multiplexers, front-end processors, and communications media. Part II also discusses data transmission codes and protocols before describing communications software packages. A new chapter on business communications services has been added.

Communications Networks

The chapters in Part III describe local area networks (LANs), wide area networks (WANs), and value-added networks (VANs). It systematically moves from an introduction to networks through to state-of-the-art packet-switching concepts, including frame relay, fast packet switching, and Global Virtual Private Networks (GVPN).

Communications Systems

Part IV explores planning and analyzing communications systems, and designing and implementing these systems. It also presents Electronic Data Interchange (EDI) concepts.

The Future of Communications

Part V discusses trends and issues and some of the newest technology. Fiber optics, wireless messaging services, and data exchange standards are covered. Part V also includes an extensive case, Fairway Department Stores, which gives the student an opportunity to apply the knowledge gained in this book in an integrated manner.

Glossary

A glossary contains definitions of the most important terms in the text. These key terms are printed in **boldface** when first introduced in the text.

CHANGES IN THE THIRD EDITION

Many topics have been added to this edition of *Data Communication for Business* to reflect new developments and changing data communications technology. Coverage of local area networks (LANs) has been greatly expanded to include wireless LANs, 10Base2, 10 Base-T, and shielded and unshielded twisted pair cabling systems. A chapter describing new business communications services available from the major common carriers has been added. Also, coverage of ISDN, mainframes, minicomputers, microcomputers, and high-speed modems has been enhanced.

Among the new or expanded topics in this third edition are cellular fax machines, MNP modems, Global Virtual Private Networks (GVPNs), frame relay, the Fiber Distributed Data Interface (FDDI), and worldwide system integration. Coverage of the growing use of Electronic Data Interchange (EDI) has been added, as well as wireless messaging, Windows Terminal, and fast packet switching, all without sacrificing the readability and clarity of the previous editions.

The Instructor's Manual includes a variety of new hands-on LAN assignments to assist students in learning first hand the important concepts of data communications.

A FINAL NOTE

The third edition of *Data Communications for Business* is written with the student in mind. As an instructor, you will find that this book is logically structured, easy to read, and easy to teach. Accompanying the text is a full support package to assist you in designing and implementing a modern course in communications.

INSTRUCTOR'S MANUAL

A comprehensive Instructor's Manual accompanies this book. The material follows the organization of the text and includes the following:

- Chapter Outline
- Learning Objectives
- Chapter Overview
- Lecture Guidelines
- Chapter Summary (including key terms)
- Exercises and Answers
- Test Questions and Answers

The Instructor's Manual also includes a comprehensive set of transparency masters and an index keying each transparency to the chapters in the text. Also provided in the Instructor's Manual is a group of project assignment sheets, which may be copied and distributed to students. These include hands-on activities conducted in a LAN environment, as well as the use of a modem to communicate with other systems.

ACKNOWLEDGMENTS

We greatly appreciate the efforts of the following individuals who reviewed the text: David Allen, San Antonio College; Mary Blyth, Detroit College of Business; Chris Carter, Indiana Vocational Technical College; Cynthia Jackson, Indiana Vocational Technical College—East Central; Chris Koone, Isothermal Community College; Martin H. Levin, Grand Valley State University; Jerry Sands, Indian Hills Community College; Larry Thomas, Highline Community College; Charles Williams, Georgia State University.

We are very grateful for their helpful suggestions. We would also like to thank the entire staff at boyd & fraser for their collective support. This third edition would not have been possible without them.

Gerald A. Silver and Myrna L. Silver
Encino, California

INTRODUCTION TO COMMUNICATIONS

OVERVIEW OF COMMUNICATIONS

LEARNING OBJECTIVES

After studying this chapter, you should be able to:

- Describe the major domains of telecommunications
- List the reasons why communications usage has expanded
- Describe major communications applications
- Discuss the growth of the communications industry
- Trace chronologically major events in the evolution of communications
- Describe the impact of personal computers on the communications industry

COMMUNICATIONS
IN ACTION

CASE PROBLEM
SHELBY INVESTMENT SERVICES

PERSONAL COMPUTERS WITH COMMUNICATIONS SYSTEMS

George and Ruth Shelby have been involved in investment services and financial planning for more than a decade. Their office is located in a midtown commercial center. Among their clients are retired postal employees, small-business proprietors, and other investors. These individuals rely on the Shelbys to assist them in their long- and short-range investment planning. The couple guides them in purchasing stocks and bonds as well as in setting up pension, retirement, and profit-sharing plans.

George and Ruth Shelby must be able to track the performance of thousands of different stock and bond issues for their clients. They must keep up to date on economic trends and financial and investment opportunities to advise their clients effectively. In addition, they must perform the computations needed to prepare profit-sharing and pension plans that meet their clients' retirement needs.

The Shelbys each have a personal computer at their desks. They have been using these machines to keep track of customer accounts, to perform computations, and for billing purposes. However, they are limited in what they can do because their machines are not equipped with communications capabilities. They find it difficult to compete with larger organizations that have greater resources. What communications capabilities might the Shelbys add to their system? At the end of this chapter you will find out how the Shelbys resolved their problem.

WITH a flick of a button, virtually anyone in the world can tune to a television station and instantly be connected, via satellite, to a global network. Images, pictures, and sounds from distant villages and major cities around the world are brought to living rooms in vivid color. Through electronic communications we are able to participate in a rap concert, watch a conflict play out in the streets, or laugh at a British comedian while seated comfortably in an armchair.

Where and when did this electronic revolution begin? Paul Revere, who saw the light in the Old North Church and then rode from house to house alerting citizens of the approach of the British Army, was an early communicator long before the advent of television. Town criers were other communicators in the early days. They strode through town, gathering people together, and then delivered the day's news verbally to the crowd.

Throughout history, people have found methods of passing information along from one to another. Before electronics, early American Indians used a system of smoke signals and drum beats, and military commanders conveyed orders to their troops in the field through the use of mirrors, which reflected sunlight. Navy commanders directed ships at sea through a system of semaphore signals, using multicolored flags.

All of these pre-electronic era methods depended on the human senses and were subject to error and miscommunication. It took weeks for news to travel across the country when our nation was first founded. Without telephones, television, personal computers, and satellite communications, the news of the meeting of the Continental Congress could not be made available to the public until many weeks after the United States was brought into being.

INCREASING USAGE OF COMMUNICATIONS

The communications industry has experienced enormous growth in the past decade. It is now a major industry, employing millions of people. Communications equipment is found in countless homes, offices, and government agencies. The breakup of AT&T has allowed the entry of dozens of competing companies into the business of transmitting information over long distances, creating a huge new industry. Further, the influx of millions of personal computers into homes and offices has generated a market for communications equipment and services. (See Figure 1.1.)

FIGURE 1.1
Personal Computer. Personal computers have expanded the communications market.

For many years the communications industry was closely regulated and controlled by the federal government. As a result, Western Union and AT&T were the principal common carriers for sending information between distant points. **Common carriers** are organizations that provide communications to the public for a fee. Today thousands of companies sell communications equipment in an industry that accounts for billions of dollars of sales in the United States. The communications marketplace is growing rapidly, with no end in sight.

THE DOMAINS OF TELECOMMUNICATIONS

The term **communications** simply means the transmission of information. A person speaking before a group is communicating information, as is one who mails a letter or talks on the telephone. **Telecommunications** is communications using electronics, fiber optics, or other specialized circuits. It is a broad field involving several major domains. (See Figure 1.2.)

FIGURE 1.2
Telecommunications Domains

Data	Voice	Video
Letters	Sounds	Pictures
Numbers	Human Voice	Images
Graphics	Radio	Television
Computers	Telephone	CATV

One major domain of telecommunications is the transmission of the human voice. The telephone and radio are examples of **voice communications**. The second major domain is the transmission of **video information**. Pictures, images, and diagrams sent over television or cable-access television (CATV) systems involve video transmissions. **Data communications**, the third major domain of telecommunications, involves the movement of alphabetic, numeric, or graphic data. This domain, which will be our major concern, transmits words, phrases, textual matter, or digital information between two or more points.

These distinctions are not clear-cut, and the domains often overlap. **Digital data** (letters, numbers, or images that have been digitized) can be transmitted over television and displayed on a screen. Digital data can also be sent over voice-grade telephone lines. Today, some businesses still specialize in selected areas of communications such as the transmission of voice (telephone), pictures (television), and numbers and characters (computer terminals). It is still useful, however, to conceptualize information transferred into these three broad areas because major facets of the industry are built around them.

It is also worth contrasting data processing and communications. The principal function of **data processing** is to increase the usefulness of data through such operations as alphabetizing, merging, sorting, storing, retrieving, or summarizing data. In communications the emphasis is on transmitting letters, numbers, or graphics quickly between two points. Data processing concentrates on the manipulation of data to improve their usefulness to the user, whereas communications relies on the prompt transmission of data.

SOME IMPORTANT DEFINITIONS

The communications field has some unique terminology. Let us review some key terms to begin developing a working vocabulary. Many of the terms discussed below will be covered in detail in later chapters.

Communication is the act of transmitting a message via a medium. The message, which may be strings of letters and numbers, is encoded as signals; the signals are sent from the sender to the receiver.

Telephony is the communication of sound or speech through a communications system.

Data communications is the transmission of alphabetic or numeric information between two points. Data communications may involve media such as microwave, telephone, radio, laser, or fiber-optic circuits to transmit information from point to point.

A **system** is a group of components or elements that interact in a regulated manner to accomplish a specific objective. Each element of a system is related to all other parts, and a change in one element affects one or more elements in the system.

A **network** is a system composed of devices that allow information to be moved about between computers or terminals. (See Figure 1.3.) A network can be tied together by telephone lines, microwave, and fiber-optic or other communications circuits.

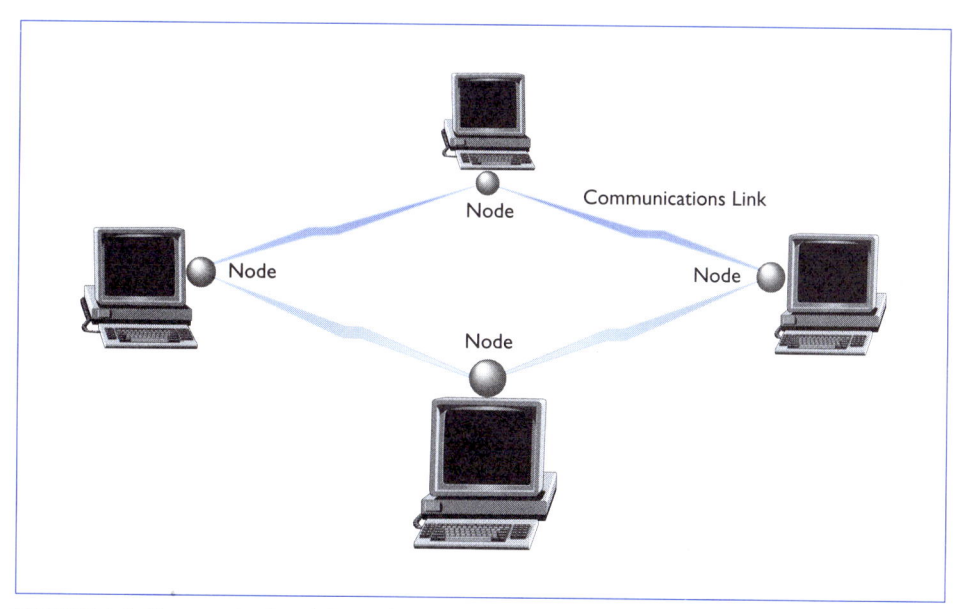

FIGURE 1.3 Communications Network

A **node** is a point in a network. It is an entry port wherein information can be input or received from the network.

A **terminal** is a device capable of receiving or transmitting information between one point and another or between a computer and a point.

A **communications link** is a means of tying together two or more points in a network, using such media as telephone wires, radio wave, microwave, or other circuits. (See Figure 1.4.)

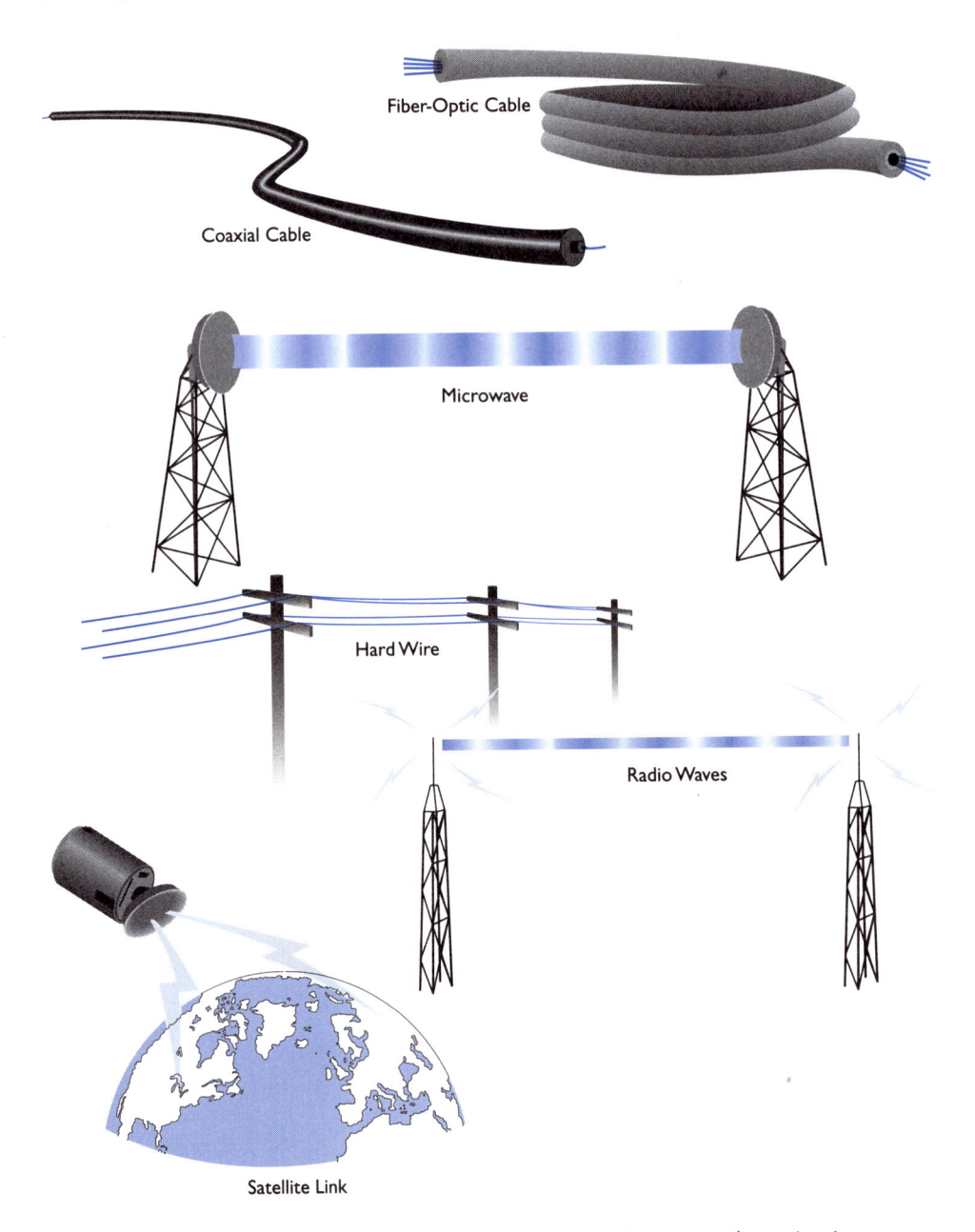

FIGURE 1.4 Communications Links. A variety of media are used to tie together points in a system.

NEED FOR COMMUNICATIONS

Many changes are taking place that have increased the demand for and reliance on communications in business and industry. The movement, storage, and retrieval of data are necessities in business today. This need is manifested by the increased use of fax machines, voice mail, computers, pagers, and cellular telephones. Let us review some of the major factors that have been the impetus for the growth of communications.

Need for Speed

When information was processed by hand, the time factor was usually measured in minutes or days. Today, businesses have installed computers to speed the processing of information. With computers, time is measured in **microseconds** (millionths of a second) or even **nanoseconds** (billionths of a second). Modern communications can move information about at speeds consistent with the demands of modern business.

Need for Greater Accuracy

Electronic communications is able to transmit information more accurately than other means. It has built-in error checking and redundancy features, making it suitable for modern business applications.

Cost Considerations

In recent years the costs of moving information about using the mails, couriers, or manual methods have risen greatly. On the other hand, electronic communications costs have dropped. Vast amounts of information can be moved quickly and inexpensively through electronic communications.

Real-Time Processing

Businesses are demanding that information be processed when a transaction occurs. This form of processing is called **real time**. Modern communications can enable an airline, for example, to book seats at the moment the request is made, regardless of the distance between points. (See Figure 1.5.) This real-time feature has many advantages over batch or delayed movement of data (such as by courier).

Increased Use of Computers

The installation of millions of computers in homes, offices, and schools has created a need for communications. **Connectivity**, the trend toward linking computers, involves coupling computers and terminals into networks, enabling them to communicate with one another.

FIGURE 1.5
Airline Reservation Terminal. This terminal is used for booking seat assignments and ticket reservations.

Courtesy of American Airlines

TYPICAL COMMUNICATIONS APPLICATIONS

Communications technology is used in many different ways in many different kinds of businesses, as well as for personal and domestic applications. Before we study the subject in more detail, let us review some of the typical tasks of communications to survey the wide utility of this growing industry.

Electronic Banking

The banking industry was one of the first to recognize the utility of communications. In the 1950s the industry developed **electronic banking** applications, which relied heavily on communications. Electronic banking is also known as electronic funds transfer system (EFTS). Today the electronic transfer of funds, rather than the physical movement of checks or debits and credits, is common. (See Figure 1.6.) A bank, for example, may have dozens of branches with hundreds of terminals and automated teller machines (ATMs), all connected. Debits and credits are posted, and funds are moved about electronically over common carrier (telephone) or private communications facilities. Banks in distant cities, as well as the Federal Reserve Bank, transfer funds between points using communications circuits.

Word Processing

Many businesses, homes, and offices generate reports, memos, and correspondence using **word processing** software and computers. (See Figure 1.7.) Many computers can be connected using communications equipment to enable them to process information quickly, then route it to other points. For instance, a document can be gener-

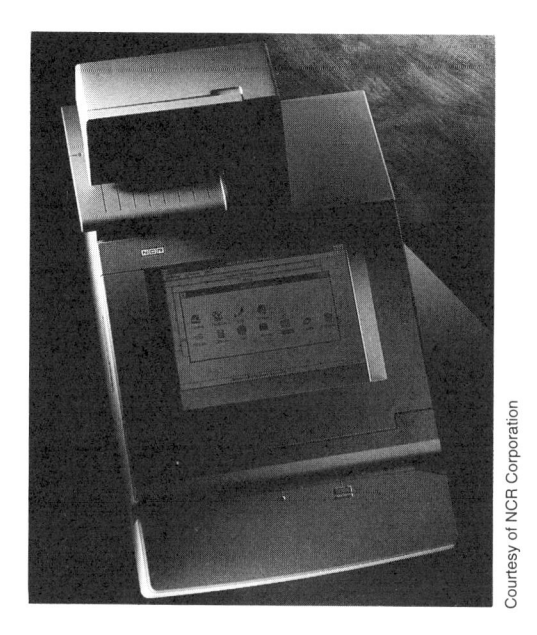

FIGURE 1.6
Bank Teller Terminal. The banking industry relies heavily on communications.

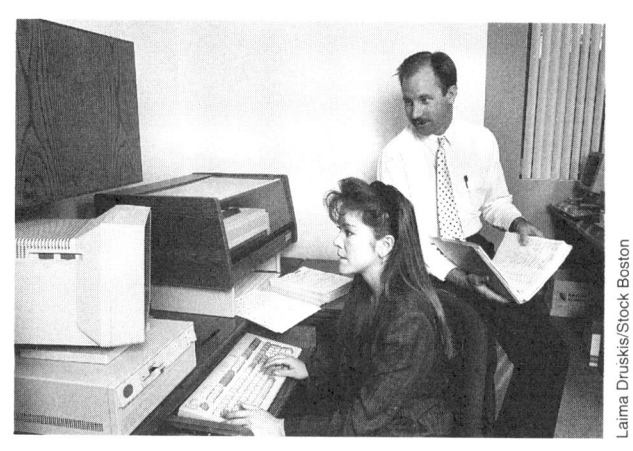

Courtesy of NCR Corporation

FIGURE 1.7
Word Processing on a Personal Computer. Reports are often generated using word processing software and then transmitted to other computers.

Laima Druskis/Stock Boston

ated in one city, reviewed or revised in another, and a final draft printed out in still another city. In electronic publishing, an entire manuscript or other lengthy document can be prepared by an originator at one location, edited elsewhere, and finally electronically transmitted to a publisher. The finished book can then be made available to readers through communications facilities. A paper copy may never be generated.

Electronic Mail

A major application of communications is the movement of correspondence between offices or cities previously served by the postal service. (See Figure 1.8.) Using **electronic mail** facilities, known as **E-mail**, a sender can keyboard a letter or memo and route it to a recipient over ordinary telephone lines. An added feature is that the same piece of mail can be routed simultaneously to hundreds, or even thousands, of recipients. As postal costs rise, the alternative of electronic mail becomes more and more attractive.

FIGURE 1.8
Electronic Mail. E-mail is routed over ordinary telephone lines rather than being physically carried from point to point.

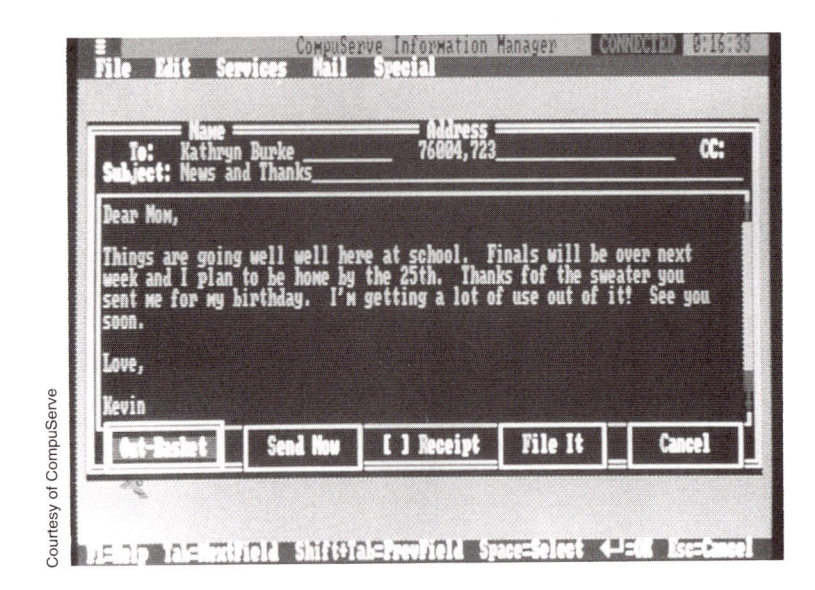

Courtesy of CompuServe

Electronic Shopping

The growth of the CATV industry has led to the development of electronic shopping. (See Figure 1.9.) In **electronic shopping**, the customer accesses an extensive list of goods for sale through a two-way data transmission over a cable television circuit or the telephone network. The shopper reads a description of the goods offered, their prices, warranties, and delivery information. Using the terminal associated with the television set, the shopper makes a selection. Choices of color, size, and other details are entered, and the goods are shipped. Electronic shopping allows the consumer to avoid crowds and is more convenient for many people than shopping in conventional retail stores.

Teletext

Teletext is another growing communications application. In the **teletext** system, newspapers or other textual matter are broadcast over television channels to homes and

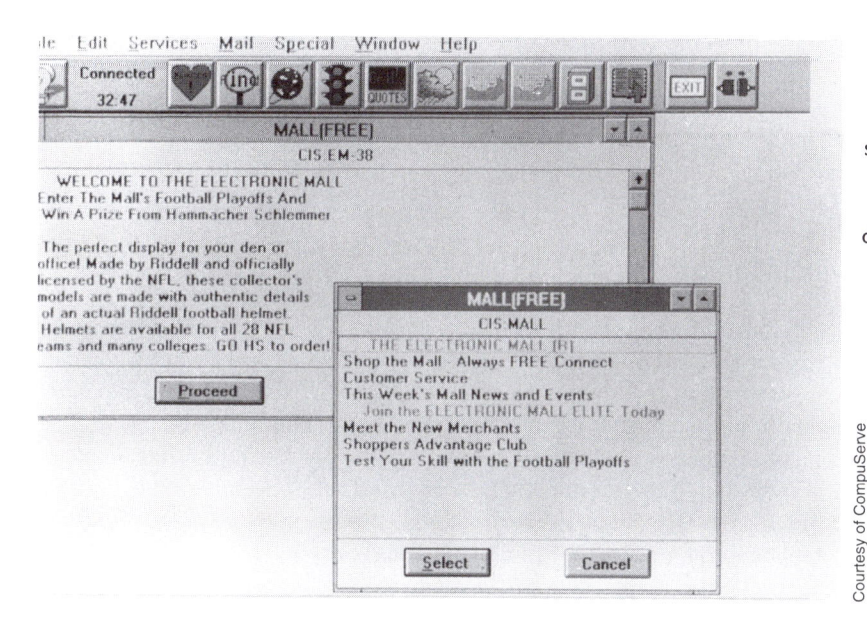

FIGURE 1.9 Electronic Shopping. Cable-access television (CATV) and the telephone network have led to the development of electronic shopping.

offices. Late-breaking stories, news of world affairs, or current events can be transmitted using the teletext system. Theater, restaurant, and motion picture reviews can be accessed through teletext systems. In a similar arrangement, known as videotex, weather reports, news, and shopping information are sent over telephone lines with the information displayed in high-resolution color graphics.

Teleconferencing

During recent years, largely because of increases in fuel prices, travel costs have greatly increased. **Teleconferencing** is a method by which individuals communicate with one another, using closed-circuit television or audio hookup, rather than physically traveling to a conference. Many businesses use teleconferencing as a substitute for business travel. These firms believe it is quicker and less expensive to have managers or executives meet via a teleconference using communications than to meet face to face.

Teleconferencing can transmit voices, pictures, charts, graphs, or visuals, as well as text matter. Some systems transmit a live action picture of the participants, while others transmit still frames and a live audio circuit. A benefit of teleconferencing is that a permanent record of the meeting can be kept on magnetic tape or disk for later reference.

Multimedia

Another recent trend is the use of multimedia. **Multimedia** involves the integration of computers, video tape, video disks (known as CD-ROMs), and communications facilities in a system capable of delivering color pictures, animation, slides, images, diagrams, or audio presentations. It is widely used for training and educational purposes and for presentations.

The system allows a presenter to structure an audiovisual session that includes a display of moving pictures, music, sound effects, and spoken dialogue. The sequence of sound and action is controlled by a computer and can be adjusted to the requirements of the audience.

Metering and Monitoring

A variety of communications applications involves **metering and monitoring** information from distant points. Some public utilities use digital transmitters to read meters recording water, gas, or electric consumption at a user's site and send the information periodically to the central office for billing. Other companies use communications equipment to monitor and protect against burglars or fire and water damage. These systems periodically or continuously scan windows, basements, attics, and other vulnerable places for intruders, fire, flooding, or other potential hazards.

The list of applications for communications continues to expand as new hardware and technologies are developed. Many new systems are being developed in conjunction with those already in place, such as existing telephone lines or cable television circuits.

EVOLUTION OF COMMUNICATIONS

Over the past hundred years, many researchers and inventors contributed ideas, innovations, and theories to the field of communications. Modern means of moving data from point to point are the result of an evolutionary process involving many disciplines. The evolution of communications is closely entwined with that of the broader field of telecommunications. Let us look at the beginnings of communications and trace chronologically the significant events, inventions, and contributions made in this field.

An early example of communications occurred when Moses carried the stone tablets containing the Ten Commandments down from the mountaintop. The essence of early primitive forms of communication was the spoken word or the physical movement of records such as clay tablets, parchment scrolls, or paper documents. Information was inscribed on the surface and then carried from point to point by a messenger or courier. Even modern postal systems and overnight couriers rely on the physical movement of documents.

ENTER ELECTRONICS

A breakthrough in communications occurred when electronics entered the picture. Electronics eliminated the physical carrier on which information is inscribed and made possible the subsequent transmission of data at the speed of light. Telegraph, microwave, and satellite relay systems are infinitely faster than physically moving records about.

Many early scientists experimented with electricity and contributed to communications. (See Figure 1.10.) Samuel Morse, Alexander Graham Bell, Thomas Edison, Benjamin Franklin, Sir William Cooke, and others delved into electronics and made valuable contributions to this growing field.

FIGURE 1.10
Early Inventors. Samuel Morse and Alexander Graham Bell were valuable contributors.

In 1837 Samuel Morse patented a functioning telegraph system. (See Figure 1.11.) A few years later a telegraph line was installed, linking Baltimore and Washington. The practicality of sending information by using a sending key and a sounder was established, and the telegraph soon became a major means of transmitting information. As railroad rights of way expanded, they were quickly followed by a network of telegraph wires sending information down the tracks from station to station.

By 1856 the Western Union Telegraph Company was formed, and it quickly expanded its lines to many cities. The Pony Express dashed onto the scene in 1860. Riders carried letters and messages for a distance of almost 2,000 miles, using a system of hundreds of horses and riders. But the Pony Express could not compete with the telegraph and soon fell on hard times. By 1861 a transcontinental telegraph system was in use, and soon thereafter the Morse key and sounder were replaced by a typewriter device that transmitted alphanumeric data. In 1866 the first successful, permanently installed transatlantic telegraph cable was installed.

But people did not want to send only letters and numbers; some dreamed of sending the human voice over a wire. This dream became a reality through the efforts of Alexander Graham Bell. Building on the work of others, Bell conceived of a system that would send an **analog signal** (continuously rising and falling voltages) over a wire to transmit and reproduce the human voice. In 1876 Bell filed an application for his invention with the patent office, and so voice transmission, the telephone, began. (See Figure 1.12.)

14 PART I / INTRODUCTION TO COMMUNICATIONS

FIGURE 1.11
Morse Telegraph Machine

FIGURE 1.12
The Evolution of Telephones

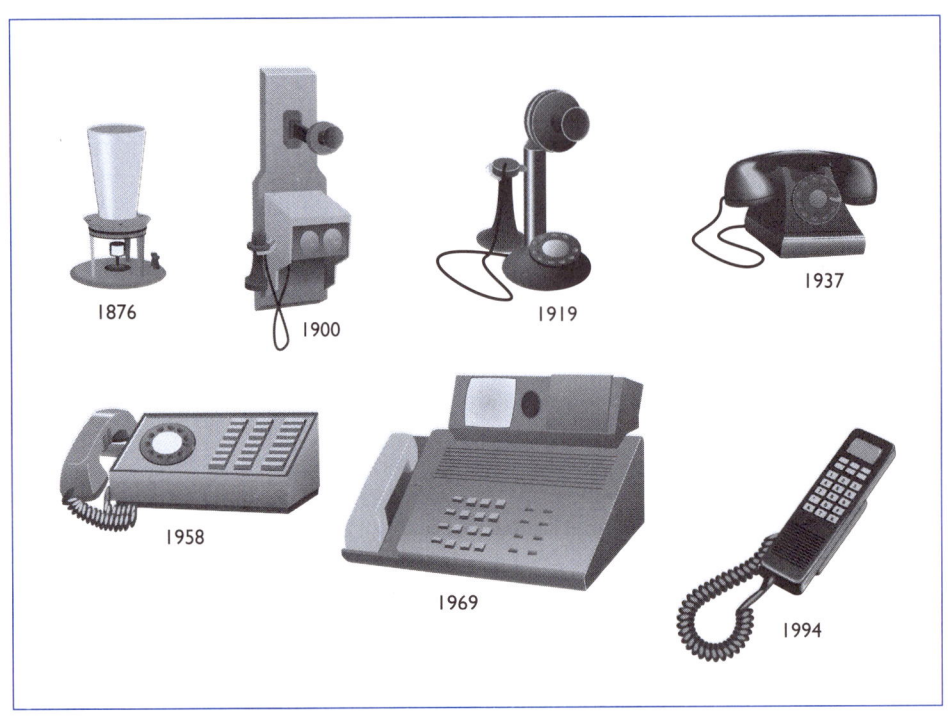

1876

1900

1919

1937

1958

1969

1994

The Bettman Archive

Telephone circuits were installed between New York and Boston in 1883. Telephone lines, following the population as it expanded to the western United States, reached all the way to Chicago by 1892. By 1915 it was possible to talk by telephone from New York to San Francisco. Early telephone systems were primitive and required the manual switching of circuits by human operators. (See Figure 1.13.) By 1919 a breakthrough was made with the introduction of the Strowger **step-by-step (stepper) switch**, which allowed an automatic connection between subscribers without the intervention of an operator. (See Figure 1.14.) Today virtually every little village worldwide can be reached by telephone. Hundreds of millions of telephones are installed around the world. (See Figure 1.15.)

FIGURE 1.13
Early Telephone Switchboard Operator. This switchboard required manual switching of circuits.

FIGURE 1.14
Bank of Strowger Step-by-Step Switches

FIGURE 1.15
Some Famous Telephone Numbers

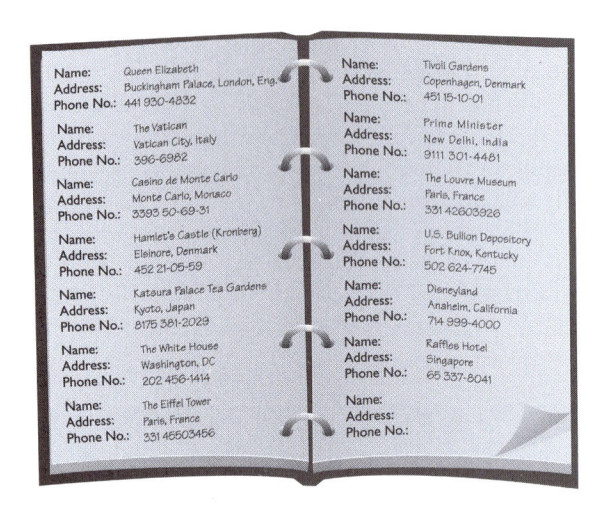

Name:	Queen Elizabeth
Address:	Buckingham Palace, London, Eng.
Phone No.:	441 930-4832

Name:	The Vatican
Address:	Vatican City, Italy
Phone No.:	396-6982

Name:	Casino de Monte Carlo
Address:	Monte Carlo, Monaco
Phone No.:	3393 50-69-31

Name:	Hamlet's Castle (Kronberg)
Address:	Elsinore, Denmark
Phone No.:	452 21-05-59

Name:	Katsura Palace Tea Gardens
Address:	Kyoto, Japan
Phone No.:	8175 381-2029

Name:	The White House
Address:	Washington, DC
Phone No.:	202 456-1414

Name:	The Eiffel Tower
Address:	Paris, France
Phone No.:	331 46503456

Name:	Tivoli Gardens
Address:	Copenhagen, Denmark
Phone No.:	451 15-10-01

Name:	Prime Minister
Address:	New Delhi, India
Phone No.:	9111 301-4481

Name:	The Louvre Museum
Address:	Paris, France
Phone No.:	331 42603926

Name:	U.S. Bullion Depository
Address:	Fort Knox, Kentucky
Phone No.:	502 624-7745

Name:	Disneyland
Address:	Anaheim, California
Phone No.:	714 999-4000

Name:	Raffles Hotel
Address:	Singapore
Phone No.:	65 337-8041

ENTER RADIO TRANSMISSIONS

In the 1800s, communications systems relied on electrical signals sent through copper wires. Obviously, a means of transmitting information without the expense of laying more wire was needed. An early effort at sending radio waves was based on a number of experiments and the work of several inventors. Joseph Henry experimented with high-frequency oscillations, and Heinrich Hertz worked with electromagnetic waves.

In 1895 Guglielmo Marconi perfected a method of sending **electromagnetic waves** from an antenna to ships at sea. By 1901 he was able to send signals across the Atlantic Ocean. A few years later in 1904, another step in communications was taken when Arthur Korn developed **telephotography**, a means of sending wire photos or radio photos. His system enabled newspapers to send pictures from one office to another using telephone or radio circuits. (See Figure 1.16.)

INDUSTRY REGULATION

By 1912 many business entrepreneurs and inventors were entering the marketplace and marketing communications equipment. It soon became evident that the broadcast bands were a limited resource and that some government regulations were necessary. In 1912 Congress passed the United States Radio Act, which would allow transmissions to occur only from stations licensed by the Department of Commerce. This legislation was necessary to prevent interference by the many stations sending signals to ships at sea. Many radio broadcasters now provided news and entertainment to the public. In the 1920s it became obvious that even more regulation was necessary, particularly to control transmissions of radio waves over land.

FIGURE 1.16
Wire Photo Machine. These early devices were able to send pictures over radio and telephone circuits.

Bettman Newsphotos

The 1930s was a decade of moderate growth in the communications industry. **Teletype**, later known as **TWX** (pronounced twix), and **Telex** services came into use. TWX was used domestically and Telex internationally. Many offices, radio stations, and newspapers installed Teletype equipment, which allowed digital data (letters, numbers, or alphabetic characters) to be sent over telephone lines.

In 1934 Congress established the **Federal Communications Commission (FCC)**. Its charge was to allocate the electromagnetic spectrum and to regulate all radio, cable, telephone, and telegraph companies. This development is significant because it began an era of regulation and tight control over the communications industry. This tight grip was not to be broken until almost 50 years later when Congress sought to deregulate the communications industry.

In 1956 another breakthrough in long distance communications occurred. In that year a transatlantic telephone cable was installed between Scotland and Newfoundland. This cable was laid underwater and used repeaters to amplify or increase the signal along the way. Hundreds of telephone calls, as well as digital data, could be sent back and forth across the Atlantic.

While all of this development in voice and data communications was taking place, what was to become a giant in the communications industry was being born. Vladimir Zworykin and others envisioned the day when moving pictures and sounds of people would be sent over the air. (See Figure 1.17.) Television had its beginning in several inventions. In 1907 Lee DeForest patented a **triode electron tube,** a device capable of amplifying electrical signals. J. L. Baird and C. F. Jenkins pioneered a mechanical means of transmitting pictures by television.

FIGURE 1.17
Vladimir K. Zworykin

In 1923 Zworykin developed the **iconoscope tube**, which was able to transmit pictures on a device with no moving parts. The following year he patented the **kinescope**, a television receiver tube. Together, these two nonmechanical devices enabled pictures to be sent and received electronically. Interest in television as a means of communication continued to grow steadily through the late 1930s and early 1940s. By the late 1950s many families were purchasing television sets, and the world would never be the same again. (See Figure 1.18.)

THE GROWTH OF THE TELECOMMUNICATIONS INDUSTRY

The late 1940s and early 1950s saw a period of innovation and growth in the telecommunications industry. The post-World War II years saw an increased demand for communications equipment and facilities. New businesses, which needed telephones, switchboards, digital transmission equipment, and mobile telephones, were opening. The new postwar households fostered even more demand for telephones.

In 1946 the first **microwave radio link** was established by the American Telephone and Telegraph Company. This link facilitated the transmission of hundreds of phone circuits between relay stations. Microwave relay stations, spaced up to 25 to 30 miles apart, proved to be a better means of expanding the communications network than ground lines. The important new technologies of radar and telemetry gave even more impetus to the communications industry.

The first application of remote communications was the Semi-Automatic Ground Environment (SAGE) air defense system, a network of thousands of miles of communications circuits that monitored our defense perimeter in the late 1950s. It proved the

FIGURE 1.18
Early Television Receiver. Television in the 1950s was received on small-screen sets such as this.

Courtesy of RCA/Thomson Consumer Electronics

dependability of remote data transmission for military use and pointed the way to civilian applications. The marriage of computers and communications was now clearly established.

In 1962 a nationwide airline reservation system, Semi-Automatic Business Research Environment (SABRE), was instituted. The SABRE system used a large central computer, connected through communications lines to thousands of ticket terminals located in airline offices around the country. It was the first major application of business communications facilities on the domestic scene.

In the same year the United States launched Telstar, a **communications satellite** designed to relay telephone and television signals between the United States and Europe. Telstar proved the practicality of communications satellites. There have been a number of successors to Telstar, including Syncom and Intelsat. The Intelsat satellite (see Figure 1.19), built by Hughes Aircraft Company, can simultaneously relay 20 television channels, or 11,000 voice channels, worldwide. In addition, two Westar satellites, operated by Western Union, provide domestic satellite service, relaying 12 television circuits, or 7,000 voice circuits, simultaneously. By the 1990s dozens of communications satellites were in orbit around the earth.

During the 1960s, the use of computers increased dramatically because of their reduced cost and greater ability to take on more complex processing tasks. This period saw the expansion of the use of mainframe computers. These large computers, which often had hundreds of remote terminals tied to them, were used extensively in banking, hotel, motel, and airline reservation systems. Terminals were tied to the main processor using multiplexers, modems, data concentrators, and other specialized devices, discussed in more detail later.

FIGURE 1.19
Intelsat Satellite. Satellites such as this opened a new era in communications.

Courtesy Hughes Aircraft

During this period, many businesses installed large internal telephone systems. These **private automatic branch exchanges (PABXs)** handled the switching of both computer terminals and voice instruments more efficiently. Frequently, companies installed terminals and used their PABXs to access outside computers, heralding the growth of the time-share industry. In time sharing, many remote users share one computer. Thereafter several large companies entered the marketplace, selling computer time over ordinary telephone lines.

THE ERA OF DEREGULATION

Prior to 1956, **interconnecting** non-Bell equipment (then called "foreign" devices) to telephone company facilities was not allowed. Thus, the Bell system had the exclusive right to interconnect communications equipment to the existing telephone network, giving it a monopoly.

In 1956 this monopoly was challenged in the courts by the Hush-a-Phone Co. Hush-a-Phone sought to market a device that blocked the ambient noise entering the telephone's mouthpiece thus providing quieter communications. The courts ruled in favor of Hush-a-Phone, opening the way for the interconnection market.

In another historic decision in 1968, the FCC expanded the interconnection right, allowing the Carterfone Company to interface to the Bell network. The Carterfone was a device that enabled a call to be placed from a vehicle in motion to a base station, where it was forwarded over telephone lines.

The decision in favor of Thomas F. Carter gave his company the right to legally connect non-Bell mobile communications equipment to the telephone network. The telephone company objected, claiming that it would degrade the quality of the system if companies such as Carterfone were allowed uncontrolled access to the switched network. The effect of the decision was to expand the interconnect industry even further. And so began competition with AT&T for the communications equipment market.

In 1969 Microwave Communications, Inc. (MCI) received permission from the FCC to install a microwave link between St. Louis and Chicago and to offer lower long distance rates between major cities than AT&T. Soon other common carriers entered the marketplace and also began to compete directly with AT&T's "Long Lines" division.

AT&T had been instrumental in developing much of the new computer and communications technology. The FCC then began looking into alleged antitrust violations by AT&T. In 1971 the FCC's First Computer Inquiry report allowed AT&T to sell computer equipment, but it recommended that parts of AT&T's operations still remain regulated.

During the 1970s dozens of companies entered the field, selling telephone and data transmission devices that could be substituted for AT&T equipment. But they were largely at the mercy of the still giant AT&T. Clearly, changes in the rules of monopoly regulation were needed, but these would not come into effect until a decade later.

In 1970 IBM introduced its **System Network Architecture (SNA)**. SNA was important because it offered an approach that allowed IBM customers to deal with the incompatibility of communications products. IBM customers could expand their communications and computer equipment in a more systematic way, based on a standard network architecture. Also in 1970, AT&T introduced the **videophone**, a means of sending a television picture and the human voice over the same line. The system involved a Touch-Tone® telephone, display unit, camera unit, and loudspeaker. The videophone system, though technologically practical, has not gained widespread acceptance.

By 1970 the TWX and Telex systems were merged, forming a giant data transmission network in place alongside the expanding telephone communications system. By the mid-1970s, the entire concept of close regulation of the communications industry was undergoing extensive reevaluation. The FCC launched several investigations into the wisdom of continuing its long-established practice of closely regulating the industry and limiting the interconnection of foreign equipment. Some analysts suggested that all common carriers should be allowed to compete on an equal basis and that AT&T should be divested. They also proposed that the industry be **deregulated**.

The Second Computer Inquiry (completed in 1981), as well as a consent decree agreed to by the Justice Department and AT&T, attempted to address these concerns. AT&T was to be broken down into smaller competing units, and it could now engage in the computer industry. The plan spurred competition in the communications industry and deregulated parts of the field. As a result, AT&T was forced to divest itself of its local operating companies. It was permitted to keep Western Electric and Bell Laboratories, its research and development arm. This decision dramatically changed the way long distance calls were switched.

In recent years, many firms have entered the common carrier business, providing alternatives to AT&T. These competitors include MCI, Sprint Communications, GTE, ITT, RCA, American Satellite, and others. In the post-deregulation era, these firms were allowed to establish a **point of presence (POP)**. The POP provided alternate routing of calls through non-AT&T equipment.

THE IMPACT OF PERSONAL COMPUTERS

The 1970s saw the advent of the minicomputer, and the 1980s and 1990s the growth and widespread use of **personal computers**. The invention of the **large-scale integrated (LSI)** circuit meant that an entire microprocessor could be manufactured on a small silicon chip. The **microprocessor** performs logical comparisons and computations and is the heart of the computer system. (See Figure 1.20.) These tiny computers could now be placed in handheld communications devices, greatly expanding their capability.

FIGURE 1.20
Large-Scale Integrated (LSI) Circuit. An entire microprocessor is manufactured on a small chip of silicon.

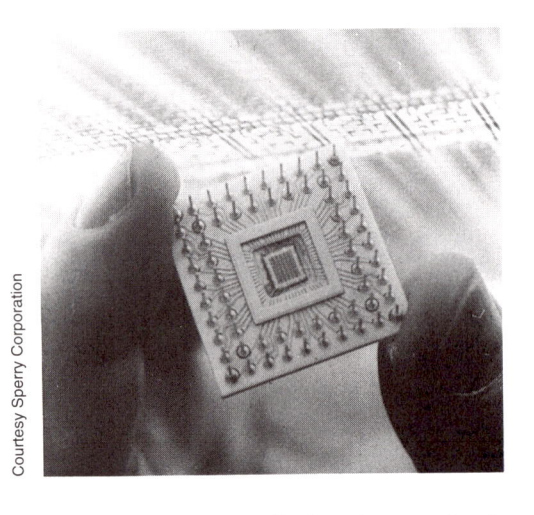

Courtesy Sperry Corporation

Millions of personal computers were purchased and installed in homes, businesses, and offices. The owners of these computers required communications facilities so that their computers could be linked with other machines over telephone lines. Because of this demand, many companies saw a growing market not only for communications equipment but for access to large commercial **databases** as well. H & R Block, Dow Jones, Dun & Bradstreet, Reader's Digest, Mead Corporation, and other companies that maintained large databases of information began marketing access to businesses and private users. This, in turn, meant that even more computer terminals and personal computers were installed, requiring still more communications facilities.

Cellular radio has come into its own during the 1990s. (See Figure 1.21.) Prior to cellular radio, mobile phone usage was very limited. Generally, because a large

FIGURE 1.21
Cellular Radio Telephone. Handheld cellular radio telephones are small enough to be carried about.

John Coletti/Stock Boston

geographic area was served by only one relay transmitter, only a few people could use their mobile phones at one time. With cellular radio a large geographic area can be broken up into cells as small as three or four square miles. Each cell is served by a low-power radio transmitter. All transmitters in the region are controlled by a central computer system. As a result, thousands of users can simultaneously access their mobile phones in a broad geographic area without interference. Cellular radio will allow both voice and data transmissions.

Today, one need only push a few buttons to move data along for hundreds or even thousands of miles and to hundreds or even millions of people. Letters and numbers can be moved on a beam of light or on a radio circuit with a wavelength only a fraction of an inch long. The movement of information has gone from the shuffling of paper to the flash of an electron.

SUMMARY

Communications is the movement of alphabetic or numeric information between two points. It began with primitive means of moving data and now uses sophisticated transmission systems. *Telecommunications* includes the domains of *voice*, *video*, and *data*.

A *communications link* is one means of tying together two points in a network. A *network* is a group of stations that enable information to be moved between computers. A *node* is an entry point in a network wherein information can be input or received from the network. A *terminal* is a device capable of receiving or transmitting information between one point and another or between a computer and a point. A *system* is a group of related parts that interact in a regulated manner. In *real-time processing*, transactions are handled at the moment they occur.

Deregulation has brought about competition in the communications industry. *Electronic mail*, or *E-mail*, involves the movement of correspondence between locations electronically. In *teleconferencing*, individuals communicate over circuits sending pictures, charts, or TV images.

Public utilities use communications circuits to *meter and monitor* services. *Word processing* involves the generation of reports, memos, or correspondence using computers and communications equipment. In *teletext*, textual matter is sent to homes and offices much like an electronic newspaper. *Multimedia* involves the integration of computers, video tape, video disk, and communications facilities into a system capable of delivering color pictures, slides, images, diagrams, or audio presentations.

Data communications stresses the movement of *digital data* between two points. *Data processing* stresses the manipulation of data to improve their usefulness to the user.

The *telegraph* was an important breakthrough in communications. In the late 1890s and early 1900s the telephone network expanded coast to coast. Communications and *radio photos* are sent using *electromagnetic waves*.

The *Federal Communications Commission (FCC)* was established in 1934 to regulate the communications industry. *TWX* and *Telex* systems came into use in the 1930s to move digital data. In the late 1940s *microwave radio links* were established to move data. In the early 1960s *communications satellites* were launched.

IBM's *System Network Architecture (SNA)* was introduced in 1970 to allow IBM users to deal with equipment incompatibility. The invention of the *LSI* circuit brought about the introduction of the growing *personal computer* market. *Cellular radio*, introduced in the 1980s, improved mobile phone communications. In the future, businesses will rely more on *teleconferencing* as a substitute for business travel and to increase interaction between employees.

EXERCISES

1. Contrast the major domains of telecommunications.
2. List five demands for communications.
3. Describe how communications is used in the banking industry.
4. Describe how electronic shopping is conducted.
5. Describe how teleconferences are conducted.
6. Describe how the teletext system operates.
7. List several individuals who made important contributions in the early days of communications.
8. What conditions led to the formation of the Federal Communications Commission?
9. Trace briefly the growth of communications satellites.
10. Explain how the communications industry was affected by the Carterfone decision.

HANDS-ON PROJECTS

- Visit the manager at your local bank. Discuss communications and determine what types of communications are used at the bank.

- Interview the proprietor of a small business. Discuss communications with the owner. Determine what type of telephone system is installed and how it is used in his or her business.

- Interview a manager of a small business and determine what word processing, electronic mail, or teletext systems are in use in the firm.

- Write a short essay describing the work of such communications leaders as Samuel Morse, J. L. Baird, or Vladimir Zworykin. Refer to a set of encyclopedias for information.

- Interview a friend or neighbor who owns a personal computer. Discuss communications and determine the kind and type of communications equipment and programs on the system and their capability.

CASE SOLUTION
SHELBY INVESTMENT SERVICES

COMMUNICATIONS IN ACTION

The Shelbys upgraded their existing personal computers to include communications capabilities. (See Figure 1.22.) Each system is now equipped with a communications device known as a modem. (See Figure 1.23.)

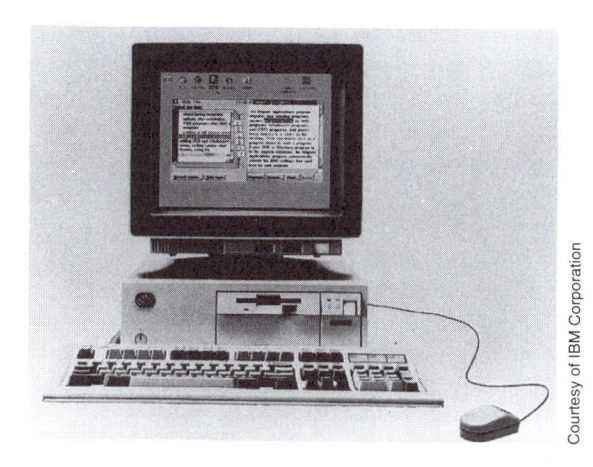

FIGURE 1.22 IBM Personal Computer

Courtesy of IBM Corporation

These modems allow each computer to communicate over a voice-grade telephone line with other computers. The software allows the Shelbys to dial outside databases and remote computer facilities. Among the databases they are now able to access directly from their offices are the Dow Jones News/Retrieval, Dun & Bradstreet, and Quotron Financial Services.

FIGURE 1.23
Modem

With a relatively small investment, the Shelbys have added connectivity to their system. The system allows them to keep track of current Wall Street trends and to obtain historical data on various stocks and bonds, money market and treasury-bill rates, mutual funds, and more. Thus, they have a reliable and accurate source of information at their fingertips. The systems operate over ordinary telephone lines and allow the Shelbys to receive data files and electronic mail from other computers. Armed with communications capability, the Shelbys can compete effectively against larger organizations that have greater resources.

FUNDAMENTALS OF COMMUNICATIONS

LEARNING OBJECTIVES

After studying this chapter, you should be able to:

- Describe the basic communications model
- Contrast analog and digital communication
- Describe how data transmission rate is measured
- Discuss communications channels, circuits, and lines
- Describe the basic telephone system
- Describe the Integrated Digital Services Network (ISDN)

COMMUNICATIONS IN ACTION

CASE PROBLEM
GREENE AND SINGER CONSULTANTS

DIGITAL BRANCH EXCHANGE

Greene and Singer is a consulting firm specializing in running political campaigns. The firm's employees make contacts with the media, write news releases and advertising copy, and handle other promotional activities for their clients. There are five consultants and six research assistants in the office who maintain contact with editors, reporters, talk show hosts, community leaders, and others. The employees spend much of their time on the telephone setting up speaking engagements and interviews for candidates.

Periodically, the firm undertakes extensive public opinion and market research polls. This effort involves making numerous phone calls to assess public attitudes on candidates and issues.

Telephone charges are a major expense in Greene and Singer's operations. The consultants place virtually all long distance telephone calls through the local AT&T operator, resulting in expensive toll charges. The system does not rely on foreign exchange (FX) lines, which provide reduced rate calling to other zones. Also limiting the productivity of Greene and Singer's personnel is the physical telephone equipment installed at their desks. This system, which consists of multiline telephones with hold buttons, was installed many years ago. (See Figure 2.1.)

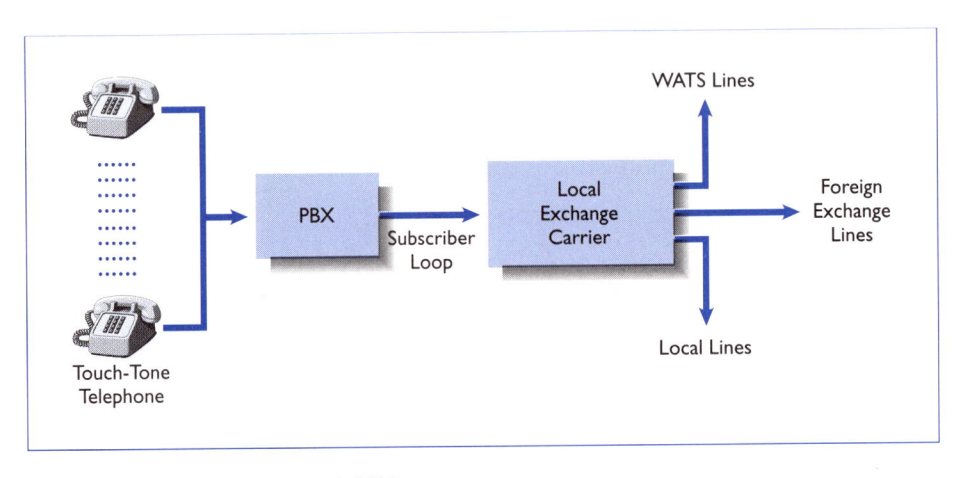

FIGURE 2.1 Existing System with PBX

What approach would you take to improve Greene and Singer's telephone system? What features should be installed? Describe the benefits of a new system. Refer to the end of this chapter to see how Greene and Singer resolved their problem.

MOST people take the telephone so much for granted that they overlook the wonder of being able to talk to a friend, relative, or business associate anywhere in the world. The computer is quickly beginning to run a close second in products that are taken for granted in our lives. Most of us don't take the time to study how these devices work and to understand their principles of operation. However, understanding them is a necessity for anyone who wishes to work in the communications field.

In this chapter we will review some of the fundamentals of the telephone—its circuitry and how messages are routed from point to point. We will look at transmission rates, communications channels, the expanding Integrated Services Digital Network (ISDN), and private branch exchanges (PBXs). We will also describe two basic modes in which information can be classified and transmitted and discuss some key terms that the student will encounter in communications.

THE BASIC COMMUNICATIONS MODEL

All communications involve a **sender** and a **receiver**. Whether the message is sent by telephone lines, between a computer and a terminal, or through a cable-access television system, someone must originate an idea and communicate it to someone else. The idea must be reduced to a **message**. The message must then be sent over some communications **medium**, such as radio waves, electrical waves, or even the printed page. At the other end, the receiver extracts the message from the medium and reconverts it to an idea. (See Figure 2.2.) Once the message is received, it is acknowledged. The confirmation of the receipt is an important part of the process because it provides **feedback** to the sender.

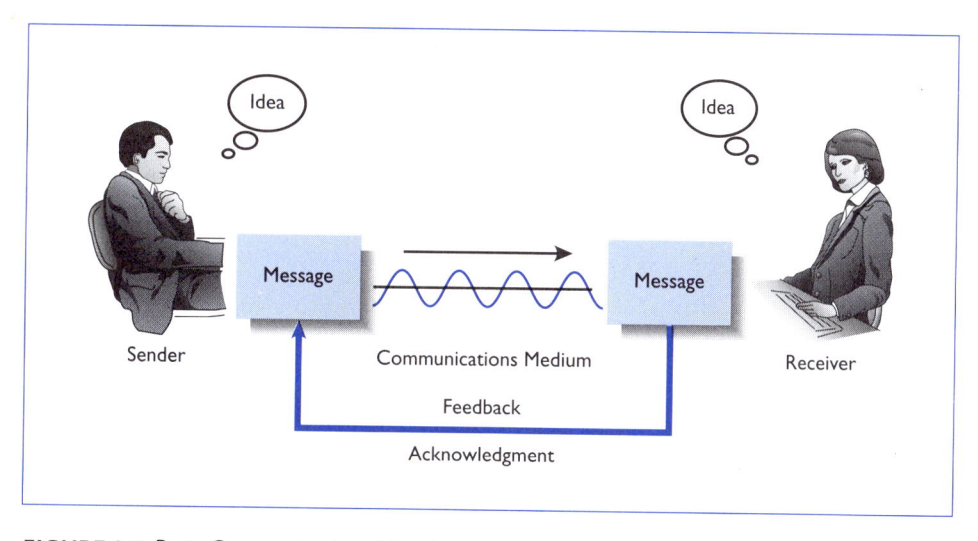

FIGURE 2.2 Basic Communications Model

This communication process takes place in many forms all about us. Friends who wish to invite us for dinner reduce the idea to a message that can be sent by the telephone or through the mails. A detergent manufacturer or seller of automobiles reduces an idea to a message that is carried by a communications medium (broadcast) to many receivers.

An integral part of all communications is the communications medium. This medium is a link or pathway that ties two points together. In this book we will discuss the various communications links, or media. For the moment, the student should know that telephone lines, microwave circuits, satellite relay stations, radio circuits, and beams of light serve as communications media.

ANALOG AND DIGITAL SIGNALS

There are two basic modes by which information can be sent over communications media. Messages may be transmitted as:

- Analog signals (rising and falling voltages)
- Digital signals (pulses of fixed voltages)

It is important to understand these two major methods of transmission because they are involved in one form or another in virtually all communications systems. Let us begin by looking at analog signals.

Analog Signals

An **analog signal** may be represented by a sine wave. (See Figure 2.3.) A **sine wave** consists of a rising and falling crestlike pattern. These shapes are much like the wave forms on the surface of the ocean—they rise and fall. Sine waves can be represented as an increasing and decreasing electrical voltage or a sound wave, changing in intensity. A beam of light that grows brighter or dimmer on a continuum is also an example of an analog signal.

FIGURE 2.3
Sine Wave

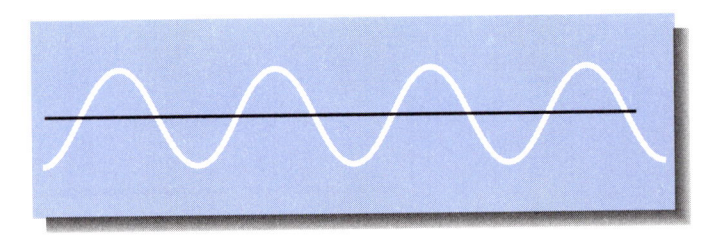

Sound waves provide a good example of an analog signal. An increase in the intensity of a sound is represented by an increase in the height, or **amplitude,** of the wave. If one strikes the middle C key on a piano with a light touch, the vibrating strings will emit an analog wave shape, such as in Figure 2.4A. If the same key is struck with more force, the string will emit a wave shape of greater amplitude (see Figure 2.4B). The string vibrating with a greater intensity will cause more air molecules to move about.

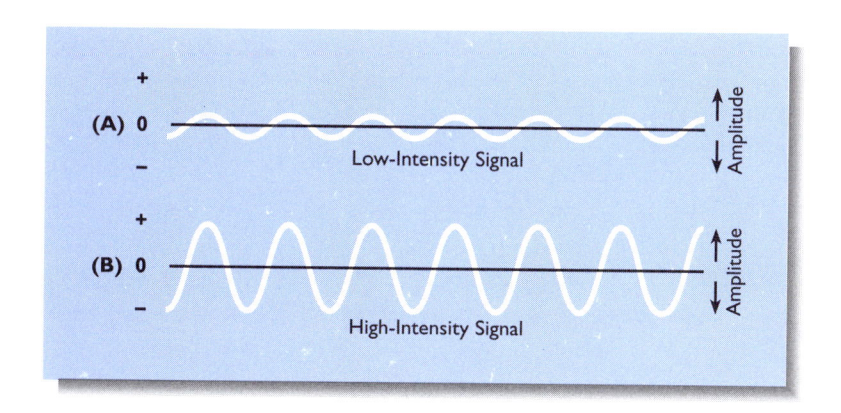

FIGURE 2.4
Low- and High-Intensity Sine Waves

The only difference between Figures 2.4A and 2.4B is the amplitude, or height, of the signal. Because the same key is struck, we would perceive the same tone, except that one would seem louder.

Another characteristic of analog signals is frequency. **Frequency**, or pitch, is noted as a difference in spacing between crests of the sine wave. Frequency is a function of the number of times a sine wave repeats itself in one second. In Figure 2.4A, middle C was struck, emitting a sound of approximately 277 cycles per second. This means that the sine wave repeats itself 277 times in one second. However, if the C key one octave below middle C is struck, it will emit a frequency of approximately 138 cycles per second. Compare Figures 2.5A and 2.5B. Both have the same amplitude, but the spacing is considerably different; the reason is the difference in frequency.

The human voice, the sounds of a violin, or even the backfire of a truck are analog in form. These sounds would be shown as wave forms that vary in amplitude (intensity) and width (frequency).

When we speak on the telephone, our vocal cords emit varying **sound pressure levels (SPLs)**, which are picked up by the telephone transmitter. The transmitter, in turn, converts the SPL into an electrical sine wave, varying in amplitude and frequency. (See Figure 2.6.)

FIGURE 2.5
Spacing of Crests Affects Frequency. Lower frequencies are represented by widely spaced crests.

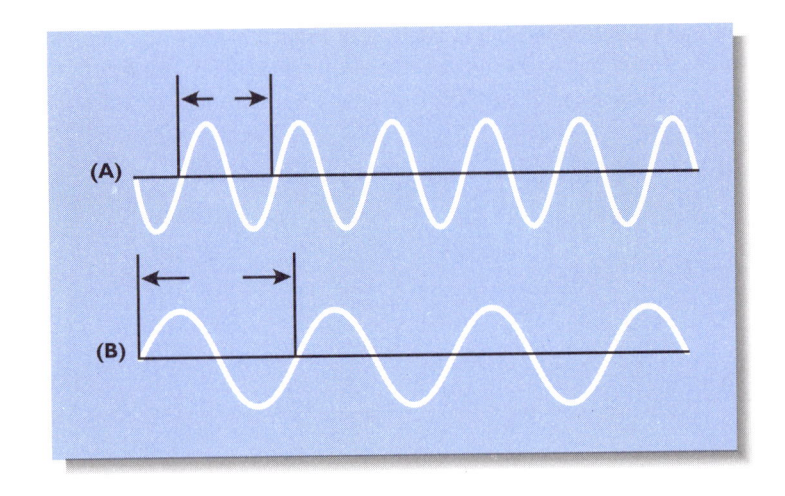

FIGURE 2.6
Telephone Signals. SPL is converted into an electrical sine wave of varying amplitude and frequency.

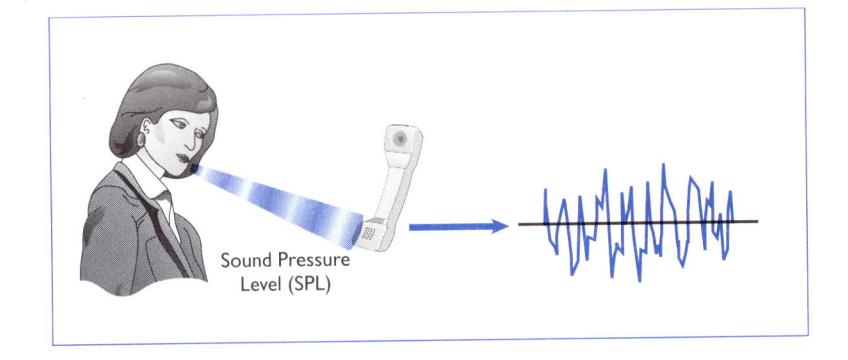

Analog signals of sound are generated by television sets. (See Figure 2.7.) The television loudspeaker receives an electrical sine wave. This, in turn, is converted into SPLs, or varying pressure patterns, which our ears perceive as sounds. They are in reality changes in frequency (pitch) and intensity (amplitude).

Analog signals require the accurate transmission of the wave shape for our ears to perceive the transmitted sound without distortion. Because of the nature of many electrical devices, however, analog wave shapes are sometimes distorted when they are transmitted and amplified. For some applications a slight distortion may not be a serious problem. High-fidelity sound systems may permit a distortion level of less than 1 percent. For data transmission, however, distorted analog signals create many problems.

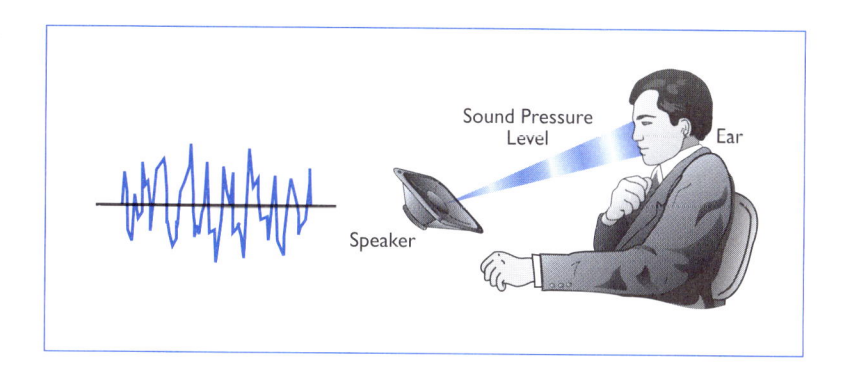

FIGURE 2.7 Television Sound System. Electrical sine waves are converted to SPL by the loudspeaker.

Digital Signals

A second fundamental way to transmit information is through digital signals. A **digital signal** is one that has a finite number of possible states. One common form of digital signal is a binary signal. A **binary signal** is a two-state signal that represents only two conditions: on and off, or ones and zeros. (See Figure 2.8.) Sometimes binary signals are in the form of electrical pulses. For example, 5 volts of direct current may represent an on pulse and no voltage the absence of a pulse. In Figure 2.8, a 5-volt square-wave pulse is shown. In digital signals the pulses are usually of the same height, or amplitude, and the same width, or frequency.

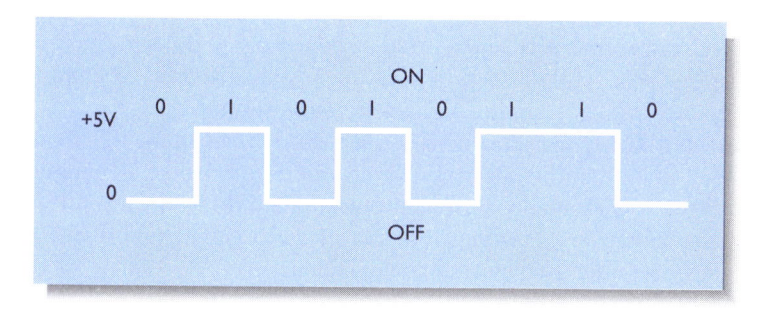

FIGURE 2.8 Binary Signal. Two conditions are represented.

Information can be impressed on a string of digital pulses, all having the same amplitude and frequency. This is done by a system wherein the presence of a pulse represents a one and the absence a zero. This system is known as binary representation, because only two states, ones and zeros (on and off), are recognized. Figure 2.8 illustrates a number being represented, using these two-state, or binary, pulses. Various coding systems, composed of binary bits, are used to represent letters and numbers. These systems are described in Chapter 8.

Another form of digital signal is illustrated in Figure 2.9. In this instance, three conditions may exist. The presence of a positive 15-volt signal represents an on or logical zero condition. The presence of a negative 15-volt signal represents an off or logical one. The absence of a voltage represents an undefined state. This form of digital signal is used in many different types of communications equipment.

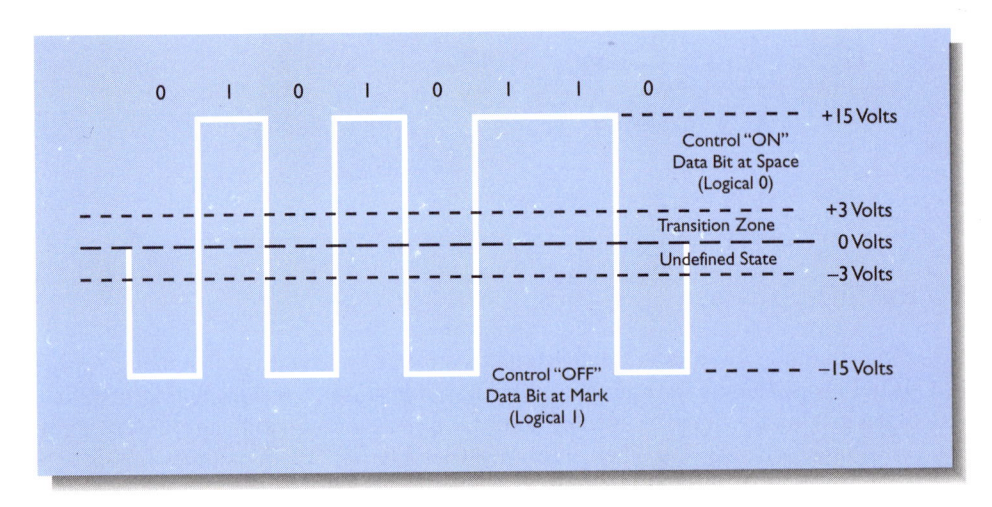

FIGURE 2.9 Digital Signal. Three conditions are represented.

Using digital signals, especially binary, rather than analog, has many advantages, particularly for transmitting data. Because binary signals deal with only two conditions, there is less likelihood that a signal will be distorted or misread. Digital signals can be regenerated using a repeater, while analog signals must be boosted by an amplifier, which increases distortion. Thus, digital signals are more reliable.

Figure 2.10A represents a binary signal without noise. Figure 2.10B shows the same signal with a great deal of noise and distortion. But even with this extreme amount of noise it is possible to discern each pulse. With appropriate electronic circuitry it is possible to clean up wave shapes and eliminate the distortion. It is much more difficult to clean up or reconstruct a badly distorted analog signal.

One of the advantages of binary signals is their compatibility with computer processing. Computers by their nature are two-state devices. A transistor is conducting or it is not, a light is on or off, a relay or switch is open or closed. Further, computers perform their mathematics using the base 2 (binary), ones and zeros, numbering system. Little if any information is processed internally in computers as an analog signal.

The term **bit** describes one **binary digit**, either a one or a zero. The collection of bits that represent a letter or a number is called a byte. A **byte** is simply a collection of binary bits, usually eight, that represent a letter, number, or special character.

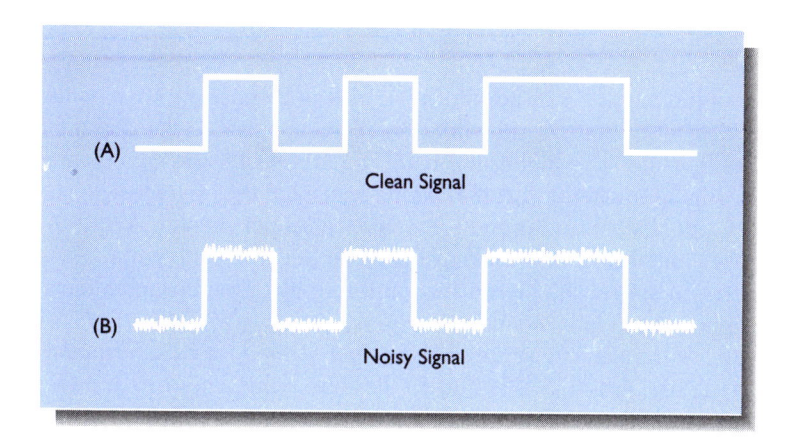

FIGURE 2.10 Signal Noise

(A) Clean Signal

(B) Noisy Signal

Phase Shift

The concept of phase shift is important to an understanding of digital signals. **Phase shift** describes the point at which a cycle begins. Figure 2.11 illustrates four different cycles that begin in separate phases. In the left figure, the cycle begins with a rising positive voltage. In the second figure, a declining positive voltage begins the cycle. In the third, a declining negative voltage begins the cycle, while in the last example, a rising negative voltage begins the cycle. These differences in cycle starts, or phase shift, are very useful for transmitting information.

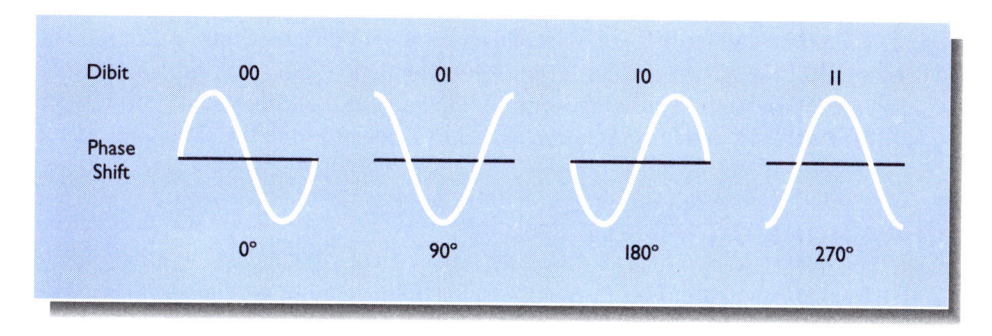

| Dibit | 00 | 01 | 10 | 11 |
| Phase Shift | 0° | 90° | 180° | 270° |

FIGURE 2.11 Phase Shift Keying

Two digits, known as a **dibit**, are used to describe the phase shift. For instance, a rising positive voltage is represented by a dibit consisting of two zero digits. A phase shifted 90 degrees is represented as a 01 dibit. Electric circuitry is available that can detect a phase shift and output dibit signals. Thus, phase shifts can be used to transmit groups of digits that convey useful information. Phase shifts and how they are used are discussed in more detail in Chapter 4.

TRANSMISSION RATES

In the data transmission industry, the **baud** and **bps (bits per second)** have come into use as basic measures of the rate of transmission. The baud rate is the speed at which a signal changes its state. The higher the baud rate, the faster the signals are changing their states. A signal transmitted at 300 baud means that the system switches back and forth between signal states, ones and zeros, 300 times per second. A 2,400-baud signal switches back and forth 2,400 times per second. Because each switch represents a transition between states, the higher the baud rate, the greater the amount of information that can be sent in one second.

Another way to state the transmission rate is in bits per second, or bps. Common bit rates are 300, 1,200, 2,400, 4,800, 9,600, and 19,200 bps. Sometimes two or more bits, called dibits or tribits, can be sent with each change of state. In this instance the bit rate will exceed the baud rate. Therefore, the bps measure is the preferred and more widely used measure in the data transmission industry. In both cases the higher the bit rate, the greater the amount of information that can be sent in one second.

Differentiating between the terms bps and baud can be confusing. In a low-speed system each change of state can represent one bit. Thus, a signal at 300 baud sends 300 bps. However, in a high-speed system a more complicated arrangement may be used, transmitting up to four bits or more with each change of state. In this case there would be a difference between baud rate and the number of bits sent.

Perhaps an analogy will make the difference clear. Suppose you flashed your automobile headlights on and off ten times per minute to send a signal to a friend some distance away. Each flash of the headlights (change of state) equals one bit transmitted. Now suppose we separate the two headlights so that one can flash slightly ahead of the other. Let the time lag, or difference in phase, represent different bits. A 25 percent lag between the first and second flash represents the digit 1, a 50 percent lag the digit 2, and so on. While both headlights would be flashing at the same rate (10 times per second), four times as much information would be transmitted in the same time span.

COMMUNICATIONS CHANNELS

Discussions of communications frequently refer to lines, circuits, and channels. Let us define some of these terms as they are used in the industry.

A **line** is the physical wire or metallic or optical path that exists in a cable connecting two points. A **circuit** is the pathway over which information is sent and received. A circuit can be a physical pair of wires or a transmitted frequency. A **channel** is a communications path and is sometimes used synonymously with circuit. On some circuits, one or more channels can exist for sending voice, video, or digital data. These are called **subchannels**. Electronic devices, described later, allow hundreds of channels to exist on one circuit.

Economies exist when several channels are sent over one circuit. For example, it would be possible to purchase a communications circuit between Los Angeles and New York and then establish, with appropriate hardware, dozens of subchannels over which information can be sent. Some common carriers charge for each circuit provided, and others may make an arrangement based on the number of subchannels provided.

THE BASIC TELEPHONE SYSTEM

The student of communications should be familiar with the principles of **telephony**, telephone **networks**, and switching. Our modern **electronically switched** telephone system is the product of many years of evolution and development. Since its early introduction in the late 1800s, relatively few changes were made in the telephone system. It remained an analog transmission network until recently. Each subscriber is connected to the system through a dedicated pair of wires. The bulk of voice transmissions are sent as analog signals, though there is a shift toward transmitting voice and data in a digitized form by packet-switching systems.

To understand the system, one must consider the technology used before divestiture and the methodology employed after the AT&T monopoly was broken up.

Figure 2.12 illustrates a simple pre-divestiture telephone system having only one station at each end and no switching or dialing capability. At each end of the circuit there is a telephone set. The set includes a **receiver** (earpiece), **transmitter** (mouthpiece), and an **induction coil**, also known as a side tone coil. The transmitter, or mouthpiece, uses a **variable resistor**, which contains finely ground carbon granules held in a chamber. (See Figure 2.13.)

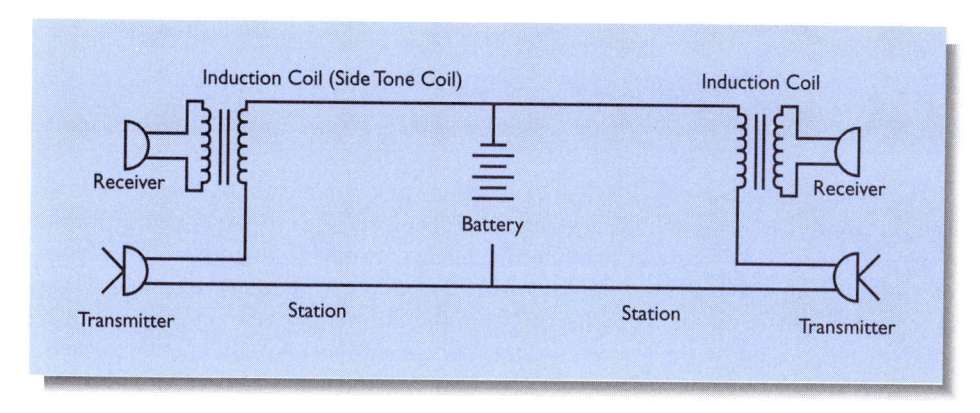

FIGURE 2.12 Simple Telephone System

As the speaker talks into the transmitter, the changes in sound pressure level cause a change in the resistance of the carbon granules in the transmitter. This change in resistance causes the current in the lines to rise and fall. The current is analogous to the sound impressed on the transmitter. At the receiving end the reverse takes place. The receiver is constructed from a small electric coil and core placed in close proximity to a metal diaphragm. (See Figure 2.14.) As the varying currents flow through the circuit, the coil and core create an electromagnetic effect, which causes a movement of the metal diaphragm. The movement of the receiver's diaphragm is directly proportional to the varying currents flowing through the circuit.

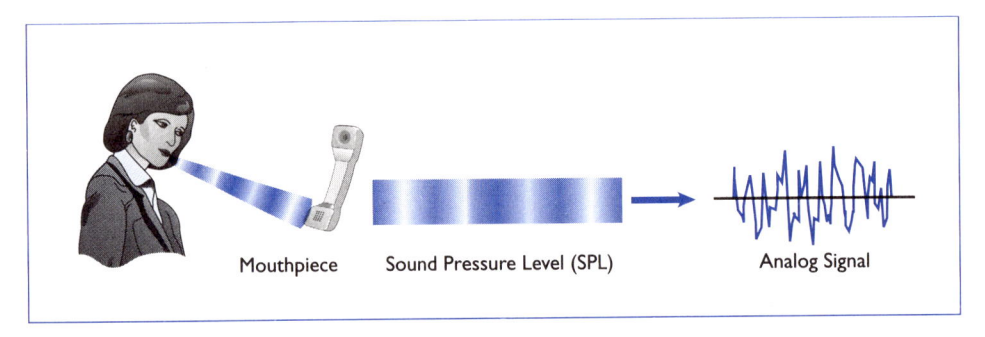

FIGURE 2.13 Telephone Transmitter. Audible sounds are converted into analog electrical signals.

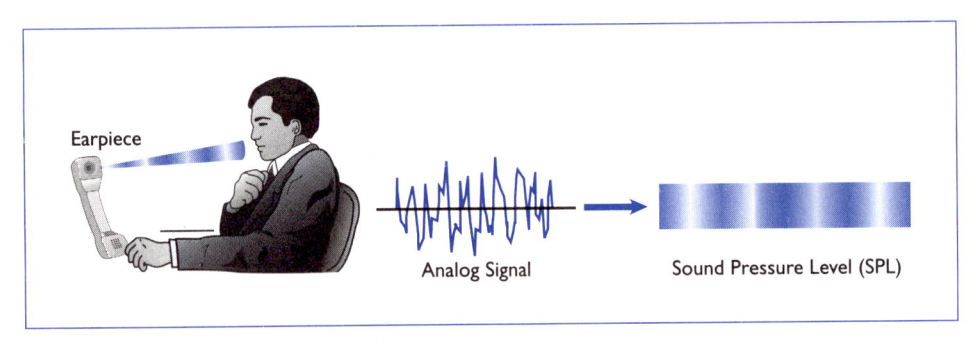

FIGURE 2.14 Telephone Receiver. Analog electrical signals are converted into audible sounds.

This simple arrangement allows two people to speak to one another over the same electric circuit because each has a sender and receiver. The electrical energy for the system is provided by a battery or other direct-current source. Modern telephone systems still use large storage batteries to provide the energy to operate the system. These batteries are constantly being recharged from the alternating-current power supply. This recharging is one of the reasons that a telephone system may still operate for some time even though the alternating-current power source is cut off from the building.

Switching

In the previous example, we illustrated a two-station telephone system in which all equipment was owned and operated by one carrier. As a practical matter, many telephone systems had hundreds or thousands of stations, all connected to one **central office (CO)**, also known as an **end office**. Each station had to be able to contact any other station selectively as well as reach stations connected to other central offices. This contact was accomplished through a system of switches.

In the early days of telephony, an operator took each call and physically connected the circuits between each station. This proved expensive, and so a system of **step-by-step switches** (see Figure 2.15) was developed. These switches automatically connected one subscriber to another. Some central offices still are equipped with this early type of switching equipment; one occasionally hears the distinctive clicks in the earpiece when placing a call through this kind of office. Later, more efficient **crossbar switches** were installed to speed up switching. Still later, **solid-state switching** arrangements were developed, using computers. These **Electronic Signal Switch (ESS)** offices are reliable, fast, and automatic. Because of computers, ESS offices can provide such features as call waiting and call forwarding to subscribers.

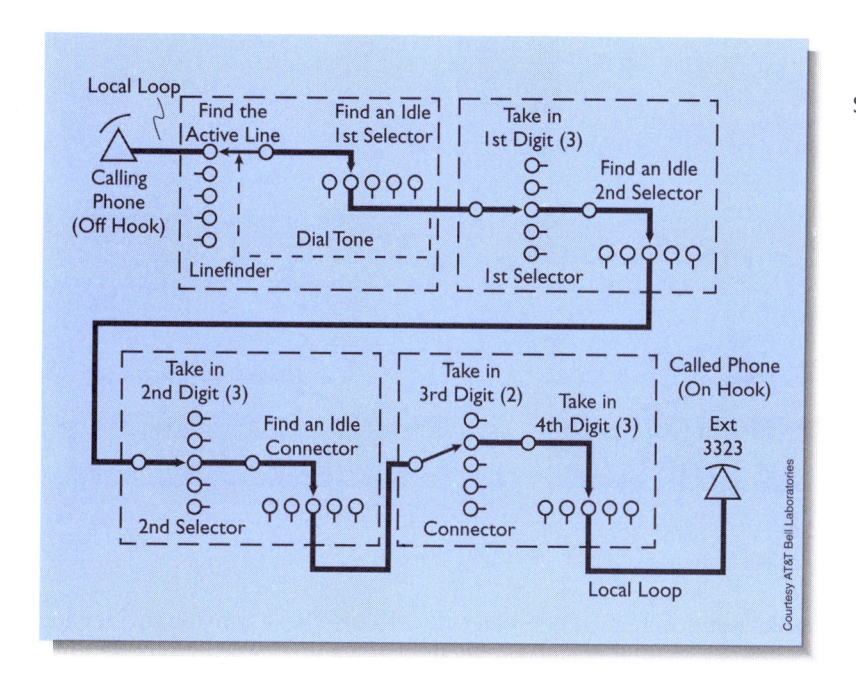

FIGURE 2.15
Step-by-Step Switch. Switches such as these were used to connect one subscriber to another.

Let us see how the switching function was accomplished prior to the entry of divestiture and the introduction of competing common carriers. Figure 2.16 illustrates two cities, each with an end office connected to a network of toll offices. An individual pair of wires connected each subscriber to an end office. This pair of wires was called a **subscriber loop** or **local loop**. An individual subscriber loop had to be provided between each subscriber and an end office, as well as for each instrument on the premises that was to be used simultaneously.

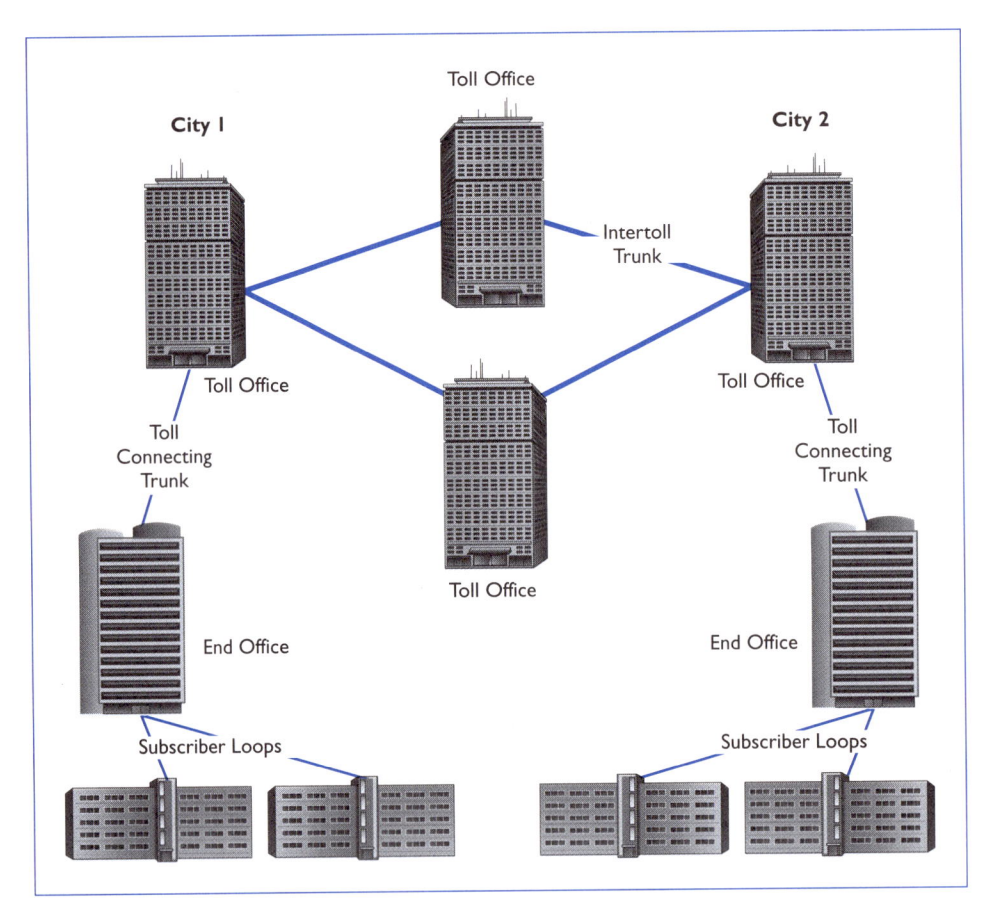

FIGURE 2.16 Switched Network

Intertoll trunks were connected between **toll offices**. These trunks provided the circuits between offices. Suppose one **subscriber** wished to talk to another subscriber and that both were connected to the same end office. Each had a subscriber loop to that office. When the subscriber lifted the receiver and dialed a given number, his or her instrument emitted a group of dialing pulses. These signals traveled over the subscriber loop to the end office. Some instruments simply opened and closed a switch, whereas others, such as Touch-Tone devices, emitted oscillations or frequencies used for dialing. The end office was equipped with circuitry that detected the dialing signals and, in turn, opened and closed circuits that connected the two stations. Because both were connected to the same end office, the calls were switched without being routed outside the end office. Once the switching was accomplished, the end-office equipment was available to switch other calls.

If a subscriber in one end office wished to talk to a subscriber connected to an end office in another city, then a different arrangement was used. The end office received the dialing signal, and the call was routed through a toll-connecting trunk to a toll office. There, more switching circuitry routed the call over an intertoll trunk to another toll office. In turn, the call went to an end office and ultimately to a receiving station.

In the early days of telephony, intertoll trunks consisted of twisted pairs of wires physically routed between offices. Later, these trunks were replaced by microwave relay stations or coaxial cables that allowed a large number of calls to be handled over one circuit. Some intertoll circuits were handled through satellite relay stations.

Post-Divestiture Switching

After AT&T was broken up, many common carriers began to compete for long distance service; this development required special switching arrangements. Figure 2.17 illustrates post-divestiture switching. A region is broken up into a group of **local access transport areas (LATAs)**. LATAs are geographic areas served by local telephone companies. Telephone companies that provide local calling services within a LATA are known as **local exchange carriers (LECs)**.

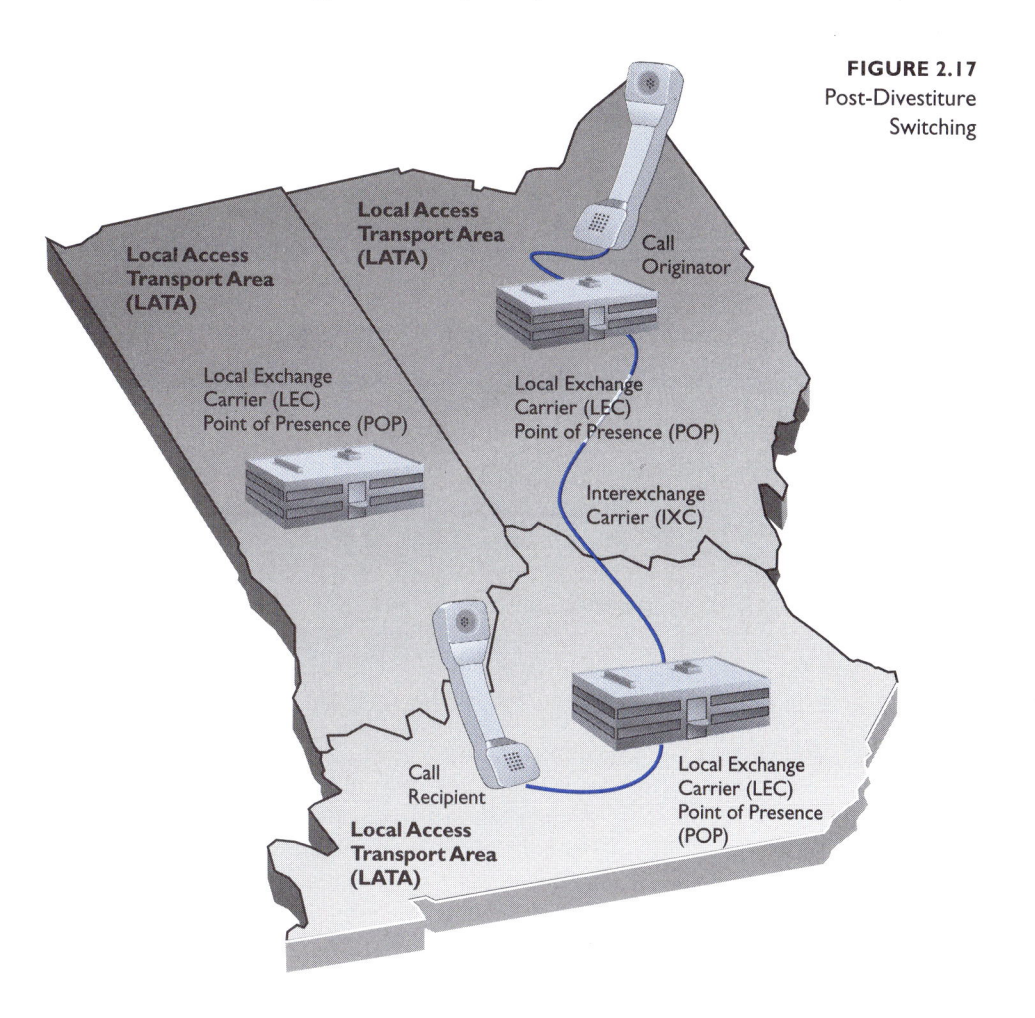

FIGURE 2.17 Post-Divestiture Switching

Within each LATA these LECs provide a **point of presence (POP)**. The POP is the transfer point in a LATA where long distance calls are routed out of the LATA through any competing common carrier network to another LATA. This arrangement allows a call to be switched from an individual subscriber in a LATA, through a POP, and then on to another LATA and POP, using any competing common carrier.

These common carriers are now known as **interexchange carriers (IXCs)**. This arrangement allows a subscriber to use an IXC, such as MCI and Sprint, or the long-established AT&T network. The IXCs route calls over microwave, fiber-optic, or satellite circuits.

Local calls placed within a LATA are still switched exclusively over the local telephone company or LEC equipment since they do not involve movement through IXCs.

PRIVATE BRANCH EXCHANGES

Some organizations have hundreds of telephones located on the premises. These individual stations must be connected to one another, or they must be able to reach stations through the LEC. This switching is performed by a **private branch exchange (PBX)**. (See Figure 2.18.) Internal calls can be switched within the organization through the PBX without going over the subscriber loop to the LEC. Such calls do not bear toll charges.

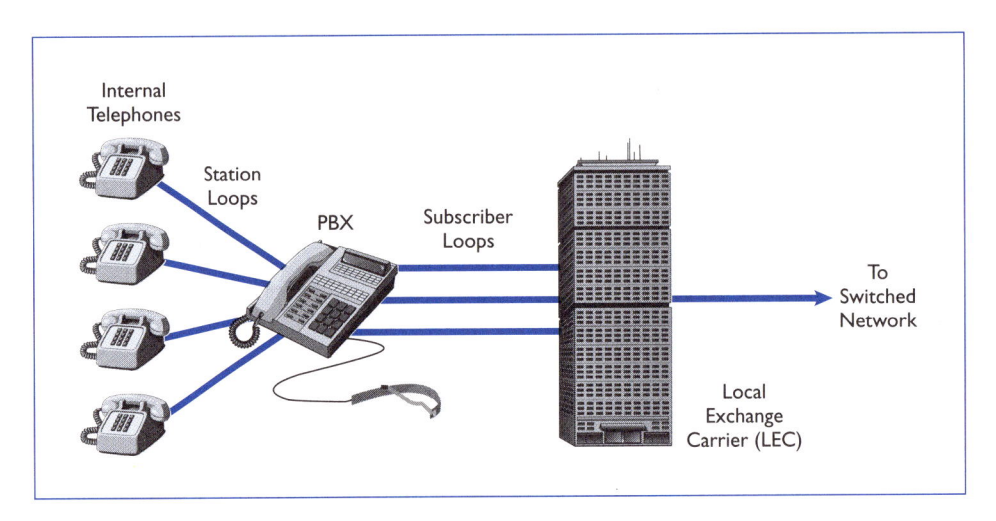

FIGURE 2.18 Private Branch Exchange (PBX)

There are several different types of switchboards in use. Some, such as the PBX, require operators to plug in cords. Others, such as the **private automatic branch exchange (PABX)**, replace connector cords with a system of manually operated switches. Still others, such as the **digital branch exchange (DBX)**, perform switching under the direction of a microcomputer. The term PBX is often used as a generic reference to all types of private switchboards. In this text, specific references are used, depending on whether the exchange is manual or computerized.

One or more subscriber loops may be provided between a switchboard and the LEC. Computerized switchboards provide automatic switching between stations, paging services, data and voice transmission services, call waiting, call forwarding, and other options. Any station connected to a switchboard can be switched automatically through a subscriber loop to an LEC. Once a call has been connected through the switchboard to the LEC, it is then routed through a POP to any IXC.

Before divestiture, all long distance calls were routed through a subscriber loop to a telephone company end office and then exclusively to AT&T lines. Today, the system provides access to AT&T lines, as well as to competing common carriers, through subscriber loops that are capable of switching and routing digital signals. Both voice and data can be handled by the same system. (See Figure 2.19.) In these systems, the switchboard can direct outgoing calls through the most inexpensive route, whether it be AT&T or a competing common carrier.

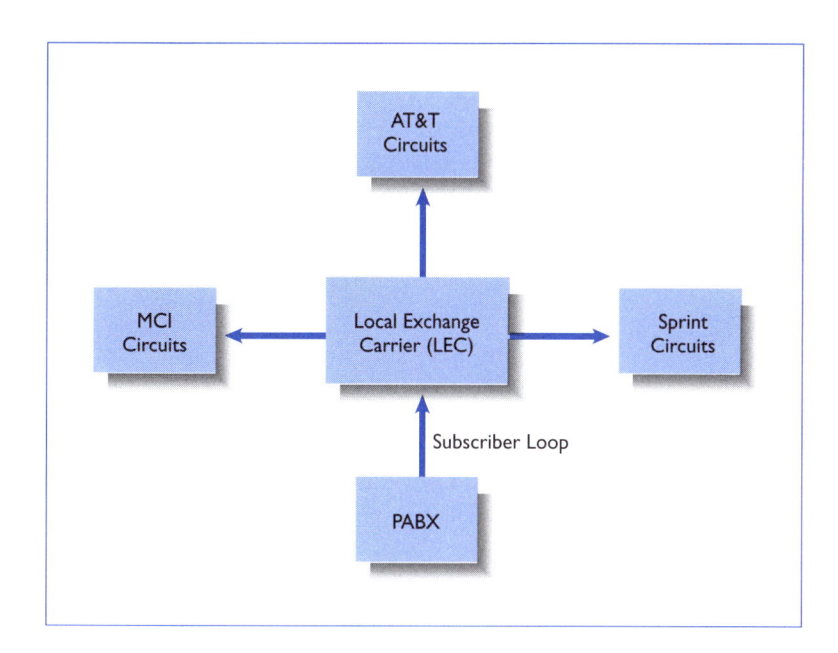

FIGURE 2.19
Private Automatic Branch Exchange (PABX)

Once a channel has been established between one station and another, digital or analog information can be sent over the circuit. Voice is converted to digital signals through a process known as **digitizing**. The various techniques for transmitting voice, data, or video information are described in more detail in Chapter 8.

THE DIGITAL TELEPHONE SYSTEM

Much communications today consists of analog transmissions. As we will see in Chapter 5, it is possible to place a modem (modulator/demodulator) at each end of the line and transmit digital signals on an analog circuit, using the existing switched network just described. However, a much more efficient and flexible means of transmitting data is via digital transmissions. Telephone companies across the country are installing digital central offices (DCOs) equipped with digital switches. Let us discuss this growing aspect of the communications world.

INTEGRATED SERVICES DIGITAL NETWORK

The **Integrated Services Digital Network (ISDN)** is a system that provides volume users with voice, data, and video services over a fully digital network. AT&T took the lead in developing the national system using computerized circuitry and more than 380 4ESS switches. These switches, together with special circuits, enable users to transmit voice, data, and other information from one point of the network to another without using modems or analog circuitry.

The ISDN is based on an international CCITT transmission standard that lets users, local and interstate carriers, and others all over the world transmit data in a common format. Most metropolitan areas in the United States have ISDN circuits now in use. In addition, the 15 countries listed below are connected to the AT&T international switched network:

Australia	France	Japan
Belgium	Germany	Netherlands
Bermuda	Hong Kong	Singapore
Canada	Italy	Sweden
Finland	Jamaica	United Kingdom

ISDN provides a common worldwide standard to move data between countries using differing systems. The full economies of the network will be realized as more and more nations join the system.

System Features

The ISDN provides users with all the services normally available on the analog network. Data can be compacted and transmitted with other data; PBX and central switchboards may be connected; faxes, personal computers, and local area networks, discussed in Chapter 3, can also be attached. (See Figure 2.20.) The system enables video teleconferencing to take place, including voice and video transmission, without expensive special circuits or modems.

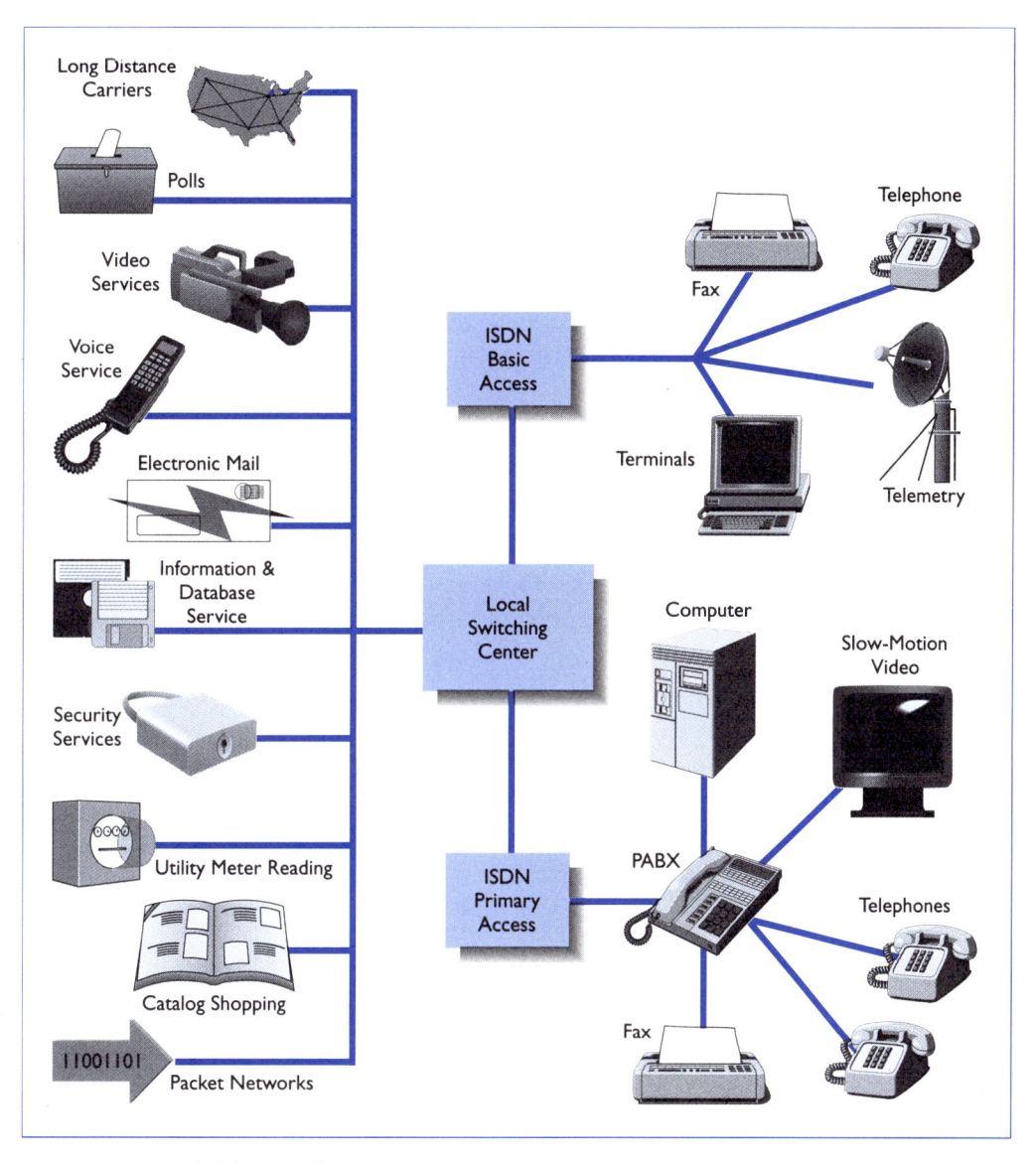

FIGURE 2.20 ISDN Network Services

Computers tied to the system can be accessed, and data can be routed from one computer to another. Among the other ISDN features are the ability to monitor alarms and back up data files at various points in the network, with cost savings over the use of the analog network.

Key system advantages are:

1. *Call management.* Call and billing details are available, enabling a business to track calls and trace their costs back to specific departments or units.
2. *Greater productivity.* Calls are handled more quickly because signaling and routing information are not mixed with the data being sent.
3. *Compatibility.* The system is compatible with local and foreign ISDNs, providing worldwide productivity.
4. *Economy.* Because only transmission time is billed, the user benefits from high-speed digital service without the costs of private lines.
5. *Flexibility.* Both voice and digital data can be transmitted simultaneously without interference over the same circuit.

System Design

The AT&T ISDN is constructed from a group of 380 4ESS switches and a network of communications lines. (See Figure 2.21.) Electronic Signal Switches (ESSs) are high-speed, computer-controlled devices that rapidly route signals throughout a network.

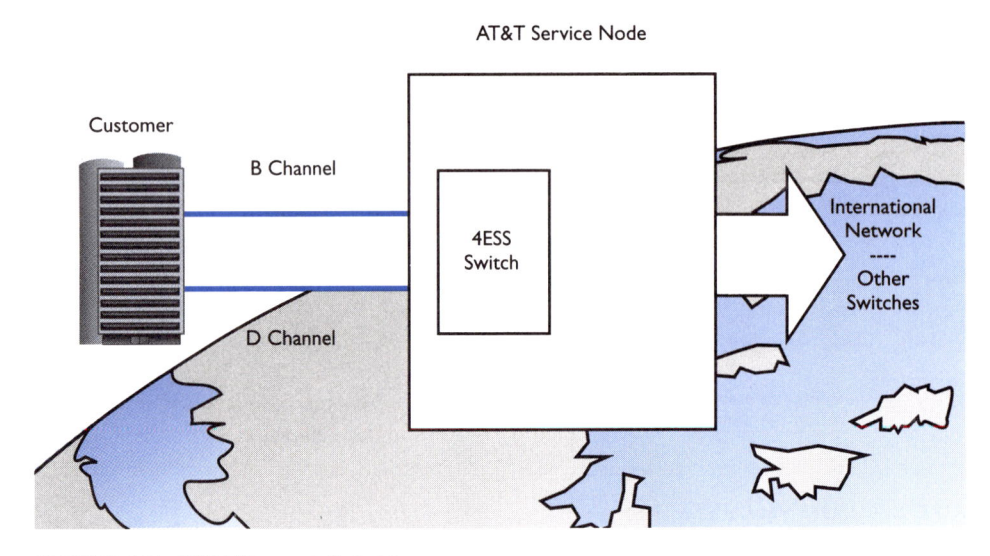

FIGURE 2.21 ISDN Network Switching

Data in the system are routed over T1 circuits. These high-volume circuits move digital data at the rate of 1.544 Mbps. They form the backbone of the network and work in conjunction with the 4ESS switches.

Users access the network with either the **Basic Rate Interface (BRI)** or the **Primary Rate Interface (PRI)** network standard. (See Figure 2.22.) The BRI interface is accessed primarily by small-volume users. The PRI interface is accessed by high-volume users who must move large amounts of data.

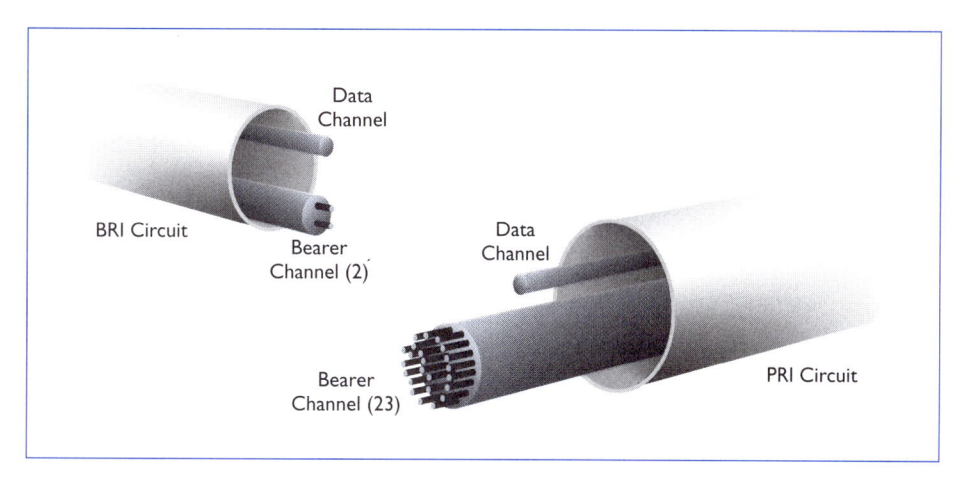

FIGURE 2.22 BRI and PRI Circuits

Two kinds of information are moved over the network in separate channels. The D, or data channel, carries signaling information, call routing, and caller identification data. The B, or bearer channel, moves digitally encoded information, such as voice, text, or other data.

Basic Rate Interface. The basic rate interface (BRI) links telephones and desktop terminals to one of the ISDN 4ESS switches. The BRI consists of two 64 Kbps B-channels and one 16 Kbps D-channel. Known as a 2B+D circuit, this circuit connects the user through a local loop, carrying either voice or data at 64 Kbps, over each of the bearer channels. The 16 Kbps D-channel is used exclusively for carrying control signals.

Primary Rate Interface. The primary rate interface (PRI) connection is provided to high-volume users and connects trunk lines, central office facilities, and network switches to the system. The PRI has 23 B-channels and one D-channel. This circuit, known as a 23B+D, supports data transmission at the rate of 1.544 Mbps. Just as in the BRI, the bearer channel moves the customer's information and the data channel the signaling and administrative information.

Price Structure

Users accessing the AT&T ISDN pay a $3,000 installation charge for the D-channel and a monthly $400 connect charge, in addition to other line costs. Once connected, error-free data transmission is assured between personal computers. Callers may use color picture phones, digitized voice, or 7.1 Khz audio on the circuit.

As greater volumes of data are moved over communications circuits, the ISDN will no doubt expand. More and more cities are being added to the network, and other common carriers are joining the system. In the years ahead, digitally switched networks will take prominence over conventional central office analog switching systems because of their greater capability and speed.

In this chapter we have seen how data can be transmitted in either an analog or a digital form. We have described how the basic telephone system works and the major elements of a communications system. We have reviewed the structure of the ISDN and discussed its advantages. In Chapter 3 we will move on to a more detailed discussion of communications hardware.

SUMMARY

A *communication* involves both a *sender* and a *receiver*. An acknowledgment provides *feedback* to the sender. The *message* is sent over a *communications medium* such as a radio, microwave, or telephone link. *Analog signals* are represented by *sine waves*, consisting of rising and falling wavelike patterns. *Digital signals* have a finite number of possible states. *Binary signals* are represented by two-state conditions, such as a *pulse* or absence of a pulse, a one or a zero.

Amplitude and *frequency* are used to describe the characteristics of a sine wave. A *binary digit* is either a one or a zero and is referred to as a *bit*. Several bits make up a *byte*, or character. *Baud* and *bps (bits per second)* are basic measures of the rate of transmission.

A *circuit* is a pathway, such as a physical line, over which data may be sent. Several communications channels can exist on one circuit. A *receiver, transmitter*, and *induction coil* are basic elements in a telephone handset.

Prior to divestiture, *switching* of telephone calls was handled by a *central office (CO)*. *Intertoll trunks* connected *toll offices*, which were, in turn, connected to *end offices* and ultimately to *subscribers*. Today, a long distance call is switched from an individual subscriber in a *LATA*, through a *POP*, to an *IXC*, to another POP, and then onto its destination. *Crossbar*, solid state, and *Electronic Signal Switch (ESS)* are common means of routing calls through a *switched network*.

A PBX is a private branch exchange, or switchboard, located on the customer's premises. A *subscriber loop* connects the end office to the customer. Individual stations may be switched using a *private branch exchange (PBX)*, *private automatic branch exchange (PABX)*, or a *digital branch exchange (DBX)*.

The *Integrated Services Digital Network (ISDN)* is a communications system capable of transporting voice, digital, and video information. The ISDN enables analog signals to be sent over a digital network, including voice and color pictures. Two interfaces are offered on the ISDN. The *BRI* has two B-channels and one D-channel. The *PRI* has 23 B-channels and one D-channel.

EXERCISES

1. What are the major elements in the basic communications model?
2. What is the difference between a sine wave's amplitude and frequency?
3. Describe how analog signals are represented.
4. Describe how digital signals are represented.
5. Define the term baud rate.
6. List three types of telephone switching equipment.
7. What is the function of a private branch exchange?
8. List several advantages of the ISDN.
9. Describe the BRI connection standard.
10. Describe the PRI connection standard.

HANDS-ON PROJECTS

- Visit a business establishment equipped with a modern telephone system, including multiple stations. Discuss the telephone system with the proprietor. List the features available on the system and discuss how they meet the needs of the enterprise.

- Inspect the telephones at your place of employment. Determine how many stations are available and whether they are connected to computers or other communications equipment.

- Visit a business that has a PBX, DBX, or other switchboard available. Discuss its function with an operator and make a list of its features.

- Contact your local telephone company and discuss available telephone equipment and services, including installation and monthly costs.

- Visit a computer laboratory on your campus. Determine the kind and type of microcomputers available and whether they are connected to communications equipment.

CASE SOLUTION
GREENE AND SINGER CONSULTANTS

COMMUNICATIONS IN ACTION

The president of Greene and Singer, Sidney Greene, hired a specialist who assisted the company in designing and installing a new communications system. (See Figure 2.23.) The new system is a digital branch exchange (DBX) with many features, including full call accounting and least-cost routing.

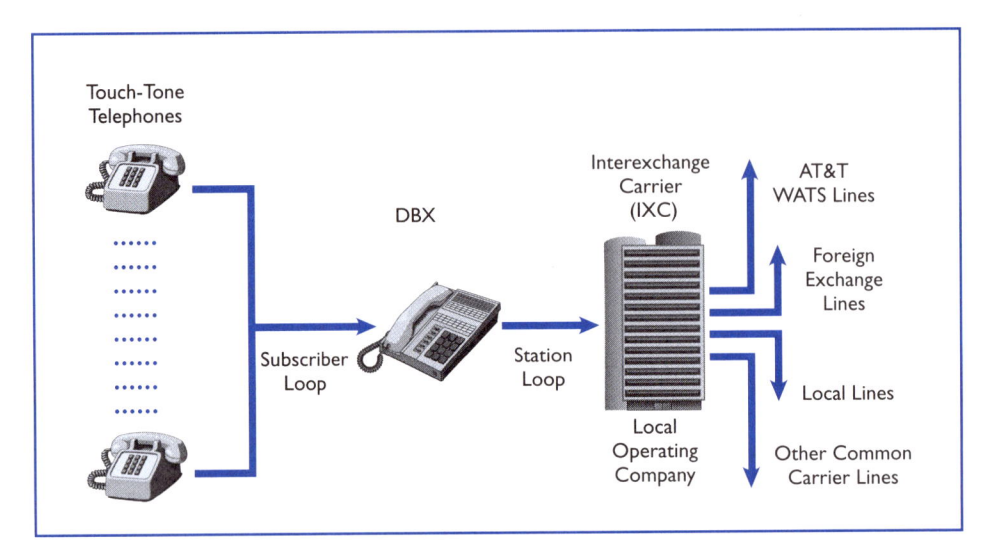

FIGURE 2.23 New System with DBX

When a consultant makes an outgoing phone call, the DBX automatically selects the lowest cost common carrier. Thus, some calls are routed over AT&T WATS lines, others over foreign exchange (FX) lines, and still others over Sprint, MCI, or another common carrier. The FX line, which gives local calling rates for distant communities, is provided by the telephone company. The computer not only routes the call by the most economical means, but also maintains a log of all calls placed by each employee. This log records the time, duration, and destination of each call. This information is essential for billing clients.

The telephone instruments installed at each desk have many features not available on the old system: automatic redialing, time and date display, and speaker-phone capability. In addition, the new system allows consultants to set up conference calls, page employees, and even lock out outgoing calls when personnel are away from their desks.

The new system has sharply reduced long distance charges to Greene and Singer because calls can be routed through the least expensive common carrier. In addition, a complete accounting record is kept of all toll charges, allowing the firm to charge calls to specific clients more accurately. The use of competing common carriers, in conjunction with WATS lines and FX lines, makes these cost reductions possible.

Productivity of the staff has increased greatly since the new system was installed. Employees no longer have to keep redialing numbers that are busy because the computer does it for them. The speaker-phone feature gives personnel hands-free operation, and the time and date feature allows them to monitor the length of each telephone call to maintain better work schedules. Conference calls are easier to arrange without the assistance of an outside operator. The lightweight handsets are more comfortable to hold, and employees are happier with the new system.

II

HARDWARE, MEDIA, AND SOFTWARE

COMMUNICATIONS HARDWARE

LEARNING OBJECTIVES

After studying this chapter, you should be able to:

- Describe major pieces of voice transmission equipment
- Discuss dual-tone multifrequency dialing
- Describe major switchboard equipment
- Describe major data transmission equipment
- Describe various communications terminals
- Contrast mainframe, minicomputer, and microcomputer systems

COMMUNICATIONS
IN ACTION

CASE PROBLEM
LARSON ADVERTISING AGENCY

FACSIMILE TRANSMISSION SYSTEM

Larson Advertising Agency is a large company with many major accounts all over the country. The agency, specializing in creative services, writes advertising copy and designs visuals and layouts for its customers. It places advertisements in local as well as national publications. In the preparation of its ads, the company's artists and designers work closely with account executives and clients.

The designer first prepares several rough layouts and then discusses them with the executive assigned to the account and others. After a satisfactory rough layout is selected, several more detailed, finished layouts are prepared. These are reviewed by the account executive and others in the agency and then are submitted to the client for approval. The process may involve redevelopment of many pieces of artwork. At any one time, hundreds of drawings, sketches, and graphics may be moving between creative designers, account executives, and clients.

Larson Advertising Agency must have an efficient method of circulating artwork, sketches, and renderings in-house as well as sending them to its clients. In addition to artwork, typed copy and galley and page proofs must be routed frequently. Because many ads must be prepared in time to meet publication deadlines, it is crucial that delays be minimized.

In the past, Larson used courier services, messengers, and the U.S. Postal Service to send drawings and sketches. (See Figure 3.1.) In addition, one employee, a mail clerk, was assigned the task of carrying artwork and graphics from office to office within company headquarters. In this process, delays were often experienced and artwork sometimes misrouted.

If you were a manager at Larson Advertising Agency, what improvements would you make in the communications system to help route artwork, copy, and graphics between offices more easily? Refer to the end of this chapter to see how Larson's management resolved this problem.

STUDENTS of communications should have a grasp of the major types and pieces of physical equipment used to transmit both voice and data. This chapter describes the major pieces of communications hardware, such as telephone instruments, switchboards, terminals, mainframes, minicomputers, and microcomputers, all of which form the basic building blocks used to construct communications systems. Later chapters describe the operating principles, electronics, and software that underlie these machines and devices.

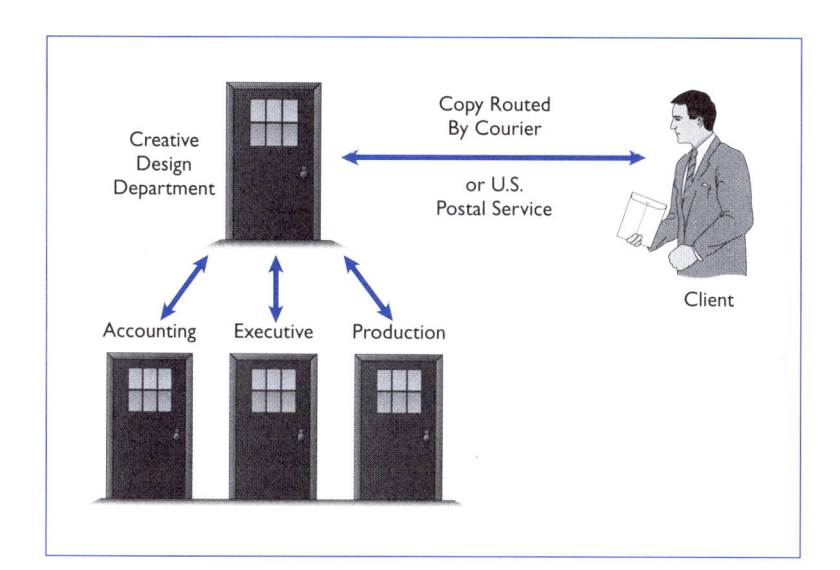

FIGURE 3.1 Old System Using Couriers

VOICE TRANSMISSION EQUIPMENT

A large amount of data are transmitted, switched, and received over ordinary voice transmission facilities. The telephone and the private branch exchange (PBX) are found in many offices and institutions, serving both voice and data communications. This dual capability makes this hardware indispensable to many business, government, military, and educational enterprises.

Telephone Instruments

Telephone instruments were first introduced to transmit the human voice. They are still the principal method used to move analog information. Telephone instruments fall into three major categories: rotary dialing; dual-tone multifrequency (DTMF), also known as Touch-Tone®; and computer-controlled telephones. Let us look at each of these three types of instruments in more detail.

Rotary Dial Telephone. The **rotary dial telephone** became popular in the 1930s when many telephone company branch offices converted to automatic switching equipment. The telephone shown in Figure 3.2 is the Model 500 rotary dialing instrument, which replaced earlier magneto-type and old candlestick-like instruments. It is equipped with a rotary dial, electrical circuitry, pulse contacts, transmitter (mouthpiece), and receiver (earpiece). The transmitter and receiver are called the handset.

When a user wishes to place a call, he or she lifts the handset from the instrument. This action switches in a set of dial pulse contacts. The dial is then rotated, causing the telephone to emit a series of pulses over the line. These **rotary dialing pulses** (see

FIGURE 3.2
Rotary Dial Telephone, Model 500

Figure 3.3) are emitted at the rate of ten per second. Each number on the dial emits a different set of pulses. For instance, a five emits five pulses, a seven emits seven, and the zero emits ten. These pulses are actually contacts opening and closing; they are carefully timed in both duration and spacing. The rotary dial mechanism allows the user to send the pulse signal to the telephone company or a local exchange carrier (LEC), where the call is routed through the switched network. Once the call is routed, the dialing circuitry is removed from the line and an ordinary analog transmission takes place. Millions of rotary telephones are still in use in many underdeveloped countries around the world. Most, however, have been replaced with newer push-button telephones.

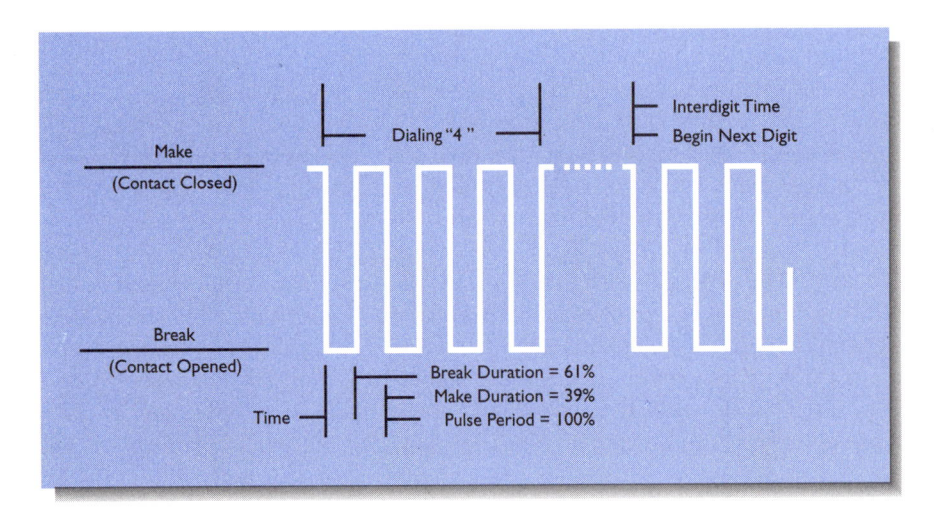

FIGURE 3.3 Rotary Dial Pulses

Dual-Tone Multifrequency Telephone. In the 1960s AT&T introduced a new telephone that used a push-button system to replace the rotary dial. (See Figure 3.4.) AT&T sold these **dual-tone multifrequency (DTMF)** dialing instruments under the name of Touch-Tone. The Model 2500 Touch-Tone telephones are the instruments of choice in most homes and offices. They offer greater dialing convenience and speed and are suited to digital switching arrangements.

FIGURE 3.4
Dual-Tone Multifrequency Telephone, Model 2500

The basic model Touch-Tone has some similarities to the rotary dialing instrument. Both contain a transmitter, receiver, and bell-ringing circuitry. However, on the Touch-Tone instrument the rotary dial has been replaced with a series of 12 buttons. When a button is pressed, two tones of different frequencies are emitted. (See Figure 3.5.) This pair of tones is sent over the line to control the automatic switching equipment at the telephone company's end office.

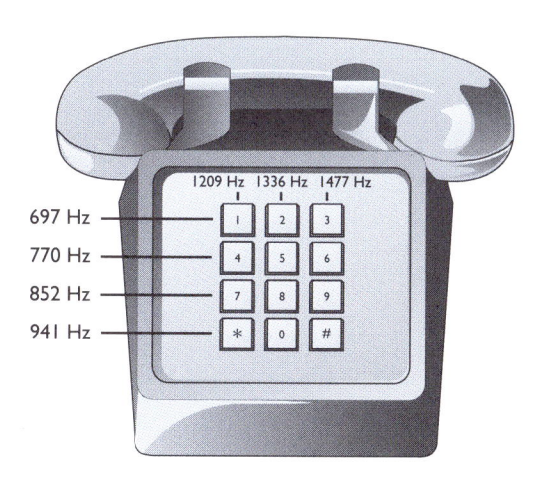

FIGURE 3.5
Touch-Tone® Dial Frequencies

Each dual-tone multifrequency telephone is equipped with a solid-state **oscillator circuit** that emits a unique pair of tones for each button pressed. When the number five button is pressed, for example, a 770 Hz and 1336 Hz tone are simultaneously sent over the line. This pair of tones is sensed by automatic switching equipment at the end office, and the call is routed accordingly. In addition to the ten numeric digits, the asterisk and number symbols are on the remaining two buttons. These nonnumeric buttons can be used for special-purpose signaling, such as automatic redial or entering numbers into memory.

Telephone companies offer customers two types of access arrangements. The rotary dial circuit accepts only rotary pulse dialing, while a dual-tone multifrequency circuit accepts either rotary pulses or Touch-Tone signals. Some common carrier companies are able only to route calls placed on Touch-Tone style instruments; their dialing circuitry is not equipped to switch rotary pulse calls.

Digital Key Telephone System

The advent of the low-cost microcomputer has led to the development of **digital key telephone systems (DKTS)**. (See Figure 3.6.) These devices are equipped with Touch-Tone dialing and have a microprocessor, which provides many additional features for the telephone user, integrated into each instrument. These instruments are capable of storing telephone numbers in memory and can automatically redial if a number is busy. They feature call forwarding, conference calling, intercom, and paging, as well as hold and line control. The line control screens outgoing calls and limits calling to selected area codes or regions, thereby restricting toll calls.

FIGURE 3.6
Digital Key Telephone System (DKTS)

Courtesy of Rolm Corporation

Figure 3.7 lists numerous features available on one digital key telephone system. Improvements in digital switching technology allow many features on instruments serviced by only three pairs of wires. Older, non-digital equipment required dozens of pairs of wires in a single thick cable to provide similar features.

DKTS-*plus* Features

1A2 compatibility	DTMF/Rotary	Private line
Account codes	End-to-end signaling	Recall - stations and lines
Auto-answer outside line	Exclusive hold	Remote system access
Automatic hold	Executive override (barge-in)	Ringing line preference
Automatic incoming line select	2-way external page interface	Secondary hold recall
Automatic preselect	Flexible softkey programming	SMDR interface
Automatic route select (ARS)	Flexible line ringing	Speakerphone
Background music	Group listen	(standard on all stations)
Call back-station/line	Handsfree voice announce	1000 speed dial numbers
Call forward	Headset capability	2500 type stations
7-call pick-up groups	Hearing aid compatible*	Speed dial - single key press
Call split	Intercom—non blocking	Station speed dial
Call transfer	Last number redial	Status display LED
Call waiting	Loop current sensing	Station wall mount capability
Camp-on	Message center	System programming from
Central office line supervision**	Microphone mute	telephone
Common audible interface	Multiple line keys	System programming from
Conference calling	Music/Tone on hold	terminal
Consultation hold	Night answer service	System speed dial
Day/Night restrictions	Non square operation	Tenant service
Default programming	Off hook CO ringing	Toll restrictions—6 digit
DTMF/Dial pulse	Off premise extension	Unsupervised conference
Digit insertion/deletion	Off premise call forward	User programmable
Directed call pick-up	Paging - all page, 8 zones	feature keys
Direct station selection	Pause	Variety of faceplate colors
Discriminating ringing	Pooled line groups	Volume control
Distinctive ringing	Power failure relay	Voice call deny
Do not disturb (DND)	22 programmable timers	Wall mount capability
Doorbell/Alarm inputs	Prime line	
DSS console	Privacy	

NOTE:
*Hearing aid compatible handsets are standard equipment on all proprietary station sets.
**Responds to open loop disconnect provided by local central office.

Courtesy SunMoonStar Group

FIGURE 3.7 DKTS Telephone Features

Local Switching Equipment

Most organizations that have more than a few telephone instruments may need some form of in-house switchboard arrangement. These switchboards are either owned or leased by the organization and serve a variety of functions. They enable calls to be switched between telephones within an organization and facilitate conference calling, intercom, and paging.

Three basic types of local switchboards that have come into use are described next. All three are designed primarily to switch analog communications. Some of the newer types of computer-controlled switchboards are designed to move voice communications in the form of digitized packets. This technique is described in more detail later in this book.

Private Branch Exchange. A **private branch exchange (PBX)** is a central switchboard operated by an organization where the switchboard itself is on their premises and controlled by a local operator. (See Figure 3.8.) Private branch exchanges, the earliest form of local switching systems, then consisted of a panel containing many jacks and cords. A group of trunk lines are connected to the PBX so that the operator can switch calls from outside the organization through the trunk line. Each telephone instrument in the organization has a pair of wires connected to the PBX. In a manual PBX the operator physically connects circuits by plugging in cords that patch jack to jack or jack to trunk line. Manually operated systems have been almost universally replaced by automated switchboards.

FIGURE 3.8
Private Branch Exchange (PBX)

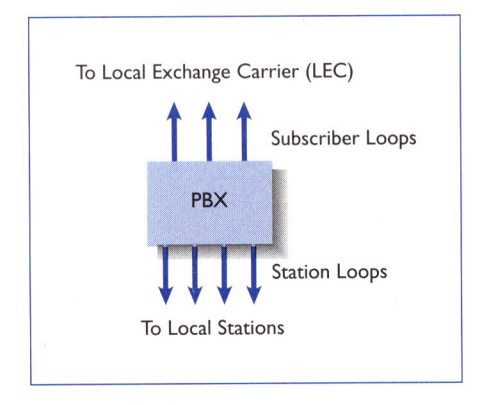

Private Automatic Branch Exchange. The **private automatic branch exchange (PABX)** is an outgrowth of the PBX. The manual jack and plug method is replaced by a system of switches. In this arrangement, as in the PBX, trunk lines and circuits to each instrument are routed to the board. Calls are then switched automatically between instruments or to the trunk lines. Some private automatic branch exchanges allow stations to call outside by dialing seven, eight, or nine to access a trunk line. Private automatic branch exchanges allow calls to be transferred within an organization and conference calls to be set up without operator intervention.

Digital Branch Exchange. A **digital branch exchange (DBX)** is an automatic switchboard that contains a microcomputer to handle switching automatically. (See Figure 3.9.) The DBX provides all the features of the PABX, plus computer control. The memory capacity and logic of the computer have been applied to local switching. The computer also plays an important role in managing toll charges by screening and routing toll calls. The computer can be programmed to limit calls to selected dialing areas. It can also route calls via the most economical common carrier and provide accounting information as well.

FIGURE 3.9
Digital Branch Exchange

Courtesy of Northern Telecom

A variety of DBX equipment is available. **Digital Centrex** is a decentralized calling system in which each instrument on the system is assigned its own unique telephone number. Stations can receive incoming calls directly from a common set of incoming trunks. The DBX can establish conference calls and avoid call overloads commonly found in centralized systems. The Meridian Digital Centrex system, offered by Northern Telecom, is a sophisticated computerized switchboard. It has a microcomputer that provides a variety of switching, call-forwarding, call-waiting, conferencing, and toll-call control features.

The switchboards discussed thus far are designed to switch and route voice-grade calls consisting of analog signals. They control analog messages using computers and digital circuitry. Some of the latest DBX equipment handles all calls in only digital form. These systems convert analog information, such as voices, to digital packets of information that are routed through the system. Communications already in the form of digital information are integrated with the digitized voice signals and routed together over the same system. All-digital systems have many advantages. Information can be moved faster and more efficiently. Both digital and analog information are moved about in the same form, thus increasing flexibility.

DATA TRANSMISSION EQUIPMENT

This section describes equipment and devices designed to move only digital information. The major pieces of equipment in the category include terminals, microcomputers, interface devices, and facsimile machines. A terminal is sometimes referred to as a piece of **data terminal equipment (DTE)**. DTEs may be teleprinters, video display terminals, or the other devices described in this chapter. DTEs are sometimes connected to computers or other communications equipment, called DCEs. "DTE" and "DCE" are frequently used in describing communications hardware.

Terminals

A **terminal** is a device capable of receiving or transmitting information between one point and another, for example, between a computer and a terminal. The wide variety of terminals on the market are used in many general and special-purpose applications.

Terminals may generate hard-copy output or a visual display on a screen. A **hard-copy** terminal generates a permanent copy of the output or message. It prints information on paper and draws lines and graphs, resulting in a document that can be filed, copied, or kept permanently.

A display monitor generates information in a nonpermanent form. The information may be output on a cathode ray tube or liquid crystal display (LCD). Machines in this category are known as video display terminals (VDTs). Still other terminals generate audible sounds. A voice synthesizer unit generates music and sounds or simulates the human voice. Let's look at these types of terminals more closely.

Teleprinter. **Teleprinter** machines were used in communications for many years. One of the earliest was the Teletype, which was equipped with a keyboard for inputting data and a printer for printing hard-copy output. A few Teletypes, including the Model ASR 33, are still in use, though they are rapidly becoming obsolete.

When a key on a teleprinter keyboard is struck, digital pulses are emitted from the machine and are sent over a communications line. The teleprinter is an example of a hard-copy terminal.

Machines in this category are sometimes referred to as **dumb terminals** because they include only the basic functions of input, output, and communications. (See Figure 3.10.) Because they do not include a microcomputer, these terminals are not capable of logic, storing data, reformatting information, or altering the coding system used to transmit information. Nonetheless, dumb terminals provide an important communications function at relatively low cost. Teleprinters are still used in the Telex and TWX communications systems.

FIGURE 3.10
Terminal, Block Diagram

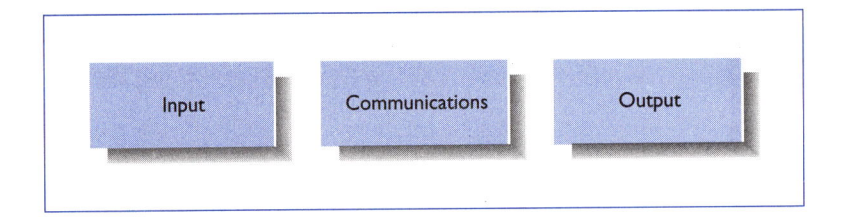

Terminals that contain integrated computers are referred to as **intelligent terminals**. These intelligent, or smart, devices, shown in Figure 3.11, are capable of many functions not provided by dumb terminals. Intelligent terminals are equipped with input, output, and memory facilities and a microprocessor. (See Figure 3.12.) The microprocessor in the terminal allows data to be stored within the machine or to be reformatted or transmitted in a variety of different codes.

FIGURE 3.11
Intelligent Terminal

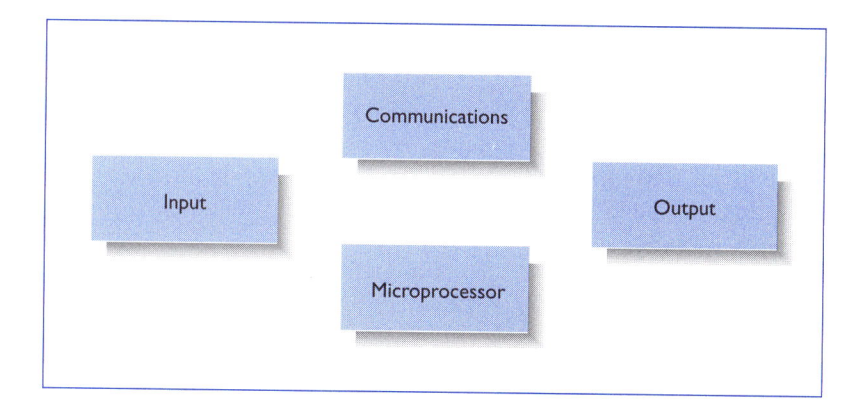

Courtesy of Hewlett-Packard

FIGURE 3.12
Intelligent Terminal, Block Diagram

Video Display Terminals. A **video display terminal (VDT)** allows digital data, drawings, or images to be output on a television-like screen. (See Figure 3.13.) Video display terminals are less expensive to operate than teleprinters because they do not require paper, ink, or ribbons. The displays, however, do not create a permanent image. An advantage of VDTs is their speed. Thousands of characters can be displayed on a screen in a second or two. These devices are more reliable than teleprinters because they have few moving parts or mechanical devices to break down.

VDTs are equipped with a keyboard just as a teleprinter is. When a key is pressed, a digital code representing the character to be transmitted is sent over the line. When a character is received by the VDT, it may be displayed on the screen by a moving electron beam, much like the image on an ordinary television screen. Other terminals, especially portable hand-held units, use liquid crystal displays (LCDs) because of their low power requirements.

FIGURE 3.13
Video Display Terminal

Special-Purpose Terminals

Dozens of special-purpose terminals have been designed to be used in many different types of systems. These systems run the gamut from simple point-of-sale (POS) terminals, found in retail establishments, to complex remote-job-entry (RJE) terminals capable of inputting and outputting a large volume of data to computers. Let us review some of the more common special-purpose terminals in use today.

Administrative Terminals. Administrative terminals are found in offices and are available to executives, administrators, and supervisors. (See Figure 3.14.) An **administrative terminal** is capable of displaying information or receiving input. Administrative terminals allow executives or managers to access information stored in their organization's database. Some devices are equipped with touch screens that allow the user to make choices by pressing areas on the screen with a finger. Many managers depend on administrative terminals to access personnel, production, and financial data at a point in the business cycle when an important decision must be made quickly.

Another function of administrative terminals is the routing of messages and information between individuals within an organization. Using an administrative terminal, an executive can send messages by electronic mail to other offices equipped with similar terminals. Memos, letters, and correspondence are routed quickly to individuals within the organization, frequently at less cost than through conventional mail or courier service.

FIGURE 3.14
Administrative Terminal

Data Collection Terminal. **Data collection terminals** are designed to receive input from a variety of sources and forward the data to a central station for processing. Data collection terminals are located in shops, factories, manufacturing plants, freight yards, or hazardous areas where information must be gathered and sent to a central point. (See Figure 3.15.)

FIGURE 3.15
Data Collection Terminal

Data collection terminals can collect data on the amount of fuel loaded into a tanker truck, record the number of hours worked by an employee, or input the amount of paper, glass, wood, plastic, or other materials used in the manufacture of goods. Sometimes these terminals are connected directly to a flow meter or other counting device. They are thus able to record the number of gallons delivered or the number of units taken from stock. Data may also be input by keyboard, bar-code reader, or optical character scanning device.

You are probably already familiar with some common data collection terminals. Perhaps you have seen a clerk in a supermarket or drug store scanning a bar code, using a portable data collection terminal. The wand scans the bar code and enters the product number, and the clerk keys in the physical inventory. In some communities, a meter reader moves from house to house, entering data on water, gas, or electricity consumption into a terminal. This information is used to generate bills or reports.

Remote-Job-Entry Terminals. Some computer systems are equipped with **remote-job-entry (RJE) terminals**. (See Figure 3.16.) RJE terminals read magnetic tape, floppy disks, or other computer input media and convert the information into pulses that are sent over a communications line to a computer for processing. These terminals are also equipped with a variety of output devices, including high-speed line printers, magnetic disks, and magnetic tape drives. RJE terminals provide full input and output ability to a computer from remote points, thus bringing the capability of a large central computer to branch offices without the expense of duplicating computers. RJE terminals, however, are not computers in themselves; they rely on a central computer to perform computations or other data processing tasks.

FIGURE 3.16
Remote-Job-Entry (RJE) Terminal

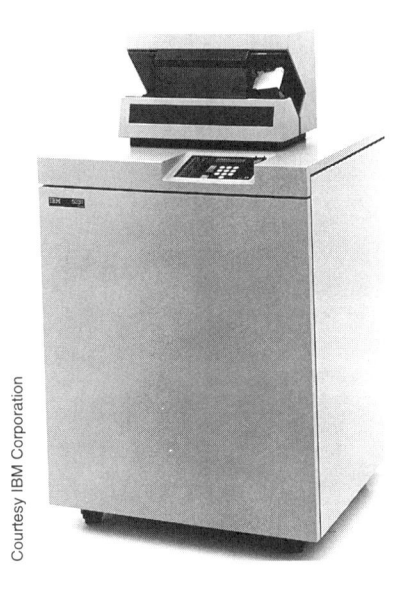

Courtesy IBM Corporation

Credit Authorization Terminals. **Credit authorization terminals** are special-purpose devices designed to read credit cards or information input from a keyboard to check customer credit. (See Figure 3.17.) Millions of transactions are processed each year by department stores, service stations, supermarkets, specialty shops, and other retailers on goods sold on credit. To minimize losses, these retailers must be able to check a customer's credit rating quickly before approving a purchase. Credit authorization terminals are found in many of these retail establishments and service organizations.

FIGURE 3.17
Credit Authorization Terminal

Credit authorization terminals usually have provisions for reading customer account data from a magnetic stripe on the back of a plastic credit card. Other devices require the retailer to enter the customer account data via a keyboard. Some have provisions for automatically dialing a central credit-checking agency. These terminals authorize credit when the account is in good standing and has not exceeded the approved credit limits.

Transaction Terminals. **Transaction terminals**, located in retail establishments, are similar to cash registers. These terminals provide functions ranging from credit authorization to the preparation of customer bills and invoices. They also post payments to accounts, issue credits, verify account balances, and display account activity and similar information.

A variety of transaction terminals are used in the retailing industry. (See Figure 3.18.) These **point-of-sale (POS) terminals** input data from tickets, tags, bar codes, or keyboards. They print out receipts and forward information to a central processing computer. There each sale is recorded, and an inventory record may be updated as well. Many retailers use this type of terminal to enter the transaction and later generate a bill or statement, which is sent to the customer from a central accounting office.

Bank Teller Terminals. Virtually the entire banking industry has converted to computerized accounting, and bank employees rely heavily on teller terminals. **Bank teller terminals** provide a full range of banking facilities. (See Figure 3.19.) They post debits and credits, display account balances, process deposits, withdrawals, loan and mortgage payments, and perform other similar functions.

FIGURE 3.18
Transaction Terminal

FIGURE 3.19
Bank Teller Terminal

Some banks operate hundreds of branches located in many cities across the country. The availability of teller terminals allows customers to make deposits and withdrawals and process routine transactions at any branch in the system.

A specialized form of banking terminal is known as an **automatic teller machine (ATM)**. (See Figure 3.20.) ATMs located in supermarkets, shopping malls, and in other high-traffic areas are designed to offer bank customers 24-hour service. Customers can make deposits or even withdrawals at any hour of the day or night, including weekends and holidays, through these specialized terminals. They have greatly expanded and made convenient the services offered by many banks while also lowering operating costs.

FIGURE 3.20
Automatic Teller Machine (ATM)

EMULATORS

Hundreds of different types of terminals are in use and are connected to various computers. Frequently, a microcomputer is needed to serve as a terminal on a mainframe computer. To carry out this function, emulator software is used. An **emulator** is a computer program that enables a terminal, microcomputer, or other communications device to simulate a physical terminal connected to a mainframe. Many different emulators are available to connect devices to a mainframe and facilitate this microcomputer–mainframe connection. These are known as VT series emulators because they create virtual, rather than physical, terminals.

VT100 Emulator

The VT100 series emulators enable readily available, low-cost microcomputers to be connected to Digital Equipment Corp. (DEC) mainframe computers. With appropriate software and circuit boards, these microcomputers duplicate all the functions normally available on a DEC remote terminal. The use of this emulator greatly increases the flexibility of the system.

IBM 3270 Emulator

Thousands of IBM 3270 terminals are physically wired to large IBM mainframe systems. It is possible to connect a microcomputer to an IBM mainframe, using IBM 3270 software and appropriate interface circuitry. This connection eliminates the need for additional IBM terminals and allows microcomputers to access a mainframe. Once the proper hardware and software are installed, the microcomputer behaves just like a permanently connected terminal. Data can be sent back and forth between computers, and processing can be handled by the mainframe.

FACSIMILE DEVICES

There is often a need to send drawings, sketches, photographs, handwritten documents, or other printed or graphic material from one place to another quickly. A **facsimile machine** is a device that scans a physical document, converts it to electrical pulses, and sends it over a communications line instantly. (See Figure 3.21.) The number of fax machines in use has increased dramatically; at present millions of facsimile machines are in service in the United States alone. Thirty million units are expected to be in operation by the year 2000.

FIGURE 3.21
Facsimile Machine

A facsimile system requires two machines, one at each end of the line, or a computer equipped with fax capability. Black and white areas or shades of gray are converted to electrical signals for transmission. At the other end, another facsimile machine receives the signals and recreates the same values as are on the original.

Facsimile machines may operate attended or unattended. Some are capable of storing 20 pages or more of documents and then transmitting them at one time over ordinary voice-grade telephone lines.

Facsimile machines convert physical documents into signals that can be relayed over ordinary telephone lines. Thus letters, drawings, or memos can be sent from office to office, eliminating the time and expense of conventional mail. Facsimile machines are used to transmit loan applications, credit reports, engineering drawings and designs, and product specifications. They are ideally suited for sending copies of contracts, sales orders, and confirmations. Because facsimile machines transmit an image of the original, the original document may be kept intact without the fear of loss. Another advantage of facsimile transmission is that one facsimile machine can transmit a document to many receiving stations simultaneously. Thus, a copy of a document can be generated at several points at the same time.

Four generations of facsimile machines have evolved. These categories or groups have been standardized by the Consultative Committee on International Telephone and Telegraph (CCITT), an organization that sets worldwide communications standards.

The major facsimile groups are:

Group 1. *Low-speed terminals*, whose standards were established in 1976, capable of sending a business letter-size page in four to six minutes.

Group 2. *Medium-speed terminals*, capable of sending one page in three minutes.

Group 3. *Faster terminals*, using the 1980 CCITT standards, capable of transmitting a page in one minute or less.

Group 4. *High-speed facsimile machines* that can transmit one page in ten seconds or less.

Group 5. *Machines under development* that will transmit millions of bits per second and enable multipage documents to be sent in only a few seconds.

Fax Cards

Personal computers can be equipped with facsimile capability by inserting a **fax card** into a computer. This addition gives the machine fax capabilities, enabling it to transmit files generated on the computer to fax machines over ordinary telephone lines. The computer can also receive fax messages and display the information on a monitor or print out a copy of a fax message on the printer.

The acquisition of a fax card eliminates the need to buy a separate fax machine. The fax card provides all the capabilities of a stand-alone machine, including automatic sending and receiving of faxes and multiple fax communications.

COMPUTERS AND COMMUNICATIONS

During the past decade there has been a great increase in computer and communications usage. The large number of computers and terminals in use has created a need for more communications facilities. Most offices are equipped with computers that route and switch telephone calls, text files, and other data. Many computers are interfaced to telephone lines and stations.

The distinction between computers and communications is becoming blurred. Individuals working in the communications field need a thorough understanding of computer fundamentals.

COMPUTER SYSTEMS

Large, permanently installed computer systems are referred to as mainframes. Smaller, more portable desktop systems are known as microcomputers. Those in between in size are known as minicomputers. Throughout the communications industry, large and small computers are integrated into systems known as networks.

A **computer network** is a system that connects computers, terminals, and communications equipment into a functioning whole. Some computer networks, such as hotel and motel reservation systems, have hundreds of terminals tied to one large computer. Other systems integrate many stand-alone microcomputers. Still others use small minicomputers, placed ahead of large mainframes, to balance or reduce work loads.

The computers described below may operate as self-contained units or be connected to terminals, such as those described earlier in this chapter. The balance of this chapter presents an overview of mainframe, minicomputer, and microcomputer systems and how they are integrated into communications systems.

MAINFRAME COMPUTERS

Throughout the computer industry, large high-speed computers capable of processing vast amounts of data have been installed. These permanently installed systems are known as **mainframes**. Mainframe computers can input large amounts of data, which can be stored, classified, summarized, retrieved, and output.

Figure 3.22 illustrates the major blocks typical in all computer systems. It shows a central processing unit (CPU) connected to secondary storage and input and output systems. Regardless of their size, computers all possess these major components.

FIGURE 3.22
Computer, Block Diagram

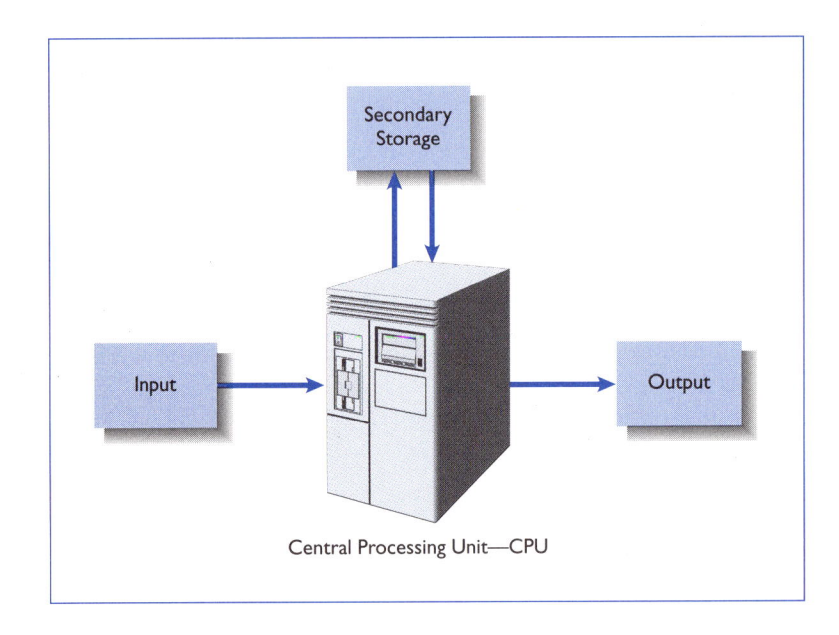

Central Processing Unit

The heart of the computer is the **central processing unit (CPU)**. The computer's CPU performs three major functions. Its primary memory system is designed to store millions of characters (bytes) of information. This is the portion of the machine that stores the program or other instructions being processed. Computer instructions are written in languages such as BASIC, COBOL, C, or assembly.

The control portion of the machine handles the timing of the system and the switching in and out of peripheral devices. It includes a system clock that emits millions of pulses per second, accounting for the system's high speed. The control unit includes various electronic counters and keeps track of each instruction, processing them in sequence.

The arithmetic and logic unit (ALU) is composed of solid-state circuitry that stores numbers and gates that are able to manipulate data. The ALU performs arithmetic and logical comparisons and returns the results to the system for output. All these operations are conducted under the direction of a program that is entered by a programmer.

Input System

The computer's **input system** is designed to receive information from keyboards, magnetic tape, or other media and transmit it to the CPU for processing. It is much like the eyes and ears of the computer. The input devices convert optical characters, magnetic ink characters, and holes or magnetized areas on tape into digital pulses. These pulses are sent to the CPU for processing.

Output System

The computer's **output system** is designed to convert electrical pulses sent to it from the CPU into a form useful to people. Output devices include line printers, video display units, voice or audio synthesizers, and similar devices. In all instances these machines receive pulses that emerge as printed documents or letters displayed on a screen or are recorded on media such as magnetic tape or disks. A computer's input and output units are referred to collectively as I/O devices.

Sometimes it is desirable to locate one or more of the computer's I/O devices at some distance from the CPU. For instance, a terminal may be connected to a computer located many miles away. (See Figure 3.23.) The terminal is an I/O device capable of receiving or outputting information processed remotely by the CPU. Therefore, data transmission circuits are needed between the terminal and the CPU. The communications circuit may be a dedicated pair of wires, a telephone line, microwave circuit, or other facility. These are described in more detail in Chapter 6.

FIGURE 3.23
Computer and Terminal

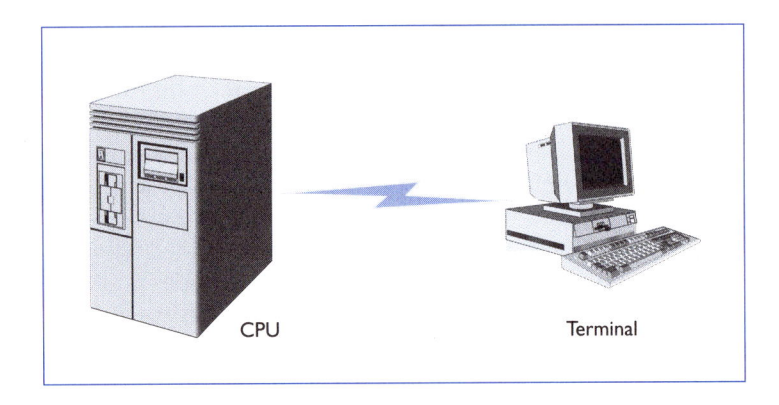

CPU   Terminal

Secondary Storage

All mainframe computers are equipped with **secondary storage devices**. These include magnetic disks, magnetic tape, or other machines that can store billions of characters of data and make them available for almost instantaneous retrieval.

Secondary storage differs from primary memory. The primary memory in the CPU holds information to be processed immediately. It must, therefore, be very fast. Data for more permanent storage, such as lengthy files, are usually stored on magnetic disk or tape. These systems have greater capacity but are slower than primary memory.

MINICOMPUTER SYSTEMS

A precise definition of a minicomputer is difficult to give. A **minicomputer** is a computer bigger than a microcomputer but smaller than a mainframe, usually costing less than $20,000, frequently used in data communications applications. Minicomputers are full-scale computers in every sense of the word except size. They have I/O capability, a CPU, and secondary memory. Their reduced size and lower cost make them attractive as switching or controlling devices for mainframe computers. In this application they are known as front-end processors (FEP).

Front-End Processors

Front-end processors (FEPs) are designed to handle the communications, switching, and security and access control for the mainframe, referred to as the **host computer**, reducing the processing demands on the mainframe. A front-end processor (see Figure 3.24) is installed ahead of the host computer and between the communications lines serving the terminals.

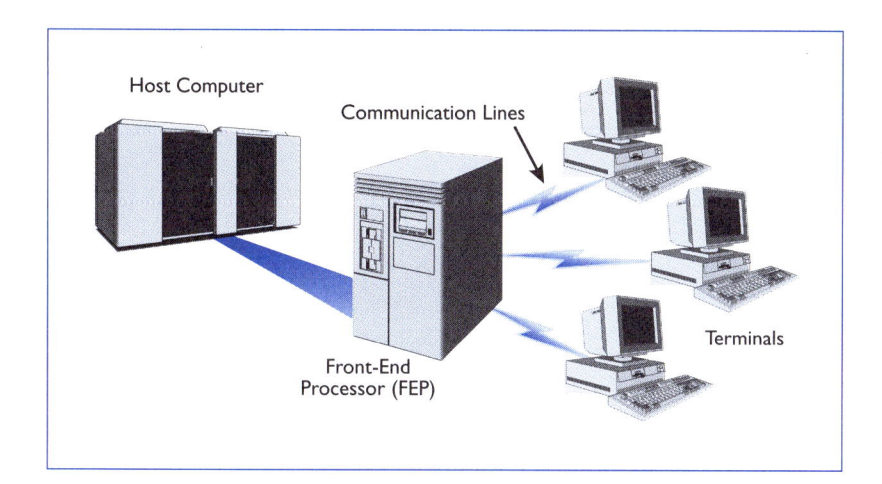

FIGURE 3.24 Front-End Processor. The FEP handles switching and communications tasks.

FEPs check passwords, convert data transmission codes, switch communications lines in and out, allocate host computer resources, and maintain an accounting of system usage. These functions are performed outside the host CPU, thereby enabling the main computer to use its full capacity on computations, rather than communications tasks.

Suppose several hundred terminals are to access one mainframe computer. This arrangement would create a substantial processing burden on the mainframe. To reduce the work load, a minicomputer, serving as an FEP, could be assigned the task of switching and managing incoming and outgoing data transmissions. Figure 3.24 illustrates a host computer, FEP, communications lines, and several terminals. The figure shows the computers connected directly to the communications line. As a practical matter, front-end processors or additional circuitry and equipment are necessary to connect a terminal or CPU physically to a line. These devices, including **modems (modulator/demodulators)**, data concentrators, and multiplexers, play an important role in data transmission. These devices are discussed in Chapter 4.

MICROCOMPUTER SYSTEMS

The microcomputer has the ability to store data, make logical comparisons, and branch accordingly. Microcomputers are operated either as stand-alone units or as terminals in a network system. A **microcomputer** is a small, tabletop device, usually costing less than $2,000, that includes a central processing unit (CPU) and input and output devices. (See Figure 3.25.) Microcomputers can be operated as stand-alone machines or, with communications equipment, can serve as a terminal.

FIGURE 3.25
Microcomputer

Courtesy of Zeos Corporation

In the late 1970s, Apple, Radio Shack (Tandy), and others introduced microcomputer systems. But it was not until 1981, when IBM introduced its personal computer (PC), that great growth in microcomputer usage began. Microcomputers store millions of bytes of data in primary memory. These systems are equipped with magnetic disk storage devices and other peripherals similar to mainframe systems.

Because of their small size, microcomputers are frequently integrated into communications systems. To function as part of a network of computers, a microcomputer may be equipped with a modem and communications software. We will discuss these items in Chapters 5 and 9. Because of their low cost, speed, and reliability, microcomputers are an important part of most communications systems.

In this chapter we have discussed modern communications hardware, including computers. Before studying how these elements are used in complex communications systems, we must look more closely at communications channels and how information is moved over circuits. The next chapter will discuss transmission modes, modulation, and multiplexing, all important concepts needed to understand data communications.

SUMMARY

Rotary dial telephones route calls through a *dial pulse* contact switch. *Dual-tone multifrequency (DTMF)* dialing telephones route calls by emitting a pair of electrical tones. *Digital key telephone systems (DKTS)* are able to store numbers, redial, forward calls, and perform other functions.

A *private branch exchange (PBX)* is a central switchboard operated at the user's premises. A *private automatic branch exchange (PABX)* allows automatic switching of calls from a switchboard located at the user's premises. A *digital branch exchange (DBX)* controls switching by using a microcomputer and performs other functions including screening and routing toll calls.

A *terminal* is a device that sends data from one point to another or between a computer and a point. *Hard-copy* terminals generate a printed copy of the output or message. *Teleprinters* produce permanent hard-copy output. *VDTs* display output as visual images on a screen. A variety of special terminals are in use, including *administrative, data collection, RJE, credit authorization, bank teller,* and *transaction terminals.*

An *emulator* is a computer program that enables a terminal, microcomputer, or other communications device to simulate a physical terminal connected to a mainframe.

Facsimile machines scan documents and transmit pulses to a receiving machine, which produces a copy of the original document. *Fax cards* can be added to microcomputers to give them facsimile transmission capability.

A *computer system* is composed of *input*, central processing unit, *output*, and *secondary storage* systems. Input systems receive data from keyboards or other media and send them to the *central processing unit (CPU)* for processing. The CPU incorporates arithmetic and logic, primary memory, and control units. Output systems receive data from the CPU and convert them into printed documents or images on a screen. Common secondary storage devices include magnetic disks or tape that can store millions of characters.

A *mainframe* is a large, permanently installed computer system, whereas a *microcomputer* is a small, desktop system that can be easily moved. A microcomputer contains a CPU, input and output devices, and, often, communications facilities. *Minicomputers* play an important role in communications. As *front-end processors (FEPs)*, minicomputers are located ahead of host computers and handle formatting, switching, and file security tasks.

EXERCISES

1. Describe the rotary dialing system.
2. Describe the dual-tone multifrequency dialing system.
3. List three types of private branch exchanges.
4. Contrast mainframes and microcomputers.
5. Describe the function of administrative terminals.
6. Describe the function of credit authorization terminals.
7. Discuss the function of a front-end processor.
8. Describe the function of the CPU.
9. List several examples of computer input and output devices.
10. Describe how facsimile machines transmit documents.

HANDS-ON PROJECTS

- Visit the sales office of your local telephone company. Discuss available equipment and prices. Make a list of equipment features.

- Inspect the telephones available in a local business office. Discuss the features and locations of various instruments.

- Visit a business office equipped with a local switchboard. During a break or slow period, discuss the type of switchboard in use and its features with the operator.

- Visit a local computer store and review the types of computers that are available. Make a list of features and input/output devices for various machines.

- Visit a local business office equipped with a facsimile machine. Observe the process by which documents are transmitted and received.

COMMUNICATIONS IN ACTION

CASE SOLUTION
LARSON ADVERTISING AGENCY

The management at Larson Advertising Agency considered a number of communications options. They ultimately settled on a group of facsimile machines that were installed in their offices. (See Figure 3.26.) These machines were located in the account executives' offices as well as in the creative design department. Many of the company's larger accounts already had facsimile machines that could receive copy and artwork over ordinary telephone lines.

FIGURE 3.26
New System with Facsimile Terminals

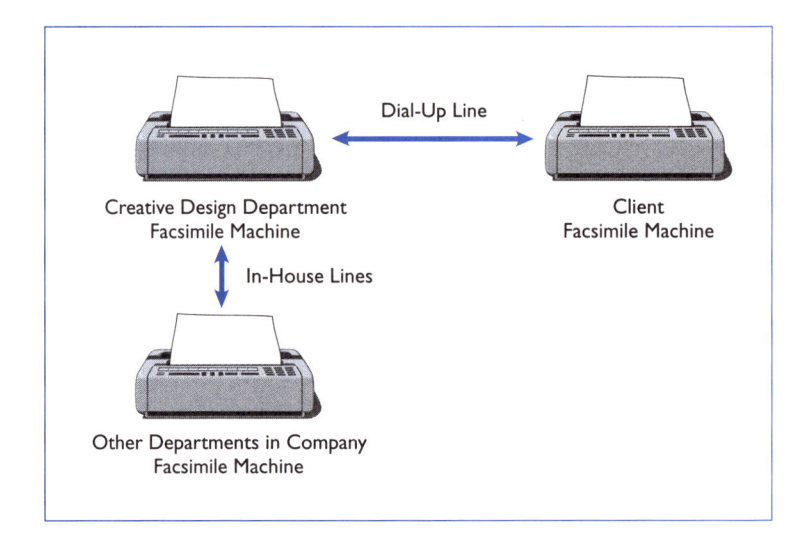

Now when designers wish to send a piece of artwork to another department, they place it in the facsimile machine. The machine reduces the graphics to a string of digital pulses that are sent to other offices over the in-house telephone system. At the receiving end, a facsimile machine generates a copy of the drawing or sketch. The copy closely matches the original. Typewritten copy, line drawings, layouts, and even photographs can be sent this way.

It is possible to send the same graphics or copy to several different departments at one time. The facsimile machines can send the graphics over ordinary telephone lines to clients who have similar machines. The system can both send and receive copy, greatly facilitating changes and alterations.

The new system is faster, less expensive, and more reliable than the couriers. Inclement weather doesn't affect speed of delivery, and important drawings and layouts are not lost or misrouted, as they never leave the designer's office. Duplicate illustrations can be sent to several offices at one time, thus speeding up the approval process. Because the facsimile machines can reduce copy, it is possible to transmit oversized drawings more easily.

The new system allows Larson Advertising's staff and its clients to study a piece of artwork concurrently. If changes or alterations are required, they are made on the facsimile and then routed back to the creative design department, greatly increasing the productivity of the staff and reducing the amount of time it takes to prepare an advertisement for publication.

FUNDAMENTALS OF COMMUNICATIONS CHANNELS

LEARNING OBJECTIVES

After studying this chapter, you should be able to:

- Discuss the frequency spectrum
- Describe the elements used to evaluate transmission channels
- Contrast serial and parallel data transmission
- Discuss the principles of modulation and demodulation
- Describe the principles of multiplexing
- Describe the operation of data concentrators

COMMUNICATIONS
IN ACTION

CASE PROBLEM
FIDELITY BANK

ELECTRONIC BANKING SYSTEM

Fidelity Bank is a full-service banking institution. It processes loans, issues credit cards to customers, and provides credit authorization services to retailers. The main office serves several branches located in town. Fidelity also handles payroll processing for some of its customers. The bank has thousands of customers, many of whom prefer to do business during non-business hours and on weekends. Competing banks have installed automatic teller machines (ATMs) located outside each bank or in shopping centers and malls. To remain competitive, Fidelity must maintain a system for processing all its transactions promptly.

Fidelity must be able to serve its branches, ATMs, and customers quickly and efficiently and so requires an extensive communications network. In addition, Fidelity must also serve hundreds of retail establishments by checking credit and issuing authorizations through point-of-sale terminals located in stores and shops.

Fidelity's tellers must have access to its database and the balances and records of all its customers. The bank also requires a reliable electronic funds transfer system to process many transactions. For instance, some of its customers send their payrolls directly to the bank and each employee's paycheck is deposited electronically without physically moving checks.

What kinds of communications facilities would you suggest that Fidelity Bank install to serve its customers, business accounts, and others? Refer to the end of the chapter to see how this problem was handled.

MOST people can walk into a travel agent's office and book flights, hotel rooms, and automobile rentals virtually anywhere in the world. This service is taken for granted. Few clients stop to think about the intricate circuitry that makes it possible to transmit thousands of characters around the world over communications lines in a few seconds.

This chapter explains how digital data are encoded and sent over circuits to many distant points. It also describes the frequency spectrum and modes of data transmission, including the principles of multiplexers and data concentrators. The chapter focuses on the most vital link in the communications process, the channel that carries information between two points.

THE FREQUENCY SPECTRUM

It has been said that Enrico Caruso, a great opera singer of the past, could shatter a wine glass with his voice at 20 paces. Why was Caruso able to perform this feat, while others failed? The answer lies in his ability to control the frequency of his voice. It is our ability to control frequencies that enables us to tune a radio to one station while blocking out all others.

You may remember from a previous discussion that sounds emitted from a piano, or spoken words, are vibrations that appear at repetitive intervals. The frequency at which a sound level rises and falls creates the pitch that we hear. **Frequency** and **wavelength** are used to describe the behavior of all sound, light, and electromagnetic waves. (See Figure 4.1.)

TYPE OF WAVE	FREQUENCY	WAVELENGTH
Sound Waves		
Human ear	16 Hz–20 kHz	
Human voice (male)	30 Hz–10 kHz	
Harp	32 Hz–3.1 kHz	
Bass viola	41 Hz–246 Hz	
Trombone	80 Hz–493 Hz	
Trumpet	164 Hz–880 Hz	
Violin	196 Hz–2.1 kHz	
C flute	293 Hz–2.1 kHz	
C piccolo	587 Hz–3.5 kHz	
Radio Waves	3 kHz–300 GHz	0.1 mm–100 km
Very low frequency VLF	3 kHz–30kHz	10 km–100 km
Low frequency LF	30 kHz–300 kHz	1 km–10 km
Medium frequency MF	300 kHz–3 MHz	100 m–1 km
High frequency HF	3 kHz–30 MHz	10 m–100 m
Very high frequency VHF	30 MHz–300 MHz	1 m–10 m
Ultra high frequency UHF	300 MHz–3 GHz	10 cm–1 m
Super high frequency SHF	3 GHz–30 GHz	1 cm–10 cm
Extremely high frequency EHF	30 GHz–300 GHz	0.1 mm–0.1 cm
Infrared Waves	1,000 GHz–10^5 GHz	3 μm–300 μm
Visible Light Waves		0.3 μm–1 μm
Red light		0.69 μm–1 μm
Orange light		0.62 μm–0.69 μm
Yellow light		0.57 μm–0.62 μm
Green light		0.52 μm–0.57 μm
Blue light		0.47 μm–0.52 μm
Violet light		0.3 μm–0.47 μm
Ultraviolet Waves		10^{-5} μm–0.3 μm
Soft X-ray Particles		10^{-5} μm–10^{-3} μm
Hard X-ray Particles		10^{-7} μm–10^{-5} μm
Gamma Ray Particles		10^{-7} μm–10^{-6} μm
Cosmic Ray Particles		10^{-12} μm–10^{-7} μm

FIGURE 4.1 Frequency Spectrum

The **frequency spectrum** is divided into parts. At the lowest end of the spectrum are the audio frequencies. These are the sound waves that we can hear. The human ear is able to detect changes in air pressure and interpret them as sounds having a pitch. These changes are known as **sound pressure levels (SPLs)**. We hear a flute as having a higher pitch than a bass viola or bass tuba because a flute vibrates at a higher frequency than a bass viola string; hence, it is placed higher on the frequency spectrum.

Engineers describe sounds according to both their frequencies and wavelengths. Frequency is measured in cycles per second, which are called **hertz (Hz)**. Low-frequency sounds may be in the neighborhood of 30 to 40 Hz and are almost inaudible, and high-frequency sounds are in the range of 8,000 to 10,000 cycles, or Hz. The range of human hearing is roughly from 16 Hz to almost 20 kHz (kilohertz).

Wave forms are described by their length. Some wavelengths are very large—about 100 kilometers—from a given point on one wave to the corresponding point on the next wave. (See Figure 4.2A.) Others are so small that the wave measures only a few millionths of a meter, end to end. (See Figure 4.2B.) The common measures of wavelength are the kilometer, meter, centimeter, millimeter, and micrometer. (See Figure 4.3.)

FIGURE 4.2
Wavelengths

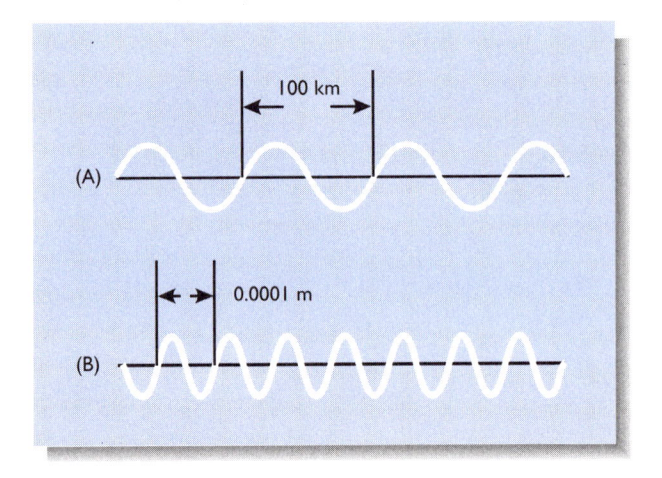

Positioned next on the frequency spectrum are **radio waves**, a form of **electromagnetic waves**. They range from very low-frequency signals (3 kHz) to extremely high-frequency signals (300 GHz). The human ear is not sensitive to these levels or types of frequency, but radio waves are the basis for radio and television broadcasting.

Positioned above radio frequencies are **infrared waves**, which are in the range of 1,000 GHz. Our bodies can feel infrared waves as heat on the skin. Above infrared on the spectrum are the **visible light frequencies**. The lowest visible frequencies produce red light; then come orange, yellow, green, blue, and finally violet. The human eye is sensitive to this part of the frequency spectrum.

Going higher on the spectrum are the **ultraviolet (uV) waves**. Although we are not aware of waves at this frequency, their effects are felt by anyone who has been sun

FIGURE 4.3 Abbreviations and Measurements

Multiple			Prefix	Symbol
1 000 000 000	=	10^9	giga	G
1 000 000	=	10^6	mega	M
1 000	=	10^3	kilo	k
100	=	10^2	hecto	h
10	=	10^1	deka	da
1	=	10^0		
0.1	=	10^{-1}	deci	d
0.01	=	10^{-2}	centi	c
0.001	=	10^{-3}	milli	m
0.000.0001	=	10^{-6}	micro	μ
0.000.000.001	=	10^{-9}	nano	n
0.000.000.000.001	=	10^{-12}	pico	p

Terms That Describe Time:

Seconds	1	s
Milliseconds	1/1 000	ms
Microseconds	1/1 000 000	μs
Nanoseconds	1/1 000 000 000	ns
Picoseconds	1/1 000 000 000 000	ps

Terms That Describe Distance:

Meter	=	1	m
Centimeter	=	1/ 100	cm
Millimeter	=	1/1 000	mm
Micrometer	=	1/1 000 000 (micron)	μm

Terms That Describe Frequency:

		Cycle Per Second	
Hertz	=	1	Hz
Kilohertz	=	1 000	kHz
Megahertz	=	1 000 000	MHz
Gigahertz	=	1 000 000 000	GHz

burned at the beach on an overcast day. This phenomenon occurs because uV waves can penetrate cloud cover.

Still higher on the frequency spectrum are **X-rays, gamma rays**, and finally **cosmic rays**. These have wavelengths as small as one millionth of a meter (one micron). It is both the frequency and the wavelength that distinguish X-rays from light rays, or radio waves from audible sounds.

An understanding of the frequency spectrum is useful because it allows us to categorize wave patterns and differentiate between them. A great deal of time and research has been spent on certain areas of the sound spectrum, in particular the range of the human voice. (See Figure 4.4.) Most of the energy emitted by the human voice is concentrated within the 300 to 3,000 Hz range, allowing intelligible human voices to be transmitted over a system capable of handling this range. Virtually all telephone equipment is designed to pick up, transmit, amplify, and receive sounds between 300 and 3,000 Hz. At the same time, telephone circuitry is designed to exclude sounds outside this range, limiting the use of frequencies beyond 3,000 Hz to switching purposes.

FIGURE 4.4
Human Voice Spectrum

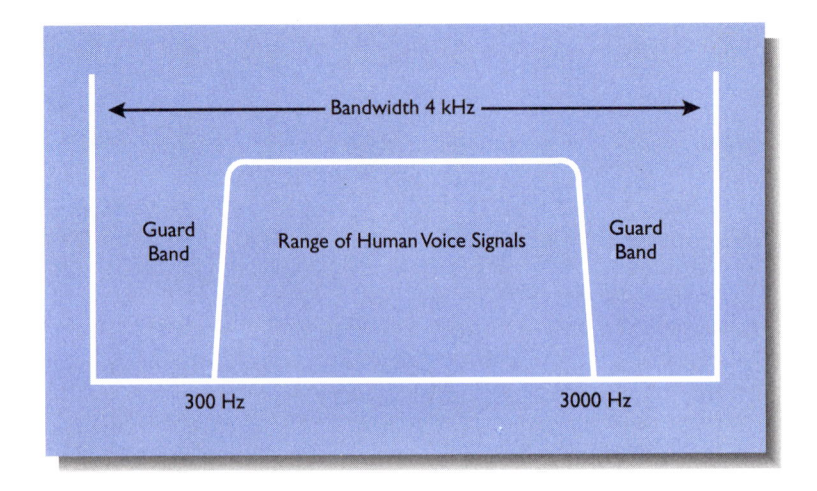

Bandwidth 4 kHz

Guard Band — Range of Human Voice Signals — Guard Band

300 Hz — 3000 Hz

EVALUATING TRANSMISSION CHANNELS

Communications channels, whether they are a twisted pair of copper wires, a microwave link, or a broadcast circuit, possess their own unique attributes. Circuits differ in their ability to transmit data, and their speed and capacity are a function of their physical and electronic characteristics. Because the communications link is vital, the reader should understand the criteria by which links are evaluated. The major characteristics that are evaluated when comparing communications channels are:

- Bandwidth
- Transmission rate
- Direction of data flow
- Medium or circuitry used
- Circuit conditioning

The range of frequencies in a circuit is known as its **bandwidth**. The bandwidth of a signal includes all of the frequencies transmitted within the band. Conversely, the bandwidth of a receiving device is the range of frequencies that it may receive and process. In human voice transmission, a basic bandwidth of 2,700 Hz (the difference between the 300 and 3,000 Hz limits of the range) is necessary to transmit intelligible communication. Telephone circuits are therefore provided with a nominal 4,000-cycle bandwidth. The extra space is provided to prevent interference from adjacent channels and is called the guard band, shown in Figure 4.4.

If several telephone channels are to be established on one circuit, then each channel must have a bandwidth of 4,000 Hz. A television set, for example, must be designed to handle all frequencies within a 6 MHz range because each TV channel requires a 6 MHz bandwidth to include both the picture and sound. The electrical characteristics of a circuit, including resistance, capacitance, and other factors, greatly affect bandwidth. The greater the bandwidth of a circuit, the greater its capacity to handle information.

A second measure of a circuit's capability is the rate at which data may be sent over it. Data transmission rate is measured in either the baud rate or **bps (bits per second). Baud rate** is based on the speed at which a signal changes states. Bps indicates how many bits can be transmitted over a channel in one second. Narrow bandwidth channels may be able to handle only 300 bits of information per second. Wide-band circuits, on the other hand, may be able to handle 9,600 bps or more. Obviously, the higher the baud or bps rate, the greater the ability of a channel to move data.

Another means of evaluating circuits is by the direction of data flow. Some circuits may be made to accept a flow in one direction only, whereas others can simultaneously send and receive data. Three common forms of directionally related signal flow are described below. These designations are often seen on terminals, modems, and other communications devices.

Simplex Operation

A **simplex circuit** is capable only of sending or receiving data. (See Figure 4.5.) The all-too-familiar "This is your principal speaking," heard over a high school loudspeaker system, is an example of simplex communication. This is one-direction-only communication, as students cannot answer back over the public address system. Radio and television broadcasts are examples of simplex operations, as are news wire services. These systems deliver information in one direction only.

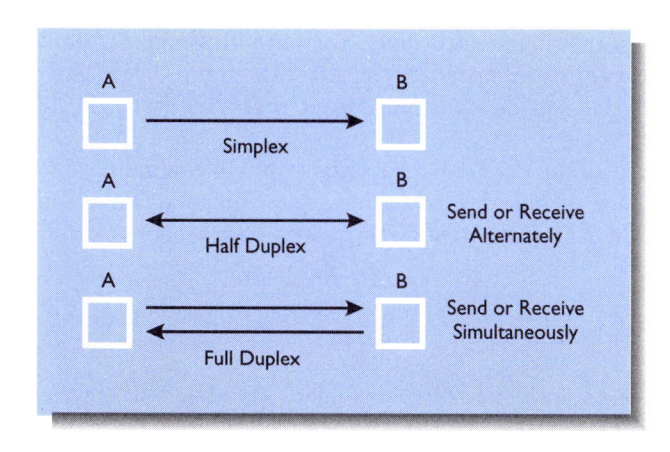

FIGURE 4.5
Communications Channels

Half-Duplex Operation

A **half-duplex circuit (HDX)** is designed to allow the sending or receiving of data alternately. A ship-to-shore radio or citizen band communication is an example of half duplex. Either the radio operator speaks, while those on shore listen, or vice versa. A computer may send data to a terminal, or receive data, but not at the same time if it is operating at half duplex.

Full-Duplex Operation

A **full-duplex circuit (FDX)** allows data to be sent and received simultaneously. It is the most flexible arrangement of the three described. The telephone is a good example of a full-duplex audio system. It allows you to talk on the line even if the person at the other end is also speaking. In full duplex, a computer can send data to a terminal for display while, at the same time, the operator keys in information that is sent back to the computer.

The physical communications medium also defines the characteristics of the channel. A variety of media can be used to transmit information. One common medium is the hard-wire circuit. In this arrangement, information is sent over a metallic pair of conductors in the form of an electrical signal. In radio transmissions, signals are sent by broadcasting electromagnetic waves. In fiber optics, a beam of light is sent through a fine glass filament housed in a sheath with other filaments. Each medium possesses its own unique characteristics. These and other media are described in more detail in Chapter 6.

The **conditioning** of a circuit greatly affects its capabilities. Conditioning is done by changing the electrical characteristics or by changing the position or spacing of conductors. Some circuits are conditioned to reduce selected frequencies, a process known as **attenuation**. Your stereo set probably has a low-frequency attenuation button. Activating this circuit filters out signals below 50 Hz, thus reducing turntable rumble.

The amount of attenuation is measured in **dB** units. The term dB stands for **decibel**, a unit for expressing the relative intensity of a signal. If a circuit has a 10 dB attenuation at 100 Hz, it means that sounds are reduced by 10 decibel units in the 100 Hz range.

We have described only some of the major characteristics used in evaluating communications channels. Other more technical factors, such as rejection of unauthorized signals and error detection software, are often used to describe communications circuits.

HYBRID CIRCUITS

A discussion of communications channels and direction of flow would not be complete without a description of **hybrid circuits**, two- and four-wire circuits, and **repeaters** (also known as line amplifiers), as well as **echo suppression** equipment.

The basic telephone system, described in Chapter 2, contains a transmitter and receiver wired together in a simple two-wire circuit using induction coils. In this arrangement, information can be simultaneously sent and received by the person at each end of the line. Two-wire circuits, though practical for short distances, are not satisfactory for sending voice and data over long distances. Such simple systems are prone to generating echoes, and the signal strength deteriorates over distance. You have probably made long-distance telephone calls in which you hear an annoying echo of your voice on the line. Sometimes you can hardly hear the person at the other end. Echoes and deteriorating signal strength over long distances have been problems for telephone companies. Engineers have corrected these difficulties by designing hybrid transformers, composed of four-wire circuits, repeaters, and echo suppressors.

Modern telephone systems use hybrid transformers located at the central office. (See Figure 4.6.) The hybrid transformer splits the two-wire circuit from the subscriber's local loop into two two-wire circuits. One two-wire circuit is dedicated solely to sending a signal from east to west, and the second two-wire circuit is dedicated solely to sending signals from west to east. Another hybrid transformer, located at the other end of the line, recombines the four-wire circuit into a two-wire loop.

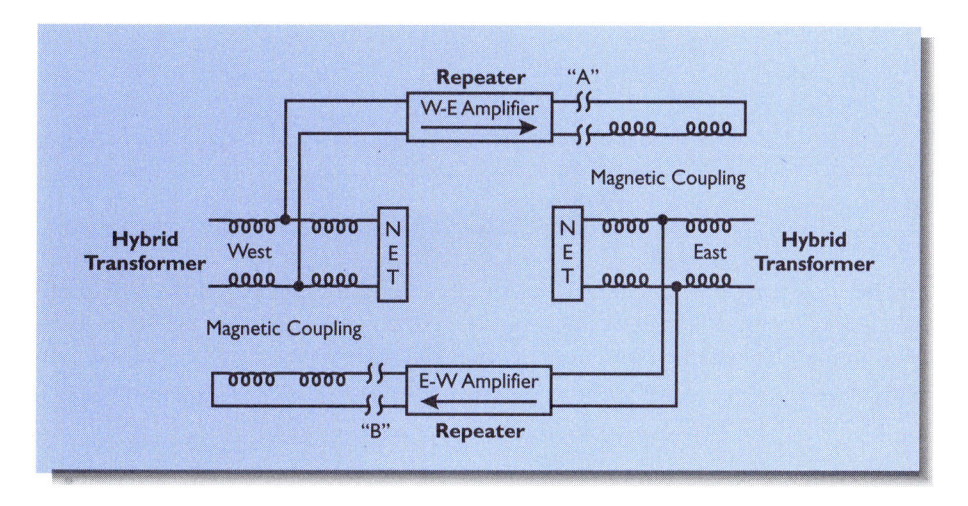

FIGURE 4.6 Repeater Amplifiers

Separating the sending and receiving signals into different circuits in full-duplex operations has many advantages. Such arrangements enable repeaters to be placed in the line to boost signal strength. A repeater is a line amplifier placed in a communications circuit to increase its signal strength. (See Figure 4.7.) Because of the inclusion of repeaters, the strength of a signal at the end of a long-distance circuit may appear to be just as loud as at the point of origin. (See Figure 4.8.)

You can understand how a repeater works if you think of a row of people standing in line spaced 20 feet apart. You say something to the first person in line. That person then repeats the message to the next person in line. As your message is relayed from person to person, its diminished strength is boosted at regular intervals, because each person outputs the message at the same strength. Someone listening to your words at the end of the line would hear them at virtually the same strength as the original utterance.

FIGURE 4.7
Repeater. This repeater, or line amplifier, boosts signal strength.

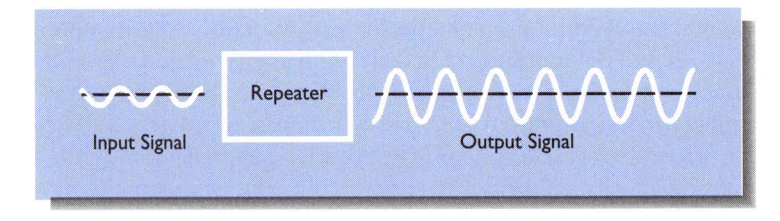

FIGURE 4.8
Series of Repeaters. Several repeaters may be placed in a circuit when long distances are involved.

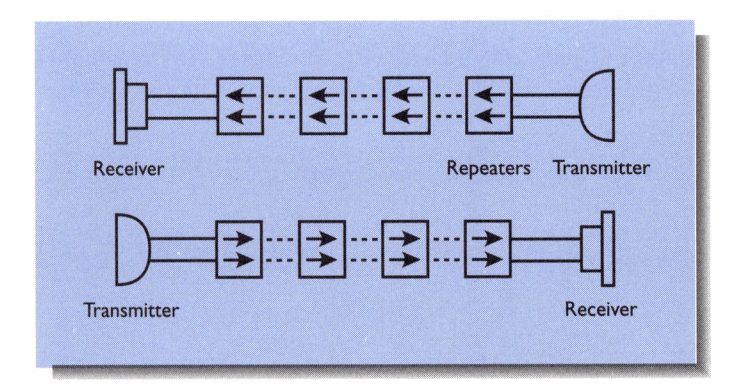

Finally, four-wire circuits allow echo suppressors to be placed on the line. Echo suppressors reject signals in one direction while passing those going in the other. Thus, voice or digital data can be boosted many times by repeaters down the line with virtually no echo.

SERIAL AND PARALLEL TRANSMISSION OF DATA

Information can be sent over communications channels in either of two fashions: serial or parallel transmission. The arrangement chosen affects the amount of information that can be sent over a circuit in a given period of time. There are also substantial cost differences in hardware between serial and parallel transmission. Early devices, such as Teletype machines, relied mainly on serial transmission, whereas many modern computers use parallel transmission between the CPU and output devices.

Serial Transmission

In **serial transmission** only one channel, or electrical pathway, is used, and all data are sent in sequence. (See Figure 4.9.) Even though it is slow, serial transmission is used for virtually all communications involving distance. You will learn in Chapter 5 that letters and numbers can be reduced to a binary bit pattern. These bits can be sent in serial fashion over a circuit. (See Figure 4.9A.) This method allows characters (bytes) to be transmitted one at a time until the entire message is sent.

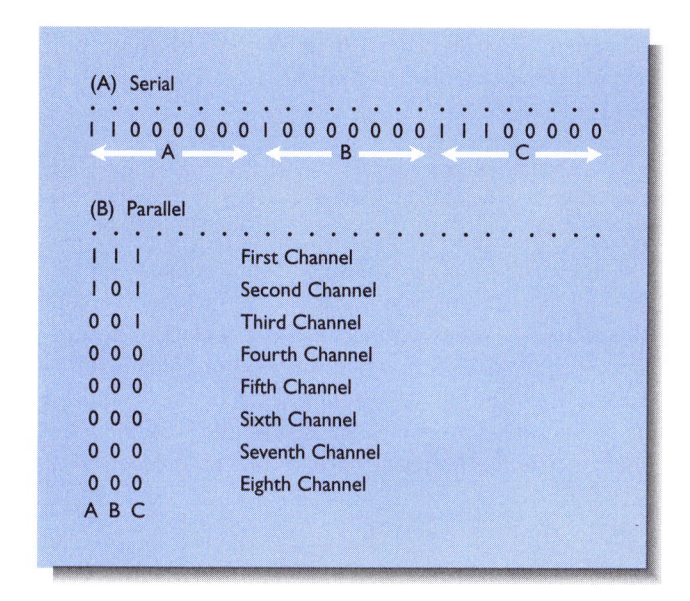

```
(A) Serial
. . . . . . . . . . . . . . . . . . . . . . .
1 1 0 0 0 0 0 0 1 0 0 0 0 0 0 0 1 1 1 0 0 0 0 0
  ←— A —→   ←— B —→   ←— C —→

(B) Parallel
. . . . . . . . . . . . . . . . . . . . . . .
1  1  1        First Channel
1  0  1        Second Channel
0  0  1        Third Channel
0  0  0        Fourth Channel
0  0  0        Fifth Channel
0  0  0        Sixth Channel
0  0  0        Seventh Channel
0  0  0        Eighth Channel
A  B  C
```

FIGURE 4.9
Serial and Parallel Transmission

Serial transmission is much like a column of soldiers crossing a river using a footbridge wide enough for only one person at a time. It would take a substantial period of time to move 100 soldiers across the bridge one at a time. However, it would require only a narrow, inexpensive bridge to allow access to the other side.

Serial transmission has been used for many years because it requires only simple and relatively inexpensive equipment at both the transmitting and receiving ends. Its biggest limitation is its low speed. It does not take advantage of the full bandwidth of many circuits.

Parallel Transmission

In **parallel transmission** the bit pattern representing one letter or number (byte) is simultaneously sent over several parallel channels. (See Figure 4.9B.) If we return to our analogy of the soldiers crossing the river, we see that we could greatly speed up the flow of troops by widening the bridge so that they can cross eight abreast. Parallel transmission uses this principle.

An 8-bit pattern representing one character (byte) can be transmitted simultaneously over eight channels. If 16 channels are used, then two bytes can be sent at the same instant. Thus, a 16-bit parallel transmission would be 16 times faster than a single-channel serial transmission.

Most modern computers take advantage of this fact in their design. Data are routed throughout the CPU and secondary storage devices in a parallel mode. Some computers are equipped to send data to printers in the parallel format. The high internal processing and transmission speed of many computers is obtainable because 8, 16, or even 32 parallel circuits are used to move data. Although parallel transmission increases the hardware cost, the expense is justified by the higher speed. Almost all communications systems use 8-bit circuits, while 16- and 32-bit circuits are used internally by computers.

TRANSMISSION MODES

Timing is an important factor in data transmission. By carefully timing signals, the volume of data sent over a channel can be greatly increased. Two systems have evolved: one based on carefully timed pulses and the other without regard to a clock. The simplest arrangement, known as stop-start, or asynchronous transmission, places information on the circuit without regard to timing. It is generally used in low-speed systems. The other arrangement, synchronous transmission, places information on the line at carefully timed intervals. It is used for high-speed data transmission.

Asynchronous Transmission

One of the earliest methods of sending information over a channel was an asynchronous arrangement. (See Figure 4.10.) In **asynchronous transmission** one start bit (zero pulse) is sent at the beginning of each byte or character transmitted, thereby alerting the circuitry that a pulse pattern, representing a character, is about to be sent. After the character is transmitted, a stop pulse is sent, indicating the end of the character. All characters sent over the line are embedded in start and stop bits, without regard to the spacing or distance between characters. This system requires ten pulses, including the eight pulses of data. The advantage of the system is that the receiving equipment can be free-running and does not have to be synchronized with the transmitting unit. Such equipment is relatively inexpensive to manufacture and does not require elaborate clock systems.

Synchronous Transmission

Very soon the limitations of the asynchronous system were realized because each 8-bit byte required two additional bits of overhead. This need wasted 20 percent of the transmission time sending non-intelligence information. This situation is avoided with **synchronous transmission** systems. (See Figure 4.11.) In the synchronous system, both the transmitter and receiver are locked in a carefully timed operation. Either precision dual clocks are installed or clock signals are sent over the line. Intelligence bits are sent only when triggered by the clock pulses, and they are received on equipment carefully timed to the same clock. Because both devices operate in the same phase, no stop-start pulses are required, and a high volume of data can be transmitted.

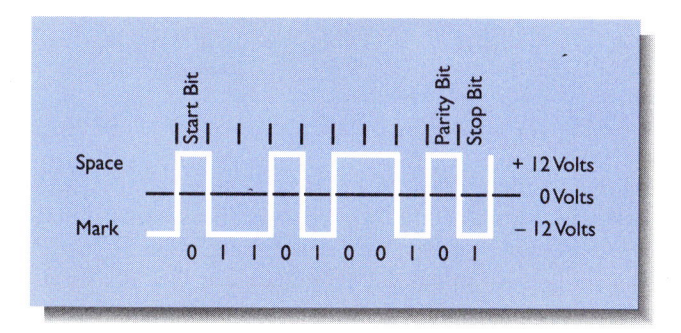

FIGURE 4.10
Asynchronous Transmission

FIGURE 4.11
Synchronous Transmission. Units of data are always sent in relationship to timed pulses.

To better understand the differences between the synchronous and asynchronous systems, visualize two people throwing a ball back and forth over a high wall. Neither player can see the other. To time a catch, the person throwing the ball must cry "ready" before each throw. Once the ball is received, the catcher must yell "okay." This arrangement limits the number of throws per hour because each player must wait to hear the other call out. However, if each player possesses a carefully synchronized watch, a ball can be thrown back and forth at five-second intervals, or even less, greatly speeding up the number of throws per hour. Thus, synchronous transmission is used as the primary mode in high-speed data transmission equipment, but it requires more expensive hardware than asynchronous devices.

DATA ENCODING

The purpose of data transmission equipment is to place messages on a circuit, send them over a distance, and then remove the information and make it available at the receiving end. (See Figure 4.12.) These functions involve data **encoding** and **decoding**.

FIGURE 4.12 Data Encoding and Decoding

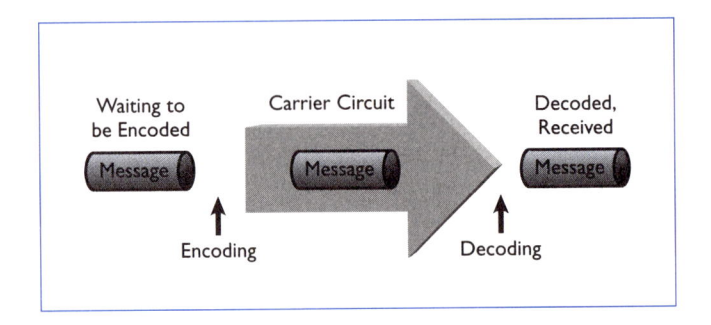

Encoding should not be confused with **encryption**. In encryption, secret messages are coded into symbols or words with scrambled letters that can be understood only by those possessing the encryption key. The key consists of the algorithm, or set of rules, that transforms the message into a meaningful communication. This process is known as **decryption**. Military and government communications are often sent as encrypted data to prevent foreign agents from reading the contents of the message.

The function of data encoding is to place a message on a medium in a manner that facilitates communication in the most efficient manner, as opposed to sending secret messages. Information can be encoded in different ways, depending on the medium of transmission. Probably the best known medium in our history was the method used to let Paul Revere know how the British were coming. Is there anyone who does not know what "one if by land and two if by sea" means?

A modern-day example of encoding and decoding is the telephone. When you pick up the phone and talk to a friend, your sound waves are encoded on an electrical signal in analog form. They are encoded as rising and falling electrical voltages that are sent over the line to the receiver. At that end, they are decoded, that is, converted back to audible sound waves.

For short distances, a simple on-off circuit can be used to encode information in a digital or binary form. An open switch (no pulse) represents a zero. A closed switch (a pulse) represents a one. By opening and closing the switch repeatedly, a string of pulses, called a **pulse train**, could be used to send a flow of digital data. (See Figure 4.13A.) A simple arrangement of opening and closing a circuit would not work for long distances because of resistance on the line. (See Figure 4.13B.) The clearly defined pulse train in Figure 4.13A would probably look like the distorted pattern in Figure 4.13C if the signal were transmitted over a long distance. It would also become distorted if the pulses were sent at a very high speed. It is therefore necessary to find a more practical means of encoding data, one that would allow information to be sent with great accuracy over long distances and at high speed.

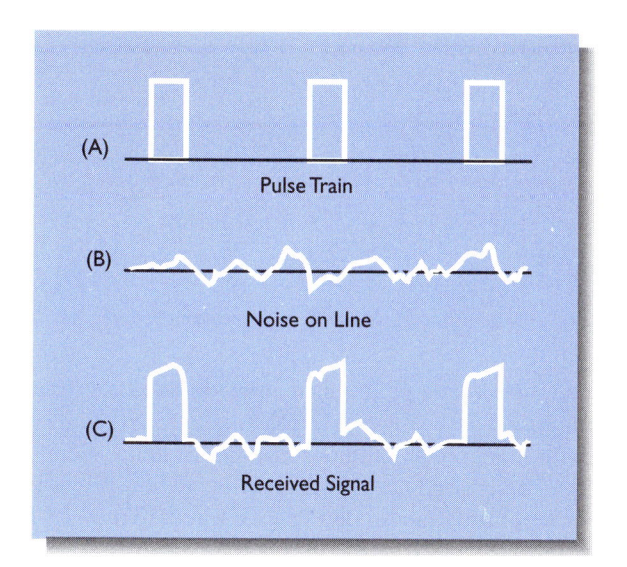

FIGURE 4.13
Pulse Train and the Effects of Noise

(A) Pulse Train

(B) Noise on Line

(C) Received Signal

MODULATION

In the early years of radio, information was sent by Morse code. A string of pulses was transmitted over the air. But radio engineers quickly discovered that transmission speeds were limited by how quickly the operator's hand could move. Further, the human voice and music could not be encoded in this system. The problem was solved by transmitting a modulated carrier wave frequency. The process became known as **amplitude modulation (AM)** and quickly became the standard of broadcasting in the 1920s. It is important to understand how frequency carriers work and how they are modulated because they hold the key to much data transmission hardware and software.

Amplitude Modulation

An **unmodulated carrier wave** is shown in Figure 4.14. You will recognize this as a sine wave, or rising and falling pattern, which was discussed in Chapter 2. Carrier waves are generated by circuits called oscillators. An unmodulated carrier wave is simply a tone or regular pattern of rising and falling voltages that does not contain or carry any message or communication. It is much like a stuck automobile horn that is creating an annoying sound. However, horns are used to convey meaningful information. A driver may toot the horn to signal a friend or press the horn button repeatedly to warn of impending danger.

FIGURE 4.14 Unmodulated Carrier Waves

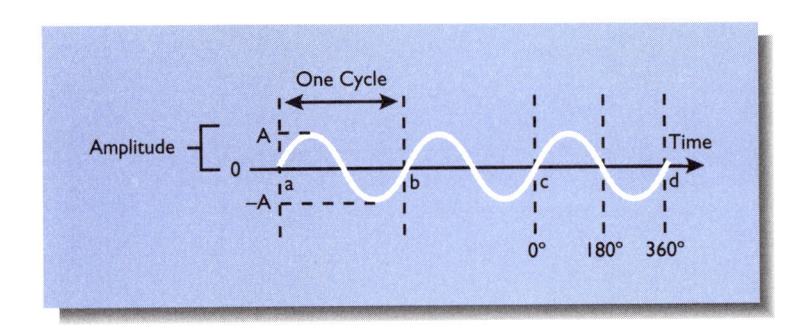

Broadcast stations use this concept to transmit programs to an audience. AM radio stations broadcast signals by modulating a carrier wave, which is generated at a frequency assigned by the Federal Communications Commission (FCC). Then a second signal, representing voice or music, is impressed or encoded on the carrier, generating a combined signal known as an amplitude modulated carrier wave. Figure 4.15 illustrates an unmodulated carrier wave, the voice signal that is impressed on it, and the resulting combined amplitude modulated carrier wave. At the receiving end the carrier wave is demodulated, and an accurate replica of the original signal recreated. AM modulation is widely used in broadcasting.

FIGURE 4.15 Voice Modulated Carrier Wave

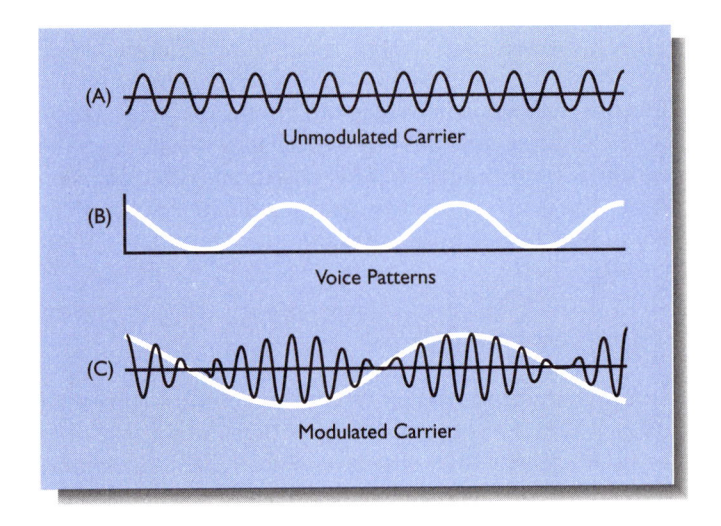

The same amplitude modulation principles used for voice and music can be applied to impressing digital signals on a carrier wave. (See Figure 4.16.) Digital encoding devices generate a carrier frequency that is sent over radio waves, telephone lines, microwave circuits, or other channels. A binary pulse train, representing digital data, is impressed on a carrier, thus modulating it and enabling digital pulse trains to be sent over great distances. At the receiving end the carrier is demodulated, and a digital pulse train is recreated that accurately reflects the original signal.

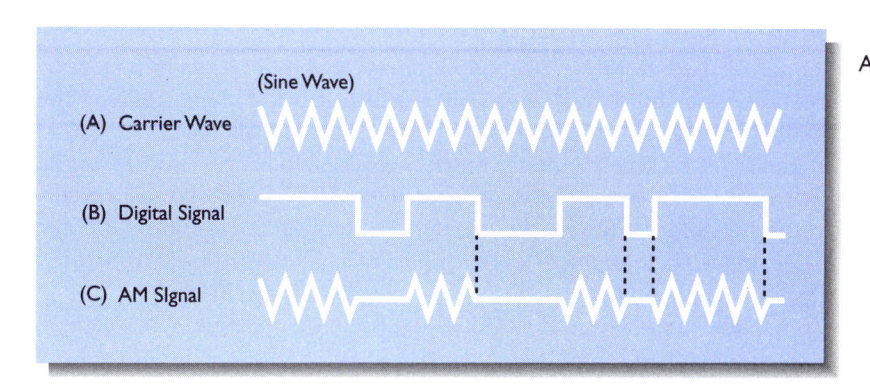

FIGURE 4.16
Amplitude Modulated Carrier Wave

(A) Carrier Wave (Sine Wave)

(B) Digital Signal

(C) AM Signal

Modems

A **modem**, or **modulator/demodulator**, is an electronic device that connects a terminal or computer to a communications line. Modems convert the binary bit pattern generated by computers or terminals into electrical signals that can be transmitted over telephone lines or other analog communications circuits. They rely on modulating a carrier wave. The method by which this is done is explained in detail in Chapter 5.

There are many different types of modems on the market. They may use different types of modulation principles, but they are always connected between a communications link and a computer or terminal. (See Figure 4.17.) The most common slow-speed modems use frequency modulation, while faster modems rely on phase modulation principles.

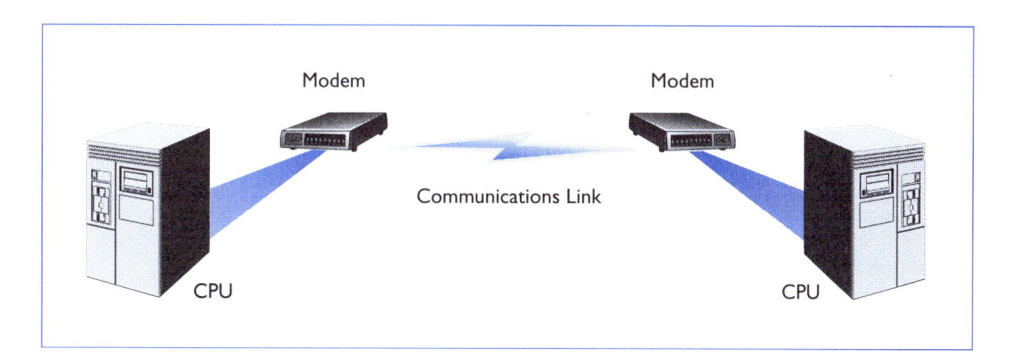

FIGURE 4.17 Modem. A modem is used between a CPU or terminal and a communications link.

Frequency Modulation

One of the weaknesses of AM transmissions is that they are prone to noise pickup and static. Changes in signal strength at the transmitter also affect the quality of AM broadcasts and digital transmissions. The allocation of available AM frequencies led to the development of **frequency modulation (FM)**. FM is used to modulate a carrier with either analog or digital data. It does not rely on increasing and decreasing the amplitude or strength of the transmitted carrier as does AM. Instead, the amplitude of the sine wave remains the same, but the frequency of the carrier is changed.

Figure 4.18 illustrates an unmodulated FM carrier, which looks very similar to the unmodulated AM carrier. The figure shows a digital signal being impressed on the carrier; this is done by modulating the frequency, not the amplitude. Each digital pulse representing a one changes the frequency of the carrier. As long as a one is impressed on the carrier, its frequency remains the same, say, 1,000 Hz. When the one is removed, the frequency changes to 1,200 Hz. In the figure, a high-pitched tone represents a zero and a low-pitched tone a one. Note that the height or amplitude of the carrier remains the same; only its frequency changes. FM is widely used in data transmission and is sometimes referred to as **frequency shift keying (FSK).**

FIGURE 4.18
Frequency Modulated Carrier Wave

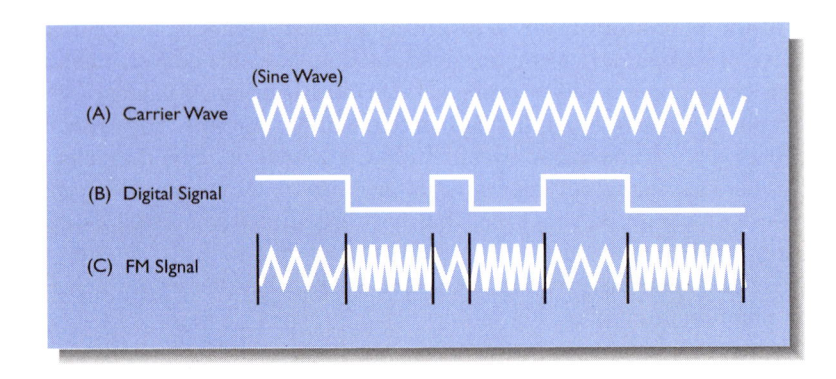

At the receiving end, the changes in the carrier frequency are detected, and the signal is demodulated, once again recreating the same binary pulse pattern that was impressed on the transmitted carrier. FM is widely used—not only for broadcasting, but for sending digital data over circuits—because it requires simple circuitry and is less prone to atmospheric disturbances.

Phase Modulation

For some applications still another means of modulating the carrier is used. In **phase modulation (PM)**, the phase of the transmitted cycle is changed to represent data. (See Figure 4.19.) In PM a carrier wave is transmitted, just as in AM or FM. However, the phase, or point where a complete cycle is begun, changes when the carrier is modulated. It is this change in phase, or beginning of a new wave cycle, that actually carries the information. At the receiving end a detector recognizes the change in the phase of the carrier. Thus, the original signal is demodulated and recreated in its original form.

FIGURE 4.19
Phase Modulation (PM)

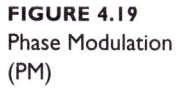

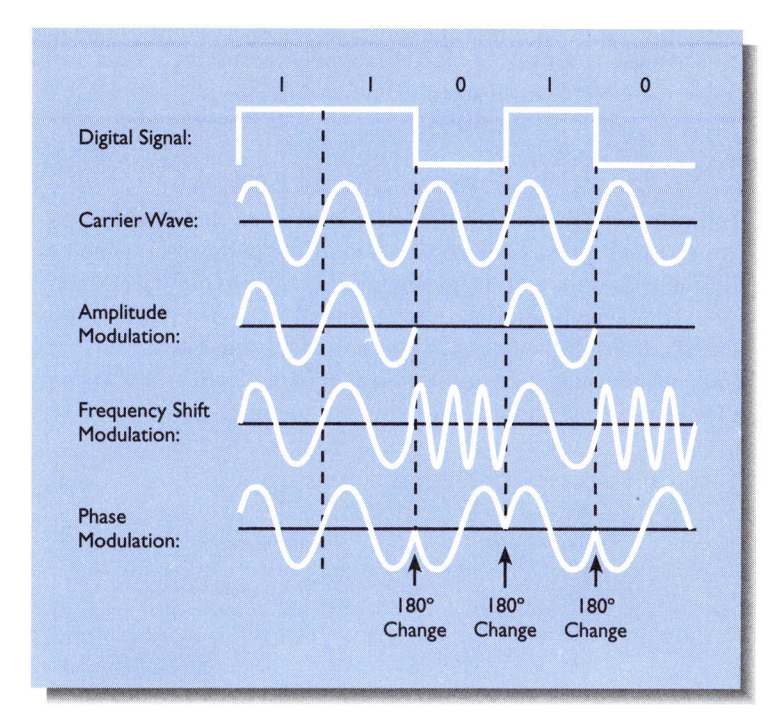

Several different phase modulation techniques are in use. In the example shown in Figure 4.19, two phases are shown, 0 and 180 degrees. Other systems are in use that rely on 0, 90, 180, and 270 degree phase shifts. Still other systems use eight phases. The technical differences are unimportant here. What is important to understand is that differences in phase shift can be used to encode digital data on a carrier wave. The advantage of the four- and eight-phase systems is speed. Much more data can be transmitted using a four- or eight-phase modulated carrier than a two-phase carrier.

The modulation techniques described above play an important role in the design, not only of modems, but also of communications devices known as multiplexers. Both modems and multiplexers are described in more detail in Chapter 5. However, to understand how these devices work, we need to study the concepts of multiplexing.

MULTIPLEXING PRINCIPLES

In the early days of communications, there was relatively little demand for long distance services. Most businesses served a relatively small number of local customers, many of whom were connected to the same central office. As the number of users increased, it soon became evident that communications channels would be overloaded. Telephone lines, Teletype circuits, and other communications utilities could not provide an individual pair of wires for each call that was placed. This fact led to the development of methods of sharing existing communications circuits with many users. Today a variety of devices, known as multiplexers and data concentrators, enable many customers to share one circuit.

Multiplexers

Multiplexers (muxes) are electronic devices that enable two or more channels to exist on one circuit. They establish multiple pathways on one line. (See Figure 4.20.) Multiplexers reduce transmission costs because one circuit can be shared by many users. For example, several dozen terminals may need to access one computer in a distant city. It would be expensive to provide a separate circuit for each terminal. If all terminals are connected to a multiplexer at one end, and the computer to a multiplexer at the other, then line requirements are reduced.

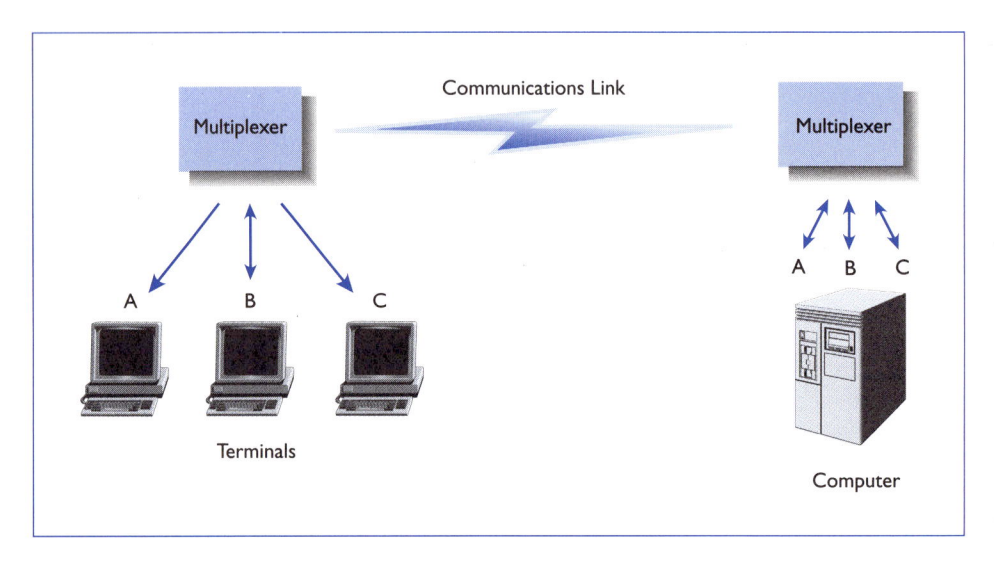

FIGURE 4.20 Multiplexer Circuit

Multiplexing principles not only are applied to sharing communications channels between distant points, but are also used in connecting computer input/output devices to central processors. By multiplexing, many low-speed terminals can be connected to a high-speed central computer. These sharing principles are fundamental to an understanding of communications.

There are two common means of sharing a circuit. In **time division multiplexing (TDM)**, each user is allocated a small fraction of the time on the circuit. In **frequency division multiplexing (FDM)**, each terminal shares the line but uses a different bandwidth to send or receive data.

Frequency Division Multiplexing

One common means of sharing a circuit is by dividing the bandwidth into several frequencies or subcarriers. In **frequency division multiplexing (FDM)** each channel on the circuit is created by assigning a group of frequencies within the band. These frequencies are spaced far enough apart so that they do not interfere with one another. The difference is referred to as a **guard band**. In Figure 4.21, four terminals are connected to a multiplexer at one end of the line. The multiplexer assigns a different frequency to each device. At the receiving end, another multiplexer separates the signals into four distinct channels. This arrangement enables different information to be sent over each of the four channels at the same time.

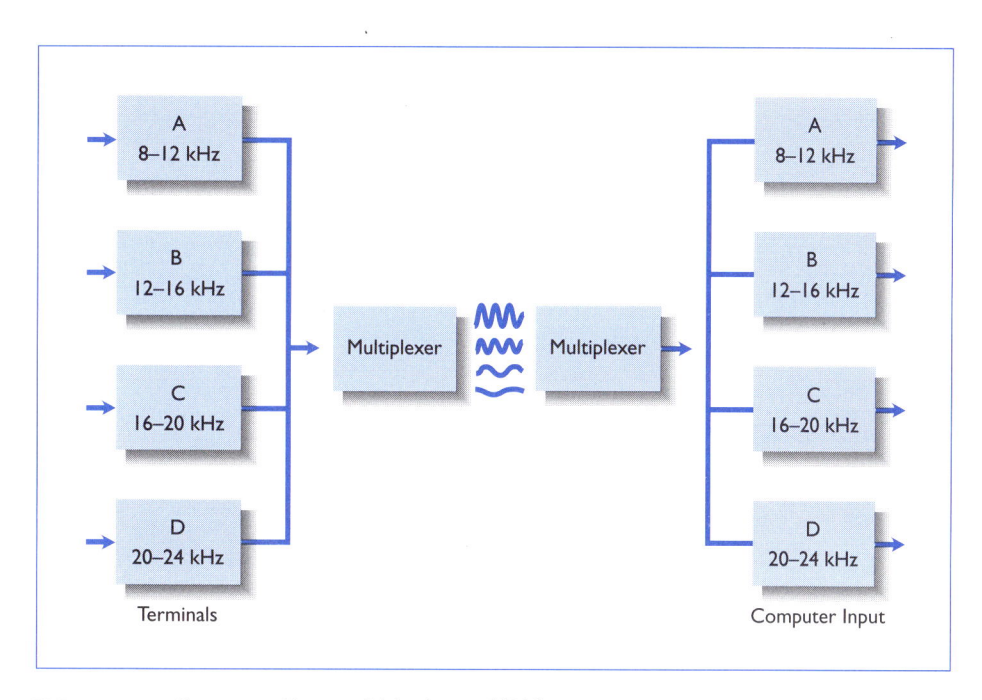

FIGURE 4.21 Frequency Division Multiplexing (FDM)

The FDM principle is used in the design of some slow-speed modems. The reader will often see references to Bell-type modem designations. These labels originally identified equipment manufactured by a Bell subsidiary, Western Electric Company. Today, these modem types are manufactured by many different firms and may carry the Bell reference, even though they may not be sold by the Bell Telephone Company. Most modern modems are identified by CCITT designations, rather than Bell designations. Industry standard designations are discussed in Chapter 5.

By assigning different frequencies, it is possible to provide full-duplex operation over one line. Figure 4.22 illustrates how one channel is divided between a send and a receive signal. One frequency, 1,170 Hz, is assigned to transmit information from point A to point B, and a second frequency, 2,125 Hz, is assigned to send information from point B to point A.

FIGURE 4.22
Bell 103/113 Channel Assignments

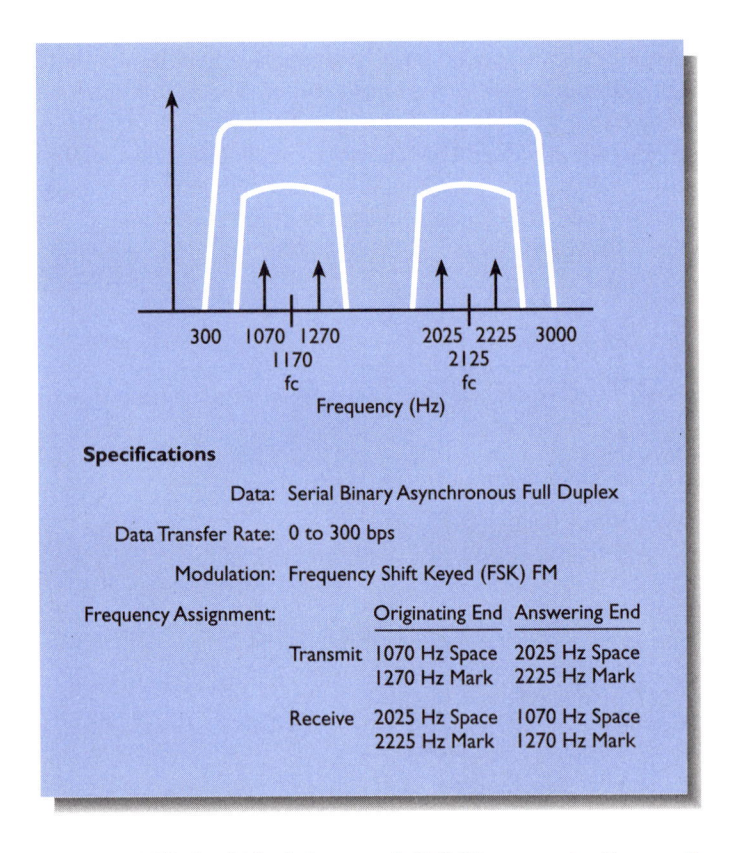

```
                    300  1070 1270    2025 2225 3000
                           1170         2125
                            fc           fc
                           Frequency (Hz)
```

Specifications

Data:	Serial Binary Asynchronous Full Duplex	
Data Transfer Rate:	0 to 300 bps	
Modulation:	Frequency Shift Keyed (FSK) FM	
Frequency Assignment:	Originating End	Answering End
Transmit	1070 Hz Space	2025 Hz Space
	1270 Hz Mark	2225 Hz Mark
Receive	2025 Hz Space	1070 Hz Space
	2225 Hz Mark	1270 Hz Mark

In practice, the frequency 1,170 Hz is shifted down to 1,070 Hz to send a "space," representing a zero, and it is shifted up to 1,270 Hz to send a "mark," or one. Where B sends to A, the 2,125 Hz is dropped to 2,025 Hz to send a space and shifted up to 2,225 Hz for a mark. Thus, simultaneous full-duplex operation is ensured without conflict.

Time Division Multiplexing

A second means of multiplexing several devices on one circuit is through **time division multiplexing (TDM)**. In TDM, bytes from several devices are interleaved and sent over a line in sequence. In effect, each gets its own time slot. In Figure 4.23, devices A, B, C, D, and E are connected to a single line via a multiplexer, which interleaves the data and sends them to the second multiplexer, which again sorts them out into five separate channels. Thus, both ends of the channel must be equipped with time division multiplexers.

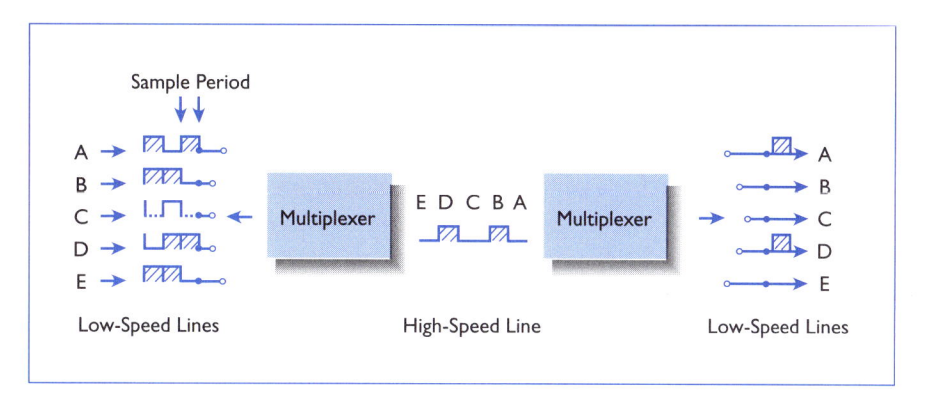

FIGURE 4.23 Time Division Multiplexing (TDM)

The difference between FDM and TDM is significant, even though they achieve the same objectives. FDM allocates different frequencies on one circuit, whereas TDM allocates different time slots. Using TDM, the more popular method, one second may be broken up into many hundreds of parts and each part allocated to a different device. Techniques such as this enable many low-speed devices to share one line without raising transmission costs.

Multiplexers are used to send vital data from orbiting spacecraft back to earth. Data on body temperatures, blood pressures, cabin temperatures, fuel supplies, electrical voltages, and more, are all sensed and then placed on one communications circuit. Each piece of data is assigned its own time slot. At the earth tracking station, another multiplexer sorts out the data and recreates a continuing stream of information.

Statistical Time Division Multiplexing

A **statistical time division multiplexer (STDM)** allocates communication line time to a group of devices, based on the activity of the devices, and has the ability to store or buffer information. It is unlikely that all terminals connected to a line will be transmitting at one time. Statistically, the odds are that one or more terminals, while connected to a circuit, may not be sending or receiving information at once. This fact is used to advantage.

Suppose a 9,600 bps circuit is available, and five 2,400 baud terminals must be connected. At first glance, it would appear that only four of the terminals can be connected to the line at one time. However, all five terminals can be serviced, using STDM principles.

This apparent increase in line capacity is achieved through the use of a buffer. A **buffer** is a circuit that stores data until it is needed later. As a practical matter, pauses or gaps exist in most transmissions and represent underutilization. These pauses can be used to support extra terminals. In the unlikely event that all five terminals must transmit at once, then the STDM's buffer holds data until line capacity is again available.

DATA CONCENTRATORS

Data concentrators condense or concentrate data emanating from several different sources. They are used where many low-speed devices must share one circuit. A data concentrator can store groups of bits emitted by low speed and then transmit them as a block at high speed. This method increases the volume of data and number of devices that can use one circuit. Data concentrators rely on STDM principles.

In both the FDM and TDM principles discussed above, it was assumed that the information to be transmitted would be available at the multiplexer at the proper instant, ready for transmission. But this is not always the case. Suppose information from a group of low-speed terminals was to be sent over one line by TDM. The operators at each keyboard would have to send keystrokes at exactly the right instant to fit their assigned time slots. This obviously would not be a practical arrangement because operators are used to typing at their own speed and timing. This problem could be resolved by using a data concentrator.

Figure 4.24 illustrates the data concentrator principle. Characters are sent to the concentrator from the terminal keyboards (or any transmitting device) without regard to timing. Once the concentrator has stored sufficient bytes from the device, it sends them over the line in their proper time slot. Concentrators differ from TDM devices by their ability to store characters and time their release for transmission.

FIGURE 4.24
Data Concentrator

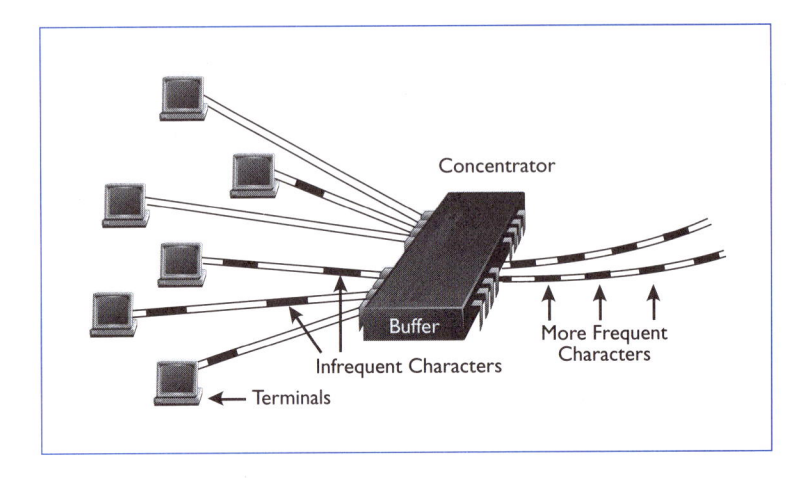

In this chapter, we reviewed some of the theories behind multiplexers, data concentrators, and transmission channels. We have seen that information can be encoded on a line in many different forms and combined with other signals for transmission efficiency. In the next chapter we will apply modulation concepts to a group of devices known as modems.

SUMMARY

Frequency and *wavelength* are used to describe sound, light, and *electromagnetic waves*. The *hertz (Hz)* is the standard measure of frequency. *Bandwidth* describes the range of frequencies that can be handled on a circuit. A *simplex circuit* is capable of only sending or receiving data. A *half-duplex circuit* can alternately send or receive data. A *full-duplex circuit* allows data to be sent and received simultaneously.

In *serial transmission* all data are sent bit by bit in sequence. In *parallel transmission* bits are sent simultaneously over several parallel channels. In *amplitude modulation (AM)* information is impressed on the carrier by changing its *amplitude*. In *frequency modulation (FM)* information is impressed on the *carrier* by changing its frequency. In *phase modulation (PM)* information is impressed on the carrier by changing the phase or point where a complete cycle is begun.

FDM divides a circuit's bandwidth into several frequencies or *subcarriers*. *TDM* divides a circuit's bandwidth into time slots and interleaves data over a line in sequence. *Data concentrators* are *multiplexers* that store bytes and release them at carefully timed intervals. A circuit is *conditioned* by modifying its electrical characteristics in order to change its transmission capability. *STDM* relies on unused line capacity to service additional devices.

Echo suppressors are placed on communications lines to diminish echoes that would interfere with communication. *Hybrid transformers* split two-wire circuits into four-wire circuits, and vice versa. *Repeaters* are placed in communications circuits to boost signal strength. The human ear converts *sound pressure levels (SPLs)* into sounds having a pitch. *Wave forms* are described by their length and may range from 100 kilometers to only a few millionths of a meter.

EXERCISES

1. List the major wave and particle forms in the frequency spectrum.
2. List some of the terms that describe frequencies.
3. Describe the major characteristics used to evaluate communications channels.
4. Summarize the three forms of data flow.
5. Describe the function of hybrid circuits.
6. Contrast serial and parallel transmission modes.
7. Contrast asynchronous and synchronous data transmission.
8. Contrast data encoding and decoding.
9. List three major forms of modulating a carrier.
10. List two common forms of multiplexing.

HANDS-ON PROJECTS

- Obtain a listing of your local radio stations and their broadcast frequencies. Review this list and determine how far apart each station is spaced.

- Visit your campus computer center and discuss data transmission. Does the center use synchronous or asynchronous transmission modes?

- Visit a local telephone office or retail outlet that sells telephone equipment. Discuss full- and half-duplex operation with a technician.

- Visit a local television station and discuss bandwidth and frequencies with an engineer. What frequency is the station assigned? How close is this frequency to that of a neighbor station?

- Visit a local computer retailer and discuss modems and frequency assignments. Look at the equipment on display and determine what type of multiplexing is used.

COMMUNICATIONS IN ACTION

CASE SOLUTION
FIDELITY BANK

The managers of Fidelity Bank recognized they had a major communications problem. As a result, they contracted with a communications consultant who developed an extensive communications system. It consists of a network that ties together all of its branches, retail merchants' point-of-sale terminals, and other banks. (See Figure 4.25.) This system also includes automatic teller machines that are connected by telephone lines at shopping centers and malls.

The heart of Fidelity's electronic banking system is a central computer with front-end processing capability located in its main office. This computer maintains customer credit records, account balances, and other data. The central computer is tied to other banks through a nationwide common-carrier network. Each branch is connected to the central computer by leased lines. (See Figure 4.26.) Terminals and a remote computer with disk storage are located in each branch.

Many of Fidelity's customers are retailers whose customers use credit cards. Under the new system, when a retailer wishes to check a customer's credit, the credit card is inserted into a point-of-sale terminal, which automatically dials the central computer and checks the transaction. Authorization is then either issued or withheld. In a similar manner, customers may make a withdrawal during non-business hours by using a remote ATM. To do so, the customer keys in an identification number and password, inserts the bank card, and is able to make cash withdrawals or deposits.

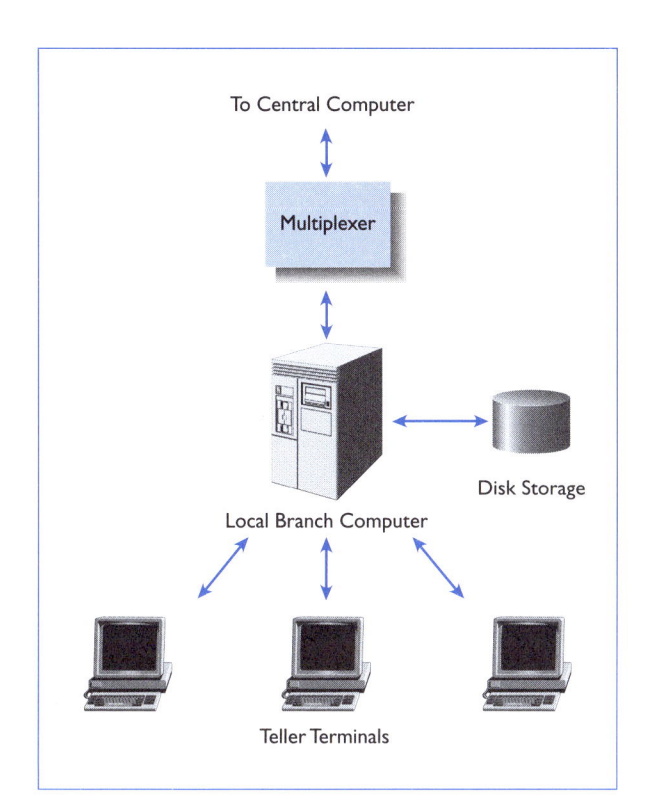

FIGURE 4.25
Electronic Banking System

Some businesses pay their employees through the bank's payroll-processing system. Each payday, employers transmit payroll information to the bank over dial-up telephone lines. Then the bank either prepares and mails checks or credits the funds directly to the employee's account. Some customers use a similar system to authorize the bank to pay their bills for them.

Using the electronic funds transfer system, Fidelity is able to move large amounts of money between points in the network electronically. The system has reduced the need for messengers and the U.S. Postal Service. The system is efficient, enabling merchants to check credit quickly and easily. Employers have reduced their payroll-processing costs. Customers have the benefit of 24-hour banking services. All this has helped make Fidelity a leading bank in the community.

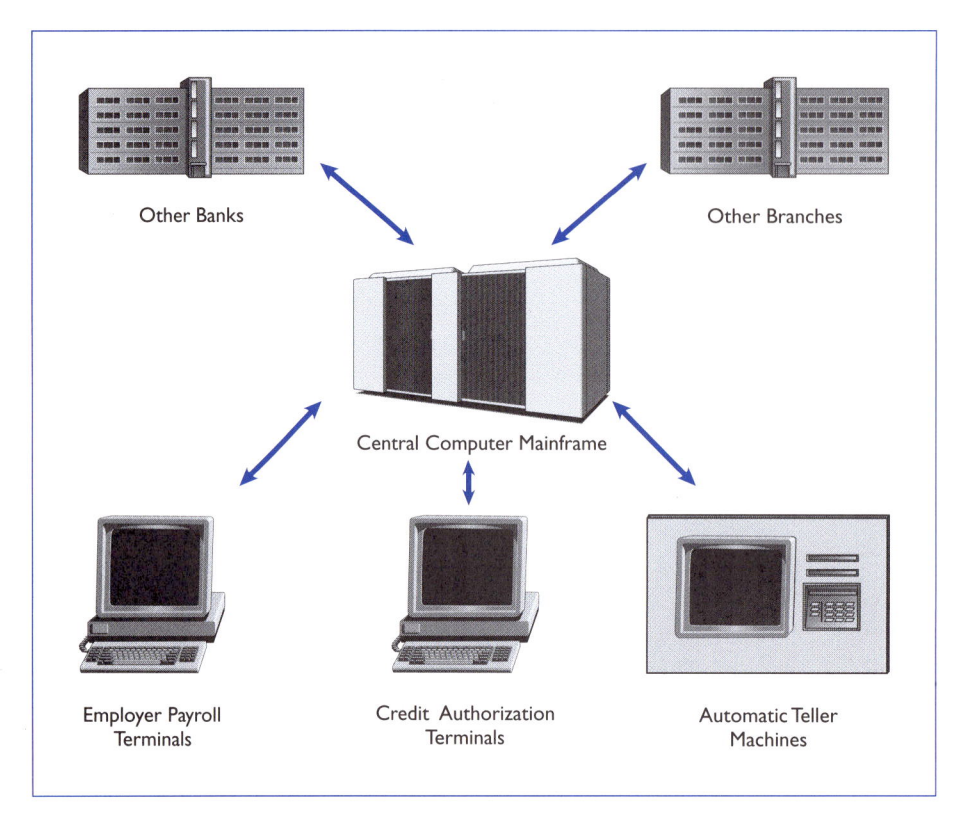

FIGURE 4.26 Branch Bank System

MODULATORS/ DEMODULATORS (MODEMS)

LEARNING OBJECTIVES

After studying this chapter, you should be able to:

- Contrast dial-up and leased lines
- Discuss conditioned and unconditioned telephone lines
- Describe the function of a universal asynchronous receiver/transmitter (UART)
- Discuss smart modem features
- Describe the MNP modem protocol
- Summarize the major CCITT standardized modems in use

COMMUNICATIONS
IN ACTION

CASE PROBLEM
BANCROFT MERCHANDISING

ELECTRONIC MAIL SYSTEM

Bancroft Merchandising purchases gift items from manufacturers located in the United States and abroad. Bancroft makes large purchases in anticipation of holiday seasons and schedules many orders to be drop-shipped directly to customers. Bancroft's customers include large department stores, small retailers, mail-order companies, and others. The company must remain in contact with more than 110 different manufacturers and several thousand customers.

Each year the owner, Bill Bancroft, travels to his manufacturers to establish buying contacts. These trips involve a substantial amount of correspondence, not only between the manufacturers and Bill Bancroft, but also between Bancroft's customers and his staff of six purchasing agents. One of the major reasons for the success of the company is its ability to keep in constant contact with customers and suppliers.

The use of conventional mail for moving correspondence has proved to be too slow. Bancroft's buyers and sales staff have been using ordinary typewriters, copy machines, and regular postal service for most of their letters, which must be typed, copied, and posted. For correspondence going abroad they use air mail. But if deadlines must be met, a more expensive Telex communication is used. Bancroft needs a better way to handle its correspondence and reduce costs.

Refer to the end of this chapter to see how Bill Bancroft solved his problem.

MODEMS are one of the most prevalent pieces of equipment used in communications. They are associated with data terminals and are wired to tens of thousands of personal computers, as well as to minicomputers and mainframes.

Anyone who has used an automatic teller machine (ATM) has probably used a modulator/demodulator (modem) without being aware of it. These pieces of electronic circuitry are located between the ATM and the bank's central computer. They communicate with each other, encode the amount of your deposit or withdrawal, and, in a flash, send the information over phone lines to alert your bank to the transaction. Modems are frequently installed between point-of-sale terminals, teller terminals, and virtually every remotely located terminal and the communications line.

We will now take a closer look at the electrical characteristics of modems and learn how they function and serve to connect communications equipment to communications lines. We will also discuss universal asynchronous receivers/transmitters (UARTs), serial ports, and various types of lines that serve communications equipment.

MODEMS

Except for distances of only a few feet, the use of an on/off circuit to send digital data is not practical on telephone circuits. When digital data are to be sent over long distances, the information must be encoded on a carrier wave and then decoded at the receiving end. (See Figure 5.1.)

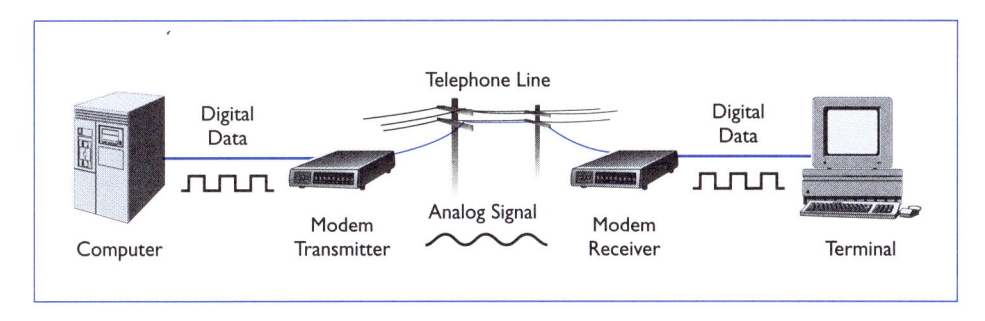

FIGURE 5.1 Digital Data Transmission. Modems transmit and receive data by converting digital data to analog signals and vice versa.

The process of **modulating** and **demodulating** is performed by a device known as a **modulator/demodulator (modem)**. Modems are sometimes known as **interface devices**. They allow digital data to modulate a carrier wave by changing its amplitude, frequency, or phase. A **carrier wave** is a transmitted signal that is capable of having information impressed on it. Modems make it possible to send thousands of characters per second over ordinary telephone lines between terminals and computers. The process of modulating a carrier wave was discussed in detail in Chapter 4.

The use of modems is expected to decline as integrated digital transmission systems become more prevalent. Digital networks such as the ISDN allow terminals and computers to be connected to communications lines without the use of modems, thus reducing the cost of a connection and eliminating hardware that may fail. However, because an enormous amount of traffic is still routed over voice-grade lines using modems, it is essential that the student understand their use and characteristics.

TYPES OF TELEPHONE CIRCUITS

Circuit characteristics determine the speed at which data can be sent over a line. Before discussing modems, we need to discuss telephone circuits since they greatly affect the type of modem that can be placed on a line and thus the amount of information that can be transmitted.

Several basic types of telephone lines are widely used in the communications industry to send and receive information. You are already familiar with one of them, the ordinary voice-grade **dial-up telephone line**. If you order a telephone installed in your home or office, your local exchange carrier (LEC) will provide you with a

voice-grade telephone circuit unless instructed otherwise. This circuit is called a **subscriber loop** or local loop and is basically a twisted pair of copper wires connected between your home or office and the LEC. This line terminates at the local office's switching equipment. (See Figure 5.2.)

FIGURE 5.2
Switched Network

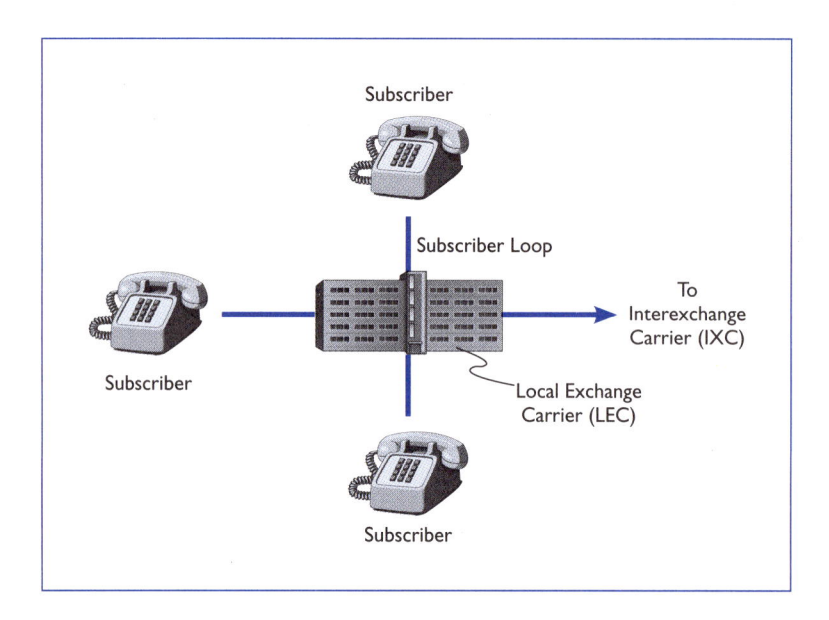

Because of this connection you are able to use the equipment to call virtually any telephone number in the world. Dial-up lines are connected directly to switching equipment, giving you dialing capability. As a result, different circuits and switches may be used each time a call is placed. Ordinary telephone lines are limited in the amount of data that can be sent over them.

Voice-grade dial-up lines have a **bandwidth** of 2,700 Hz. Both voice and data can be sent over this type of line. However, to send digital data, modems are required at each end of the line. Charges for dial-up lines may be based on a flat fee or on usage, such as the number of calls placed or length of calls.

When calls are routed through the switched network there is no way to control the quality of the line. In effect one must take what is available and accept whatever electrical and bandwidth characteristics are assigned when the call is switched. The lines assigned are known as **unconditioned circuits**. On the other hand, if one purchases a leased line, it can be **conditioned** with certain bandwidth or other electrical characteristics.

A second category of telephone lines available to users is called **leased**, or **dedicated, lines**. Leased lines do not connect the user to the local exchange carrier's switching equipment. Instead, they are routed through special banks of circuits to other LECs in the LATA and, finally, to other dedicated subscriber loops. (See Figure 5.3.) Leased lines do not go through the **switched network** and equipment. They are circuits that are permanently connected between two points and that do not allow the user to dial other telephone numbers. Leased lines are paid for via a monthly fee, usually based on airline miles between two points.

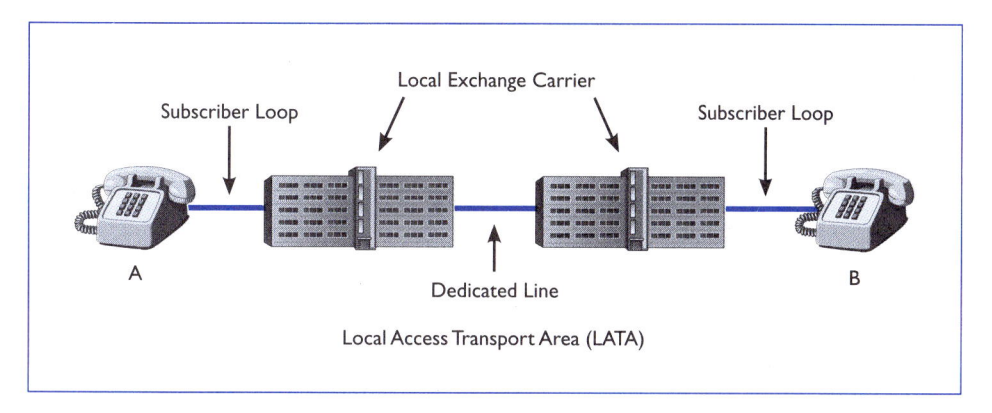

FIGURE 5.3 Leased Lines

Ordinary voice-grade lines are called unconditioned **3002 circuits**. These circuits can be conditioned and are then known as 3002-C1, 3002-C2, 3002-C4, etc., conditioned circuits. The prices for leasing various conditioned circuits depend on the quality of the circuit desired and its distance. The higher the degree of conditioning, the greater the line charges, and the greater the volume of data that can be sent.

A third type of telephone line is known as a **T1 circuit**, which is reserved exclusively for the transmission of digital information. As a result, modems are not required on the T1 network. T1 circuits have the capacity to transmit 24 separate 64 Kbps channels on one circuit. If voice is to be sent on a digital circuit, the analog signal must be digitized. Thus, one circuit can transport voice, video, computer, and facsimile information. (See Figure 5.4.) The combined T1 circuit will transmit 1.544 Mbps and is known as a **DS1 circuit**. These circuits are described in greater detail in Chapter 7.

UNIVERSAL ASYNCHRONOUS RECEIVER/TRANSMITTER

Some data terminal equipment (DTE) and data circuit-terminating equipment (DCE) can send and receive data in parallel fashion. It is faster to send a character, or byte, in parallel because all the bits in the byte are sent at one time over several parallel channels.

For economic reasons, most digital transmission is done on one channel in serial rather than parallel form. It is therefore necessary to convert parallel bits into a serial stream before they can be sent over a circuit. Thus, most modems expect a serial stream of data that will be used to modulate the carrier wave. At the other end, a modem receives the serial transmission and converts it back to parallel.

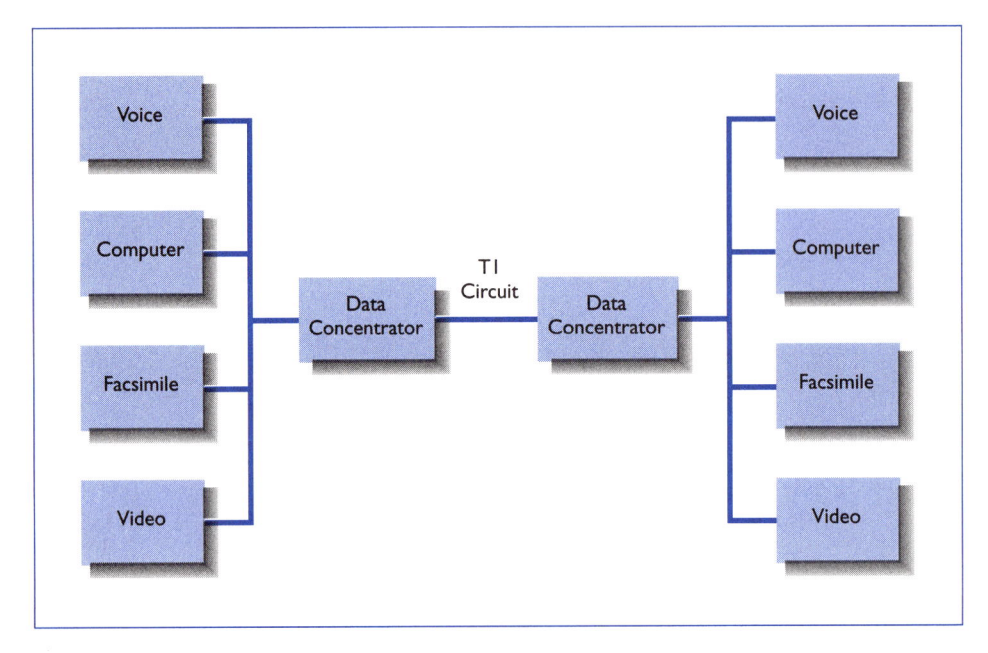

FIGURE 5.4 Digital Network Connection

Many personal computers are equipped with a serial port. The **serial port** consists of a circuit card placed in the computer that conveniently and easily connects a modem to the computer. The serial port is designed to take parallel data bits processed by the CPU and output them in serial fashion. (See Figure 5.5.)

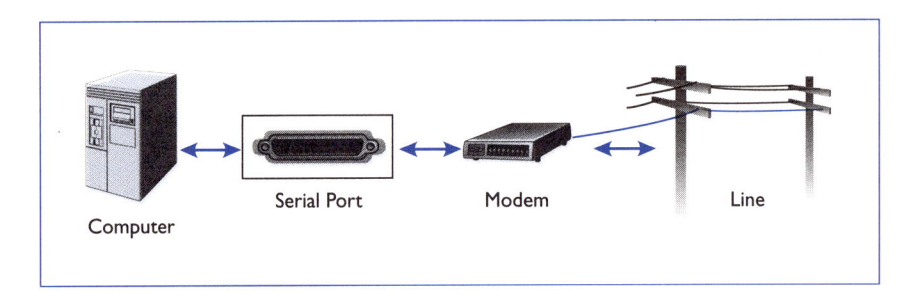

FIGURE 5.5 Serial Port Connection

The actual conversion from parallel to serial is done using a **universal asynchronous receiver/transmitter (UART)**. This electronic device is in the circuit between the modem and the computer or terminal equipment. (See Figure 5.6.)

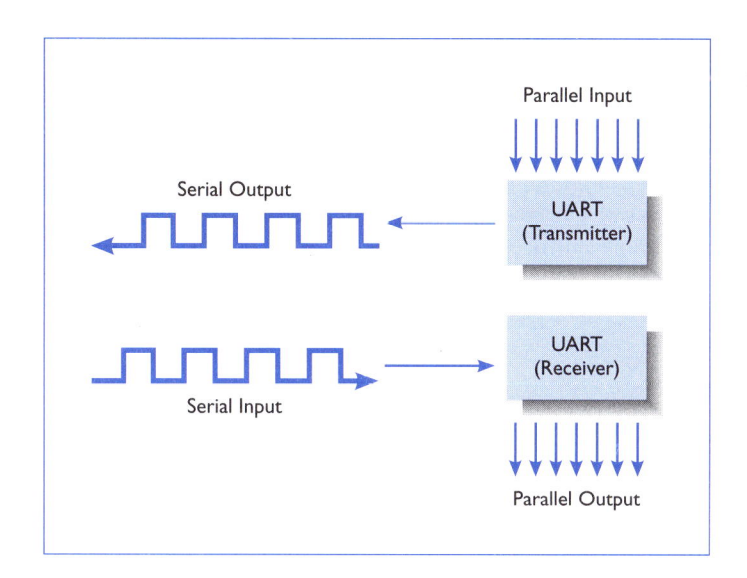

FIGURE 5.6
Universal Asynchronous Receiver/Transmitter (UART)

The function of a UART is to convert parallel bits into a **serial stream** at the transmitting end and from a serial stream into a **parallel stream** at the receiving end. UARTs are not necessary if parallel circuits are available to transmit all bits in a byte. UARTs perform only serial-to-parallel or parallel-to-serial conversions.

The physical hardware used to implement UART circuitry is usually an integrated circuit chip mounted on a printed circuit board. These chips, manufactured by several different companies, are small enough to be physically integrated into data terminal equipment or computers.

INDUSTRY-STANDARD MODEM DESIGNATIONS

Over the past several decades, a number of industry standard designations have come into use that describe modem performance and characteristics. Industry standards were originally based on a series of modems designed by Bell Laboratories, referred to as Bell 103A, Bell 202C, etc. The numbers described a basic circuit configuration, and the letter following the numbers described specific models and features.

Later, Hayes Microcomputer Products introduced a modem that could be easily programmed, using a series of two- or three-letter attention (AT) codes. These attention codes established a de facto design standard that was followed by many other vendors. Modems that conform to the Hayes design are known as Hayes-compatible modems.

Recently, more complex modems were developed that integrate many operations directly into hardware, rather than via software. These modems, developed by Microcom Systems, Inc., set the stage for yet another round of standards. These include a network protocol known as **Microcom Network Protocol (MNP)**.

Today many firms, including Hayes Microcomputer Products, ZyXEL U.S.A., Practical Peripherals, and others, manufacture and sell modems, while Bell and

AT&T have left the modem marketplace. Nevertheless, the Bell, Hayes, and Microcom de facto standard designations remain in use.

However, the major work toward industry standardization was done by the **Consultative Committee for International Telephone and Telegraph (CCITT)**. This international standards organization publishes standards for modem design and characteristics. These are known as V. modems (pronounced "vee dot"). Some of the older **Bell-type** modems conform to the new **CCITT V. standards**. The CCITT standard modems, which are used worldwide, are listed in Figure 5.7. The CCITT and Bell-type standards are basically different, although there are similarities.

FIGURE 5.7
Modem Classifications

SPEED (bps)	CCITT DESIGNATION	BELL DESIGNATION
300	V.21	Bell 103
1200	V.22	Bell 212A
2400	V.22bis	
1200	V.23	Bell 202
2400	V.26	Bell 201
4800	V.27	Bell 208
9600	V.29	Bell 209
9600	V.32	
14.4k	V.32bis	
14.4k	V.17	

Modems can be classified by transmission mode, such as **full-duplex (FDX)** or **half-duplex (HDX)**, whether they transmit data **synchronously** or **asynchronously**, and by transmission speed. The modems in Figure 5.7 range from relatively slow devices, such as the CCITT V.21, which transmits at 300 bps, to the CCITT V.32, which can transmit up to 9,600 bps or more. Further, these modems are classified according to whether they are designed to operate on dial-up or leased lines and whether they conform to the CCITT, Hayes, or Microcom MNP standards.

Modems are designed to operate in specified bandwidths and transmit and receive data on agreed-upon frequencies. Modems manufactured by different firms are compatible with each other as long as they follow the same frequency standards. Similarly, CCITT modems are compatible with each other, but they may not be compatible with all Bell-types.

MODEM FEATURES AND DESIGN

In designing and manufacturing modems, a variety of special features may be included. Some modems contain **microprocessors** that control their function; others do not. Some modems are designed for direct connection or acoustic use. Some modems implement transmission protocols in software, while others do it in hardware. Modem features include auto-answer, auto-dial, and field selectable transmission rates. Let us look at some of these features.

Microprocessor-Controlled Modems

For many years modems were manufactured as stand-alone pieces of gear. These devices did not include any internal computers or logic and could not reformat data, dial phone numbers, or be directed by programs or software located in computers or terminals. As a result, these devices perform only the limited functions of sending and receiving data.

A new generation of **smart modems**, pioneered by Hayes Microcomputer Products, has emerged. (See Figure 5.8.) Smart modems, built with microprocessors and primary memory capability, are able to operate under the control of program software. These modems are directed by attention (AT) commands, issued by a computer. Smart modems are able to communicate with a line even though the host computer is shut down. These devices can detect the incoming signal speed and then automatically switch to that speed. They are able to store names and telephone numbers in a directory that can be updated, revised, and have its contents displayed.

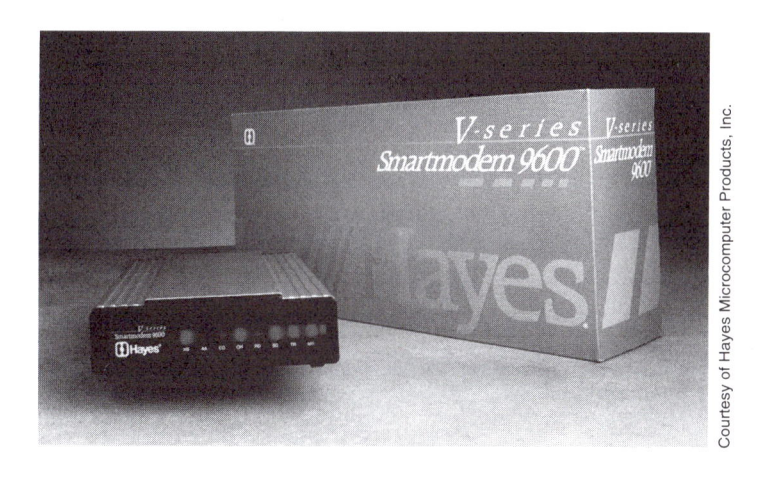

FIGURE 5.8
Smart Modem. This modem is directed by the AT command set.

Smart modems can be programmed to change modes, originate or answer calls, or perform other functions. These functions are enabled by sending various AT command prefixes to the modem. Modems using the Hayes standard respond to the attention code AT, followed by other letters. For example, AT DP 555 1212 directs the computer to originate a call using pulse dialing. The command AT DT 555 1212 causes the modem to call the number using Touch-Tone dialing.

Smart modems can use either pulse dialing or dual-tone multifrequency (DTMF) dialing. Microcomputer-controlled smart modems are able to answer calls automatically or wait for a certain number of rings before answering. They can check user passwords and communicate with other modems. They are able to reformat data, insert check bits, and keep track of how many times a number rings before hanging up.

Transmission Speeds and Formats

Some modems are equipped with **field selectable switches** that allow the modem to operate at any of the standard speeds up to its maximum capacity. This feature allows, for example, a CCITT V.26, which normally operates at 2,400 bps, to operate at only 300 bps, thus enabling it to communicate directly with a CCITT V.21 modem.

Virtually all modern modems are software-driven, which means their speed and function can be altered by issuing program commands, rather than manipulating switches. A few modems have a switch that allows them to be shifted into either full- or half-duplex mode. Both the originating and answering modem must be in the correct mode if they are to function properly.

To operate at maximum speed, some modems must be connected to specially conditioned lines, to a dedicated non-switched line, or a pair of lines. If such conditioned lines are not available, at the user's option, a lower speed may be selected and an unconditioned single line used.

Modes

Modems are designed to operate either in the **originate** or the **answer** mode. Figure 5.9 illustrates the frequency assignments for a Bell-type 103 modem. A full-duplex, two-way data transmission can be established within the 2,700 Hz bandwidth available on ordinary telephone lines. If 1,070 Hz and 1,270 Hz are selected to transmit the 1 and 0, respectively, then the answer modem must be designed to receive the 1,070 and 1,270 frequencies.

FIGURE 5.9 Originate and Answer Modes

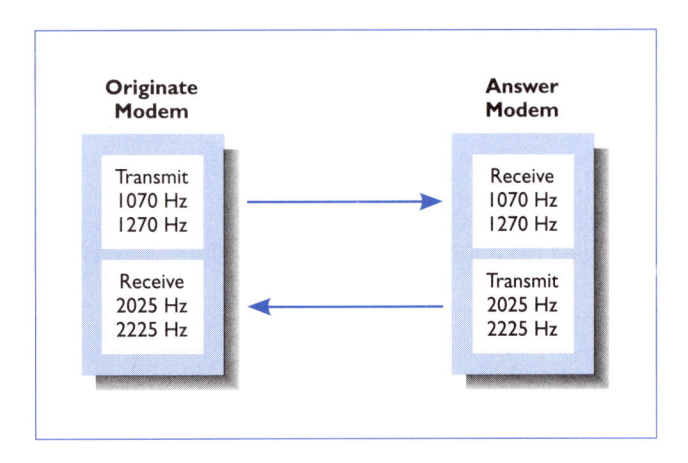

Originate Modem
- Transmit 1070 Hz / 1270 Hz
- Receive 2025 Hz / 2225 Hz

Answer Modem
- Receive 1070 Hz / 1270 Hz
- Transmit 2025 Hz / 2225 Hz

Because full-duplex involves a two-way transmission, the originate modem must be adjusted to receive signals at 2,025 and 2,225 Hz, as those are the frequencies that will be transmitted. Note that full-duplex operation can be achieved on one voice-grade circuit because low-speed modems require little bandwidth. As we shall see later, some high-speed modems require two separate circuits.

Most modems can automatically answer as well as originate calls. The appropriate send and receive frequencies must be selected by the user. Generally, modems used with terminals or personal computers in the field are assigned the originate mode. Those at the receiving end, usually a large computer or mainframe, are directly connected and assigned the answer mode.

Dialing Features

A modem may be built with **auto-dialer** capability. This capability enables the device to dial telephone numbers automatically. When driven by a computer and appropriate software, such modems are able to dial one or more telephone numbers. After the call is answered, and on receipt of the appropriate handshake signals, the modem then proceeds to transmit and receive data.

Other modems may be equipped with **auto-answer** capability. These devices can detect ringing on the telephone line and are able to answer the phone when it is unattended. After handshake signals are exchanged, the modem is then able to send and receive information. Thus, a computer with an auto-dialer modem can call another computer with an auto-answer modem and establish a two-way communication without human assistance or intervention.

MICROCOM NETWORK PROTOCOL

Some of the newest modems have error-correcting, flow control, and data compression logic built directly into the hardware. These devices implement the Microcom Network Protocol (MNP) and CCITT V.42 data compression standards. Modems equipped with the MNP and CCITT V.42 standards are able to establish more reliable connections and pass data more efficiently than those that implement error-correction and data compression algorithms in software.

The MNP links two modems, detecting and correcting transmission errors automatically through a system of **data frames**. A data frame contains a header, the data to be transmitted, and a frame-checking code. The frame-checking code is created by the sending modem and checked by the receiving modem for each frame of data sent. As long as the two checking codes match, the data are accepted; if not, they are retransmitted.

The MNP provides six levels of service. Level 1 is a half-duplex block protocol, in which the sending modem transmits a block of data and then waits for an acknowledgment. It is slow and usually used between terminals, not for computer-to-computer communications.

Level 2 is a bidirectional, full-duplex protocol in which data are transmitted in a stream. It is not widely used because it offers no gain in throughput.

Level 3 strips the stop and start bits from data packets before they are transmitted. These bits are reinserted by the receiving modem. The result is the synchronous movement of data from information available in asynchronous format. Level 3 increases throughput about 10 percent over non-MNP modems.

Level 4 reduces information in the header frame and increases the frame size, thus improving throughput by about 5 percent over ordinary modems.

Level 5 invokes data compression logic. Substantial increases in throughput are gained because redundant data are reduced to fewer bits before being transmitted.

Level 6 achieves the maximum speed because it relies on transmitting a high volume of data in one direction at a time. It has the greatest throughput of the six levels described.

As soon as a reliable connection is established between two MNP modems, they automatically negotiate the highest level of service available between them, and data flow begins. This procedure is carried out automatically through a handshaking process, completely devoid of operator intervention.

ATTENTION COMMAND SET

The **attention (AT) command** set, originally developed by Hayes Microcomputer Products for its modems, has become the standard by which other modems are programmed as well. Modems that use the AT command set can be programmed to change their configuration by sending AT commands from the computer. The operating mode, flow control, or baud rate can be adjusted by issuing the proper AT command.

Both Hayes-compatible and MNP modem functions can be programmed using AT commands. Figure 5.10 illustrates a group of AT commands and the functions they control for a particular modem. These commands, of course, only respond in modems designed to interpret them.

MODEM HARDWARE

Modems are made by many different manufacturers, and the physical size and configuration of a modem may take many forms. The circuitry may be housed in a small stand-alone box, as shown in Figure 5.11. This unit can be placed anywhere near a terminal or table-top computer. Many manufacturers produce modems on a single printed circuit board. (See Figure 5.12.) This board may be mounted within a personal computer or in a rack with other data transmission equipment.

FIGURE 5.10 AT Command Set

Select Operating Mode:

AT\N0 = Normal mode – buffered – no error detection (NOT "Hayes compatible" mode)
AT\N1 = Direct mode – not buffered – no error detection – default ("Hayes compatible" mode)
AT\N2 = MNP Reliable mode – buffered – error detection
AT\N3 = MNP Auto-Reliable mode – buffered – error detection – fallback

Serial Port Flow Control Selection:

AT\Q0 = Disables all flow control on serial port – default
AT\Q1 = Enables XON/XOFF flow control on serial port
AT\Q2 = Sets unidirectional hardware flow control
AT\Q3 = Sets bidirectional hardware flow control using RTS/CTS

Modem Port Flow Control Selection:

AT\G0 = Disables XON/XOFF flow control on modem port
AT\G1 = Enables XON/XOFF flow control on modem port

XON/XOFF Pass Through:

AT\X0 = Process XON/XOFF characters do not pass through
AT\X1 = Process XON/XOFF characters and pass through

Set BPS Rate Adjustment:

AT\J0 = Rate adjust OFF; DTE/DCE and DCE/DCE rates independent
AT\J1 = Rate adjust ON; DTE/DCE adjusts to rate of connection

MNP Extended Result Codes:

AT\V0 = Extended MNP result codes disabled
AT\V1 = Enable extended MNP result codes

Set Break Characteristics:

AT\K$n$ = See tables in modem manual

Transmit Break:

AT\B$n$ = n = 1 to 9 × 0.1 second

MNP Level 5 Compression:

AT%C0 = MNP Level 5 compression is OFF
AT%C1 = MNP Level 5 compression is ON – default

Miscellaneous MNP Commands:

AT\S = Display two-page modem parameter list
AT%R = Display the contents of all 27 S-registers
AT%Bn = Explicitly set the bps rate of the modem port

FIGURE 5.11
Stand-Alone Modem

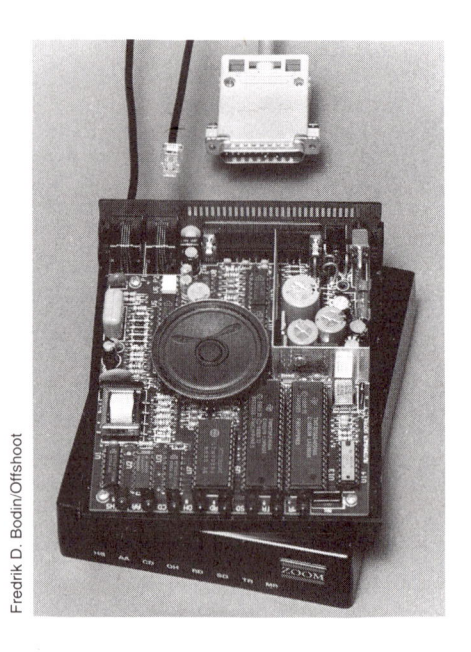

Fredrik D. Bodin/Offshoot

FIGURE 5.12
PC Modem Card

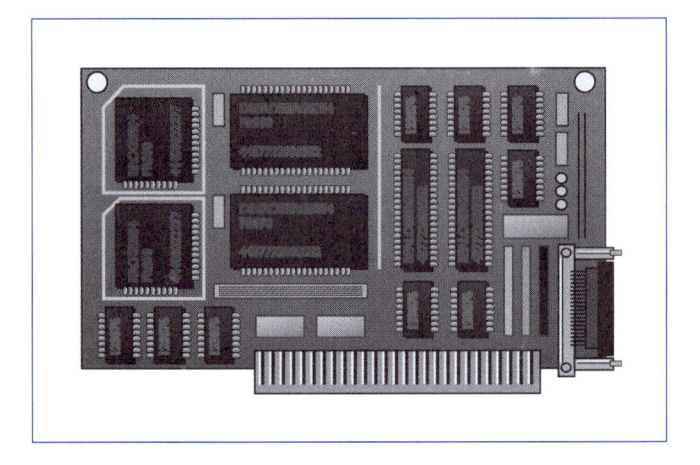

The balance of this chapter describes the specifications, physical design, and frequency assignments of these common CCITT and Bell-type modem devices. These range from CCITT V.21, capable of speeds of up to 300 bps, through CCITT types able to handle speeds up to 14.4 Kbps.

CCITT MODEM STANDARDS

We will review CCITT modem standards in the order of their speed and data-handling capacity, then discuss Bell-type modems. The Bell-type designations have been largely abandoned in favor of the international CCITT standards. The reader should be aware of both designations because much earlier equipment bears only Bell-type designations.

CCITT V.21—300 bps Modems

The international standard for the 0 to 300 bps modem is the **CCITT V.21** device. Modems in this category are able to send and receive data at speeds of up to 300 bps, using frequency shift-keying (FSK) modulation, in either the originate or answer mode. They are in service on both dial-up and leased lines and provide full- or half-duplex operation on a single channel. CCITT V.21 devices are generally used where low-speed asynchronous transmissions are required. These devices are being rapidly replaced by higher speed modems, although many still remain in use.

In the V.21, two center frequencies, 1,080 Hz and 1,750 Hz, are assigned to send and receive data. The originate modem transmits a **space** (0) on 980 Hz and a **mark** (1) on 1,180 Hz. It receives a space on 1,650 Hz and a mark on 1,850 Hz. The complementary answer modem is designed to transmit and receive data on the opposite set of frequencies. (See Figure 5.13.) In this arrangement full-duplex operation is established on two channels well within the 2,700 Hz bandwidth available on voice-grade lines.

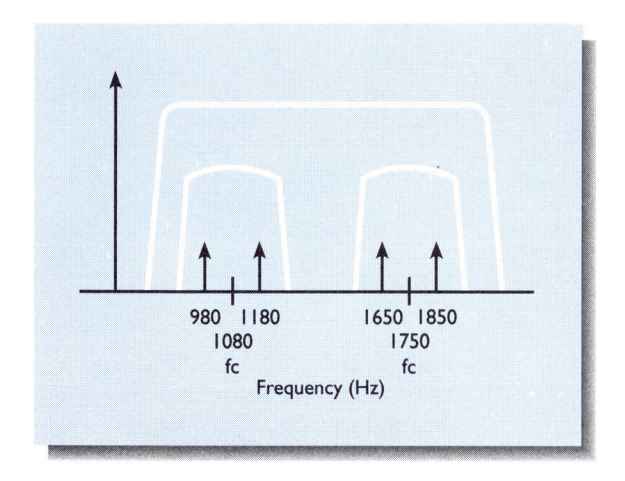

FIGURE 5.13
V.21 Frequency Assignments

CCITT V.22—1,200 bps Modems

CCITT V.22 modems are able to transmit up to 1,200 bps asynchronously or synchronously. At 1,200 bps a **dibit phase shift-keying (DPSK) system**, which represents shifts in phase, is used. A **dibit** is a two-bit number that represents a **phase shift**. The relationship is shown in Figure 5.14. These modems also transmit up to 300 bps, using conventional frequency shift keying (FSK). The frequency assignments for the V.22 modem are shown in Figure 5.15.

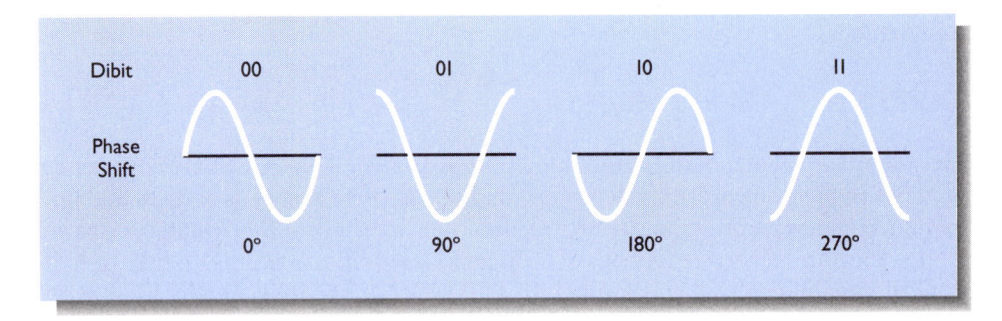

FIGURE 5.14 Dibit Phase Shift Keying (DPSK)

FIGURE 5.15
V.22 Frequency Assignments

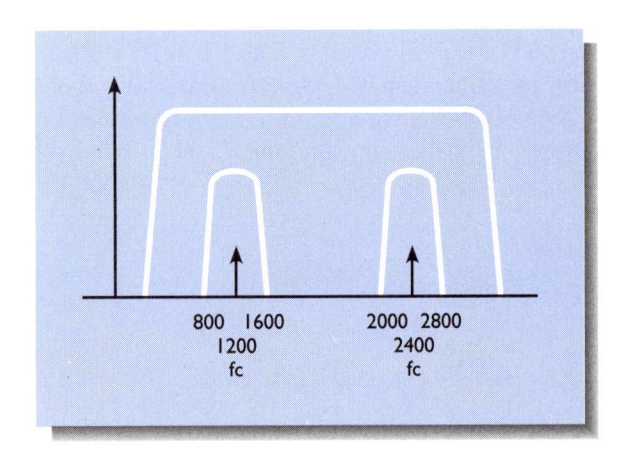

CCITT V.22 bis—2,400 bps Modems

The **CCITT V.22 bis** modem is similar in characteristics to the CCITT V.22 modem and can operate either synchronously or asynchronously. It uses the same frequency and channel assignments as the CCITT V.22 modem. Its greater speed is achieved by using two two-wire circuits.

CCITT V.23—1,200 bps Modems

The international standard for the 600/1,200 bps modem is the **CCITT V.23** device. The center frequency assigned for the main channel is 1,700 Hz and for the reverse channel, 420 Hz. A mark is sent at 1,300 Hz and a space at 2,100 Hz. The reverse channel's center frequency is 420 Hz, with a mark at 390 and a space at 450. At 600 bps, 1,500 Hz is used as the center frequency, with a mark at 1,300 and a space at 1,700. The same frequency assignments are used for the reverse channel at 600 and 1,200 bps. (See Figure 5.16.)

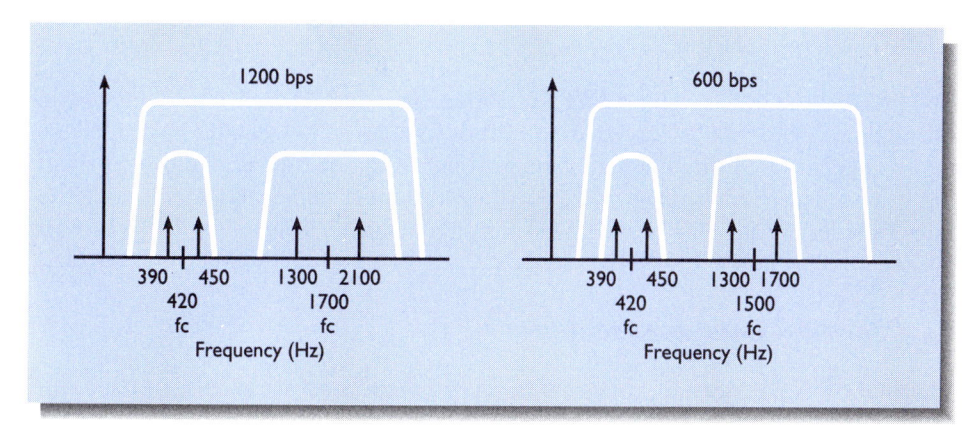

FIGURE 5.16 V.23 Frequency Assignments

CCITT V.26—2,400 bps Modems

Medium-speed modems in the **CCITT V.26** group transmit information on a frequency of 1,800 Hz. They operate in either the full- or half-duplex mode, using dial-up or leased lines and DPSK (see Figure 5.17). The 2,400 bps modems are able to operate on ordinary voice-grade dial-up lines and are frequently found on personal computers or in organizations that must move moderate amounts of data over ordinary telephone lines.

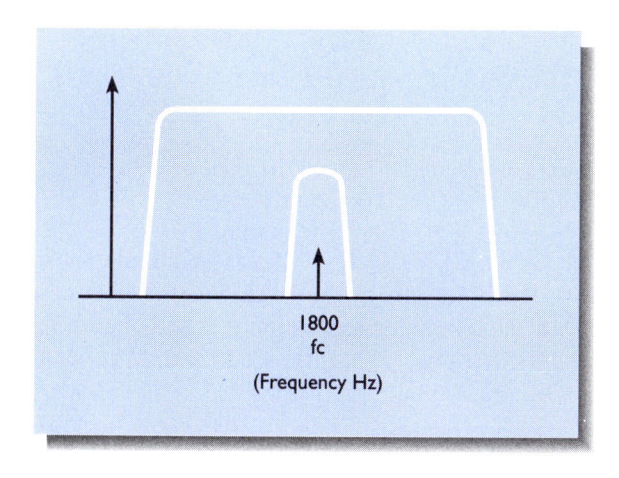

FIGURE 5.17 V.26 Frequency Assignments

CCITT V.27—4,800 bps Modems

CCITT V.27 modems operate at medium to high speeds and can transmit and receive up to 4,800 bps, using synchronous transmission techniques over leased or dial-up lines. A band between 1,000 Hz and 2,600 Hz is used, with a center frequency of 1,800 Hz. This higher speed modem requires a bandwidth of 1,600 Hz.

CCITT V.29—9,600 bps Modems

The CCITT has published the **CCITT V.29** standard for high-speed modems capable of sending 2,400, 4,800, 7,200, or 9,600 bps over leased or conditioned telephone lines. They are used where a high volume of data must be transmitted over specially conditioned leased lines. They operate in the full-duplex mode and are preferred when large volumes of data must be sent. V.29 devices operate on a center frequency of 1,700 Hz and a bandwidth of 2,400 Hz, covering the spectrum from 500 Hz to 2,900 Hz.

CCITT V.32—9,600 bps Modems

The **CCITT V.32** modem provides 9,600 bps data transmission over ordinary dial-up lines. (See Figure 5.18.) It does not require dedicated or conditioned lines. V.32 modems are manufactured by many firms and have become very popular because they provide high-speed economy and utilize existing switched network lines.

FIGURE 5.18
CCITT V.23 Modem

Courtesy of Hayes Microcomputer Products, Inc.

Even higher speeds are attained using the **CCITT V.32 bis** standard. These modems achieve speeds as high as 14.4 Kbps. They rely on sophisticated error-correction logic and achieve a high speed using two two-wire ordinary telephone lines.

CCITT V.17 Fax Modems

All fax machines include built-in modems and are designed to convert text, drawings, or graphic images into bit patterns that are transmitted over ordinary telephone lines. Several standards are in use, depending on the speed of the fax machine.

Reliance on the **CCITT V.17** fax standard is growing. This protocol enables documents to be transmitted or received at 14,400 bps. It is this high speed that enables the rapid transfer of printed or typeset documents over ordinary telephone lines.

BELL-TYPE MODEMS

Bell-type modems have been largely supplanted by CCITT standards. A brief review of Bell-types is presented because some of these devices are still in use.

Bell-Type 103 Modems

The **Bell-type 103** modem is designed to transmit information at speeds of up to 300 bps in either half- or full-duplex. It may be used to interface computer terminals or a computer with a transmission line. The Bell-type 103 is an asynchronous modem using FSK modulation. Two center frequencies, 1,170 Hz and 2,125 Hz, are assigned to send or receive data. (See Figure 5.19.) The originate modem transmits a space on 1,070 Hz and a mark on 1,270 Hz. The originate modem is designed to receive a space on 2,025 Hz and a mark on 2,225 Hz.

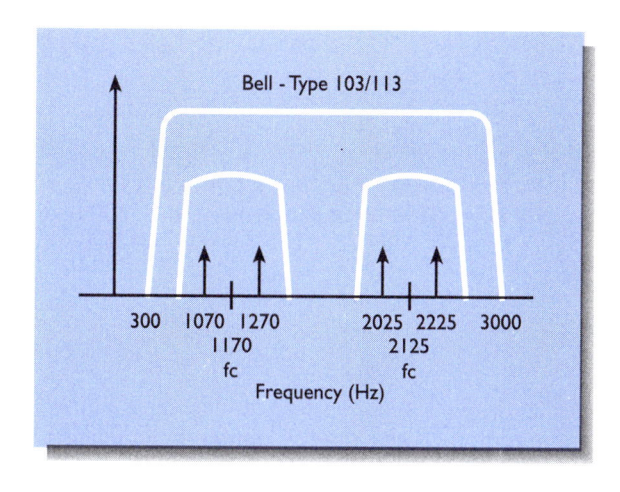

FIGURE 5.19 Bell-Type 103 Frequency Assignments

Bell-Type 201 Modems

The **Bell-type 201** series of modems transmits information over ordinary voice-grade lines in serial form, using DPSK. A dibit phase shift system similar to the one used by the 1,200 bps modem is employed to encode data at speeds up to 2,400 baud. Each dibit sent over the line specifies the phase shift. At the receiving end another modem detects the phase shift, converting it back to digital data.

Bell-Type 202 Modems

The **Bell-type 202** is an asynchronous modem that operates in the half-duplex mode on leased or dial-up lines. It can transmit up to 1,200 bps on one two-wire circuit. An optional 5 bps reverse channel, using amplitude modulation (AM), is available. These modems have been largely supplanted by faster devices.

Bell-Type 208 Modems

The **Bell-type 208** series of modems is designed to send and receive data at 4,800 bps. They are synchronous modems that may be operated in either full- or half-duplex mode on leased or dial-up lines, depending on the model. These modems are used where medium-speed transmissions are required over ordinary voice-grade, non-conditioned phone lines.

Bell-Type 209 Modems

The **Bell-type 209** is a high-speed modem designed to transmit up to 9,600 bps. They are used where a high volume of data must be transmitted and D1 conditioned lines are available. The Bell-type 209 is operated in full-duplex synchronous operation over leased lines. Ordinary dial-up lines cannot be used because these modems require special line conditioning to transmit 9,600 bps.

Bell-Type 212A Modems

The **Bell-type 212A** is a modem designed to operate in either the synchronous or asynchronous mode. In the asynchronous mode, up to 300 bps can be sent over ordinary dial-up lines, using FSK. In the synchronous mode it can send up to 1,200 bps, using DPSK.

MODEM CONNECTIONS

A modem may be either hard-wired or acoustic. The hard-wired modem uses a direct physical connection between the computer or terminal and the communications line. (See Figure 5.20.) **Acoustic modems** do not make electrical connections, but transmit sound waves between the device and the communications line. This feature enables terminals taken into the field to send signals over an ordinary telephone handset without direct connection.

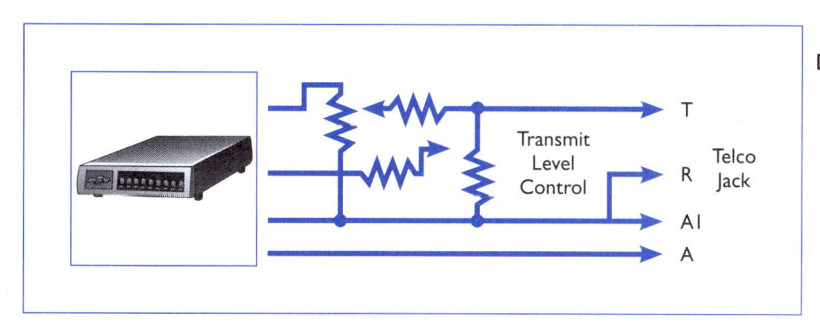

FIGURE 5.20 Direct Modem Connection

Most users prefer hard-wired modems because of their lower noise and improved performance. The highest speed modem performance is obtained through a direct hard-wire connection. In this arrangement the modem is physically wired to the phone line. In the past, such direct connections were greatly restricted by telephone companies.

Today approved equipment can be connected directly to the telephone line, using a **modular plug** and **jack**. The most common is the four-conductor RJ-11 plug and jack, shown in Figure 5.21, frequently found in many homes and offices. An eight-conductor RJ-45 plug is also used for this purpose.

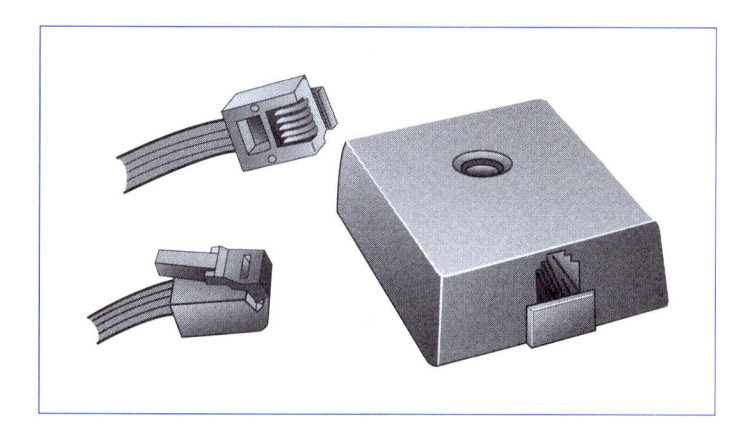

FIGURE 5.21 RJ-11 Modular Plug and Jack

Much higher transmission speeds and a better coupling between the modem and the phone line are achieved through direct connection. There is less chance for an accidental disconnect, and extraneous room sounds cannot enter the system as with acoustic modems. Direct connection arrangements may limit the portability of equipment, especially if a public phone is being used. If no modular jack is available, one must be installed.

THE MODEM/COMPUTER INTERFACE

Because many different types of modems can be connected to many different types of computers, a standard is needed so that similar devices can communicate with one another.

Many modems use the common **EIA-232-D interface standard** to connect the device to a computer. The EIA-232-D interface standard, adopted in 1987 by the Electrical Industries Association (EIA), replaces the older RS-232-C designation.

This standard describes the voltage and signal lines that connect modems to computers. According to the standard, a space (zero) is shown on the line as a positive voltage between +3 and +15 volts. A mark (one) is shown as a negative voltage between −3 and −15 volts. (See Figure 5.22.)

FIGURE 5.22
EIA-232-D Voltages

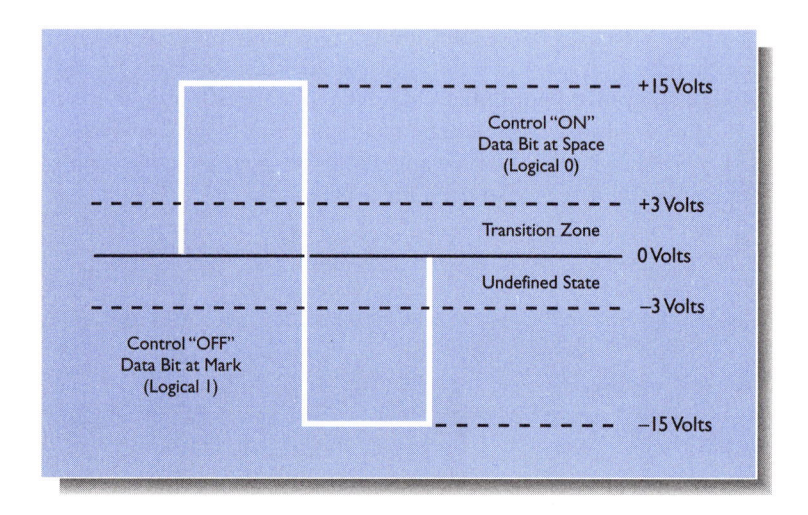

Using the presence of a positive or negative voltage from either the data terminating equipment (DTE) or data circuit-terminated equipment (DCE), the modem is able to modulate a carrier wave, thus sending a mark or space (one or zero) down the line.

The modem is physically connected to either the terminal or the computer using a standard 25-pin connector. (See Figure 5.23.) Although 25 pins are present in the connector, fewer than a dozen actually carry signals when used in a Bell-type 103 modem. (See Figure 5.24.) Data are transmitted on pin 2 in serial form. Data are received on pin 3 in serial form. Pin 1 is a protective ground, whereas other pins carry signals that indicate clear to send, data set ready, signal ground, carrier detect, and so forth.

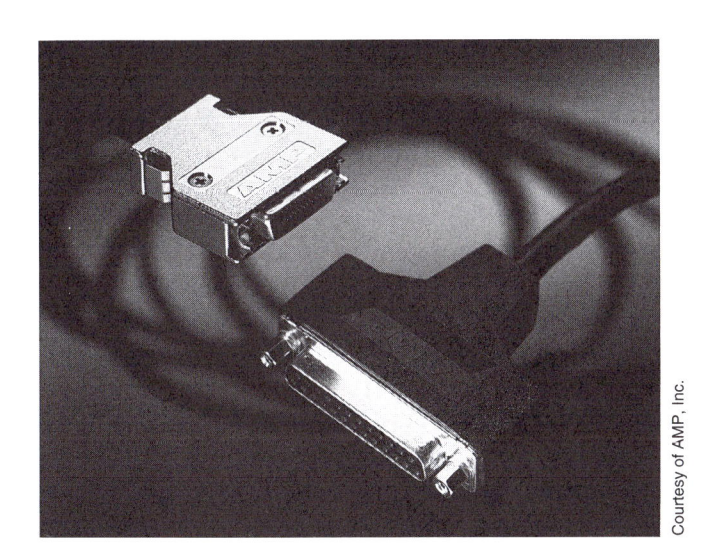

FIGURE 5.23
25-Pin Connector

FIGURE 5.24
Bell-Type 103 Pin Assignments

PIN	CIRCUIT	I\O	FUNCTION
1	AA	–	Protective Ground
2	BA	I	Transmitted Data
3	BB	O	Received Data
4	–	–	–
5	CB	O	Clear to Send
6	CC	O	Data Set Ready
7	AB	–	Signal Ground
8	CF	O	Carrier Detector
9	Reserved		
10	Reserved		
11	–	–	–
12	–	–	–
13	–	–	–
14	–	–	–
15	–	–	–
16	–	–	–
17	–	–	–
18	–	–	–
19	–	–	–
20	CD	I	Data Terminal Ready
21	–	–	–
22	CE	O	Ringing Indicator
23	–	–	–
24	–	–	–
25	–	–	–

Before a data transfer can take place, a **handshake procedure** is carried out by the modem. A handshake procedure consists of sending signals back and forth between the modem and the terminal or computer. The purpose is to ensure that the modems on the sending and receiving ends of the line are both turned on and properly connected to transfer data.

A variety of handshaking procedures are used, depending on the type of modem. Figure 5.25 illustrates one such handshaking procedure. The figure is read from top to bottom. It describes the signals that are sent between the modem at the computer end and the modem at the terminal end. Although the actual sending of signals back and forth is done automatically you should be aware that this procedure takes place.

COMPUTER END		Handshaking Sequence	TERMINAL END	
Computer	Modem		Modem	Terminal
		1		Operator Dials Number
	←RI	2		
DTR→		3		
	Modem Answers	4		
	←DSR	5		
RTS→		6		
	Modem Turns On Transmitter	7		
		8	DSR/RLSD→	
	←CTS	9		
Transmission Begins		10		

FIGURE 5.25 Handshake Procedure

In this chapter we have studied a variety of modems, ranging from low-speed devices to those capable of transmitting up to 9,600 bps or more. Modems find their principal use in sending data over leased or voice-grade telephone lines. In the next chapter we will look at the many forms of circuits and transmission media used to send data.

SUMMARY

Modems perform the task of *modulating* and *demodulating* a carrier wave. *Dial-up telephone lines* are *voice-grade* lines that connect to switching equipment. *Leased lines* are routed point to point and do not go through switching equipment. Voice-grade lines come in various degrees of *conditioning*.

A *serial port* provides a direct connection from a computer to a modem. A *UART* converts *parallel* bits into a *serial* stream and vice versa. Modems may be either *full-* or *half-duplex* in operation. Modems may transmit data *synchronously* or *asynchronously*. Modems without microcomputers cannot reformat data or dial telephone numbers and cannot be programmed by computers.

Smart modems can be directed by a computer and can reformat data, dial numbers, check passwords, and more. These modems, pioneered by Hayes Microcomputer Products, can be programmed to change modes, originate or answer calls, and perform other functions on receipt of various commands. They use the *attention (AT) command set*.

A direct-wired modem is physically connected to the telephone lines. *Acoustic* modems pass sound only between the modem and the telephone handset. *Originate* modems operate on frequencies assigned to the origin of a signal. *Answer* modems operate on frequencies assigned to the receipt of a signal. *Auto-dialer* modems are capable of automatically dialing telephone numbers. *Auto-answer* modems can detect a ring and answer an unattended telephone line.

FSK modulation is used in low-speed modems. A reverse channel is capable of sending information in the opposite direction from the main channel. *DPSK* represents shifts in phase to send signals. Medium-speed modems are in the 2,400 bps class. High-speed modems send data at 9,600 bps or more.

Modems that use the *MNP* standard implement error-checking and data compression logic in the modem's hardware, to greatly increase reliability and throughput.

T1 circuits are reserved exclusively for the transmission of digital information. T1 circuits have a capacity to transmit 24 separate 64 Kbps channels on one circuit. The combined T1 circuit will transmit 1.544 Mbps and is known as a *DS1 circuit*.

EXERCISES

1. Describe the T1 circuit.
2. Why are UARTs used in a communications circuit?
3. How do smart modems gain their intelligence?
4. What are the disadvantages of acoustic modems?
5. What is the function of auto-dialer and auto-answer circuits?
6. Explain how marks and spaces are sent over a line via a modem.
7. List some common low-speed modems.
8. List some medium-speed modems.
9. List some high-speed modems.
10. Describe the common interface used between modems and communications equipment.

HANDS-ON PROJECTS

- Review a manual for a modem available in your school or place of work. Read the document carefully. Determine the modem's type and speed.

- Visit a business establishment equipped with communications facilities. Determine the number and types of modems available.

- Visit a computer store and look at various modems. What types are available? Make a list of their features and prices.

- Assume you are to install several computer terminals and modems. Make a list of modem types you might need.

- Prepare a drawing showing a layout for the placement of the terminals and modems discussed in item 4, above.

COMMUNICATIONS IN ACTION

CASE SOLUTION
BANCROFT MERCHANDISING

Bill Bancroft analyzed his accounts and their needs very carefully. He discovered that many of his customers and suppliers were already using electronic mail. This led him to install an electronic mail system in his company. (See Figure 5.26.) Bancroft's system consists of a group of personal computers, which are located at the desks of buyers, sales people, and executives. These computers are connected to ordinary dial-up telephone lines, using modems. A large amount of Bancroft's electronic mail is now handled through a common-carrier telemail service, such as GTE's Telemail. The common carrier provides both local and international destinations.

FIGURE 5.26 Electronic Mail System

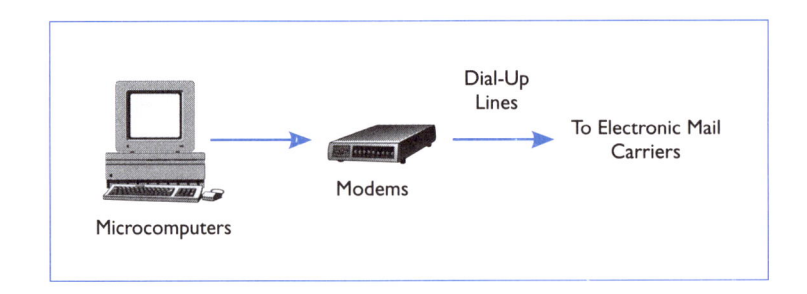

Bancroft still uses the U.S. Postal Service to send local mail. Correspondence sent to distant customers is delivered to their electronic mailboxes, allowing recipients to call for messages at their convenience. When necessary, messages can be delivered in printed form directly on remote terminals.

Urgent communications are put at the top of the recipient's mailbox queue so that they will be seen first. Some mail can be labeled "private" to ensure that it is read only by the person for whom it is intended. This labeling is done by use of a password. Other messages are sent registered, which initiates a response when they are picked up, assuring Bancroft of their receipt.

Bancroft Merchandising has experienced many benefits from the new system. The staff can communicate more quickly and inexpensively with foreign and domestic suppliers. Many of the letters are typed directly on a computer and immediately routed over the electronic mail networks. There is no longer a need to type paper documents, photocopy them, prepare envelopes, and take them to the post office. Permanent copies of all correspondence are saved electronically, using a word processing program. Electronic storage has reduced the need for filing cabinets and made more space available in the office. There is also less misfiled and lost correspondence.

COMMUNICATIONS MEDIA

LEARNING OBJECTIVES

After studying this chapter, you should be able to:

- Describe major forms of hard-wire circuits
- Describe how radio circuits are used to transmit digital data
- Describe cellular radio telephone systems
- Describe microwave relay systems
- Describe satellite transmission systems
- Describe fiber-optic cable systems

COMMUNICATIONS IN ACTION

CASE PROBLEM
AARONSON DISTRIBUTORS

TELECONFERENCING NETWORK

Aaronson Distributors is a large vendor of food products, coffee, tea, and other grocery items. Its product line is prepared in five major plants located around the country and in several smaller subsidiary packaging facilities. New products are pioneered in its research and development department, located at company headquarters. The U.S. sales territory is divided into five regions, each of which has its own manufacturing plant. (See Figure 6.1.) Other major divisions include the international marketing and distribution departments. Key decisions are made at Aaronson Distributors by a group of executives from marketing, research and development, and corporate finance.

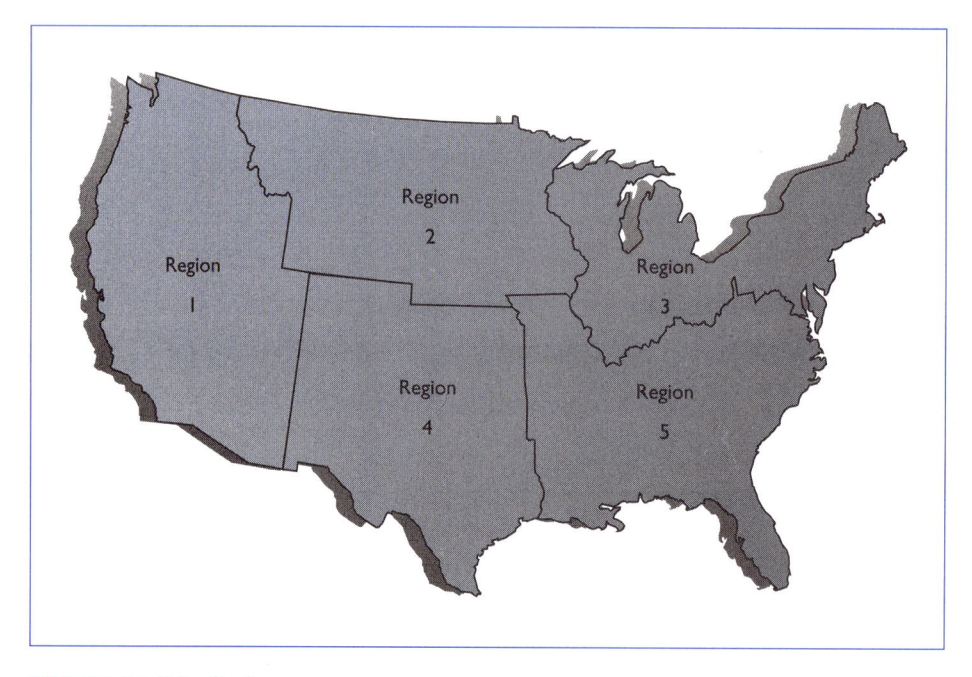

FIGURE 6.1 Sales Regions

Aaronson Distributors competes with many other major food purveyors. The company must continually develop new items. Decisions involve millions of dollars and are based on input from managers who work in the five plants. These decisions must be made quickly and efficiently.

Aaronson Distributors requires much face-to-face discussion among its executives, involving a good deal of travel. Although some travel is done in the corporate jet, the costs of operating the aircraft continue to increase. Regular commercial air travel for executive meetings means being at the mercy of airline schedules, as well as incurring hotel and other travel expenses. Many executives cannot take the time away from their home bases for meetings.

What kind of communications system would you propose for Aaronson's management? The system must provide face-to-face contact and the ability to exchange video and audio information as well as graphics.

Turn to the end of this chapter to see how the management of Aaronson Distributors solved the problem.

COMMUNICATIONS has come a long way since military commanders launched balloons or flocks of homing pigeons to send messages from behind enemy lines to their headquarters. As primitive as these communications may seem, they were the most practical means available less than 100 years ago. Today not only the military, but also industry, government, and educational institutions use a variety of communications media. Some are so sophisticated that they involve space-age communications technology—orbiting satellites or bursts of light that streak down fine strands of glass for thousands of miles.

In this chapter we will look at major communications media, including hard-wire telephone and coaxial cable circuits, radio wave transmission, microwave relay circuits, fiber-optic cables, earth-orbiting satellites, and other media. These media form the link that facilitates the flow of vital data in business, government, military, and educational institutions.

Chapter 7 will round out our discussion by exploring the wide variety of communications services provided by AT&T and other communications companies over these links.

THE COMMUNICATIONS LINK

The common element in all communications systems is the communications link. (See Figure 6.2.) A **communications link** is the pathway over which voice, video, or digital information can be transmitted. Circuits reserved for transmitting digital data are usually called **data links**. A data link is any pathway that enables discrete data, such as letters or numbers, to move from one point to another.

FIGURE 6.2
Communications Link. The common link in all communications systems is a communications circuit.

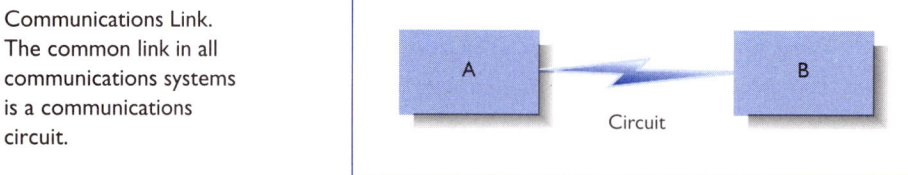

You are already familiar with many common voice and data communications links. When you tune to your favorite AM or FM radio station, you are tuning to a communications link that sends audio information. When you watch a television show, you tune to a channel that links you and the broadcasting station with both video and audio information. A telephone call to a friend involves another form of communications link: the common telephone service, or twisted pair. In the industry this link is irreverently called **Plain Old Telephone Service (POTS)**.

For many years, AT&T had a monopoly on ground-based voice communications links. Virtually all telephone calls were handled over AT&T lines, and Western Union essentially monopolized all land-based digital communications with its Telex and TWX services. During the last several decades there has been a great increase in the number of competing common carriers offering communications links to users. Some of the companies in this marketplace include US West Communications, American Satellite Corporation, MCI Communications Corporation, Sprint Communications, RCA Corporation, Southern Pacific Communications Company, and others.

These firms offer both surface (terrestrial) and satellite services domestically. International common carriers that offer voice and data communications services include AT&T, MCI Communications Corporation, Sprint International, ITT World Communications, Inc., and Western Union International, Inc.

Many organizations provide a diverse range of communications and data links to business, education, government, and the military. Companies such as RCA moved from computers into communications. Others, such as AT&T, have moved in the other direction. Recently AT&T purchased NCR Corporation, a major computer manufacturer. This merger creates a giant company, with both computers and communications capabilities, offering integrated services.

The great growth in the communications industry in the last several decades has spawned many common carriers that provide **leased** or **dedicated lines** to end users. These companies, including Southern Pacific, ITT, and others (see Figure 6.3), offer an alternative to existing AT&T **switched network** services. Still others provide even more expanded services known as value-added networks. These companies not only provide communications links, but offer access to databases, computer services, and distributed data processing capability. These firms include Tymnet, Sprint Communications, and others.

```
                        LEASED NETWORKS
        ┌───────────────────┼───────────────────┐
   Sub-Voice Grade      Voice-Grade           Broadband
   (0-150 bits/sec)    (300-9600 bits/sec)   (above 10,000 bits/sec)

   AT&T Series          AT&T Series 3000      AT&T Series 5000 and
   1000 Channels        Channels (MPL)        8000 Channels

   Western Union        Satellite (W.U., RCA, DDS (56 kilobits/sec and
   (Standard and        American Satellite)   1.544 megabits/sec)
   Datacom)
                        Western Union         Western Union
   MCI, Southern        (Standard and         (Standard and Datacom)
   Pacific, ITT,        Datacom)
   and Others                                 Satellite (W.U., RCA,
                        DDS (2400, 4800,      American Satellite)
                        9600 bits/sec)
                                              MCI, ITT, Southern
                        MCI, ITT, Southern    Pacific, and Others
                        Pacific, and Others
```

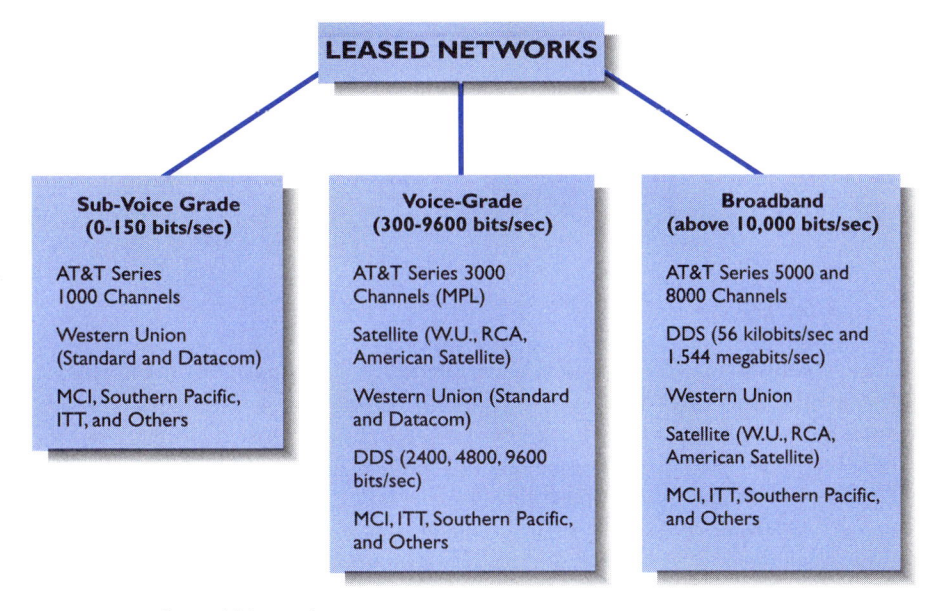

FIGURE 6.3 Leased Networks

Hard-Wire Circuits

Hard-wire circuits, also known as twisted pairs, are the backbone of the communications industry. **Hard-wire circuits** are constructed from copper wire conductors. They are usually strung as **twisted pairs** and are often grouped into cables that run from one point to another. AT&T has for many years used 22 to 26 American Wire Gauge (AWG) size wire for this purpose. If you have a telephone, you probably have a 22 or 26 AWG twisted pair linking your home with your local exchange carrier.

Hard wires are suitable for sending either digital or analog data through the switched network. Ordinary telephone calls are routed through the **Direct Distance Dialing (DDD)** network and can handle speeds of 9,600 bps or more. Other services are available on these lines, including **AT&T's Wide Area Telephone Service (WATS),** which moves voice or data at speeds up to 9,600 bps and, with data compression, up to 14.4 Kbps. WATS lines provide outbound calling. Charges are billed on a bulk rate basis with time, day, and volume usage discounts. AT&T's 800 service is designed for subscribers who receive large volumes of incoming long distance calls. Data and voice can be moved at speeds up to 9,600 bps, with incoming calls billed to the receiver on a bulk rate basis. Chapter 7 explores these services in greater detail.

TWX circuits can move digital data at speeds of up to 150 bps, and **Telex** circuits handle digital data at 50 bps. (See Figure 6.4.) All of these services allow the user to dial a telephone number to access another point. They differ from the leased networks, shown in Figure 6.3, which do not provide switching capability.

FIGURE 6.4
Switched Networks

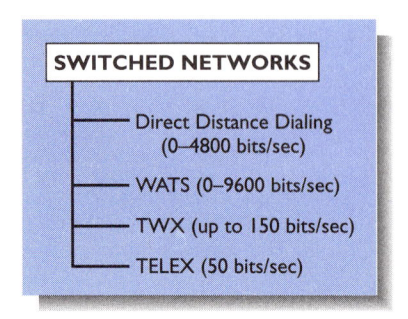

SWITCHED NETWORKS
- Direct Distance Dialing (0–4800 bits/sec)
- WATS (0–9600 bits/sec)
- TWX (up to 150 bits/sec)
- TELEX (50 bits/sec)

The basic unit of AT&T's hard-wire telephone system is the **unconditioned voice-grade line**. This line possesses limited data-handling characteristics because of its limited bandwidth of 2,700 Hz. Nevertheless, it is a basic building block of the switched network. The line can be used to send both digital and analog information.

Other circuits possessing more closely controlled electrical characteristics are also available from AT&T. (See Figure 6.5.) These are known as conditioned circuits and they include C1, C2, C3, C4, and C5 conditioning. Conditioned circuits allow data to be transmitted more reliably than do unconditioned circuits and include other features that reduce signal distortion and delay.

Unloaded Circuits

For many applications, the standard hard-wire circuit or conditioned lines are not acceptable because the circuit includes **line amplifiers** and other reactive components that load the circuit. Whenever line amplifiers are in a circuit, they compensate for signal loss but exclude signals above 300 and below 3,000 Hz. To eliminate this problem, **unloaded lines** known as AT&T 3010 lines, or 11,000-type lines, can be ordered from AT&T. Lines in which loading coils and amplifiers have been removed do not have the same bandwidth or frequency limitations as do other lines; however, they can be used only over short distances because there are no amplifiers to compensate for transmission loss. Unloaded lines are used when a high volume of data is to be transmitted and special high-speed modems are available.

Voice-grade lines, WATS, and 800 service utilize the same inter-trunking, toll, and access facilities. They are all switched network services with the same physical characteristics. Dedicated leased facilities access a LEC just as switched services do. Local loops are modified to meet transmission requirements in a process called conditioning. The inter-trunking and common carrier facility have switched services running through at the same time.

The 20-Mil Current Loop

Figure 6.4 lists several digital switched circuits, referred to as TWX and Telex. These services, which transmit digital data exclusively, serve teleprinter devices known as **Teletype machines**. Devices such as these, sometimes found in business offices, are used to send typewritten messages through a switched network from one point to another, using a **20-milliampere current loop**.

	ATTENUATION DISTORTION (FREQUENCY RESPONSE) RELATIVE TO 1004 Hz		ENVELOPE DELAY DISTORTION	
Channel Conditioning	Frequency Range (Hz)	Variation (dB)	Frequency Range (Hz)	Variation (microseconds)
Basic	500–2500	–2 to + 8	800–2600	1750
	300–3000	–3 to + 12		
C1	1000–2400	–1 to + 3	1000–2400	1000
	300–2700	–2 to + 6	800–2600	1750
C2	300–3000	–3 to + 12		
	500–2800	–1 to + 3	1000–2600	500
	300–3000	–2 to + 6	600–2600	1500
			500–2800	3000
C3 (access line)	500–2800	–0.5 to + 1.5	1000–2600	110
	300–3000	–0.8 to + 3	600–2600	300
			500–2800	650
C3 (trunk)	500–2800	–0.5 to + 1	1000–2600	80
	300–3000	–0.8 to + 2	600–2600	260
			500–2800	500
C4	500–3000	–2 to + 3	1000–2600	300
	300–3200	–2 to + 6	800–2800	500
			600–3000	1500
			500–3000	3000
C5	500–2800	–0.5 to + 1.5	1000–2600	100
	300–3000	–1 to + 3	600–2600	300
			500–2800	600

FIGURE 6.5 Conditioned Circuits

Teletype machines do not modulate carrier waves to transmit data. Instead they open and close a switch contact, resulting in a serial bit pattern transmitted down the line representing a given character. The Telex network uses a 5-bit code system; the TWX system uses a 7-bit plus parity ASCII code. Circuits that transmit open and closed pulses using this arrangement are referred to as 20-mil current loops. They are still in use on Teletype machines and in Telex or TWX digital data services in some countries.

Coaxial Cable

A twisted pair of metallic conductors, such as those discussed above, has several advantages. Twisted wire is inexpensive to manufacture and easy to install. However, its major drawback is its inability to transmit high frequencies, limiting its data transfer rate. Twisted pairs of wires are very susceptible to noise pickup and interference from outside electrical sources. The longer the twisted pair, the greater its susceptibility to noise and the greater its line loss.

To overcome these limitations, **coaxial cable**, often called simply coax, is used for long distance circuits. A coaxial cable is composed of a wire surrounded by an insulator and a shield. The inside conductor is a straight, centered lead enclosed in an outer solid or braided conductor. This shield protects the inner conductor from noise and electrical disturbance. The inner wire is kept properly centered by plastic disks, a tube of Teflon, beads, or other material. (See Figure 6.6.) Coaxial cables may be made up of only one pair of wires, or they may be grouped into cables with eight or more pairs. (See Figure 6.7.) Sometimes a physical-support cable is placed in the center of a group of coaxial cables to relieve strain when the cable is strung over distances. When buried underground, an armored sheath may be placed around the cable.

FIGURE 6.6
Coaxial Cable Construction

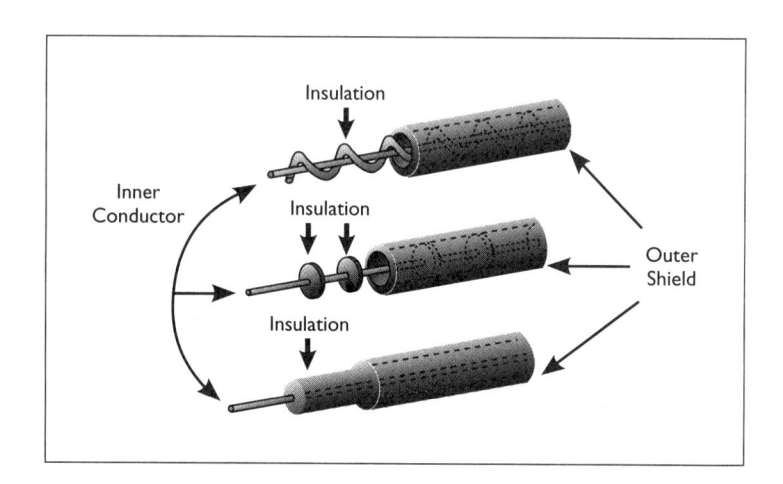

FIGURE 6.7
Coaxial Cable Cross-Section View

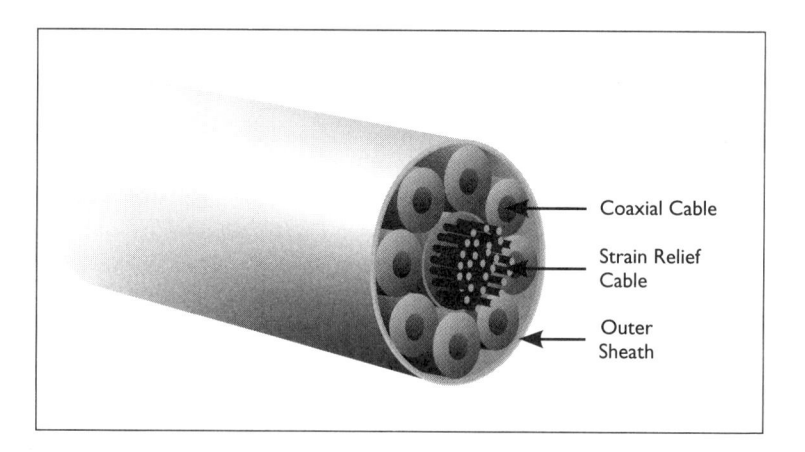

Coaxial cables are used as the major conductors to distribute television signals over cable-access television (CATV) systems. If you live in an area that is served by cable TV, you are probably already familiar with coaxial cables. Coaxial cables are more expensive to install and manufacture than twisted pairs. However, they possess several important advantages. First, they are able to transmit much higher frequencies because of their greater bandwidth. Second, the outer shield protects the inner lead from noise and other electrical interference. Coaxial cables also suffer substantially less line loss when the cable is strung over long distances.

The development and engineering that went into designing cable-access TV systems have been applied to hooking up local area networks (LANs). The same coaxial cables, switches, connectors, and other hardware used to install digital data links were used in video cable systems. These cables string together computers, printers, and communications equipment.

RADIO CIRCUITS

For many years radio was the principal means of providing communications links when hard-wire cables were not feasible. Ship-to-shore radio, transatlantic telephone service, and conventional AM and FM broadcasts used **radio frequency links**. (See Figure 6.8.) Radio signals have many advantages over land lines. They can transmit analog or digital data over short and long distances inexpensively, without the need to string wires from point to point. Radio transmissions, however, are subject to noise pickup, static, and interference. Transmissions can also be intercepted by unauthorized individuals.

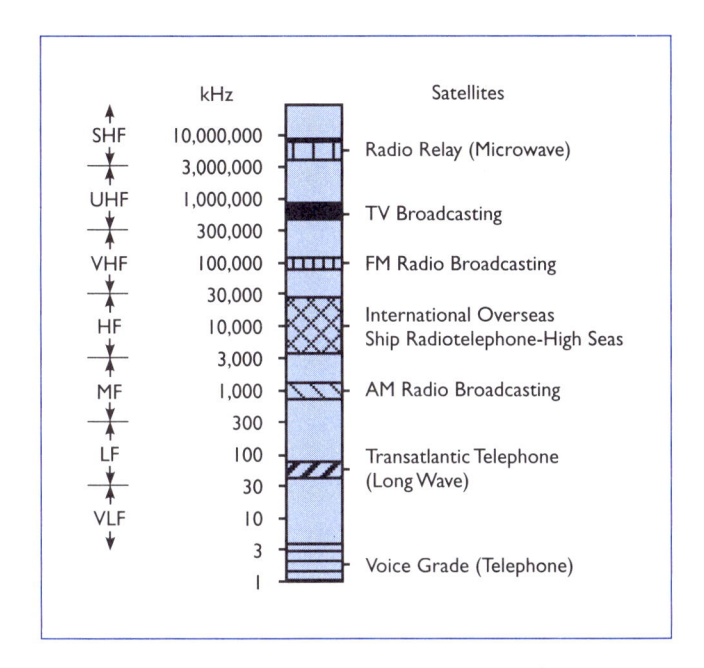

FIGURE 6.8
Frequency Spectrum

Band	kHz	Use
SHF	10,000,000	Satellites
	3,000,000	Radio Relay (Microwave)
UHF	1,000,000	
	300,000	TV Broadcasting
VHF	100,000	FM Radio Broadcasting
	30,000	
HF	10,000	International Overseas
	3,000	Ship Radiotelephone-High Seas
MF	1,000	AM Radio Broadcasting
	300	
LF	100	Transatlantic Telephone
	30	(Long Wave)
VLF	10	
	3	Voice Grade (Telephone)
	1	

Let us review some of the more important forms of radio communications links.

Medium-Frequency AM Radio

AM radio has been used to broadcast digital as well as analog information for many years. The FCC has assigned specific frequencies of the electromagnetic spectrum for commercial radio broadcasts. AM radio occupies the medium-frequency band above and below 1,000 kHz. Other frequencies have been reserved for amateur radio and various forms of telegraphy, facsimile, TV, and so on. (See Figure 6.9.) Some of these frequencies are used by radio amateurs to send **continuous wave (CW)** Morse code signals.

Frequency Band	Emissions
kHz	Type
1800-2000	A1,A3
3500-4000	A1
3500-3775	F1
3775-3890	A5,F5
3775-4000	A3,F3
7000-7300	A1
7000-7150	F1
7075-7100	A3,F3
7150-7225	A5,F5
7150-7300	A3,F3
14000-14350	A1
14000-14200	F1
14200-14275	A5,F5
14200-14350	A3,F3

Frequency Band	Emissions
MHz	Type
21.000-21.450	A1
21.000-21.250	F1
21.250-21.350	A5,F5
21.250-21.450	A3,F3
28.000-29.700	A1
28.000-28.500	F1
28.500-29.700	A3,F3,A5,F5
50,000-54,000	A1
50,100-54,000	A2,A3,A4,A5,F1,F2,F3,F5
51.000-54.000	A0
144-148	A1
144.100-148.000	A0,A2,A3,A4,A5,F0,F1,F2,F3,F5
220-225	A0,A1,A2,A3,A4,A5,F0,F1,F2,F3,F4,F5
420-450	A0,A1,A2,A3,A4,A5,F0,F1,F2,F3,F4,F5
1215-1300	A0,A1,A2,A3,A4,A5,F0,F1,F2,F3,F4,F5
2300-2450	A0,A1,A2,A3,A4,A5,F0,F1,F2,F3,F4,F5,P
3300-3500	A0,A1,A2,A3,A4,A5,F0,F1,F2,F3,F4,F5,P
5650-5925	
10000-10500	A0,A1,A2,A3,A4,A5,F0,F1,F2,F3,F4,F5
21000-22000	A0,A1,A2,A3,A4,A5,F0,F1,F2,F3,F4,F5,P

Type A0 – Steady, Unmodulated Pure Carrier
Type A1 – Telegraphy on Pure Continuous Waves
Type A2 – Amplitude Tone-Modulated Telegraphy
Type A3 – AM Telephony Including Single and Double Sideband, with Full, Reduced, or Suppressed Carrier
Type A4 – Facsimile
Type A5 – Television
Type F0 – Steady, Unmodulated Pure Carrier
Type F1 – Carrier-Shift Telegraphy
Type F2 – Audio Frequency-Shift Telegraphy
Type F3 – Frequency- or Phase-Modulated Telephony
Type F4 – FM Facsimile
Type F5 – FM Television
Type P – Pulse Emissions

FIGURE 6.9 Frequency Assignments

Radio amateurs pioneered many early forms of digital data transmission. Today a large volume of digital data is sent not only by radio amateurs but by commercial services. They send signals over AM radio, using Teletype machines similar to those discussed in the section, "The 20-Mil Current Loop." This service is known as **RTTY**, short for **radio Teletype**.

High-Frequency Radio

In recent years a good deal of interest has evolved around high-frequency (HF) radio circuits for transmitting digital data. This interest has led to the development of **packet radio networks**, which use either a central radio transmitter or a distributed system of radio repeaters. (See Figure 6.10.) A system using packet radio, developed by the University of Hawaii, was put into service in 1970. The network, called **ALOHANET**, tied together various campuses of the University of Hawaii, using radio frequency signals. ALOHANET uses two channels—one for sending and the other for receiving digital data—in frequencies above 400 MHz. The system transmits data by radio waves at speeds up to 9,600 bps. The digital information is transmitted as a packet from point to point. It is received, amplified by a repeater, and transmitted to the next station. A system such as this allows large volumes of data to be transmitted reliably over water, where twisted wire conductors or other physical connections would not be practical.

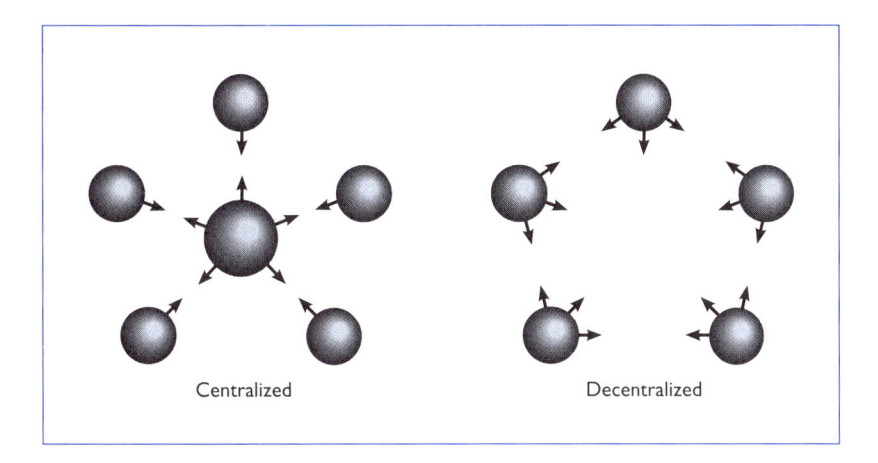

FIGURE 6.10 Packet Radio Networks

Centralized   Decentralized

FM Radio

FM radio provides another form of digital, as well as analog, communications link. FM radio is relatively free from static and interference. Signals can be broadcast over great distances at relatively low cost. You have probably sat next to someone in a movie theater or at a party and heard his or her paging beeper go off. These **paging systems** use **FM radio signals** to send both analog and digital signals.

A central FM transmitter broadcasts analog or digital data over a wide geographic area. Receivers located within the region pick up the analog or digital signals and trip a beeper that alerts an individual to a message being sent. FM radio systems can send digital data such as names and telephone numbers that can then be stored in the pager's memory. These data can be displayed or saved at the option of the person carrying the pager.

Many metropolitan police departments rely on digital FM systems rather than voice-radio networks for communications. The cliche "calling all cars," crackling over the police radio, has been replaced by a modern digital terminal in the police vehicle. The remote terminal enables police officers in the field to search a database and print out a search warrant. Information on suspects can be transmitted to headquarters, and an immediate reply can be received in the police vehicle and acted on.

The Los Angeles Police Department, for example, has installed an FM radio system that sends digital data between police cars and the central station. Crime reports, data on stolen vehicles, and information on missing persons, for example, are received by the police cars' radios and displayed on monitors. Police officers in the field can keyboard data for transmission by FM radio back to headquarters.

FM radio is used in air traffic control. Aircraft equipped with devices known as altitude encoding transponders can pick up radar signals from air traffic centers that are then echoed back to the controller. These transponders encode the aircraft's altitude. The digital data are then displayed on the air traffic controller's radar screen, enabling the operator to track the aircraft.

Wireless Message Center

The union of the personal computer and the wireless paging system has given birth to the wireless message center. The system links computers and pagers, allowing electronic mail messages, including both business and personal communications, to be routed quickly and easily without wires.

Suppose a sales manager wishes to send an immediate message to a salesperson, who is in transit between two clients. The manager sits in front of her personal computer and keyboards the text of the message. It is then routed through her modem over telephone lines to a local paging service. (See Figure 6.11.) There the digital message is sent to an orbiting satellite and bounced back to a local transmitter, which broadcasts the message to a moving vehicle. The salesperson is alerted to the incoming message by a beep on the portable wireless receiver. (See Figure 6.12.) There the digital message is displayed. The salesperson may then respond to the message, call the office, or take whatever action is appropriate.

CHAPTER 6 / COMMUNICATIONS MEDIA   149

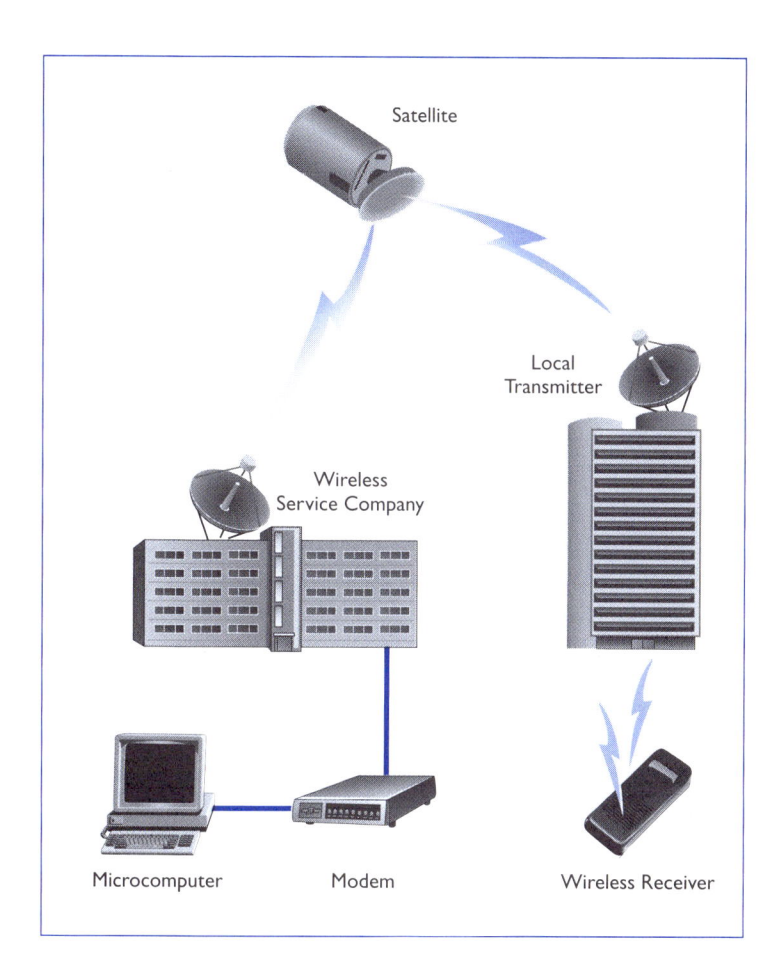

FIGURE 6.11
Wireless Message Center

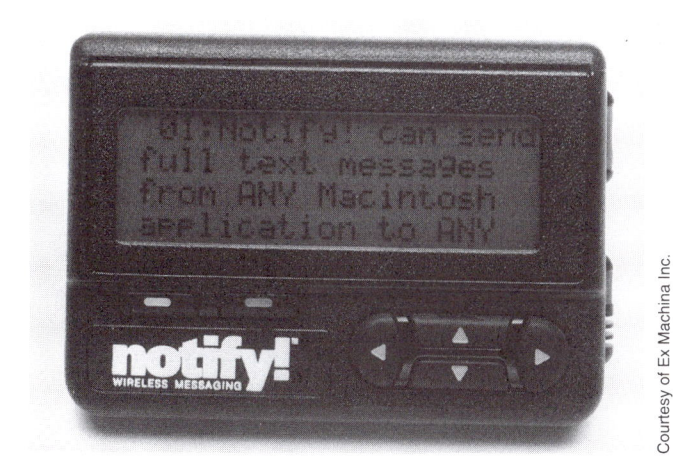

FIGURE 6.12
Wireless Receiver

Courtesy of Ex Machina Inc.

The wireless message center is able to route messages to multiple pagers, to airplanes in flight, or to radio-equipped computers with portable modems. Messages can also be sent to MCI Mail or CompuServe. These systems, in turn, send the message on to other computers or generate a hard copy that is delivered by messenger. Wireless message systems allow news media, business executives, service managers, and others to be in direct communication with their home offices at all times.

Multiplexed Radio

Many FM stations transmit digital information over the same carrier waves used to broadcast music or other regular programming. A communications link is established on a subcarrier of its regular modulated frequency. Using one transmitter and its primary carrier, an FM station is able to multiplex digital data from several channels. These **subchannels** are sold to other organizations for paging purposes.

The basic operating costs are paid for by paging users who use the subchannels. Additional revenue may be obtained from advertisers who sell their products over the FM station's primary carrier. Collectively, these two services allow a broadcaster to operate profitably.

Cellular Radio Telephones

A prominent innovation in radio communications is **cellular radio telephone** service. This service provides private individuals, as well as businesses, with mobile telephones located in cars, trucks, buses, and other vehicles. It also serves hand-held instruments that may be carried in a purse or clipped to a belt.

In cellular radio a region is broken down into a honeycomb-like grid. (See Figure 6.13.) A relay station, known as a **repeater,** is located in the center of each cell of the honeycomb. It picks up a low power signal, such as a signal from an automobile telephone or hand-held transceiver, and relays it to a local telephone office. As an individual drives through the region, the call is handed off from one repeater to the next. This new system allows thousands of mobile telephones to be in use simultaneously.

Cellular radio has opened up many new communications possibilities. For example, cellular telephone service has been implemented along highway Interstate 10 between Houston and New Orleans, a distance of 350 miles. (See Figure 6.14.) Drivers equipped with cellular telephones may send or receive calls anywhere along the route. As a vehicle leaves one cell and enters another, the call is handed off to a different repeater without any interruption in service.

In earlier radio telephone systems, many users had to share one channel that covered a large geographic area. However, in cellular radio, low-powered transmitters that cover short distances are used. Thus, many mobile phones can operate in one region because each is operating on low power and communicating with a nearby relay station in the center of each cell. Cellular telephone service is widely used for voice transmissions. However, it can also handle digital data as well.

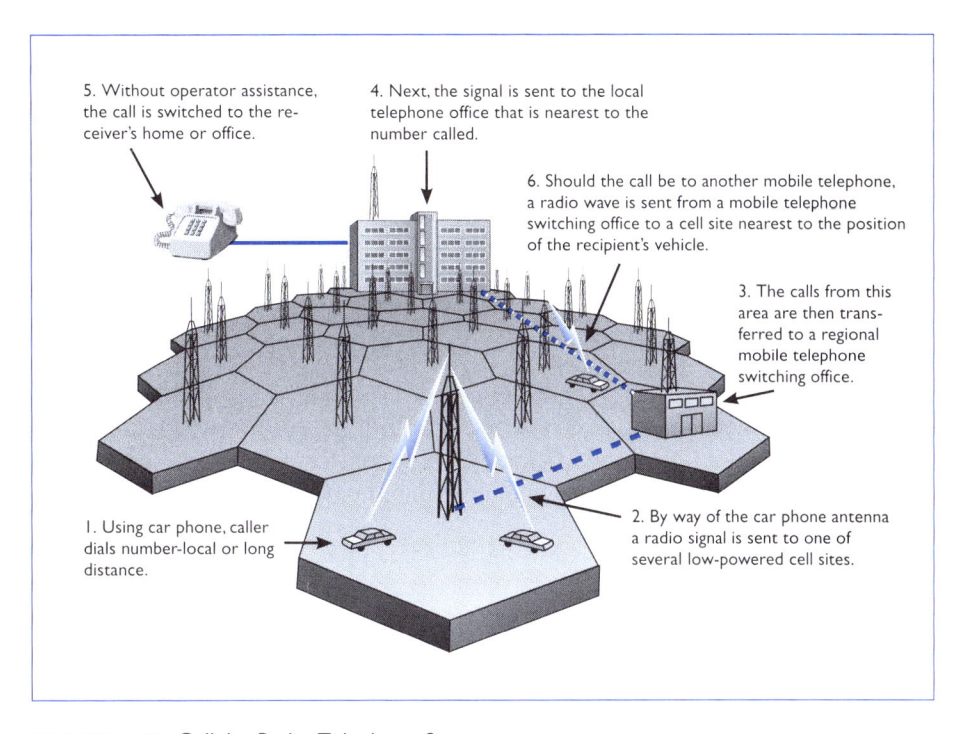

FIGURE 6.13 Cellular Radio Telephone System

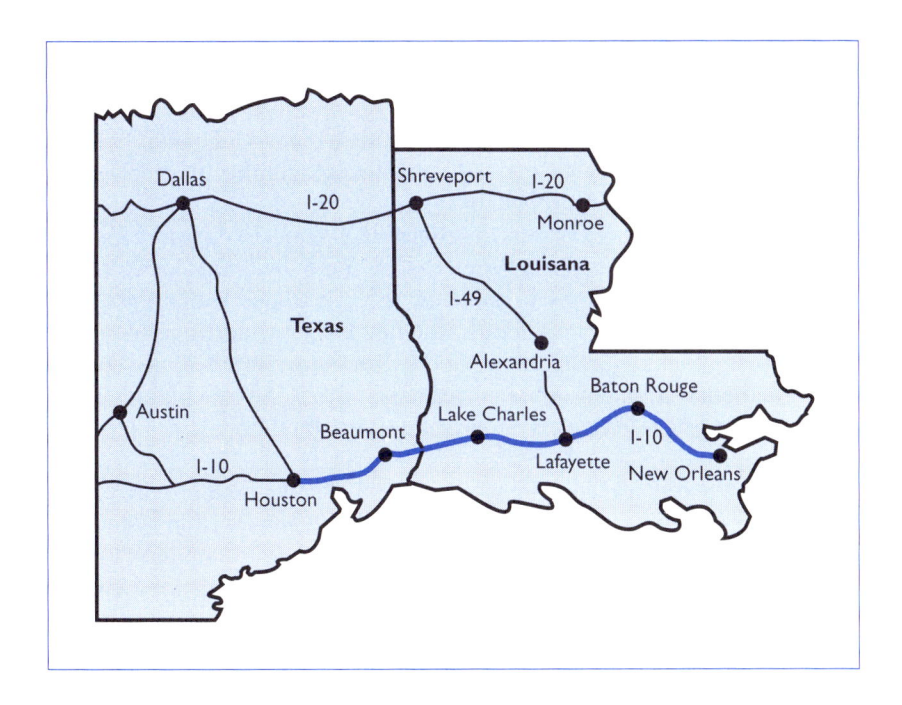

FIGURE 6.14 Cellular Radio Along Interstate 10

Cellular radio is particularly advantageous in rural or remote areas by allowing telephone service in homes or temporary sites where a cable is not present. It also provides service where an existing cable has reached full capacity. Cellular radio service is an excellent backup for police, fire, medical, and other services where a disruption to a cable could create severe communications problems.

Cellular radio calls, like any other form of broadcast signal, can be intercepted by unauthorized individuals. Unless a scrambler is used, anyone can monitor the band and listen to calls.

Cellular Fax Machines

Battery-operated fax machines may be connected to cellular telephones. In this arrangement, documents can be transmitted from the field to other fax machines located in homes and offices. The system allows signed orders to be faxed into an office, or a hard-copy printout can be obtained from the fax unit in the field or from a motor vehicle, train, or boat.

The system is wireless, as opposed to conventional fax machines, which use telephone lines. The portable fax machine converts a page of text, drawings, or images into a stream of binary bits. These bits, in turn, modulate a carrier wave, transmitting the material over the cellular telephone to another fax machine. The second fax machine may be connected to the switched telephone network or may also be a portable cellular fax machine.

Videotex and Teletext

Videotex and teletext systems are in widespread use in Europe and the United States. **Videotex** systems transmit digital data over telephone lines or coaxial cables to be displayed on television screens. Current events, news, weather reports, community bulletins, and more, are sent over videotex systems. In **teletext**, similar information is broadcast over the air and received by television sets.

Some retailers are using videotex systems to sell goods. Prospective customers see goods displayed on a screen and then make purchases by sending digital signals back over closed-circuit coaxial cable. Many homes now receive videotex data via their already-in-place CATV system. Sports, news, theater reviews, and features are received in homes, sometimes replacing newspapers as a news source. Many hotels offer news, travel, and entertainment options over cable TV. Some provide detailed descriptions on the use of the telephone system, television, or other services offered to hotel guests.

A large volume of teletext is already being transmitted over TV. You are probably familiar with the CC, or closed caption, logo; it indicates that the television station is broadcasting digital text on a subcarrier of its main channel. Hearing-impaired viewers can receive these signals and, with the proper decoder, superimpose the text over the picture on the screen.

MICROWAVE RELAY SYSTEMS

A large volume of analog and digital information is handled through **microwave transmission links**. Microwaves consist of high-frequency electromagnetic waves in the range of 1 GHz to 23 GHz. Both analog and digital data can be encoded on a carrier wave that is transmitted from point to point using highly directional microwave beams.

Before the advent of satellites, microwave systems formed the backbone of long distance telephone communications. Figure 6.15 illustrates a parabolic antenna used for microwave transmission. Microwaves, directional in nature, behave very much like beams of light. A microwave beam can be projected through space, reflected around a corner, or channeled through tubelike guides. Long distances are covered by transmitting microwave signals from tower to tower, each in sight of the other. (See Figure 6.16.) The spacing between towers ranges from 20 to 35 miles. As microwave signals move through the atmosphere, they diminish in strength. Each tower is equipped with a large horn-shaped receiving antenna. The electrical signal is picked up and fed through **waveguides**, hollow tubes that reflect and direct the high-frequency radio signals, to an amplifier.

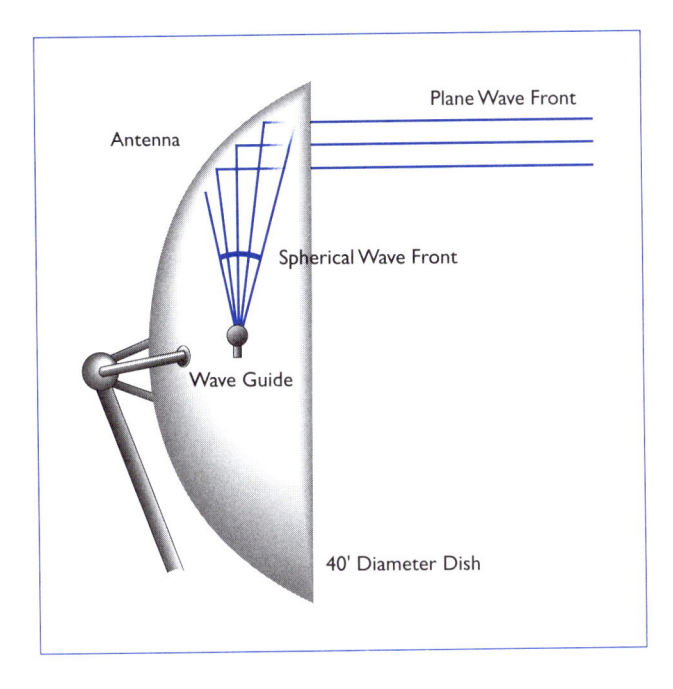

FIGURE 6.15
Parabolic Microwave Antenna. Specially shaped antennas receive microwave signals, channel them through waveguides, amplify the signals, and send them on to the next antenna.

FIGURE 6.16
Microwave Relay Tower

After the signal is amplified, it is fed back to the tower and then transmitted on another antenna down to the next station. Systems that move a high volume of traffic use a full-duplex arrangement. This arrangement requires a separate transmitting and receiving antenna, operating on different frequencies, on each tower.

If there is not a clear line of sight between towers, due to mountains or terrain, then the transmitting and receiving antennas must be spaced more closely together, greatly increasing the cost of the system. As more earth-orbiting satellites are put into space, the use of ground-based microwave systems to transmit and receive information will diminish.

SATELLITE TRANSMISSIONS

Some of the most spectacular advances in communications technology have been in the field of **satellite communications**. Today, earth-orbiting satellites form an important part of the world's communications system. They link together ground stations around the globe, using **geosynchronous satellites** positioned at strategic points over the earth. A geosynchronous satellite rotates around the globe in a fixed position with respect to the earth. (See Figure 6.17.)

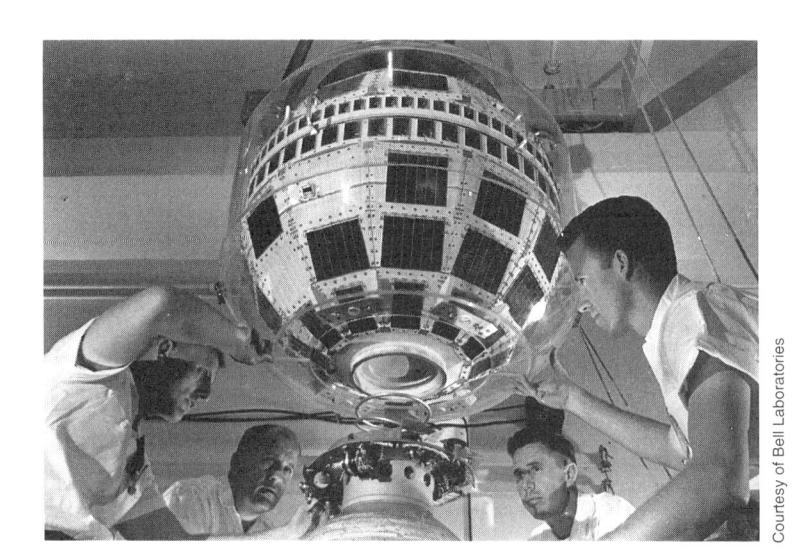

FIGURE 6.17
Telecommunications Satellite

The first communications satellite, Telstar, was launched in 1962. It was an earth-orbiting satellite placed in a synchronous orbit around the globe. Three strategically placed satellites can effectively cover the entire globe. An earth station transmits a signal to the orbiting satellite. (See Figure 6.18.) The satellite receives the signal, amplifies it, and then transmits it back to earth. The pathway from the first earth station up to the satellite is called the **uplink**, and the signal sent back to earth is called the **downlink**. By placing a series of geosynchronous satellites around the globe, it is possible to establish worldwide communications without the need to string wires or construct microwave relay stations.

Communications satellites are sophisticated and complex pieces of equipment. (See Figure 6.19.) They must be able to remain in a precise orbit for many years and receive, amplify, and retransmit signals, using an onboard transponder. The transponder receives a signal from earth on the uplink channel, amplifies it, and transmits it back to earth on the downlink channel. Satellites are also equipped with receiving and transmitting antennas that can be precisely positioned with respect to earth stations. In addition, they must also contain their own electrical generating system. Solar panels, which convert sunlight to power that energizes the transponder circuitry, are an efficient means of generating electrical energy.

Today there are hundreds of communications satellites orbiting the earth, relaying data, voice, and television signals all over the globe. Certain frequencies have been set aside for satellite communications. The **C Band** uses 6 GHz for its uplink and 4 GHz for its downlink. This provides numerous wideband communications links on one circuit. Because of its frequency, relatively large receiving antennas, called **dishes**, are required.

The **Ku Band** utilizes the 14 GHz and 12 GHz frequencies. Even shorter wavelengths are used. The **K Band** uses the 30 GHz and 20 GHz frequencies. These higher frequencies use sending and receiving dishes of smaller diameters and allow more satellites to be stationed in orbit without interfering with one another. Higher frequencies mean less expensive dishes and greater portability of equipment.

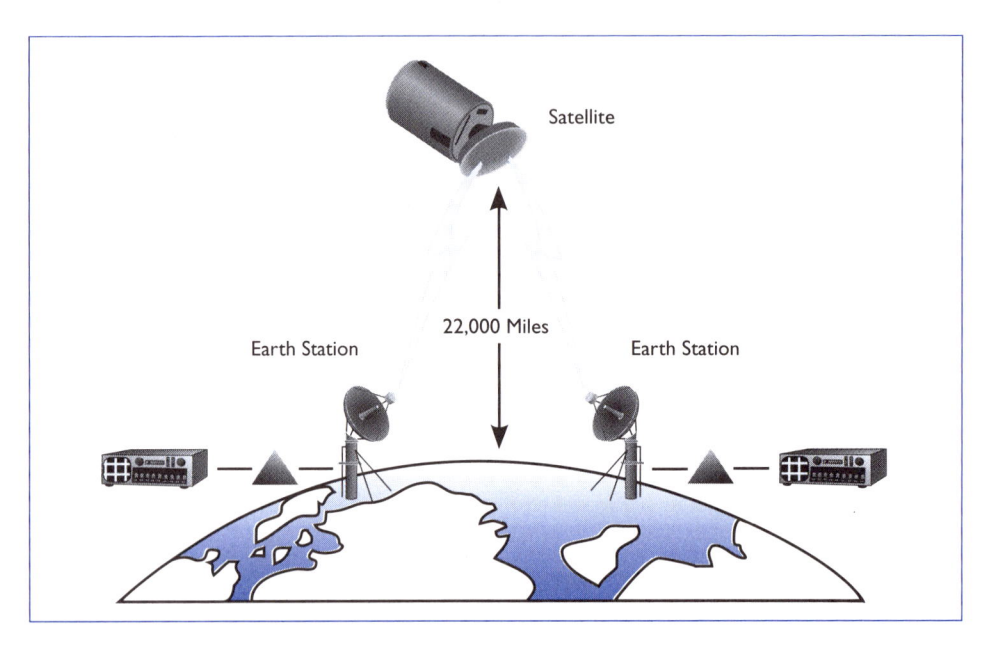

FIGURE 6.18 Earth Stations with Orbiting Satellite

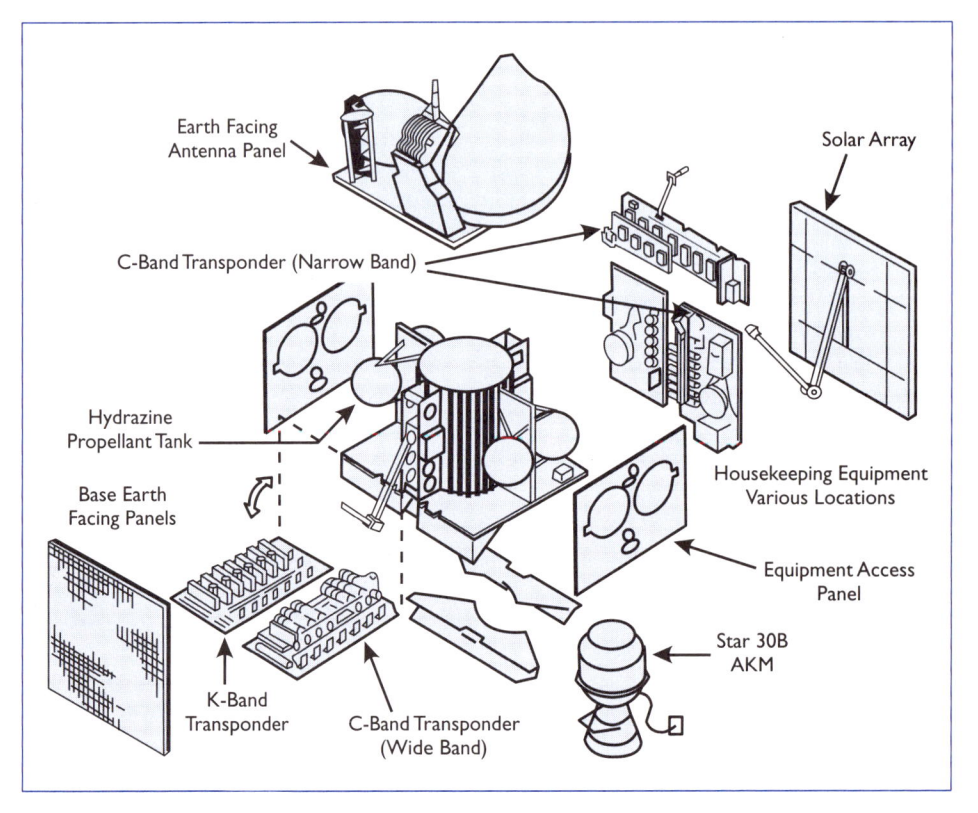

FIGURE 6.19 Satellite Construction

A great deal of research and development continue to go into satellite communications. Once the satellites are in place, they provide a reliable and inexpensive means of worldwide communications. Their initial costs are, however, extremely high, involving millions of dollars in engineering costs and a substantial investment in the rocketry needed to place the satellite in proper orbit. Failed satellites have been retrieved, repaired, and placed back in orbit.

FIBER-OPTIC TRANSMISSION

Another rapidly growing technology is **fiber optics**. Millions of dollars are being spent on research and development, as well as the installation, of fiber-optic cables between cities and between continents. A light signal can be sent down a thin filament of glass and thus transmit information. Almost no light loss occurs when a beam of light is passed through a strand of glass perhaps four or five miles in length. This capability forms the basis for fiber-optic transmission. Cables consisting of dozens of filaments of fine glass fibers are woven into a bundle, which is then covered with a protective plastic shield. Fiber-optic cables provide a pathway for moving light beams. (See Figure 6.20.)

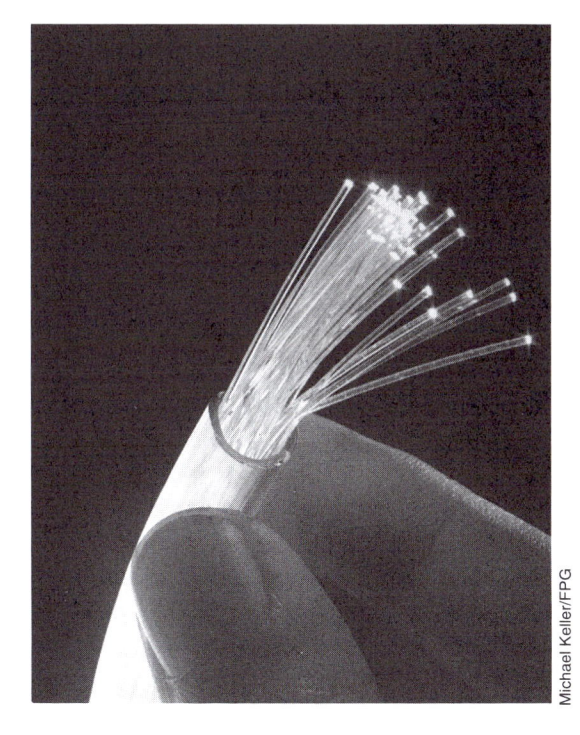

FIGURE 6.20
Fiber-Optic Cable

Michael Keller/FPG

The Bell companies and other organizations worldwide are rapidly moving toward a digital loop carrier system designed to handle traffic on a **synchronous optical network (SONET)**. International standards have been developed for the transfer of information over fiber-optic cables. The SONET standards specify a frame structure, header information, and data transfer speeds. North American fiber-optic systems send data at rates in excess of 51.84 megabits per second. Other networks are developing systems to move data well in excess of 139 megabits per second, and as high as 500 megabits per second. Further development promises rates in excess of 1.5 gigabits per second. This rate is substantially faster than conventional transmission systems.

AT&T is racing against its competitors to provide fiber-optic cable service worldwide. (See Figure 6.21.) AT&T is competing with British Telecommunications PLC, which is establishing a worldwide fiber-optic network. Neither MCI Communications, Sprint Corporation, nor AT&T have developed a program as extensive as British Telecommunications PLC. The winner of this race will no doubt command the position of global supercarrier leader in the next decade.

FIGURE 6.21
Installation of Underground Fiber-Optic Cable

A major advantage of fiber-optic transmission is its extreme bandwidth. Fiber-optic cables are able to pass signals of up to 500 MHz or more; this means that tens of thousands of telephone calls or digital data transmissions can be sent through a single fiber-optic circuit. Signals move through the glass filaments as pulses of light and are not susceptible to noise or interference from electrical circuits. Fiber optics are also used to send signals under water. Because glass will not rust, it is particularly suited to underwater links between cities where microwave towers cannot be installed.

The reliability and bandwidth of fiber optics, especially in undersea service, have made it a major competitor to orbiting satellites. Once an undersea cable is laid, it remains in place and is much easier to service than orbiting satellites.

Information sent down a fiber-optic cable is not easily intercepted by unauthorized persons as it is in satellite or radio broadcast communications. However, as with any cable system, fiber-optic cables are subject to damage and vandalism. Fiber-optic transmission also offers a high degree of clarity for voice communications. You may have seen the TV commercials that claim, "You can hear a pin drop!" for systems that rely on fiber-optic transmission networks.

AT&T has invested millions of dollars in a 21,000-mile domestic fiber-optic network. (See Figure 6.22.) This network moves voice, data, and video across the country from New England through the South and up the West Coast. MCI, Sprint, and other common carriers have also invested heavily in domestic fiber-optic transmission.

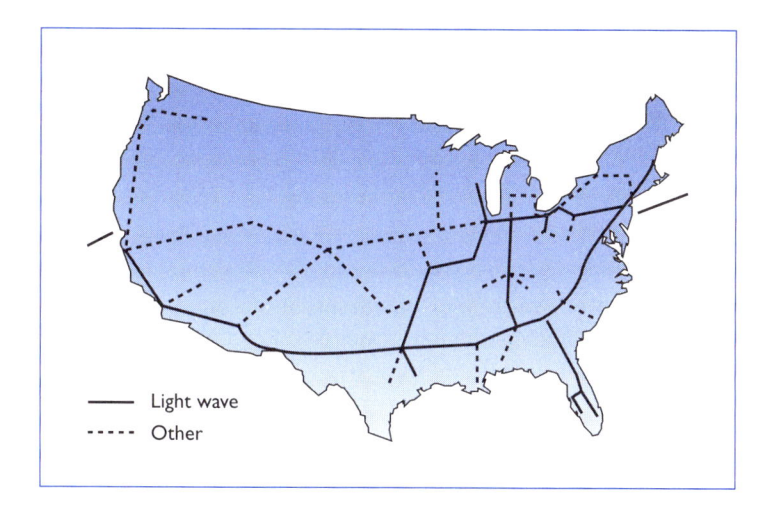

FIGURE 6.22 AT&T Fiber-Optic Network

Laser Beams

Laser beams are used to send analog and digital information through fiber-optic cables. The term laser is an acronym for Light Amplification by Stimulated Emission of Radiation. A **laser beam** is a high-intensity, focused path of coherent light. Laser beams do not spread like ordinary beams of light. (See Figure 6.23.) If one were to shine a high-intensity flashlight beam of ordinary white light at a great distance, the resulting spot would probably cover many feet; this occurs because light energy is scattered as it moves through the atmosphere. On the other hand, a laser light beam focused on an object many miles away would spread only a fraction of an inch.

These tightly focused beams of coherent light are used to transmit signals over long distances through fiber-optic cables. Laser beams have a high degree of communications security because the beams are not intercepted as easily as radio signals. Laser beams have wide bandwidth, thus offering high transmission rates.

FIGURE 6.23
Laser Beams. A laser beam does not spread like an ordinary beam of light.

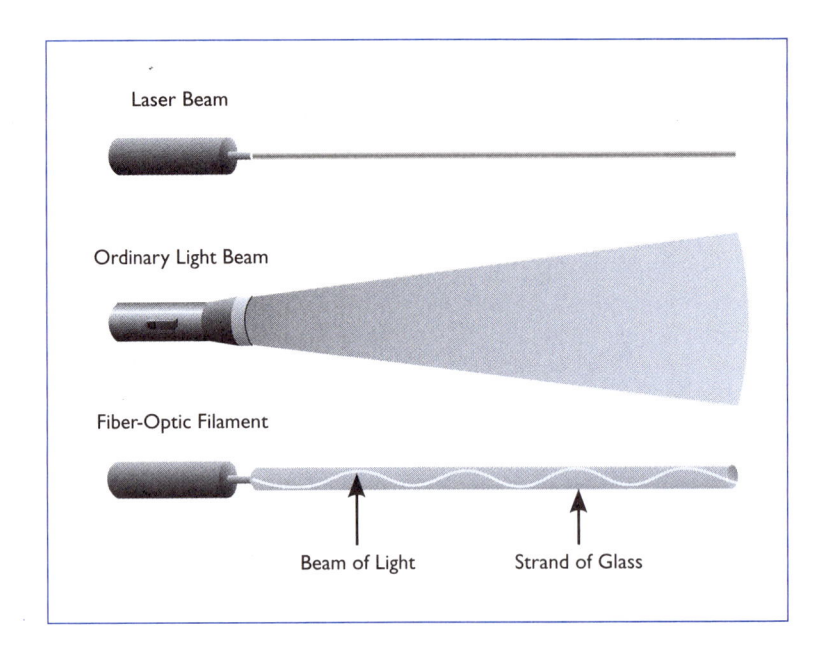

- Laser Beam
- Ordinary Light Beam
- Fiber-Optic Filament
  - Beam of Light
  - Strand of Glass

In this chapter we have reviewed traditional communications media, such as twisted pairs of wires, and described some of the new space-age technology. Research is being done on still other media, such as infrared transmission systems. Now that we have reviewed common communications media, we will move on to study communications software packages.

SUMMARY

The *communications link* is a common element in all communications systems. Communications links are sometimes known as *data links*. *Common carriers* make their communications services available to all users for a fee. Ordinary telephone calls are routed through the *Direct Distance Dialing (DDD)* networks.

An *unloaded circuit* has its *conditioning* changed by the removal of *line amplifiers*. A *20-milliampere current loop* is generally used to communicate with *Teletype* machines. A *coaxial cable* is composed of a single conductor surrounded by a shield. Coaxial cables have less line loss than *twisted pairs* and are used for long distance circuits.

The union of the personal computer and the wireless paging system has given birth to the *wireless message center*. The system links computers and pagers, allowing electronic mail messages, including both business and personal communications, to be routed quickly and easily.

Radio frequency links are used to send digital data as well as voice communications. *Packet radio networks* use high-frequency carrier waves to transmit digital data.

Frequency modulated carriers are often used to send digital data. An additional channel can be *multiplexed* on a radio transmission by using a *subcarrier*. In *cellular radio* a region is broken down into a grid and signals are sent to vehicles as they move from cell to cell.

Cellular radio telephone systems allow many callers to share frequencies in a small geographic area, using *repeaters*. Portable fax machines can transmit text or graphic images through cellular radio telephones to other fax machines.

Videotex is able to transmit digital data to television sets located in homes and offices, while *teletext* broadcasts similar data over the air waves. *Microwaves* in the range of 1 GHz to 23 GHz are used to transmit analog and digital data over distances. *Geosynchronous satellites* are able to receive information from earth stations, amplify them, and send them back to earth.

Fiber-optic cables, using thin filaments of glass, can transmit information over long distances. *Laser beams*, using a high-intensity, focused path of light, can be used to transmit information through fiber-optic cables.

EXERCISES

1. List the major forms of communications links.
2. Describe the unloaded circuit.
3. Describe how paging systems operate.
4. Describe how teletext systems operate.
5. Contrast the function of uplinks and downlinks.
6. List three common bands used for satellite communications.
7. What are the advantages of fiber-optic circuits?
8. Contrast laser beams with ordinary light beams.
9. Describe how laser beams are used to send signals through fiber-optic cables.
10. Describe the makeup of coaxial cable.

HANDS-ON PROJECTS

- Visit a local communications company that sells cellular telephones. Make a list of the features and prices of different cellular phones.

- If you have a friend or neighbor whose automobile is equipped with a cellular telephone, ask to inspect the system. Determine the usage pricing system and how the phone is installed in the automobile.

- Refer to your local Yellow Pages. Count the number of establishments offering microwave, fiber-optic, or satellite communications services. What conclusions can you draw?

- Visit the engineer at a local radio station and discuss the communications system, use of satellites, and remote services.

- Visit a local television station. Discuss satellite communications with an engineer. Make a list of the station's different communications modes.

COMMUNICATIONS IN ACTION

CASE SOLUTION
AARONSON DISTRIBUTORS

The solution to Aaronson's problem was the installation of a teleconferencing network. (See Figure 6.24.) The organization set up conference rooms in its major plants and equipped them with a variety of audio and video facilities. This arrangement enables the five conference rooms to be connected together, using satellite transmission and common carrier circuits.

Those in attendance sit at a conference table situated before a video camera that picks up their images and voices. Each conference room is equipped with a large-screen television monitor. Pictures of participants, charts, graphs, or videotapes can be displayed on this monitor. The video cassette recorder in each conference room allows the dialogue to be taped for later review. For some less demanding conferences, still figures and graphics are acceptable, and slow-scan television is used. Executives can send charts, graphics, and still matter, as well as the spoken voice and video pictures, over the system.

Aaronson's executives now rely heavily on teleconferencing rather than extensive personal travel. They hold high-level planning meetings without leaving their home bases. Marketing managers can discuss new product ideas with research and development personnel and others by video conferencing. Because direct eye contact can be made and gestures and facial expressions can be seen, communication among company executives improves.

Travel in the corporate jet has been reduced, as have hotel and other expenses. Better decisions are made because executives are more responsive and can act quickly. Morale is higher as executives are not faced with extensive and tiring travel schedules and time away from their families. The video cassette recording capability enables conferences to be replayed, thus giving managers a better picture of other people's points of view. Charts, tables, and graphics can be reviewed at any time after the conference.

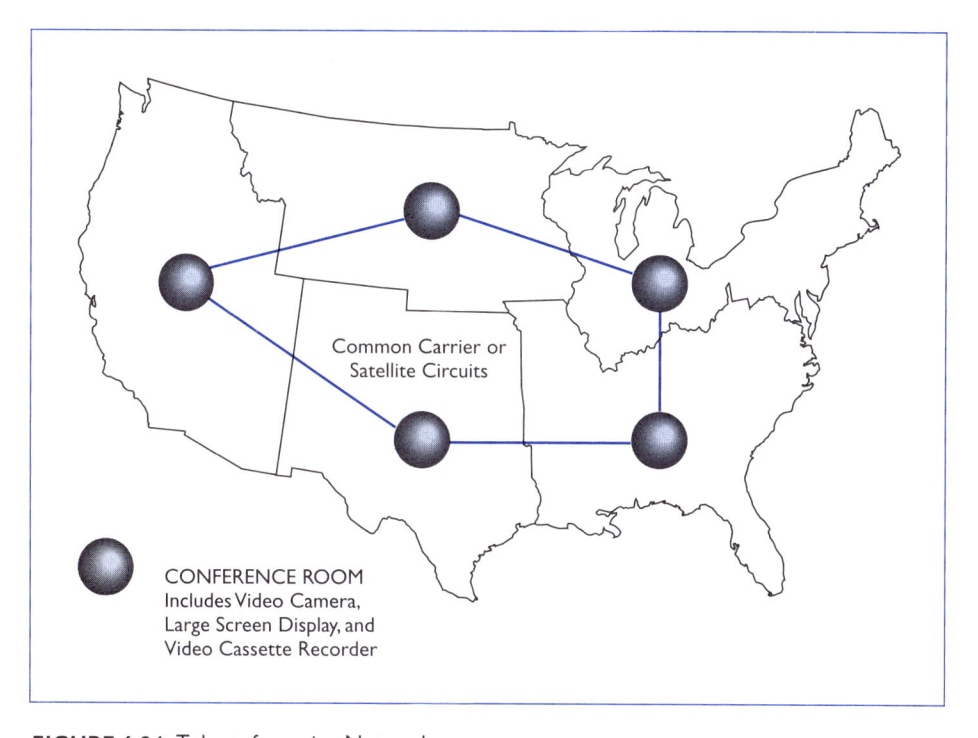

FIGURE 6.24 Teleconferencing Network

BUSINESS COMMUNICATIONS SERVICES

LEARNING OBJECTIVES

After studying this chapter, you should be able to:

- Describe the Integrated Services Digital Network (ISDN)
- Describe outbound common carrier services
- Describe inbound common carrier services
- Discuss various ACCUNET digital services
- Describe satellite and video services
- Discuss teleconferencing and messaging services

COMMUNICATIONS IN ACTION

CASE PROBLEM
WORLD SPORTS TODAY

INTEGRATED SERVICES DIGITAL NETWORK

World Sports Today is a weekly national magazine devoted to reporting worldwide sports activities. Each week, the publication contains over 100 pages of color pictures and artwork, reporting on worldwide sports events. The publication has both domestic and worldwide subscribers.

Because of competition from newspapers and television, it is essential that *World Sports Today* report scores, sports news, and tournament results promptly. It is able to maintain its subscription base because of the large number of color pictures in each edition. Many readers prefer to obtain sports news through this colorful publication rather than other media. As a result, *World Sports Today* prints hundreds of color pictures, always produced under a deadline.

The editorial offices are located in one major city, the advertising offices are in another city, the design department is in a third city, and the printing plant is in yet a fourth location. Consequently, production problems abound. The page layout, artwork and graphic design, advertising production, and preparation of color separations needed for printing are done in different cities.

After the publication has been assembled, color proofs of the pages are checked by both the editorial staff and the advertising staff. After corrections are entered by the design staff, the finished pages are sent to the large midwestern printing plant, where the publication is printed and mailed.

Until recently, *World Sports Today* transmitted copy, artwork, color-separated photographs, and other production items among the four cities, using 9.6 Kbps modems, via ordinary dial-up telephone lines. As a result, transmitting a four-color page from point to point could take as long as an hour and 15 minutes. It required a 24-hour period to transmit the entire publication. Faster results could be obtained using point-to-point leased lines. This alternative could be expensive because much of the time the dedicated lines would sit idle.

If you were the communications manager for *World Sports Today*, how would you speed up the production process and reduce costs? Refer to the end of this chapter to see how the *World Sports Today* communications manager analyzed the problem and planned a new communications system.

OVER the past several decades, business communications services have expanded greatly. Once there was only one telephone company; it offered local and long distance services and gave customers a choice of telephone type, as long as it was black. Today, the communications industry has changed tremendously. Now, dozens of common carriers offer a vast array of long distance services, including satellite, fiber-optic, and mobile paging services.

Hundreds of companies sell telephones, switching equipment, PBXs, answering machines, voice mail devices, and ordinary telephones, usually in a wide variety of colors. The student of data communications should be able to maneuver through this vast array of communications equipment and services.

This chapter focuses principally on the business communications services offered by common carriers. AT&T provides the most comprehensive long distance, ISDN, satellite, and video services of any common carrier. However, AT&T is not exclusive in the long distance market. It has two major competitors, MCI Communications Corporation and Sprint Corporation.

This chapter provides an overview of network capabilities and business services offered not only by AT&T, but by its two major competitors. A comprehensive Business Communications Services Guide is available from the AT&T Customer Information Center in Indianapolis, Indiana. Similar product reference guides are available from both Sprint and MCI. This chapter provides a sampling of the broad range of services offered by these common carriers.

OVERVIEW OF SERVICES

There are many different ways to classify the hundreds of circuits, message handling and routing services, switching capability, and products offered by common carriers. AT&T categorizes its services according to several basic categories, which include the ISDN network, outbound services, inbound services, and information services, among others. (See Figure 7.1.) This chapter is organized around this logical structuring of services.

Integrated Services Digital Network (ISDN)
Outbound Services
Inbound Services
Information Services
Digital Services
Unified Network Management Architechture (UNMA)
Satellite Services
Video Services
Teleconferencing Services
International Services
Voice Messaging Services
Consumer Communications Services

FIGURE 7.1
AT&T Service Offerings

INTEGRATED SERVICES DIGITAL NETWORK

AT&T has pioneered the **Integrated Services Digital Network (ISDN)**, designed to offer end-to-end digital communications service. Today, Sprint and MCI support the ISDN. The ISDN eliminates the need for modems and allows voice, data, and other signals to be sent simultaneously over a line. The ISDN is part of a growing worldwide network.

ISDN offers customers two services:

1. *Basic Rate Interface (BRI)*—two 64 Kbps bearer channels and one 16 Kbps data channel
2. *Primary Rate Interface (PRI)*—twenty-three 64 Kbps bearer channels and one 16 Kbps data channel, supporting 1.544 Mbps transmission speed

The PRI interface, which connects to 4ESS switches, supports WATS lines, 800 service, international service, and virtually all the common carrier services described later in this chapter. The ISDN offers high transmission speeds, cost savings, and the ability to track calls and their costs.

The AT&T Primary Rate Interface costs $400 a month and bears a $3,000 installation charge. In addition, a high-volume T1.5 access connection is required. MCI and Sprint have a similar pricing structure.

OUTBOUND SERVICES

AT&T, MCI, and Sprint offer a wide variety of outbound services, one of the most basic components of the communications industry. This market was once held exclusively by AT&T. As a result of deregulation, many common carriers have entered the market, offering lower priced long distance service.

AT&T Outbound Services include a group of long distance services, Corporate Calling Cards, single- and multiple-line WATS service, as well as high-volume WATS service. **Outbound Services** are specially priced long distance volume calling arrangements that provide discount prices on outgoing calls. These services do not affect the price of incoming calls.

The most basic outbound call, known as Long Distance Service, is placed over ordinary telephone lines for small volume users. Charges are based on distance, day and time, and duration of call. Rates are determined by airline miles between telephone company rate centers.

AT&T's Corporate Calling Cards are issued to businesses that allow users to place long distance calls directly, with charges being billed to the corporate account. Calls can be placed to more than 250 countries or to the United States from more than 150 international locations. The Corporate Calling Card uses a magnetic stripe, eliminating the need for handling change.

A variety of **Wide Area Telephone Service (WATS)** is available. Outbound long distance calls can be made at a discount; WATS is suited for businesses with monthly charges below $5,000. (See Figure 7.2.) WATS lines are used by telemarketing, recruiting, market research, and credit collection agencies. Single WATS lines offer a discount on outgoing calls, with a 30-second minimum, billed in 6-second increments.

FIGURE 7.2 WATS Charges

AT&T WATS (EFFECTIVE 3-1-92)

Service Group Charge (Per service group): $12.00 monthly

Access Line Charges (Per access line arranged for service areas): $75.00 monthly

(Connection charge per access line): $266.50 nonrecurring

Rate Schedule

INTRAMAINLAND AND MAINLAND – HAWAII AND ALASKA

Rate Mileage	Initial 30 Seconds or Fraction			Each Add'l 6 Seconds or Fraction		
	Day	Evening	Night	Day	Evening	Night
0–55	$.1125	$.0775	$.0650	$.0225	$.0155	$.0130
56–292	.1200	.0825	.0680	.0240	.0165	.0136
293–430	.1260	.0875	.0720	.0252	.0175	.0144
431–925	.1260	.0875	.0720	.0252	.0175	.0144
926–1910	.1300	.0915	.0775	.0260	.0183	.0155
1911–3000	.1300	.0915	.0775	.0260	.0183	.0155
3001–4250	.1300	.0915	.0775	.0260	.0183	.1055
4251–5750	.1300	.0915	.0775	.0260	.0183	.0155

HAWAII – ALASKA

Rate Mileage	Initial 30 Seconds or Fraction			Each Add'l 6 Seconds or Fraction		
	Day	Evening	Night	Day	Evening	Night
1911–3000	$.3150	$.2290	$.1810	$.0630	$.0458	$.0362
3001–4250	.3310	.2400	.1900	.0662	.0480	.0380

(Source AT&T Business Communications Service Guide)

The AT&T PRO WATS, WATS, and MEGACOM WATS services provide multiple lines with a variety of discounts on outgoing calls. The MEGACOM WATS service is used by high-volume businesses, such as resellers of telephone services, hotels and motels, and telemarketing firms. It is most attractive to businesses making more than 320 hours of long distance calls per month.

The benefits of using WATS lines include discounts over ordinary long distance rates and the availability of free call detail reports. These reports, available on magnetic tape or in a hard copy, break down calls by customer, time, originating or terminating numbers, and other factors.

INBOUND SERVICES

Many companies use **800 service**, which enables business firms to pay long distance charges for incoming calls so that customers can reach them toll free. AT&T, MCI, and Sprint all offer 800 service. This inbound service is the complement to the WATS outgoing service.

Many businesses rely on this service to build customer satisfaction and good will. Customers can call sales or service departments without incurring any charge. Market testing firms, mail order companies, and organizations that disseminate public information are primary users of 800 service. AT&T publishes a toll-free 800 directory.

AT&T commands a 75 percent share of the 800 service market. By 1997, it is estimated that its share will drop to 64 percent, as MCI Communications Corporation and Sprint Corporation expand their market shares. (See Figure 7.3.) Much of this shift is due to recent FCC policies regarding the portability of 800 numbers.

FIGURE 7.3
U.S. 800 Services Market, 1991 and 1997

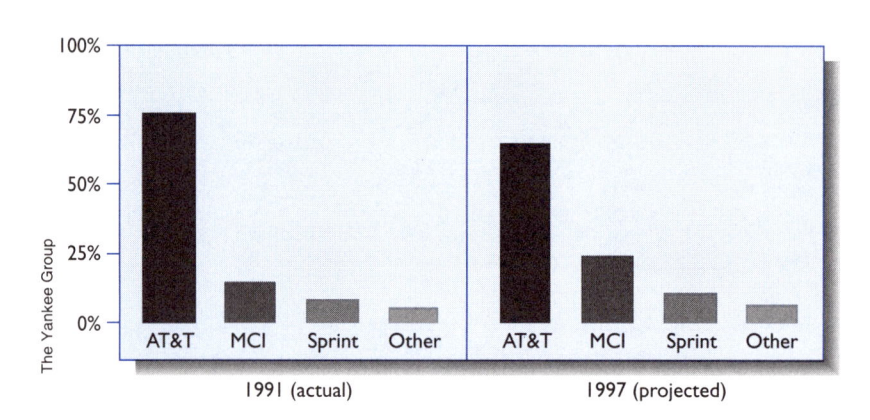

The FCC has directed common carriers to issue 800 numbers directly to customers. These numbers become the property of the customers. As a result, 800 users can switch from one common carrier to another without changing 800 telephone numbers. Many companies have invested huge sums of money in advertising and promoting their particular 800 numbers; they now can shop around for the best price and service. This factor will spawn much competition between common carriers.

AT&T offers its 800 service by geographic region. These service areas allow inbound calls from other states, but not from within the subscriber's home state. Special arrangements can be made with local Bell companies to provide in-state incoming call options. The AT&T 800 service requires a minimum of one access line. Once installed, the service allows customers to receive voice and data up to 9.6 Kbps. Users of the service receive Call Detail Reports, which are much like those provided on WATS lines to describe usage statistics.

Figure 7.4 illustrates how the AT&T 800 service is implemented. The caller dials an 800 number, which is routed through an end office to a computerized 4ESS switch. There the call is routed over the switched network to another 4ESS switch, and then to the firm's PBX. Sprint and MCI offer similar arrangements.

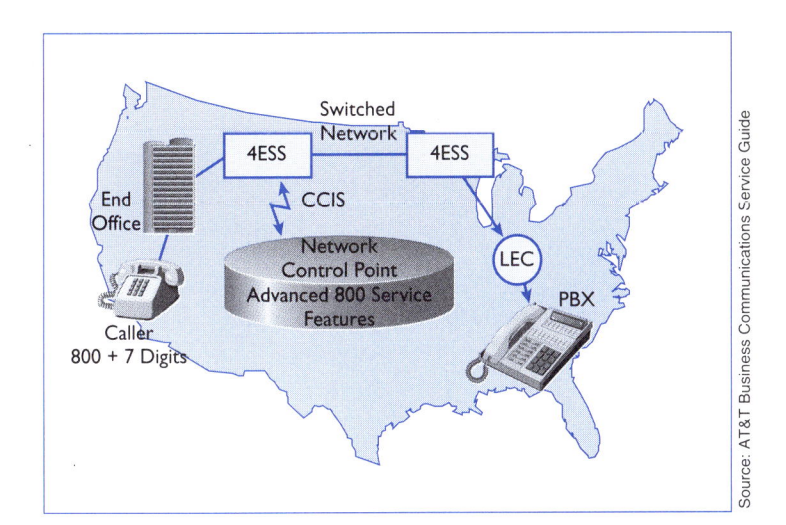

FIGURE 7.4 AT&T 800 Service

Source: AT&T Business Communications Service Guide

INFORMATION SERVICES

The past decade has seen a great growth in the use of information services, also known as **900 service**. The **AT&T MultiQuest** service, for example, enables callers to dial a 900 number to obtain information, cast a vote, or listen to a public service message.

AT&T can handle up to 108,000 calls per minute. The 900 phone numbers are used by radio stations, political analysts, and companies to sample opinions on products, events, or political viewpoints. Callers are charged by the minute for these calls. Sometimes two 900 numbers are used, one for yes and the other for no responses.

Figure 7.5 shows a typical AT&T MultiQuest application. Both domestic and international callers dial a 900 number and are connected to a 4ESS switch. The call is then routed to an announcement distribution system that can be accessed by the 900 line sponsor. The system will not accept collect calls or those from coin telephones.

The 900 numbers have become controversial. Because calls are charged to the caller, with fees of $1 to $2 or more per minute, substantial charges can be incurred. Children have accessed adult telephone lines or have repeatedly called for sports results, generating large bills for their parents. Some states require that customers be allowed to block the service to preclude such abuses. The service nevertheless remains very popular for obtaining stock and bond prices, movie and entertainment reviews, nationwide sports results, and even personal counseling on help lines.

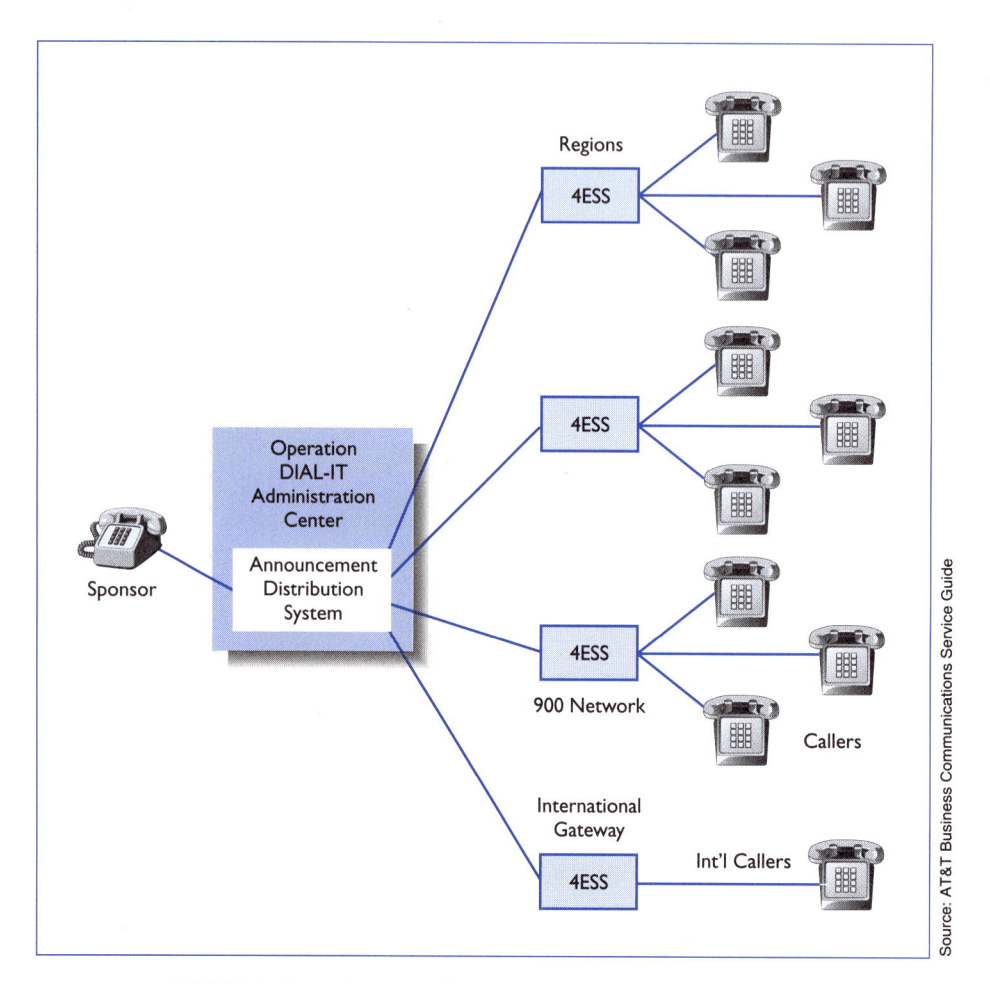

FIGURE 7.5 AT&T MultiQuest Broadcast Service

DIGITAL SERVICES

AT&T, MCI, and Sprint are major digital common carrier providers. AT&T remains the dominant vendor in this area, and the AT&T **DATAPHONE Digital Services (DDS)** now operates out of virtually every AT&T office in the United States. DDS is composed of a group of all-digital, private line, dedicated services known collectively as **ACCUNET.** ACCUNET serves interstate, intrastate, and international point-to-point and multipoint users. DDS operates at speeds between 2,400 bps and 56 Kbps. Because 85 percent of the DDS network is fiber optic, it offers a reliable and fast means of moving digital data over dedicated lines.

Many types of businesses use the DDS, including wholesale and retail firms, data collection, and credit collection companies. Health care companies, insurance firms, publishers, hotel reservation centers, and banks also rely on this service.

The DDS ACCUNET system is actually a collection of digital and analog services, ranging in speed that include:

- Analog
- Digital (9.6 bps, 56 Kbps, 64 Kbps)
- T1.5
- T45

Accessing the Network

The DDS services can be accessed using modems and an ordinary analog telephone line or special T circuits. (See Figure 7.6.) These lines access an **ACCUNET Spectrum of Digital Services (ASDS)** central office. From there, special **DS1 circuits** route the communications throughout the digital network. DS1 circuits, the building block of the network, transmit up to 1.544 Mbps. These DS1 circuits are composed of a group of DS0 circuits, each of which can carry 64 Kbps. Most low-volume users do not require or access DS1 facilities directly.

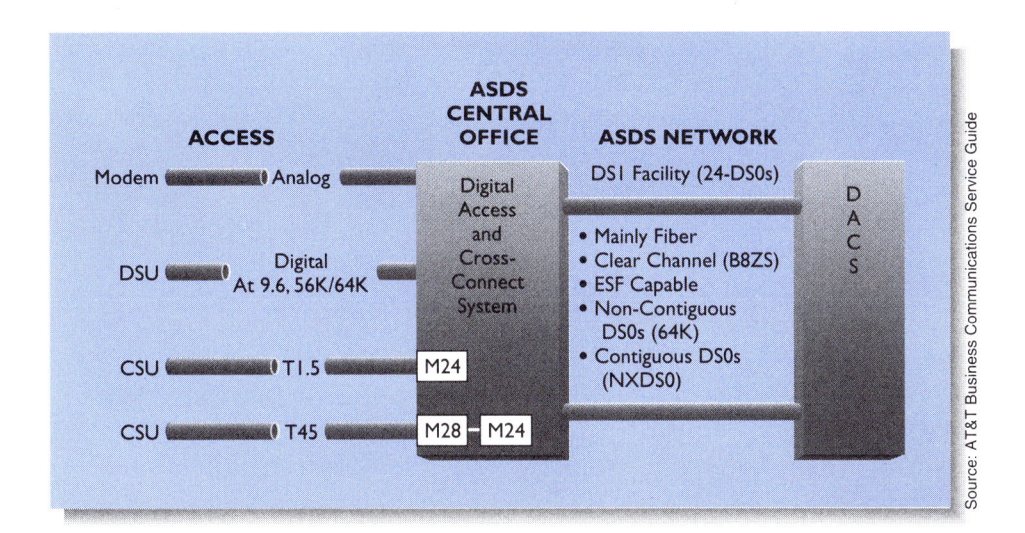

FIGURE 7.6 ACCUNET Circuits

Network users are able to access the system at differing speeds, depending on their needs. The following are the major ASDS access modes.

1. *Voice-Grade Private Line (VGPL).* This serves analog users at speeds up to 9.2 Kbps. Connections are made to the ASDS central office via modem.
2. *Digital Data Local Channel (DDLC).* This serves users at 9.6 or 56 Kbps. It is often used as a line for transmitting graphics or as a high-speed link between subscribers.
3. *ACCUNET T1.5 with M24 multiplexing.* This service, sometimes called fractional T1, connects users to the ASDS. It allows multiplexing and allows subscribers to buy only pieces or part of a full DS1 circuit. This option enables businesses to expand, eventually increasing their communications in steps until they need the full capacity of one DS1 circuit. The T1 carrier is capable of transmitting up to 1.544 Mbps of data over 24 multiplexed channels. This M24 multiplexing function enables subscribers to access each one of the 24 channels, transmitting up to 64 Kbps on each. (See Figure 7.7.)
4. *T45 access with M28 and M24 multiplexing.* This access arrangement connects high-volume subscribers to the central office and includes multiplexing capability. The M28 multiplexer splits the channel into a group of T1.5 circuits. The M24 multiplexer, in turn, splits each T1.5 circuit into 24 smaller 64 Kbps channels.

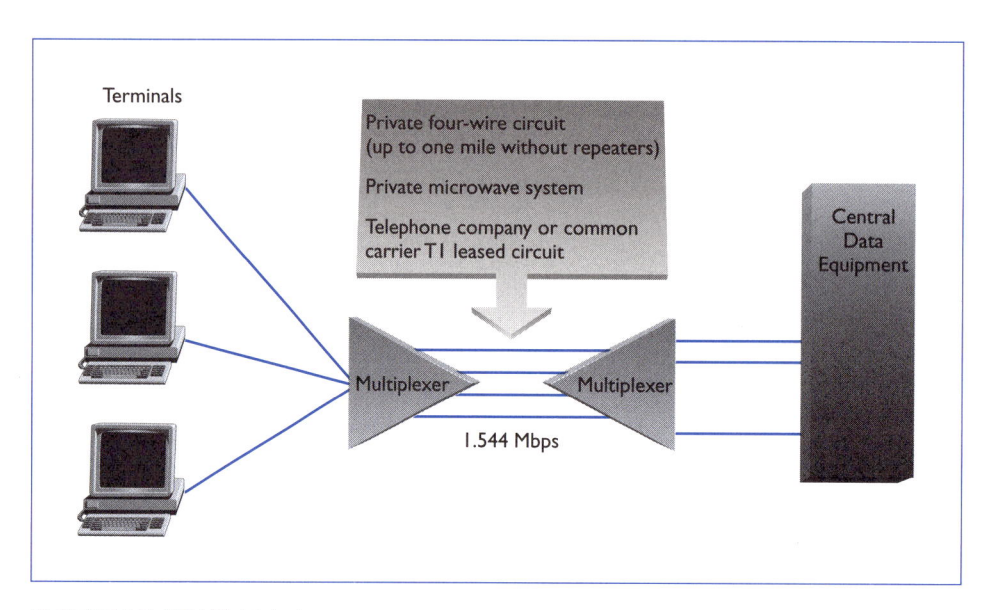

FIGURE 7.7 M24 Multiplexing

ACCUNET Switched Digital Services

AT&T offers a group of switched digital services that provide high-volume digital communications to subscribers who wish to use dial-up arrangements. These services, known as ACCUNET Switched 56 Service, 64 Service, 384 Service, and 1536 Service, provide high-volume data transfer without the cost of dedicated lines. Subscribers access the network through the dial-up switched network. The 56 Service derives a 56 Kbps access line from a 1.544 Mbps circuit, usually through a connection to a 4ESS switch. The other switched services operate at speeds of 64 Kbps, 384 Kbps, and 1536 Kbps, all over dial-up lines.

UNIFIED NETWORK MANAGEMENT ARCHITECTURE

Unified Network Management Architecture (UNMA), another service provided by AT&T, is designed to address the growing complexity of large multiterminal, multicomputer, voice, and digital networks. Many large organizations have difficulty managing their internal networks and access arrangements to common carriers. UNMA is a service that provides for the orderly growth of a system and for its most efficient management. Similar services are offered by Sprint and MCI.

The services included are:

- Configuration management
- Fault management
- Performance management
- Accounting management
- Security management
- Network planning
- Operations planning
- Programmability
- Integrated systems control

Collectively, these services are aimed at managing networks in a way that provides for orderly growth, with optimum performance. The system deals with accounting and network security and emphasizes the integration of all elements into the most efficient configuration of people, circuits, and hardware. The system generates administrative reports, billing reports, and traffic volume reports; it even includes testing and circuit diagnostic programs.

SATELLITE SERVICES

Today, many communications networks rely on earth-orbiting satellites. These systems include satellite links that can relay digital information, broadcast color video conferences, or serve as a backup for terrestrial-based networks. They are used for sales rallies, business meetings, stockholders' annual meetings, real estate auctions, and even for legal testimony.

The AT&T **SKYNET Digital Service** offers a non-preemptible digital satellite network that can link two ground stations. (See Figure 7.8.) Each ground station is equipped with microwave dishes that transmit or receive information from the satellite, using uplinks and downlinks. Systems such as these are widely used in the printing and publishing industries, where newspaper or magazine pages must be sent from an editorial office to a printing plant some distance away.

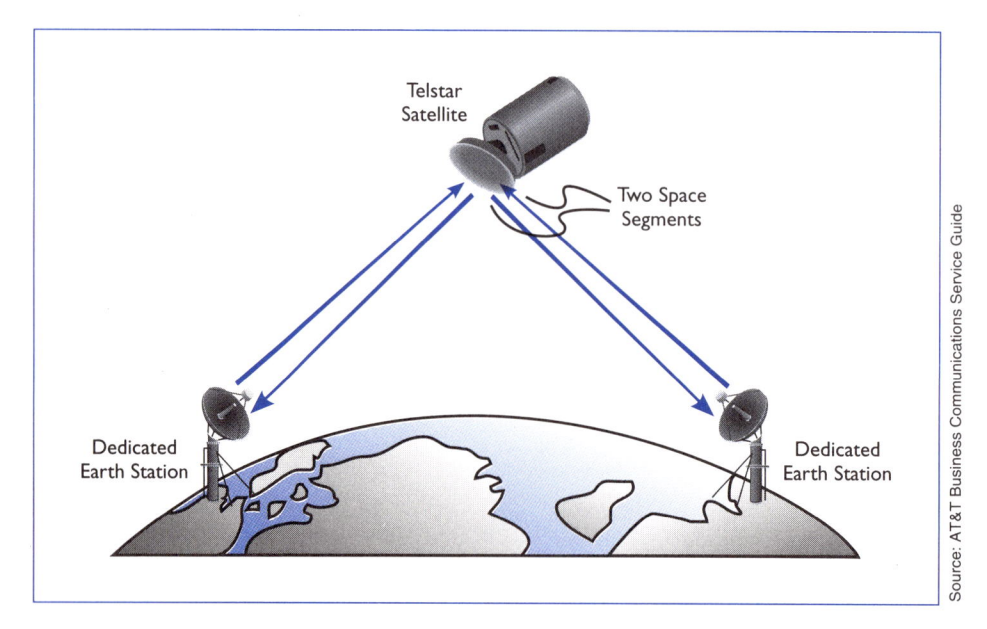

FIGURE 7.8 AT&T SKYNET Digital Service

An **uplink** is an earth station with a transmitting antenna aimed at a satellite. It sends information to the satellite. A **downlink** is an earth station that receives a signal, usually in the 1.8 to 2.4 meter band, from a satellite.

System Components

The SKYNET Digital Service is constructed from a group of building blocks that include these items:

1. *Dedicated earth stations.* These are located on the subscriber's premises and have uplinks and downlinks to a satellite.
2. *Shared earth stations.* These are operated by AT&T and serve many subscribers.
3. *Transportable earth stations.* These are mobile stations that can be placed on a subscriber's property and used at sporting events, national conventions, and so on.

4. *Transponder.* Located on the satellite, the transponder's function is to filter, amplify, convert frequency, and retransmit a signal back to earth.

5. *Operations management center.* This involves a land-based computer system that monitors satellites and earth stations, detects faults, and assures trouble-free operations.

Satellite Operations

Voice, data, or video signals are received from earth stations and echoed back to earth at speeds of from 56 Kbps to 1.544 Mbps. Signals may be simplex or duplex or may involve broadcasting a one-way transmission.

The system uses a C band satellite, which receives signals from earth stations in the 6 GHz band. After the signals are reamplified by a transponder, the satellite sends them back to earth in the 4 GHz band.

Figure 7.9 illustrates the SKYNET Direct Service in use. It replaces land lines and uses a Ku band satellite. It is cost-effective for video conferencing, holding press conferences, or training sessions, where participants are located at widely distant points. On the Ku band, earth stations transmit at 14.0 to 14.5 GHz and receive data from the satellite at 11.7 to 12.2 GHz.

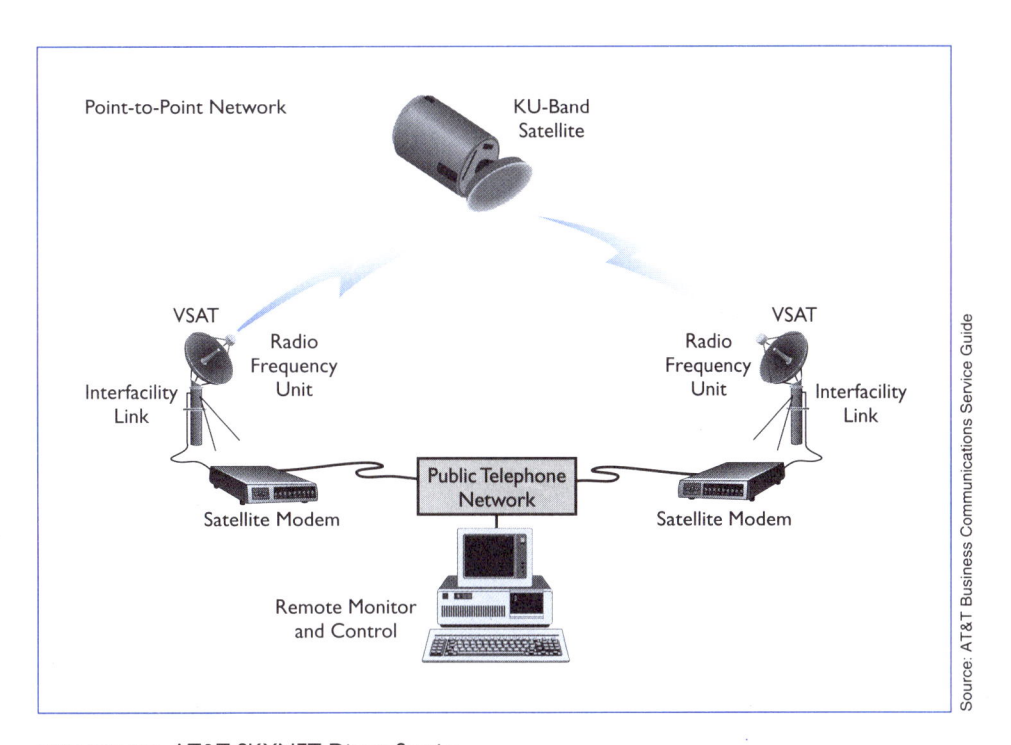

FIGURE 7.9 AT&T SKYNET Direct Service

Because satellites are located approximately 22,000 miles above the earth, there is a slight delay in information sent over these systems. A delay of one-eighth of a second may occur on the uplink, and another eighth of a second on the downlink, accounting for the slightly noticeable pause in an international television interview. Once a question is asked, it takes a fraction of a second for the interviewee to receive the query and then respond.

VIDEO SERVICES

The growth of the television industry has spurred a worldwide global video communications service. Today, thousands of hours of video programs, video conferences, and video training sessions are transmitted over Sprint, MCI, and AT&T circuits.

For example, the AT&T **Global Business Video Services (GBVS)** consists of a group of digital service offerings that move video images and audio from point to point or multipoints at speeds between 56 Kbps and 1.5 Mbps. Using this service, businesses are able to link meeting sites via video. The service is used to conduct job interviews, present training sessions, and hold project team, sales, and management meetings.

The international GBVS network links up to 21 countries, from Australia, the United States, and Canada, to Taiwan and the United Kingdom. The broadcast capability allows a video program to originate in a site in one country and to be broadcast to hundreds of other sites in many different countries.

TELECONFERENCING SERVICES

The high cost of business travel has led many businesses to rely on teleconferencing. The AT&T **Teleconference Services** link many telephone callers into a live forum worldwide. (See Figure 7.10.) The services are available 24 hours a day, seven days a week, at as many as 500 different locations.

FIGURE 7.10
Teleconferencing. Participants can engage in a live forum, using conference call facilities.

Teleconferencing provides two-way communications across time zones with as few as three people. The system automatically adjusts sound level. The service can be used on demand or via a reservation to set up a conference at a fixed time. The broadcast feature enables one or more speakers to address large audiences in many different cities.

To use the service, the originator dials a 700 number. Each domestic telephone number is keyed in. As each conferee answers, he or she is greeted and then joins the conference. Once all participants have been added, the originator joins the conference. The system requires a Touch-Tone telephone.

Before the Meeting

As in face-to-face meetings, planning ahead is the best way to be sure all teleconferencing goals and objectives are met. Depending on the conference's size and scope, advance planning can include simply distributing a list of conferees and telephone numbers ahead of time, publishing a formal meeting agenda, and/or developing a series of visual aids to enchance the exchange of ideas as well as following these suggestions:

- Hosts should use the AT&T TeleConference Service that best matches their needs. AT&T TeleConference Specialists are ready to assist at any time.
- Participants should receive all written information (graphs, charts, and studies) ahead of time.
- Participants should be ready for the conference a few minutes ahead of time.
- If hosts have any questions or special requirements, they should notify the TeleConference Specialist prior to the conference.
- When arranging AT&T ALLIANCE Attendant or Meet-Me conferences, hosts always should schedule enough time to ensure the completion of the meeting before the reserved time elapses. Additional resources might not always be available.

During the Meeting

When conducting a teleconference, the conference host should do the following:

- Start on time; waiting seems to take longer on the telephone than in person
- Set the tone by opening either formally or informally
- Take roll call
- Begin with an overview and/or ground rules for the teleconference
- Advise participants that putting their telephones on "hold" will interrupt all parties on the call since music is heard quite often
- Tell conferees using speakerphone equipment to mute their microphones when they're not speaking
- Focus on main topics first
- Encourage participation
- Stimulate discussion
- Direct questions to specific individuals or locations
- Summarize key points

For larger and more complex meetings, the conference planner should do the following:

- Establish site leaders
- Plan frequent breaks
- Schedule participants' presentations
- Use audio/graphic equipment when appropriate

Participants in a teleconference should do the following:

- Act naturally
- Speak naturally
- Identify themselves when speaking
- Pause for others to comment
- Direct questions to individuals or locations
- Spell out unusual terms, names, and numbers

The host should arrange for a follow-up teleconference while all the participants are still on the line.

Source: AT&T Business Communications Service Guide

FIGURE 7.11 Conducting a Teleconference

Teleconferencing is widely used by law firms, banking institutions, engineering firms, retailers, and government. As a rule, participants in conference calls should be given written information in advance and should be ready for the conference call a few minutes ahead of time. To facilitate such conferences, the host should follow some basic rules. (See Figure 7.11.)

Charges for this service are based on a $10 setup cost per **leg**, a connection between a host and a conferee. Minute charges are established for usage on each leg. Charges are billed to the host, a calling card, or a third party. Sprint and MCI offer similar services and pricing.

INTERNATIONAL SERVICES

As worldwide trading agreements have expanded and economic common markets have been formed, the volume of worldwide digital and analog communications has increased dramatically. International communications introduces many complexities, including differing time zones, a multitude of languages, and a patchwork of laws and regulatory restrictions. Adding to the problem are differing technical standards, terminal speeds, broadcast frequencies, and data encoding systems. In spite of all this, common carriers have entered this market aggressively.

International communications provides a common denominator by which government, business, banking, and marketing organizations can exchange vital data. The types of organizations that rely heavily on worldwide communications include the following:

- Airlines
- Banking and finance firms
- Brokerage companies
- Car rental companies
- Commodity traders
- Diplomatic corps
- Educational institutions
- Exporting and importing firms
- International customs, commerce, and energy organizations
- Legal firms
- Marketing companies
- Publishers
- Travel agencies

Let us look at the major AT&T services that address the digital and analog needs of organizations located in more than 250 countries around the globe. Sprint and MCI offer similar services.

AT&T Business International Long Distance Service

The AT&T **Business International Long Distance Service** provides users with direct dial capability 24 hours a day to 175 of the 250 countries served. To place an international long distance call, the caller dials: 011, the international access code plus the one- to four-digit country code plus the one- to five-digit city code plus the local telephone number.

A call placed to the center of London, direct-dialed from the United States, is:

011	**44**	**71**	**xxxx**
International Code	Country Code	City Code	Local Number

International long distance rates are determined by the time of day at the point of origination. They include a minimum one-minute period, plus additional minute rates. At the end of the billing period, the customer may receive call detail reports, listing the city alphabetically or by area code of the city called. Exceptions, such as those calls over 30 minutes, may be reported separately.

Other AT&T International Services

Virtually all the domestic services AT&T offers are offered internationally. These include Corporate Calling Card, MEGACOM WATS, 800 service, switched digital service, and ACCUNET digital services. In addition, SKYNET International Service provides satellite capability, and the AT&T International Facsimile Service allows faxes to be sent worldwide.

ACCUNET's international service is built on two major undersea fiber-optic circuits: the Atlantic link, which connects the United States and Europe, using undersea fiber-optic cables; and the Pacific link, which connects the United States, Hawaii, and Japan.

Figure 7.12 illustrates the existing digital services for the Pacific link. It shows both the existing and planned network, using undersea fiber-optic cables, which can carry 280 Mbps on each of two fiber-optic paths. Other international common carriers are installing similar fiber-optic links.

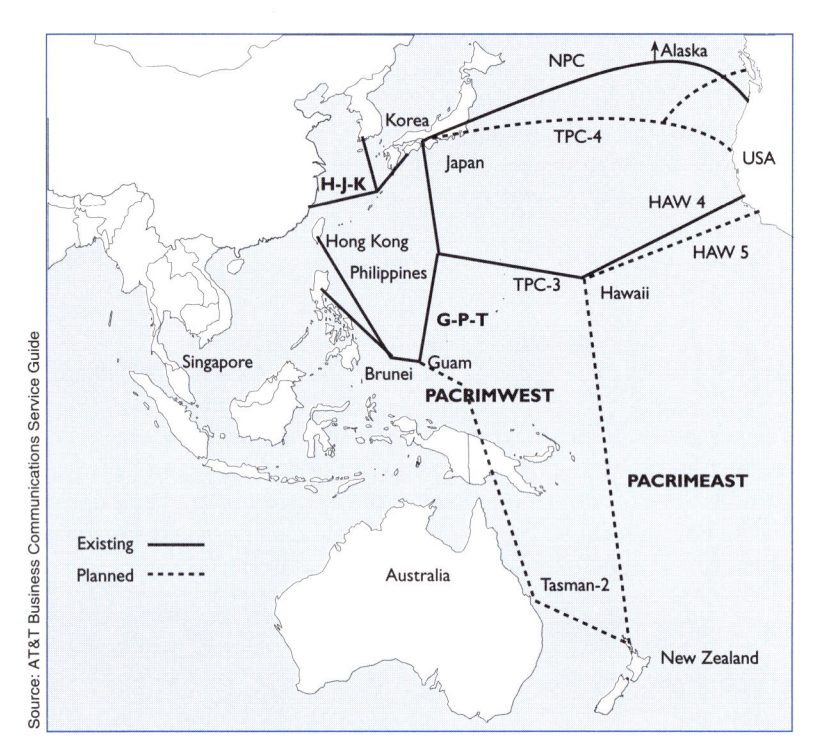

FIGURE 7.12
ACCUNET'S Pacific Link

Source: AT&T Business Communications Service Guide

VOICE MESSAGING SERVICES

Because of time pressures and increasing labor costs, many businesses are starting to rely on voice mail rather than human operators. **Voice mail** is a store-and-forward technology that moves voice messages without human intervention. It allows subscribers to create, store, forward, broadcast, or receive recorded messages through a Touch-Tone telephone.

Voice mail ensures that messages are handled in a timely manner and allows companies to be more responsive while reducing costs. Studies show that three-quarters of all business calls are never completed, resulting in telephone tag as callers keep missing each other. Over half of all business calls involve one-way communications and do not require a simultaneous conversation. Frequently, messages that are taken by an operator are incomplete or inaccurate.

AT&T Voice Mail

AT&T **Voice Mail** is available as a domestic service. Customers or family members leave messages by dialing an 800 number. The subscriber can then access the voice mail messages. Messages can be up to five minutes long and are retained up to 14 days. (See Figure 7.13.)

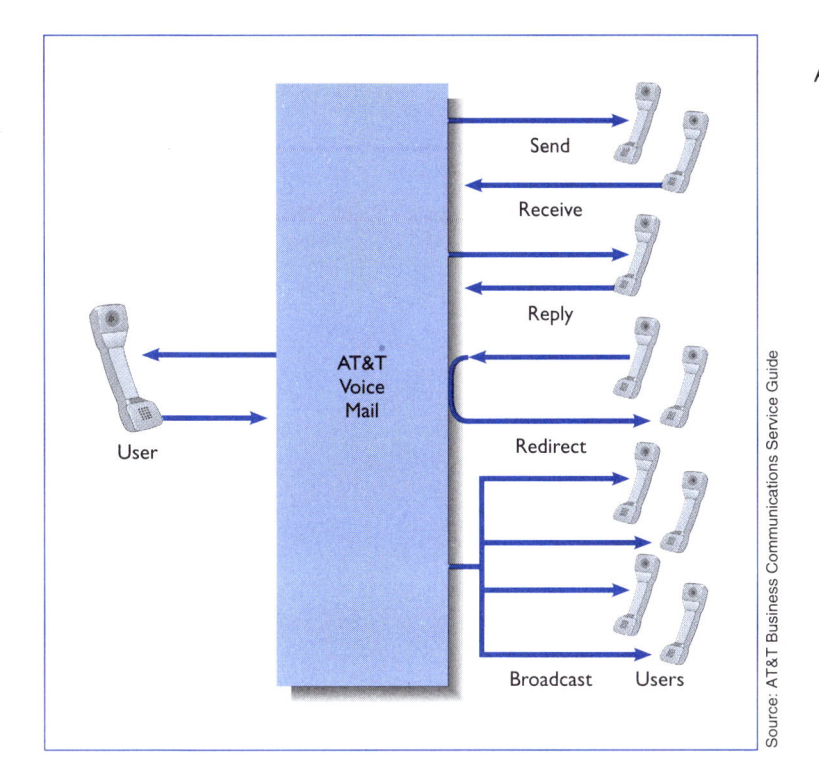

FIGURE 7.13
AT&T Voice Mail

AT&T Message Service

The AT&T **Message Service** allows callers to record a one-minute message and then have it delivered to any telephone in the United States or worldwide. Because it uses store-and-forward technology, the communication is not affected by busy signals, unanswered telephones, or poor timing, an especially important factor when calls are made to different time zones. Rates for this service are $1.75 for domestic messages and $2.50 for person-to-person delivery of each message. International messages cost between $4.50 and $11.00 each.

CONSUMER COMMUNICATIONS SERVICES

A variety of services is offered in this category, including language interpretation and translation, access to directory assistance databases across the country, and "on the road" services.

AT&T Language Line Services

The Language Line Services are especially useful in the health care, lodging, law enforcement, and business areas. When a non-English-speaking person places a call to a subscriber, the subscriber tries to identify the language. If this cannot be done, the call is routed to Monterey, California, where foreign language operators receive the call, interpret the message, and relay it back to the subscriber.

This service is available 24 hours a day, for more than 140 languages and dialects. Written translations can also be provided.

Find America Directory Service

The Find America Directory Service gives businesses online access to directory assistance databases across the country. Using a PC at the subscriber's location, the service enables the PC operator to collect listings nationwide without operator assistance. It is faster than voice directory assistance and is widely used in the banking, retail, and telemarketing fields.

The number and range of services offered by competing common carriers will continue to expand. Competition between carriers will increase for both the domestic and worldwide markets. The carrier with the widest range of services and broadest network will be able to capture the largest share of the communications market.

SUMMARY

AT&T services include the ISDN network, outbound services, inbound services, information services, video, teleconferencing, and voice mail. AT&T has pioneered the *Integrated Services Digital Network (ISDN)* that offers end-to-end digital communications service, eliminating the need for modems. Sprint and MCI offer similar services.

AT&T Outbound Services include Corporate Calling Cards, single- and multiple-line WATS service, and high-volume WATS service. *Outbound Services* are specially priced, long distance volume calling arrangements that provide discount prices on outgoing calls.

Many organizations use *800 service*, enabling them to pay long distance charges for incoming calls so that customers can reach them toll free. AT&T, MCI, and Sprint all offer 800 service.

The *AT&T MultiQuest* service, sometimes known as *900 service*, enables callers to dial a 900 number to obtain information, cast a vote, or listen to a public service message.

The AT&T *DATAPHONE Digital Services (DDS)* is composed of a group of all-digital, private line, dedicated services known collectively as *ACCUNET*. ACCUNET serves interstate, intrastate, and international point-to-point and multipoint users. DDS operates at speeds between 2400 bps and 56 Kbps. The DDS network is fiber optic and offers a reliable and fast means of moving digital data over dedicated lines.

The AT&T *SKYNET Digital Service* offers a non-preemptible digital satellite network that can link two ground stations equipped with microwave dishes that transmit or receive information from the satellite, using uplinks and downlinks. Systems such as these are widely used in the printing and publishing industries.

The AT&T *Global Business Video Services (GBVS)* consists of a group of digital service offerings that move video images and audio from point to point or multipoints at speeds between 56 Kbps and 1.5 Mbps. The service is used to conduct job interviews, present training sessions, and hold project team, sales, and management meetings.

Teleconferencing provides two-way communications across time zones with as few as three people. The service can be used on demand or via a reservation to set up a conference at a fixed time.

Virtually all the domestic services AT&T offers are offered internationally.

Voice mail ensures that messages will be handled in a timely manner and allows companies to be more responsive while reducing costs.

EXERCISES

1. Describe how the ISDN operates and contrast the BRI and PRI interfaces.
2. List the major long distance outbound services.
3. List the major long distance inbound services.
4. Contrast the difference between 800 service and WATS.
5. Describe the 900 service and give some examples of its application.
6. Discuss the different ACCUNET services.
7. Describe the SKYNET digital service.
8. Describe Global Business Video Service.
9. Discuss teleconference services.
10. Describe how voice mail operates.

HANDS-ON PROJECTS

- Visit a local communications company and discuss ISDN services, prices, and network capability.

- Assume you are going to set up a teleconference with 10 participants. Prepare an agenda and describe the steps needed to implement the conference calls.

- Visit a business establishment that uses voice mail. Discuss its features and limitations with a communications manager. Give reasons why the system was installed.

- Assume you represent a telemarketing company selling office supplies. Prepare a list of reasons why 800 service would benefit your company.

- Prepare a list of businesses or industries that might use WATS. After each name, state the benefits the WATS line provides.

COMMUNICATIONS IN ACTION

CASE SOLUTION
WORLD SPORTS TODAY

World Sports Today's communications manager considered the production and communications problems carefully. It was obvious that proofs could not be sent back and forth by messenger because this would take several days. Using modems and dial-up lines had proven too slow. Dedicated circuits between offices and the remote printing plant were too expensive because the lines would remain idle much of the time.

The solution to the problem lies in implementing the system shown in Figure 7.14. The key to the system is a connection to the ISDN. The ISDN circuits are capable of routing digital data up to 1.544 Mbps, thus providing more capacity than needed for moving the color pages.

Under the new system, copy and design layouts are routed from the editorial office to the graphics and layout office over the ISDN. Color advertisements are transmitted either from the display advertising department or directly from advertisers, also on the ISDN, to the graphics and layout department. There the pages are designed and laid out, including the placement of advertisements. Color pages are then routed back to these offices over the ISDN. After checking and final corrections have been entered, the color pages are transmitted to the printer, also over the ISDN. There machines convert the electrical signals into images on plates ready for printing.

For some applications, a 64 Kbps data transmission rate is used. For other purposes, such as transmitting entire color pages, multiple channels are aggregated to obtain higher transmission speeds. The result is a system that moves proofs and color artwork between offices at minimum cost.

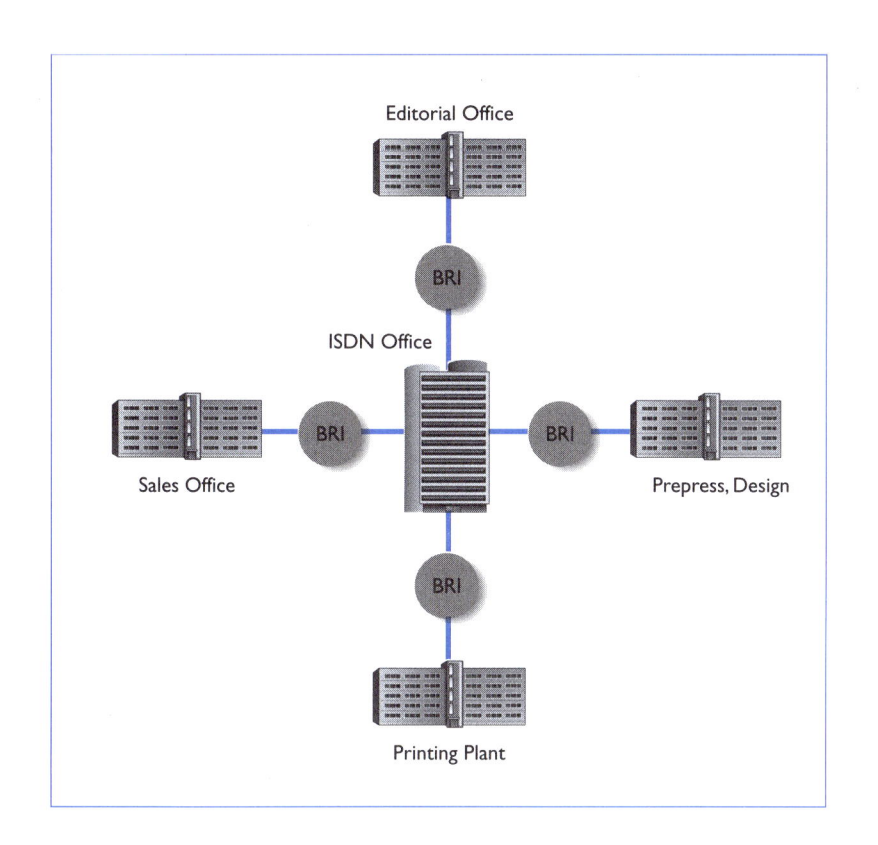

FIGURE 7.14
New System with ISDN

DATA TRANSMISSION CODES AND PROTOCOLS

LEARNING OBJECTIVES

After studying this chapter, you should be able to:

- Describe major information codes in use
- Describe the EIA-232-D interface standard
- Describe how communications equipment and terminals are interfaced
- Discuss the function of protocols and handshakes
- Discuss error-checking systems
- Describe data compression techniques

COMMUNICATIONS
IN ACTION

CASE PROBLEM
AIR RESOURCES COMPANY

INTEGRATED VOICE AND DATA NETWORK

Air Resources Company is a major manufacturer of jet engines. The firm employs hundreds of engineers, designers, and technicians in the manufacture of high-performance jet engines that must meet demanding environmental standards regarding noise and air pollution. Employees are in frequent contact with one another. They exchange reports, drawings, and data, and often discuss in detail design features of engines under development. The telephone and the computer have become indispensable in their work.

Air Resources Company must be able to handle both voice and data communications efficiently. In the past, the company had two separate but parallel systems. (See Figure 8.1.) A conventional switchboard and telephone were in place. The phones were installed throughout the organization and were used by engineers, designers, and others in the firm to stay in touch with one another. As computers came into use in the company, a separate system was installed, involving a network of cabling that connected small computers and terminals to the company's mainframe computer.

FIGURE 8.1
Old Parallel System

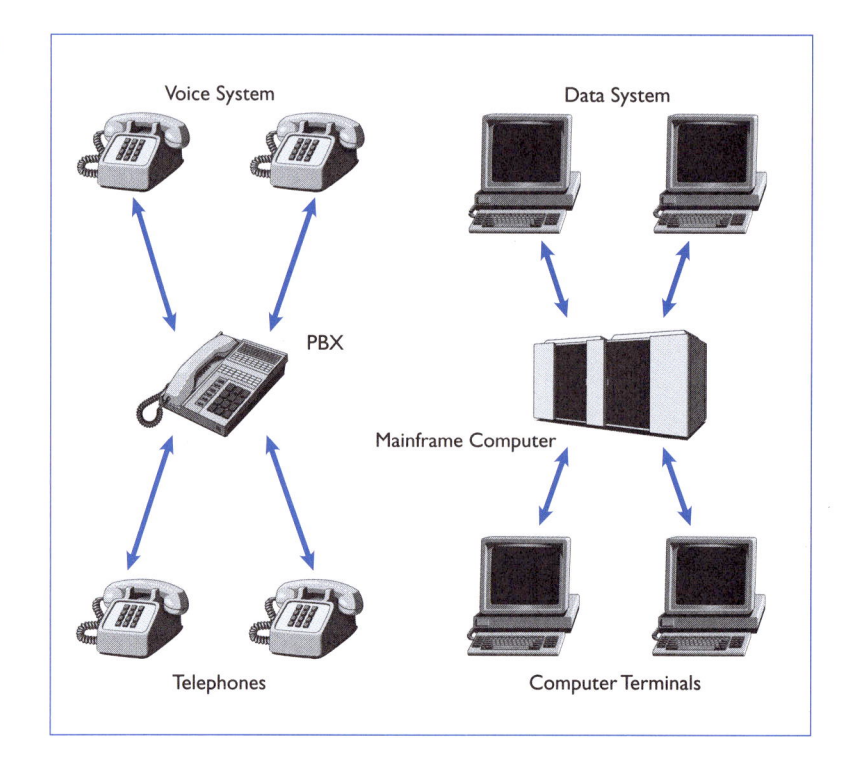

When new offices were opened, the dual installation was expensive. Air Resources Company's problems were made worse when it purchased another manufacturing company. The new subsidiary was adequately wired with plenty of telephone circuits throughout the building. But the company faced a major expense in wiring the building with data circuits for computers. How would you resolve Air Resource Company's communications dilemma? Refer to the end of this chapter to see how management solved the problem.

PICTURE a small dusty town somewhere in the western United States. It is the late 1800s, and we are watching an operator hunched over his telegraph set in the train station, laboriously copying a message. The sharp clicks and clacks tell the operator that another family is moving out west to seek a better life. The telegraph operator is the first one to hear the news. Long before the train has screeched its way into the station, half the town will know about the new arrivals. This was life in the early days of telecommunications.

Messages were sent from point to point, from one telegraph office to another. The early telegraph system used the wires strung along the railroad right of way. Towns and hamlets not fortunate enough to be on the rail line had to use Pony Express, courier, or stagecoach routes to send messages.

Early telegraph systems were simple. They required only a sending key, a sounder, and an operator who could learn the telegrapher's code. When the operator made a mistake the damage was usually minimal: no one would be at the station to greet Aunt Sally when she arrived, or perhaps, the relatives were there and Aunt Sally was not.

Telecommunications today is considerably different. Not only has the technology changed, but so has our reliance on communications. Today billions of dollars are transmitted by government and industry over communications lines. The fate of millions of people, or entire nations, may rest on the accurate transmission of messages. A mistake made in transmitting a diplomatic communique could have enormous political consequences.

Modern communications systems are made up of a network of different types of devices. These include terminals, computers, and analog and digital communications machines, operating at various speeds and manufactured by different companies. Thus, modern communications must deal with an electronic Tower of Babel.

This chapter discusses data transmission codes and the means by which information is sent over communications lines. It describes the methods and procedures that enable machines of different makes, speeds, and business environments to communicate effectively with one another. It also describes error-checking protocols and data compression techniques.

DATA CODES

Many different systems have been used to encode data to be sent over communications circuits. One of the earliest means of sending words and phrases was through **international Morse code**. (See Figure 8.2.) This simple system of dots and dashes could be used to send characters over a line, one after another in a serial fashion. Although it is still used by amateur radio operators, international Morse code does not serve the needs of modern technology. At best, a good operator could send up to 30 words per minute, and the code had no built-in error detection capability.

FIGURE 8.2
International Morse Code

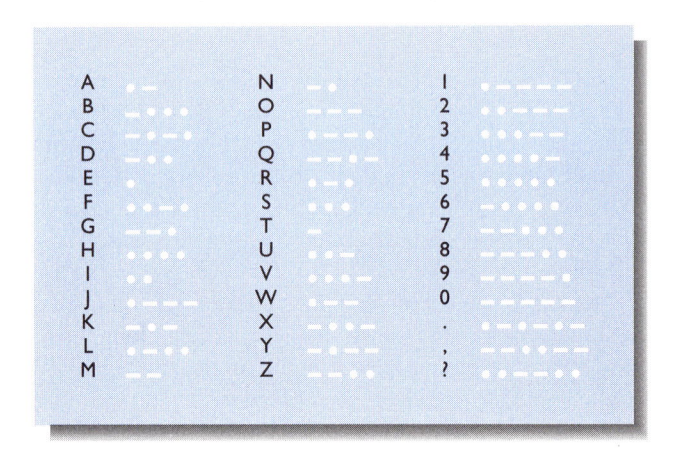

Many of the codes used to transmit data are standardized, and approved versions have been published by such organizations as **American National Standards Institute (ANSI)** and **International Standards Organization (ISO)**. Other communications standards have been published by the **Electronic Industries Association (EIA)**, the **Institute of Electrical and Electronic Engineers (IEEE)**, and the **Consultative Committee for International Telephone and Telegraph (CCITT)**. These and other standards organizations have helped lay out universal codes and procedures that have greatly facilitated the development of integrated international standards that are used worldwide.

Baudot Code

One of the first data coding systems was developed by Jean-Maurice-Emile Baudot. (See Figure 8.3.) In the Baudot code, each letter of the alphabet is represented by a 5-bit code combination. The **Baudot code** was used as the international telegraph alphabet code for many years. Because only 32-bit combinations are possible, it is necessary to include two additional characters, LTRS (letters) and FIGS (figures). If a letter is to be transmitted, the LTRS character must be sent first to signal that a letter, or a space, carriage return, or line feed, is desired. If, however, the FIGS character is sent first, the bit combination is interpreted as a numeric digit. Thus, by sending either the LTRS or FIGS character first, two different sets of characters can be transmitted.

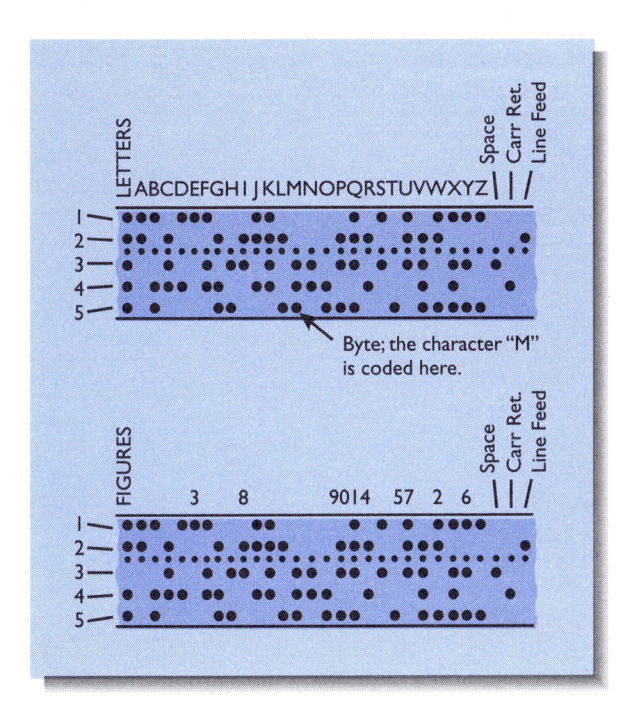

FIGURE 8.3
Baudot Code

Using the Baudot code along with the figures and letters characters, 57 different letters, numbers, or special characters could be sent. The system is known as a five-level code because five bits are present. It was widely used on early Teletype machines that used paper tape to send and receive messages.

The Baudot code has largely been replaced by other coding systems for several reasons. First, there are many instances in which more than 57 characters are needed. Second, the code has no built-in system to ensure that bits are not inadvertently changed in transmission. What was needed was a system that would keep track of all bits transmitted. These error-detection systems are known as parity-bit checks or error-checking routines. Before discussing these routines in detail, let us review the major transmission codes in use.

Binary Coded Decimal Code

Another important code to come into use was the **Binary Coded Decimal (BCD)** code. (See Figure 8.4.) The code contained six bits for transmitting characters, plus an additional parity bit. The function of parity bits is explained a little later in this chapter. The bits are numbered 1, 2, 4, 8, A, B, and C. This code can transmit 64 different characters and was used in early IBM computer systems. BCD was the first major code in use that included a parity bit with each character transmitted. An even- or odd-parity check system can be used in the BCD code. (See Figure 8.5.) Bits 1, 2, 4, 8, A, and B transmit characters; the C bit is the check bit.

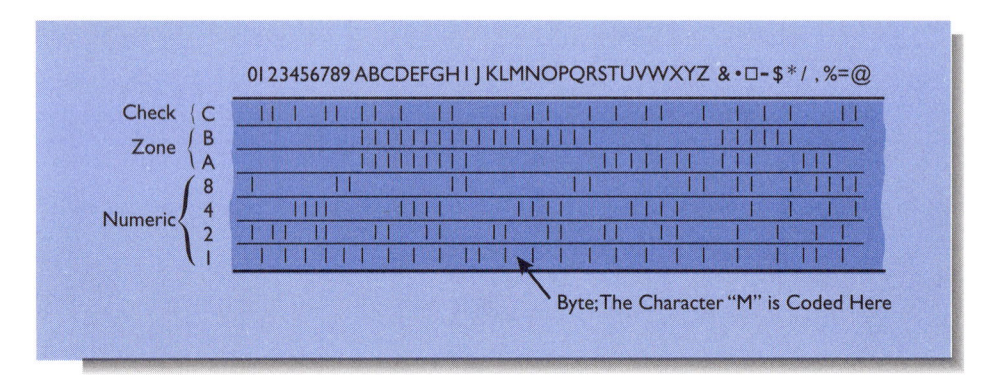

FIGURE 8.4 Binary Coded Decimal (BCD) Code. This is an example of an even-parity check.

FIGURE 8.5 Parity Check Bits. This figure illustrates the letter A encoded with odd parity (top) and even parity (bottom).

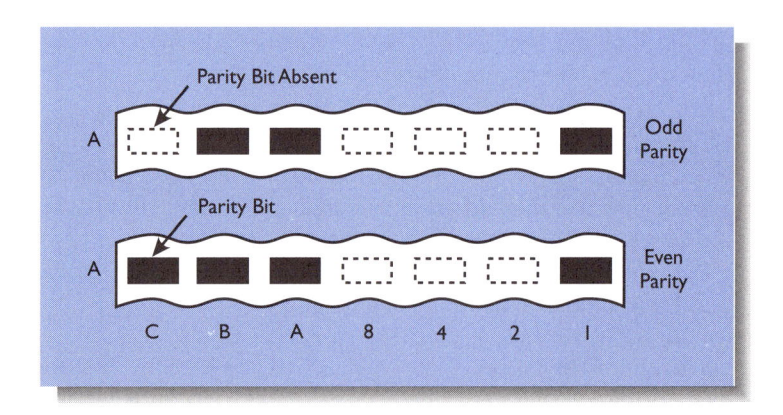

American Standard Code for Information Interchange

The need for a transmission code that could send more characters led to the development of the **American Standard Code for Information Interchange (ASCII)**. In the ASCII (pronounced ask-key) code, seven bits are used to transmit a character and the eighth is reserved for the parity bit. (See Figure 8.6.) ASCII is a standard code published by the American National Standards Institute (ANSI). Using ASCII, it is possible to transmit 128 different characters. The ASCII code is used on many pieces of communications equipment and on many computers and terminals.

The ASCII code can be either even- or odd-parity, depending on the system selected. Most computer terminals and communications equipment provide an even- or odd-parity check option. Figure 8.7 illustrates the full 128 character ASCII code.

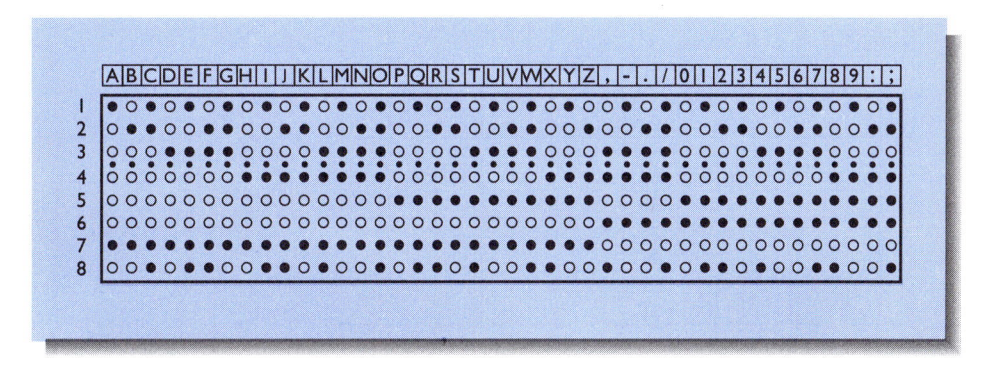

FIGURE 8.6 American Standard Code for Information Interchange (ASCII). This is an example of even parity.

Extended ASCII

Most microcomputers are able to handle 9-bit codes easily. That is, the microcomputer hardware is able to manipulate an 8-bit code with an additional parity bit. This development posed an interesting dilemma for computer designers. While microcomputers could handle 9-bit codes, the ASCII 8-bit code (seven information bits and one check bit) was greatly underutilized. Further, many computer users needed a 256 character set, not the 128 provided by the standard ASCII. In effect, only 128 of the possible 256 code combinations are actually used in ASCII.

As a result, many computer manufacturers and software developers use a non-standard ASCII set of extended characters. These engineers and designers use the first 128 standard ASCII characters and then assign a second group of 128 characters, making a total of 256 characters. This step has resulted in much confusion. Because the upper 128 characters are not standardized, a given 8-bit combination may represent different characters, depending on its usage.

Computer software, such as WordPerfect, PageMaker, Ventura Publisher, and Microsoft Word, are all widely used in industry. These programs all treat the first 128 character combinations in the same way, but each produces different results when the extended 128 characters are used.

ASCII Codes and Controls

b7 →					0	0	0	0	1	1	1	1
b6 →					0	0	1	1	0	0	1	1
b5 →					0	1	0	1	0	1	0	1
Bits	b4	b3	b2	b1	Column row ▼ 0	1	2	3	4	5	6	7
	0	0	0	0	NUL	DLE	SP	0	@	P		p
	0	0	0	1	SOH	DC1	!	1	A	Q	a	q
	0	0	1	0	STX	DC2	"	2	B	R	b	r
	0	0	1	1	ETX	DC3	#	3	C	S	c	s
	0	1	0	0	EOT	DC4	$	4	D	T	d	t
	0	1	0	1	ENQ	NAK	%	5	E	U	e	u
	0	1	1	0	ACK	SYN	&	6	F	V	f	v
	0	1	1	1	BEL	ETB	/	7	G	W	g	w
	1	0	0	0	BS	CAN	(	8	H	X	h	x
	1	0	0	1	HT	EM	)	9	I	Y	i	y
	1	0	1	0	LF	SUB	*	:	J	Z	j	z
	1	0	1	1	VT	ESC	+	;	K	[	k	{
	1	1	0	0	FF	FX	,	<	L	/	l	;
	1	1	0	1	CR	GS	–	=	M	]	m	}
	1	1	1	0	SO	RS	.	>	N	> .	n	~
	1	1	1	1	SI	US	/	?	O	—	o	DEL

Character Codes

1. Standardized groupings of bits (ones and zeros) to represent alphanumeric and control information.
2. American Standard Code for Information Interchange (ASCII) – ANSI X3.4
   a. A 7-bit code which yeilds 128 possible combinations or character assignments.
   b. Ninety-six graphic, i.e., printable or displayable, characters.
   c. Thirty-two control characters, including
      1) Device-control characters such as Line Feed, Carriage Return, Bell, etc.
      2) Information-transfer control characters such as ACK, NAK, etc.

ASCII Control Characters

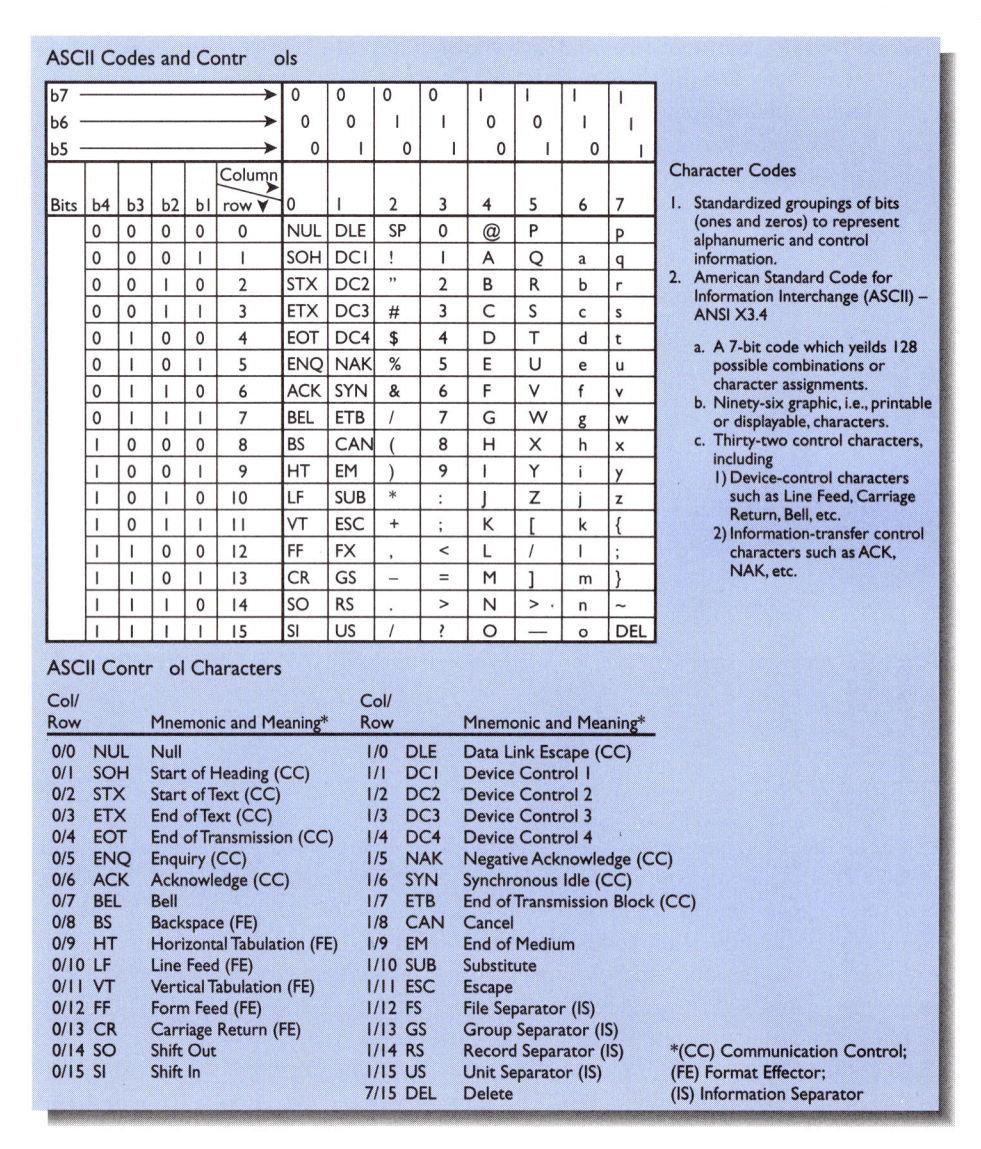

Col/Row	Mnemonic and Meaning*	Col/Row	Mnemonic and Meaning*	
0/0 NUL	Null	1/0 DLE	Data Link Escape (CC)	
0/1 SOH	Start of Heading (CC)	1/1 DC1	Device Control 1	
0/2 STX	Start of Text (CC)	1/2 DC2	Device Control 2	
0/3 ETX	End of Text (CC)	1/3 DC3	Device Control 3	
0/4 EOT	End of Transmission (CC)	1/4 DC4	Device Control 4	
0/5 ENQ	Enquiry (CC)	1/5 NAK	Negative Acknowledge (CC)	
0/6 ACK	Acknowledge (CC)	1/6 SYN	Synchronous Idle (CC)	
0/7 BEL	Bell	1/7 ETB	End of Transmission Block (CC)	
0/8 BS	Backspace (FE)	1/8 CAN	Cancel	
0/9 HT	Horizontal Tabulation (FE)	1/9 EM	End of Medium	
0/10 LF	Line Feed (FE)	1/10 SUB	Substitute	
0/11 VT	Vertical Tabulation (FE)	1/11 ESC	Escape	
0/12 FF	Form Feed (FE)	1/12 FS	File Separator (IS)	
0/13 CR	Carriage Return (FE)	1/13 GS	Group Separator (IS)	
0/14 SO	Shift Out	1/14 RS	Record Separator (IS)	*(CC) Communication Control;
0/15 SI	Shift In	1/15 US	Unit Separator (IS)	(FE) Format Effector;
		7/15 DEL	Delete	(IS) Information Separator

FIGURE 8.7 American Standard Code for Information Interchange (ASCII). This example is the complete code.

Figure 8.8 illustrates the characters assigned to each code combination by one software system, ANSI Windows. The first 128 characters are assigned the usual representations for letters, numbers, and punctuation. Those with assignments above 128 are unique to ANSI Windows.

0–31	***	60	<	89	Y	118	v	147	***	176	°	205	Í	234	ê
32	space	61	=	90	Z	119	w	148	***	177	±	206	Î	235	ë
33	!	62	>	91	[	120	x	149	***	178	2	207	Ï	236	ì
34	"	63	?	92	\	121	y	150	***	179	3	208	Ð	237	í
35	#	64	@	93	]	122	z	151	***	180	'	209	Ñ	238	î
36	$	65	A	94	^	123	{	152	***	181	µ	210	Ò	239	ï
37	%	66	B	95	—	124	|	153	***	182	¶	211	Ó	240	ð
38	&	67	C	96	`	125	}	154	***	183	·	212	Ô	241	ñ
39	'	68	D	97	a	126	~	155	***	184	,	213	Õ	242	ò
40	(	69	E	98	b	127	***	156	***	185	¹	214	Ö	243	ó
41	)	70	F	99	c	128	***	157	***	186	º	215	—	244	ô
42	*	71	G	100	d	129	***	158	***	187	»	216	Ø	245	õ
43	+	72	H	101	e	130	***	159	***	188	¼	217	Ù	246	ö
44	,	73	I	102	f	131	***	160	***	189	½	218	Ú	247	·
45	-	74	J	103	g	132	***	161	¡	190	¾	219	Û	248	ø
46	.	75	K	104	h	133	***	162	¢	191	¿	220	Ü	249	ù
47	/	76	L	105	i	134	***	163	£	192	À	221	Ý	250	ú
48	0	77	M	106	j	135	***	164	¤	193	Á	222	Þ	251	û
49	1	78	N	107	k	136	***	165	¥	194	Â	223	ß	252	ü
50	2	79	O	108	l	137	***	166	¦	195	Ã	224	à	253	ý
51	3	80	P	109	m	138	***	167	§	196	Ä	225	á	254	þ
52	4	81	Q	110	n	139	***	168	¨	197	Å	226	â	255	ÿ
53	5	82	R	111	o	140	***	169	©	198	Æ	227	ã	256	end of set
54	6	83	S	112	p	141	***	170	ª	199	Ç	228	ä		
55	7	84	T	113	q	142	***	171	«	200	È	229	å		
56	8	85	U	114	r	143	***	172	¬	201	É	230	æ		
57	9	86	V	115	s	144	***	173	-	202	Ê	231	ç		
58	:	87	W	116	t	145	'	174	®	203	Ë	232	è		
59	;	88	X	117	u	146	'	175	¯	204	Ì	233	é		

FIGURE 8.8 ANSI Windows Character Set. Characters above 128 do not conform to standard ASCII assignments.

Extended Binary Coded Decimal Interchange Code

When IBM introduced its new series of computers in the 1960s it also introduced a 9-bit code system known as the **Extended Binary Coded Decimal Interchange Code (EBCDIC).** The EBCDIC (pronounced ebb-see-dick) code can represent 256 different characters. (See Figure 8.9.) It allows both uppercase and lowercase characters and many special symbols to be transmitted.

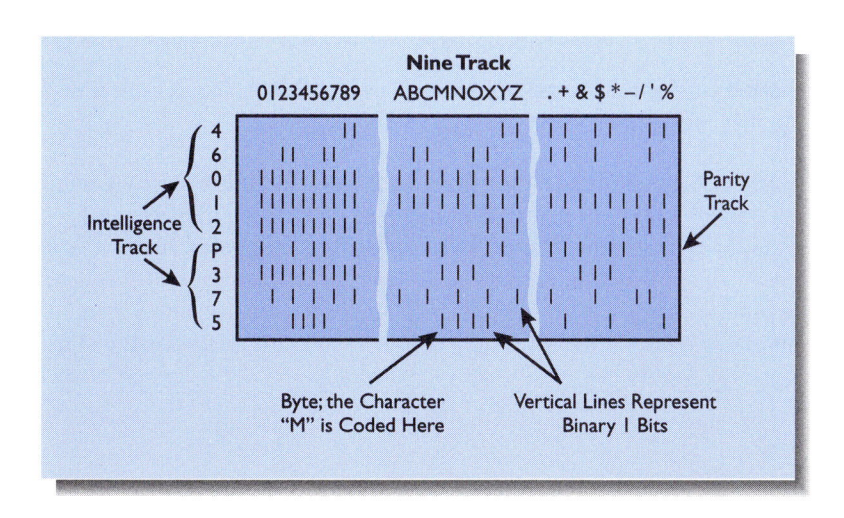

FIGURE 8.9 Extended Binary Coded Decimal Interchange Code (EBCDIC). This is an example of odd parity.

The EBCDIC consists of eight bits to transmit characters and one parity bit, for a total of nine bits. The bits are labeled 0, 1, 2, 3, 4, 5, 6, 7, and P. It is likely that EBCDIC will remain the standard for IBM mainframe equipment because of the large number of characters that can be represented. Capital letters, lowercase letters, punctuation marks, and dozens of special symbols and control characters can be represented using this code. Figure 8.10 illustrates the EBCDIC in entirety. EBCDIC and ASCII are the two most widely used codes in data transmission.

Hex 1		00				01				10				11			Bits 0,1
Bits 4567		00 0	01 1	10 2	11 3	00 4	01 5	10 6	11 7	00 8	01 9	10 A	11 B	00 C	01 D	10 E	11 F	2,3 Hex 0
0000	0	NUL	DLE			SP	&	-									0	
0001	1	SOH	SBA					/		a	j			A	J		1	
0010	2	STX	EUA		SYN					b	k	s		B	K	S	2	
0011	3	ETX	IC							c	l	t		C	L	T	3	
0100	4									d	m	u		D	M	U	4	
0101	5	PT	NL							e	n	v		E	N	V	5	
0110	6			ETB						f	o	w		F	O	W	6	
0111	7			ESC	EOT					g	p	x		G	P	X	7	
1000	8									h	q	y		H	Q	Y	8	
1001	9		EM							i	r	z		I	R	Z	9	
1010	A					¢	!	|	:									
1011	B					.	$	,	#									
1100	C		DUP		RA	<	*	%	@									
1101	D		SF	ENQ	NAK	(	)	—	'									
1110	E		FM			+	;	>	=									
1111	F		ITB		SUB	|	—	?	"									

*An 8-bit code yielding 256 possible combinations or character assignments

*Absence of certain functions not usable by 3270 products (e.g., paper feed, vertical tab, backspace) which would show up in EBCDIC code charts for other products that might make use of them

FIGURE 8.10 Extended Binary Coded Decimal Interchange Code (EBCDIC). This example is the complete code for the IBM 3270 product family.

Control Characters. Several of the codes described above include a series of special nonprinting characters known as **control characters**. Printing characters transmit letters, numbers, or punctuation marks that appear on the printed page or are displayed on a screen. Their function is to relay a message or transmit text. Control characters, on the other hand, are a set of special characters used to control special functions. For example, a control character may delete a character, indicate the start of text, or signal the end of the transmission. Other special characters ring the bell and provide line feed, form feed, backspace, vertical tabulation, horizontal tabulation, and various file and record separators. These and other control characters can be embedded in a text message to call out the functions required.

ERROR-DETECTION SCHEMES

Several of the data transmission codes just discussed include provisions for detecting errors. These codes use a check bit in each byte. The check bit is either a one or a zero, depending on whether even or odd parity is used. Systems such as these are known as **vertical redundancy checks (VRCs)**.

Vertical Parity

In the **even-parity system**, each character transmitted has a fixed number of bits in each byte, including a check bit. If the byte has an odd number of one bits, then a one check bit is assigned in the check bit position to make the number of one bits even in the transmitted bit package. At the receiving end, the equipment checks to see if the bits received add up to an even number. If a bit is accidentally changed, and a one becomes a zero, then the receiving equipment will detect an uneven number of bits and will report the error. This arrangement allows millions of characters to be transmitted, with even one error in a million detected by the electronic circuitry.

In the **odd-parity system**, each byte transmitted also contains a fixed number of bits. If the character transmitted contains an even number of one bits, then a one bit is assigned as the check bit.

Longitudinal Parity

The even- and odd-parity check systems are called vertical parity checks because they check only one byte at a time. It is also possible to check the parity at the end of a transmitted block. This is called horizontal or **longitudinal redundancy check (LRC)**. (See Figure 8.11.)

In the **longitudinal parity check**, a check bit is transmitted at the end of the block to ensure that the correct number of bits has been transmitted. If both a horizontal and vertical check system are used, redundancy takes place, giving an even greater assurance that the loss or gain of one bit in millions of bytes transmitted will be detected. Several sophisticated longitudinal parity check systems have been developed. These will be described next.

FIGURE 8.11
Longitudinal Parity

Byte Parity Check

Longitudinal Parity Check

Longitudinal Check Character

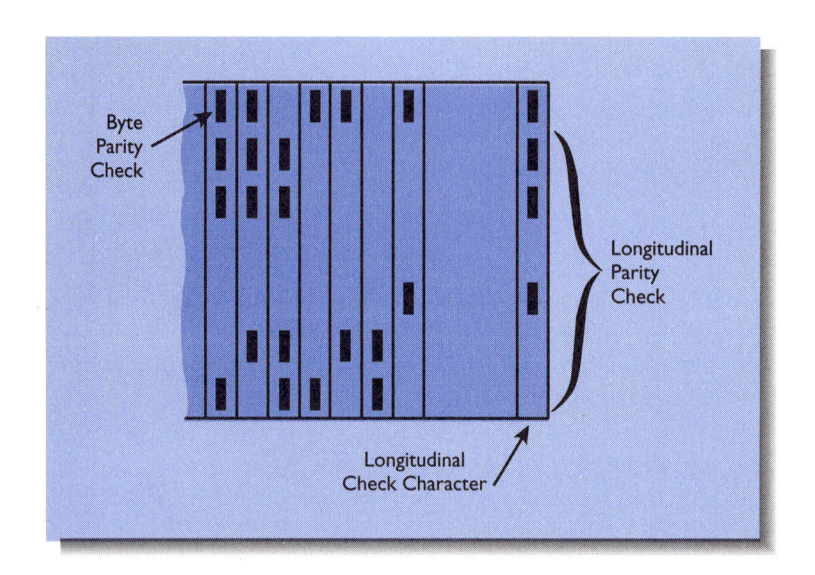

X-ON/X-OFF Flow Control

For many years, early Teletype equipment regulated the flow of information between devices using a simple **X-ON/X-OFF** file transfer system. The purpose was to assure that a device was ready to receive information and that the flow of data was regulated.

A Teletype machine, for example, ready to receive data, would send an X-ON signal to the computer to initiate the process. After the computer transmitted a volume of information, the Teletype sent back an X-OFF signal, telling the computer to stop sending data. After the information was printed out on the Teletype, it would again send an X-ON signal, indicating it was ready to receive more data.

This relatively primitive system was adequate where small amounts of information were to be transmitted between similar types of devices. Today, the X-ON/X-OFF flow control system has largely been replaced by the more efficient schemes we shall discuss next.

XMODEM Error Checking

For microcomputers the **XMODEM** error-checking system, developed by Ward Christensen, is widely used. The Christensen system achieves a high transmission accuracy rate because it checks the received block of data. In this method, 128 bytes of data are sent. Upon receipt, an acknowledge signal is transmitted. (See Figure 8.12.)

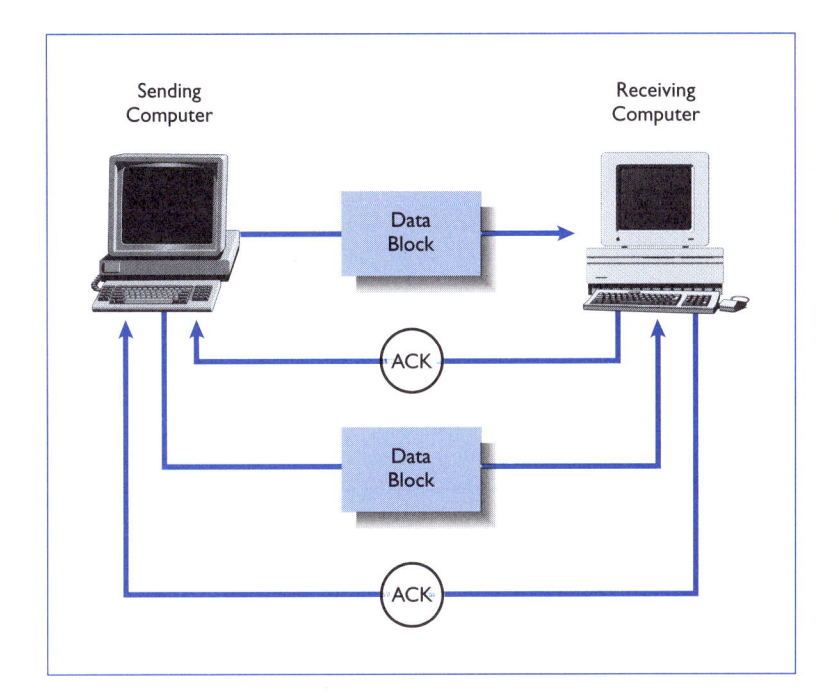

FIGURE 8.12 XMODEM Protocol. Blocks of 128 bytes are transferred, followed by an ACK signal.

First the receiving computer sends a **negative acknowledgment (NAK)** signal, which indicates that it is ready to receive data. (See Figure 8.13.) The receiver continues to transmit the NAK signal every 10 seconds, waiting for the sending computer to begin transferring blocks of data. A 128-byte block of data is then sent to the receiving computer. If the parity checks correctly, an **acknowledgment (ACK)** signal is transmitted. Then another 128-byte block is transmitted. The process continues, with an ACK signal being transmitted to the sending computer on the correct receipt of each block of data.

If a block of data is received incorrectly, that is, if the parity check does not agree, then a NAK signal is transmitted, causing the sending computer to retransmit the block. After the sending computer transmits the last block of data, it sends an **end of transmission (EOT)** signal to the receiving computer, which then sends an ACK signal, thus completing the transaction.

On microcomputer systems, a period (.) is displayed on the screen each time a 128-byte block of characters is received without error. If an error occurs in transmission, an R is displayed on the screen and the block is retransmitted. Although the XMODEM check has not been standardized, it has become the de facto standard for small systems.

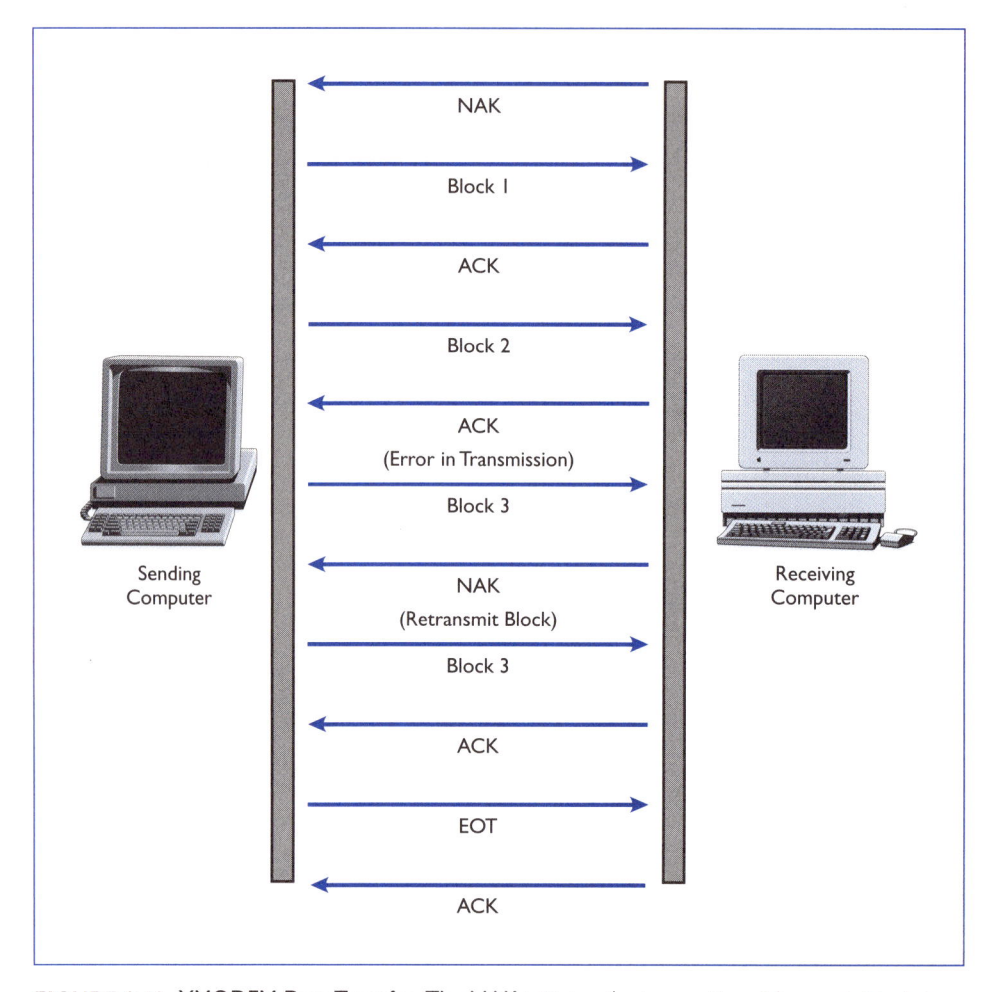

FIGURE 8.13 XMODEM Data Transfer. The NAK initiates the transaction. After each block is received correctly, the receiving computer transmits an ACK to the sending computer.

XMODEM-1K

A substantial increase in transmission speed is obtained when larger blocks of data are sent before an acknowledgment. The **XMODEM-1K** error-checking system transmits 1024 bytes of data instead of the 128 in the XMODEM system.

YMODEM

The **YMODEM** system is based on the XMODEM-1K, but includes additional features. It allows multiple files to be transmitted as a single batch. It is suitable for transmitting groups of files without additional operator intervention.

ZMODEM

The **ZMODEM** transfer system finds applications in moving files over packet-switched networks. It contains many advanced error-checking features that eliminate waiting for acknowledgments as in the XMODEM system. It is able to vary the size of each block to compensate for noise on the communication line.

Cyclic Redundancy Check

Another widely used system is the **cyclic redundancy check (CRC)**. In the CRC system, a block of data is transmitted together with additional checking bits. The number of checking bits, usually two, three, or four, is determined by the length of the block chosen for the system. When the message is received, the system compares the checking bits against the transmitted block. If no bits are changed, it is assumed that the data have been transmitted without error. If the check bits do not agree, the block is retransmitted. Systems such as this are commonly used on large computer networks.

KERMIT Error Checking

KERMIT is another common error-checking system. It finds its widest applications in linking microcomputers to mainframes, both IBM and non-IBM equipment. It uses a seven or eight data bit system with blocks up to 1024 bytes in length. In full-duplex mode, KERMIT sends a continuous stream of data.

The X.25 Standard

The CCITT has adopted the **X.25 standard**, which specifies the interface between data terminals operating in the packet-switching mode on public networks. (Packet switching is discussed in Chapter 13.) If many users are to access a packet-switched network, there must be a standard to ensure that information is presented in a uniform format with approved destination headers. When all devices on the system conform to this standard, which includes error-checking features, error-free transmissions occur. Because all data packets moving through a network have a common format, switching equipment can route packets through to their destination. The X.25 standard assures users that regardless of the make of equipment, all messages will be properly transmitted error-free through the network.

In addition to the systems discussed above, communications software vendors, such as Hayes Microcomputer Products, Inc. and others, have developed proprietary error-checking systems. These typically transfer 128 to 1,024 bytes in each block.

DATA COMPRESSION SCHEMES

A discussion of error-detection schemes would not be complete without a review of data compression and decompression techniques. **Data compression** involves a concentration in the number of characters or data bits that represent information in order to reduce the number of bytes stored or transmitted. **Decompression** involves the expansion of compressed data back into its original form.

Transmitting a line of text containing a string of blank characters or spaces, such as a line spaced out to the right margin, would not be efficient. Instead, the number of blank spaces is counted and then represented by a short compression code. Once received, a decompression algorithm adds the necessary blank spaces to fill out the line.

Data-compression schemes are often integrated with error-detection systems so that data move not only error-free, but in the most condensed and compact manner. Data compression allows large volumes of data to be transmitted over a channel using a minimum amount of time and resources. There are many techniques and algorithms used to compress data. For example, short code combinations may be used to represent lengthy sequences of characters, or a two-digit byte may represent a lengthy word or phrase.

Programs that perform these functions are known as squeezers and unsqueezers. They are used not only for compressing data to be transmitted over a communications circuit, but for storing data on a hard disk drive or floppy disk. Such programs are able to reduce the size of a file by 60 percent or more, depending on the nature of the contents.

INTERFACE STANDARDS

An **interface** is a common boundary between two or more pieces of communications equipment. (See Figure 8.14.) It is the junction or point where different pieces of equipment are linked together. Two categories of equipment are usually interfaced: **data terminal equipment (DTE)**, which may be a microcomputer, video display terminal, teleprinter, or other device, and **data circuit-terminating equipment (DCE)**, which may be modems, concentrators, multiplexers, or similar devices. The common boundary between these two groups is the interface.

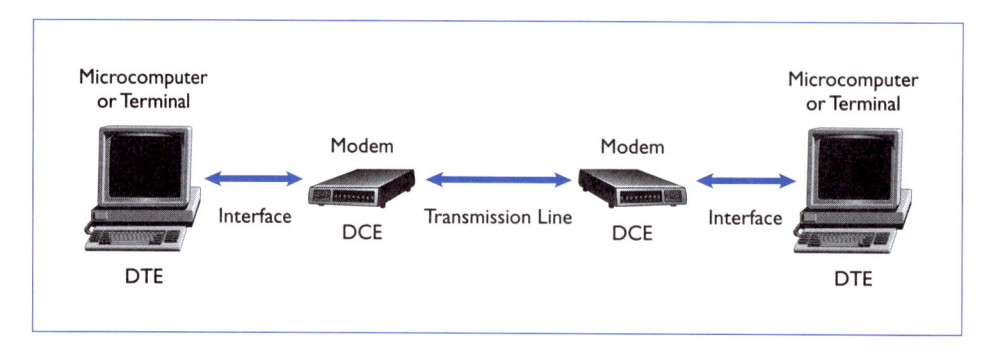

FIGURE 8.14 Communications Interface

An interface standard is the agreed-on facilities, including the formats, transmission speeds, and physical wiring arrangement that enable the terminals (DTEs) to communicate with the modems or other DCEs. In the absence of a standard interface arrangement, chaos would exist in the industry and no two pieces of equipment would be able to communicate with each other.

The EIA-232-D Standard

To facilitate interfacing and the connection of dissimilar devices, the Electronic Industries Association (EIA) has published a standard interface connection arrangement known as the **EIA-232-D**. (See Figure 8.15.) The standards established by the EIA-232-D have become the universal circuit arrangement by which virtually all external modems, data terminals, and other devices are physically connected to a communications line.

Interchange Circuit	C.C.I.T.T. Equivalent	Description	Gnd	Data From DCE	Data To DCE	Control From DCE	Control To DCE	Timing From DCE	Timing To DCE
AB	102	Signal Ground/Common Return	×						
BA	103	Transmitted Data			×				
BB	104	Received Data		×					
CA	105	Request to Send					×		
CB	106	Clear to Send				×			
CC	107	DCE Ready				×			
CD	108.2	DTE Ready					×		
CE	125	Ring Indicator				×			
CF	109	Received Line Signal Detector				×			
CG	110	Signal Quality Detector				×			
CH	111	Data Signal Rate Selector (DTE)					×		
CI	112	Data Signal Rate Selector (DCE)				×			
DA	113	Transmitter Signal Element Timing (DTE)							×
DB	114	Transmitter Signal Element Timing (DCE)						×	
DD	115	Receiver Signal Element Timing (DCE)						×	
SBA	118	Secondary Transmitted Data			×				
SBB	119	Secondary Received Data		×					
SCA	120	Secondary Request to Send					×		
SCB	121	Secondary Clear to Send				×			
SCF	122	Secondary Received Line Signal Detector				×			
RL	140	Remote Loopback					×		
LL	141	Local Loopback					×		
TM	142	Test Mode				×			

FIGURE 8.15 EIA-232-D Standard Interchange Circuits by Category

In late 1986, EIA approved the EIA-232-D standard, which was intended to replace the widely followed RS-232-C standard. There are only minor differences between the two standards, and the EIA-232-D is compatible with the RS-232-C. Even though the new standard has been adopted, some manufacturers still refer to it as RS-232-C. The EIA-232-D standard serves the United States; although CCITT has approved the same arrangement for international use, it is known abroad as the V.24 standard.

The EIA-232-D standard also describes the physical pin connections and voltages on a given circuit. It does not specify the data code that is used to actually send information. Thus, the Baudot, BCD, ASCII, or EBCDIC codes may all be used on the EIA-232-D circuit at speeds of up to 20,000 bits per second.

The EIA standard specifically defines voltages that will be present on the line. In many computers a zero voltage is used to represent the binary digit zero and a +3 voltage to represent the binary digit one. Other systems use different negative or positive voltages to represent binary ones and zeros. Thus, it was necessary for the EIA to specify a standard set of voltage conditions.

In the EIA-232-D, a binary zero is represented by a positive voltage ranging between +3 and +15 volts. A binary one is represented by a negative voltage between –3 and –15 volts. Therefore, any direct-current pulse between +3 and +15 volts represents a binary zero, and the complementary negative pulse represents a binary one.

25-Pin Connector

The EIA-232-D standard specifies the 25-pin physical connector, in which each pin is reserved for a specific function. (See Figure 8.16.) Pin 1 is reserved for connecting to the physical grounded frame of the equipment. Pin 2 transmits data from the terminal to the modem. Data are received from the modem on Pin 3. Pin 4 is used for a request to send a signal to the modem, Pin 5 for clearance to send, etc. Thus, each pin carries a standard signal both in voltage and type, enabling all EIA-232-D compatible equipment to be interfaced.

The RS-449 Standard

Although the EIA-232-D has become the virtual standard in communications, it has not become an absolute. The American National Standards Institute (ANSI) has not accepted this standard, nor has the United States government strongly favored it. As a result, another standard, **RS-449**, has been developed. The RS-449 interface, because of different electrical and physical characteristics, is able to operate over longer distances and at higher speeds. It requires a 37-pin connector rather than the simpler and less expensive 25-pin used in the EIA-232-D. The U.S. government has stated its intent to acquire new equipment based on the RS-449 standard.

Pin Number	Circuit	Description
1	– –	Shield
2	BA	Transmitted Data
3	BB	Received Data
4	CA	Request to Send
5	CB	Clear to Send
6	CC	DCE Ready
7	AB	Signal Ground
8	CF	Received Line Signal Detector
9	–	(Reserved for Data Testing)
10	–	(Reserved for Data Testing)
11		Unassigned
12	SCF/CI	Secondary Received Line Sig. Detector/Data Signal Rate Select (DCE Source)
13	SCB	Section Clear to Send
14	SBA	Secondary Transmitted Data
15	DB	Transmitter Signal Element Timing (DCE Source)
16	SBB	Secondary Received Data
17	DD	Receiver Signal Element Timing (DCE Source)
18	LL	Local Loopback
19	SCA	Secondary Request to Send
20	CD	DTE Ready
21	RL/CG	Remote Loopback/Signal Quality Detector
22	CE	Ring Indicator
23	CH/CI	Data Signal Rate Selector (DTE/DCE Source)
24	DA	Transmit Signal Element Timing (DTE Source)
25	TM	Test Mode

FIGURE 8.16 EIA-232-D Standard Interface Connector Pin Assignments

PROTOCOLS AND HANDSHAKES

A **protocol** is a formally prescribed set of rules or conduct that governs an event. A commonly observed protocol is the handshake of two people meeting for the first time. The handshake says, "I recognize your presence, and you have my attention." At parting, the handshake is repeated, to signify the meeting is at an end and each party can resume his or her affairs. Protocols also govern our timing of events. One example is the protocol used in a restaurant. Generally, a glass of water is served and a menu handed to the customer on being seated. This action says "Hello" and tells the customer to prepare to order the meal. When the waiter returns and asks "May I take your order?", the customary protocol is to recite one's food order.

Handshakes and protocols are needed in communications and have been incorporated in many standards. **Handshake procedures** establish an orderly sequence for initiating a transmission, a method to avoid contention on a line, and a signal to show that a message has been received.

When a DCE such as a modem is to communicate with a terminal (DTE), it follows an orderly handshake procedure using the standard EIA-232-D pin arrangement. Before data are sent, a request to send a signal must be put on the line. Then, a "clear to send the signal" is received. Next, the "data set ready" signal is transmitted. These signals must be communicated and received before the actual message is sent over the line.

The handshake ensures that information will not be sent to a terminal that is unplugged or not ready to receive data. It also ensures that the timing of the message is correct and that leading characters will not be lost because the receiving device is not active.

As a practical matter, a variety of different handshake procedures are used on different systems. The type of equipment, speed of data transmission, information coding system, and format of the data sent influence the specific handshake procedure.

In this chapter we have looked at various coding systems, error-detection schemes, and handshaking protocols. In Chapter 9 we will look at the specific programs and computer software that implement many of these functions. Unless a standard is implemented in a program, it remains only that—a standard. It is when these standards become widely accepted that they enable the efficient flow of information between widely differing types of machines and devices.

SUMMARY

Early messages were sent *point to point*, routed from one telegraph office to another.

Communications standards are published by *ANSI, ISO, EIA, IEEE*, and *CCITT*. The *Baudot code* consists of a five-bit combination without parity checks. The *BCD* code contains six bits and one *parity bit check*.

Even-parity systems transmit an even number of bits in each byte. *Odd-parity* systems transmit an uneven number of bits in each byte. *Longitudinal parity* checks the parity at the end of the transmitted block.

The *ASCII code* contains seven bits and a parity bit check and can represent 128 different characters. The *EBCDIC code* contains eight bits and a parity bit check and can represent 256 different characters. *Control characters* are nonprinting characters that perform special functions.

The *X-ON/X-OFF* protocol assures that a device is ready to receive information and that the flow of data is regulated. For microcomputers the *XMODEM* error-checking system achieves a high transmission accuracy rate. The *XMODEM-1K* error-checking system transmits 1,024 bytes of data instead of the 128 in the XMODEM system.

In the *cyclic redundancy check (CRC)* a block of data is transmitted with two, three, or four checking bits, determined by the length of the block. *KERMIT* finds its widest applications in linking microcomputers to mainframes, both IBM and non-IBM equipment.

The *YMODEM* protocol transmits large files and uses a cyclic redundancy check to monitor errors. The *ZMODEM* transfer protocol finds applications in moving files over packet-switched networks. The *X.25 standard* specifies the interface between data terminals operating in the packet-switching mode on public networks.

An *interface* is a common boundary between two or more communications devices. The *EIA-232-D* is a common standard for interfacing *DTEs* and *DCEs*. A DTE may be a microcomputer, CRT, or teleprinter. A DCE may be a modem, concentrator, or multiplexer.

A *protocol* is a prescribed set of rules that governs a communications transaction. *Handshake procedures* establish an orderly sequence for beginning and terminating a communication.

Data compression is the concentration of the number of characters or data bits that represent information in order to reduce the number of bytes. *Decompression* is the expansion of compressed data back into its original form.

EXERCISES

1. List the major organizations involved in establishing data transmission standards.
2. Describe the Baudot code.
3. Describe the BCD code.
4. What is the function of the longitudinal parity check?
5. Describe the ASCII and extended ASCII codes.
6. Describe the EBCDIC code.
7. Describe the EIA-232-D standard.
8. Describe the function of a protocol.
9. Contrast the XMODEM and other error-checking protocols.
10. Describe the function of data compression software.

HANDS-ON PROJECTS

- Review the manual for the printer associated with a computer. Determine what type of interface and connection exists between the computer and the printer.

- Obtain several different types of communications connectors. Study them carefully and determine their type.

- Study the connectors and jacks on the back of your computer. Determine their type and function.

- Obtain several different pieces of communications software and determine what type of error-detection protocols are used.

- Obtain a copy of the EIA-232-D standard interface. Review the document and determine the kinds of information in it.

COMMUNICATIONS IN ACTION

CASE SOLUTION
AIR RESOURCES COMPANY

Air Resources Company installed an integrated voice and data system. (See Figure 8.17.) All conventional telephone switchboards were replaced by a digital branch exchange (DBX). This switchboard is able to route both telephone calls and data transmissions over any of the organization's already in-place telephone wiring. Ordinary telephones were replaced by

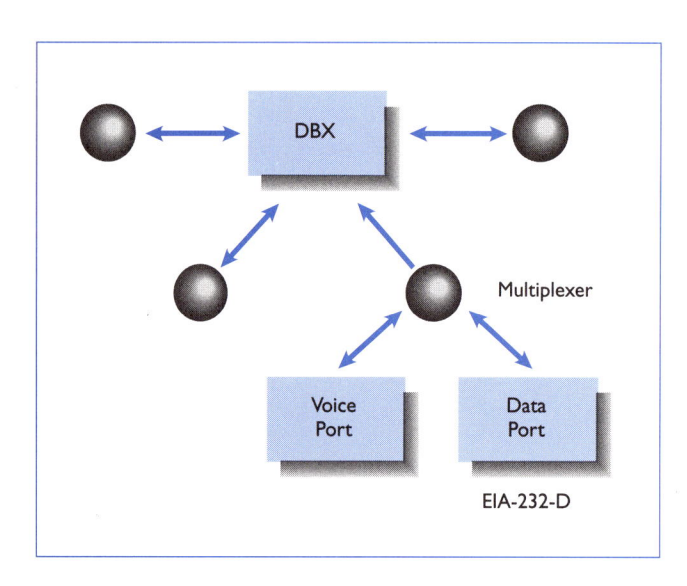

FIGURE 8.17 New Integrated DBX System

new combination instruments that had EIA-232-D connectors for computers or data terminals. These devices enabled individuals to place telephone calls to anyone in the company just as before, but now they could also multiplex data over the same circuits.

The biggest cost saving was realized when Air Resources Company acquired the new subsidiary. The thousands of feet of telephone wiring already in place served as the basis for the new integrated system. The new arrangement is very flexible. Managers can relocate or move their offices or facilities at minimal expense. As long as an ordinary telephone twisted pair is available, the office can be served by both voice and data systems. Because each multiplexer box has an EIA-232-D jack, any standard terminal, printer, or CRT can be connected.

The personnel at Air Resources Company like the new system. They see a digital display when the telephone rings. The telephone terminal shows the name of the calling party, the point of origin, and whether the call has been forwarded from another station.

COMMUNICATIONS SOFTWARE PACKAGES

LEARNING OBJECTIVES

After studying this chapter, you should be able to:

- Describe mainframe communications packages
- Discuss the function of front-end processors
- Describe the function of front-end software
- Contrast several different microcomputer communications packages
- Discuss user-supported software packages
- Describe the operation of bulletin board services (BBSs)

COMMUNICATIONS
IN ACTION

CASE PROBLEM
MICROS 'N STUFF

ELECTRONIC BULLETIN BOARD

Bob Gordon owns Micros 'n Stuff, a retail shop selling microcomputers, software, printers, and supplies. His store sells hardware and software to educational institutions, students, and business and home computer users.

Gordon employs six salespeople in his store. Much of their time is spent demonstrating computers and software, explaining how to hook up equipment and diagnose routine problems. Sometimes customers come to Micros 'n Stuff for after-sales service, carrying in their equipment. Others seek help and guidance over the telephone.

Some of Micros 'n Stuff's business consists of selling used equipment. Gordon often takes in used computer systems as down payments on new systems. He must then find buyers for the used equipment.

As business has expanded, Bob Gordon is concerned about the time his staff spends answering the same questions over and over. They are constantly having to explain how to solve routine problems, and they spend a lot of time providing basic problem diagnosis. Gordon must also determine what to do with the used computers stacked up in his storeroom. Gordon wants to find a way to make his staff more productive, without cutting back on service to his customers. He must also find a way to sell the used equipment he takes as trade-ins.

What communications facilities would you recommend that Bob Gordon install to solve his problem? At the end of this chapter you will find out what he did.

A VARIETY of communications software packages have been developed to facilitate the flow of information between computer and computer, computer and terminal, and terminal and terminal. This chapter describes some of the software packages available from computer manufacturers and software firms, as well as user-supported free software. This chapter also explains how programs and data files are transferred from one computer to another.

First we discuss mainframe communications software, then move on to a discussion of communications software packages available for microcomputers. The chapter concludes with a description of bulletin boards and virus protection software.

A communications software package is a collection of one or more programs designed to facilitate communications between computers and terminals. Software packages enable computer users to interact with programs on a large computer, dial computers through the switched telephone network, transfer programs from one system to another, and perform message switching, routing, and data security functions.

MAINFRAME SOFTWARE

In the early 1960s programmers of large mainframe computers recognized the need for **communications software packages** to ease the programming task. Without communications software, programmers writing programs for payroll, billing, or other applications had to understand thoroughly the hardware details and unique characteristics of each terminal and device tied to the system. Figure 9.1 illustrates an applications program that communicated with a remote terminal through the computer's operating system without the presence of communications software. Programming in this environment was very difficult. The programmer not only had to understand the problem to be solved and write an appropriate program, but also had to write instructions (called driver routines) for each different type of terminal on the system.

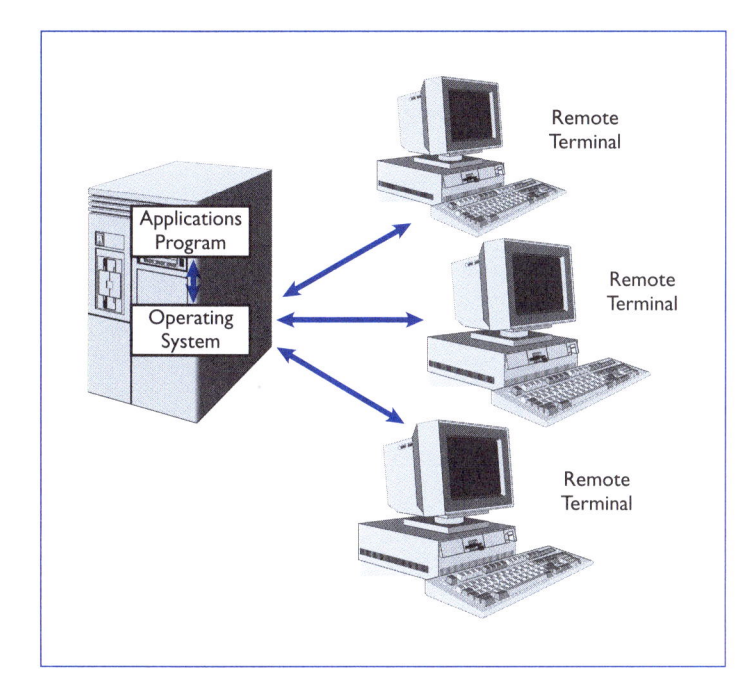

FIGURE 9.1
Host Computer Without Communications Software. An applications program communicates with terminals directly through an operating system.

This arrangement also created an excessive load on the **mainframe** or **host computer**. It required the host computer to handle all the routine switching, line control, error-checking, and message-buffering functions in order to support the terminals.

To address these problems, computer manufacturers introduced communications software to relieve the programmer of the burden of writing unique instructions for individual terminals.

Figure 9.2 illustrates how a mainframe package, developed by IBM Corporation, facilitates communications between terminals and applications programs. The package shown in the figure, called **Basic Telecommunications Access Method (BTAM)**, eliminated the need for the programmer to code detailed instructions to communicate with specific types of terminals. The BTAM package and the others discussed here greatly simplified and eased the applications programmer's task by allowing programs to be written without concern for the particular terminals connected to the system.

FIGURE 9.2
BTAM Communications Package. BTAM resides in the host computer.

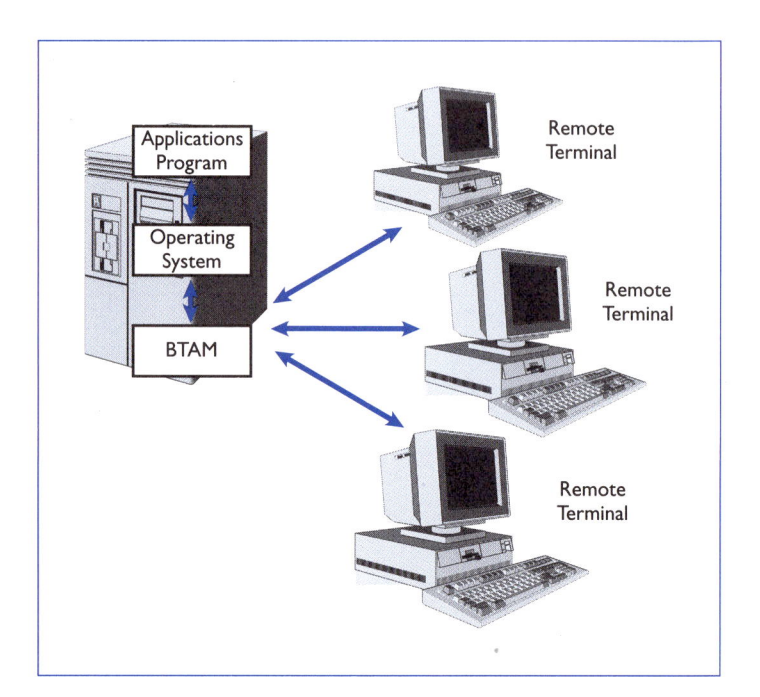

FRONT-END PROCESSORS

Special-function computers, known as **front-end processor (FEPs)**, were developed and installed in front of host computers to relieve the load on mainframes. (See Figure 9.3.) The front-end processor is a stand-alone computer designed to handle communications tasks. (See Figure 9.4.) The FEP frees the mainframe from routine housekeeping tasks, shifting the burden of buffering, error checking, and switching to a separate computer, thus greatly increasing the speed and capacity of the mainframe.

One of the most widely used FEPs on the IBM system is the IBM 3725. Several models of this device are available. When equipped with appropriate software, the front-end processor is able to take full responsibility for routing and switching data between devices on the system. The FEP handles error recovery in case messages need to be retransmitted or interruptions occur on the line. The FEP also detects terminal transmission speeds and recognizes different transmission codes.

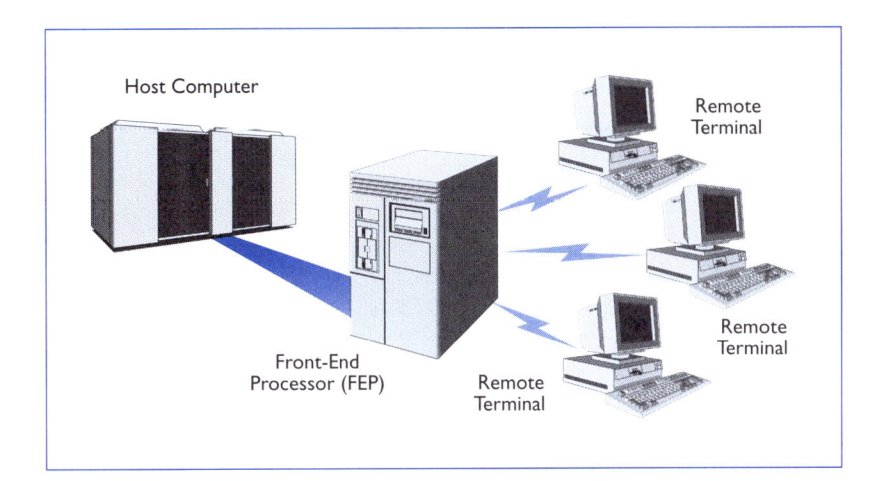

FIGURE 9.3
Front-End Processor (FEP). The FEP handles communications tasks for the host computer.

FIGURE 9.4
Front-End Processor (FEP) Functions

Outgoing Call Dialing
Code Conversion
Message Switching
Log Communications
Terminal Polling
Error Detection
Queue Tasks
Incoming Call Answering
Device Contentions Resolution
Report Usage Statistics
Message Header Reading, Message Routing
Display System Status

Controllers are often installed in systems to facilitate communications. (See Figure 9.5.) A **controller** is a hardware device that connects a terminal to a communications line. On some systems, a controller is simply a circuit card that handles the timing and error-checking routines between a device and a communications line. These controllers may cost less than several hundred dollars. On other computer systems, such as those that tie together dozens of terminals and high-speed communications devices, a sophisticated controller may be required. These devices, costing thousands of dollars, may occupy several racks of equipment and have connectors and cabling for dozens of devices.

FIGURE 9.5
Controller Card. This controller connects terminals to a communications line.

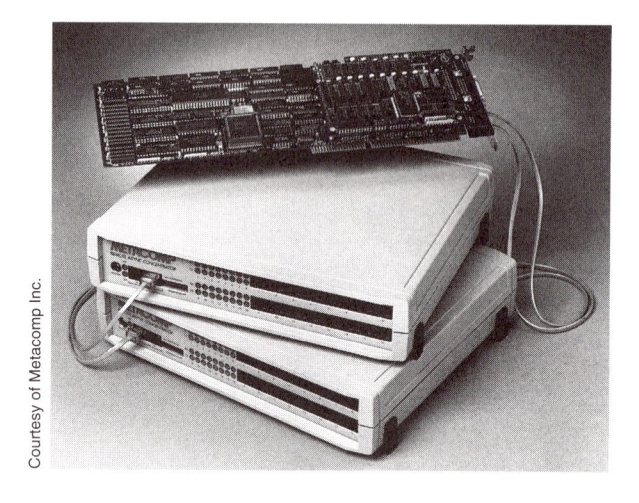

Courtesy of Metacomp Inc.

FRONT-END SOFTWARE

Soon after BTAM was introduced, it became apparent that other tasks needed to be performed by communications software. Thus more sophisticated versions of BTAM were developed. These include **Queued Telecommunications Access Method (QTAM)**, which not only handled line switching and error checking as did BTAM, but also analyzed message headers and routed communications to specific applications programs. QTAM also logged the time and date of each message or request coming into the mainframe and kept them waiting in a queue until mainframe resources were available to process them.

As more computing tasks involving communications were placed on host computers, more advanced software packages were needed. One of the most flexible packages available for the IBM 370 series, for example, is **Virtual Telecommunications Access Method (VTAM)**. (See Figure 9.6.) VTAM resides in the host computer's main memory, serving as an interface between the applications program and the front-end processor. With a **Network Control Program (NCP)** running in the front-end processor, an applications program can communicate with hundreds of devices operating at various bps rates and using different protocols and transmission codes. When applied to IBM equipment, the entire system is known as System Network Architecture (SNA).

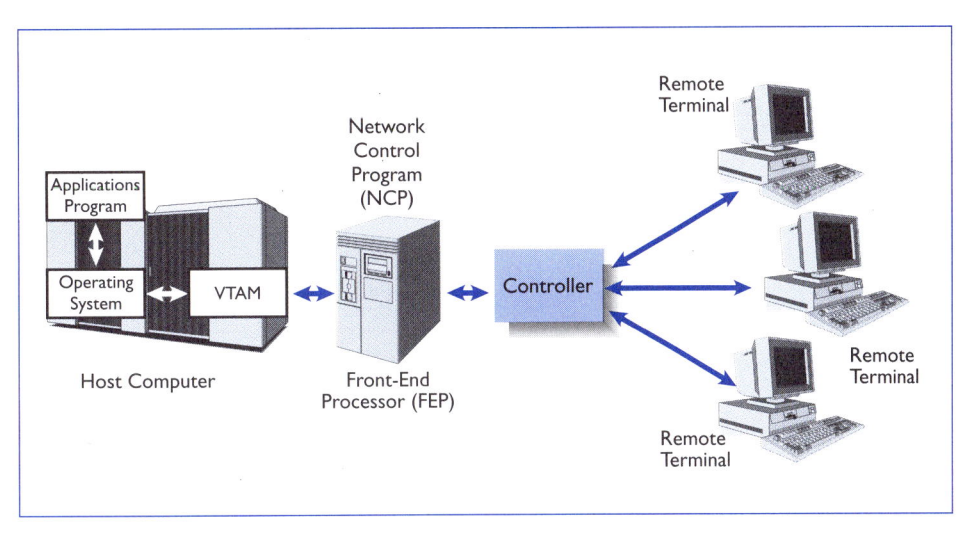

FIGURE 9.6 Virtual Telecommunications Access Method (VTAM).

SYSTEMS NETWORK ARCHITECTURE

The IBM **System Network Architecture (SNA)** is a proprietary set of specifications written by IBM Corporation, designed to integrate communications software and hardware into a package. The architecture has become popular because of IBM's major penetration in the communications marketplace. Today, SNA is the leading large system network software.

SNA is constructed from a group of **nodes**. A node is an entry point in a network and may be a computer mainframe, a front-end processor, or a group of terminals. The devices on the network are addressable, which means they can be called in by specific location. Three types of **network addressable units (NAUs)** are on the system:

1. *Physical units (PU)*. These are the physical nodes, such as a particular terminal or front-end processor.
2. *Logical units (LU)*. A logical unit may be an applications program, a disk drive, or even a portion of a system treated as an entity. LUs are generally created by software.
3. *System services control point (SSCP)*. An SSCP is a point in the network that switches logical and physical units.

SNA defines a group of software layers that assist in the physical flow of data. These layers provide for:

- The detection of errors and provisions for transmission protocols
- Routing of communications through the network
- Selection of the logical channel over which a communication is sent

- Establishment of communications between several devices and assurance that communications have been initiated and terminated properly
- Coordination of data flow and grouping related data into units
- An interface to the system and a mechanism for using the network

The IBM SNA is discussed in more detail in Chapter 12.

CUSTOMER INFORMATION CONTROL SYSTEM

Computer manufacturers have developed many sophisticated communications control programs. For example, IBM's **Customer Information Control System (CICS)** resides in the host computer together with VTAM, providing high-level monitoring of the entire communications process. It interfaces between a group of terminals and an applications program. CICS takes over the functions of terminal control, providing systems management, job priority, task scheduling, and other jobs.

CICS can be customized to suit the needs of a particular user. Much of the utility of CICS lies in its ability to control different types of terminals. The system maintains a table of various terminals wired to the system. CICS deals with the unique attributes of each terminal, allowing many different applications programs to serve terminals of differing speeds and characteristics.

Another advantage of CICS is its ability to allow access to many databases by various terminals on the system. Both sequential and direct-access files are accessible, as well as databases generated by software other than IBM's. CICS thus enables simultaneous operation of numerous terminals, accessing different types of databases and applications programs. It is a key piece of front-end software.

Although we have discussed just some specific IBM software packages, similar pieces of software have been developed by other manufacturers for their mainframes. In addition, a competitive marketplace has led software houses to design and market similar communications packages.

MICROCOMPUTER-TO-HOST SOFTWARE

One of the most common terminals connected directly to the IBM mainframe computer is the IBM 3270 terminal. With the great increase in the use of personal computers, many small machines are now connected directly to large mainframes. With the appropriate **microcomputer-to-host** software and controller card, virtually any microcomputer can emulate this IBM terminal.

Listed below are three common PC-to-host connections.

PC-to-IBM Host

A PC-to-IBM host connection is implemented in hardware by inserting a controller card in the PC and connecting it directly to a mainframe. (See Figure 9.7.) Using appropriate 3270 emulation software, the PC behaves exactly like a standard IBM 3270 terminal. It can upload and download files, access information, and print out reports, among other tasks.

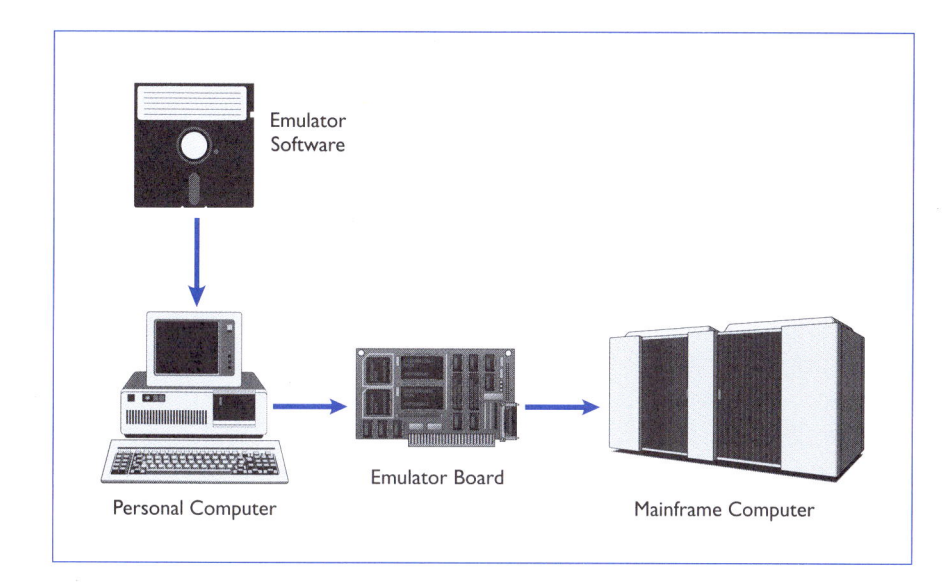

FIGURE 9.7 PC-to-Mainframe Host

Macintosh-to-IBM Host

The Apple Macintosh computer can also be interfaced to an IBM mainframe by installing a 3270 emulator board in the Macintosh and equipping it with appropriate software. This interface allows Macintosh users to develop programs with Macintosh graphics on an IBM mainframe—a particularly challenging goal because the IBM and Macintosh worlds are very different.

This PC- or Mac-to-IBM host connection adds greater capability to the microcomputer. With emulator boards installed, both the Macintosh and the PC still function as stand-alone microcomputers as the need arises; in effect, they can operate in two different environments.

PC-to-DEC Host

Digital Equipment Corporation (DEC) has sold many **VT series terminals** that are connected to DEC mainframes. Because of the popularity of these terminals, many microcomputer owners use their PCs to emulate VT series terminals by using **VT emulator software**. Both the VT52 and VT100 emulators are widely used. When this software is running, the keyboard key assignments all conform to those of standard VT terminals.

Other emulators are available that allow PCs to emulate Televideo, ADDS, Texas Instrument, and even TTY terminals. Many of these emulators are built into the microcomputer communications software packages that are discussed next.

MICROCOMPUTER COMMUNICATIONS PACKAGES

Up to now we have described computers in which the mainframe, front-end processor, controllers, and terminals are all integrated in a single system. In these instances, the communications manager has a relatively high degree of control over the physical hardware, programs, and applications run on the system.

Let us now turn to more loosely constructed systems involving microcomputer communications. In Figure 9.8, a number of microcomputer users access many different host computers or other microcomputers in a much more loosely structured environment. This accessing is done through the use of ordinary dial-up telephone lines, direct lines, or common-carrier facilities. The microcomputers, communications facilities, and host computers may all be under the control of different organizations or entities.

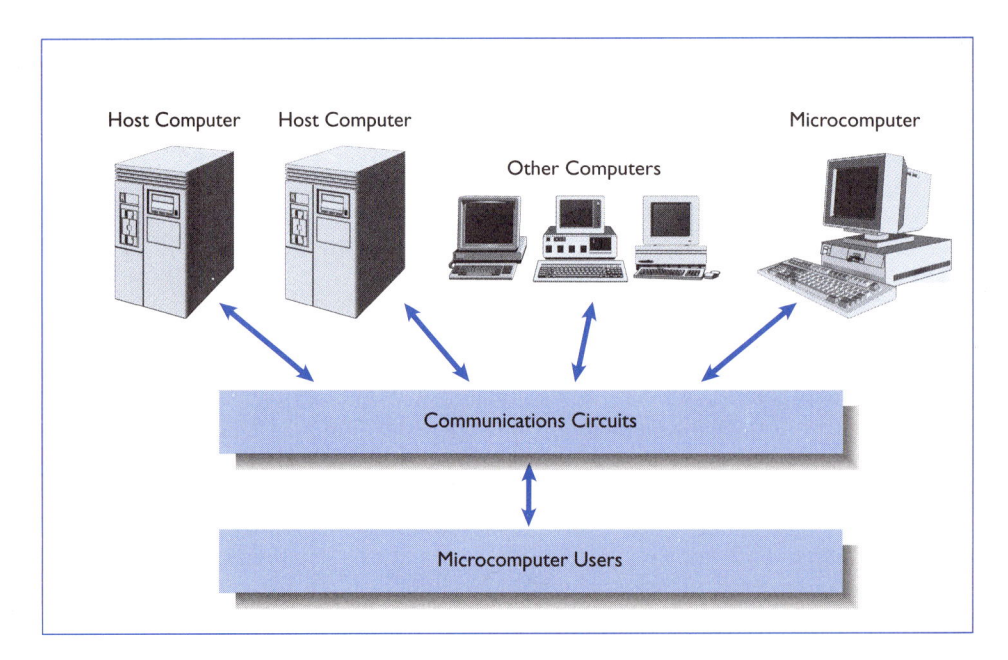

FIGURE 9.8 Microcomputer Communications Environment. Many microcomputers communicate with a variety of host computers and microcomputers through common-carrier or leased lines.

In the microcomputer communications world, dozens of different brands of machines can communicate with many separate mainframes, using various communications software and protocols. These machines may be located in schools, large and small businesses, or private homes. Microcomputer communications packages have been developed specifically for these environments. Figure 9.9 illustrates a system in which a communications software package is loaded on the microcomputer, usually from disk, enabling the user to access other systems through the dial-up network.

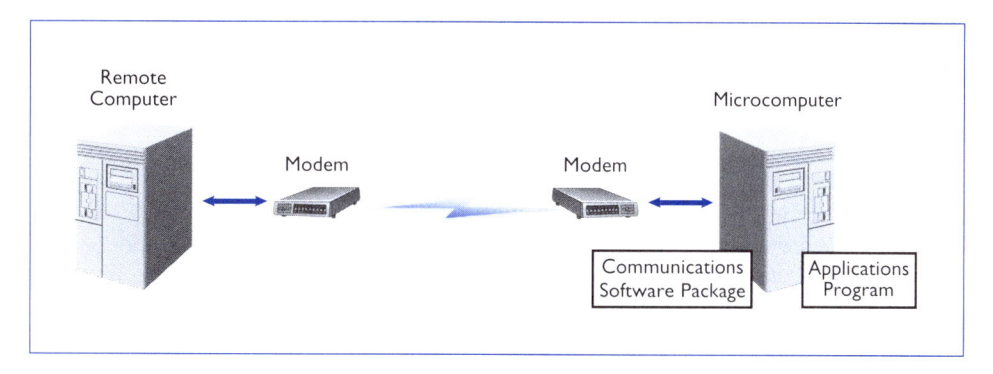

FIGURE 9.9 Microcomputer Communications Package. Communications software resides in the microcomputer and directs a modem which, in turn, communicates with a remote computer.

Hayes Microcomputer Products, Inc. developed one of the earliest microcomputer communications packages. It was designed to operate in conjunction with a sophisticated modem that was directed by software commands. In Chapter 5 we discussed the Hayes smart modem Attention (AT) commands that established a de facto standard for small computer modems and software. The Hayes Smartcom III software became widely used in conjunction with its modems.

Later, other microcomputer communications packages came on the market, including Crosstalk XVI from Digital Communications Associates, Inc., that were sold to the commercial market. In addition, several **user-supported packages** became popular, including PC-TALK and QMODEM. Both were available through free distribution channels, with donations requested from users.

The popularity of specific microcomputer software packages is mercurial, changing as new and improved software packages are developed. One of the most popular packages available today is Procomm Plus, produced by Datastorm Technologies, Inc. Both DOS and Windows versions are available.

A new entry to the communications software market is Terminal, a communications package that runs under Windows 3.1. This software, available from Microsoft Corp., is gaining wide acceptance because millions of copies of Windows have been sold. For the Apple Macintosh computer, AppleTalk is a leading communications package.

Let us review some of the major communications software packages, the services they provide, and the functions they make available to the small-system user.

WINDOWS TERMINAL

Windows Terminal is becoming a leading microcomputer communications software package, because Terminal is provided without additional cost with every copy of Windows Microsoft sells. Together with a serial port, modem, and telephone line, Terminal is able to transmit and receive files between a microcomputer and other systems connected to a modem.

Software Operation

Terminal runs under Windows, a graphical user interface (GUI). This means that functions are executed by using a mouse to move a pointer about a screen. Terminal software is started by double-clicking on the Terminal icon; the Terminal window then appears. (See Figure 9.10.) Using a mouse, the operator makes a selection from the menu bar at the top of the screen.

FIGURE 9.10
Windows Terminal

Before a communication is initiated, various settings are selected. (See Figure 9.11.) By clicking on the appropriate button, the user selects baud rates from 110 to 19,200 Kbps. From 5 to 8 data bits can be chosen, including the number of stop bits. Various parity check options are given, including no parity, odd, and even.

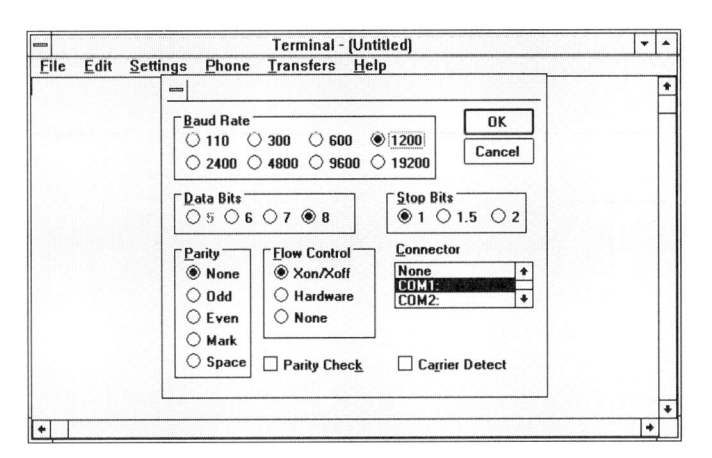

FIGURE 9.11 Communications Setting Window

After the communications settings have been entered, the telephone number to be called is entered into the Phone Number dialog box. (See Figure 9.12.) This phone number can be saved in a file for later reuse. The operator can also specify other choices, using different window screens that allow DEC VT52 and VT100 series terminals to be emulated.

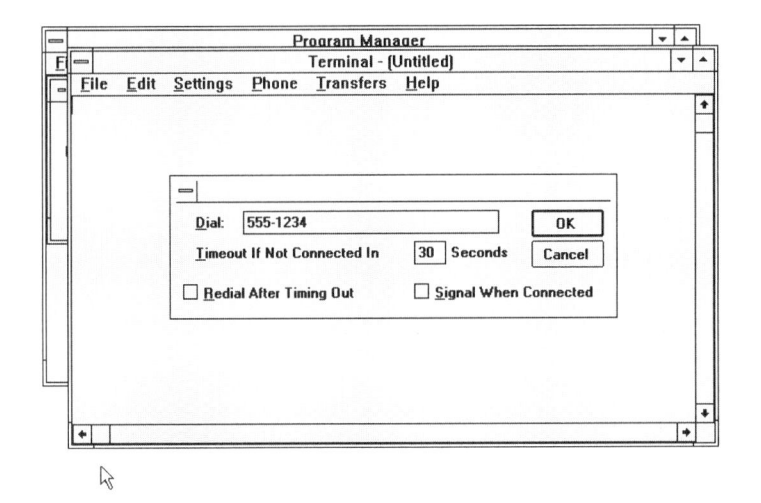

FIGURE 9.12 Phone Number Dialog Box

To initiate a communication, the operator selects Dial, the phone number from the Phone menu, and the communications link is automatically established. Files can be transferred either in text or binary form. To send a file, the Send Text File option is selected and the OK button pressed to begin transmission. To receive a file, the Receive Text File option is selected. Once the file is received, it can be saved on disk or sent to the printer. The session is finished by selecting the Quit Terminal option.

Although Windows Terminal does not contain as many features as other communications packages, its wide availability is making it popular.

PROCOMM PLUS 2.0

Procomm Plus software was developed by Datastorm Technologies, Inc., Columbia, Missouri. It is a user-friendly communications package that uses a **pull-down menu**. It supports many functions, including sending and receiving files, viewing files, and maintaining a dialing directory. The software includes an editor and provides automatic redial capability.

Procomm Plus illustrates how communications software handles the uploading and downloading of files. A file is **uploaded** when it is sent from one microcomputer to another microcomputer or to a mainframe. A file is **downloaded** when it is received from another computer and stored on disk or primary memory in the microcomputer.

Most communications software provides a variety of file transfer protocols. The protocol performs the necessary handshaking procedures when a file transfer is started. All file transfers follow these basic steps:

- The protocol is agreed on by both systems.
- The receiving system is directed to start transmitting or receiving the file.
- The calling system is directed to begin receiving or transmitting the file.
- The transfer protocol checks to see that no errors are present and will retransmit corrupted data in a file.

Files can be uploaded using XMODEM, YMODEM, ASCII, KERMIT, and several other formats. Procomm Plus can download files received in the same format. Its ease of use and low cost has made this software very popular among both commercial and domestic users.

Software Operation

A command menu shows all the Procomm Plus functions; it is brought up by using the Alt and Z keys. (See Figure 9.13.) Procomm Plus commands are grouped into five functions: Before, During, After, Set Up, and Other. Specific functions are executed using the Alt key and a character or function key.

When first beginning Procomm Plus, the operator must enter system parameters via several setup screens. Figure 9.14 illustrates the Modem Command Options screen, in which AT commands, initialization strings, and other commands are entered.

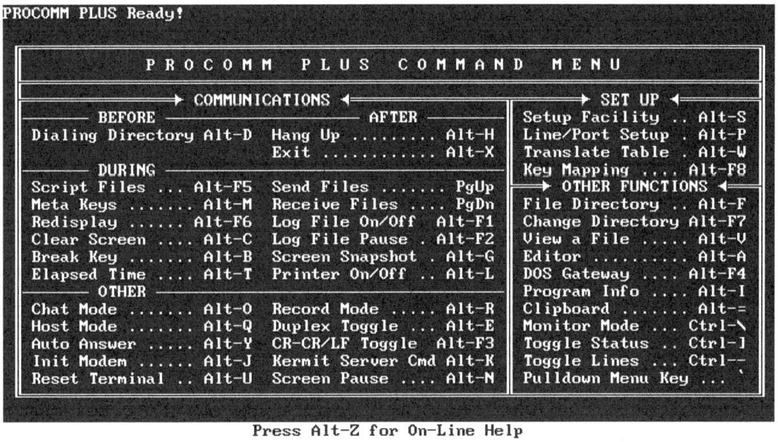

FIGURE 9.13 Procomm Plus Command Menu

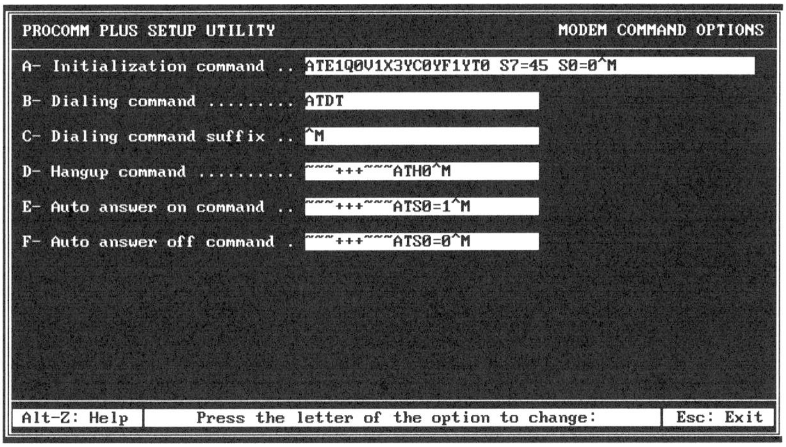

FIGURE 9.14 Procomm Plus Modem Command Options Screen

The Terminal Options screen (see Figure 9.15) is used to enter the type of terminal emulation, flow control, and other features. Once these parameters are entered, the telephone numbers to be called are entered into the dialing directory. (See Figure 9.16.)

Figure 9.15
Procomm Plus Terminal Options Screen

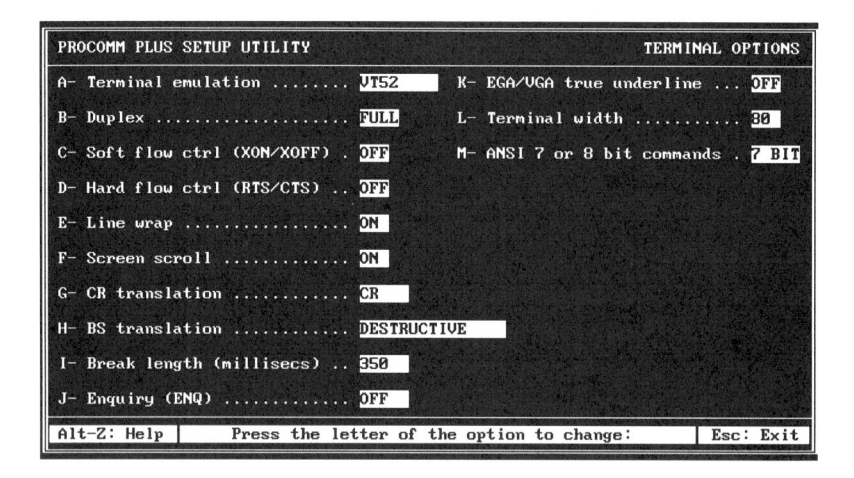

Figure 9.16
Procomm Plus Dialing Directory Screen

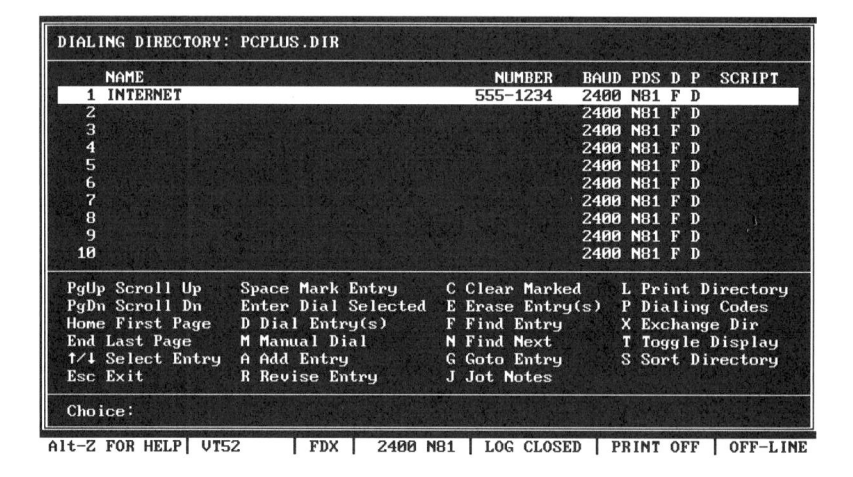

To go online, the operator selects a phone number from the directory list, and the auto-dialer feature initiates the call, transmitting the correct AT command, baud rate, and other parameters. To download a file, the operator selects the Files Section on a bulletin board and initiates the transfer with the PgDn command in Procomm.

A useful feature of Procomm Plus is its ability to generate and save script files. A **script file** is a stored sequence of commands, including passwords and security and file protection commands, that can be passed back and forth between computers. As a result, one or two keystrokes can activate a script file that then logs onto a remote computer, enters a password, and allows information to be exchanged automatically. Script files not only can initiate a communication but can transfer data, conclude the communication, and sign off from the remote computer automatically.

Procomm Plus provides a special language, known as Aspect, for writing script files. Aspect script files are executed quickly and are helpful where the user wishes to carry out a series of repetitive communications.

SMARTCOM III

Smartcom III software, available from Hayes Microcomputer Products, Inc., is designed to run on IBM PCs or compatible systems. The software is provided on 3 1/2- or 5 1/4-inch floppy disks. 640K of RAM and a hard disk are recommended. Once loaded, Smartcom III is able to provide the following functions:

- Dial or answer computer calls automatically
- Create and display information files
- Send and receive data files
- Send data to the microcomputer's printer
- Set up and provide unattended operation of microcomputer communications
- Manage and maintain a file of parameters (records of telephone numbers, transmission speeds, and other pertinent data related to a computer communication)
- Provide a system of error-free file transfer
- Store commands for automatic execution at a later time
- Emulate other devices such as the VT52 terminal
- Provide data security and protection
- Facilitate transfer between voice and data communications

Software Operation

Smartcom III is a **menu-driven** piece of software, which means that the user is able to select specific functions from a group of choices presented in a menu. (See Figure 9.17.) Among the choices is the ability to initiate a communication session, that is, start the dialing and data transmission process, receive files, send files, and more. The Smartcom III software will support modems at speeds between 300 and 9,600 baud. It allows keys on the microcomputer keyboard to be programmed for specific applications and provides password protection.

Before initiating a call between a microcomputer and another system, Smartcom III must be configured. This process is done by selecting the connection settings options. (See Figure 9.18.) The user enters such information as phone number, transmission speed, character format, and flow-control protocol. Smartcom III then stores this data in a **communications parameters** file, which contains the telephone number of and other pertinent information on the connection to be called.

Parameter files are much like pages in your personal telephone book. They list phone numbers, names, and other key data that must be accessed quickly. The user displays the parameter option menu and then enters the connection type, keyboard definitions, access telephone number, and passwords. This set of parameters is then saved on a disk and is called up whenever a call is placed to that particular telephone number and computer. A directory can be displayed listing the saved parameter files. Initiating a computer data call involves simply loading the parameter set and selecting the "begin communication" option. The software then directs the modem to place the call, conduct the handshake protocol, and begin exchanging data.

FIGURE 9.17
Smartcom III Main Menu

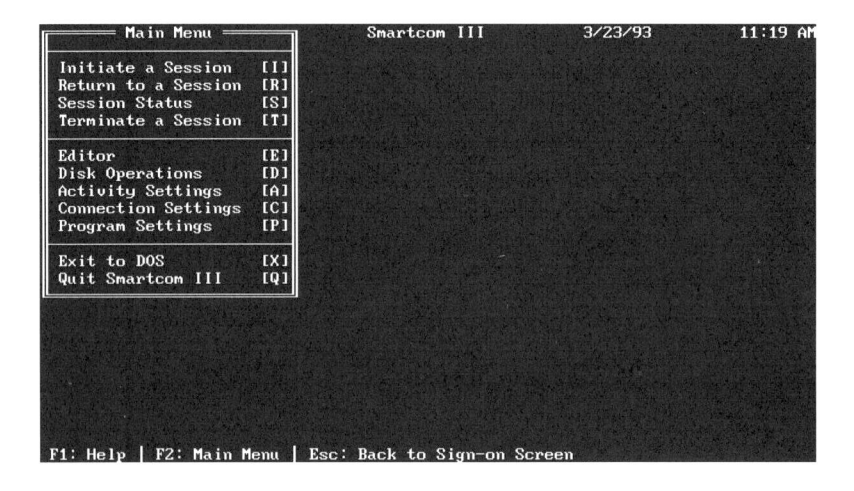

FIGURE 9.18
Smartcom III Connection Settings Menu

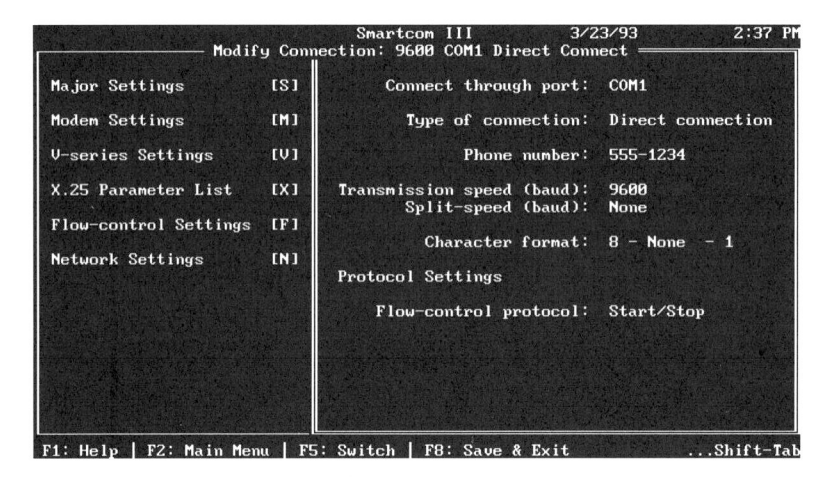

Smartcom III software provides emulation capability for the microcomputer. The **emulator** causes the computer to emulate VT102 and VT52 series terminals. The emulator feature allows the microcomputer running Smartcom III to appear to be a remote terminal to the mainframe. The software also includes the X.25 protocol which allows a device to be connected to a network, and the CCITT V.42 error-correction and data-compression protocols.

CROSSTALK XVI

Crosstalk XVI software, developed by Digital Communications Associates, Inc. (DCA), is used on many microcomputers to provide communications capability. Crosstalk XVI supports full microcomputer communications capability and also can emulate remote terminals, such as the DEC VT52, VT100 series, and others.

Software Operation

Crosstalk XVI differs from the previously discussed communications package in that it is **command-driven** rather than **menu-driven**. Figure 9.19 illustrates the command screen displayed when Crosstalk XVI is first brought up. Crosstalk XVI lists two-letter commands. The user enters his or her choice at the bottom of the screen. To illustrate, communications parameters such as SPeed or PArity are changed by keying in a two-letter command and entering the appropriate information. Once the communications parameters have been entered, including the number to be called, the information can be saved or acted on immediately. Entering GO causes the computer to actuate the modem, which in turn dials the number and begins the communication according to the specified parameters.

FIGURE 9.19
Crosstalk XVI Status Screen. This screen displays commands available to the user.

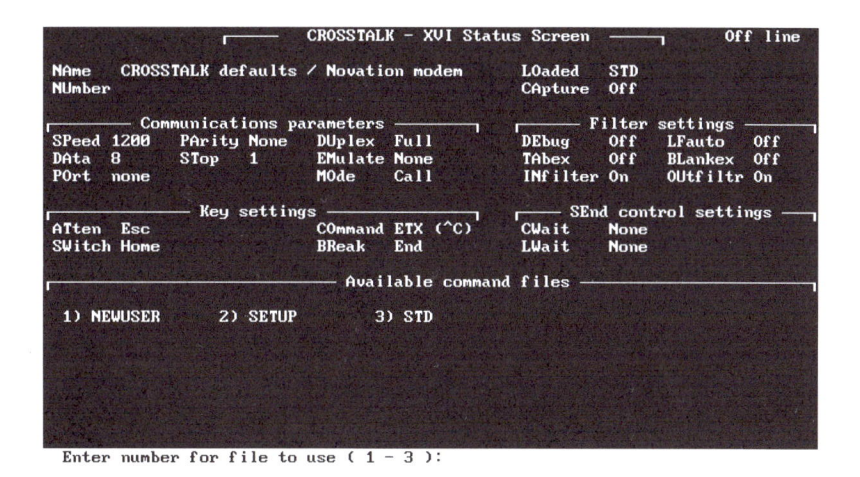

```
┌──────────────── CROSSTALK - XVI Status Screen ────────────────┐ Off line
 NAme    CROSSTALK defaults / Novation modem      LOaded   STD
 NUmber                                           CApture  Off
 ┌──────── Communications parameters ────────┐ ┌──── Filter settings ────┐
 SPeed 1200    PArity None    DUplex  Full     DEbug   Off   LFauto   Off
 DAta  8       STop   1       EMulate None     TAbex   Off   BLankex  Off
 POrt  none                   MOde    Call     INfilter On   OUtfiltr On
 ┌────────── Key settings ──────────┐ ┌──── SEnd control settings ────┐
 ATten  Esc         COmmand ETX (^C)   CWait   None
 SWitch Home        BReak   End        LWait   None
 ┌─────────────── Available command files ───────────────┐
  1) NEWUSER     2) SETUP      3) STD

 Enter number for file to use ( 1 - 3 ):
```

Crosstalk XVI can store sets of parameters for different calls that are saved as script files on disk in the microcomputer. A directory of script files can be called up, new parameter sets saved, and others erased as needed.

Crosstalk XVI supports the XMODEM, KERMIT, and Crosstalk (XTALK) protocols. Using Crosstalk XVI software and the XMODEM protocol, a binary file transfer is begun by selecting the RX option from the file transfer menu.

OTHER MICROCOMPUTER COMMUNICATIONS PACKAGES

The packages discussed here are widely used in the communications industry for commercial applications on small computers. They are purchased from software outlets or licensed for use on one or more individual computers.

With computer users' increased interest in communications, **user-supported software** has become available through user-supported distribution channels. These packages are distributed without charge through computer bulletin boards and other sources. Once users have tried the software, they are asked to pay for the program by sending the author of the software a modest fee. This distribution system works for a category of software known as **shareware**.

PC-TALK

PC-TALK was developed by Freeware, in Tiburon, California, and is distributed without charge to users. Freeware requests that users make a $35 contribution after their trial use. PC-TALK, which has become widely used by computer hobbyists, requires a minimum of 128K of primary memory on a microcomputer. It allows files to be downloaded or uploaded, and it supports the XMODEM file transfer protocol. Communications parameters can be saved and stored on disk as well.

QMODEM

QMODEM, developed by the Forbin Project in Cedar Falls, Iowa, is available from Mustang Software. The QMODEM package supports data transfer at speeds of up to 9,600 baud using even or odd parity and can upload and download files. Communications parameters can be saved on disk, and an index is displayed. Because of its low cost and capability, QMODEM has gained its share of users.

ELECTRONIC BULLETIN BOARDS

The widespread use of microcomputers in homes and offices has led to the development of **bulletin board service (BBS)**. BBSs are privately owned information databases maintained on small computers by individuals and business organizations that are open to the public or selected groups. They are widely used by business and government agencies to provide important support services.

Originally, hobbyists started BBSs to share information. Today, many hobbyists still spend hours playing on the bulletin boards or, as they call it, "working the boards." But the utility of BBS has greatly expanded, especially for commercial applications.

For example, many hard drive manufacturers make BBS available 24 hours a day. Customers can call in and obtain technical specifications and formatting information. (See Figure 9.20.) Computer and controller card manufacturers also make information available on BBS. Jumper and switch settings, product specifications, warranty information, operating instructions, and similar data are available on these systems. These services greatly reduce the need for personnel to answer telephones, repeat information, and take messages. BBSs automate these functions and make information available to customers at any hour of the day and night.

FIGURE 9.20 Commercial Bulletin Board

There is usually no charge for the use of a bulletin board, and individuals are free to log on to these computers, download and upload files, or pass along bulletins and information. Virtually any microcomputer can be operated as a bulletin board if it has enough disk storage, an answer-mode modem (one able to answer calls automatically), and an appropriate bulletin board software package.

Types of Bulletin Boards

Hundreds of bulletin boards are available to users across the country. Some are accessed through local telephone lines, while others offer 800 lines. These bulletin boards may be categorized in many different ways. Some serve government agencies, schools, or hobbyists; others appeal to specific areas of professional interest, such as medicine, law, history, or politics.

BBSs can also be categorized by the type of computers they serve. For example, many bulletin boards offer software and programs for Apple, IBM, Amiga, or Macintosh systems.

Bulletin Board Networks

Bulletin board operators have joined their individual systems into loosely constructed networks that can store files and move them from one bulletin board to another. A bulletin board located in one calling area may be able to route a message to the next zone without toll charges. By placing these systems in tandem, moving messages across the country from one bulletin board to another—without charge—is possible.

UNIX Network. DEC computer users have enjoyed the ability to move messages great distances at minimal cost over the UNIX network. Private citizens, schools, and businesses may use their computers to access a local UNIX machine, which in turn dials a neighboring computer and forwards the message. Because of overlapping toll zones, messages are routed at great distances without cost.

FidoNet. FidoNet, an informal bulletin board network started by Tom Jennings, has been in existence for almost ten years. His bulletin board was able to call another bulletin board and move messages across the country. Soon, Fido nodes sprung up in other locations. Most of these systems utilize low-cost long distance night rates. Local system operators usually absorb these operating expenses.

Using a Bulletin Board

To access a bulletin board, the user must have a personal computer, modem, telephone line, and a communications software package, such as those discussed earlier in the chapter. Once the user enters a telephone number, the software initiates the call to the bulletin board. The bulletin board answers the call and requests log-on information. Once the user has successfully logged on and entered a password, an opening menu is displayed.

Figure 9.21 shows an opening menu from a bulletin board that displays a variety of options. The user can access bulletins placed on the system by the **system operator (sysop)**, enter messages, or join a conference. Conferences are round-robin communications meetings by computer on virtually any topic of interest to users. Conferees contribute comments, which are then stored on file. A board user can scan messages, view a conference, or direct communications to others.

FIGURE 9.21
BBS Main Menu

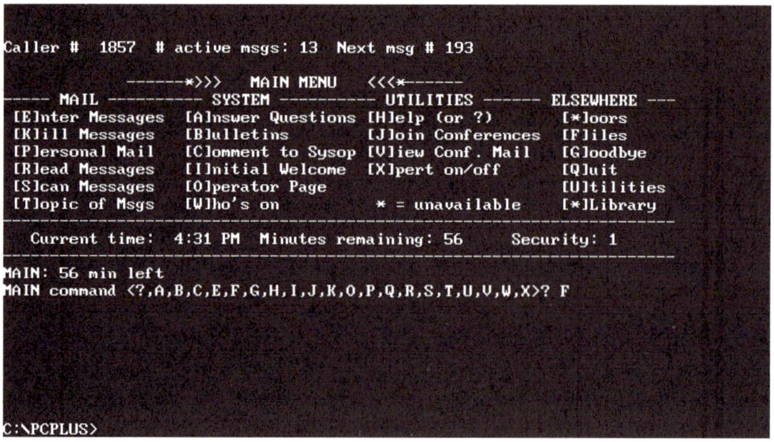

A typical BBS provides various options and utilities, including the selection of baud rate, reporting of statistics on system usage, and more. The file menu shown in Figure 9.22 presents the options for transferring files. By selecting the download option, a user can transfer a file from the bulletin board database to his or her computer. The U option allows data to be uploaded, that is, moved from the user's computer to the bulletin board. Other file menu options allow programs and files to be listed and files searched, among other functions.

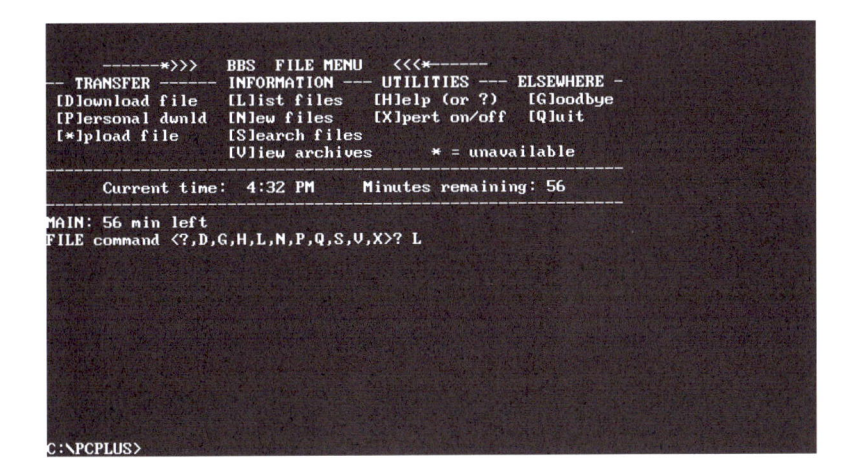

FIGURE 9.22
BBS File Menu

PUBLIC DOMAIN SOFTWARE

The availability of free **public domain software** has increased the popularity of bulletin boards. Figure 9.23 is a partial listing of some of the programs and software available on one BBS. Major categories include business applications programs, communications programs, and games. In addition, a variety of utility programs that are able to squeeze, compress, or reconstruct data files are available. These **squeezers** and **unsqueezers** are useful for compacting programs so that they occupy less space in memory when stored or transmitted.

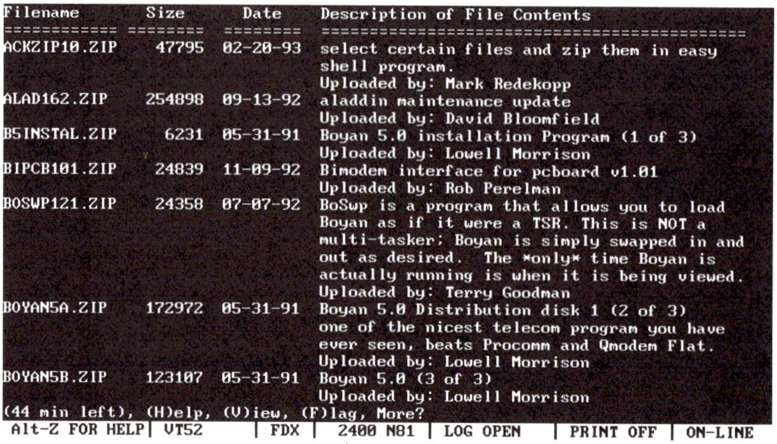

FIGURE 9.23
Public Domain
Software on BBS

```
Filename        Size     Date       Description of File Contents
============    ======   ========   ============================================
ACKZIP10.ZIP    47795    02-20-93   select certain files and zip them in easy
                                    shell program.
                                    Uploaded by: Mark Redekopp
ALAD162.ZIP     254898   09-13-92   aladdin maintenance update
                                    Uploaded by: David Bloomfield
B5INSTAL.ZIP    6231     05-31-91   Boyan 5.0 installation Program (1 of 3)
                                    Uploaded by: Lowell Morrison
BIPCB101.ZIP    24839    11-09-92   Bimodem interface for pcboard v1.01
                                    Uploaded by: Rob Perelman
BOSWP121.ZIP    24358    07-07-92   BoSwp is a program that allows you to load
                                    Boyan as if it were a TSR. This is NOT a
                                    multi-tasker; Boyan is simply swapped in and
                                    out as desired. The *only* time Boyan is
                                    actually running is when it is being viewed.
                                    Uploaded by: Terry Goodman
BOYAN5A.ZIP     172972   05-31-91   Boyan 5.0 Distribution disk 1 (2 of 3)
                                    one of the nicest telecom program you have
                                    ever seen, beats Procomm and Qmodem Flat.
                                    Uploaded by: Lowell Morrison
BOYAN5B.ZIP     123107   05-31-91   Boyan 5.0 (3 of 3)
                                    Uploaded by: Lowell Morrison
(44 min left), (H)elp, (V)iew, (F)lag, More?
Alt-Z FOR HELP| VT52   | FDX | 2400 N81 | LOG OPEN | PRINT OFF | ON-LINE
```

COMPUTER VIRUSES

The growth of BBSs and communications has been hampered by computer viruses. A **computer virus** is an unwanted and difficult-to-detect program that erases or destroys valuable data. Viruses are transmitted from system to system, and they may not be detected until after they do their damage. A virus may remain dormant in a system until a particular program is run a given number of times. The virus then goes into action, doing anything from placing a humorous message on the screen to erasing all data on a hard disk.

Viruses are rarely found in original software distributed by manufacturers. Programs transferred from one bulletin board to another, however, are particularly susceptible. Therefore, users are advised to keep backups of all data files, not to share disks, and to be alert to the virus threat. Some software manufacturers market virus detection software that scans software for viruses and protects systems against data loss or damage.

This chapter has reviewed communications software packages for mainframes and microcomputers as well as those geared for hobby or commercial use. Some of the most innovative and creative new public domain software is being developed by computer hobbyists who are actively engaged in creating new communications concepts and techniques.

SUMMARY

Specialized software packages have been developed to facilitate communications. A *host computer* is a *mainframe* that performs data processing. *Front-end processors* are installed in advance of host computers to relieve the communications load. A *controller* is a hardware device that connects a terminal to a communications line.

BTAM, QTAM, and *VTAM* serve as software interfaces between applications programs and a front-end processor. *CICS* software enables a computer to serve many different types of terminals, applications programs, and databases.

Windows Terminal is provided with every copy of Windows. Together with a serial port, modem, and telephone line, Terminal is able to transmit and receive files between a microcomputer and virtually any other system connected to a modem.

Procomm is a user-friendly, menu-driven communications package. It supports many functions, including sending and receiving files, viewing files, and maintaining a dialing directory.

The XMODEM protocol transfers data in binary form between computers. In *menu-driven* software, the user selects specific functions from a group of choices presented in a menu. Communications parameters are stored as files that specify the details for a particular call or communication. A *command-driven* program presents options by allowing the user to enter two-letter commands. *User-supported software* is distributed through bulletin boards and can be tested free of charge. The QMODEM is a user-supported microcomputer communications package. *BBSs* are available to the public without charge.

Much *public domain software* is available free on bulletin boards. *Squeezer* software compresses data files so that they can be stored compactly. *Unsqueezer* software reconstructs data files to their original form.

A microcomputer can simulate a remote terminal by using *emulation software*. Smartcom III is an example of menu-driven software; Crosstalk XVI is an example of command-driven software. PC-TALK and QMODEM are examples of user-supported software.

BBSs are widely used by business, government, and private individuals to transfer data and make files available to the general public. *Viruses*, sometimes detected in software, are unwanted programs that will erase or destroy data. Viruses are found on bulletin board software because these programs are shared by many users and run a greater risk of infection.

EXERCISES

1. What is the function of a front-end processor (FEP)?
2. List some software packages for mainframes.
3. Describe the function of CICS.
4. Describe how Smartcom III options are selected.
5. Describe how Crosstalk XVI options are selected.
6. What is a communications parameter?
7. What is meant by downloading?
8. What is meant by uploading?
9. Describe a script file.
10. What is meant by user-supported software?

HANDS-ON PROJECTS

- Visit your campus computer center. Make a list of the types of communications software used.

- Visit a local computer software house. Determine the kinds and types of communications software available.

- If a computer and software are available to you on campus, log on to the system and explore some of the features of its communications software.

- Log on to a bulletin board. Carry out the file transfer protocol for downloading a file.

- Log on to a bulletin board. Carry out the file transfer protocol for uploading a file.

COMMUNICATIONS IN ACTION

CASE SOLUTION
MICROS 'N STUFF

Bob Gordon found an excellent solution to his problem: he decided to set up a bulletin board. He selected a desktop computer equipped with a high-capacity hard drive and 640K of RAM that was sitting in his storeroom. He equipped the machine with an auto-answer modem and installed an additional voice-grade telephone line to service the machine. (See Figure 9.24.)

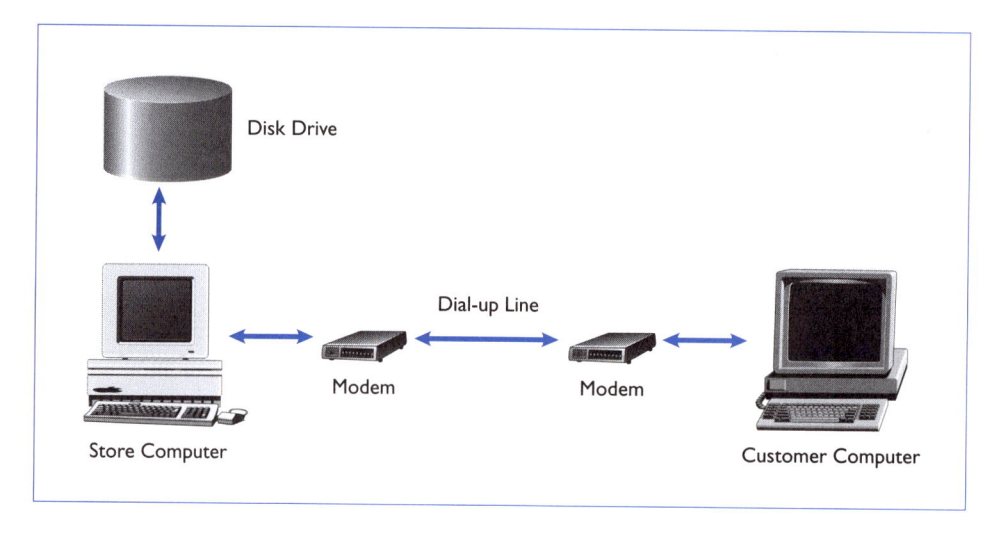

FIGURE 9.24 Micros 'n Stuff Communications System

He then selected a bulletin board software package available on a local BBS that he often used for personal purposes. After he installed and checked out the BBS on his system, he opened it to customers. He placed the telephone number in a local newspaper advertisement as well as on his store window and business cards.

The bulletin board maintains several files. One file, updated daily, lists Gordon's used computer equipment along with the prices. Other files provide answers to questions customers frequently ask. Any customer whose machine is equipped with a modem can now call Micros 'n Stuff and immediately access the bulletin board.

As a result of installing the BBS, sales of used equipment have increased markedly. The profits exceed the cost of the computer, modem, and telephone line Gordon allocated to the system. Another advantage of the BBS is that Gordon's sales force now has more time to concentrate on selling instead of answering routine questions.

The BBS has worked out so well for Bob Gordon that he plans to expand the system to include 800 service. This addition will allow customers out of his immediate area to call the BBS without charge; he expects this move to stimulate sales of used equipment.

III

INTRODUCTION TO COMMUNICATIONS NETWORKS

INTRODUCTION TO NETWORKS

LEARNING OBJECTIVES

After studying this chapter, you should be able to:

- Discuss the need for the Open Systems Interconnection model
- Summarize the function of each layer of the Open Systems Interconnection (OSI) model
- Contrast distributed and centralized data processing
- Describe different network topologies
- Contrast baseband and broadband technologies
- Contrast synchronous and asynchronous transmission protocols

COMMUNICATIONS
IN ACTION

CASE PROBLEM
PIZZA HEAVEN RESTAURANTS

DISTRIBUTED DATA PROCESSING NETWORK

Bill Fantuzzo opened his first pizza restaurant 15 years ago; it soon expanded to a chain of three restaurants in his hometown. Later he franchised his restaurants and now has more than 100 Pizza Heaven Restaurants in operation.

When Fantuzzo opened his first restaurant, he and a friend wrote a restaurant management and accounting program. This program monitored foodstuffs, table linen, laundry, paper goods, and other operating costs. The program enabled him to track profits, cash flow, and food preparation costs carefully.

In the beginning, restaurant managers sent their cost and management information to Pizza Heaven's home office. There the information was keyboarded, and several operating reports were generated. The reports were mailed back to each of the restaurant managers in the franchise. A database was maintained at the home office containing information on each of Fantuzzo's franchises. Later, microcomputers equipped with modems and dial-up lines were installed in each restaurant. At the end of each business day, cost and management information was sent via modem to the home office for processing.

The system worked well until the chain expanded to more than 100 restaurants. It became obvious that the centralized information processing system with modems and remote microcomputers could not handle future needs.

If you were Bill Fantuzzo, what changes would you make in the communications system? Refer to the end of this chapter to see how he improved his communications and data processing operations.

A SIGNIFICANT amount of the growth and development in communications has taken place in the field of networks. In previous chapters we discussed the dial-up telephone network and long distance services, including common carrier digital networks.

This chapter presents an introduction to basic network concepts. It discusses network architecture and design principles. After we explore fundamental concepts, local area networks (LAN), wide area networks (WAN), and value-added networks (VAN) are introduced; discussion of the networks is expanded in later chapters. This chapter also describes efforts to standardize networks, including the Open Systems Interconnection (OSI) model. Chapters 11, 12, and 13 cover these topics in greater detail.

BASIC NETWORK CONCEPTS

A **network** is composed of a group of stations, computers, or terminals, wherein information can be moved between points, or nodes, within the system. The term network describes an interrelated group of elements that functions as a whole. A network may be as simple as two computers linked with a communications circuit, or as complex as a worldwide system with thousands of terminals, fiber-optic cables, satellite links, and more.

Networks can be categorized as one of three types:

1. *Local area network (LAN).* Networks capable of serving multiple terminals within a five-mile geographic radius.
2. *Wide area network (WAN).* Networks capable of serving multiple terminals over vast geographic distances, without enhancing the quality or nature of the data transmitted.
3. *Value-added network (VAN).* A system capable of serving multiple terminals over a wide geographic area, with the ability to enhance or add value to the data being transmitted.

Before we explore these three types of networks, we must consider the evolution of data processing from centralized to distributed systems; this evolution sets the foundation for networks. Today, more data than voice moves over communications circuits, thus greatly influencing network design.

DISTRIBUTED DATA PROCESSING

In the early years of data processing, usually *one* computer was found in an organization. All data or information to be processed was physically carried to the computer, and the results were carried back to offices or other locations. Therefore, there was little need for communications or remote processing techniques.

Centralized data processing departments began to expand their services by locating terminals, known as remote-job-entry (RJE) devices, some distance from the central computer. These input and output devices were connected via communications circuits, forming the beginnings of a digital network. (See Figure 10.1.) These systems concentrated their data processing in one location.

FIGURE 10.1 Centralized Data Processing Network. In this system, data files are maintained and processed at a central point.

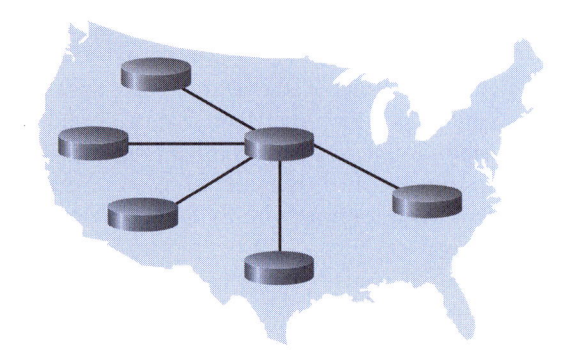

Soon, organizations found that centralized data processing was neither functional nor economical. Often, several computers were linked together to handle the processing load. (See Figure 10.2.) This step led to the development of a decentralized, or distributed, system.

FIGURE 10.2 Distributed Data Processing (DDP) System. In this arrangement, each CPU can access data from the others.

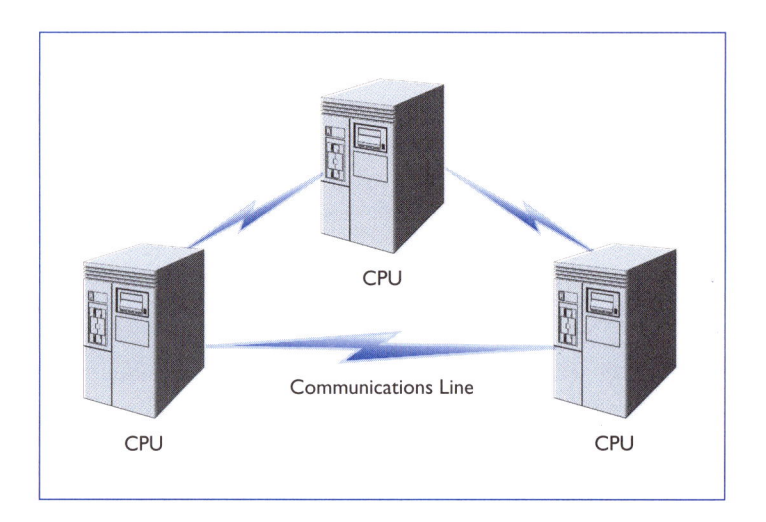

In a centralized system, data are maintained and processed at a central point but may be accessed from many locations. In a **distributed data processing system,** data files are stored at many different locations, usually close to where the information is generated. They are also processed at many points in the system. Figure 10.3 illustrates a distributed data processing system.

The convenience and benefit of a distributed data processing system laid the groundwork for still another form of network. After the introduction of microcomputers, many organizations needed to link the independent machines into small, localized groups, a step that led to the development of the local area network (LAN).

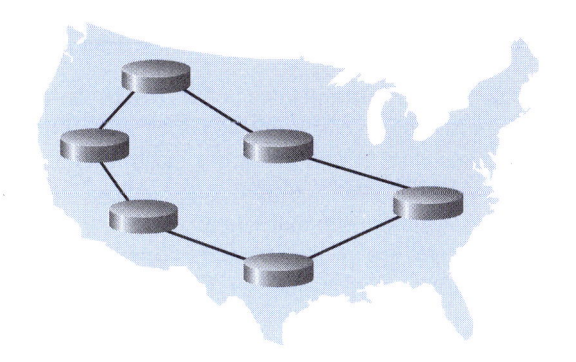

FIGURE 10.3 Distributed Data Processing Network. In this system, data files are stored at many different locations.

LANs provide an integrated and relatively inexpensive means of tying together all of an organization's microcomputers, printers, and other devices within a limited geographic area. A LAN environment reduces costs and makes more computing facilities available to a greater number of users at greater speed than distributed or centralized systems.

Using LANs, organizations are able to distribute their data processing capability over points up to five miles apart, or throughout many buildings at one site. (See Figure 10.4.) Each LAN, in turn, may be linked together in even wider networks.

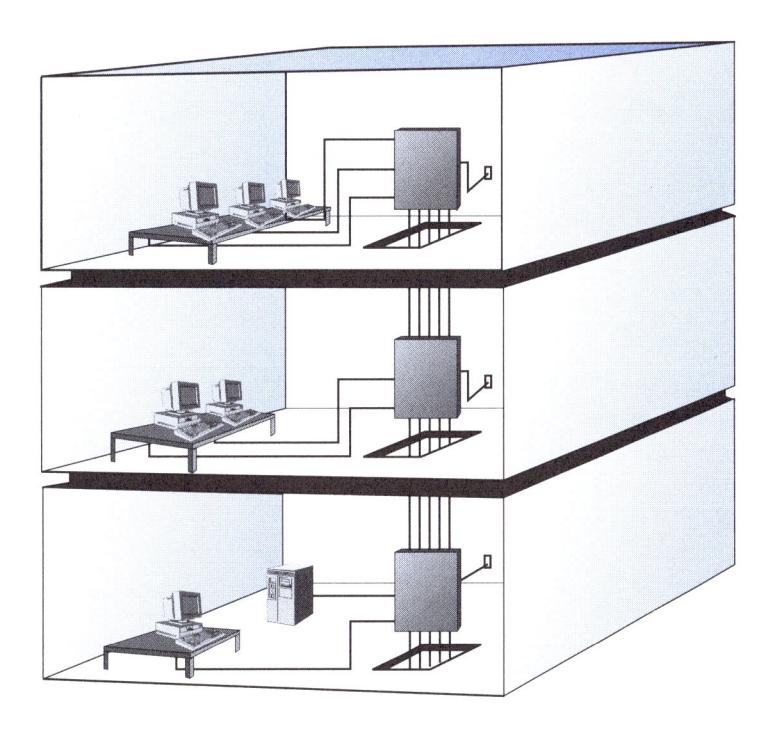

FIGURE 10.4 Local Area Network (LAN). LANs integrate computers into a single system.

INTRODUCTION TO LOCAL AREA NETWORKS

One of the most rapidly expanding areas of communications is the **local area network**. In local area network systems, stand-alone computers are integrated into networks where machines share a database and access the resources of other computers. (See Figure 10.5.) In the LAN environment, each computer can share secondary storage and input/output devices on the system. Each machine is also equipped with communications facilities and specialized software and programs that enable network operation and provide security and access controls. Chapter 11 is devoted to this topic.

FIGURE 10.5 Sharing Resources on a LAN. Stand-alone computers are integrated into networks in which machines share databases and resources.

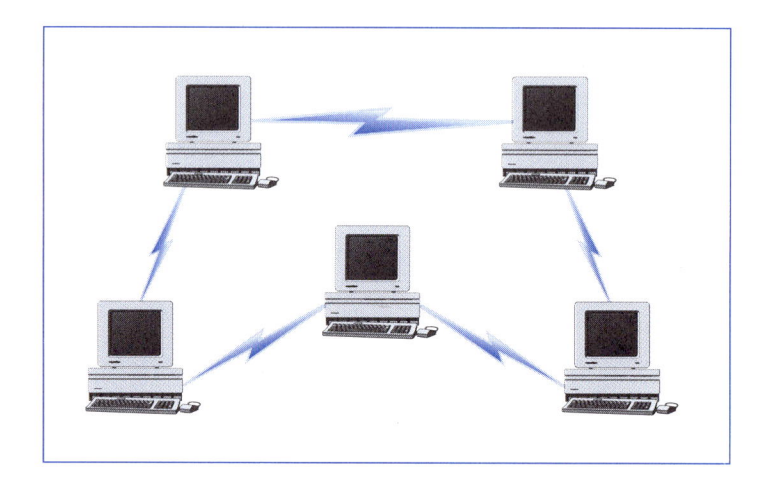

LANs may be classified into two broad categories: baseband coaxial LANs and broadband coaxial LANs.

Baseband Coaxial LANs

Baseband coaxial systems are often used in LANs. In these systems, digital signals are fed directly to the coaxial cable. It is a low-voltage, low-frequency transmission, similar to those sent over a twisted pair of telephone wires. The system does not allow multiplexing, and no high-frequency carrier is used. Baseband is able to send up to 50 million bps over a single circuit at distances of as much as several miles.

Broadband Coaxial LANs

In **broadband coaxial systems**, a high-frequency carrier is used, much like those used for a TV video cable. Coaxial cable can transmit carriers with bandwidths of 4,000 MHz or more. As a result, up to 200 million bps can be sent over distances of several hundred miles. Thus, broadband has greater capacity and distance capability than baseband. Both broadband and baseband technology, using coaxial cables, are described in more detail in Chapter 11.

INTRODUCTION TO WIDE AREA NETWORKS

If only two devices (such as a computer and a terminal) are to be tied together using a single communications link, then only a simple network architecture or design is required. Figure 10.6 illustrates a **point-to-point** architecture. In this example, two devices are connected with a single communications link. Because only one terminal is on the line, there is no problem of device identification or selection, and there is no contention for the use of the communications link.

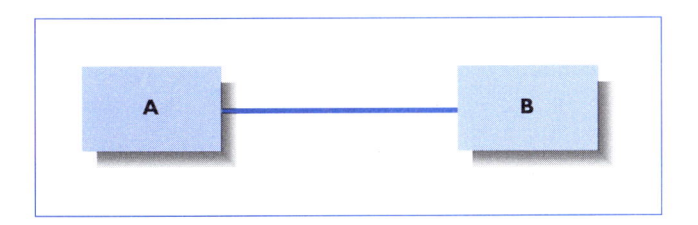

FIGURE 10.6
Point-to-Point Architecture

Most communications networks are not simple point-to-point arrangements, such as the one shown in Figure 10.6. Instead, they involve dozens, or even hundreds, of devices connected to one or more communications links. Systems such as these are known as **multidrop** or **multipoint** configurations. (See Figure 10.7.) Connecting many devices to a single communications link introduces several problems. Switching, device addressing, and contention for the use of the line all contribute to the need for a more complex design or architecture.

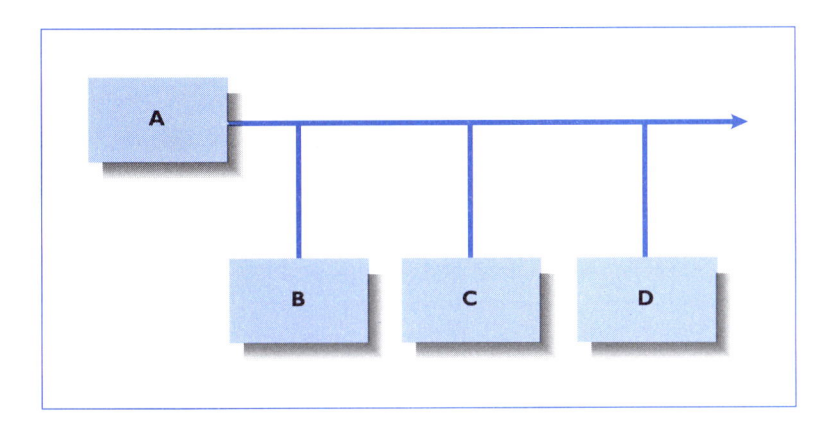

FIGURE 10.7
Multidrop Architecture

Early network architecture used a central computer to control switching, contention between competing devices, and message timing. However, using a computer just to handle traffic flow added cost and complexity and often slowed down the system.

NETWORK TOPOLOGY

The layout, design, or structure of a network is known as its **topology** or **architecture**. Let us discuss some of the common network topologies in use.

The Star

The **star** topology takes the form of spokes projecting from a central hub. (See Figure 10.8.) The star relies on a central computer to control all the traffic in the system. Because all devices are switched in and out by a master controller, failure of the central computer would cause total system failure. Further, the system is limited by the capacity of the central controller to handle the traffic. Star networks that cover many miles require all communications to be routed through the hub of the star, thus adding complexity and transmission line costs to the system.

FIGURE 10.8
Network Topologies

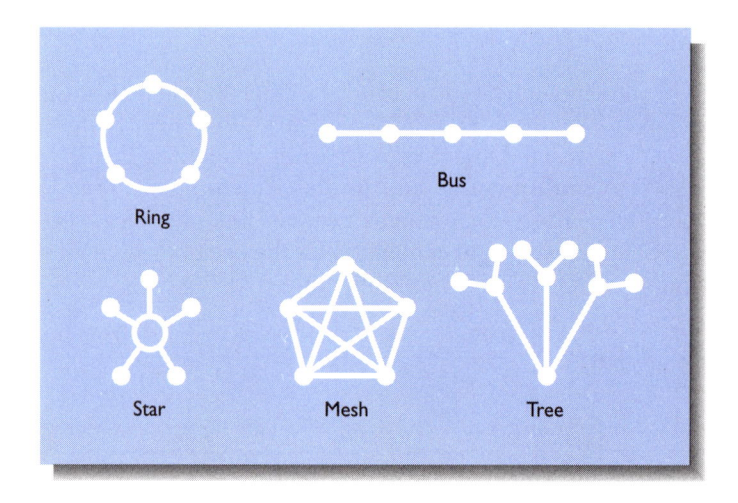

The Ring

A **ring** architecture is sometimes used in a network. In this arrangement, all nodes or devices are arranged around the perimeter of a circle. (See Figure 10.8.) Switching is not handled by a central controller; instead, traffic is routed around the ring from device to device. This system has the advantage of high-speed data transmission, but a break in the line anywhere around the ring might cause a failure of the entire system. With each node added to the ring, the chance of failure increases. A major advantage of the ring is that two points close to one another can communicate without being routed through a central hub.

The Mesh

Still another architecture, the **mesh**, involves wiring all nodes in the network together in an interwoven grid. (See Figure 10.8.) In the mesh, also called point-to-point topology, each element in the network is wired to all other elements. This process provides multiple pathways and does not require a central controller. Although systems such as these are practical for small networks, they are unwieldy when a large number of nodes are used.

The Tree

An architecture shaped much like a **tree** is sometimes used in network design. (See Figure 10.8.) Communications are routed along branches until they reach a controlling switch. Then they are moved down one of the branches until they reach another branch. This movement continues until the final destination is reached. No central computer is required; instead, a network of switches controls the system.

The Bus

One of the most common forms of network architecture is the **bus**. (See Figure 10.8.) The bus is a single line or highway down which data travel. Each node has equal access to the bus. Additional nodes can be conveniently added to the system by simply connecting them at any point along the bus. Because no master controller is required, the failure of any one node does not shut down the entire network.

The selection of a specific architecture depends on many factors: the number of terminals or nodes to be connected, physical distance between nodes, availability of a central computer able to control switching, speed of the traffic, and wiring and installation costs. Many modern networks use either the bus or ring configuration, largely because a good deal of money and research have been invested in these architectures and standards have been published that further expand their utility.

THE OPEN SYSTEMS INTERCONNECTION MODEL

As thousands of computers, terminals, and pieces of communications equipment came into use over the past few decades, it became evident that additional standards and interface connections were needed. Hundreds of different firms were manufacturing computers, terminals, modems, multiplexers, and other devices, and the possibility that these various types of equipment would not be compatible was real. Further, organizations needed an orderly plan to facilitate the growth of their communications systems.

A major development in the standardization of communications networks came in 1977 when the **International Standards Organization (ISO)** Special Committee 97 began work on the problem. The committee sought to develop a comprehensive model that would include protocols, electrical interface connections, and general methods and procedures that could be used by virtually all manufacturers and users of data transmission equipment.

The result of this committee's efforts was the publication of the seven-layer **Open Systems Interconnection (OSI) model**. (See Figure 10.9.) The initials may be a bit confusing; therefore, an explanation is in order. ISO, the International Standards Organization, developed OSI, the Open Systems Interconnection model. As a result, OSI is a product of ISO. The work on this model is ongoing, and not all details of each level have been fully defined. Nevertheless, this model has become the most important definition of standards in use today.

FIGURE 10.9 Open Systems Interconnection (OSI) Model

LAYERS OF THE OSI

The OSI model organizes communications between devices within a network into seven layers. (See Figure 10.10.) Each layer establishes a protocol or format for information handled at that level. At the bottom of the hierarchy is a primary layer that concerns itself with the physical circuits and bit codes that send data. At the top of the hierarchy are the application layers that deal with end-user programs, local needs, and the way the system is accessed. The OSI model recognizes the data transmission codes, discussed in previous chapters, as the most basic elements of the system. Let us look at the layers of the OSI model in some detail.

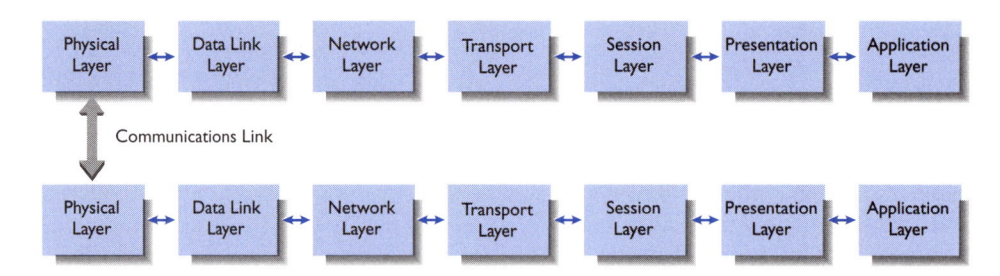

FIGURE 10.10 OSI Layers

Layer 1 (The Physical Link)

Regardless of where a message originates or the data code used, it must be reduced to an electrical signal of specified voltage and characteristics, microwaves, or light signals for transmission. Layer 1 of the OSI model is much like the standard that specifies electrical voltages in households throughout the country. You can plug radios, lamps, or television sets into a wall socket with the assurance that the plug will physically fit and that the correct voltage will be present to operate the equipment properly.

Layer 1 of the OSI model covers the voltages, physical circuitry, timing, and wiring arrangement actually used to send characters. The first layer of the OSI model is the most basic and specifies how a terminal is physically connected to the data transmission equipment. The model takes advantage of the already existing EIA-232-D interface standard. Because devices connected to the system generally use the same voltages and physical wiring arrangements, many are interchangeable.

The OSI standard for layer 1 defines both the electrical and functional characteristics of devices tied to a system; it also encompasses the international standards V.24 and V.28, developed by the Consultative Committee for International Telegraph and Telephone (CCITT). As a result, thousands of terminals already in use in the United States under the EIA-232-D standard, and worldwide under the CCITT's V.24 and V.28 standards, were immediately compatible with each other. This layer also accepts the Electronic Industries Association's standard RS-449, the 37-pin connector arrangement that supplements the older 25-pin RS-232-C, as well as the newer EIA-232-D.

Layer 2 (The Data Link Layer)

Layer 2 concerns itself with the actual transmission of characters and the sequence in which they are transmitted. A major function of this layer is an accuracy check to see that transmissions are error-free. For transmission, messages are broken up into **frames**, blocks of characters that are sent over a line. Once the frame has been transmitted, the receiving station sends an acknowledging signal.

Another function of the layer is to account for speed differences between devices. Layer 2 sets up a buffer to hold characters from low-speed devices. Once the buffer is full, the characters are sent at a high speed. **Data link controls (DLCs)** and message formatting are important parts of the second layer.

Several formats can be used to transmit data over a line. Data can be transmitted asynchronously or synchronously. Under the synchronous format, two methods are commonly used: Synchronous Data Link Control (SDLC) and Bisynchronous Control (BSC). Let us first discuss asynchronous transmission, and then describe the two commonly used synchronous modes.

Asynchronous Transmission. The earliest format in use was **asynchronous transmission**. (See Figure 10.11A.) In this mode, characters are transmitted without regard to a clock. A letter or number is placed on the line and immediately transmitted. Each byte begins with a start bit, followed by several bits representing the character, perhaps a parity bit, and finally, one or more stop bits. The start bit signals the beginning of a character and the stop bit the end. The communications equipment at the receiving end is set up to detect the start bit and recognize that a character is being sent. The trouble with this arrangement is its inefficiency, because start and stop bits must be sent with each character, greatly reducing the number of characters that can be sent in a given time.

FIGURE 10.11
Asynchronous Data Transmission

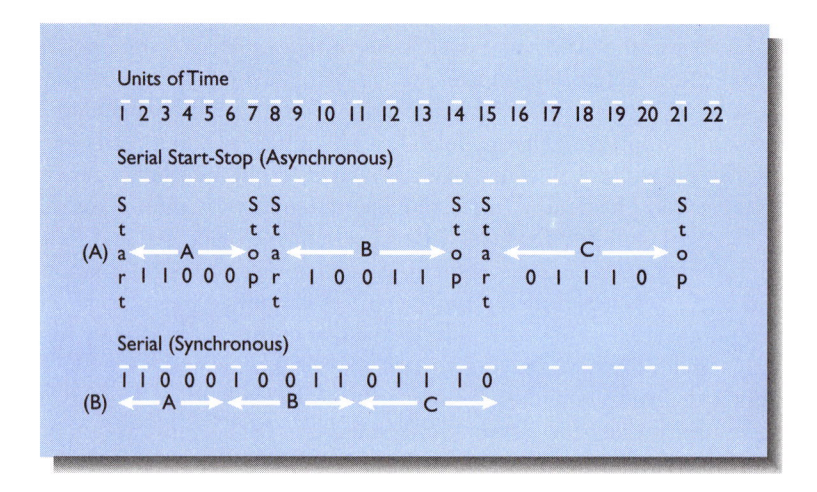

```
Units of Time
1 2 3 4 5 6 7 8 9 10 11 12 13 14 15 16 17 18 19 20 21 22

Serial Start-Stop (Asynchronous)

        S           S S                    S S                      S
        t           t t                    t t                      t
(A)     a  ← A →    o a  ←    B    →       o a  ←   C    →          o
        r  1 1 0 0 0 p r  1 0 0 1 1        p r  0 1 1 1 0           p
        t               t                  t

Serial (Synchronous)

        1 1 0 0 0 1 0 0 1 1 0 1 1 1 0
(B)     ← A →    ←  B  →    ←  C  →
```

Asynchronous transmission is used today on many pieces of equipment because it is simple and inexpensive. Printers and some computer terminals are examples of asynchronous transmitting devices.

Synchronous Transmission. A more efficient means of transmitting a high volume of data is through **synchronous transmission**. (See Figure 10.11B.) The key to the synchronous system is in timing when pulses are sent. An electronic clock is located at each end of the line; the two clocks operate synchronously. The clock at the transmitting end emits pulses at specific intervals. The receiving clock samples the incoming signal to detect the presence or absence of a pulse and thus the receipt of a character. This sampling can be done at speeds of up to 20,000 times per second. (See Figure 10.12.) The sampling rate is much faster than the actual character transmission rate because each pulse is sampled many times before it is recognized.

FIGURE 10.12
SDLC Bit Sampling. Bits are sampled thousands of times per second to detect presence or absence of a pulse.

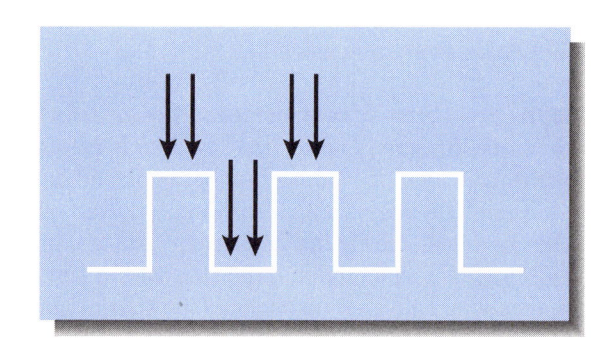

When a block of data is to be sent synchronously, two or more SYN signals are transmitted first. (See Figure 10.13.) This transmission causes the receiving equipment to start sampling data. Because both the receiver and transmitter are operating at the same sampling frequency, a high volume of data can be transmitted. No time is wasted sending stop and start pulses.

FIGURE 10.13 Synchronous Byte

| SYN Byte | SYN Byte | User Information Bytes | SYN Byte |

The two common forms of synchronous transmission are Synchronous Data Link Control (SDLC) and Bisynchronous Control (BSC).

Synchronous Data Link Control. The **Synchronous Data Link Control (SDLC)** uses a standard transmission frame. (See Figure 10.14.) Each SDLC message begins with a **flag**, a standard 8-bit recognizable binary pattern (01111110). Next follows an address, control information, and then the message. After the message, a frame check sequence and a closing flag are sent.

FIGURE 10.14 Synchronous Data Link Control (SDLC)

| Flag | Address | Control | Message | FCS | Flag |

Frame Check Sequence

Bisynchronous Control. Another means of transmitting information at the second layer is **bisynchronous control (BSC)**. In this arrangement, each message is preceded by a message header, which contains a start of heading (SOH) byte, control characters, and a start of text (STX) signal. Next follows the message, which can be of any length. At the end of the message, a trailer is sent that includes an end-of-text (ETX) signal and a block check-character. (See Figure 10.15.)

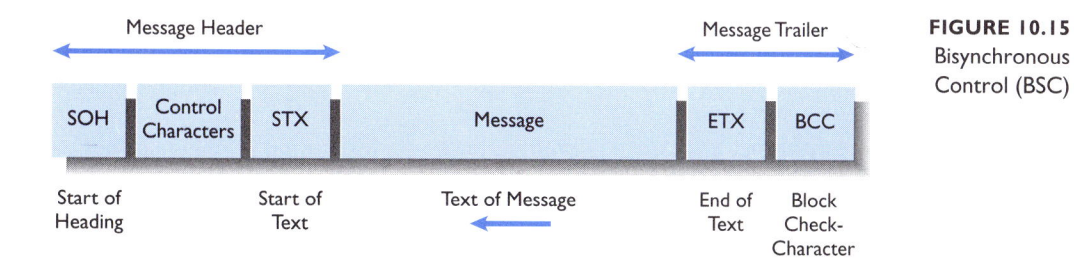

FIGURE 10.15 Bisynchronous Control (BSC)

Message Header | Message Trailer

| SOH | Control Characters | STX | Message | ETX | BCC |

Start of Heading | Start of Text | Text of Message | End of Text | Block Check-Character

Layer 3 (The Network Layer)

The third layer defines message addressing and routing methods. As communications networks expanded, it became necessary to establish switching arrangements that would route data end-to-end through various communications networks.

Layer 3 routes a communication by the most logical path through a switched network. This layer handles the connection of lines and the signing-off of circuits, as well as line accounting, which involves tallying loads and volumes, gathering statistical information, and charging various users according to the amount of services consumed.

The Burstiness Problem. In the early days of data transmission, the problem of network switching was minimal because loads were light and there were few stations to be connected. As more users began to rely on public networks, such as AT&T lines, it became necessary to improve switching methods and to deal with the problem of messages that contain many pauses or extended gaps.

In a typical voice communication, many pauses occur: one person listens while the other speaks, then the listener responds. This process creates gaps in communication, a phenomenon known as **burstiness**. Bursty communications, those that involve bursts in transmission followed by pauses, are very inefficient and waste communications resources. A person can pick up a telephone, dial a few digits, and command the exclusive use of millions of dollars of switching equipment, communications lines, and perhaps a channel on a satellite relay station. When you consider the millions of telephone conversations and data transmissions going on all over the world at any given moment, burstiness produces a lot of dead air time.

Burstiness led to the development of packet-switching technology. Layer 3 of the OSI defines packet-switching protocols and specifies how characters will be saved and transmitted as a packet or block without unnecessary pauses or gaps. Packet switching allows both voice and data to be moved efficiently over communications lines.

Fundamental Packet-Switching Concepts. **Packet switching** reduces a message to small segments, called **packets**, that are routed through a communications network. Upon receipt, the packets are reassembled back into the original message. Packet switching differs from techniques used in the switched network, described earlier, to route ordinary telephone calls through dial-up lines. As you will recall, the switched network opens and closes circuits that establish a continuous pathway dedicated to the uninterrupted transmission of one message. Local phone calls and **Direct Distance Dialing (DDD)** establish an exclusive end-to-end circuit for each call. (See Figure 10.16.)

In packet switching, a message is broken down into individual segments or packets. (See Figure 10.17.) Each packet is assigned a header that describes its destination. The packet is then sent over the network and is routed through one junction to another until it reaches its destination. (See Figure 10.18.)

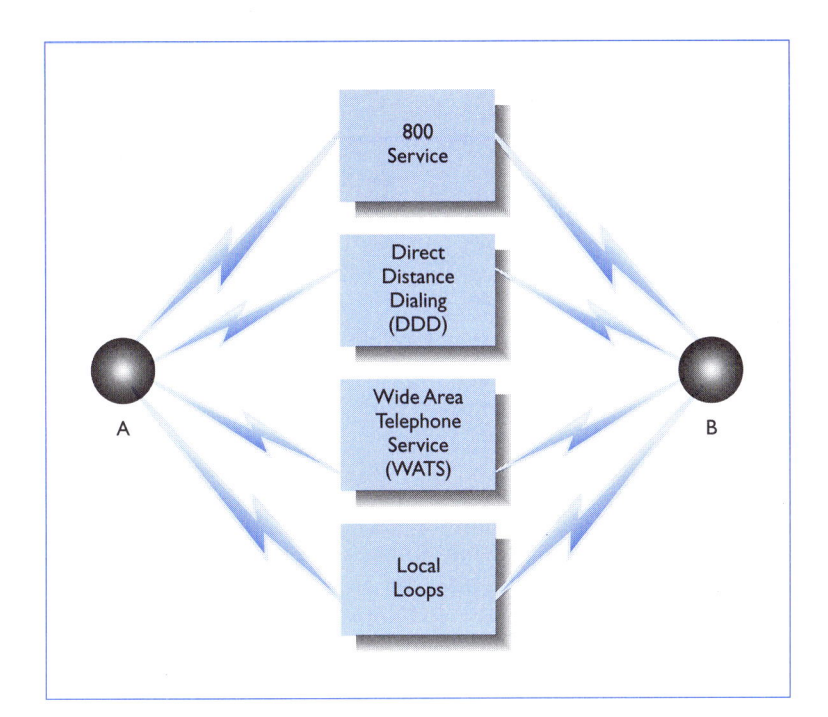

FIGURE 10.16 Switched Network Options

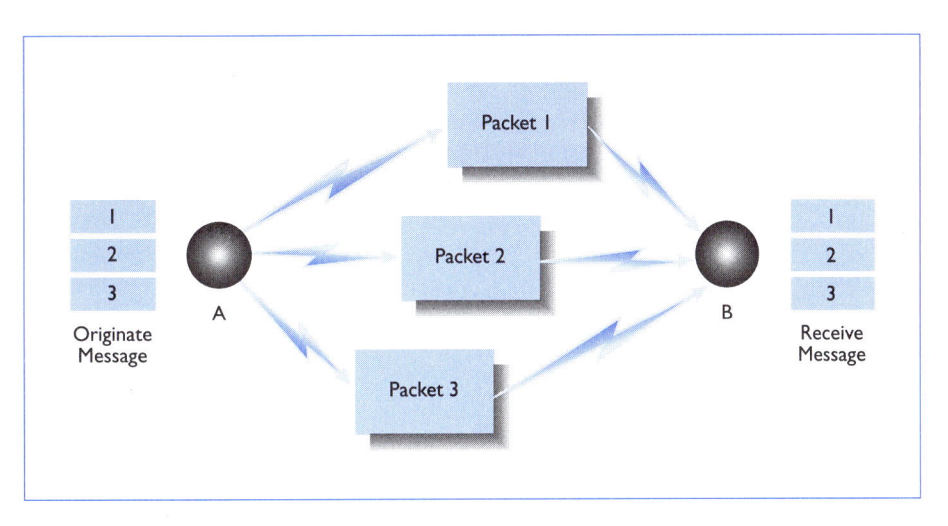

FIGURE 10.17 Message Packets. In packet switching, a message is broken down into segments and routed to a destination.

FIGURE 10.18
Packet-Switched Network

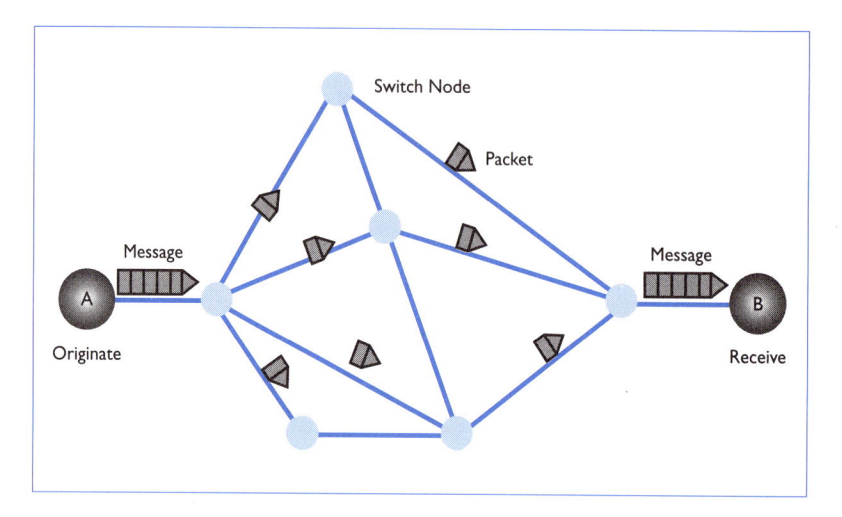

Figure 10.19 illustrates this process in detail. Information from a terminal enters a storage buffer and is then encapsulated in a packet envelope. Next, routing information is added, and a frame envelope created. From there, the packet moves to another storage buffer, and then through error control before being sent through the network. Upon arrival at its destination, the frame and packet envelopes are removed, and the data packet finally arrives at the host computer destination. The envelopes just described are not physical records, but electronic signals that contain routing and other information. These electronic signals are no longer needed after the packet has arrived and are therefore discarded from the data packet.

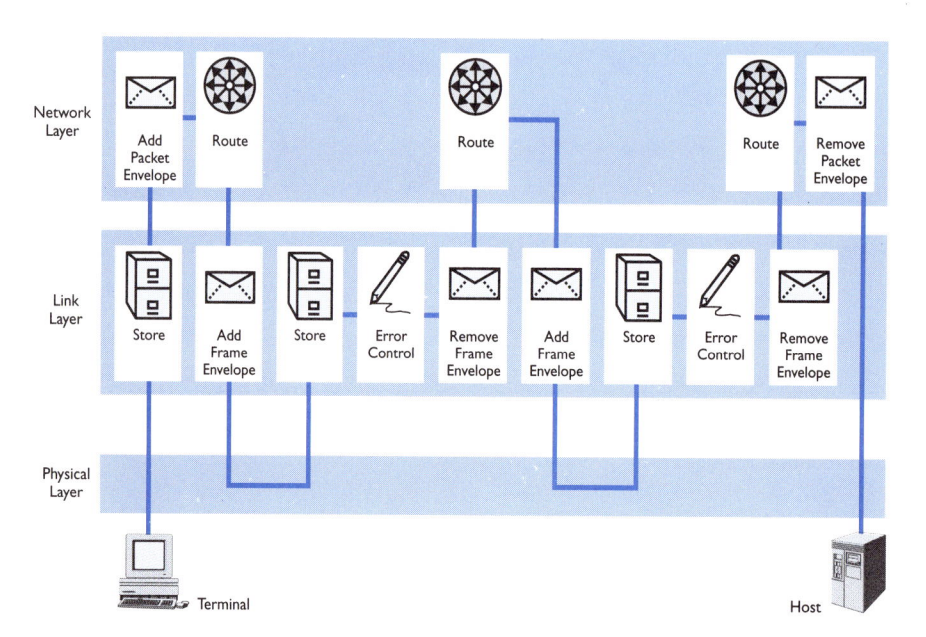

Figure 10.19 Packet Frame Envelopes

In the example just described, only the first three layers of the OSI model are used. All routing information is handled by the network layer. We will look at packets in greater detail in Chapter 11.

Sometimes a packet is lost in routing as it moves through the network. Therefore, **error-control** mechanisms are provided to deal with this contingency and retransmit the lost data. As in any system, traffic flow must be regulated to keep messages from bunching together. Regulating traffic requires balancing loads on nodes and monitoring the entire system.

The X.25 Standard. Packet switching requires a standard to ensure that information is presented to the network in a uniform format. Each packet must possess approved routing headers. The CCITT has adopted the **X.25 standard** for this purpose. It specifies the data packet frame structure for information moving between data terminals operating in the packet-switching mode on public networks.

The X.25 packet is based on the standard frame shown in Figure 10.20. The information to be transmitted is moved as a **data packet**. The data packet has a header, a user data field, and variable information and is encapsulated in a larger **information frame**. The information frame contains a start-of-frame flag, frame header, the

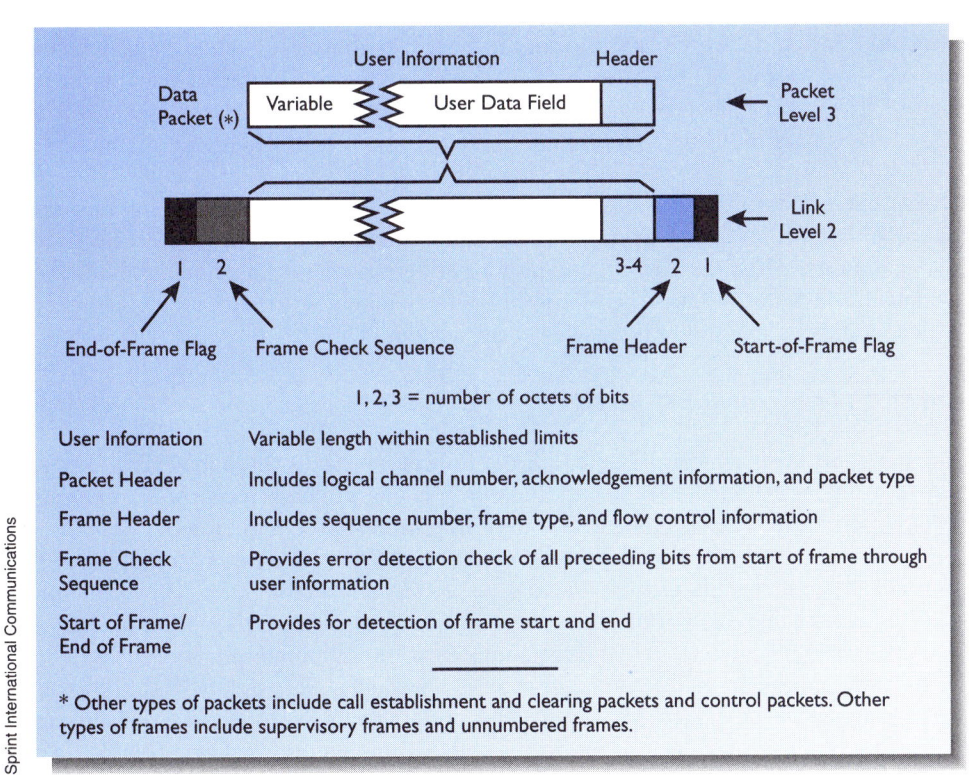

User Information	Variable length within established limits
Packet Header	Includes logical channel number, acknowledgement information, and packet type
Frame Header	Includes sequence number, frame type, and flow control information
Frame Check Sequence	Provides error detection check of all preceeding bits from start of frame through user information
Start of Frame/ End of Frame	Provides for detection of frame start and end

* Other types of packets include call establishment and clearing packets and control packets. Other types of frames include supervisory frames and unnumbered frames.

FIGURE 10.20 X.25 Standard

data packet with the user data field, followed by a frame sequence check and end-of-frame flag. Thus, the entire packet contains all the information needed to route the data from one point in a network to another.

A packet-switching system does not establish an exclusive direct link from one point to another. Rather, it routes the message in smaller segments over the most direct route and over different circuits; this process means that messages arrive at their destination in parts, with packets going through different routes. At the receiving end, the packets are reassembled and the headers and end-of-frame flags removed, thus reproducing the original data frame intact. Breaking up the message and reconstructing it are handled so quickly and automatically that the message appears to be routed over an exclusive direct circuit. Packet switching eliminates dead air and resolves the burstiness problem.

For the system to work, all nodes and terminals on the network must conform to the X.25 standard. Because all packets moving through the network have a common format, switching equipment can route them through to their destination easily. The X.25 protocols assure users that regardless of the make of equipment, all messages will be properly transmitted through the network.

Messages can be routed through the packet network in either of two modes, the virtual or the datagram form.

Virtual Mode. In the **virtual mode**, the system performs sequence control. Once the packets are routed, they are held at the receiving end until all packets have arrived. The network then reorganizes the packets into their proper sequence, regardless of the timing of the arrival.

Datagram Mode. In the **datagram mode**, sending and receiving stations are responsible for routing and switching. This mode is available, but it is rarely used. In the datagram mode, the only function performed by the network is that of moving the packets through the system. The reordering of the packets into their correct sequence is done under the control of the user, not the system.

Layer 4 (The Transport Layer)

The transport layer concerns itself with the flow of messages through several different networks. It establishes protocols and controls and provides for **data security** as information moves through the various networks from source to recipient.

This layer is sometimes called host-to-host or end-to-end. The programming and software to facilitate this task are usually located in a host computer. The OSI standard defines a common interface between networks. It also sets priorities for messages and error-recovery systems when large amounts of information are lost.

A common protocol in the transport layer is a system developed by IBM known as the System Network Architecture (SNA). This system deals with such face-to-face elements as data security, message priorities, data flow control, and routing of data between networks. The SNA and other Layer 4 protocols are discussed in more detail in Chapter 11.

Layer 5 (The Session Layer)

Layers 5 through 7 have not been defined to the same extent as the preceding layers. Layer 5, the session layer, deals with the organization of a logical session. It sets up resources, coordinates equipment, handles the transfer of files, and recognizes users, allowing them to log on and log off the system. This layer also sets priorities for traffic and does various accounting and billing tasks for the end user.

Layer 6 (The Presentation Layer)

The presentation layer handles the **formatting and display** of information, such as that on a monitor. This layer transforms messages or reformats them. It adjusts for variations in file format and accounts for different line widths and page depths. Code conversion and the transformation of information from file to file is managed at this level. Details of this layer are still under development.

Layer 7 (The Application Layer)

Layer 7 is loosely defined and is open-ended. It deals with the specific industry or end-user programs available on the system. Its parameters are general, and it focuses on end-user needs. For example, layer 7 may deal with how an organization uses its own database, distributed between several points throughout a network. Because of the differences among users and flexibility of this layer, a single standard is not easily developed.

BENEFITS OF THE OSI MODEL

With the adoption of international standards it is now possible to move data worldwide across computer systems through many differing networks. We have agreement on transmission codes, flow control protocols, and data formats.

By relying on the OSI model, communications managers can expand their systems in an orderly manner. They are assured that data structures will be consistent with those of other users. Most important, with agreed-upon standards, equipment from different suppliers can be used to build a system with a degree of assurance that each vendor's products will be compatible with the network.

Much time and effort will continue to be spent on improving and developing the OSI model. The ultimate goal is to generate protocols and standards that will allow any end user to communicate with any other, implementing virtually any piece of communications equipment and routing messages over many different types of circuits and networks. Many of the functions performed by the OSI model are not visible to the user even though they provide for the efficient, error-free flow of a large volume of data.

SUMMARY

Distributed data processing involves storing and manipulating data files at many different locations.

A *network* is composed of a group of stations, computers, or terminals, wherein information can be moved between points, or nodes, within the system.

Multidrop systems connect many devices to a single circuit. The *star topology* is shaped like spokes projecting from a hub. The *ring* topology has *nodes* arranged around the perimeter of a circle. In the *mesh* topology all nodes are tied together in an interwoven grid. In the *tree* topology communications are routed along branches to their final destination.

Baseband coaxial systems use low-voltage, low-frequency transmissions sent over a twisted pair of wires. *Broadband* coaxial systems use *carrier frequencies* to send information through coaxial cables.

The *OSI model* organizes communications between devices within a network into seven layers. Each layer establishes a *protocol* or format for information handled at that level. At the bottom of the hierarchy is a primary layer that concerns itself with the *physical circuits* that send information. At the top of the hierarchy are the *application layers* that deal with end-user programs, local needs, and the way the system is accessed.

Asynchronous transmissions send characters in serial fashion without reference to a clock. *Synchronous* transmissions send characters in a manner carefully timed by clocks at both the sending and receiving ends. *Bisynchronous control (BSC)* sets up a protocol of message headers and control characters that facilitate transmission of data.

Packet switching reduces messages to segments called *packets* and routes them through a *network*. *Error-control* mechanisms handle misrouted or lost data contingencies. In the *virtual mode*, the system performs sequence control. Once the packets are routed, they are held at the receiving end until all packets have arrived. In the *datagram mode*, sending and receiving stations are responsible for routing and switching. The only function performed by the network is that of moving the packets through the system. The *X.25 standard* specifies the interface for terminals using packet-switched networks.

EXERCISES

1. List the major layers in the OSI model.
2. Contrast synchronous and asynchronous transmissions.
3. Describe the X.25 standard.
4. Describe how packet-switching networks operate.
5. Describe virtual mode sequence control.
6. Describe the function of an error-control mechanism.
7. Discuss the burstiness phenomenon and how it affects communications.
8. Explain the purpose of message headers and end-of-frame flags.
9. Contrast centralized and distributed data processing.
10. Contrast network topologies.

HANDS-ON PROJECTS

- Visit your campus computer center. Discuss the Open Systems Interconnection model with a staff member. Determine which layers are in use at the facility.
- Draw a simple ring network and include five nodes.
- Draw a tree network with eight nodes.
- Place a telephone call to two friends and discuss data communications. Using a stopwatch, make an approximation of the amount of dead air or time lost during the conversations. Compare the two phone calls.
- Prepare a list of reasons why a packet-switching network has advantages over direct telephone connections.

COMMUNICATIONS IN ACTION

CASE SOLUTION
PIZZA HEAVEN RESTAURANTS

It became clear to Bill Fantuzzo that his centralized data processing system, using remote microcomputers, could not handle his future expansion requirements. His present system placed all data processing demands on a central computer in the home office.

To solve this problem, Fantuzzo developed a program that could be run independently on a group of decentralized microcomputers. (See Figure 10.21.) The programs were installed on a microcomputer in each restaurant to allow individual managers to generate their own reports.

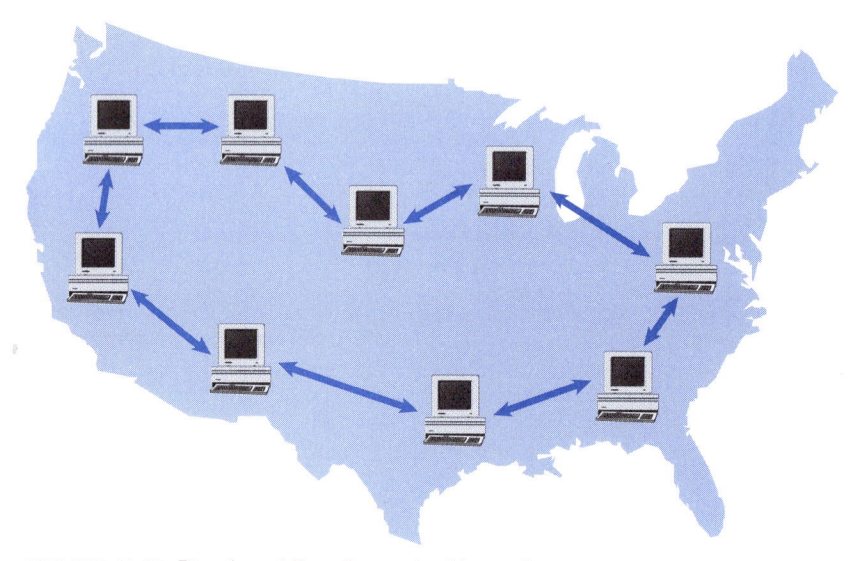

FIGURE 10.21 Distributed Data Processing Network

The system includes polling capability, which allows a central computer to automatically communicate with each remote device in the system and initiate a data transfer. This feature results in a decentralized information processing system that gives direct control to each restaurant manager while still providing centralized reports for Fantuzzo.

Each night the central computer goes online with the remote computers and accesses files. The system uses ordinary dial-up lines; data is transferred in bursts during late evening hours when toll charges are at a minimum. The decentralized system solved Fantuzzo's expanding network problems without incurring substantial increases in costs.

LOCAL AREA NETWORKS (LANs)

LEARNING OBJECTIVES

After studying this chapter, you should be able to:

- Describe the LAN environment
- Describe LAN cabling systems
- Discuss the components of a LAN
- Describe message collision and avoidance systems
- Describe the function of a network bridge
- Describe the function of a network gateway

COMMUNICATIONS
IN ACTION

CASE PROBLEM
LAW OFFICES OF PARKER AND PARKER

LOCAL AREA NETWORK

The law offices of Parker and Parker specialize in personal injury litigation. Each year the firm, operated by the partnership of Dan and Robert Parker, is involved in litigating or settling claims regarding automobile accidents, personal injuries, or product liability cases. This litigation entails the preparation of legal briefs, pleadings, and an extensive amount of correspondence directed to clients, attorneys, and litigants.

At any given time Parker and Parker has dozens of cases pending, which are handled either by the general partners or the associates. Law clerks research cases, prepare legal briefs, summarize points of law, and check authorities and other documents. All of this material is reviewed by senior partners and then sent to clients or other attorneys. In addition, the staff prepares many letters, responses, and memos. In this process, documents undergo extensive revisions. Parker and Parker must be able to make changes literally up to the moment their attorneys enter the courtroom.

The attorneys and researchers at Parker and Parker require simultaneous access to a number of different pieces of software. Word processing is a major application program used for preparing briefs, pleadings, and other documents. Law clerks and researchers also use spreadsheet software to prepare settlement offers and financial accountings. Database management software is also needed to maintain inventories, lists, and reports for clients.

What kind of communications system should be installed in the law offices to handle the variety of required applications? Refer to the end of this chapter to see how Parker and Parker solved the problem.

INTEREST in local area networks (LANs) has grown as more and more microcomputers have come into use. Many organizations recognized the need to link all their computer equipment at one location, or within a limited geographic area, into a single integrated system. The availability of sophisticated and often expensive laser printers further established the need to link computer hardware.

This chapter explains the fundamental principles of local area networks and how they work. It describes LAN standards, baseband and broadband systems, and how devices access networks. The chapter also covers how message collisions and contention are handled when multiple users are on one circuit.

Xerox Corporation; IBM Corporation; Novell, Inc.; Datapoint, Inc., and other companies have invested heavily in LAN software and hardware systems. They offer off-the-shelf LAN components or software that can be used to construct an integrated system. Numerous schools, universities, and businesses, both large and small, and government institutions now rely on local area network systems.

THE LAN ENVIRONMENT

A **local area network (LAN)** is a privately operated communications system that interconnects computers and communications equipment over a limited geographic area, usually five miles or less. (See Figure 11.1.) LANs are not regulated as are common carriers, such as the AT&T network. However, personal computers and specific LAN components that emit radio frequency energy, such as circuit cards, must comply with FCC standards. In particular, wireless LANs must meet FCC standards because they broadcast radio waves.

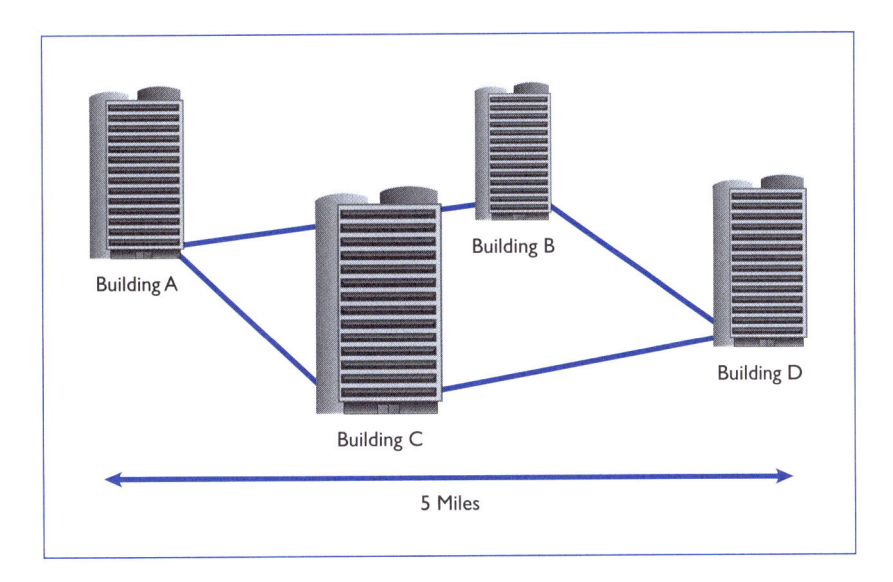

FIGURE 11.1 Local Area Network (LAN). LANs integrate computers at points as far as five miles apart.

Many organizations have found that as much as 80 percent of their communications takes place within the company. The remaining 20 percent goes outside the organization and involves the use of common carriers, telephone circuits, and other media. This fact has been the impetus behind the installation of many new LANs.

LANs may utilize twisted pairs of wires, coaxial, or fiber-optic cables and may tie together printers, computers, terminals, disk storage devices, or communications equipment that can also access other networks.

LANs have several inherent features. First, they allow sharing of resources such as printers, disk storage devices, and other pieces of hardware. The purchase of expensive, high-speed, or specialized devices may be justified in a LAN environment because these devices are shared by many microcomputers. Second, a LAN facilitates the transfer of files between microcomputers or mainframes, thus eliminating the need to maintain duplicate files or transport disks or other storage media between computers. Third, specific records in a common file can be accessed or modified from many different computers using a LAN. This activity requires some form of record or field lock to prevent records from being simultaneously modified by two or more users.

LAN ADVANTAGES

LANs have a number of characteristics that make them attractive for many business and commercial applications. Let us look more closely at their advantages:

1. Because numerous devices can be attached to a single system, LANs provide reliability. For instance, several printers may be available to back up one another.
2. LANs are easily modified because they are wired together using inexpensive cabling systems. Changes and relocation of devices in a system are easily accomplished by simply adding or removing devices from the network.
3. Because the network is privately owned, management can change or modify the system at will without recourse to a common carrier.
4. LANs provide flexibility. Different users with different needs may be served simultaneously. Thus, word processing, spreadsheet, database management, CAD/CAM, and graphics can be provided at one time.
5. Access can be controlled, limiting the type and kinds of users on the system.
6. LANs offer greater security. LAN services can be handled in a closely controlled environment in which system security and integrity must be maintained.
7. LANs provide economy. Systems costs are reduced where many microcomputers can share an expensive input/output device, high-speed printer, or mass storage device.
8. LANs facilitate connectivity. LANs enable microcomputers to communicate with similar machines or networks.
9. LANs offer standardization. Agreed-upon standards ensure that components can be tied to the system and will function properly as part of a network.
10. LANs provide easy expandability. Terminals, printers, microcomputers, and other devices are easily added to a system without requiring major system changes.

AN EXAMPLE OF A LAN APPLICATION

Let us consider a typical application that illustrates how a LAN is used. Assume that the ABC Engineering Company wants to prepare a 200-page technical report that includes figures and illustrations. The report will be drafted by a staff engineer who has access to a LAN workstation. The tables and graphics will be prepared by a different engineer who also has access to a workstation. A draft will be reviewed at several stages by a supervisor and a manager. A final draft, incorporating changes and revisions, will be generated. Then the report will be output in final form on a laser printer and prepared for duplication.

The individuals working on this project are located in different buildings, all within a five-mile radius. The final draft is to be checked by the manager, who is located in a plant at the company's headquarters in another city. The steps that will be followed in generating the final document follow:

1. The original draft of the text is keyboarded by the staff engineer at a workstation. The draft is displayed on the monitor for proofing. After the engineer is satisfied that the draft is ready for checking, it is routed via the network to a file server, where it is stored.

2. Later, a second engineer calls up the text from the file server and routes it to a local workstation through the coaxial cable. Then he adds charts and tables to the draft. When he is finished, the text is sent back to the file server, where it is stored on disk.

3. The supervisor now displays the draft and makes additional changes. When she is finished, the draft is routed back to the file server.

4. After all of the engineers have checked and approved the draft, it is then routed to the manager via the communications server, which sends the draft over common-carrier lines to the company headquarters. There it is received by another LAN and routed through a communications server to a file server. Now the manager accesses the draft at a workstation. His additional changes are incorporated into the draft. The final revised draft is then routed back to the originating engineer, where it is stored by the file server on disk.

5. The last step is to direct a laser printer, located in the firm's duplicating department, to generate a final printout. After this is done, a typeset-quality report is then made available for copying and distribution.

These five steps were taken using the LAN—and avoid couriers and out-of-town mail. The system allows all concerned parties to check the draft as it evolves and to make necessary changes. Only a minimum of time and effort is required, and the entire process is completed in a matter of hours or days, not weeks.

OTHER APPLICATIONS

Much of the popularity of LANs is due to their capacity to handle a diverse range of applications. **Resource sharing**, the ability to access common files and to share major applications software, is particularly valuable for schools, business offices, engineering and design firms, and others. Here are some typical environments that have found LANs to be of great value.

Educational Uses

Numerous schools and colleges have installed LANs. These networks allow students in many different courses to share printers, software, databases, and other resources. A school that could not justify the purchase of 20 laser printers may easily afford a single laser printer, shared by many students in a laboratory on a LAN.

For example, a student in a sociology course may share resources on a LAN for research purposes. The student may access a database on population demographics and then prepare a statistical report for a course. Students from other disciplines may share the same database and use it in different ways.

Business Offices

Many business offices use a laser printer, which may be equipped with many type fonts. By connecting the printer to a LAN, anyone on the network can have access to typeset-quality printing. By placing an imagesetter on the network, many people can share a single expensive output device. An imagesetter can generate pages that include detailed photographs, type, and graphics either on paper printout or as a film negative or positive.

LAN operations allow many users in one office to share one or more databases. (See Figure 11.2.) Instead of each user maintaining his or her own database, a common database may be used, thus avoiding inconsistencies and redundancies.

Some business software costs thousands of dollars. Businesses may save money by implementing a network version of an applications program on a LAN, making it available to multiple users. This implementation is more economical than purchasing several copies of the software.

Design Applications

Today, the computer has become an almost indispensable tool of the designer. It replaces manual drafting and speeds up the design and creation of many products. A LAN can facilitate a design effort because more than one person can access drawings, proposals, engineering change orders, and other items simultaneously.

FIGURE 11.2 LAN Workstation

Fredrik D. Bodkin/Offshoot

Larger or smaller plotters may be connected to a LAN. (See Figure 11.3.) These instruments may cost several thousand dollars and may be used only occasionally by a draftsperson. Connecting the plotter to the system as a print server allows many draftspersons to share the machine and use its capabilities.

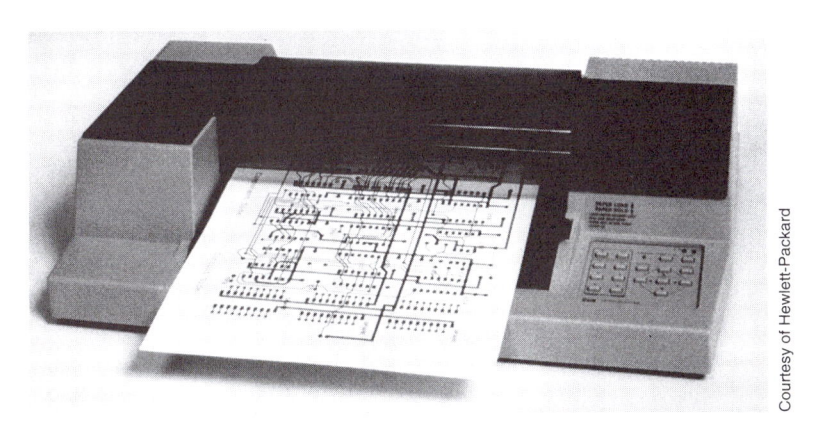

Courtesy of Hewlett-Packard

FIGURE 11.3 LAN Plotter

Computer-Aided Manufacturing

LANs have made their way into manufacturing plants because they enable many departments to access manufacturing data simultaneously. For example, terminals on a LAN may be placed throughout a manufacturing plant to allow stockroom keepers, machine tool operators, shipping department personnel, and maintenance people to access a common database. Everyone within the span of the LAN can be apprised of new orders received, goods shipped, or materials held on back order. Without access to common information, producing a given product would take much longer.

BASIC COMPONENTS OF A LOCAL AREA NETWORK

The LAN is a system and, as such, is composed of subsystems or parts that enable it to function as an integrated whole. Figure 11.4 illustrates the basic building blocks of a typical LAN. These include file servers, print servers, workstations, interface cards, connectors and cables, and network software.

FIGURE 11.4
Basic LAN Components

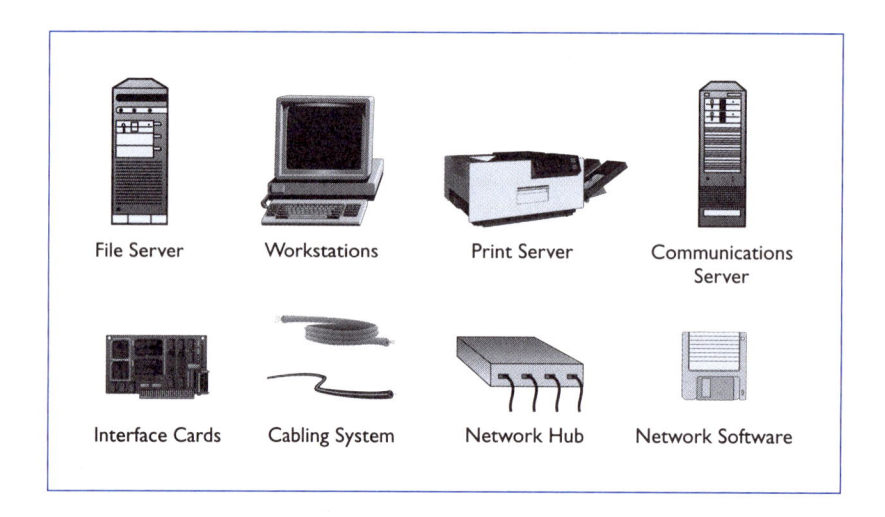

File Server   Workstations   Print Server   Communications Server

Interface Cards   Cabling System   Network Hub   Network Software

The specific selection of components and types of devices depends on the hardware vendor, the system requirements, and budget considerations. The number and types of users and their locations also play a part in component selection.

Let us now look at the components of a LAN more closely.

The File Server

A **file server** is a microcomputer with a magnetic storage device, usually a disk, designed to provide high-volume storage for the system. The server is the heart of the LAN. It can store millions of bytes of data input from any of the workstations on the network. The server holds the essential network software that integrates all other elements of the network.

Some networks may be constructed from a group of workstations without a single dedicated file server. Each workstation, equipped with its own disk storage, is able to function as part of the network without relying on a central server. These systems are known as **peer-to-peer networks**.

Workstations

A **workstation** is a device that provides a point where an operator communicates with the network. It is a **node**, or entry point, to a network. (See Figure 11.5.) A node may be a microcomputer, terminal, printer, or secondary storage device. A workstation is usually a microcomputer that contains a keyboard, monitor, disk storage, and perhaps a printer. (See Figure 11.6.) Each workstation on the network contains an interface, or controller, card. The **interface card** physically connects the microcomputer and its peripheral devices to the cabling system.

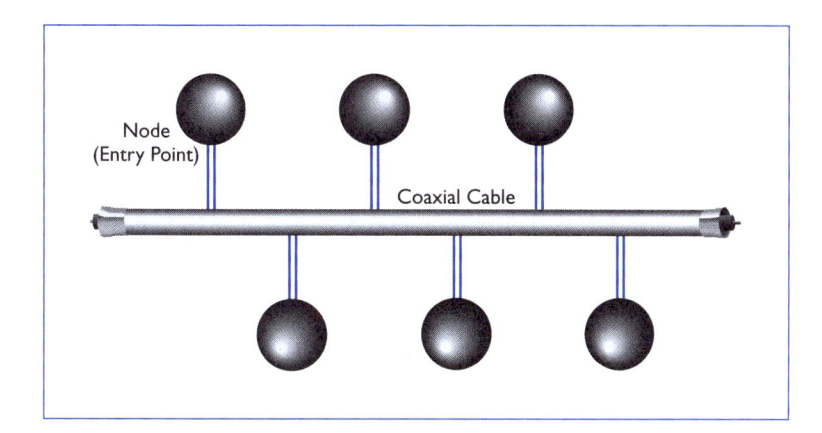

FIGURE 11.5
System Node

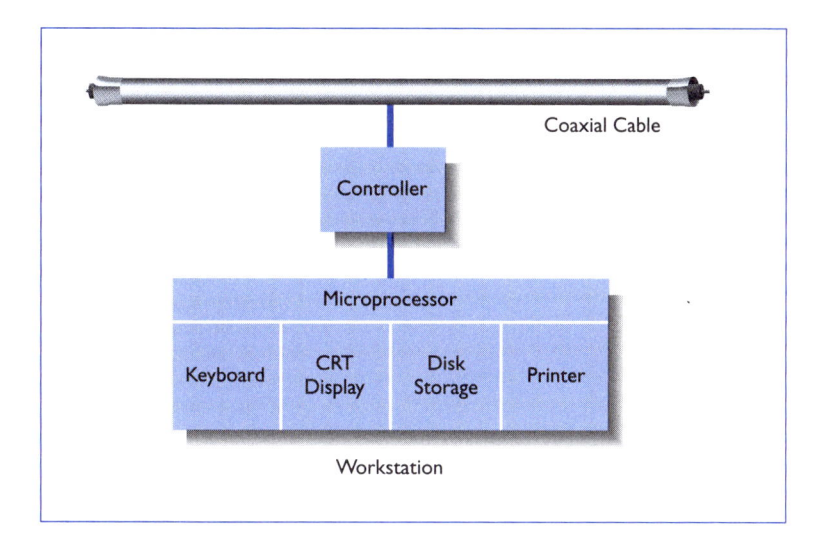

FIGURE 11.6
Workstation Diagram

Workstations can operate as independent stand-alone computers or as part of a LAN. In the stand-alone mode, data can be keyed in, stored on disk, processed, displayed, or output on the local printer. In the online mode, the workstation can access all devices on the network.

The Print Server

Many tasks performed on the network require high-quality or high-speed output, a requirement that may be met with a **print server**. (See Figure 11.7.) Print servers are printers containing interface cards that link them to the cabling system. Laser printers are often used as print servers to generate reports and hard-copy documents. One print server may meet the needs of many workstations, providing fast, high-quality laser output on the LAN.

FIGURE 11.7
LAN Print Server

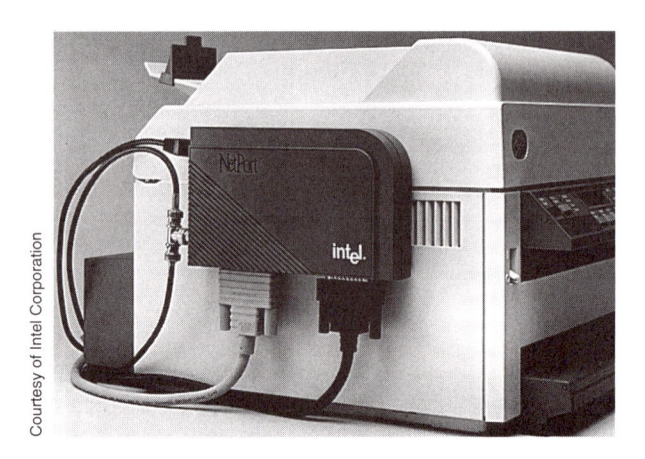

The Communications Server

The **communications server** is a device connected to a network that provides an interface to other systems. Most communications servers provide EIA-232-D capability, which means serial port devices can be connected via common carriers to other networks or remote host computers.

Interface Cards

Interface cards are also known as adapter cards, network interface cards (NIC), or controller cards. Interface cards are physically inserted into microcomputers, printers, or other devices on the network. (See Figure 11.8.) They provide the physical connection between the device and the cabling system. For example, a file server would be connected to the cabling system via an interface card. The interface card handles timing and switching functions and allows the workstation to go online when it is cleared to do so.

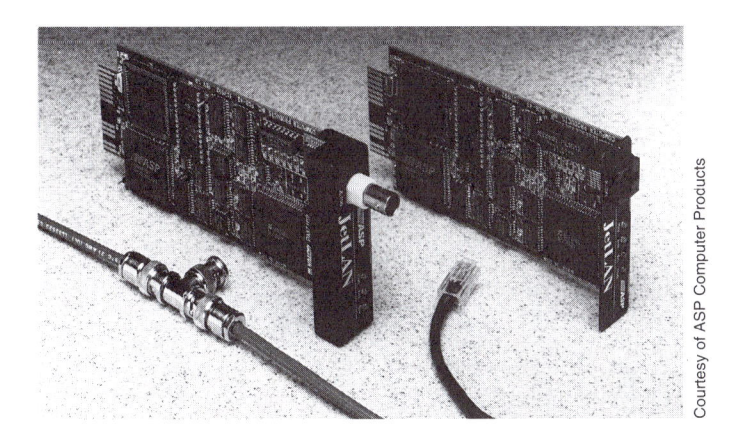

FIGURE 11.8
Interface Card

Courtesy of ASP Computer Products

Cabling System

The most fundamental element of a LAN is its **cabling system** or communications medium. This may be a coaxial cable, twisted pair, or fiber-optic cable. Cables are strung into networks to which are attached computers, printers, and disk storage devices. In some systems a coaxial cable is strung from point to point to interconnect all physical components on the system. The coaxial cable may be strung through walls or partitions, or it may be routed through ceilings or even underground.

Network Hub

A **network hub** is a common device to which workstations, print servers, and other equipment are connected. It provides the physical connection to which other devices are physically cabled. It is much like a multiplug outlet socket that one might use in a living room to connect several different appliances. Network hubs conform to standards such as the 10Base-T and IEEE 802.3, discussed later in the chapter.

The hub is a multiport repeater that provides error detection and correction and is able to identify and isolate malfunctioning components that are tied to the hub. This feature prevents a problem in one device from shutting down the entire network.

Network Software

Network software, essential to the operation of a LAN, performs many functions. Network software coordinates devices on the system, performs error checking and correction, allocates resources, resolves device contentions, and controls system access and security. Its important tasks are to back up and restore data and provide system management information. The specific software selected must be coordinated with the network hardware.

CABLING SYSTEM

The physical wiring used to connect elements in a LAN is known as the **cabling system**. Common cabling systems used in LANs are shown in Figure 11.9. They are listed below.

1. *Unshielded twisted pair (UTP)*. A twisted pair of metallic conductors without a shield to protect them from outside electrical interference.
2. *Shielded twisted pair (STP)*. A twisted pair of metallic wires within a braided or foil shield that protects them from outside electrical interference.
3. *Coaxial cable (Coax)*. A single metallic conductor within a braided metallic shield that protects it from outside electrical interference.
4. *Fiber-optic cable*. A pair of fine strands of glass surrounded by a fiber jacket and shield that protects the inner strands.

Let us look more closely at these common LAN wiring systems.

Unshielded Twisted Pair

Many LANs are built from **unshielded twisted pair (UTP)** systems, which may be constructed from 22, 24, or 26 AWG wire. These circuits are able to transmit data at speeds as high as 16 Mbps. Major limitations of twisted pair cabling are its susceptibility to noise and electrical interference, as well as its limited bandwidth. Twisted pairs of wires are suitable for LAN cabling provided that distances over five miles are not involved. The twisted pair system is becoming widely used due to its ease of interfacing with existing circuits, such as twisted pair telephone wiring. In effect, buildings that have been prewired with ordinary telephone cables are ready for LANs.

A common specification for this type of circuit is known as **10Base-T**. The 10Base-T uses a 22 or 24 AWG unshielded twisted pair of wires. A single link or segment may be as long as 100 meters (328 feet).

The common connectors for UTP circuits are the RJ-11, RJ-12, and RJ-45 modular plugs. You are probably already familiar with the four-conductor RJ-11 connector if you have a telephone that can be plugged into a wall jack.

Shielded Twisted Pair

Many LANs, including those marketed by IBM, are based on the shielded twisted pair wiring system. It is similar to the UTP, except that the **shielded twisted pair (STP)** of conductors is covered by a foil shield that protects them from electrical interference. Various IBM specifications have been written for this wiring; they are known as Types 1, 2, 3, 6, and 9.

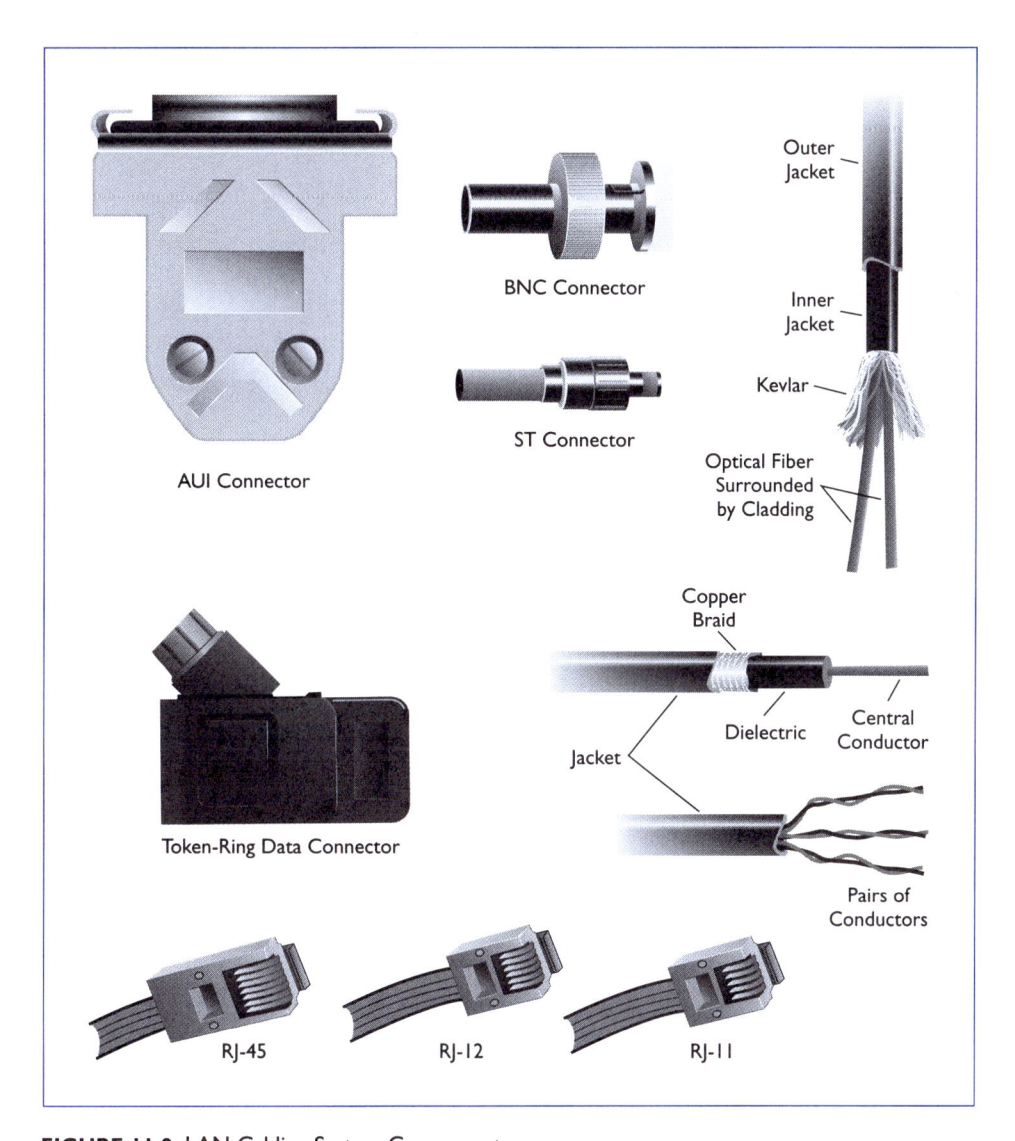

FIGURE 11.9 LAN Cabling System Components

Coaxial Cables

Coaxial cables provide another means of wiring devices together in a LAN. Coaxial cable is particularly suited as a LAN cabling system because of its wide bandwidth. Coaxial cable hardware is readily available, and cables can be installed relatively inexpensively using off-the-shelf connectors and fittings already widely used in CATV cable systems.

Coaxial cable systems can move data at rates as high as 10 Mbps. They use common wires specified as RG-58/U, 10Base5, or 10Base2. It is desirable for a cabling system to allow nodes to be easily added or removed from a system without expensive connectors, fittings, or rewiring. An inexpensive coaxial clamping device is suitable for this purpose. (See Figure 11.10.)

FIGURE 11.10
Ethernet Clamp

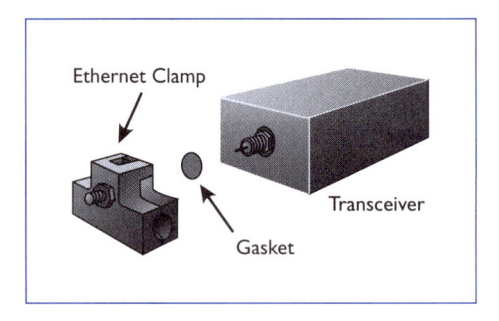

The common connector for coaxial cable is the BNC connector, shown in Figure 11.9. Two common wiring specifications define coaxial cable LANs:

1. *10Base5 (Standard Ethernet)*. This system consists of coaxial cable connecting devices. The maximum data transfer rate is 10 Mbps. The maximum length of a single link is 500 meters (1,640 feet). No more than 100 connections are allowed per segment.
2. *10Base2 (ThinNet Ethernet)*. This system consists of coaxial cable connecting devices. The maximum data transfer rate is 10 Mbps. The maximum length of a single link is 185 meters (607 feet). No more than 30 connections are allowed per segment.

Fiber-Optic Cables

Fiber-optic cables are also used in LANs. They are not subject to electrical interference or static and are able to transmit a large volume of data because of their wide bandwidth. They offer more security because tapping a fiber-optic line is very difficult. Fiber-optic systems are more expensive to install than coaxial cables, and additional nodes cannot be added as easily as they can with hard-wire systems.

The common specification for this system is known as the ANSI X3T9.5 **Fiber Data Distributed Interface (FDDI)**. Devices on the network are connected by fiber-optic cable and are able to move data at speeds up to 100 Mbps. The FDDI is commonly used on IBM's token-ring network. The standard connector for fiber-optic cable is the ST connector, shown in Figure 11.9.

CABLING SYSTEM BANDWIDTH

Two distinctly different LAN systems have evolved based on the bandwidth of the cabling system. Baseband systems use low-voltage unmodulated carriers to send data, whereas broadband systems use radio frequency modulated carriers. Both broadband and baseband systems are widely used in LANs.

One of the initial questions that must be asked when selecting a LAN is whether to use baseband or broadband technology. The two systems are not compatible, and deciding which to select is based on cost, volume of data to be transferred, expandability, and whether the organization seeks to integrate its voice and data communications into a single network. Another factor affecting this decision is whether existing wiring, such as telephone lines and switchboards, is already available. Such wiring would be suitable for baseband but not broadband systems.

Baseband Systems

Baseband LANs operate at low frequencies and allow only one signal to be placed on the medium at one time. Baseband hardware is relatively inexpensive and involves sending only digital pulses over a circuit, without the use of a modulated carrier. Baseband systems do not utilize the full bandwidth of the coaxial cable and are thus less efficient than broadband systems. Because only one signal can be placed on a line at a time, the amount of information that can be passed between nodes is limited. Using a baseband system, it is not possible to multiplex analog and digital data on the same circuit.

Broadband Systems

Broadband LANs take full advantage of a circuit's bandwidth. Broadband systems use radio frequency carriers that are modulated and placed on the cable, establishing a number of channels over one circuit. Data can be time division multiplexed (TDM) or frequency division multiplexed (FDM), thus sending more data over a circuit than with a baseband system. Further, analog and digital data can be transmitted on one circuit. This advantage is particularly important to organizations that require computers, telephones, and video equipment to share the same facilities.

WIRELESS LANS

Because of the cost of installing physical wiring systems, some LAN designers have turned to wireless systems. A **wireless LAN** is a network constructed from elements that are linked by a broadcast or infrared light system rather than physical wiring. Wireless LANs communicate by transmitting information between devices over FM radio frequencies or through waves of light in the infrared spectrum.

Radio frequency LANs can connect components that are located at distances up to 800 feet. Infrared LANs are restricted to line-of-sight conditions; that is, the receiving sensor on each device must be in direct view of the infrared emitting device.

Wireless LANs have many advantages. They are less expensive to install because wires do not have to be laid through attics or under floors. Workstations and other devices may be moved about easily without requiring rewiring. However, such systems are subject to electrical interference or interference from other networks. For some installations, wireless systems are preferred over hard-wire or coaxial systems.

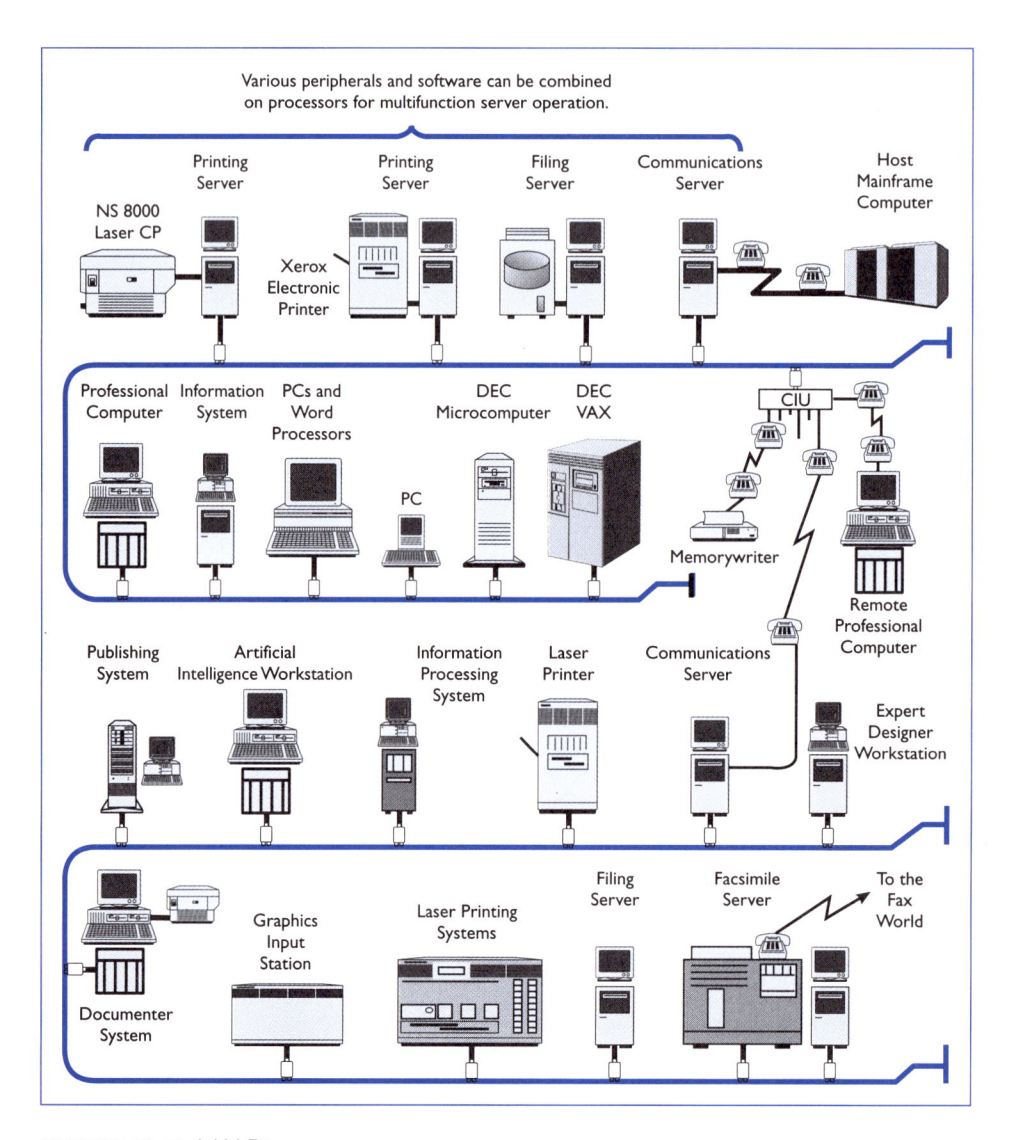

FIGURE 11.11 LAN Diagram

AN EXAMPLE OF A LAN CONFIGURATION

The arrangement in Figure 11.11 is an example of a flexible and expandable LAN system. It has many components, including a cabling system, file servers, workstations, and connections to other networks. Not all LANs are as complex as this example.

The communications server provides access to totally separate LANs located thousands of miles away by using telephone lines. If any workstation on the LAN needs greater processing capacity, it can call on a remotely located computer. The system allows data to be moved through a communications server to WATS lines, microwaves, and satellite communications links. Included in the system are a high-speed laser copy machine with collating capability and fax machines.

The system includes word processors and a publishing system that outputs final pages, ready for printing or reproduction. Systems such as these can be changed or modified as the needs of an organization evolve.

OTHER SYSTEM CONFIGURATIONS

We next present a group of examples that illustrate various LAN designs.

Figure 11.12 shows several host computers tied to Ethernet, LocalTalk, and Token-Ring LANs.

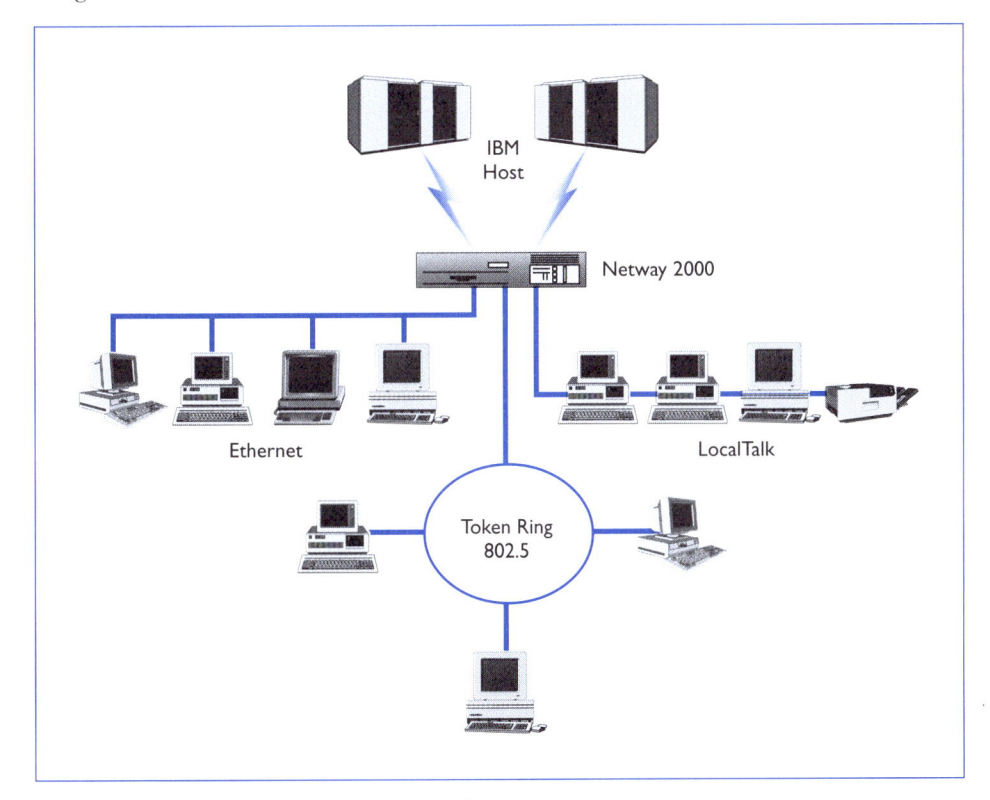

FIGURE 11.12 Three LANs and Two Host Computers

Figure 11.13 shows an IBM host computer connected to two Token-Ring LANs and one Ethernet LAN.

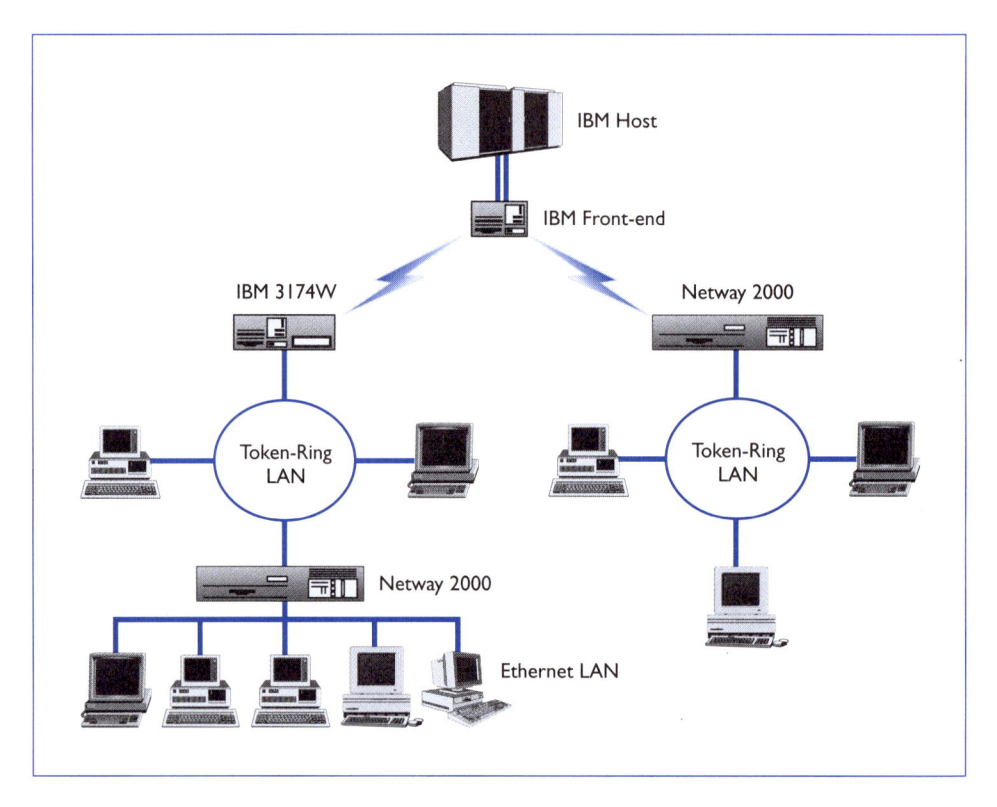

FIGURE 11.13 Three LANs and One Host Computer

Figure 11.14 shows a LAN using a fiber-optic cable with several work groups and remote sites. This system uses the Hewlett-Packard EtherTwist LAN facilities.

NETWORK SOFTWARE AND SECURITY

Simply physically connecting all devices in a network does not create a LAN. To function properly, a LAN must have a variety of software, starting with system network software. In addition, the individual microcomputers must load a LAN BIOS, which provides *b*asic *i*nput and *o*utput *s*ystem functions. Finally, applications software must be put on the LAN and made available to users. Programs such as WordPerfect, dBASE, and Lotus 1-2-3, to name only a few, must be accessible from each workstation.

CHAPTER 11 / LOCAL AREA NETWORKS (LANs) 283

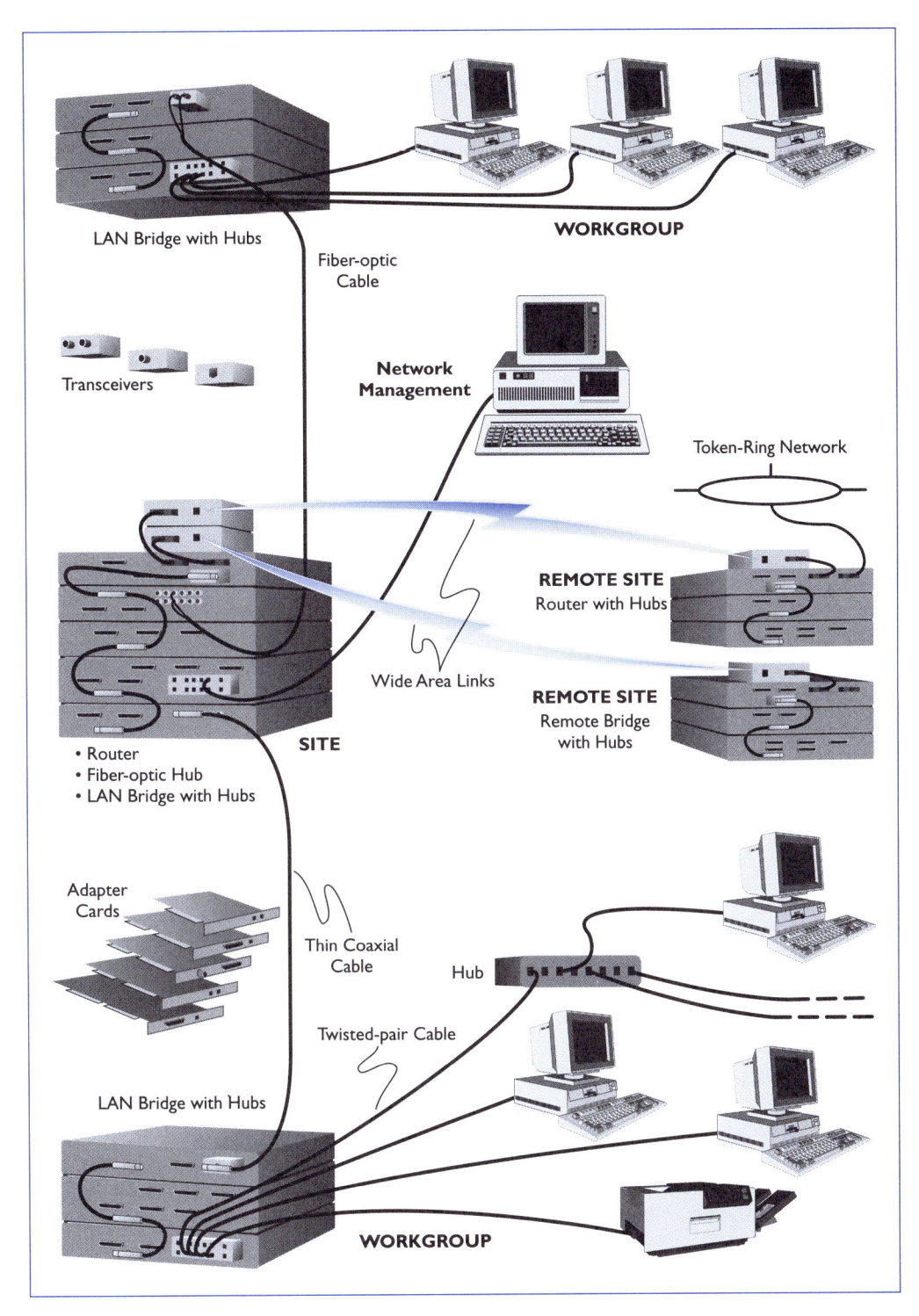

FIGURE 11.14 HP EtherTwist Network

Novell NetWare

Many software packages support LANs. Novell markets many LAN software products and is a leader in this field. Novell's NetWare product line is widely used on both large and small systems.

Novell NetWare software includes a number of utilities: a file management system, file server statistic reporting, and features that allow files or directories to be copied from one machine to another. It also includes an E-mail system, allowing messages to be sent throughout the system or even to third parties.

Novell has several major LAN systems available:

1. *NetWare Lite.* NetWare Lite is a DOS-based network operating system. It includes security features such as encrypted passwords, user account restrictions, resource access rights, and audit trails. It is the simplest and most inexpensive of Novell's peer-to-peer network solutions.
2. *NetWare V.2x.* This is a 16-bit network operating system for small offices or work groups. It includes all of NetWare Lite's features, has more capacity, and supports from as few as 5 to as many as 100 users.
3. *NetWare V.3x.* This is Novell's most fully featured 32-bit network operating system. It supports DOS, Windows, OS/2, UNIX, and Macintosh computers. It is designed for large offices where many workstations will share files, printers, scanners, disk space, and applications software. V.3x supports work groups with as few as 5 users to as many as 250. It is best suited for 386-based microcomputers and also includes 32-bit multitasking, allowing several concurrent operations to take place.
4. *NetWare V4.x.* This is Novell's newest and most fully featured LAN product. It is currently under development and is aimed at the large system user.

Other Software Vendors

A number of companies are competing for the LAN software market. Other major LAN software products include Microsoft Corporation's OS/2 LAN Manager and 3COM Corporation's 3+Open network operating system. Each addresses a slightly different customer base.

Licensing Considerations

Most software licensing agreements allow a program, such as WordPerfect or Lotus 1-2-3, to be run on a single machine. If these or other programs are to be run on a LAN, then LAN versions must be acquired and special licensing agreements negotiated that permit multiple users to simultaneously access software legally. Further, these network versions are specifically designed to avoid system conflicts that may appear when several users simultaneously access a particular application program.

Network Security

A LAN provides opportunities for unauthorized users to access the system. In some instances, authorized users may gain access to unauthorized files. Abuses such as these must be anticipated and prevented through the network software. A software and/or hardware system can control access to workstations, requiring passwords, user numbers, or other authorizations.

The software may provide record, file, or volume locks, which allow only certain users, with previously established clearance, to access a particular record, file, or group of files. Maximum security is achieved because the software is able to track not only authorized users, but those who seek unauthorized access.

NETWORK STANDARDS

A LAN requires the interconnection of dozens of different devices into a system. Without standards, the possibility of connecting incompatible devices or those that could not communicate with one another is real. Obviously, some form of standardization is necessary. The IEEE has been engaged in the development and publication of communications standards. It recently released several standards for LANs; equipment manufacturers have designed and marketed components that meet these standards.

The first LAN standard published was known as the IEEE 802.3, which described a bus type of architecture. The Ethernet system, developed and marketed by Xerox Corporation, is built around this topology. It uses a common bus to feed data among all nodes in the network.

The second standard published, now gaining widespread interest, is the IEEE 802.5 token-passing configuration. This system, heavily marketed by IBM for its new office LANs, uses a ring architecture, placing all devices in a loop. Before we describe these two topologies in more detail, it is necessary to understand the problems of message collision, detection, and avoidance.

The IEEE is considering adopting other LAN standards. Figure 11.15 summarizes some of the major LAN standards that have been approved.

ACCESS PROTOCOLS

Whenever two or more devices are connected to a network that does not have a master controller, **message collisions** are possible. This can happen if two workstations, for example, go online and simultaneously transmit data at the same time and frequency, creating a collision that garbles both messages. If hundreds of devices are on the network at the same time, the possibility of message collision and contention for resources grows even greater. A **contention** occurs when two or more users wish to access the same resource at the same time.

FIGURE 11.15
IEEE LAN Subcommittees

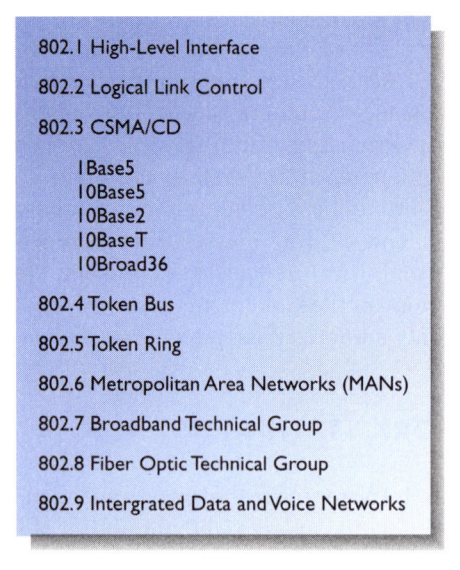

> 802.1 High-Level Interface
>
> 802.2 Logical Link Control
>
> 802.3 CSMA/CD
>
>   1Base5
>   10Base5
>   10Base2
>   10BaseT
>   10Broad36
>
> 802.4 Token Bus
>
> 802.5 Token Ring
>
> 802.6 Metropolitan Area Networks (MANs)
>
> 802.7 Broadband Technical Group
>
> 802.8 Fiber Optic Technical Group
>
> 802.9 Intergrated Data and Voice Networks

To help understand the problems of message collisions, consider what happens when a room full of people all wish to speak at once. Without someone to moderate the discussion, chaos would ensue and no one would be heard or understood. The problem could be solved in several ways. One method would involve employing a moderator, who would call on only one individual at a time. No two people would speak at once because they would all be under the control of the moderator. This solution is not as practical as others as it involves the expense of a full-time moderator.

A better solution might involve the use of a baton, or token, that is passed around the room from one person to another. Only the person holding the baton is allowed to speak, and no moderator is needed.

There is still another means of handling the contention. Each person in the room is instructed not to speak unless the room is quiet. This scheme works well as long as only one person chooses to speak. If two people speak at once, there will be a message collision. To deal with this, speakers are asked to refrain for given periods of time before speaking again. The speaker must first listen and then refrain from speaking if another person is speaking. This arrangement gives all speakers an opportunity as long as they listen for another voice before speaking.

In LAN architecture, an arrangement involving a single master controller (moderator) is not as functional as other configurations. Systems of this design require additional circuitry and the cost of a dedicated computer. Constructing networks without a central controller is possible, but it requires some method of collision avoidance. Two LAN systems, based on the IEEE 802.3 and 802.5 standards, are becoming widely used. These are known as the carrier sense multiple access/collision detection (CSMA/CD) and the token-passing systems.

CARRIER SENSE MULTIPLE ACCESS/COLLISION DETECTION

A widely used implementation of the IEEE 802.3 standard is **Ethernet**. (See Figure 11.16.) This system, pioneered by Xerox Corporation, uses the **carrier sense multiple access/collision detection (CSMA/CD)** system. Ethernet uses a bus topology and is constructed from nodes that are physically wired to a single coaxial cable or twisted pair of wires. The nodes may be workstations, print servers, communications devices, and other pieces of equipment.

FIGURE 11.16
CSMA/CD Frame

| PRE | SFD | DA | SA | LEN | LCC Frame | PAD | CRC |

Any device on the network has access to any other device through the bus. The device must listen to the line and detect whether a carrier is present. If the bus is open, the device may access it. All devices, including the one transmitting, monitor the carrier. The transmitting device has exclusive use of the bus until another device chooses to access it. When it does so, a collision occurs, and the information on the bus is garbled. The collision causes both devices to stop transmitting and wait a length of time before again accessing the bus. The length of the waiting period is selected at random, making it very unlikely that both will come online at the same time. This carrier detection and monitoring mechanism allows many nodes to share the bus at once.

Consider what happens when no carrier is present on the bus and two nodes, simultaneously detecting the absence of a carrier, begin to transmit at the same instant. They create a collision that both devices will detect, causing each to refrain from transmitting. If each waits a different period of time, one will then be able to access the bus and begin transmitting. If the demand on the bus at a given instant is not large, this carrier detection system works well. It would not be practical if a majority of devices connected to the bus tried to access it simultaneously. Numerous message collisions would occur, and much time would be wasted while nodes waited for one another to clear the bus. Fortunately, on most systems a large number of terminals do not demand access at the same time. A well-designed system can use carrier detection as a functional way of interfacing many nodes without the necessity for a central controller, with its inherent delays and expense.

TOKEN-PASSING ACCESS

Another popular LAN standard is based on the IEEE 802.5 definition. In this arrangement, dozens of devices are connected to a single ring. All nodes access the same ring, allowing information to be moved between computers, printers, and storage devices. There is no potential for a collision because the system uses a token that is passed from node to node. A device can access the system only while it holds the token.

The 802.5 standard recommends transmission over ordinary unshielded twisted pair wire, at speeds up to 4 Mbps. As many as 72 workstations may be installed on each ring.

Systems built on the **token-passing protocol** are IBM's Token-Ring network, Nestar's Plan Systems, and Datapoint's ARCnet. In these systems, a device cannot commandeer the ring and begin transmitting information unless it possesses the token. The token is a block of data, consisting of binary bits of information, that is electronically passed from device to device. When the token is received, the node can transmit data; then it sends the token on to the next terminal. If the next device does not need to transmit data, it simply passes the token on. Because there is only one token, no two devices ever transmit at the same instant.

GATEWAYS

Up to now we have been discussing LANs as though they were stand-alone entities that did not connect or interface with other systems. In practice, two or more dissimilar LANs may be interfaced into a larger system or they may be linked together. These LANs may use different technologies, for example, broadband or baseband media, and may mix both token-passing and CSMA/CD elements. Therefore, standard **protocols** and procedures are necessary to allow different types of LANs to interface in one network.

Suppose a broadband LAN is to be connected to a non-LAN network. The independent LAN is connected to a long-haul network via a **gateway** interface. This gateway contains electronic circuitry and protocol software that enables LANs to communicate with the long-haul network, which may include long distance lines, common-carrier circuits, and microwave facilities. Figure 11.17 illustrates how this connection is made.

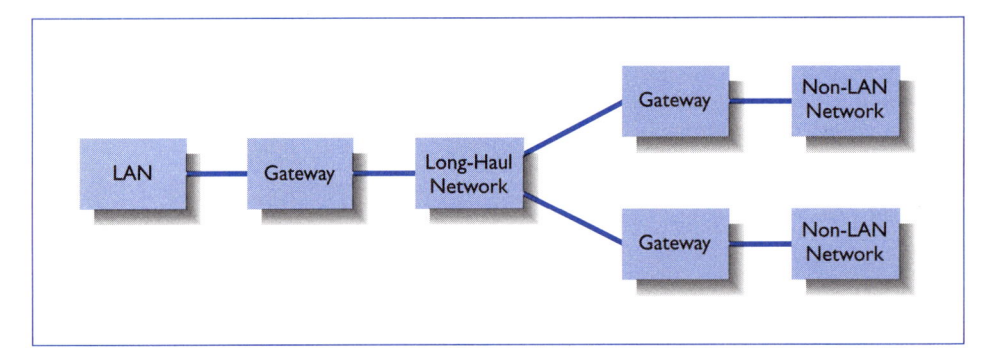

FIGURE 11.17 Gateway Interface

Mixing of LANs with non-LAN systems is facilitated by the X.25 standard, published by CCITT. This standard, which describes common characteristics for equipment using public data networks, is becoming the common element by which many LANs are interfaced. Other standards, such as IBM's System Network Architecture (SNA), are also used to establish universal standards between elements in a network.

BRIDGES

Dissimilar LANs may be interfaced in a single network using a **bridge interface**. (See Figure 11.18.) In this instance, a LAN interfaces with a bridge interface. At the other end of the line, another bridge interface provides a connection to the dissimilar LAN. Thus, bridges are used to connect dissimilar LANs, while gateways connect LANs to non-LAN networks.

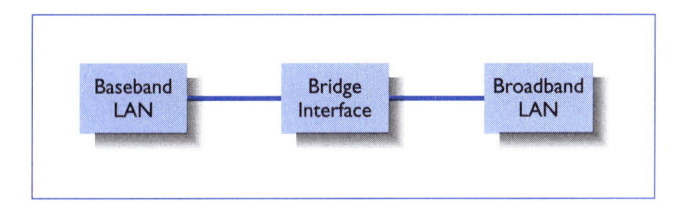

FIGURE 11.18
Bridge Interface

Let us use an illustration to show how the bridge interface system works. Suppose a workstation in a CSMA/CD LAN wishes to access a data file in a different LAN that uses a token-passing ring access system. The first workstation accesses its local bus using a carrier-detection arrangement. Once it has accessed the bus, it can send a request for information down the line. The request for information is received by the bridge interface, which in turn relays the transmission through to another bridge. There it is received by the bridge interface at the receiving LAN. This bridge accesses the ring LAN, using the token system. When the token is received by the bridge interface, the necessary secondary storage device is accessed. The data that have been sought are then put on the ring, relayed back through the bridge, through the originating bridge, and finally to the node requesting the information. All of these operations take place automatically, without direction by the user.

ACQUIRING A LAN

A wide range of LAN hardware, software, cables, and connection equipment is available on the market. A business or organization wishing to install a LAN should carefully evaluate its budget, its needs, and its applications before purchasing a LAN. Among the criteria that should be considered in making a LAN selection are:

- Kind and types of messages and traffic handled

- Cost factors
- Need to share specific pieces of hardware, such as plotters or special printers
- Equipment capability
- Software capability
- System flexibility and expansion capability
- Reliability and provision for backup facilities
- Operator training costs
- System maintenance costs
- Ability to integrate LAN into other organizational communications facilities

After a careful review of these and other factors, the organization may select specific LAN hardware and software. If the proper facilities have been chosen, the system can be easily changed or modified and will serve the organization well. It should allow terminals, print servers, and file servers to be added or removed, and wiring changes to be made inexpensively.

In this chapter we have seen how hundreds of different devices may share common resources in a limited geographic area by using local area networks. We have also learned how contentions and message collisions are handled or avoided. The chapter discussed how widely separated geographic LANs are integrated through gateways. In the next chapter we will go beyond LANs and study much broader networks. These networks, known as wide area networks (WANs), transport data over wide geographic areas. They are becoming an increasingly important part of the communications industry.

SUMMARY

LANs are privately owned communications systems that integrate computer facilities. *Coaxial cables* are particularly suited to wiring together devices in a LAN. *Fiber-optic cables* may be used to tie together elements of a LAN. *Wireless LANs* do not use cables, but instead broadcast radio frequencies. *Baseband LANs* operate with only one signal on the circuit at a time. *Broadband LANs* operate at radio frequency and place several signals on the circuit at one time.

A *network* ties together all elements of a system and allows devices to interact with one another. A *workstation* is a microcomputer or other device with I/O capability. An *interface card* is used to connect microcomputers or other devices physically to a cabling system. *File servers* provide high-volume storage, usually on disk, for LANs. *Print servers* provide high-speed printing output for the LAN. A *communications server* connects the LAN to other networks or incompatible equipment.

The physical wiring used to connect elements in a LAN is known as the *cabling system*. This system may be composed of *unshielded twisted pair (UTP)*, *shielded twisted pair (STP)*, *coaxial cable (Coax)*, or *fiber-optic cable*.

The IEEE has published several standards for the design of LANs. The *CSMA/CD* system, used by *Ethernet*, handles the problem of *contention* for network resources. The *token system*, used by IBM, is able to handle the problem of contention for network resources.

Common LAN applications include educational, business, and design programs, as well as computer-aided manufacturing. LANs should be selected on the basis of traffic handled, organization needs, software and hardware capability, and other factors.

A *gateway* contains electronic circuitry and protocol software that enables LANs to communicate with the long-haul network. Dissimilar LANs may be interfaced in a single network using a *bridge interface*.

EXERCISES

1. How do baseband LANs differ from broadband systems?
2. List the major components of a LAN.
3. Describe the function of network software.
4. List some common network security problems.
5. How does CSMA/CD deal with message collision?
6. Describe how the token-passing system is used to access a line.
7. What is the function of a controller card on a LAN?
8. What is the function of a bridge interface?
9. Describe a file server and its function.
10. Describe the function of the communications server.

HANDS-ON PROJECTS

- Visit a distributor that markets an Ethernet LAN. Review the product literature and discuss system features.

- Visit a distributor that markets a token-passing LAN. Review the product literature and discuss system features.

- Visit your campus computer center and discuss local area networks. Is a LAN in use? What types of systems and hardware are employed?

- Draw a diagram of a LAN for a small commercial business. Include one file server, several terminals, and one or more printers.

- Draw a diagram of a LAN that includes a gateway. Show how the LAN is connected to other systems through the gateway.

COMMUNICATIONS IN ACTION

CASE SOLUTION
LAW OFFICES OF PARKER AND PARKER

Parker and Parker decided to install a local area network (LAN) to fully automate their office and paperwork operations. (See Figure 11.19.) The LAN that was purchased connects a group of workstations by coaxial cable throughout the law offices. Workstations are located at the desks of law clerks, attorneys, and senior partners. From any workstation, an attorney or law clerk can access word processing, spreadsheet, and database software.

The LAN is equipped with a high-speed electronic printer connected to the coaxial cable by a print server. A disk storage device is connected to the system via a file server, which acts as a buffer to store millions of characters of text. The network is able to access other LANs through a communications server, also connected to the coaxial cable.

When a brief, legal document, or piece of correspondence is prepared, it is first entered by a law clerk or legal secretary at a workstation. (See Figure 11.20.) After completion, the document is saved by the file server. It can then be displayed on another workstation for review. Changes or revisions may be made and a draft stored on disk. After final approval, the document is output by the print server on a line printer. The hard copy is then sent to the client. Another copy is generated for submission to the court.

CHAPTER 11 / LOCAL AREA NETWORKS (LANs) 293

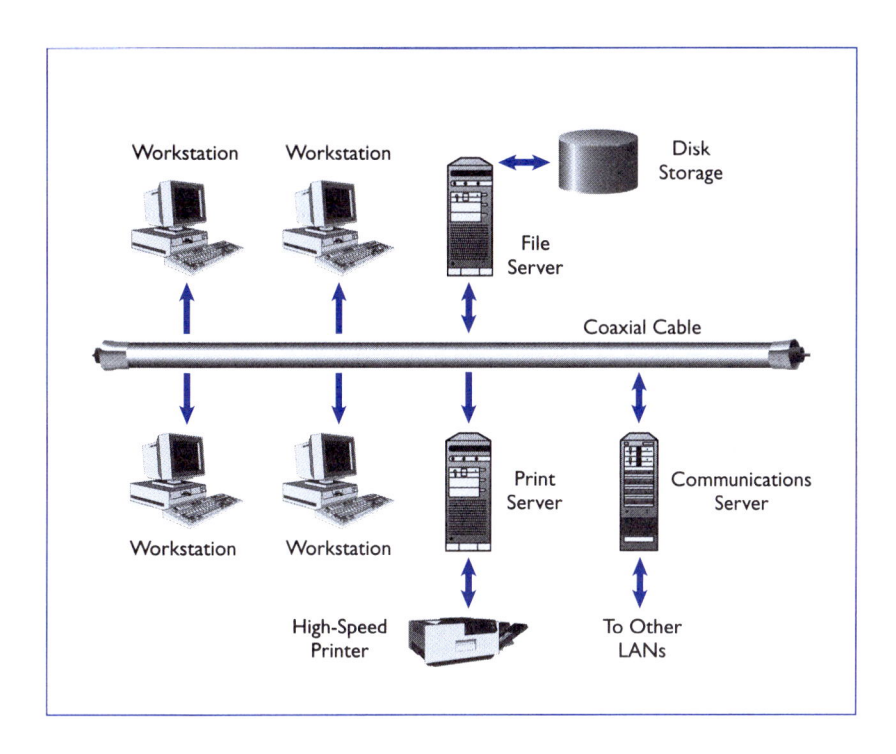

FIGURE 11.19
Local Area Network (LAN)

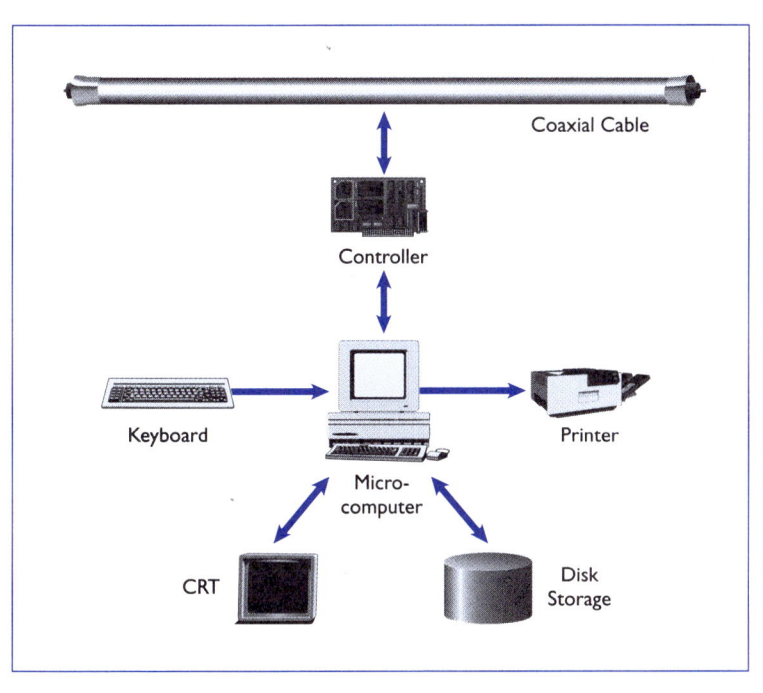

FIGURE 11.20
Workstation Configuration

Parker and Parker has become very dependent on the LAN because of its efficiency. Before it was installed, all documents were manually typed and corrections entered by hand, as required, causing much retyping. Sometimes errors crept into the final draft that were not detected.

The new system is fully integrated. It provides interoffice communications, high-speed printing, and connection to other LANs. Last-minute changes can be entered into legal documents just before filing. The output of the system is neater and better organized and enables the firm's attorneys to increase their productivity at the same time. Finally, workstations can be added or relocated easily by simply connecting them to the single LAN coaxial cable that runs throughout the offices.

WIDE AREA NETWORKS (WANs)

LEARNING OBJECTIVES

After studying this chapter, you should be able to:

- Describe wide area network topology
- Discuss IBM System Network Architecture (SNA)
- Discuss DECnet architecture
- Describe fast packet and frame relay networks
- List various private wide area networks
- Discuss messaging services

COMMUNICATIONS
IN ACTION

CASE PROBLEM
LOGAN ELECTRONICS

DISTRIBUTED DATA PROCESSING SYSTEM

Logan Electronics began manufacturing electronic test equipment many years ago. The firm has grown and expanded over the years. Today, Logan Electronics is a leader in the field of computers and automated test equipment. The company has many divisions, which specialize in electronics, computer design, and digital test equipment, located throughout the country. Logan employs thousands of engineers, designers, assembly line workers, and managers who need access to computers, databases, and extensive data processing facilities.

For many years, Logan relied on a centralized data processing system. (See Figure 12.1.) It included large central mainframe computers, extensive communications lines, and many remote batch-processing terminals. Through these terminals, divisions were able to access the extensive personnel, accounting, sales, and research and development data stored on the mainframes. Although this system worked well, it was expensive to maintain and relied heavily on costly wideband data circuits. When the mainframe computer went down, it effectively halted data processing throughout the entire organization. Logan wishes to eliminate these problems and distribute its data processing system over its many divisions.

FIGURE 12.1
Logan's Centralized Data Processing System

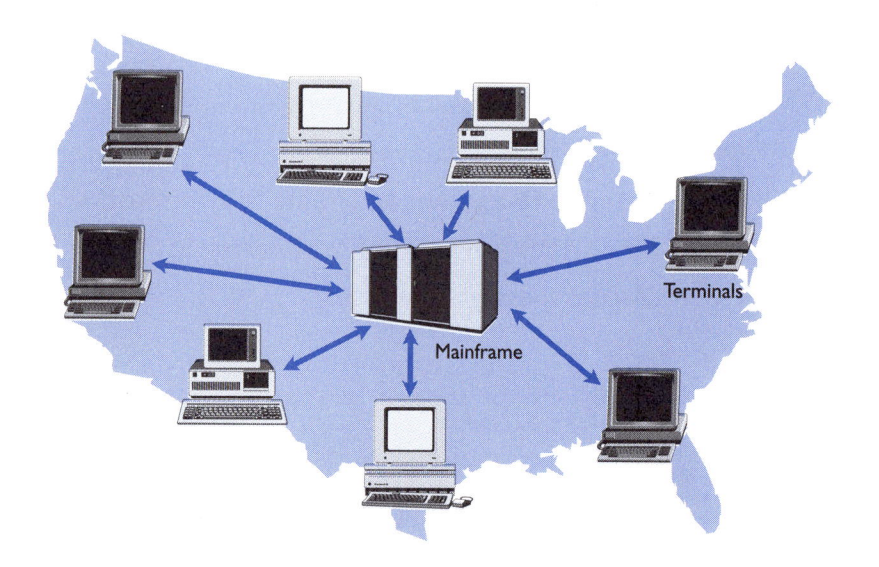

What would you do to solve Logan Electronics' problem? Refer to the end of this chapter to see how Logan's management resolved the problem.

As businesses continue to find more efficient ways to operate and expand their worldwide markets, the importance of connectivity takes on new meaning. **Connectivity**, essentially the linking together of components in a network, is crucial to the integration of an organization's personnel, production, and financial resources.

This chapter explores how wide area networks are constructed. A **wide area network (WAN)** is a privately or publicly owned communications system that is able to send and receive information between computers or workstations that may be located over great distances. Mainframes, microcomputers, terminals, and LANs can be connected together using long haul common carrier circuits, satellites, or microwave relay links.

WANs are networks that move data without any significant enhancement or change in character of the information. They differ from VANs, discussed in Chapter 13, which are able to access databases, enhance information, and provide computer services, thus greatly adding to the utility of the network. WANs differ from LANs, discussed in the previous chapter, which are limited to small geographic areas.

WANs have been operational for many years and include Telex and TWX services. They are often used by large business organizations that need to communicate with offices located in other cities, or even in foreign countries.

WIDE AREA NETWORK OVERVIEW

WANs are complex systems of high-speed electronic switches, high-capacity communications circuits, and computers. These elements can be configured in many different ways, depending on the number and types of computers and terminals in the system and the types of traffic handled.

Entry into the network occurs via a **port**, which is an entry or exit point in a network. A network may have one to as many as several thousand ports. The more ports, the greater the complexity of the switching system. Let us look at some broad examples of wide area networks.

Point-to-Point Communications System

The **point-to-point** communications system is the simplest form of network, in which only two distant points are linked together by a communications circuit. If three or more points are to be tied together, each point in the network is connected directly to all other points. (See Figure 12.2.)

One example would be a small business operator, such as a real estate agent or a sales representative, who sets up a microcomputer to access another microcomputer through a single telephone line installed for that purpose. The two computers achieve connectivity by being tied together through a communications link. The system allows data files to be moved back and forth. Operators can access information stored on either computer. Point-to-point systems are limited to a relatively few points because the mesh of interconnecting circuits becomes expensive on systems with numerous ports.

FIGURE 12.2
Point-to-Point Network

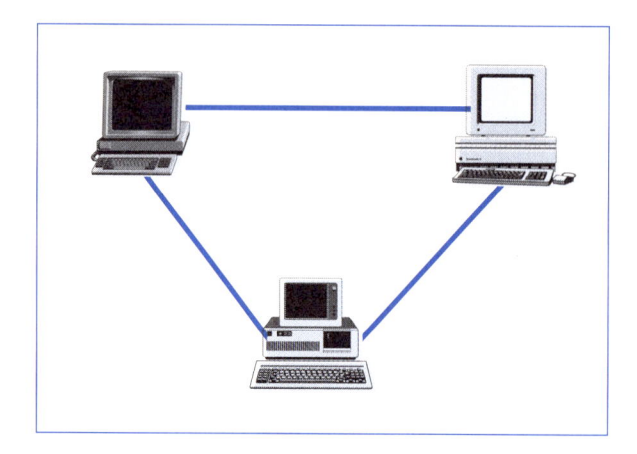

Multipoint Communications System

Figure 12.3 illustrates a **multipoint** network that has several terminals and a computer that attain connectivity by accessing a common circuit. A network such as this enables several users to share the resources of a single computer. A bank with a number of branch offices might use this type of communications system. The central computer serves all branches through a single multidrop line that is wired from one branch to another.

FIGURE 12.3
Multipoint Network

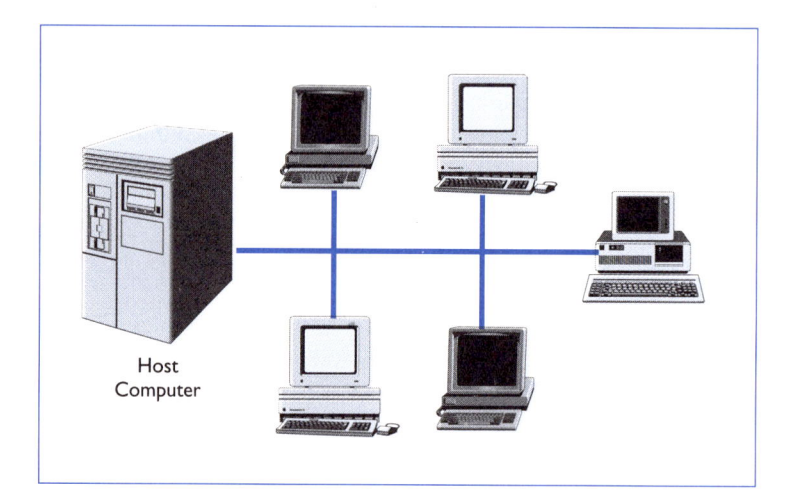

Multiprocessor Network

Figure 12.4 illustrates a **multiprocessor** network. It is composed of a system of mainframe switching computers with many remote terminals and microcomputers. A system such as this, expanded nationwide, might be used by a credit and collection agency to provide up-to-the-minute credit reports. Each major office or branch has its own computer with several connecting terminals in the local offices. The branch office computers are connected by the communications system, thus allowing a pooling of resources and an exchange of information between computers and terminals.

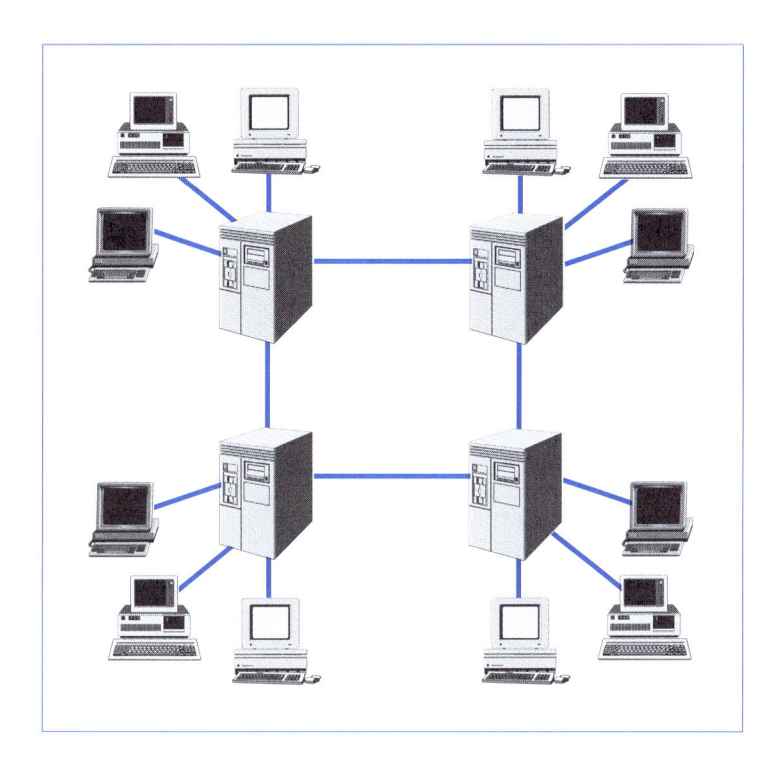

FIGURE 12.4
Multiprocessor Network

WIDE AREA NETWORK ARCHITECTURE

A number of computer manufacturers have developed proprietary WAN systems. These networks include both computers and software to enable numerous computers and terminals to be connected as an interactive system. Let us look at some of these basic WAN configurations.

IBM's System Network Architecture

In 1974 IBM Corporation announced its **System Network Architecture (SNA),** a model that spurred the development of private networks. (See Figure 12.5.) SNA was introduced to serve IBM customers at distant sites who operated mainframe computers that required a standard protocol for interfacing with their machines. SNA is a WAN that uses voice-grade and Direct Distance Dialing (DDD) circuits. It uses the **synchronous data link control (SDLC)**. SNA allows computers of various sizes and designs to operate as an integrated system.

FIGURE 12.5
System Network Architecture (SNA)

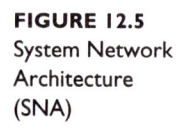

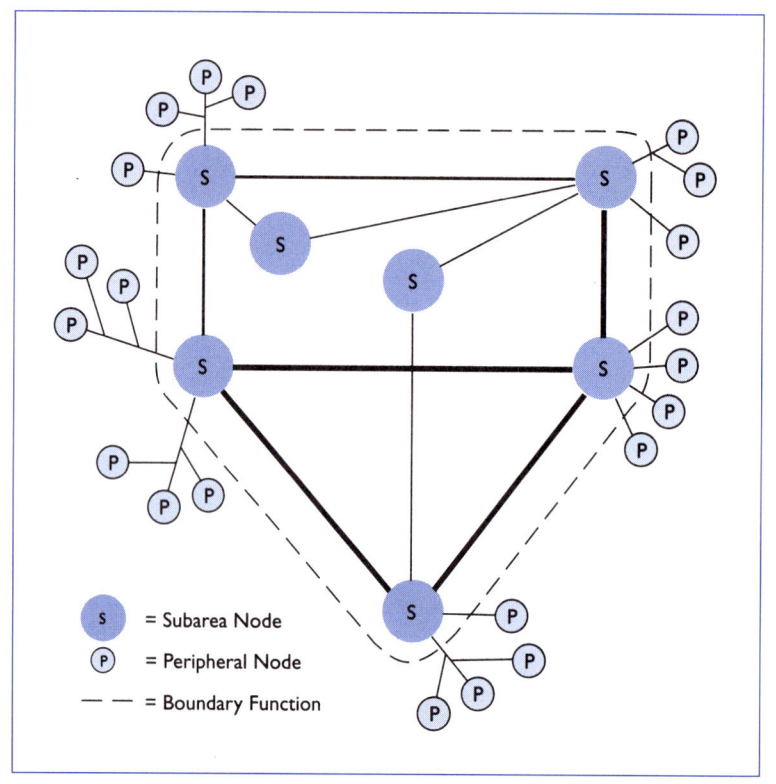

S = Subarea Node
P = Peripheral Node
— — = Boundary Function

SNA has become widely used by organizations with large-scale computers. It is estimated that there are more than 27,000 computer systems using SNA. These mainframes communicate with thousands of terminals located at remote sites. Some systems have as many as 100 host computers and 100,000 terminals in the network. Using SNA, computers can communicate with other machines in different networks, including those that require the X.25 protocol.

Network Layers. The IBM SNA is composed of seven layers that facilitate the logical, as well as physical, flow of data between nodes or network users. (See Figure 12.6.) The lowest level addresses circuitry and voltages. Intermediate layers deal with routing packets, synchronizing flow, and format. The top layer services the user's applications software. Let us look at the function of each of the seven layers in the network.

1. *Physical control.* This layer physically and electrically connects two points in a system. It addresses transmission codes and voltages.
2. *Data link control.* This layer transmits data between nodes and ensures reliability.
3. *Path control.* This layer controls traffic and manages congestion on the network. It routes data between points in the form of packets.
4. *Transmission control.* This layer enciphers data for security purposes and paces data flow to balance end-point processing.

5. *Data flow control.* This layer blocks data into indivisible units, correlates exchange, and synchronizes flow.
6. *Presentation services.* This layer coordinates sharing of resources and formats data for various presentation media.
7. *Transaction services.* This layer deals with the application software and handles such things as movement of records between network users and access to distributed databases.

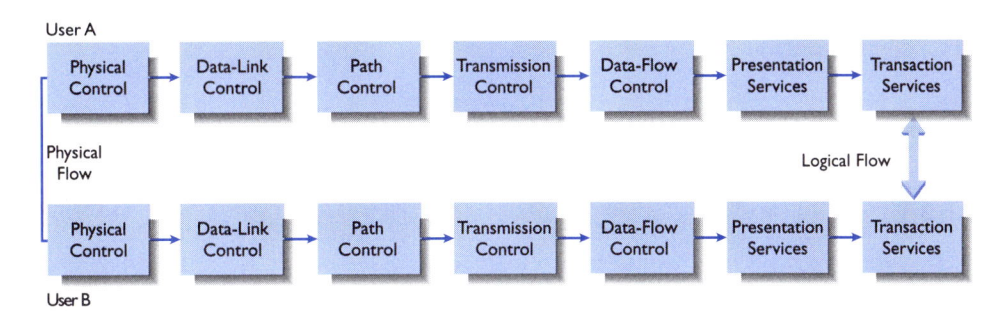

FIGURE 12.6 SNA Layers

An SNA network may utilize different programming languages and operating systems. Microcomputers, midsize, and mainframe computers may all communicate with one another without requiring master control under one host computer.

One of the weaknesses of SNA is that it was designed before the advent of LANs. IBM is working now to modify its SNA structure so that it will support LANs, such as those described in Chapter 11. Nevertheless, SNA continues to be an important standard in private communications network design.

Digital Equipment Corporation's Digital Network Architecture

Another architecture used in private WAN design is Digital Equipment Corporation's (DEC) **Digital Network Architecture (DNA)**, referred to as **DECnet**. DEC designed DECnet to allow minicomputer users to connect their machines into a large, distributed data processing system. DECnet differs from SNA in that it organizes many small minicomputers into a distributed network, whereas SNA is oriented toward large host computers, with a heavy emphasis on centralized data processing.

Local Area System. DEC has developed the **local area system (LAS)** as part of its WAN architecture. The LAS connects DEC's entire engineering network with more than 34,000 nodes in dozens of countries around the world. The system utilizes VAX 8800 computers and serves a variety of computer-aided design (CAD) workstations.

Figure 12.7 illustrates an LAS that integrates DEC's design engineering, manufacturing, and engineering services operations. Each LAS is connected to DEC's wide area corporate network. Systems such as these allow connectivity between an almost unlimited number of microcomputers.

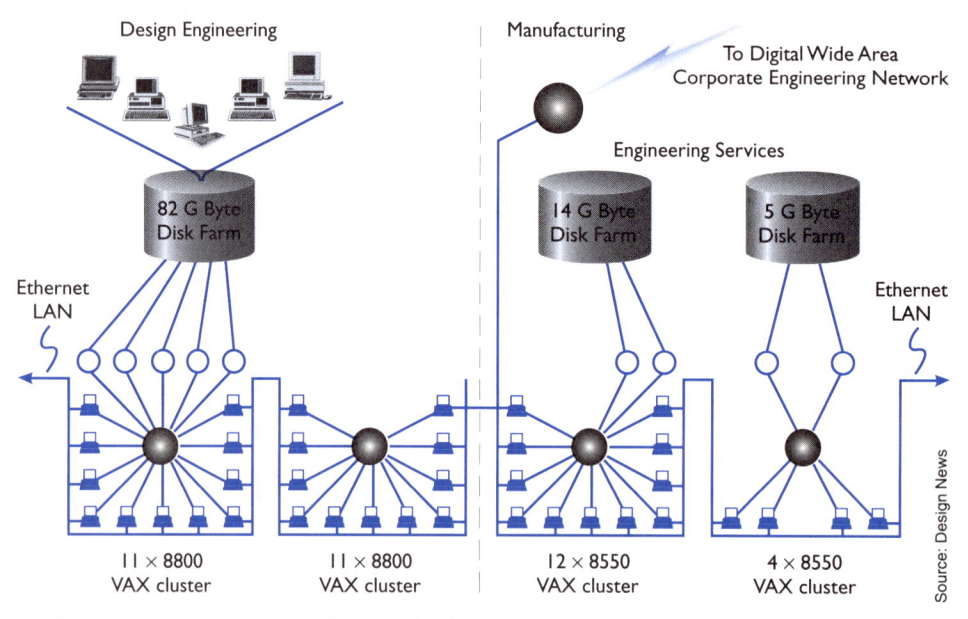

FIGURE 12.7 DEC's Local Area System (LAS)

The system uses Digital's **Distributed System Service (DSS)** software. Any workstation may use DSS and go through a VAX cluster to access either a file server or a print server. The file server consists of a cluster of disks, the **disk farm**, connected through a controller to a VAX cluster. The disk farm is a cluster of individual disk drives that appears as a single large disk storage device to terminals on the system. The print server consists of multiple printers connected through a controller to the VAX cluster. (See Figure 12.8.)

UNIX Transmission Control Protocol/Internet Protocol

The UNIX **Transmission Control Protocol/Internet Protocol (TCP/IP)** is of growing importance in the WAN world. This system architecture was designed for UNIX computers and is widely used on the Internet network. Internet was originally funded by the U.S. government in the 1970s; today it remains the major network linking schools, universities, government, and commercial establishments.

As thousands of users joined Internet, TCP/IP gained popularity. Internet is the outgrowth of the ARPANET network, discussed later in this chapter. Today, hundreds of thousands of users move data and information over Internet. Internet provides E-mail service for a multitude of users. It is now available on many non-UNIX systems and is accessed by both PCs and Macintosh computers.

This widespread usage has given great impetus to TCP/IP. The protocol has three classes of users: Classes A, B, and C. (See Figure 12.9.) Messages are routed throughout the network, using one of the three classes of message headers. Each header contains an address class, network ID, and host ID element. Early subscribers are assigned Class A addresses. Large firms are given Class B addresses, while Class C

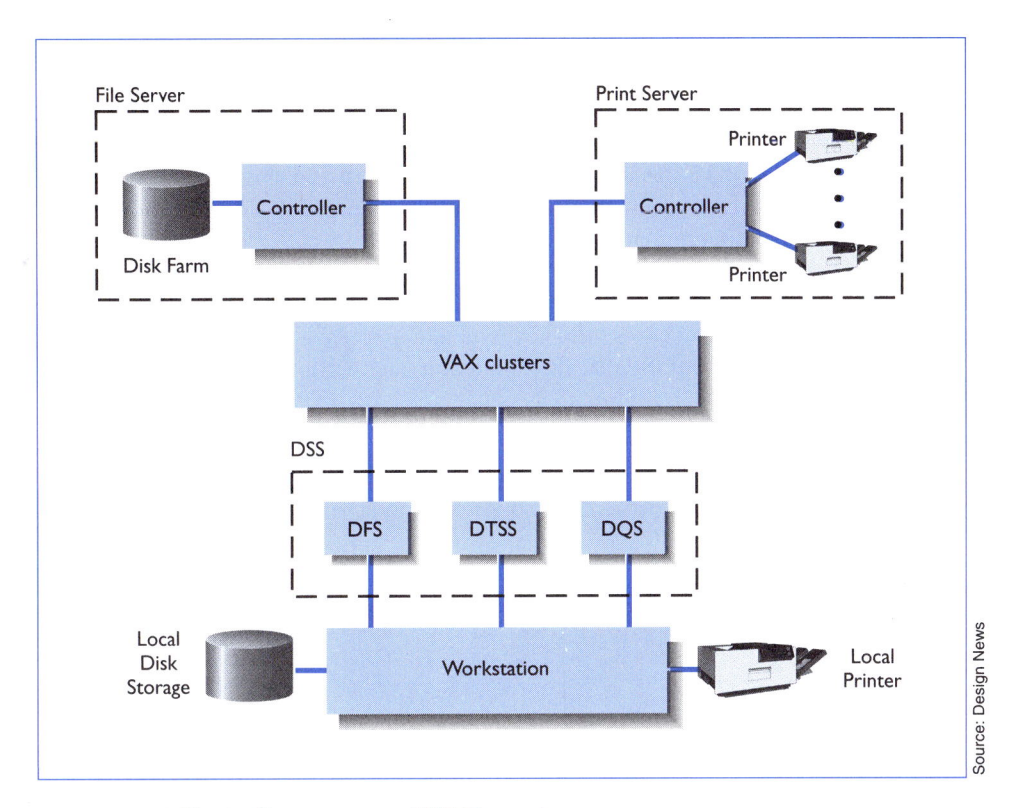

FIGURE 12.8 Sharing Resources on a DEC Network

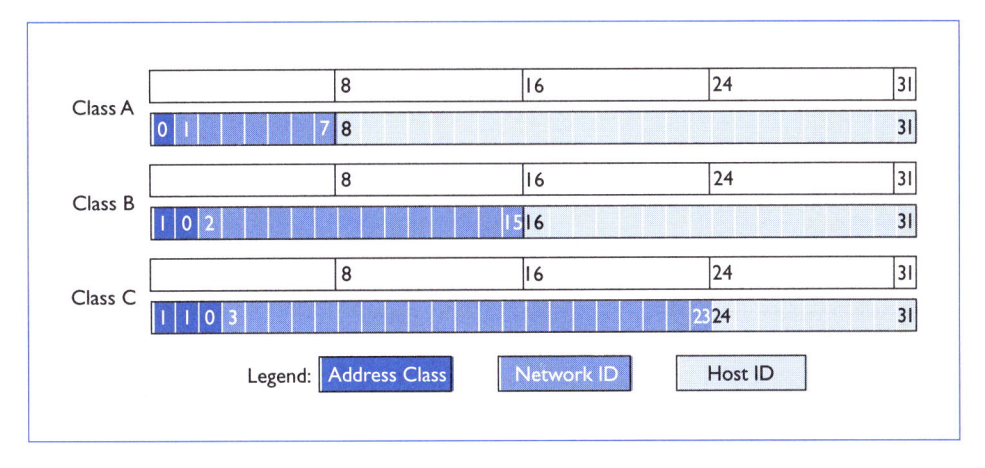

FIGURE 12.9 TCP/IP Address Header

addresses are assigned to smaller organizations. Messages move through the network from one **router** to another. The router reads the message header and transmits it along to the next switch.

CCITT X.400 E-Mail Protocol

With the widespread use of WANs have come increasing demands for E-mail. In 1984 CCITT approved the **X.400 E-mail protocol**. It is estimated that there are more than ten million users of LAN-based E-mail systems worldwide. Much of this mail is routed from one LAN to another over WANs. This internetwork communication requires a uniform communication protocol.

The X.400 E-mail address consists of four components. (See Figure 12.10.) Much like ordinary U.S. mail, the address contains a country code showing the country where the mail system operates. This is followed by a mail service address, then a company or department address, and, finally, the name of a user within the department.

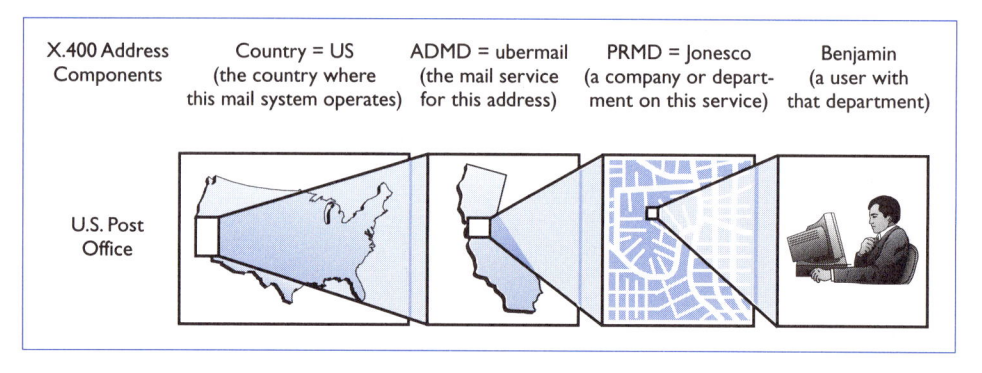

FIGURE 12.10 CCITT X.400 E-Mail Protocol

The system uses the User Agent (UA) and Message Transfer Agent (MTA) that transport the messages from one point to another. After the E-mail is created by the UA software, it is given to the MTA software. From there it is routed to the recipient or on to the next level of address. This method works much like the postal system, which delivers local mail first and then routes out-of-state mail for distribution by other centers.

NETWORKS OF MICROCOMPUTERS

The last several years have seen a great increase in the number of microcomputers connected to wide area networks. In 1992 it was estimated that almost 60 percent of all microcomputers were connected to some form of network.

Microcomputers have advantages that make them logical candidates for integration into networks. They are inexpensive, small, and do not require air conditioning. Their popularity has led to the development of a large amount of software specifically designed for microcomputers.

A microcomputer may be equipped with disk storage, laser printer, or other devices as part of a local area network; it then may be connected to wide area networks through a gateway. Figure 12.11 illustrates a token-ring network that integrates numerous microcomputers that could form a single node on a large complex WAN.

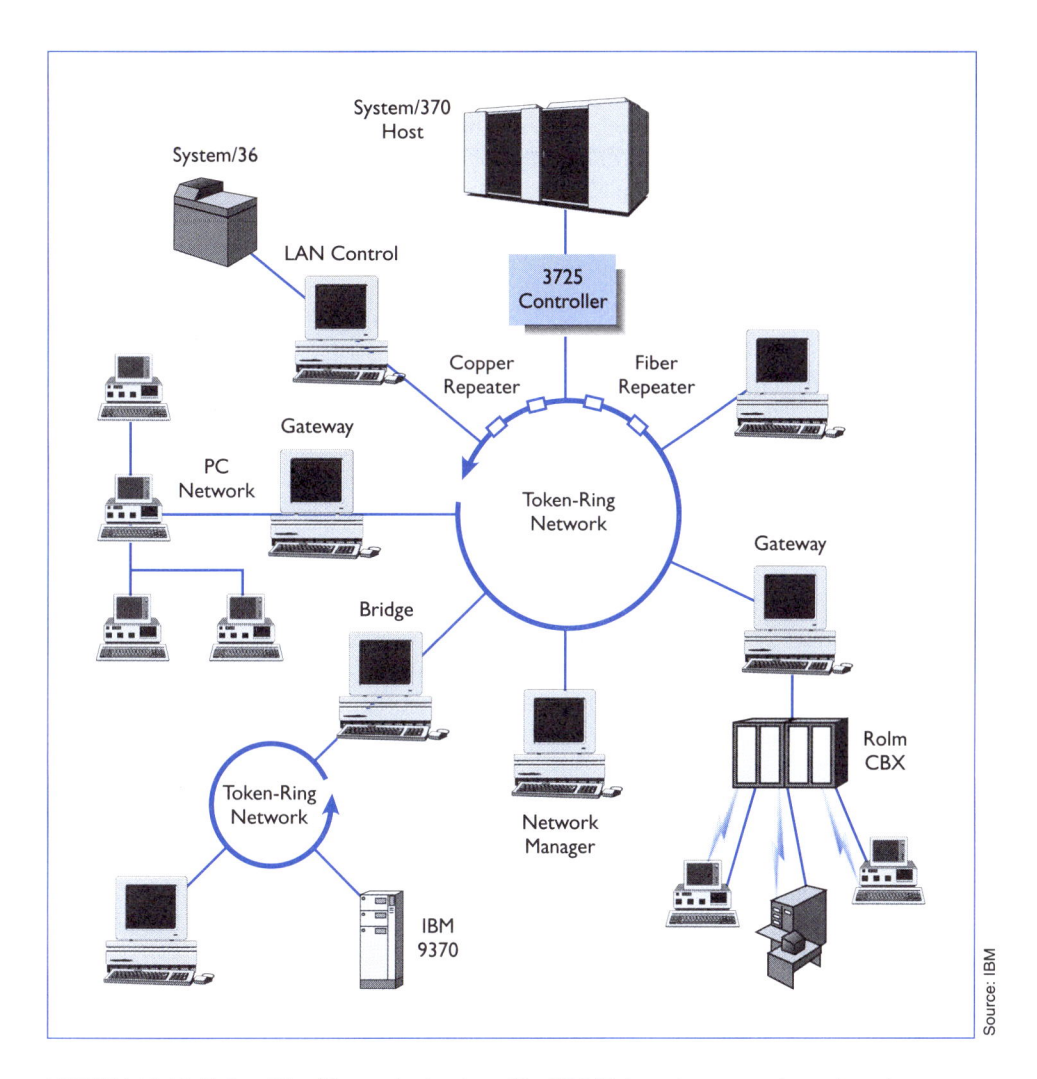

FIGURE 12.11 Token-Ring Network, developed by IBM. Token-ring networks such as these are linked together over great distances using WAN facilities.

Some microcomputers in the system are linked to the network via a gateway. Other microcomputers, themselves a token-ring network, are linked to the WAN via a bridge. Still others may be linked through a digital branch exchange (DBX) or to the network through fiber-optic repeaters.

Large systems, such as the IBM 370, may be integrated into the microcomputer network, using an appropriate controller. This approach enables personal computers to exchange information or share printers, files, or other resources with other microcomputers or even large mainframes on the system. All devices in the node are, in turn, accessible through the WAN to other networks.

PUBLIC NETWORKS

Originally, Western Union provided public access for data circuits. Later, AT&T expanded its services to include digital and message-handling facilities. MCI Communications Corp. and Sprint Communications Co. soon followed with similar services. We will now look at the Western Union, AT&T, MCI, and Sprint public network message-handling facilities.

Western Union Network

Western Union has operated an extensive network of communications lines for many years. These link the United States, Canada, and Mexico, as well as more than 150 other countries, via international carrier circuits. Western Union offers two services, Telex I and Telex II. This Western Union network transmits digital data between data terminal machines, using a non-packet-switched network.

Telex I. The Telex I system connects more than 60,000 terminals in the United States, as well as several hundred thousand more machines in countries around the world. The Telex I system routes messages through a central computer-controlled system to any subscriber on the network. It uses the 5-bit Baudot code and transmits at the rate of 66 words per minute. Once the connection is established, users are billed 38 cents per minute.

Telex II. The Telex II system was formerly known as the **TWX network**. Using Telex II, a digital message can be sent to any subscriber via the more than 35,000 teleprinters on the network; Telex II allows the same message to be sent simultaneously to as many as 100 different addresses. It uses the ASCII code and transmits at the rate of 110 words per minute. Telex II, available only in the United States, costs 43 cents per minute.

The principal difference between Telex I and Telex II is speed. Users are charged for a connection to the network based on the number of seconds on the line, which are billed in six-second increments. Telex I and Telex II are used by travel agents, importers and exporters, automobile rental agencies, and other organizations equipped to send and receive data with either Baudot or ASCII teleprinters.

Western Union has continued to expand its communications capability. After acquiring Telex and TWX from AT&T in the 1960s, Western Union became a major WAN. Originally its services were confined to moving data only. Now it is expanding its services. Telex I and Telex II subscribers are able to access extensive databases of information via their Telex terminals. Among the newer services offered is FYI Reports, which allows access to news, weather, sports reports, and data on stocks, currencies, commodities, and congressional actions. The News Alert service makes available major UPI worldwide news bulletins even before they appear in print. Fares and schedules for airlines and other forms of travel are also accessible through a database known as the Official Airline Guide (OAG).

MCI Mail

MCI Communications Corp. operates a wide area network, **MCI Mail**, designed to handle electronic mail. It enables system users to send letters, reports, contracts, and memos to other computer users or, via a link to the U.S. mails, to virtually anyone anywhere in the world.

MCI Mail consists of a group of communications services including:

1. *Electronic mail.* This service allows MCI Mail subscribers to send messages electronically to other MCI subscribers, using their PCs. These communications can be stored and read later or printed out immediately.
2. *Fax dispatch.* This service enables fax messages to be sent from a PC to any of 8 million fax machines located worldwide.
3. *Telex dispatch.* This service allows MCI subscribers to send a Telex message using a PC to more than 1.7 million Telex subscribers worldwide.
4. *Courier and postal delivery.* This service allows a message input via MCI Mail to be delivered to non-MCI subscribers, using hard copies delivered by either first-class mail or overnight couriers.
5. *Electronic bulletin boards.* This service allows thousands of individuals to access information on an MCI bulletin board, where the subscriber has access and can update the message instantly.

Mail sent through the MCI system is routed to various print centers that generate hard copies, using laser printers. These printouts are inserted into MCI envelopes and then delivered according to the option selected by the customer. Recipients who have MCI mailboxes and have been registered with MCI as customers can receive messages directly through their terminals.

SprintMail

Sprint Communications Co. operates a public message service network similar to MCI's. These services include **SprintMail**, which allows a customer to send, receive, forward, or print a message over the network. These messages can be routed from PC to PC or from a PC to a fax machine. SprintMail can also route messages through the Telex system or through the U.S. mail for delivery to customers not on the Sprint network.

AT&T EasyLink Services

EasyLink is an **electronic mail** service offered by AT&T that allows subscribers to use personal computers to send and receive messages. EasyLink can send electronic mail at speeds up to 9,600 bps. EasyLink allows users to bypass conventional mail and courier systems to route corporate communications, marketing, accounting, and purchasing data.

EasyLink messages can originate on a PC or computer terminal either domestically or internationally and then be routed through AT&T's worldwide Electronic Data Interchange (EDI) network. Messages can be output electronically and stored on a customer's computer, sent as a hard copy through the U.S. mail, or sent as a Telex or fax communication.

AT&T WAN FACILITIES

AT&T has been a leader in the development of WANs. AT&T initially pioneered land-based analog services known as AT&T Analog, Voice, and Data Service. This service, together with the AT&T Wideband Service, served as a prototype for their major digital and packet-switched network.

Let us review some of the major wide area network services developed by AT&T (discussed in detail in Chapter 7) because they provide the backbone for much of the digital transmissions as well as radio and television long distance communications. AT&T services are discussed because they are typical of those of other common carriers. However, the reader should be aware that both MCI and Sprint offer similar services and, in some instances, exceed AT&T's speed and capability.

ACCUNET T1.5 Service

The ACCUNET T1.5 Service is based on digital technology and permits a large volume of data to be transmitted. It uses high capacity 1.544 Mbps terrestrial digital circuits. It supports simultaneous user-specified applications and single-use applications users. The service is offered between AT&T communications offices and between an AT&T office and a subscriber's premises. A local channel can provide either 24 or 44 voice channels on one ACCUNET T1.5 service channel. These channels can serve digital, analog, or video applications.

ACCUNET Reserved 1.5 Service

The ACCUNET Reserved 1.5 Service is designed to support video teleconferencing. This WAN service enables businesses to conduct conferences electronically, using full motion, two-way video communications.

More than 32 public video teleconferencing nodes have been established, and more are planned. This WAN allows connection of picture processors. Businesses or individuals may reserve a conference room in any of the cities serviced. The teleconferencing is billed on the amount of time used while connected to the service. The reserved service is used for sales, marketing, advertising, and financial applications. Agencies and clients, customers and engineers, can all communicate with one another using video over the network.

ACCUNET Packet Service

The ACCUNET Packet Service is provided on the network for small-volume business users who do not need dedicated transmission lines. Data to be transmitted must meet the X.25 protocol standards. The ACCUNET Packet Service provides ports with transmission speeds of 4.8, 9.6, and 56 Kbps. This service is suited for financial institutions that must check credit or airline and travel agencies that do not need a dedicated digital circuit.

Dataphone Digital Service

The Dataphone Digital Service is designed to provide a reliable digital communications system, free of the problems found in analog transmissions. The service, available in approximately 100 U.S. cities, provides multipoint data transfer at rates of 2.4, 4.8, 9.6, and 56 Kbps. The service provides network timing and synchronization.

ACCUNET Switched 56 Service

The ACCUNET Switched 56 Service is provided between AT&T offices and customers' premises via dedicated lines. Data can be transmitted at speeds as high as 56 Kbps. The service is billed much like ordinary long distance, with a fixed monthly charge and usage based on time. The WAN utilizes DS1 circuits and 4ESS electronic switches. The network is totally terrestrial and is reached by dialing a 700 number. Among the network's applications are bulk data transfer, audio and video teleconferencing, and high-speed facsimile. The network extends to more than 64 cities.

SKYNET Satellite Service

The **SKYNET Satellite Service** provides transcontinental voice circuits, widespread broadcasting of television and radio programs, data transmissions at speeds up to 1.5 Mbps, and teleconferencing. The WAN is accessed through earth stations that lie within satellite coverage area. The SKYNET Satellite Service operates on satellites equipped with wideband transponders that are geared for high-speed data transfer.

FRAME RELAY WANS

In Chapter 10 we discussed the emerging packet-switching network. You will recall that a data packet containing information to be transmitted is forwarded over a communication line. A packet envelope and frame envelope, containing routing and message-handling data, are added to the data packet. These are routed over T1 circuits or the ISDN. At the receiving end, the packet envelope and frame envelope are removed, resulting in the delivery of the message.

While such systems are more efficient than separate voice and data dedicated circuits, they are slow and carry data routing overhead not required on dedicated circuits. They also do not use the full circuit bandwidth. These issues have led to the introduction of frame relay networks.

A **frame relay** network is constructed from special wideband circuits and high-speed switches able to route messages that conform to a frame relay standard. Figure 12.12 illustrates how a frame relay communication is handled. Note that only the physical and link layers are required; no network layer information, as in conventional X.25 packet switching, is needed.

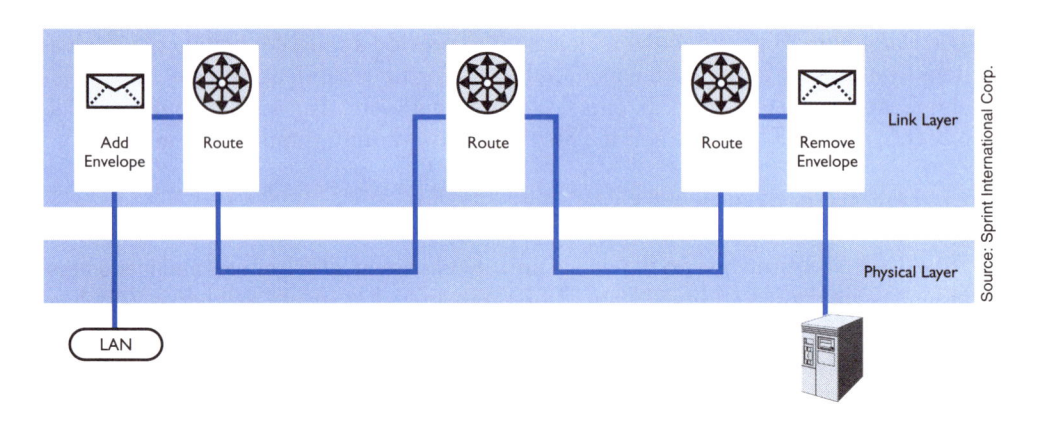

FIGURE 12.12 Frame Relay Communication

Messages sent over a frame relay network must emerge from an intelligent network, such as a LAN, and be received by a similar system. An envelope is added to the data frame, which includes a connection identifier and user information. The LAN puts this information in the envelope and then relays it from one switch to another until the envelope arrives at its destination.

Frame relay messages conform to a CCITT Q.922 frame format standard. This frame standard contains a frame check sequence, a data link connection identifier (address), and two other flags that are examined by a frame relay switch. (See Figure 12.13.)

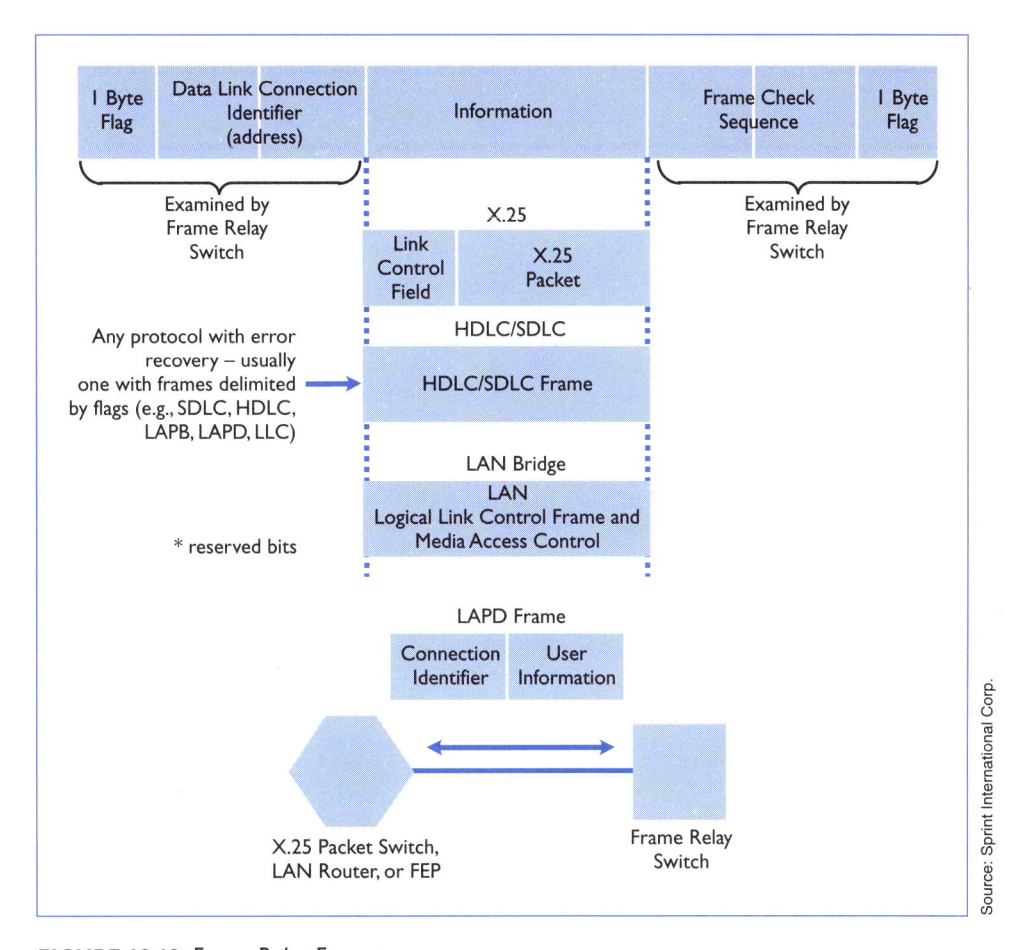

FIGURE 12.13 Frame Relay Format

FAST PACKET-SWITCHING WANS

Development is going forward on still faster packet-switching systems. Much promise is shown in the U.S. Sprint Fast Packet Switching network, a system built on a group of fast packet multiplexers. (See Figure 12.14.) When fully implemented, fast packet switching will route voice, video, and data over a single wideband circuit.

FIGURE 12.14
Fast Packet-Switching Network

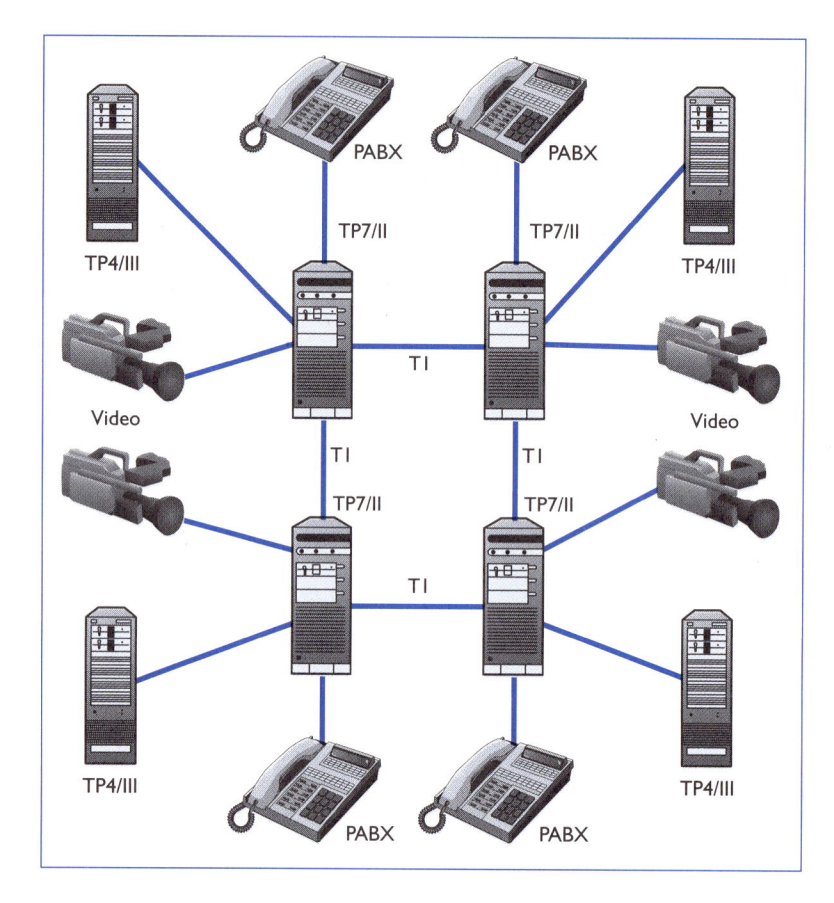

    Fast packet-switched networks eliminate the delay and overhead involved in processing frame address and routing information. They omit error-checking routines for voice and data because they expect these to be checked at the end points. This system promises cost and speed benefits and is particularly suited for LAN-to-LAN communications, where much of the error checking and processing can be handled at each end of the circuit rather than on the circuit itself.

PRIVATE NETWORKS

    Many organizations prefer to operate their own networks rather than use public facilities. These organizations have installed facilities not available to outside users that move data between company nodes. These private networks use public network links only to expand their capability. They are constructed from communications links, computers, switching equipment, and satellite facilities that route data throughout an organization. Boeing Company, Ford Motor Company, the Internal Revenue Service, and others maintain private networks. Many of these networks stem from early in-house computer systems that have been expanded to include both voice and digital data transmission capability.

ARPANET

A discussion of private networks would not be complete without reference to **ARPANET**, an important precursor to Internet. ARPANET, one of the original private networks, was placed in operation in 1968. ARPANET was a packet-switched digital system funded by the U.S. Department of Defense, Advanced Research Projects Agency (ARPA). Its purpose was to tie together host computers at many government installations and research institutions around the country. ARPANET then expanded to include hundreds of host computers, not only in the United States, but also abroad. Through ARPANET, research institutions such as UCLA, Stanford, and MIT were able to communicate with government agencies, as well as interface with the public networks described above. Today this service has been replaced by Internet.

SABRE

The **Semi-Automatic Business Research Environment (SABRE)** system was developed by American Airlines. Its purpose is to link thousands of ticket agents, travel agents, and reservation services into a ticketing network. SABRE is based on SNA and links more than 19,000 travel agents. United Airlines has a similar system called APOLLO.

SABRE has now been expanded to enable agents to book hotel and motel rooms, auto rentals, and theater tickets. At the center of SABRE are four IBM mainframe computers located in Tulsa, Oklahoma. They support approximately 65,000 terminals that are connected by leased lines provided by AT&T. These lines can move data at speeds of up to 56 Kbps. American Airlines is expanding the system so that it can utilize packet-switching technology.

Boeing Network

Boeing Company is a large diversified aircraft manufacturer with plants located all over the country. Boeing developed the **Boeing Network Architecture (BNA)** to integrate its mainframe computers, minicomputers, and numerous microcomputers into an extensive private network. The present BNA system incorporates elements of both SNA and DECnet into an overall architecture. The Boeing system includes a number of databases, large computers, terminals, LANs, and even metalworking machines and robots. (See Figure 12.15.) The system enables engineers and managers to access databases and to transfer data as well as visuals and graphics to any location throughout the organization.

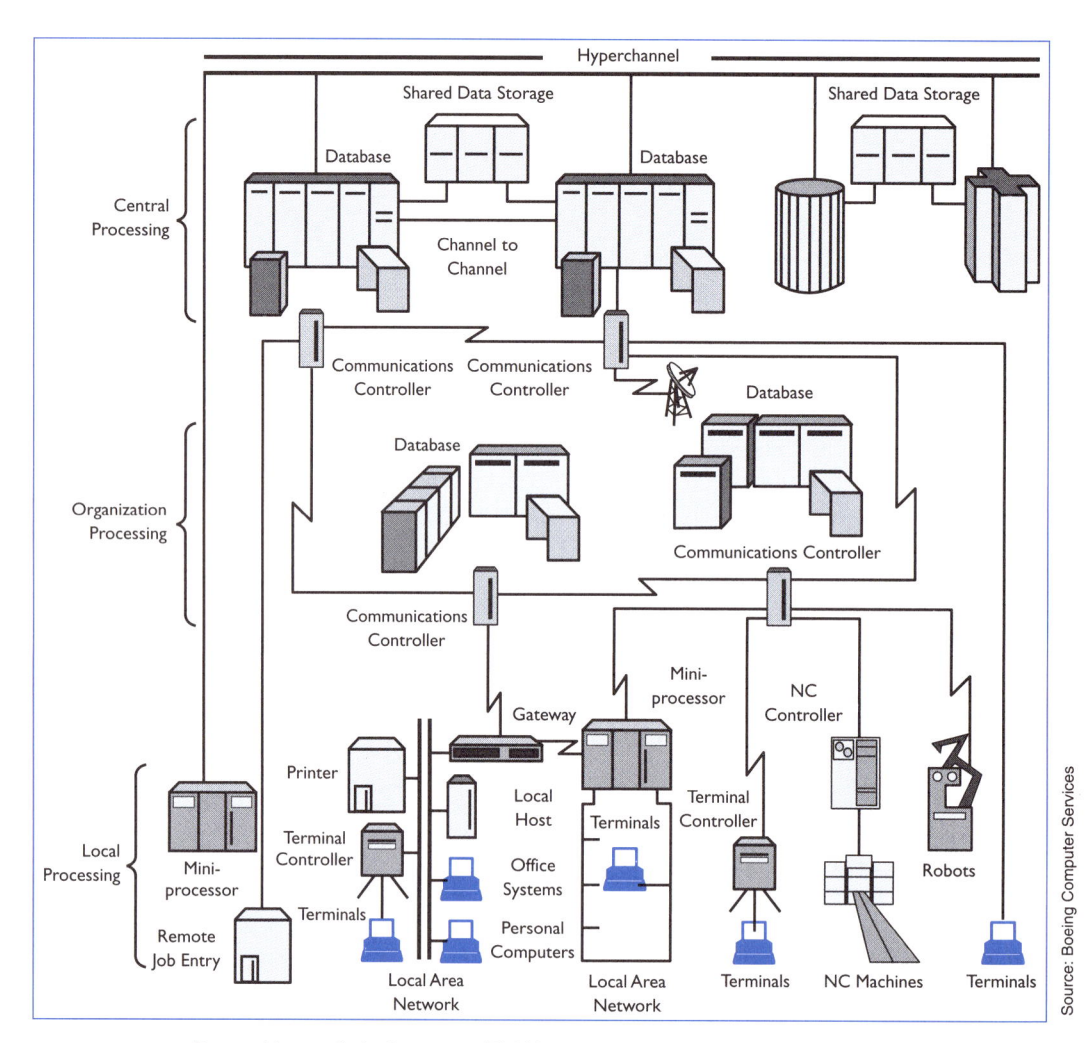

FIGURE 12.15 Boeing Network Architecture (BNA)

Bank of America Network

Bank of America operates an extensive network of 1,100 branch banks. It is the largest chain in the nation; it has designed a private network that ties together thousands of automatic teller terminals, in-house computers, remote terminals, and other facilities. Bank of America's data center has several IBM mainframes that serve the network.

Bank of America supports its **International Banking System (IBS)** through its privately owned network. This system links regional banking centers all over the world. It will soon enable personal computer users to do their banking in foreign countries and route communications through the bank's packet-switched network.

GLOBAL VIRTUAL PRIVATE NETWORKS

In the private networks just described, dedicated facilities—exclusive switches, circuits, and communications hardware—that are owned or exclusively assigned to a system are required. This results in a costly system, particularly when there are periods when only a minimum amount of traffic is being moved.

An alternative to the dedicated system is the **Global Virtual Private Network (GVPN)**. A GVPN may be either domestic or worldwide. It possesses all the capabilities of a private network except that data moves over public facilities. A virtual network is created rather than a physical network. Devices are not physically linked over dedicated circuits; instead, they rely on existing T1 and fiber-optic facilities. Sprint's GVPN provides customers with a worldwide network at a reduced cost and allows expandability without requiring installation of dedicated circuits.

In this chapter we have reviewed a wide variety of public and private networks that move data without substantially changing or enhancing their form. In Chapter 13 we will look at still another group of networks. These not only move data, but enhance them and provide processing and database services as well.

SUMMARY

Wide area networks (WANs) tie together computers and workstations that are located over great distances. They may be private or publicly owned; they move data without any significant enhancements. *Point-to-point* networks link two distant points. *Multipoint* systems enable terminals to be linked from several distant points. *Multiprocessor* networks are composed of *nodes* that link many computers and terminals into a system.

IBM's *SNA* serves as a model for many networks and uses *voice grade* and *DDD* circuits. The *X.25 protocol* may be used to interface computers to the SNA network. The SNA layers include *physical*, *data link*, *path*, *transmission*, and *data flow control*, as well as *presentation* and *transaction services*. Microcomputers, midsize, and mainframe computers may communicate over SNA without requiring master control.

The *DECnet* is a wide area network developed by Digital Equipment Corp. DECnet may include *local area systems (LAS)* in its architecture. Workstations may access the network through VAX computers.

Microcomputers are widely used on networks because of their low cost and small size. These machines may be integrated into WANs using IBM's *token-ring* network.

Telex and *TWX* were examples of early switched digital networks. AT&T and others offer a variety of WAN services. These include *ACCUNET T1.5*, *ACCUNET Reserved 1.5*, *ACCUNET Packet*, and *Dataphone Digital Service*, as well as *ACCUNET Switched 56 Service*. These network services are based on terrestrial links.

A *frame relay* is constructed from special wideband circuits and high-speed switches able to route messages that conform to a frame relay standard.

Fast packet-switched networks eliminate the delay and overhead involved in processing frame address and routing information. They omit error-checking routines for voice and data because they expect these to be checked at the end points.

Private WAN networks now in service include *ARPANET, SABRE, Boeing Network Architecture,* and the *Bank of America's International Banking System network.* Virtual private networks offer exclusive connectivity without dedicated lines.

EXERCISES

1. Contrast three generic wide area network configurations.
2. Describe the seven layers in the SNA.
3. Prepare a short summary that describes the DECnet system.
4. Describe message service routing options.
5. Describe AT&T's ACCUNET T1.5 service.
6. Discuss different types of packet-switching networks.
7. Write a short summary of the ARPANET system.
8. Write a short summary of the SABRE system.
9. Write a short summary of the BOEING network.
10. Write a short summary of the Bank of America network.

HANDS-ON PROJECTS

- Obtain a statewide road map and draw several point-to-point networks on it.
- Obtain a statewide road map and draw a multipoint network on it.
- Obtain a map of the United States and draw a multiprocessor network on it.
- Visit a local data center, such as one on your campus, and determine what types of networks link the center to other systems.
- Visit a travel agent's office and discuss the SABRE, APOLLO, or other network. Prepare a short report on your conclusions.

CASE SOLUTION
LOGAN ELECTRONICS

COMMUNICATIONS IN ACTION

Logan Electronics has developed a distributed data processing system (see Figure 12.16) to replace its centralized system. Local plants were equipped with LANs, which tied together terminals, printers, and disk storage devices at each facility. Gateways and bridges were provided so that each division could access other networks and other LANs in the company. Each division then maintained its own databases, local files, and processing capability.

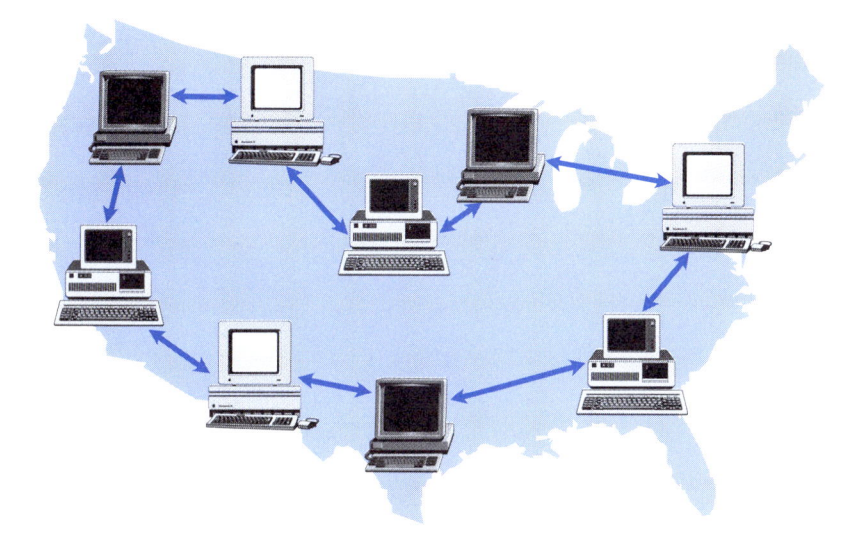

FIGURE 12.16 Logan's Distributed Data Processing System

A much smaller mainframe is now required at the central facility. The staff has been relocated to data processing operations at other plants.

The decentralized system allows widely separated divisions in the company to share data processing facilities and databases in other divisions. Now most data processing is done locally, eliminating the need for accessing the large central mainframe for many applications.

Logan has done a good job of communications planning. It has established protocols and standards for its databases and distributed data processing operations. As new divisions are opened, more computers and local area networks can be installed to meet local needs. These computers can share printers and communications facilities with other divisions or access the mainframes. As a result, the new system provides for not only expansion, but also security. The distributed databases can be accessed only through the proper user code and identification numbers.

The new decentralized system is less dependent on the central mainframes, reducing the possibility of a total systems failure. Even when circuits to the mainframe fail, local divisions can still handle their data processing needs. The costs of operating the mainframes have been reduced, and each plant is better able to address its own unique data processing needs.

VALUE-ADDED NETWORKS

LEARNING OBJECTIVES

After studying this chapter, you should be able to:

- Describe value-added networks (VANs)
- Describe network architecture
- Describe the Tymnet VAN
- List major public data networks
- Describe network control centers
- Discuss the various information services

COMMUNICATIONS
IN ACTION

CASE PROBLEM
WORLDCOM

VALUE-ADDED NETWORK

Worldcom had its early beginnings as a data processing service bureau offering remote data processing services to local users. (See Figure 13.1.) Jobs were sent to Worldcom by courier or over local dial-up telephone lines. Initially, the company offered just remote computing to customers; later it offered access to databases of proprietary information on its extensive collections of programs and software.

FIGURE 13.1
Service Bureau Operations

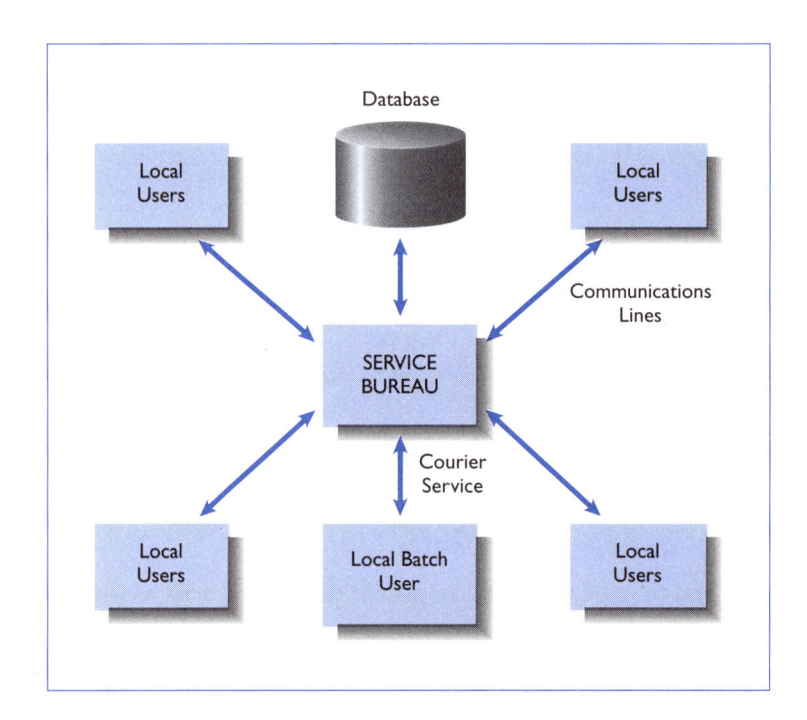

Today Worldcom is a worldwide company that serves thousands of users. Some of its customers are small businesses that utilize its large computers. Others purchase computer time and use many of Worldcom's specialized programs to solve engineering, financial, and business problems. Still others use Worldcom as a communications link to access other computers all over the country. Some of Worldcom's customers have extensive proprietary databases that they make available to other organizations through Worldcom. Thus Worldcom is a public access network, incorporating both wide area communications and value-added services.

Worldcom must have a communications network that allows it to offer its services worldwide. It must communicate with many different types of computers, terminals, and data transmission devices. In addition, it must provide packet-switching access to extensive databases and a high level of security to its users. The goal of offering these services economically can be achieved only through a carefully planned and integrated worldwide network.

What communications facilities would you recommend? Refer to the end of this chapter to see how the management at Worldcom solved the problem.

IN A CHICAGO suburb, a student accesses an encyclopedia through his personal computer and completes his homework assignment without going to a library. In San Diego, a young couple, using their microcomputer, orders theater tickets for a play they wish to see when they visit New York. In Denver, a retired teacher who enjoys dabbling in the stock market checks the earnings records of hundreds of stocks without leaving her home. These are examples of communications and value-added networks (VANs) in use.

In this chapter we will study publicly accessed databases and VANs. Through the use of VANs, people access data stored in computers around the world, sending messages and routing mail electronically. They do this by making use of computer facilities at distant points and a rapidly expanding network of communications circuits that are being installed parallel to existing telephone lines.

This chapter discusses SprintNet, Tymnet, Uninet, CompuServe, and other value-added networks. The services these networks offer have become increasingly important to business, government, and education users, as well as private citizens.

THE CHANGING NETWORK ENVIRONMENT

For many decades, digital data transmission was handled almost exclusively over AT&T's Telex and TWX circuits. AT&T offered these services, enabling messages to be sent between Teletype machines. Before the 1950s, this system routed data without computers and simply connected one terminal to another, using lines reserved for data transmission. There was no enhancement of the message, merely a relaying of text from one point to another, handled through the **AT&T switched digital network.** Although systems such as these were relatively slow, sending information at only 66 words per minute, they were adequate for many companies because few required access to databases.

When organizations first began to use computers on a large scale in the 1950s and 1960s, many turned to the already in-place public switched voice telephone network operated by AT&T for service. Using modems, early computer networks were able to route information over voice-grade phone lines, bypassing the Telex and TWX switched digital networks.

The use of the AT&T switched network to transmit modulated carriers was satisfactory when a relatively small amount of data was being sent. Many organizations still use modems and modulated carriers for their communications. In the last decade or so, organizations have turned to digital, rather than analog, transmission and, as we have seen in previous chapters, have begun to rely on packet switching. With the widespread use of computers has come a reliance on databases and networks that not only move data but enhance its characteristics.

INDUSTRY DEREGULATION

In the 1960s, changes in **regulatory policies** and rules promulgated by the FCC led to the development of new, privately owned communications networks, which grew along with the existing AT&T switched network. AT&T was forced to sell TWX and Telex, which then began operation under the control of Western Union. In 1975, General Telephone and Electric (GTE) introduced the first public access **digital data network**, known as **Telenet**. Telenet allowed users to access its private facilities to have digital data routed inexpensively all over the country, as well as to other countries. Telenet was purchased by U.S. Sprint and became known as SprintNet. McDonnell-Douglas, through its network of communications facilities, made Tymnet available.

In 1976, the FCC changed the rules regarding common carriers. After this ruling, private organizations were no longer constrained from reselling services. They could either set up their own networks or multiplex AT&T lines and sell services to others. This decision spurred the growth of networks that not only move data but offer database services, information processing, and access to enormous files of proprietary information. Today, there are many companies, including Uninet, MCI Communications, U.S. Sprint, and IBM, that have developed networks that parallel AT&T's switched analog network.

The availability of these alternative networks has spawned a new generation of services available to business, education, and government agencies, as well as private individuals. Because it is now economically feasible to utilize these networks, individuals and businesses can access local telephone numbers to reach computers holding extensive databases and offering a variety of services from distant points. In particular, packet switching has become the vehicle that makes possible electronic mail and access to financial databases, information services, national news wires, as well as hotel, motel, airline, and theater reservation systems.

NETWORKS DEFINED

A **value-added network (VAN)** is a common-carrier facility available to the public that is able to send and receive information over publicly and privately owned systems. These networks, capable of routing messages through switching equipment, provide computer services and access to databases. (See Figure 13.2.) They not only transmit information, but also change its characteristics or enhance it; this is the feature that distinguishes VANs from WANs. WANs transmit data essentially unchanged, while VANs provide supplementary databases, electronic mail, and numerous other features.

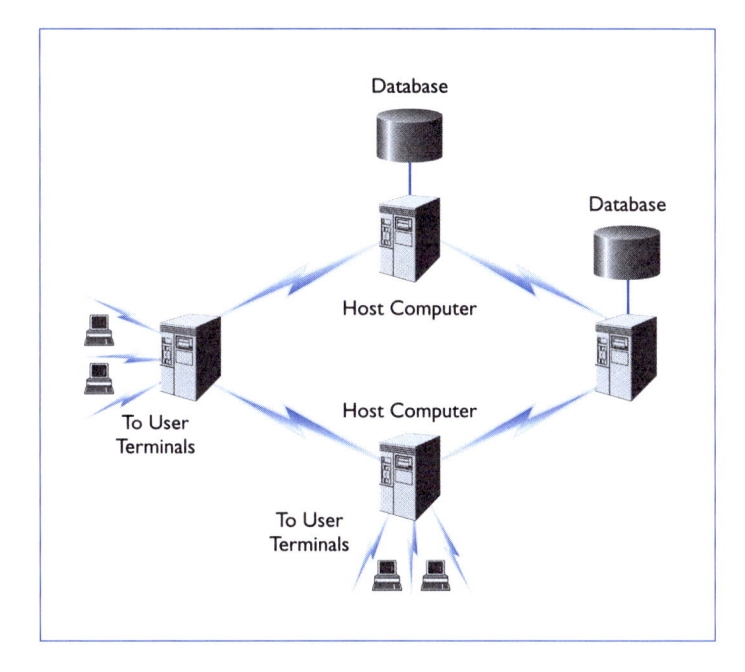

FIGURE 13.2 Value-Added Network (VAN)

VANs have grown into a multibillion dollar industry. SprintNet is a packet-switched VAN whose revenues exceed $90 million. SprintNet routes billions of characters over its lines each month. The total packet-switched VAN industry exceeds $220 billion, and the volume of traffic has continued to grow at a significant rate each year. Thousands of companies now rely on CompuServe, Dow Jones News/Retrieval, and the Official Airline Guide/Electronic Edition (OAG) to provide them with information ranging from stock market quotations and the price of sow belly futures through to the departure time of flights between Frankfurt and Geneva.

By far the largest user of VANs is the time-sharing market. (See Figure 13.3.) Time sharing consists of remote-terminal users who access large central or host computers for data processing. Fifty percent of the traffic handled by VANs involves remote time-sharing users. A second major component of the market consists of users who seek to access remote databases. These people use such databases as the Dow Jones News/Retrieval and H & R Block's CompuServe. (See Figure 13.4.)

Another growing segment of VANs consists of private organizations that operate their own networks, which are not accessible to the public. These organizations access databases, use remote processing, or maintain distributed data processing systems. These elements are linked through a VAN communications system. Examples of firms in this category are American Airlines, Bank of America, Aetna Casualty and Surety Company, Ford Motor Company, and the Internal Revenue Service.

FIGURE 13.3
Network Market Segments

- Time-sharing 50%
- Database 15%
- Communications 7%
- Other 28%

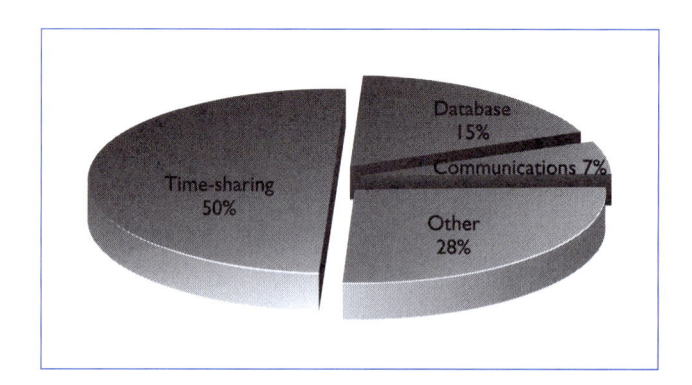

FIGURE 13.4
Major Database Vendors

LEADING ON-LINE INFORMATION COMPANIES

Excluding Providers of Stock Quotes and Other Trading Information

Company (Owner)	Number of Subscribers as of 1992
CompuServe	903,000
Prodigy	715,500
GEnie	260,000
Ziff Desktop	225,000
American Online	156,549
Videoway	154,000
Delphi	71,000 (Estimate)
The Source	—
U.S. Videotel	8,000
The Wall	7,000
Odyssey Online	5,000
Star Text	4,000
101 Online	300
Total	2,509,349

Courtesy of Digital Information Group

MAJOR VANs

The demand by business, industry, and government for information services has continued to grow over the past several decades, with increasing reliance on public networks. The advent of packet-switched networks has further stimulated this growth because they provide low-cost access to databases located at distant points.

Prior to the availability of VANs and packet switching, databases at distant points were usually accessed through expensive toll calls over analog or digital networks. For example, a user in Los Angeles who sought access to information stored on a computer in Virginia would need to place a long distance call. Today, virtually all VANs serve customers through a packet-switching system that provides access through local telephone numbers.

In this arrangement, a user in Los Angeles dials a local telephone number and is connected to a packet-switching network center. The user then accesses distant systems and uploads or downloads lengthy files through the packet-switching network. This offers substantial cost savings because many users share the same circuit. Each may pay only a nominal network connection charge of $5 or $10 per month. It is this availability of entry points through local calls that makes distant information services and databases so attractive.

Let us look at some of the major publicly accessed data networks that offer local access and support a variety of information services, discussed later in this chapter.

SprintNet

SprintNet was one of the first publicly accessed packet-switching networks to come on the scene. Started in 1975 as Telenet, it was owned and operated by General Telephone and Electric (GTE). Telenet began by serving only seven cities; it has since been purchased by U.S. Sprint and expanded its scope to include links in over 250 cities in more than 40 countries.

SprintNet is a VAN that is used by time-share companies, colleges, computer service bureaus, and other organizations to access remote databases or mainframe computers. The SprintNet system is made up of a group of major circuits known as the backbone.

Up to 56 Kbps of data can be moved on each circuit between regional centers. The circuits that interconnect various cities are controlled by switching nodes. These nodes interpret and direct the flow of data throughout the system, which is monitored at the network control center in Vienna, Virginia. (See Figure 13.5.) Each switching node is a regional distribution network that can move data at speeds of up to 9,600 bps or more. (See Figure 13.6.)

FIGURE 13.5
SprintNet Control Center

FIGURE 13.6
SprintNet Architecture

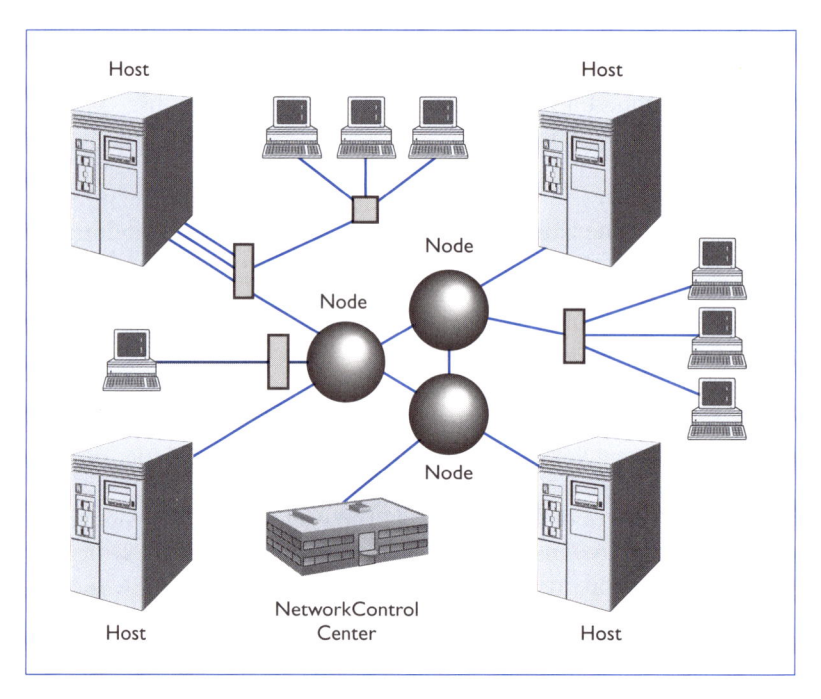

Many users maintain extensive private networks that are then connected to SprintNet. These systems are known as **hybrid networks**. In the hybrid network, shown in Figure 13.7, a user-owned system of computers, terminals, and communications equipment is treated as an entity. By connecting to the SprintNet system, any terminal or computer in the privately owned hybrid network can access outside systems.

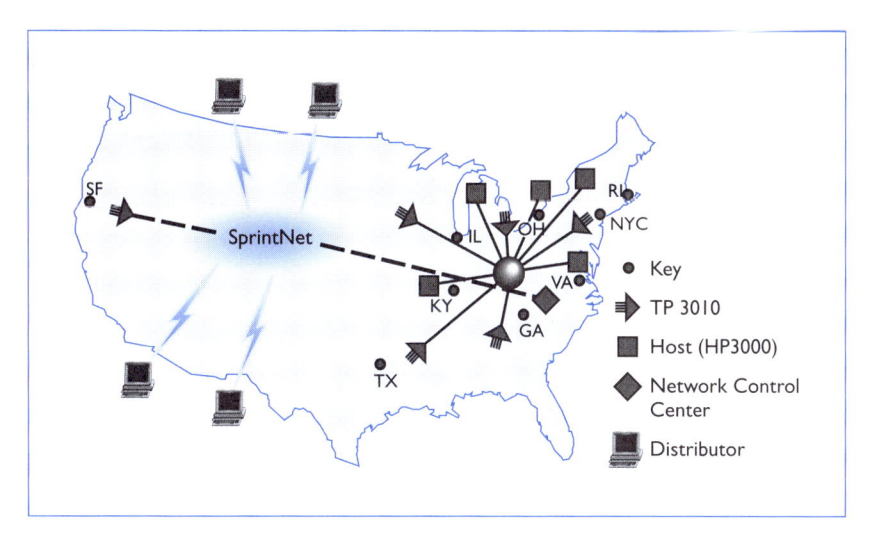

FIGURE 13.7 Hybrid Network

SprintNet has established a rate structure based on the type of access and speed of service. (See Figure 13.8.) Local dial-in service, using a low-speed device running at 110 to 1,200 bps, is charged an hourly rate of $3.90. A dedicated access facility, where the user has a direct connection to the SprintNet network at speeds of 9,600 bps, can cost as much as $1,400 per month.

These fees are network access charges only; charges are also assessed for the services provided at the other end of the line. Users who access databases, large host computers, or other facilities are also charged for central processor time, access to the database, and data storage and manipulation.

SprintNet is known as a VAN because of the enhanced services it offers, one of which is SprintMail. SprintMail, started in 1980, enables messages to be transmitted from one point in the network to another. These messages can be saved, forwarded at a later date, or sent to many addresses simultaneously. Users can access the SprintMail system through desktop or laptop computers, shown in Figure 13.9.

FIGURE 13.8 SprintNet Rate Schedule

DATA CALL PLUS®—ASYNCHRONOUS SERVICE

	Dial Location	Hourly Charge Standard	Hourly Charge 1 Year Arrangement
300–9600 bps:	Class A Access Center	$7.50	$6.00
	Class B and C Access Centers	$9.00	$7.50
	In-WATS	$15.00	$14.00

Traffic charges are included for 300 to 9600 bps.

GLOBAL DATA CONNECTION
(Dedicated X.25 Connection)

Speed of Service	Monthly Charge	Installation Charge
9600 bps	$900	$1,200
19200 bps	$1,500	$1,500
56/64 kbps	$2,475	$1,500
112/128 kbps	$3,000	$1,500
224/256 kbps	$3,525	$1,500

All Global Data Connector charges are estimates. Actual charges are dependent on local access and install charges from the local teleco.

Courtesy of U.S. Sprint

Other SprintNet services include SprintMail Fax, which allows a user to send a fax directly from a PC or terminal via SprintMail to any Group III fax machine. The system includes broadcast capability where multiple fax messages can be sent simultaneously. It automatically retries a transmission if a fax machine is busy. Each fax message is sent with a cover page that includes address information and an attention line, ensuring that the message will be routed to the proper person.

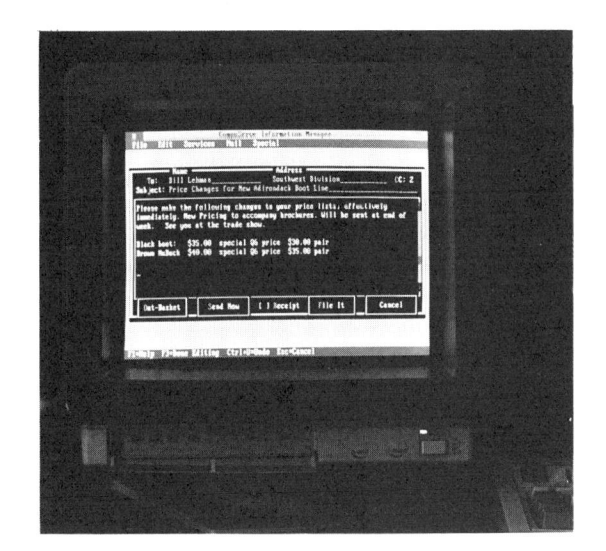

FIGURE 13.9
Accessing SprintMail

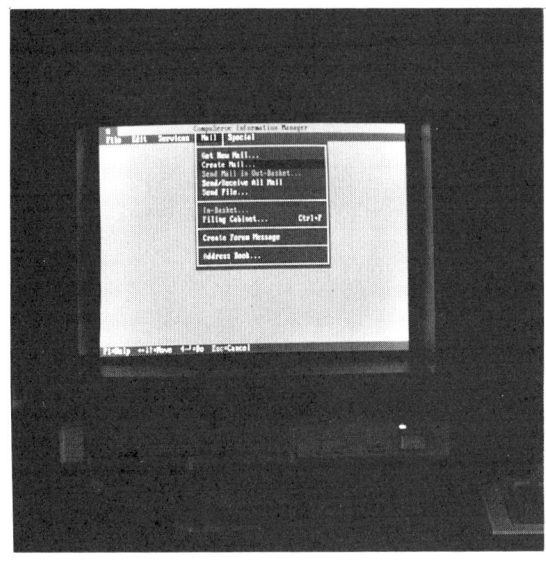

SprintMail Newsclips provides customers with access to 6,000 news stories each day that are obtained from domestic and international news wire services. It brings subscribers current news articles that are sent over United Press International (UPI), Federal News Service, Kyodo News Agency, and others. News stories are delivered directly to the customer's private mail box. Customers can filter the news feed and receive only those stories that match their predefined requirements.

Tymnet

Another major VAN that has continued to expand its packet-switching network is **Tymnet**. Tymnet serves 500 U.S. cities and more than 60 foreign countries. It was developed in 1969 by Tymshare, Incorporated to serve its remote computer users. In 1972, Tymnet opened its network to other organizations. In 1977, it became an FCC-regulated specialized common carrier. Tymnet was purchased in 1989 by British Telecommunications PLC.

The basic building block of the Tymnet packet-switched network is the **node**. In Tymnet there are more than 1,400 nodes that include communications switching computers. The nodes are interconnected by leased lines, microwave links, and satellite circuits. These circuits move data at speeds of 4.8 to 56 Kbps. The entire network is controlled by a software program known as the Network Supervisor, which monitors the system, balances loads, and is in active control at all times.

Nodes that offer access to customers are called Tymsats. (See Figure 13.10.) Tymsats allow users to send data from synchronous, asynchronous, and non-ASCII terminals. (See Figure 13.11.) The network accepts the CCITT X.25 standard as well as numerous other protocols. Terminals can be connected to the system through either dial-up or leased lines, or even directly with EIA-232-D cable. (See Figure 13.12.)

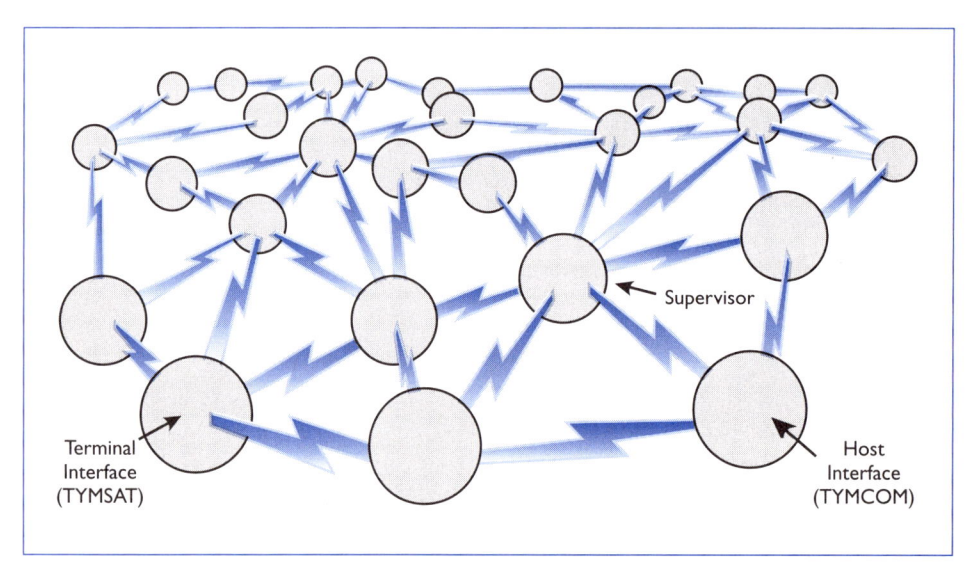

FIGURE 13.10 Tymnet Network Components

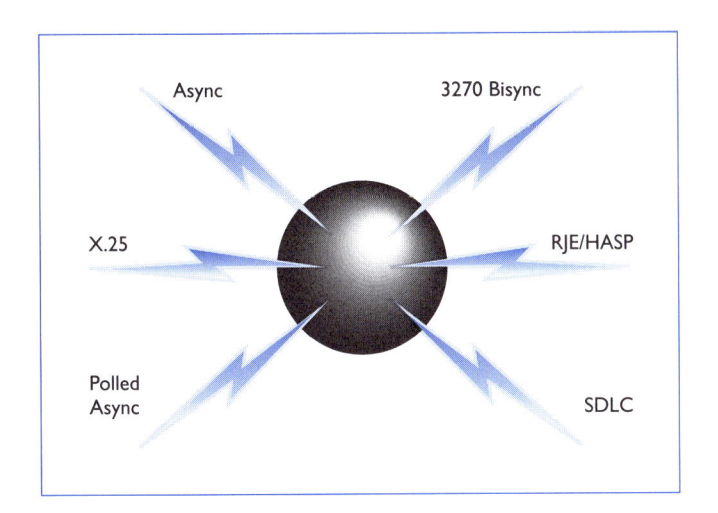

FIGURE 13.11
Tymnet Terminal Interfaces

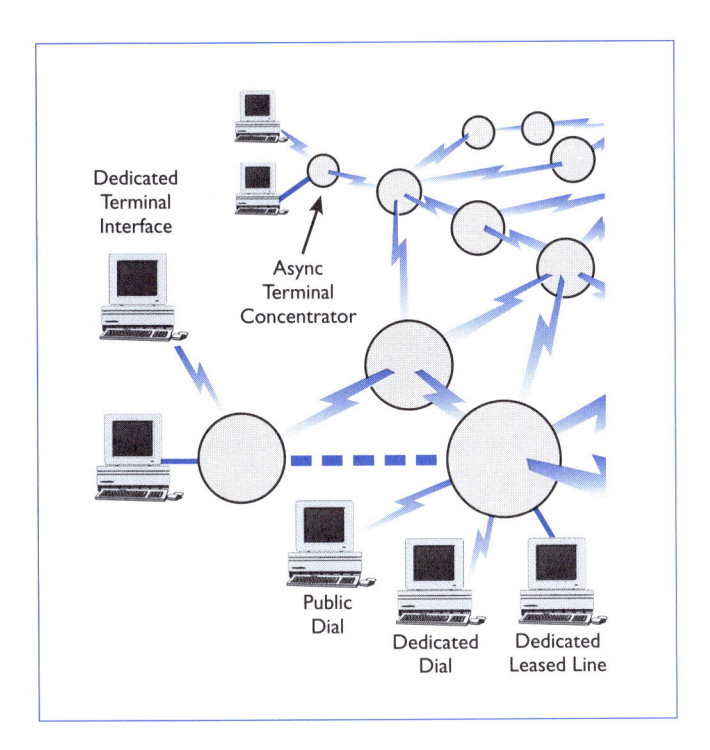

FIGURE 13.12
Tymnet Terminal Connections

Users may also connect their own host computer to these nodes through interfaces known as Tymcoms, also shown in Figure 13.10. They can access the system using the X.25 or other protocol through either dial-up or leased lines.

Tymnet offers users its Tym electronic mail service. Tym allows letters, reports, and messages to be sent through the communications network from terminal to terminal without ever using paper or generating hard copies. However, its TymGram service enables users to send messages that are routed electronically through the network and, on receipt, are converted into paper documents. These are sent to the recipient by first class mail.

The **X.PC protocol** used by Tymnet allows personal computer users to access the VAN through local dial-up lines. This service allows messages to be sent to thousands of destinations at speeds of up to 2,400 bps. The X.PC protocol is based on the CCITT X.25 standard.

Once users have accessed the network, they may be connected not only to other terminals, but to remote databases as well. For instance, the Dow Jones News/Retrieval system offers much historical and current economic news. It contains portfolio reports, ranks stocks by industry groups, provides weekly economic updates, and houses a collection of thousands of research articles. (See Figure 13.13.) These and other services are all accessed through the packet-switched network.

FIGURE 13.13
Dow Jones Reports

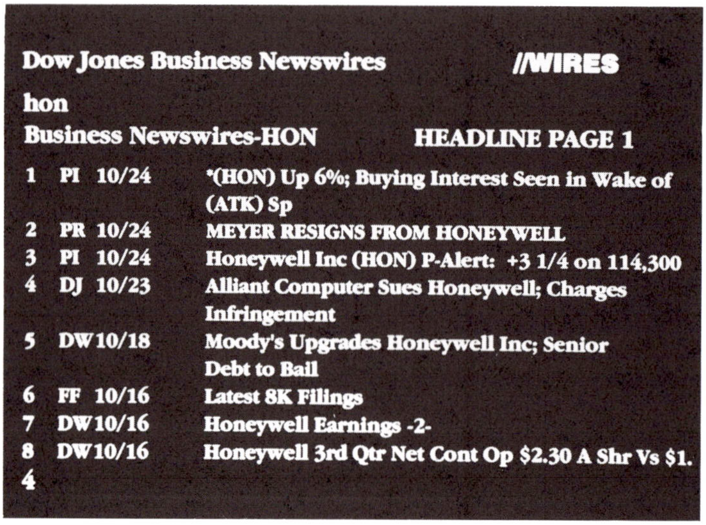

Uninet

Uninet, operated by United Telecommunications, is the third-ranking packet-switched network in the United States. It evolved from the private network created by Control Data Corporation to serve its computer time-share users. Uninet now serves more than 275 cities in the United States. The network is composed of a group of regional nodes, which are the switching centers through which packets are routed. The nodes are interconnected by digital telephone lines that can transmit up to 56 Kbps.

Devices ranging from 110 bps to 9,600 bps can access Uninet. Once a user has obtained access, he or she can route communications anywhere throughout the network. Uninet is designed to accept information using the X.25 standard and other protocols.

Uninet is one of the many VANs that allow access to CompuServe, a major database service owned and operated by H & R Block. CompuServe provides a variety of services, ranging from general news to a complete encyclopedia maintained online. InfoPlex is one of the resources CompuServe offers. InfoPlex customers are able to use the system's powerful word processing software to generate correspondence, memos, and reports. (See Figure 13.14.) These documents are edited and routed to distant points through Uninet or other public networks.

Other Networks

In addition to the networks discussed above, a number of other organizations have entered the marketplace. RCA Corporation offers its Cylix communications system to the public. Cylix operates a 56 Kbps satellite link between earth stations and its central control facility in Memphis, Tennessee. It also maintains thousands of miles of leased lines that can move data at speeds of up to 9,600 bps.

Another VAN is Automatic Data Processing's Autonet. Autonet operates more than 180 nodes, connected to more than 100 computers, all linked in a network. Its packet-switching capability accepts the X.25 and other protocols.

AT&T has operated a data transmission network for many years. Originally, it offered its **Dataphone Digital Service (DDS)**, a wide area network of high-speed digital circuits using special communications links. AT&T now offers its **ACCUNET Digital Service**, discussed in Chapter 12. The ACCUNET T1.5 Service provides a high-capacity, 1.544 Mbps, ground-based digital service for large-volume users. AT&T's ACCUNET Switched 56 Service provides transmission facilities at 56 Kbps. It is now available in dozens of cities across the country. This network is totally terrestrial and offers service only to the contiguous United States.

These and other networks are part of a rapidly growing system, available to the public, that moves billions of characters each month. They are operated alongside AT&T's conventional switched network.

Read Your Messages When it is Convenient for You. →	`InfoPlex 1B(43) -- Ready at 11:50 EST 15-Jan 94 on T11NYC`
	`1 Text file pending`
	`/retrieve`
	
	`Text file 201-44`
	`Subj: Monroe Electronics`
	
	`To: Judy Bennet`
	`Fr. John Malloy`
	
	As you know, I have been speaking with Ed Moeller of Monroe Electronics for the past few months. We are very close to finalizing the contract, But Ed would like to meet with you tomorrow, if possible, to discuss some final technical details. I realize this is very short notice, but if you could possibly fly in for the day, it would be greatly appreciated.
	
	We have a meeting scheduled for 10:00 A.M. at our office. Let me know if you can make it, and I will pick you up at the airport.
	
	Thanks,
	
	John
	
	`DETROIT for BENNET 10:35 EST 15-JAN-94 Text file 201-44`
	`[ Done ]`

Compose a Message by Simply Typing It. →	`/compose`
	`[ ready ]`
	
	John,
	
	I would be glad to meet with Ed Moeller and you tomorrow. Let me check on some flight schedules and I'll let you know when to pick me up. Looking forward to seeing you again.
	
	Judy Bennet

Send a Message Quickly and Easily, Knowing That Its Delivery is Guaranteed. →	`/store detroit`
	
	`Subj?: Monroe Electronics`
	
	`Text file 201-77 stored at 11:53 EST 15-Jan-94`

Conveniently Access the Forms Generator. →	`/form travel`

The Form Prompts for Specific Predefined Information. →	`Travel Request Form`
	`Name: Judy Bennet`
	`Department Number: 30`

Data Can Be Verified for Accuracy. →	`? Invalid reply, try again`
	`Department Number: 302`
	`Airline Reservations -`
	`Destination -`
	`To: Detroit, MI`
	`Fr: Chicago, IL`
	`Departure Date and Time: 16-Jan-94 around 8:03 A.M.`
	`Return Date and Time: 16-Jan-94 after 5:00 P.M.`
	`Prepaid or Delivered? Prepaid`
	`Rental Car? No`
	`All responses correct (Y or N)? Y`

Display the Form Once It Is Complete. →	`[ Done ]` `/type`

Information Is Sent in a Consistent Format With the Use of the Forms Feature. →	`                    Travel Reservations`
	`                    ------- ------------`
	`Name Judy Bennet                      Department Number: 302`
	
	`Destination`
	`-----------`
	
	`To: Detroit, MI`
	`Fr: Chicago, IL`
	
	`Departure Date and Time: 16-Jan-94 around 8:03 A.M.`
	`Return Date and Time: 16-Jan-94 after 5:00 P.M.`
	
	`Tickets will be: Prepaid`
	
	`Rental Car needed: No`

Information Can Be Sent on a Priority Basis. →	`% End of text`
	`/store/priority resv`
	`Subj?: Travel Reservations`
	`Text file 201-80 stored at 11:58 EST 15-Jan-94`

FIGURE 13.14 InfoPlex Word Processing System

INFORMATION SERVICES

Over the past decade, a number of companies have entered the **information services** marketplace. These firms provide a wide range of databases containing a vast amount of information available through various networks, such as Tymnet, SprintNet, and others. Companies such as CompuServe and the Dow Jones News/Retrieval have grown into extensive information networks. They focus on providing information or enhancing data, rather than merely moving messages from one point to another. These firms provide online databases covering business and financial markets, literature abstracts, book and software reviews, manufacturers' directories, and product literature.

In addition, they offer current news, as well as information on travel, weather, sports, home and family, health care, executive news services, and other topics. These systems host **electronic forums**, where users may communicate with one another on topics ranging from computer software and hardware to citizens' band radio and sports.

Another feature is their broadcast capability. Firms that seek to communicate technical information, product releases, or news bulletins to many customers or users rely on these services. VANs enable users to place a bulletin, menu, or file on the network, which can then be accessed worldwide. Such bulletins can be updated or revised instantaneously.

We shall close this chapter by reviewing some of the major information services available on VANs.

CompuServe

CompuServe is an online subscription information network. It offers its service through a packet-switching network with local telephone numbers available throughout the United States. To access CompuServe, a user dials a local number and logs on; the access is through a microcomputer and modem. First-time subscribers log on by typing AGREE. This prompts the system to provide a printed subscription agreement. Information services may be billed directly to the users through their Visa, MasterCard, or other credit card. Once logged into the system, the user is issued an exclusive password.

Service Rates. CompuServe users are charged for services based on the modem speed and the time of access. Evening or daytime rates are $6 per hour for a 300 baud connection. Rates for 1,200 or 2,400 baud modems are $12.50 per hour, day or evening. CompuServe provides service 24 hours a day. In addition to the connect rates above, a small communications surcharge is added.

There is no minimum usage charge if service is billed to a credit card. There is, however, a minimum monthly support fee of $1.50. Additional charges are incurred for electronic mail, financial stock market information, and reference to the Academic American Encyclopedia. Figure 13.15 on page 338 is a partial listing of some of the numerous information and online services available through CompuServe.

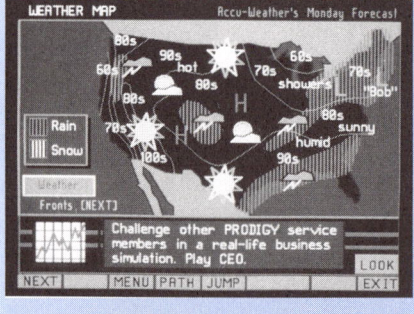

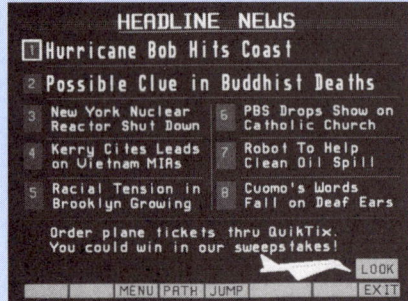

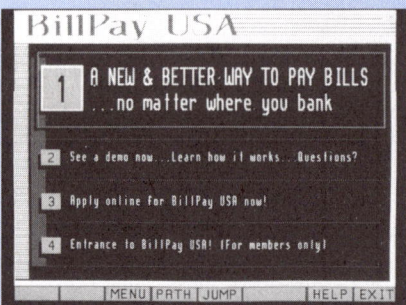

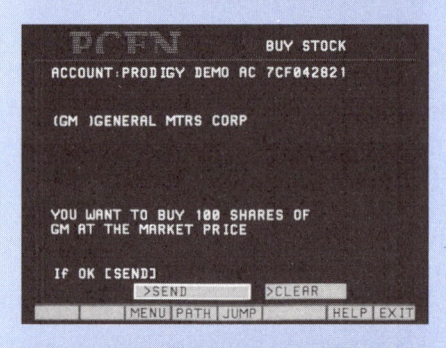

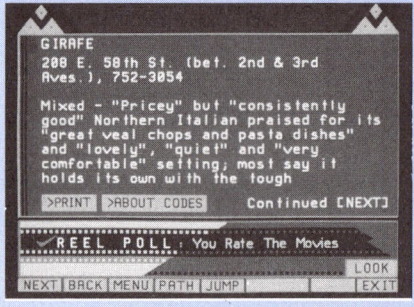

336 PART III / INTRODUCTION TO COMMUNICATIONS NETWORKS

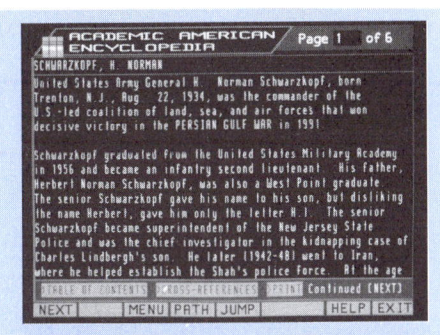

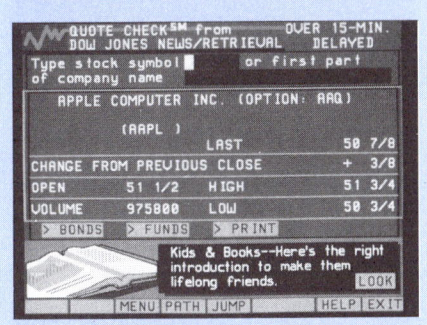

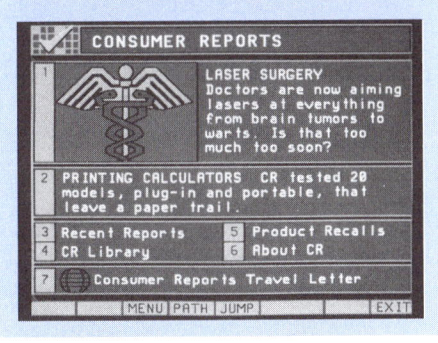

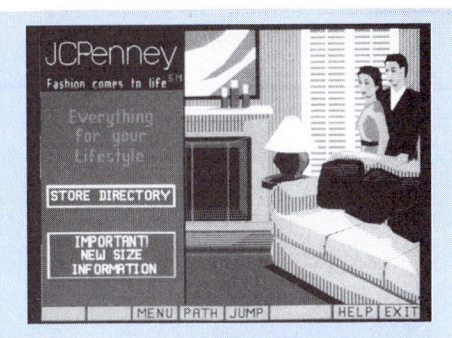

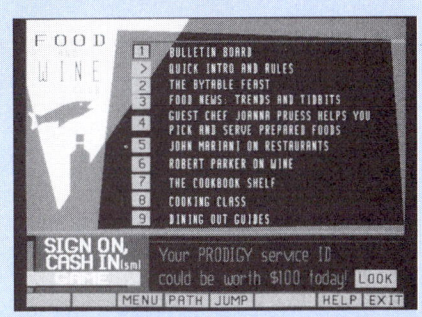

A SAMPLING OF PRODIGY SERVICES
Among the services available to Prodigy users are the headline news service, automatic bill payment, retail shopping, consumer reports, FTD florist, and E-mail.

Computer & Technology
Adobe Forum
Aldus Customer Service Forum
Amiga Arts Forum
Apple Macintosh Forum
Apple II/III Forums
Atari Users Network
Berkeley (Macintosh)
Berkeley (Windows)
Canon Support Forum
Commodore Arts & Games Forum
Compaq Connections
Computer Club Forum
Computer Language Forum
Dataquest Online
Desktop Publishing Forum
Digitalk Forum
Epson Forum
Executives Online
Graphics Developers
Graphics Support Forum
Hardware Forums
HP Peripherals Forum
IBM Applications Forum
IBM Bulletin Board
IBM New Users/Fun Forum
Intel Software Developers Forum
Logitech Forum
Lotus Spreadsheet Forum
Macintosh Developers Forum
Macintosh Hardware Forum
Macintosh New Users & Help Forum
Microsoft Access Forum
Microsoft Applications Forum
Microsoft Connection
Microsoft Windows New User Forum
Multimedia Forum
Norton/Symantec Forum
Online Today
Quick Pictures Forum
Software Forums
Tandy Users Network
Toshiba Forum
WordPerfect Users Forum
The World of Lotus

Aviation Services
NWS Aviation Weather
Weather Maps
Aviation Forum
EMI Aviation Services

Communication
CompuServe Classified
CompuServe Mail
CONGRESSgrams
Directory of Members
CB Forum

News, Weather, Sports
AIDS News Clips
AP Online
Assoc. Press Sports Wire
The Business Wire
Executive News Service
Hollywood Hotline
NCAA Collegiate Sports
Outdoors News Clips
Sports Medicine
Weather
IQuest

New/Sports Forums
Automobile Forum
Comics Forum
Gardening Forum
Health/Fitness Forum
Literary Forum
Military/Vet. Forum
Music/Performing Arts Forum
Outdoor Forum
Photography Forum
SCI-FI/Fantasy Forum

Professional Forums
AMA Medical Forum
Broadcast Prof. Forum
Computer Training
Journalism Forum
PR/Marketing
Safetynet

Travel Service
ABC Worldwide Hotel Guide
Adventures in Travel
Dept. of State Advisor.
EAASY SABRE
Hotel Information
OAG Travel Service
VISA Advisors
West Coast Travel
Worldspan Travelshopper
Zagat Restaurant Survey

Travel-Related Forum
Florida Forum
Travel Forum

Shopping Services
Shoppers Advantage Club
SOFTEX Software Sales
The Electronic Mail
Selected Mall Merchandise
Adventure in Food
Air France
American Express
Books on Tape
Brooks Brothers
The Chef's Catalog
Coffee Anyone??
Computer Express
Contact Lens Supply
Dow Jones & Co.
Executive Stamper
Figi's Gifts
Hammacher Schlemmer
Holabird Sports Discounters
The Home Finder Service
JC Penney
K & B Camera Center
Land's End
Mac User
Narada Productions
PC Sources
The Travel Club
Windstar Cruises
Z Best Electronics

Courtesy of CompuServe

FIGURE 13.15 CompuServe Subject Index (Partial Listing)

Logging On. **Logging on** to CompuServe is a simple procedure. Figure 13.16 lists the seven steps, from setting up your computer and modem through obtaining the subscription agreement, used to log on to the system.

Starting Up WinCIM

Once you have completed all the necessary setup procedures, starting up WinCIM takes you directly to the initial desktop.

What you see when you start up

Besides a menu bar, the initial desktop includes a ribbon of icons. All but one of the icons are shortcuts for frequently-used WinCIM commands.

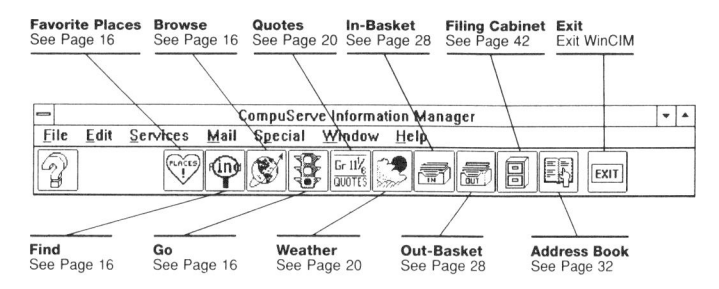

Favorite Places — See Page 16
Browse — See Page 16
Quotes — See Page 20
In-Basket — See Page 28
Filing Cabinet — See Page 42
Exit — Exit WinCIM

Find — See Page 16
Go — See Page 16
Weather — See Page 20
Out-Basket — See Page 28
Address Book — See Page 32

Automatic logon

Whenever you choose a function that requires connection to CompuServe, WinCIM connects you automatically. It is up to you to disconnect when you are through. (You can always disconnect by pressing [Control]+[D].)

> When you access some CompuServe services, the **EXIT** icon changes to a **LEAVE** icon (see the next page).

When the **question mark** icon is accessible, you can use it to get context-sensitive help information. When the icon isn't accessible, you can press [F1] or click a Help command button.

A Different Ribbon

Sometimes WinCIM uses a different Ribbon, with icons for commands that you can normally choose from the File menu:

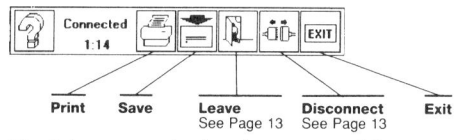

Print
Save
Leave — See Page 13
Disconnect — See Page 13
Exit

The **Print** command prints the contents of the active window. The **Save** command saves the window contents to a text file.

Courtesy CompuServe

FIGURE 13.16 Logging on to CompuServe Information Manager for Windows, WinCIM

Once signed on, the user may then go to various menus. The FIND command enables users to locate topics of special interest. The FIND command searches the CompuServe index and then lists related services.

The GO command bypasses the menu structure and goes directly to a particular file. Other CompuServe commands include:

Top	Return to the CompuServe top menu
Menu	Return to the previous menu
Next	Go to the next menu choice
EXIT	Return to a ! prompt
OFF	Disconnect from CompuServe

CompuServe can accommodate baud rates between 110 and 9,600. It can also handle different computer and terminal types, screen sizes, and number of lines per screen or characters per line. The system also includes an Online Q and A file that assists users with frequently asked questions.

Delphi

The **Delphi** information service provides information to thousands of subscribers located in more than 40 countries. The database contains business and financial news and analyses of the world currency market and more than 9,000 stocks and commodities. It offers information on tax laws, insurance, and travel (including flight and hotel reservation data), as well as an online encyclopedia and an online librarian. There is no minimum monthly fee, and customers are charged based on usage.

Dialog

The **Dialog** information service offers an extensive database on scientific, business, medical, and other disciplines. The system is actually made up of 75 different databases containing summaries of more than 35 million articles, reports, books, and conference papers.

Dialog users can monitor issues in more than 720 law journals or locate summaries of articles in more than 3,000 engineering and technical journals. The latest advances in medical, psychological, and biological research are covered.

Dow Jones News/Retrieval

The **Dow Jones News/Retrieval** information utility is aimed at the business world. Information is available on stock prices, earnings, economic forecasts, and historical trends. The service allows private investors to monitor daily stock market fluctuations. It enables them to manage their own portfolios and to make trading decisions based on current research reports. Reports written by market analysts, investment bankers, and stockbrokers are available on more than 3,000 companies and industries.

The Dow Jones News/Retrieval provides such information as price/earnings ratios, return on investment, and developing trends. In-depth coverage of specific companies or entire industries is available. The service also provides access to electronic versions of the *Wall Street Journal*, *Barron's*, and the *Washington Post*.

Subscribers to this service can also access the *Grolier's Academic American Encyclopedia*. The database includes reviews of the latest motion pictures and video tapes, as well as reviews of thousands of movie classics.

GEnie

The **GEnie** service, short for General Electric Network for Information Exchange, contains a wide variety of databases. It offers travel and shopping services, information on education and entertainment, financial services, and electronic mail. Users on this system may access American Airlines' EAASY SABRE Personal Travel Service, which reports on airline schedules and automobile and hotel rates. Stock market quotations and access to the Dow Jones News/Retrieval system are available through GEnie.

Official Airline Guide/Electronic Edition

The **OAG** is an extensive travel database that enables users to check airline fares, flight information, and dates and times prior to booking. The database contains information on more than 750 airlines worldwide and two million flights, which may be booked through the system. Hourly usage charges are waived for any session that results in a booking or cancellation of a previously booked flight.

The system is used this way: after logging on, the user is presented with a main menu, whose selections include tours, cruises, discount travel packages, frequent flyer information, and current airline schedules and fares. The Find a Fare option displays one-way and round trip fares for various destinations. The Find a Schedule option displays departure and arrival times, flight data, and more. The Check Seat Availability option indicates whether seats are available on specific flights.

In this chapter we have discussed some of the many private and public networks now in operation. We have also described how databases are accessed through networks, greatly adding to their utility and capability. Chapter 14, which opens a new section of this book, describes how companies plan and structure their communications systems to meet the needs of the changing business and organizational environment.

SUMMARY

In the 1960s, changes in *regulatory policies* and rules promulgated by the FCC led to the development of new, privately owned communications networks, which grew along with the existing AT&T switched network.

A *value-added network (VAN)* is a common-carrier facility available to the public that is able to send and receive information over publicly and privately owned systems. These networks, capable of routing messages through switching equipment, provide computer services and access to databases.

Prior to the availability of VANs and packet switching, databases at distant points were usually accessed through expensive toll calls over analog or digital networks. Today, virtually all VANs serve customers through a packet-switching system that provides access through local telephone numbers.

Electronic mail is routed through packet-switched networks. *SprintNet* and *Tymnet* are examples of major packet-switched networks. *Dataphone Digital Service (DDS)* is a data transmission network available from AT&T. *ACCUNET Digital Service* circuits move data at speeds of up to 1.544 Mbps.

CompuServe and *GEnie* are examples of online subscription *information networks*. They enable users to access databases and obtain current news, sports, financial, weather, and other information. Services are billed on *baud rate* and *connect time*. Other information services include *Delphi*, *Dialog*, and the *Official Airline Guide/Electronic Edition*.

The *Dow Jones News/Retrieval* information utility is aimed at the business world. Information is available on stock prices, earnings, economic forecasts, and historical trends. The service allows private investors to monitor daily stock market fluctuations.

EXERCISES

1. Describe the changing network environment.
2. Define a value-added network (VAN).
3. Describe the services offered by the Dow Jones News/Retrieval system.
4. Describe how information services are accessed.
5. Describe the CompuServe log-on procedure.
6. List some of the services offered by SprintNet.
7. Discuss how Tymnet is controlled.
8. List several data services offered by AT&T.
9. Describe the services offered by the OAG.
10. Discuss how packet-switching networks have reduced charges to access databases and information services.

HANDS-ON PROJECTS

- Visit your campus computer center. Determine what value-added networks are available. What services do they offer?

- Contact one of the major VANs, such as CompuServe, and request literature on their services. When you receive the material, review the literature and make a list of features.

- Using a personal computer and modem, establish a connection with a VAN such as GEnie. Access the system for services.

- Make a list of VANs that are accessible to you without toll charges. Refer to your Yellow Pages for assistance.

- Contact a local bulletin board and determine if the system is affiliated with any VANs.

CASE SOLUTION
WORLDCOM

COMMUNICATIONS IN ACTION

Worldcom solved its problem by installing the network shown in Figure 13.17. It is made up of many mainframe computers and includes a system of network nodes. Users access the mainframes through the ports connected to each node. The nodes are linked by microwave, satellite, and other circuits. These high-volume circuits are multiplexed so that many channels are established between the nodes. The entire network is controlled and monitored from a central location. Services are billed from the central office, which also does systems planning and design.

In overcoming many problems, Worldcom has gained expertise in operating large networks. The company now offers consulting services to its customers. Worldcom's consultants will study a user's sites and requirements and assist in designing private networks that can interface with Worldcom's worldwide system.

Worldcom has achieved reliable worldwide communications through the efficient use of multiplexers, data concentrators, and a variety of communications circuits. Worldcom is able to send large volumes of data between its mainframe computers less expensively than do common carriers because it also possesses packet-switching capabilities. Small-volume communications customers can access remote databases at low cost through Worldcom.

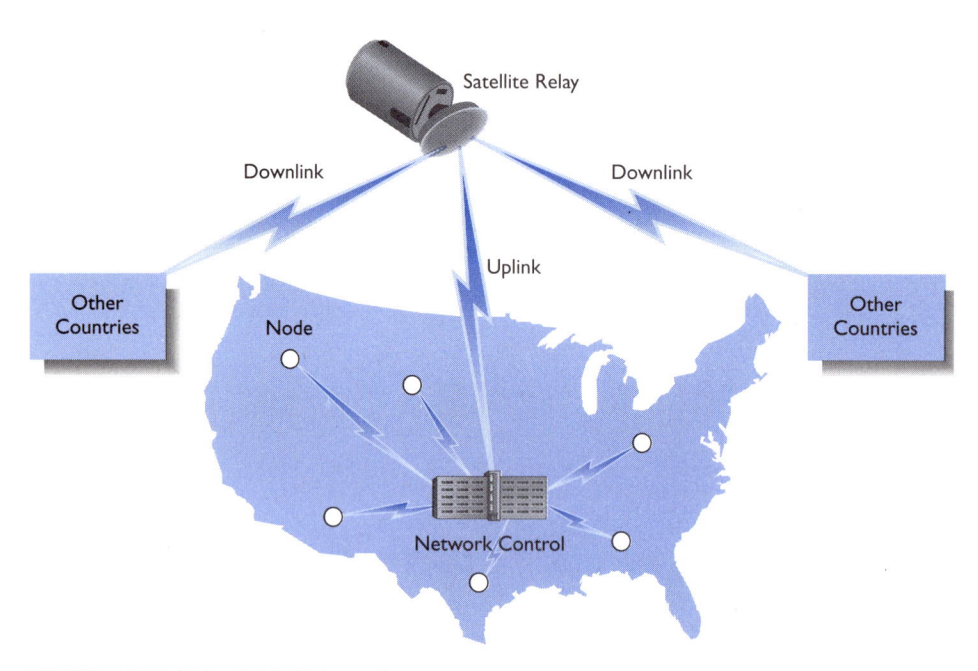

FIGURE 13.17 Value-Added Network

Because Worldcom maintains a worldwide network, it runs less risk of service interruption to its users. Because of its network's economy and reliability, Worldcom's customers rely on it rather than on other long-established common carriers.

IV

PLANNING AND DESIGNING COMMUNICATIONS NETWORKS

PLANNING AND ANALYZING COMMUNICATIONS NETWORKS

LEARNING OBJECTIVES

After reading this chapter, you should be able to:

- Describe the functions of the data communications department
- Discuss the functions of the feasibility study
- Outline the goals of the investigative study
- Describe the purpose of the final report
- Describe the major steps in systems analysis
- Describe the function of traffic analysis

COMMUNICATIONS
IN ACTION

CASE PROBLEM
FARNSWORTH PETROLEUM

GLOBAL VIRTUAL PRIVATE NETWORK

Farnsworth Petroleum is a multinational corporation with management offices located worldwide. Farnsworth operates oil drilling rigs in the southern United States, the North Sea, and other locations. Its operations consist of oil drilling, refining, and transportation of oil products. A large volume of the company's oil is processed in several locations around the globe and then transported to other sites via pipeline and barge.

Farnsworth Petroleum has more than 6,000 employees who communicate with customers, governmental agencies, and one another. Thousands of messages are routed back and forth between company offices, located in the United States, Europe, and the Middle East, 24 hours a day. These communications consist of letters, memos, reports, purchase orders, engineering drawings, and other records. Both graphic and textual material are transmitted.

In recent years, Farnsworth's department managers have begun to rely heavily on facsimile machines. This custom has resulted in increasing usage of direct-dial long distance calls and use of dedicated long distance circuits. Control of long distance charges has become a major problem for the company. Further complicating the situation is employees' demand for additional fax machines and telephone lines.

If you were a communications manager at Farnsworth, what would you do to stem the rising cost of long distance usage and still provide adequate communications? Refer to the end of this chapter to see how Farnsworth's communications manager analyzed the problem and planned a new communications system.

WHEN communications was in its infancy, business organizations had few choices and limited options. The mistakes they made were small and easily corrected. Consider a typical communications problem in the 1940s or 1950s. When the XYZ Company expanded its marketing department, more telephones were needed at the order desks. In those days there were few communications managers, and all telephones were supplied by one vendor, the Bell System. Telephones had only rotary dials, they came in one style, and most of them were black. The only decision XYZ company had to make was where to install the new phones.

Suppose the company discovers that telephones have been installed at the wrong desks or at inconvenient locations. All that was needed was a single call to the telephone company, and within a day or so an installer would drive up in a khaki-colored truck to take care of the problem.

Now, as we approach the turn of the century, the communications industry has changed dramatically. In this era of deregulation and global networks, communications services are available from dozens of companies, and hundreds of options exist. Telephones can be leased or purchased. Some systems integrate data, voice, and video. Users have a choice among common carriers, wide area networks (WANs) and value-added networks (VANs), and a host of long-haul alternatives, including fiber optics, microwave, and satellite links.

To further complicate matters, hundreds, or even thousands, of computers, terminals, modems, multiplexers, and data concentrators may be integrated into one company-owned system. Mistakes can be costly. Ineffective communications facilities mean millions of dollars of lost revenue, dissatisfied customers, misrouted or lost messages, and investment in equipment that is technologically obsolete before it has been fully amortized.

It is necessary, therefore, for organizations to plan and install communications facilities in a systematic and organized manner. In the following chapters we will look at network planning and design and learn how communications systems are implemented in the most efficient manner. The section covers how the principles of systems analysis are applied to communications networks.

NEED FOR PLANNING

Good planning involves a detailed and critical look at all aspects of a system. Most organizations today view their communications needs in a systems context, not as a group of isolated elements. A **communications system** is a collection of hardware, transmission links, personnel, policies, procedures, and facilities that function as an organized whole and allow an organization to reach its communications objectives.

Communications systems include all the elements in a network, including terminals, computers, communications circuits, telephones, switchboards, and other devices. In some organizations voice, data, and video are organized into a single system, known as an **integrated telecommunications network**.

New equipment is expensive to purchase and must be correctly specified. Duplication of facilities creates waste. Reliable and consistent communications must be provided to all levels of an organization. Modern organizations cannot afford to interrupt their flow of information. Managers, customers, suppliers, employees, and decision makers must be kept in constant communication. A properly planned network meets the immediate needs of an organization and provides for expansion and future requirements.

THE TELECOMMUNICATIONS DEPARTMENT

Some public and private organizations have gathered together all communications functions under a single organizational entity in order to be more responsive to the needs of the organization. These units are called **telecommunications departments**, data communications departments, corporate communications departments, or the like. A telecommunications department is headed by a manager who oversees the development and implementation of the organization's communications network. (See Figure 14.1.) These departments employ experts in many fields, including network planners and designers, message and routing specialists, equipment installers (Figure 14.2), network evaluators, maintenance and repair people (Figure 14.3), and engineers. The department may have responsibility for operating and managing networks throughout the entire organization. (See Figure 14.4.) Personnel must design networks that fit into the organization's strategic plans and provide secure and reliable communications at minimum cost.

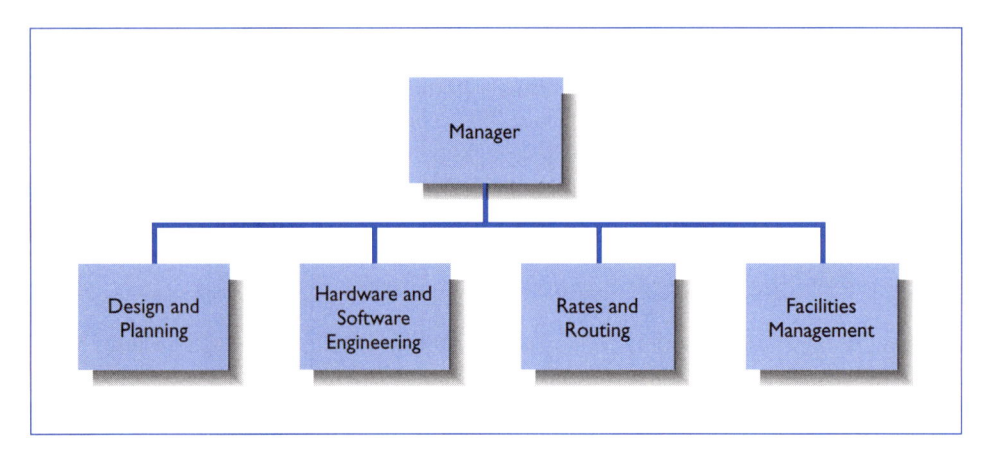

FIGURE 14.1 Data Communications Department

FIGURE 14.2
Equipment Installers

Dan McCoy/Rainbow

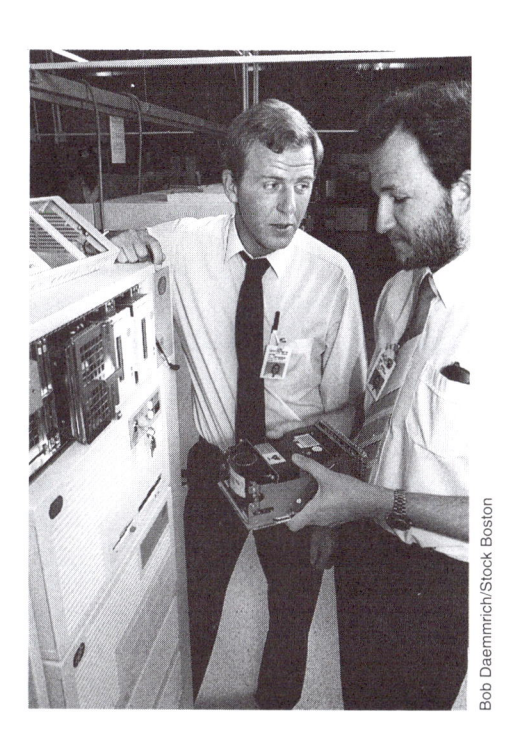

FIGURE 14.3
Maintenance and Repair Specialist

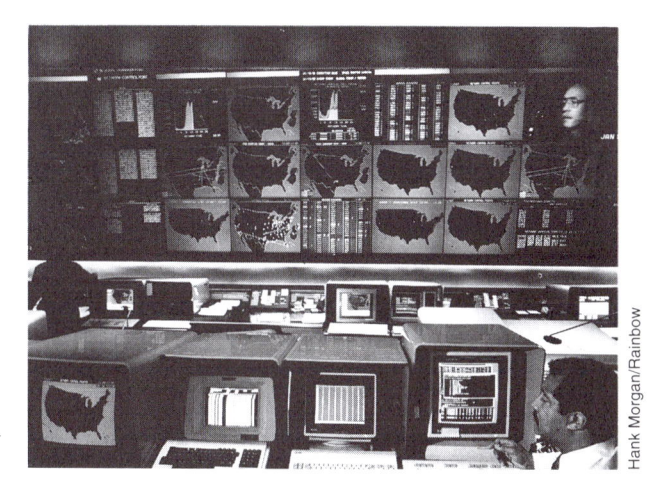

FIGURE 14.4
Network Control and Management

OVERVIEW OF SYSTEMS ANALYSIS

The planning, design, and installation of a communications system usually follows five major phases. (See Figure 14.5.) The first phase, **systems planning**, involves an early preliminary plan known as a feasibility study. Individuals who will conduct the study are selected, and systems goals are defined. Some preliminary cost estimates are made. In the second step, **systems analysis**, the in-place system is carefully studied, including the volume and types of transmissions handled.

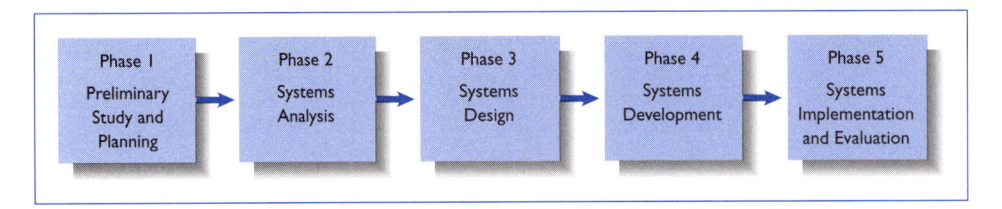

FIGURE 14.5 Systems Analysis Process

Phase 1: Preliminary Study and Planning → Phase 2: Systems Analysis → Phase 3: Systems Design → Phase 4: Systems Development → Phase 5: Systems Implementation and Evaluation

In the third phase, **systems design**, an improved system that meets the organization's needs is committed to paper. Specifications are written showing the types of equipment, services, and circuits needed.

After the system has been designed, it must actually be acquired. This is done in the fourth phase, **systems development**. Systems development involves the purchase of modems, couplers, and terminals or the signing of agreements with suppliers and common carriers.

In the last step, **systems implementation and evaluation**, the equipment is installed and the old system taken out of service. The systems analyst sees that the new equipment is properly installed, checked, tested, and maintained. Once in place, it is monitored to ensure that it is performing up to specifications.

The task of systems analysis may be delegated to a systems analyst. A **systems analyst** is an individual trained in the principles of scientific problem solving who also has a grasp of telecommunications concepts. He or she may work with communications specialists or company management to carry out the systems analysis process. Systems analysts are sometimes drawn from within the communications or operations research department of an organization, or they may be supplied by a consulting firm.

Network managers may follow the five-step approach just described to design and install new networks or to replace or upgrade existing ones. Once a network is in place, it may be turned over to others for operation. If this happens, the ongoing responsibility is transferred from the systems analysis or communications department to another department or division within the organization. The analyst is consulted only when the system needs updating or exhibits problems.

PRELIMINARY STUDY AND PLANNING

Systems planning begins with the recognition of a communications problem. That recognition can come from people at any level of the organization. It may be described by executives or managers or identified by complaints from customers or users of the system. Management may indicate that they wish to have a new communications system installed to handle the organization's data, voice, or video needs. They may even budget substantial funds to install or improve an existing system. At other times, the need is brought to the attention of the network manager by line employees or unhappy customers. Sometimes communications problems are brought to management's attention by accountants or auditors who have determined that phone or data transmission charges appear excessive or out of control.

A statement of the problem may raise many issues. Should a new system handle data, voice, and video separately, or should these elements be integrated? Who should be permitted to use the new system? What kinds of messages—and what length and type—will be routed through the system? What security and error-control requirements should be implemented? What will all of this cost?

These and other questions are answered in a preliminary investigation known as a **feasibility study**. The feasibility study determines whether a new system is, in fact, called for or whether the existing system should be modified or upgraded. It may even recommend that no action be taken and that further investigation be curtailed because of cost, time, or other factors. The feasibility study is one of the major aspects of the planning phase.

COMMUNICATIONS FEASIBILITY STUDY

The feasibility study answers many questions and lays the groundwork for further study. One of the questions answered is whether a given system will be practical and if it merits further investigation. If it does, a plan of action is then prepared. In the process, the question of who will conduct further studies is answered. Communications involves complicated hardware, facilities, and services and must be staffed with people who have specialized training and skills. Several approaches to staffing are often considered. These include appointing a communications manager, a committee or a task force, and hiring consultants.

A **communications manager** may be appointed to lead the feasibility study. These individuals are also called **project managers** and may be assigned the staff, time, and money to complete an investigation. They may even stay on beyond preliminary planning, through to final implementation and evaluation. Large organizations with extensive communications networks may permanently assign a communications manager to implement new systems or to oversee revision and updating of existing systems.

An **ongoing committee**, or team, is sometimes assigned the responsibility of conducting the feasibility study. The committee may be composed of individuals drawn from various levels of the organization, possessing many different skills. Some people may be experts in writing documentation or procedure manuals. Others may possess engineering or electronic skills. The advantage of using an ongoing committee rather than a project manager is that many individuals will be concerned with the system, bringing a diverse range of talents to the task. Also, that the committee is ongoing ensures that a long-range and consistent plan of growth will take place.

A one-time committee, known as a **task force**, may be convened and given the responsibility of updating or implementing a new communications system. The task force may be drawn from all levels of the organization and include line employees, supervisors, managers, and others. After the committee has completed the feasibility study, sometimes even aiding in its implementation, the task force is disbanded. Other task forces may be assembled to deal with new problems as they arise.

Hiring outside consulting firms to assist in feasibility studies or project development is often advisable. These organizations employ experts who possess specialized knowledge in communications hardware, network management, governmental regulations, tariffs, pricing, and so forth. Qualified consultants may have a range of experience not available within the organization and thus provide an effective alternative to the need to train in-house employees.

Later, **consultants** may be brought back to monitor the system or make recommendations for changes or improvements. Sometimes consultants are made available to organizations from systems vendors and common carriers. AT&T, MCI, and Sprint, for example, all maintain a staff of experts skilled in data transmissions who are available to organizations for consultation.

The feasibility study has three distinct parts. These include the preliminary study, the investigative study, and the final report. A positive final report directs the organization to move on to phase two, systems analysis. Let us look more closely at the three elements of the feasibility study.

Preliminary Study

A major function of the **preliminary study** is to define the benefits sought by the new system. Will new terminals, switching equipment, or a different common carrier save money? What will be the benefits in terms of increased capacity, reduced error rate, and greater reliability? Cost should always be weighed against benefits. Can adequate response times, throughput, capacity, and line speeds be achieved at a reasonable cost? Although specific purchasing details are not sought in the preliminary study, an effort is made to identify sources, vendors, and common carriers, who could provide hardware or facilities later.

A preliminary study sometimes asks whether specific pieces of equipment or an entire network should be purchased outright or leased. The decision to lease will require a different kind of investigation than will a decision to purchase equipment. These decisions rest on capital equipment requirements, tax considerations, and other factors. They are considered early on in any study.

Investigative Study

The **investigative study** takes a look at speed, cost, and capacity of a proposed system. The current system is scrutinized and weighed against alternatives. The manager seeks to determine whether a single user, multiuser, or distributed network may be needed. Various forms of network architecture are considered.

Those involved in this part of the study meet with organization personnel, vendors, consultants, common carriers, and others. The study group conducts interviews to help define and write specifications for a new system. Personnel requirements, training needs, and staffing changes required by the new system are assessed. Cost comparisons are made to determine not only the purchase price of equipment, but installation charges, plant remodeling costs, and maintenance costs.

Final Report

The **final report** of the feasibility study summarizes all the data and facts that have been uncovered. It makes vendor and supplier recommendations and lists equipment and services that may be acquired in the event the project goes forward. It may state that certain consultants will be needed and estimate what they will cost. A timetable for completing systems analysis, design, development, and implementation is included. Based on this final report, management will then decide whether to commit the necessary funds and personnel to implement the system.

ANALYZING COMMUNICATIONS NETWORKS

Before instituting a new or improved system, the manager must have a thorough understanding of the present system. The system already in place offers a benchmark or milestone by which changes or improvements are measured. A careful assessment of the existing network is extremely important because all further study, changes in the system, and acquisition of hardware, software, and circuits will be based on the information generated in this phase.

SYSTEMS ANALYSIS

Lord William Kelvin, a nineteenth century scientist, made a profound observation: he said one cannot control a phenomenon unless it can be carefully measured. The act of reducing systems, events, activities, or other phenomena to **quantitative**, measurable terms is fundamental to analyzing communications systems. Statements such as "The system works well most of the time," "The system has problems," or "Operators experience delays" are of little use in improving a system. Although these **qualitative** assessments may identify problems, they do not provide sufficiently precise data on which to base changes.

This information is gathered through the process known as systems analysis. **Systems analysis** is the systematic collection of pertinent data that describes an existing system so as to provide a foundation for changing, modifying, or creating a new and improved system. The objective of systems analysis is to measure and document all phases of a system. The process includes interviews, sampling studies, traffic analysis, a review of policy manuals and documentation, and other techniques. Throughout the process, as information is gathered, performance standards are developed, giving measurable criteria for future changes. Let us look more closely at the tools and techniques used to analyze an already in-place system.

The Scientific Method

An objective, quantifiable series of steps for solving a problem is used in systems analysis. (See Figure 14.6.) This approach, referred to as the **scientific method**, is characterized by objective observations, use of mathematical and statistical tools, a logical plan of action, and close attention to detail. Finally, it involves a critical evaluation of results.

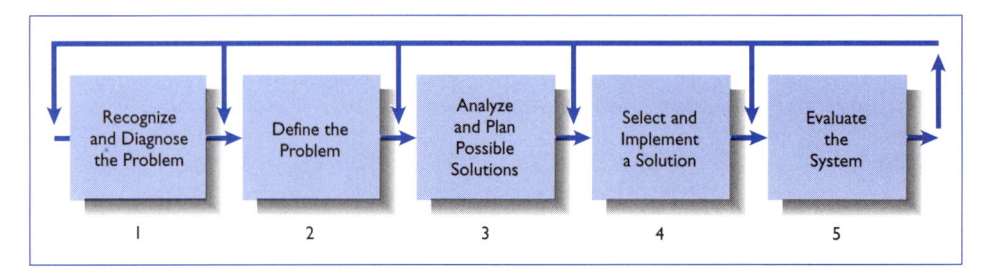

```
1. Recognize and Diagnose the Problem
2. Define the Problem
3. Analyze and Plan Possible Solutions
4. Select and Implement a Solution
5. Evaluate the System
```

FIGURE 14.6 Steps in the Scientific Method

The scientific method is based on a consideration of alternatives and a systematic selection that continually leads toward improvements in methods and procedures. It relies on "if-then" logic. If procedure A is followed, then this will result; if procedure B is followed, then that will result. To make these kinds of assessments, it is necessary to conduct a detailed system study and investigation. Let us look at how this is done.

Interviews

To understand an in-place system, the analyst conducts many **interviews** with customers, employees, managers, and other users of the network. (See Figure 14.7.) The analyst asks many questions: who is using the present system and needs access to terminals, telephones, switchboards, and so on? What types of information are sent and received? When is the data moved, and how much time is consumed in the process? Where does the data originate, and which locations are to receive the information? Why is the data sent, and for what purpose? Finally, how is the information sent? Is it keyboarded, spoken, or sent via video?

FIGURE 14.7
Conducting Interviews. Employees, customers, managers, and others are interviewed to gain insight into the communications network.

Questions such as these bring out useful information about a network and its workings. The interviewer keeps detailed notes and records, which he or she will study later to form conclusions about the current system. (See Figure 14.8.)

Present Transaction Types	
Transaction Name	Description of Transaction (include the time it takes and the means of communication)

FIGURE 14.8 Interview Form. This form is used to take notes during an interview.

Analysis of Systems Documentation

In addition to interviews, the systems manager methodically reviews all documentation on a system. This review involves the acquisition and study of policy manuals, reports, bulletins, and similar documents. An understanding of organizational policy and company needs and descriptions of already in-place computers, terminals, and communications links help define the present network. Some of the documents reviewed include complaint logs, time cards, service bulletins, repair logs, and other records.

Obviously, a new organization, or one without a communications network, will not possess this sort of documentation. In its absence, the manager will have to rely on other study techniques, such as the questionnaire.

Questionnaires

A variety of **questionnaires** may be prepared and given to users to answer. The objective of the questionnaire is to gain facts that describe the present system and the needs of users. These questionnaires may be carefully structured or open-ended. They may include fill-in answers, multiple choices, or short-answer questions. A questionnaire sent to a manager, for example, may ask what kinds of telephone calls are made or what kinds of reports or digital data are sent and received. The questionnaire may ask for a description of the data sent, and it may request a log of geographic points of origin, length of message, and other details. Questionnaires are efficient because they can be handled through the mails—or even processed through existing electronic mail systems—and thus reduce the time and expense of direct interviews.

Audits

An **audit** is an analysis of records and documents, performed by an independent investigator to gather data on a communications system. The kinds of records that may be audited include telephone charges (such as local service, message-unit cost, and long-distance fees), invoices from common carriers, payroll records, and copies of memos and reports. These audits may look into budgets, expenditures, response time, and traffic volumes.

Some audits investigate queue lengths. These investigations report on the numbers and kinds of requests that are kept waiting or delayed because a communications system cannot handle the transaction immediately. An audit may also involve a **monitor**, a computer program or hardware device that gathers meaningful data and statistics on the speed, volume, or kinds of messages processed.

Network reliability is another aspect of a communications system that is frequently audited. The auditor determines the number of times a system goes down and for how long it is unable to handle traffic. The audit may also analyze misrouted or lost messages or faults in transmission. After an examination of these and other elements, a clear picture of the in-place system begins to emerge.

Analysis of Costs

Because most organizations are profit-oriented, costs are very important. Nonprofit organizations, such as schools, government agencies, and hospitals, must also keep their costs within prescribed budgets. In **cost analysis**, accounting records are studied and conclusions drawn. Labor charges, data entry costs, fees for common carriers, and equipment installation and maintenance charges are gathered. Then they are compared to those of previous years or other departments, or even other businesses.

Some of the major costs that must be documented for an existing communications system include:

- Investment in capital equipment
- Investment in programming and software
- Installation cost
- Maintenance cost
- Common carrier fees
- Cost of backup system
- Cost for leased lines

A major portion of these costs is the purchase and leasing of communications lines. In determining the total cost of these elements, the network manager must determine how many miles of leased lines are on the system, the number of local loops, wideband charges for T1 circuits, and more.

The costs of technicians, keyboard operators, systems monitors, and maintenance staff must all be computed. In addition, the costs of providing supervision and management for the communications staff are assessed. Opportunity costs (revenue lost because funds are invested in capital equipment) must be considered. After all costs have been determined, they are documented and recorded for a specific volume of usage.

Traffic Analysis

Traffic analysis assesses the communications circuits and traffic moved throughout a network. The volume, kinds, and types of transmissions are carefully documented. (See Figure 14.9.) This documentation gathers data on circuit loading, kinds of transactions, and possible bottlenecks.

Response Time. A major element in the traffic study is **response time**, the delay between making a request and the receipt or answer to the inquiry. (See Figure 14.10.) Response time is based on transmission speeds, circuit delays, number of devices served, loading, type of computer programs, and terminal speeds. If a network is overloaded, terminal operators may have to wait many seconds, or even minutes, before a message can be handled. Often this causes a break in concentration for the operator, creating even more delay. These delays must be documented, not only for normal operating periods but peak periods as well.

Initial tests involving only parts of a network may give unrealistically fast responses. Sometimes a delay is deliberately programmed into a system to test it and give users a realistic feel for a system. By building in delays, a more accurate view of the shortcomings of the system may be obtained.

| | Day _____ Date _____ | Transaction Volume Survey |

Time Converted to a Std.	Time Starting	NUMBER OF TRANSACTIONS					
		* *	* *	* *	* *	* *	* *
PRIOR	PRIOR						
	8:00						
	8:15						
	8:30						
	8:45						
	9:00						
	9:15						
	3:45						
	4:00						
	4:15						
	4:30						
	4:45						
	5:00						
	5:15						
AFTER	AFTER						
	TOTAL						

* * Transaction Name

FIGURE 14.9 Traffic Analysis Report

Network managers should address the problem of peak traffic-flow periods throughout the day as well as throughout the year. The real acid test for many retail communications systems is the Friday after Thanksgiving, a day that traditionally places a heavy burden on communications. A system that cannot handle peaks may work well during normal periods only to fail when needed most.

Throughput. Another factor considered in a traffic study is **throughput**, a measure of the amount of usable information moved through a system in a given period of time. One of the best measures of throughput is known as the **transmission rate of information bits (TRIB)**. TRIB is a function of the volume of information sent over a line in a specified unit of time. The higher the TRIB, the greater the volume of information sent.

In computing TRIB, managers look at the number of bits per character as well as the length of block sent. TRIB is also based on the transmission speed of the modem and the number of control, or non-data, characters sent. Gaps in transmission, as well as transmission errors that require retransmitting data, also affect TRIB. (See Figure 14.11.)

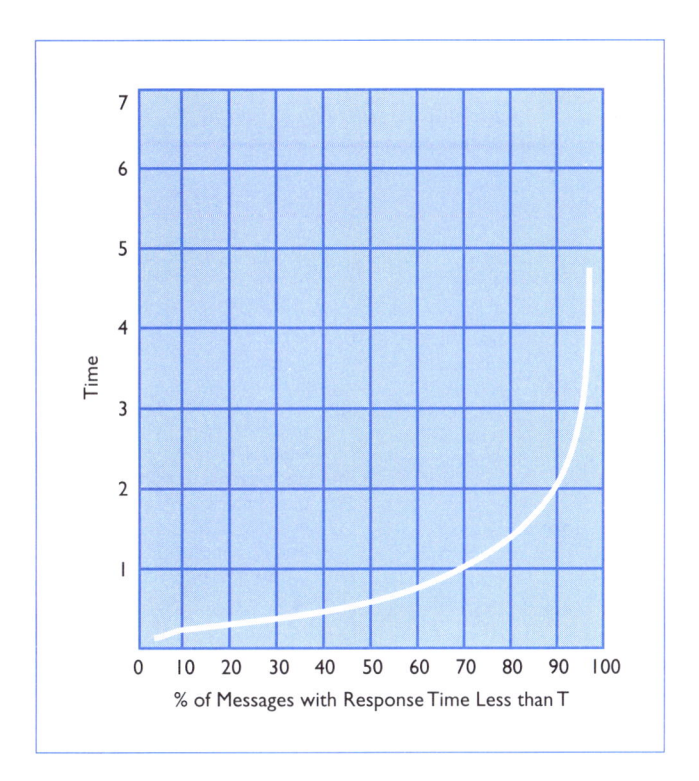

FIGURE 14.10
Message Response Time

The network manager makes an effort to document the volume of traffic at all levels of the system. The process includes determining how many terminals, computers, and other devices are on the network and the number, types, and length of lines that serve them. The type and length of messages are computed, and system peaks are analyzed. In studying the communications network, many specific details are assessed. The type of application for each terminal, as well as the number of input and output characters per transaction, is analyzed. The total transactions per day and the number, type, and speed of each modem on the system are determined. This information is particularly helpful later when the new system is designed. The new system will have to carry the traffic volume of the old system as well as provide for further growth.

In determining traffic volume, maps are drawn indicating the major points where data originate. These studies are further refined to indicate mileages between cities and the volume of traffic handled on each interconnecting circuit. (See Figure 14.12.) System loading is not an easy matter to compute in many organizations. Some businesses exhibit extreme activity cycles, meaning that the volume of traffic varies, depending on the time of year or other factors. For example, the airline industry experiences a large increase in communications traffic prior to certain holidays. Yet during the holiday itself travel falls off and the message volume drops significantly.

FIGURE 14.11 Effect of Block Length on Throughput

Half Duplex, 2-Wire Operation
Bit Error Rate = 10'
Modem Speed = 4800 bits/sec
Time interval between blocks = 3000 msec

Optimum Block Length

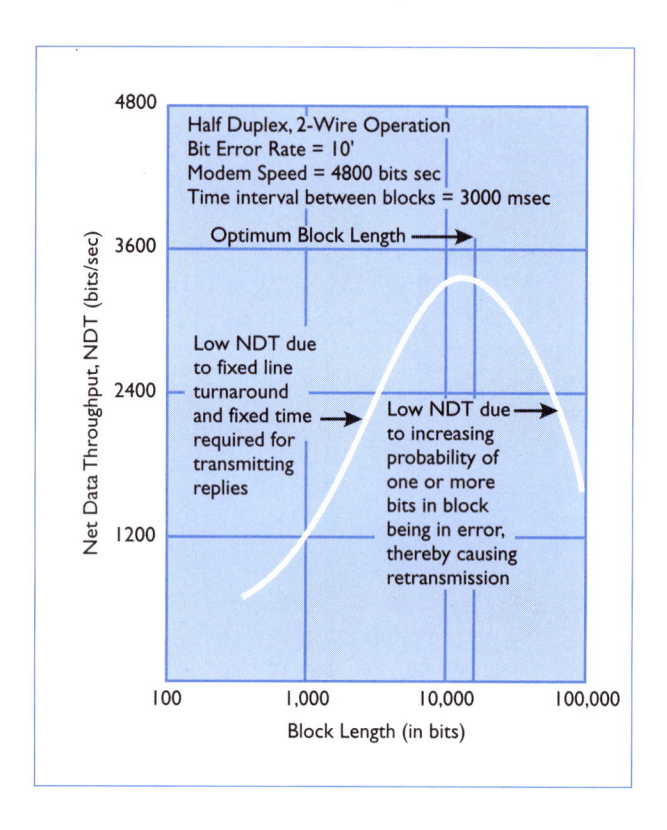

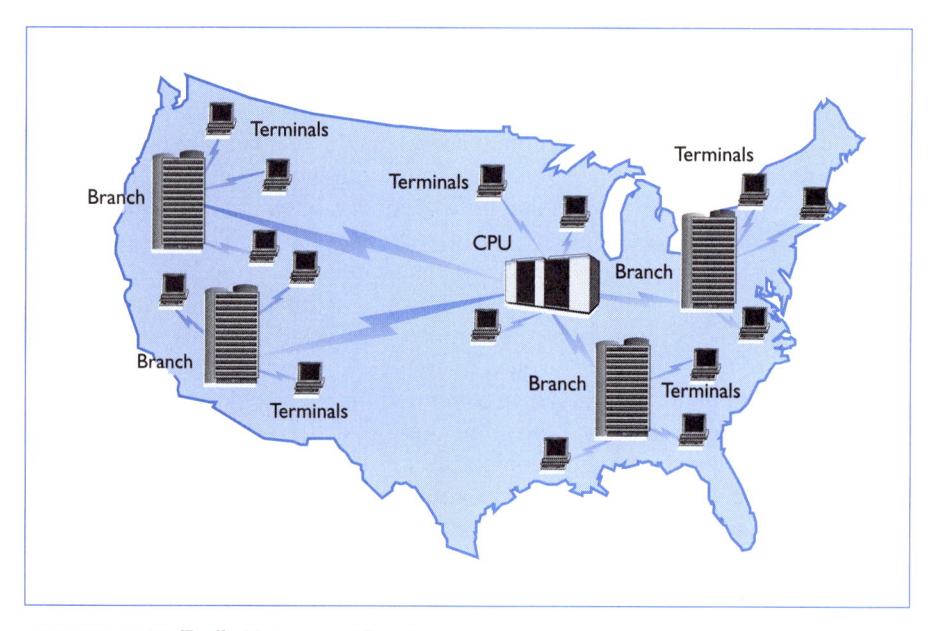

Low NDT due to fixed line turnaround and fixed time required for transmitting replies

Low NDT due to increasing probability of one or more bits in block being in error, thereby causing retransmission

Net Data Throughput, NDT (bits/sec) vs. Block Length (in bits)

FIGURE 14.12 Traffic Volume and Routing

Error Rate. Because no system is without its faults, statistics on failures must be gathered. Networks that transmit millions of characters per month experience errors in transmission. When errors occur, data must be retransmitted, which further reduces throughput and increases costs. These **error rates** depend on many factors. Shielded coaxial cable is less prone to errors than flat cable. Fiber-optic cables are less susceptible to error than data sent via radio transmissions. Error rates must be documented to measure improvements in the new system.

Another measure of breakdown is known as **mean time between failures (MTBF)**. MTBF is the average length of time between equipment failures or malfunctions. Some solid-state communications equipment may give tens of thousands of hours of reliable service without failure. Other devices, such as mechanical printers or rotary dialing equipment, may have an MTBF measured in only hundreds of hours before maintenance is required.

Equipment and Hardware Inventory

A comprehensive systems analysis involves preparing an inventory of the present physical equipment on the network. The manager determines how many modems, terminals, multiplexers, computers, and switching devices are on the system. Their speed, capacity, number of lines served, and physical location are documented. This information will be helpful in planning a new system later.

In assessing equipment, the functions of each workstation are defined. Which communications lines are needed to serve a given terminal or computer? Should they be full duplex or half duplex? Should the station be provided with backup facilities, and what priorities are assigned to each station on the network? The network manager deals with these and other hardware questions.

Personnel Requirements

Many organizations have invested thousands of dollars in acquiring and training personnel. Sometimes a choice was made to acquire personnel rather than equipment to do a particular job. The network manager must assess the numbers and types of individuals required to operate a system. Generally, this process involves checking job descriptions and personnel files and interviewing individuals to determine their function in the present system.

In addition to line personnel, supervisory and management people must be accounted for. Sometimes a new system replaces personnel, and the only way to measure the success of the new system is by comparing the personnel requirements before and after its implementation.

DISTORTIONS IN ANALYZING A NETWORK

By its very definition, a change in one part of a system affects all other parts. The individual who measures an in-place system must be aware of the critical interrelationship of all elements in a communications system. In particular, the manager must understand the Hawthorne effect, the learning curve, and the turnpike effect. Each of these has an impact on the measurement of an in-place system.

The Hawthorne Effect

In the 1920s, Elton Mayo, an industrial psychologist, studied a group of relay assembly workers at the Hawthorne plant of The Western Electric Company. Mayo was experimenting with light levels to determine the best level for maximum productivity. As he raised the light level, productivity increased, as expected. However, Mayo was surprised to find that productivity continued to increase even when he reduced the light level. Mayo's conclusion was that individuals who know they are part of a study behave differently from those who are not part of a study or who do not know they are being observed.

Network managers today are aware of the **Hawthorne effect**. Managers have seen employees speed up when their output is used to decide who will receive a bonus or fringe benefit. They have also seen output fall when productivity is measured to establish minimum output standards. Those under observation simply do not behave as they do when they are unobserved.

In terms of communications, the Hawthorne effect must be evaluated when results are gathered from a network under study. Employees who know their keyboard speeds, telephone calls, or messages are being monitored and scrutinized will often refrain from using a system the way they would when they are not being watched. As a result, a new system based on an artificial level of usage may not be able to handle the throughput or speeds that are encountered under normal conditions. The Hawthorne effect can be dealt with by conducting studies of traffic without indicating that the participants are under observation.

The Learning Curve

The network manager must take the **learning curve** into consideration when studying an existing system. The learning curve, shown in Figure 14.13, illustrates the relationship between the number of times a task is repeated and the error rate and time required to perform it. When a new operator begins a task, he or she proceeds slowly and usually makes many errors. With practice, speed and accuracy improve until a plateau is reached. Further practice will not net significant improvements in performance.

For example, a new keyboard operator, or someone unfamiliar with a terminal, may take ten minutes to enter a message. An experienced operator may perform the same task in three or four minutes. When assessing an existing system, the manager needs to be aware of the impact of the learning curve on measurements. The speed, accuracy, and proficiency exhibited are the result of many months or years of practice on the system. When a new system is implemented, the operators must relearn their jobs; thus, productivity is reduced and error rate increased. It may take many weeks or even months for users to regain their proficiency, and so the benefits of a new system may not be obvious for a long time.

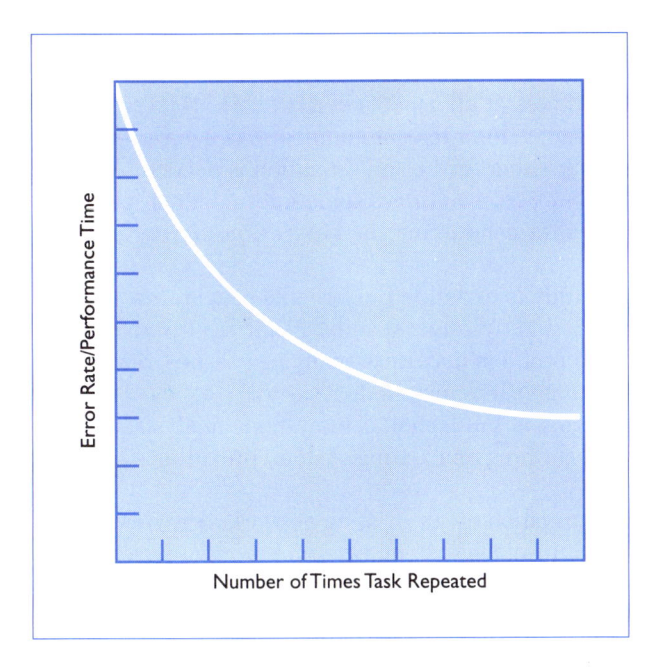

FIGURE 14.13
The Learning Curve

The Turnpike Effect

Many years ago, IBM systems engineers noticed an unexpected phenomenon whenever they installed new computers and communications systems. They called this phenomenon the **turnpike effect**, because they felt new systems behave much like newly opened turnpikes. New turnpikes were built with the assumption that people would continue to travel their old routes and use existing facilities. The intent of the new turnpike was to provide additional options and thus reduce traffic jams. However, when new turnpikes were opened, drivers stopped using the old routes and switched to the turnpikes, thus creating even greater traffic problems.

With new communications systems, users are attracted by faster circuits, lower error rates, greater throughput, or reduced costs. At the same time, other users see the advantages of the new system and abandon their old communications methods. Soon the new circuits are overloaded, and performance on the entire network may be degraded.

In assessing an existing system and looking toward a new one, the manager must consider not only the turnpike effect, but the learning curve and the Hawthorne effect as well. Failure to do so means the manager is not relying on realistic numbers, and projections may be erroneous.

In conducting the detailed systems analysis phase just described, criteria for a new system may be uncovered. As problems and weaknesses in an existing network are discovered and documented, they lead to a clearer picture of what is needed in a new or improved system. A well-written set of standards derived from the existing system will add validity to the task of network design. In Chapter 15 we will look at network design, costs versus benefits, security considerations, and alternative systems architecture.

SUMMARY

Systems analysis involves a detailed look at all aspects of a network. Data communications departments oversee an organization's telecommunications needs.

The *feasibility study* determines whether further investigation is needed. A *project manager* may oversee the study. *Ongoing committees* sometimes conduct feasibility studies. A *task force* may disband after conducting the study. *Consultants* are often hired to conduct feasibility studies.

An early function of a systems study is to define the benefits sought. *Investigative studies* look closely at speed, cost, and system capacity. *Final reports* summarize facts and findings. A statement of a problem may raise many new issues. Sometimes control of a network is relinquished after it is installed.

Measurement in *quantitative* terms is fundamental to systems analysis. *Systems analysis* is the collection of data describing an existing system, providing a basis for making changes or improvements.

Interviews are used to gather information on an existing network. A review of documentation is useful in analyzing an in-place system. *Questionnaires* are useful tools to gather information on an existing system. *Audits* are often conducted to gather data regarding costs and system usage. A careful *cost analysis* is often conducted to learn the economic parameters of an in-place system.

A *traffic analysis* study assesses the kind, type, and volume of transmissions handled by an organization. *Response time* is the delay between making a request and the receipt or answer to the inquiry. *Throughput* is a measure of the amount of usable information moved through a network in a given period of time. *TRIB* is a useful measurement of throughput.

Statistics on *error rate* indicate the accuracy of a system. The *MTBF* is a measure of the average length of time between equipment failures or malfunctions. An equipment inventory often reveals the physical hardware assigned to a network.

Network managers must be alert to the *Hawthorne effect* when making observations. The *learning curve* states a relationship between repetition, error rate, and time required to perform a task. Network managers must consider the *turnpike effect* when assessing the impact of a system.

EXERCISES

1. List some of the functions performed by the data communications department.
2. List the five phases in the systems analysis process.
3. What is the purpose of a preliminary study?
4. What is the purpose of the investigative study?
5. What is the purpose of the final report?

6. What are the advantages of using outside consultants?
7. List the key questions asked in an interview.
8. Discuss some of the items analyzed in cost analysis.
9. Describe some of the key items reviewed in a traffic analysis study.
10. How does the turnpike effect influence new systems?

HANDS-ON PROJECTS

- Develop a feasibility study for a communications system for a small manufacturing plant.
- Develop a feasibility study for a communications system for a small retailing establishment.
- Prepare a questionnaire that will assist in gathering information for a new communications system for a small retailing firm.
- Visit a business firm equipped with communications equipment. Discuss error rate and throughput with the communications manager. Prepare a short report on your findings.
- Interview a communications manager and discuss his or her responsibilities. Prepare a short report on your findings.

CASE SOLUTION
FARNSWORTH PETROLEUM

COMMUNICATIONS IN ACTION

Farnsworth's communications manager quickly realized that it would not be possible to provide unlimited fax and telephone service to all managers and individuals in the company. He also knew that modern communications technology would be required to solve the problem. The manager obtained approval to assemble a task force to study the problem and make recommendations.

A task force, made up of individuals drawn from the ranks of managers, supervisors, and line employees, was organized. The task force began a feasibility study that analyzed Farnsworth's growing communications needs, the existing communications system, and available funds. A preliminary study suggested that Farnsworth's problems could be solved by eliminating its reliance on leased circuits and dial-up lines and replacing them with a Global Virtual Private Network (GVPN). (See Figure 14.14.) The task force then entered the investigative study phase by looking at the costs, capabilities, and feasibility of a GVPN.

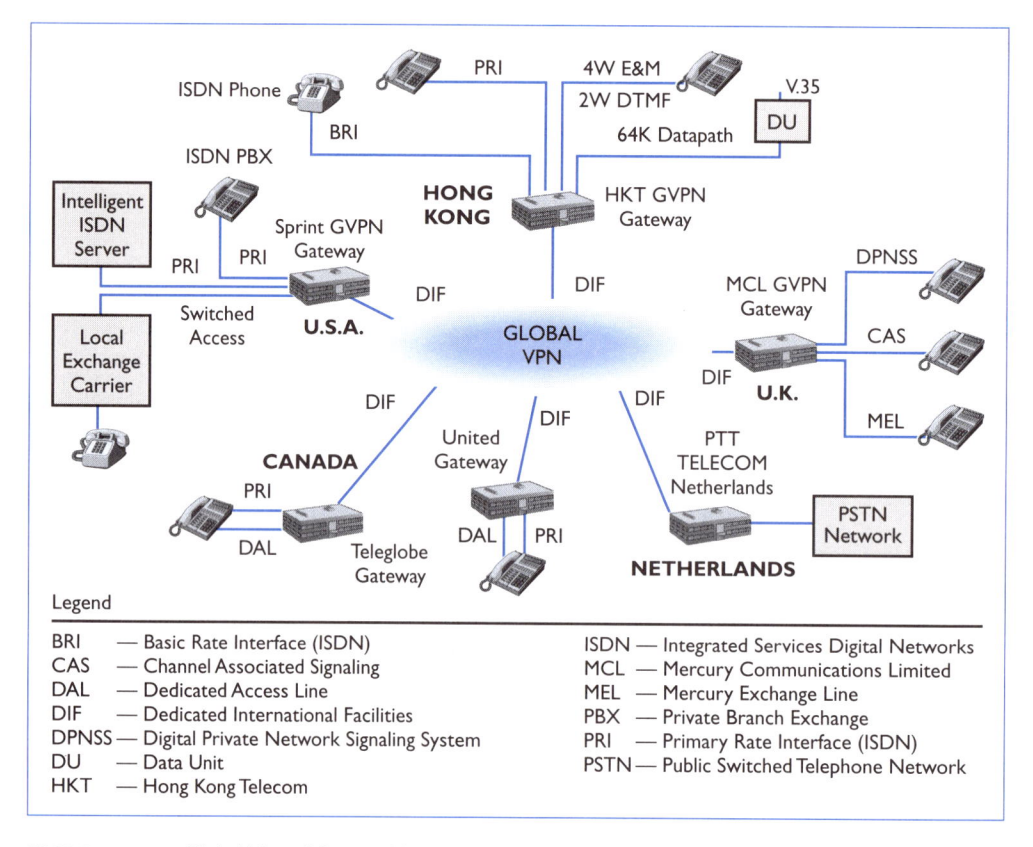

FIGURE 14.14 Global Virtual Private Network (GVPN)

Legend:

BRI	— Basic Rate Interface (ISDN)
CAS	— Channel Associated Signaling
DAL	— Dedicated Access Line
DIF	— Dedicated International Facilities
DPNSS	— Digital Private Network Signaling System
DU	— Data Unit
HKT	— Hong Kong Telecom
ISDN	— Integrated Services Digital Networks
MCL	— Mercury Communications Limited
MEL	— Mercury Exchange Line
PBX	— Private Branch Exchange
PRI	— Primary Rate Interface (ISDN)
PSTN	— Public Switched Telephone Network

The task force prepared a final report that made specific recommendations. These included shifting from dedicated and dial-up circuits to the installation of the GVPN. When the final report recommendations were implemented, Farnsworth Petroleum was able to transmit text, graphics, and voice over the GVPN. This implementation has resulted in the availability of better communications services at a substantially lower cost.

The GVPN has eliminated the underutilized dedicated circuits and replaced them with access to a common carrier's entry point. Now there is no waiting for calls to be connected, investment in switching equipment has been virtually eliminated, and the common carrier has the responsibility for upgrading the system.

DESIGNING COMMUNICATIONS NETWORKS

LEARNING OBJECTIVES

After reading this chapter, you should be able to:

- Discuss the task of communications systems design
- Describe the role of consultants in designing networks
- Describe how computers are used in communications systems design
- List the major items considered in designing a new network
- Discuss data security and systems integrity
- Describe the process of systems documentation

COMMUNICATIONS
IN ACTION

CASE PROBLEM
METRO SECURITY

SYSTEM ACCESS CONTROL

Metro Security began as an armored car transport company several decades ago. It carried cash and securities between retailers, banks, amusement parks, and other customers that required the handling of large amounts of cash. In recent years, Metro Security has expanded its operations to include industrial and plant security services, as well as home security.

Metro Security operates a large central computer monitoring system that monitors business and home, fire, burglary, and medical communications. The names and addresses of all the accounts monitored by the company are also maintained on the computer. The computer stores dates when cash shipments are to be made, notes on security procedures, and other highly confidential and sensitive data.

Metro Security employs several hundred people who must use its computer and communications system. What controls or safeguards would you recommend the company install to protect its vital data? At the end of this chapter you will see how management handled the problem.

WITH AN UNDERSTANDING of the in-place communications system, the network manager can design a new or improved network. This chapter discusses network design and the use of computers in network management. It describes the role of consultants and how costs and benefits are weighed when allocating resources and making decisions. The chapter lists the items defined in describing a new network. It also explains security and data protection mechanisms and procedures. A discussion of systems documentation is included.

DESIGNING THE SYSTEM

Systems design is the methodical consideration of alternatives and the listing of specific hardware, software, communications circuits, and personnel requirements. In the systems design phase, managers evaluate organizational needs, future growth projections, and long- and short-range plans. This evaluation serves as the foundation for designing an improved network.

In Chapter 14, we discussed the scientific method. The key to applying this procedure to communications systems lies in a careful consideration of **alternatives**. The network manager uses if-then logic to make decisions: **if** this circuit is used, **then** these terminals will be served; **if** that circuit is used, **then** those terminals will be served. The first step in the systems design process is to define all feasible ways of solving a particular communications problem. From these alternatives choices will be made. Here are some examples of the kinds of alternatives considered:

- Single-user system
- Multiuser, centralized system
- Multiuser, distributed system
- Leased-line network
- Public switched access network
- Integrated Services Digital Network (ISDN)
- Packet-switched system
- Frame relay system
- Global Virtual Private Network (GVPN)

The selection of a specific alternative is usually based on a careful consideration of the benefits versus the costs. The systems designer reviews all tangible and intangible benefits. Here is a list of some typical benefits from a new system:

- Greater throughput
- Faster message handling
- Greater security
- Reduced error rate
- Greater reliability
- Lower labor costs
- Reduced capital investment
- Easier-to-use system
- More entry ports available

These benefits may be obtained as a result of the following costs:

- Investment in training personnel
- Investment in software development
- Investment in new capital equipment
- Higher maintenance
- Additional line charges
- Installation
- Building and plant conversion
- Preparation of documentation
- Relocation of personnel

With a new system, costs may rise substantially until users and operators become familiar with the new facilities because of the learning curve, discussed in Chapter 14. Sometimes a new system will cost the organization more than the old because it attracts new users. The benefits of a new system are often intangible. Increased employee satisfaction and improved communications with customers or governmental agencies may be hard to measure in dollars and cents.

A new system may include backup facilities for handling data. Although the backup may never be used, its availability is an advantage that should not be overlooked. Only if the system fails and the backup is employed can the benefits be fully appreciated.

NETWORK DESIGN SOFTWARE

Specialized software has been developed to facilitate the design of complex communications networks. These programs run on either a mainframe or personal computer and generate a variety of maps, charts, schedules, and pricing tables. For example, Wide Area Network Design Laboratory's program called Network Planning and Analysis Tools (NPAT) is available to assist users in designing networks. It is programmed to find the most efficient arrangement of T1 circuits, multiplexers, and multipoint terminals. It finds the best combination of facilities for an integrated voice and data network.

Figure 15.1 illustrates a graphic output for a group of T1 circuits that serves a 250-node network. The software finds the most inexpensive routing and circuit configuration.

FIGURE 15.1
T1 Design for a 250-Node Network

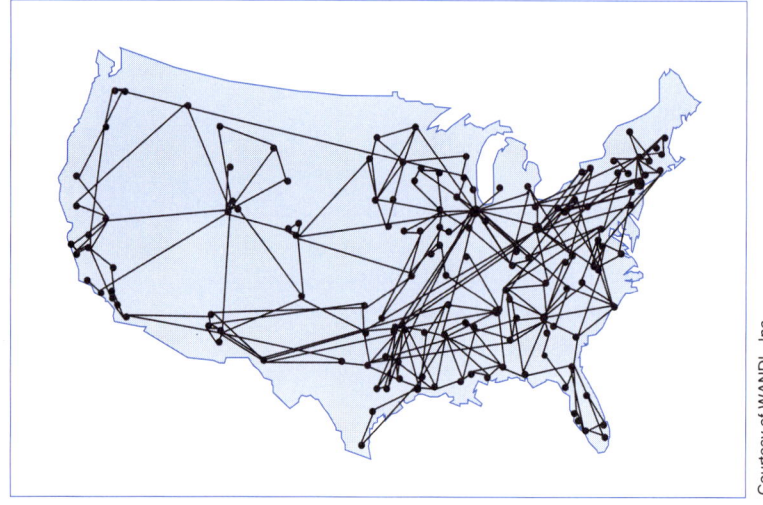

USE OF CONSULTANTS

Consultants are frequently brought in to assist in network design. They are particularly helpful when dealing with the **regulatory environment**. The Federal Communications Commission (FCC) is continually changing its rules and regulations, as are state regulatory bodies. Regulatory change has a profound effect on the design of a system. Network managers must be familiar with the thousands of pages of government rules and regulations that apply to communications. In addition, they must know about the various kinds and types of physical hardware, telephones, modems, and multiplexers that can be interconnected to common carriers. Consultants who have expertise in these areas may be brought in to assist in the systems design phase.

The pricing of services, such as WATS lines, local loops, dial-up service, and more, from local telephone companies is also controlled by state and federal regulations. Consultants can be helpful in this aspect of systems design.

Network Management

AT&T, MCI, and Sprint Communications all offer not only consulting services, but network management as well. For example, AT&T offers customers the following services:

1. *Configuration management*—Ensures users of the most efficient use of circuits and call routing plans.
2. *Fault management*—Minimizes network downtime through the delivery of alarms and status information.
3. *Performance management*—Provides traffic data, call pattern information, and performance statistics.
4. *Accounting management*—Provides call detail and billing information tailored to the specific requirements of the customer.
5. *Network planning*—Assists in site selection, call routing, and network optimization.

MCI provides its Integrated Network Management Services (INMS) to customers. This service efficiently monitors, analyzes, and controls voice and data networks, including costs of operation. The system provides alarm reports, trunk usage reports, hourly call patterns, and trouble reports. Services such as these assist the systems analyst in better managing a network.

STEPS IN A NEW DESIGN

The first step in designing a new system is to gain an understanding of the organization's communications needs. The network manager should review the volume, type, and destination of all messages routed through the system, including the points of origin, security needs, and pertinent cost factors. Future organizational needs must be taken into consideration; it would be inefficient to design a network that meets present needs but overlooks future ones. To do so could mean that the system would soon be overloaded or require replacement of expensive equipment or circuits. Let us review some of the major items to be considered in designing a new system.

Communications Hardware

After a review of equipment specifications, the network manager describes the particular size, type, and capacity of each piece of physical equipment for the new system. This is a complex task that involves the review of specifications for computers, switching equipment, multiplexers, data concentrators, and so on. The goal here is to write specifications in sufficient detail to allow vendors to price out specific pieces of **hardware**.

Communications Software

The manager must define exactly what type of **software** will be required for the new system. Sometimes software can be purchased; at other times, it must be written for the particular installation. These programs and other pieces of software may cost tens of thousands of dollars and are a significant part of the new system. Software specifications must therefore be written in sufficient detail to allow vendors to make competitive bids.

Communications Circuits

The manager must specify what kinds and types of circuits will be needed in the new system. The design criteria should include the mileage required as well as the circuit speed and bandwidth. In some networks thousands of circuits must be purchased. These include WATS lines, local loops, foreign exchange lines, microwave circuits, underground cables, and satellite circuits. All of these circuits must be acquired at the minimum possible cost consistent with communications requirements. Figure 15.2 contrasts the prices of some of these circuits.

Personnel Requirements

Virtually all communications networks require staffing. In laying out a new system the manager must specify the kinds of employees needed to operate the system. Design criteria include job descriptions that state the skill and proficiency required for each operator. Labor costs are a major expense item and must be assessed very carefully.

FIGURE 15.2
Representative Line Rates

Service	Approximate Costs (Costs Vary Considerably Depending Upon the Common Carrier)
Dial-Up Lines	$25.00/month each end (same as normal dial-up)
Local Leased Lines	$3.00/mile to $15.00/mile depending on area and distance
AT&T Leased Lines	$0.57/mile to $2.25/mile depending on distance
Unloaded Lines	$0.50/mile to $1.00/mile, no minimum billing, limited availability
Dataphone Digital Service (DDS)	Dependent on speed and service
303 Wide-Band	Dependent on speed and service

Systems Accounting

Organizations need to know their precise communications costs to compute their overall operating expenses and profit. Many also require charge-back systems that assign costs to particular departments, users, or customers. It is up to the network manager to define an accounting system that will be able to charge computer time, long distance charges, fees to access databases, and other costs back to their proper accounts. A well-designed charge-back system helps an organization allocate its costs more quickly and fairly.

Systems Costs

A major part of systems design is an assessment of full **systems costs**. Network costs include both capital investment and operating expenses. The computations should cover all direct and indirect costs, including those for converting files, preparing documentation, installing new communications lines, training operators, and installing a backup system. Maintenance costs, including repair or replacement of equipment, should also be included. A thorough analysis always contrasts the old systems costs with those of the new. (See Figure 15.3.)

Benchmark Tests

The information gathered in the systems design phase should generate quantifiable data that can be used to prepare **benchmark tests**. Benchmarks are established time or cost yardsticks that can be used to monitor a new system to ensure that it is performing properly. Benchmark tests are often established for transmission rate of information bits (TRIB) or other measures of throughput, transmission speeds, queuing or

FIGURE 15.3

Monthly Cost Analysis

Item	Old System	New System
Line Charges	$3,000	$2,000
Square Footage Rental	2,600	1,900
Utilities	150	150
Supplies	580	620
Equipment Lease	400	1,100
Salaries	2,100	1,400
TOTAL	$8,830	$7,170
Messages Handled	1,100	3,200

system delays, peak load capacity, error rate, and response time. Without these benchmarks it would be impossible to determine if the new system is performing at its best.

ALLOCATION OF RESOURCES

One of the common problems in designing a communications system is determining how to allocate a fixed amount of resources to obtain optimum results. This situation arises whenever there are alternative ways of combining limited resources. The communications system designer must determine the most effective combination of resources to optimize profits, reduce time delays, and move the maximum amount of traffic.

As an example, consider a telephone network that must cope with loads that vary throughout each day and from one day to another. The network manager must determine the most efficient and economical arrangement of operators, switches, lines, and equipment to handle the changing loads.

A system designed to serve the peak loads at all times would ensure that no customer experienced any delays on the telephone, regardless of when the call is placed. But because the system is not always at peak capacity, a large portion of the equipment and many of the operators will be idle at one time or another. Unused resources represent an economic loss to the company.

This arrangement would require a large expenditure in money, lines, equipment, and personnel to avoid all delays. To meet only the minimum needs of customers would also be unacceptable. The ideal solution lies somewhere in the range of employing less than a full complement of operators, staggered so as best to meet varying needs, and to provide less than a maximum number of lines and equipment. This arrangement would save money. It would also mean that at certain peak periods some customers would experience delays or reductions in quality of service. Situations such as these always involve compromise—the problem facing the network manager is to find the best compromise.

Linear Programming

Linear programming (LP) is a computer mathematical technique developed to determine the **best mix** of resources. It is useful when dealing with complex situations involving many variables.

In linear programming, all the elements involved in the mix—lines, switches, and multiplexers, among others—are expressed quantitatively. Then these values are fed into the computer and tested in various combinations until the one that most closely meets the stated objective is discovered.

Examples of expected results include "must handle a minimum of 100 queries per hour"; "each call must cost less than 70 cents"; or "find the best mix of equipment that produces less than one error per million transactions." Resources to be allocated are expressed as cost per personnel hour worked, cost of facilities, number of lines available, total amount of money that can be earmarked for the network, number of people that must be served, and so on. It is assumed that one or more of the resources are limited and that a change in the cost or available quantity of one of them will result in a proportionate change in the others.

Consider the difficult task of finding the best mix when hundreds of different communications devices operating at different speeds and dozens of common carriers with thousands of different routes are available. (See Figure 15.4.) LP is useful in determining the most cost-efficient mix when many choices exist.

FIGURE 15.4
Large-Scale Communications Installation

Courtesy of Hewlett-Packard

In a simple system, a manager can easily compare costs, line rates, system loading, and performance. But in a large and complex system, the task of network management is infinitely more difficult. Figure 15.5A illustrates a nationwide network that connects many lines to a central point. In a dial-up system, charges are based on toll rates, determined by airline miles. An operator could go to an airline mileage table (as in Figure 15.6) and a toll rate table (shown in Figure 15.7) and manually compute the cost of the system. However, a computer program could be used to perform the calculations and find the best mix. It could even be used to help design an improved system, using multiplexers, concentrators, and fewer circuits. (See Figure 15.5B.)

A. Before
Nationwide network implemented without multiplexing.

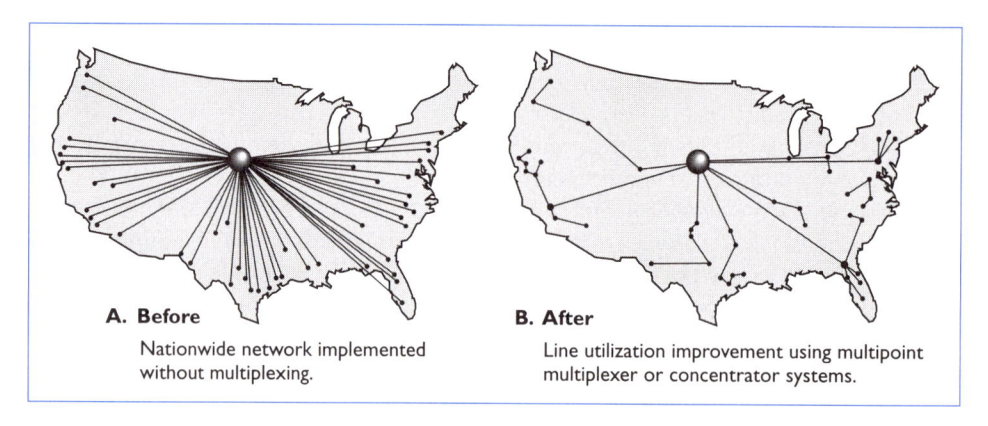

B. After
Line utilization improvement using multipoint multiplexer or concentrator systems.

FIGURE 15.5 Nationwide Network Before and After Installation of Multipoint Multiplexing Systems

FIGURE 15.6 Distances Between Cities (Partial Table)

FIGURE 15.7
Toll Rate Table

AT&T DIRECT-DIALED DAILY RATES

Mileage	Daily Rate
1–10	.20
11–22	.22
23–55	.22
56–124	.22
125–292	.22
293–430	.23
431–925	.23
926–1,910	.24
1,911–3,000	.25
3,001–4,250	.30
4,251–5,750	.33

Three Rate Periods:
(1) Business Day — 8 AM – 5 PM, Monday–Friday
(2) Evening — 5 PM – 11 PM, Sunday–Friday
(3) Night/Weekend — 11 PM – 8 AM, All Day
 8 AM – 11 PM, Saturday
 8 AM – 5 PM, Sunday

Evening Discount is 33%
Night/Weekend Discount is 48%

The computer is able to store worldwide communications rates (such as shown in Figure 15.8) as well as telephone area codes (as in Figure 15.9). The computer can then select the most efficient routing to reduce overall communications costs. It can also monitor outgoing calls and restrict calls to selected area codes or assign calls to particular common carriers, depending on their destinations. For example, some digital branch exchanges (DBXs) are equipped with an automatic route selection (ARS) program that performs these functions. Using an ARS program ensures that the rates and routes selected are always the most efficient available.

Queuing, Waiting Line Theory

Queuing, or the waiting line theory, is another communications technique related to allocation of resources. Queuing theory techniques are used to schedule assignment of resources so that they can efficiently process the requests for service that arise during any given time period. This scheduling must be flexible enough to handle not only the average number of expected requests, but also an unexpected increase or decrease in load, without involving either an economic loss or excessive waiting time.

On an order processing system, for example, if insufficient personnel are available to handle telephone requests, customers are put on hold and queues develop. If the delay is too long, customers become impatient and hang up. If too many telephone operators are available to handle the load, time is wasted and operator costs go up.

The network manager uses two mathematical techniques to estimate the expected and unexpected loads. A study of the average number of requests handled, based on the law of averages, indicates the expected normal load. The theory of probability is used to estimate the unexpected load. Briefly, this theory indicates what the chances are that an event will occur. The manager uses it to calculate such information as how often more customers than expected will call for service simultaneously. Based on the pattern that evolves from this study, the network manager schedules the resources so as to best meet the demands that will *probably* be placed on the system.

Country	Country Code	Rate	Country	Country Code	Rate
Abu Dhabi (UAE)	949	3.81	Cayman Is. (BWI)	309	3.19
Afghanistan	930	3.91	Central African Rep.	980	3.81
Ajman (UAE)	949/958	3.81	Ceylon [Sri Lanka]	954	3.19
Albania	866	3.28	Chad Rep.	984	3.81
Algeria	936	3.81	Chile	332/354/359/392	3.28
American Samoa	782	3.93	China, Peoples (Mainland)	716	3.47
Andorra	833	2.76	China, Republic (Taiwan)	785	3.19
Angola	998	3.81	Christmas Is. (Indian Ocean)	917	3.81
Anguilla (BWI)	317	3.71	Cocos – Keeling Is.	918	3.81
Antigua (BWI)	306	3.71	Colombia	396	3.28
Argentina	390	3.28	Comoros, Rep. of	942	3.47
Armenia	870	2.90	Congo, Rep.	971	3.91
Aruba (Neth. Ant.)	364/384	3.28	Congo Republic	968	3.28
Ascension Is.	920	3.91	Cook Is.	717	3.91
Australia	790	3.19	Costa Rica	303/323/343/363	3.28
Austria	847	2.76	Ivory Coast	969	3.28
Azerbaijan	914	2.90	Croatia	862	2.76
Azores (Portugal)	835	2.76	Cuba	307	3.47
Bahamas	382	2.76	Curacao (Neth. Ant.)	384	3.28
Bahrain	955	3.81	Cyprus	826	2.76
Balearic Is. (Spain)	831	2.76	Czechoslovakia	849	3.28
Bangladesh	950	3.19	Dahomey Rep. [Benin]	979	3.81
Barbados (BWI)	386	3.28	Denmark	855	2.76
Belarus	872	2.90	Diego Garcia Is.	919	3.47
Belgium	846	2.76	Djibouti, Rep.	994	3.81
Belize	310	3.47	Dominica (BWI)	304	3.71
Benin Peoples Rep.	979	3.81	Dominican Rep.	326/346/366	3.19
Bermuda	380	2.65	Dubai (UAE)	949/958	3.81
Bhutan	733	3.19	Ecuador	393	3.28
Bolivia (355/356/326)	336	3.28	Egypt, Arab Rep. of	927	3.28
Bonaire (Neth. Ant.)	384	3.28	El Salvador	301	3.28
Bophuthatswana	932	3.28	England (UK)	851	2.21
Bosnia-Hercegovina	862	2.90	Equatorial Guinea	939	3.81
Botswana	991	3.28	Estonia	875	2.90
Brazil	391	3.28	Ethiopia	976	3.81
Brazzaville (Congo)	971	3.91	Falkland Is.	319	3.91
British Virgin Is.	318	3.71	Faroe [Faeroe] Is.	853	2.76
Brunei	799	3.19	Fiji Is. [Suva]	792	3.81
Bulgaria	865	3.28	Finland	857	2.76
Burkina Faso	985	3.81	Formosa [Taiwan]	785	3.19
Burma [Mynmar]	713	3.19	France	842	2.76
Burundi	977	3.81	French Guiana	313	3.28
Caicos Is. & Turks	315	3.71	French Polynesia	711	3.19
Cambodia [Kampuchea]	720	3.91	Fujaira (UAE)	949/958	3.81
Cameroon	978	3.81	Gabon Republic	981	3.81
Canada	389	1.78	Gambia	992	3.81
Canal Zone [Panama]	328/348/368	3.28	Georgia	873	2.90
Canary Is. (Spain)	966	2.76	Germany	841/840	2.76
Cape Verde Is.	938	3.81	Ghana	974	3.81
Caroline Is. [Micronesia]	729	3.47	Gibraltar	837	3.28

FIGURE 15.8 Western Union Telex Rates (Partial Table)

State	Area Codes						State	Area Codes					
Alberta	403						North Carolina	704	919				
Anguilla	809						North Dakota	701					
Alaska	907						Nebraska	308	402				
Alabama	205						Newfoundland	709					
Antigua	809						New Hampshire	603					
Arkansas	501						New Jersey	201	609	908			
Arizona	602						New Mexico	505					
Bahamas	809						Nova Scotia	902					
British Columbia	604						Northwest Territory	403	819				
Barbados	809						Nevada	702					
Bermuda	809						New York	212	315	516	518	607	716
British Virgin Islands	809							718	914	917			
California	209	213	310	408	415	510	Ohio	216	419	513	614		
	619	707	714	805	818	909	Oklahoma	405	918				
	916						Ontario	416	519	613	705	807	905
Colorado	303	719					Oregon	503					
Cayman Islands	809						Pennsylvania	215	412	717	814		
Connecticut	203						Prince Edward Island	902					
District of Columbia	202						Province of Quebec	418	514	819			
Delaware	302						Puerto Rico	809					
Dominica	809						Rhode Island	401					
Dominican Republic	809						Monserrat	809					
Florida	305	407	813	904			St. Lucia	809					
Georgia	404	706	912				South Carolina	803					
Grenada	809						South Dakota	605					
Hawaii	808						Saskatchewan	306					
Iowa	319	515	712				Turks and Caicos	809					
Idaho	208						Tennessee	615	901				
Illinois	217	309	312	618	708	815	Trinidad	809					
Indiana	219	317	812				Texas	210	214	409	512	713	806
Jamaica	809							817	903	915			
St. Kitts Nevis	809						Utah	801					
Kansas	316	913					Virginia	703	804				
Kentucky	502	606					Virgin Islands of the US	809					
Louisiana	318	504					Vermont	802					
Manitoba	204						Washington	206	509				
Massachusetts	413	508	617				Wisconsin	414	608	715			
Maryland	301	410					West Virginia	304					
Maine	207						Wyoming	307					
Michigan	313	517	616	906			Yukon Territory	403					
Minnesota	218	507	612				St. Vincent	809					
Missouri	314	417	816										
Mississippi	601												
Montana	406												
New Brunswick	506												

FIGURE 15.9 Area Codes

Examples of the types of situations that involve fluctuating queues are file inquiry systems, telephone order systems, and reservations systems.

Figure 15.10 charts the size of the queues that develop each week in the classified advertising department of a newspaper. It shows that the queues are largest just before the deadlines for entering ads for each major edition, and shortest just after the deadlines. The classified advertising department must have a communications system designed to handle a load that varies, not only from day to day, but from week to week as well.

FIGURE 15.10
Classified Ad Queuing

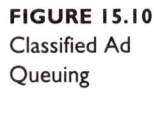

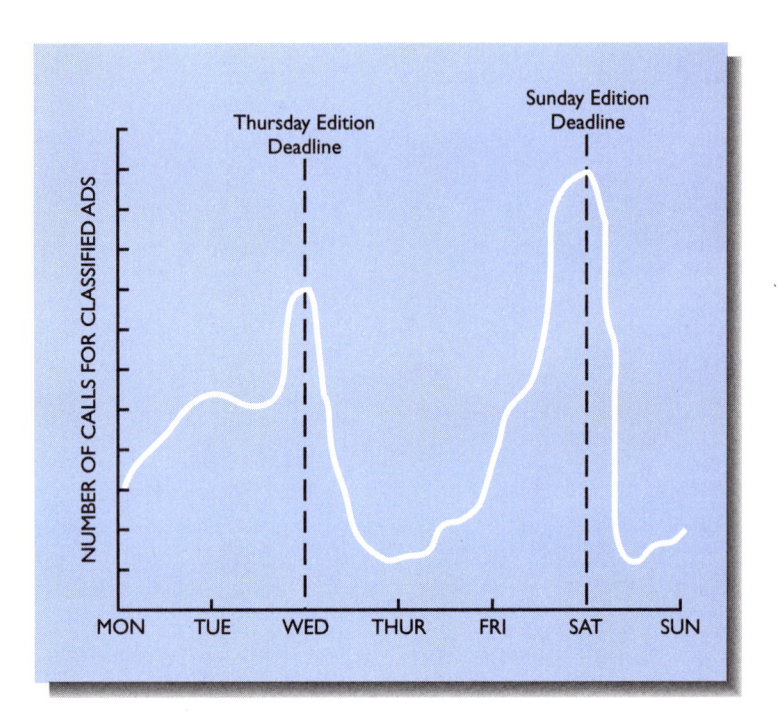

QUALITY CONTROL TECHNIQUES

In communications systems, the designer often has the responsibility of monitoring the error rate for a given network, indicating when the rate has gone beyond acceptable standards, and instituting measures to correct the problem. For example, this task could involve monitoring the various office and information processing procedures to assure that the **quality control** standards set for those processes are being maintained. These procedures might include such activities as scanning messages, reports, documents, invoices, calculations, entries in records, and other output.

To examine each message would be slow, costly, and inefficient. Instead, the network manager relies on random sampling to select a sample for analysis. The frequency of the sample depends on how closely the error rate of the sample conforms to the standard for that process.

One common quality control method is to continue sampling at a low frequency as long as the error rate is below or at the standard. If the error rate increases, the frequency of the sample also expands—a larger percentage of the messages being handled are carefully examined. If the cause of the error cannot be found, and if the error rate continues to climb, an even larger proportion of the population is examined. This process continues until the cause has been found and corrected.

In occasional instances where difficulties still occur, the sample may become as frequent as one in five, or perhaps include all messages handled. When the condition has been corrected and the error rate begins to drop, the frequency of the sample is reduced proportionally. When the error rate has again reached the standard for that process, the sample size is reduced once more to the original maintenance level. Figure 15.11 illustrates the relationship of the error rate for a process, such as keyboarding or transmitting a block of data, and the frequency of the sample taken for examination.

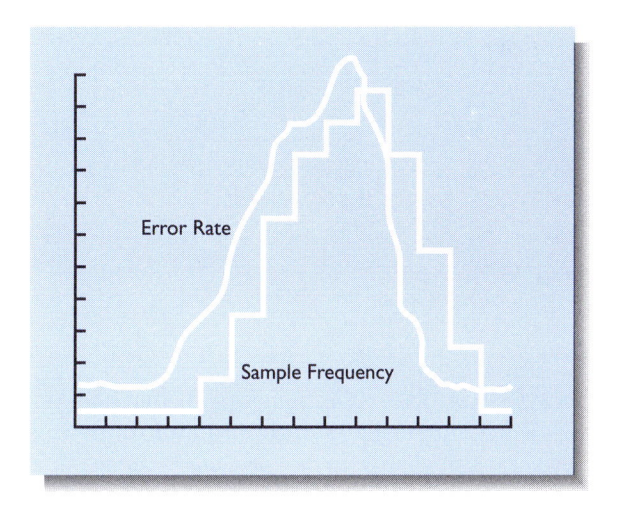

FIGURE 15.11
Error Rate vs. Frequency of Sample

Forecasting

Forecasting is a technique used to make predictions of future events based on past performance. The network manager is often asked for advice or information regarding future considerations, demands, costs, or output of a communications system, based on available knowledge and data.

Linear regression analysis is an important statistical tool in forecasting. Using past performance data, this mathematical formula will extend a given line, or sequence of events, into the future. (See Figure 15.12.) To use it, all conditions relevant to the network under study are expressed quantitatively. These include costs of personnel, equipment, line charges, time considerations, output rate, and error rate. The formula manipulates these values to produce an estimate of what results will be at a specific time in the future.

Computer programs, written to solve this formula, have increased the complexity of the situations that may be forecast and the accuracy of the results. In day-to-day communications situations, however, many factors that cannot be reduced to numbers also influence the system. Changes in competition, demand, supply, new facilities, and regulatory controls must also be considered.

The task of the network manager is to study all of the unpredictable, as well as the predictable, variables affecting a given condition and, by utilizing the appropriate mathematical techniques, make predictions that are as accurate and comprehensive as possible.

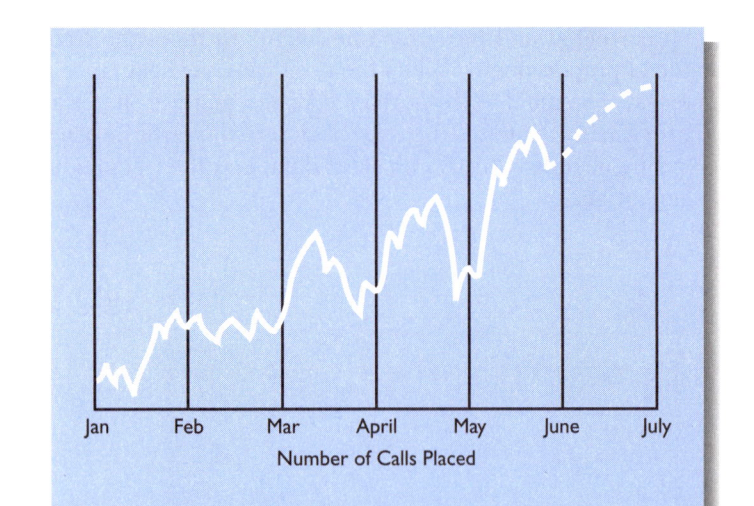

FIGURE 15.12
Forecasting

Number of Calls Placed (Jan–July)

Simulation and Modeling

Making changes in a communications system involves time, money, and effort and can lead to serious problems if the wrong changes are made. **Simulation and modeling** is a technique used to examine the effect that a change in one or more elements in a network will have on the rest of the network—without actually making the changes. It allows the network manager to experiment with various modifications or improvements to learn how each would affect a system without disrupting its normal activities.

The process of simulating a system is done by building a model—a mathematical description, not a physical construction. It is built by expressing each element in the network as a quantitative value. The simulation is performed by manipulating the values to represent the changes that would occur from modifications introduced into a system. The model is designed so that a change in one value will produce a proportionate change in the appropriate related values. Performing simulations on the computer increases the practicality and value of the technique and allows experimentation with models and modifications of greater complexity and intricacy.

A firm might run a simulation to experiment with the possibility of installing new equipment—with greater capacity, but at an increase in cost—to see how it will affect such areas as costs, output, and number of operators. Simulations can help to predict the effects of raises in material costs or salary increases. They would also be used to study what would happen if additional workstations were added in a system—before the actual changes were made.

A firm may simulate restructuring its telephone switchboard to find the arrangement that produces the best results. Without simulation techniques, it would be necessary to install a group of telephone lines, establish operator stations, rearrange office facilities, and then check the results.

Installing new terminals and switching equipment, or leasing new communications circuits, for systems that are untested or untried could be costly. However, by simulating users, destinations, circuits, messages, and hardware, the designer can experiment with a variety of alternatives. For example, a bank may develop a model of a new teller terminal system. Then, using the computer, the model can test loading, queue lengths, time delays, and even simulate transmission errors. Once the best system has been developed on the computer, it can then be constructed in the most efficient manner.

With simulation techniques it becomes feasible to study various modifications and arrangements until the optimum number of lines and workstations are determined. Only after this information has been obtained will plans for implementing the actual changes be initiated.

Program Evaluation and Review Technique

Program evaluation and review technique (PERT) is a computer scheduling technique that is useful in creating timetables for implementing complex networks. By using either PERT or a technique known as **critical path method (CPM)**, the network manager can use the computer to prepare timetables for installing a new system that will ensure completion by a specified date.

Figure 15.13 illustrates the steps in implementing a new communications system. The task will take 36 months and involves issuing plans, developing maintenance programs, negotiating with vendors, and purchasing and ordering equipment. While all of these tasks are going on, troubleshooting procedures are being developed and building sites prepared. Special terminals are being produced and operators trained.

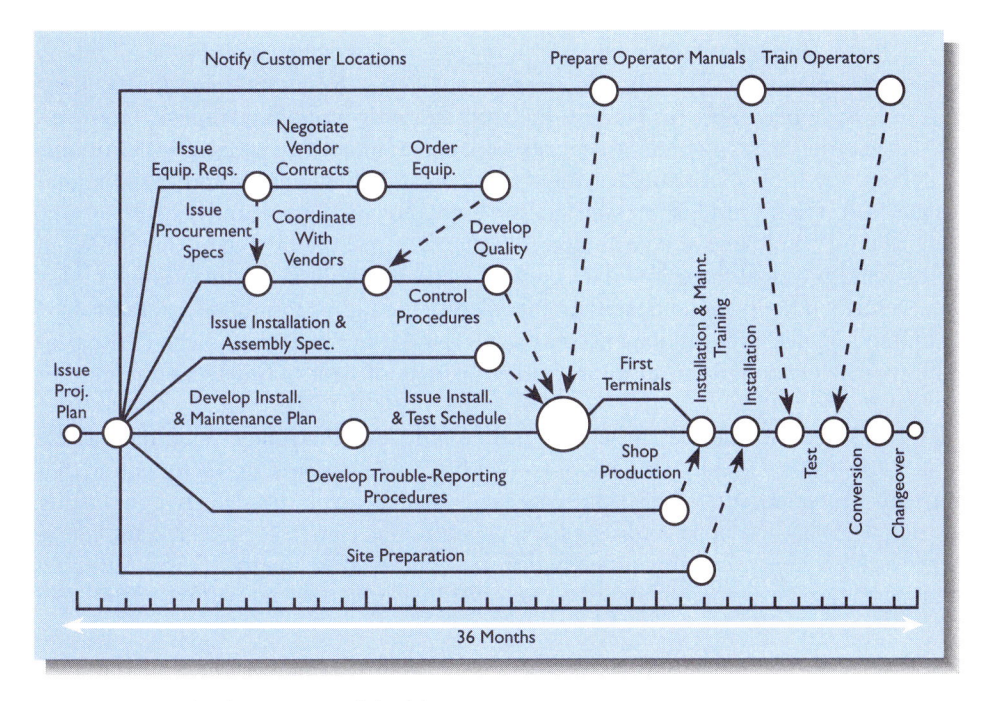

FIGURE 15.13 Implementation Schedule

If thousands of terminals and hundreds of pieces of hardware, including communications circuits, are needed, then a detailed printout of beginning and ending times for each phase, prepared by a computer, would be extremely helpful. This would ensure that no steps are inadvertently left out and that critical dates are met so that the project is completed on time.

DATA SECURITY AND SYSTEMS INTEGRITY

In designing a new system, two of the most important factors to consider are **data security** and **systems integrity**. As more and more organizations turn to distributed data processing, they place vital data in computers located at remote sites around the country. With millions of personal computers installed in homes and offices, many with communications capability, the potential for mischief, misuse, and breaches of security exists. When one considers that SprintNet, for example, has several thousand computers linked by telephone lines accessible to hundreds of thousands of users, it becomes obvious that security is a key issue.

There have been instances in which disgruntled employees have planted destructive programs into a network, timed to disrupt operations weeks or months after the employee was terminated. Such programs, sometimes known as Trojan Horses, may remain inactive for long periods of time and then become active, destroying important communications data.

Access vs. Security

One of the major goals of a communications system is to make resources available to as many people as possible. By providing broad access to computer databases, organizations have been able to increase their productivity and effectiveness. However, easy access raises the problem of security of data and unauthorized use. With millions of dollars worth of information in their files, organizations must protect their vital resources. Yet they must balance this need against providing quick and convenient services to their employees and customers. To guard against thefts of data, unauthorized access, and physical threats to data networks and computers, organizations employ data security officers and a host of methods and procedures to protect information.

Protection measures are expensive, but necessary. Let us look at some of the procedures and methods used to improve the security of data networks and computer centers.

Network security can be viewed as a series of layers that protect vital data at the center. (See Figure 15.14.) At the core are the files, data, records, and information that must be protected. Encircling the core are various levels of security, including restricted access, use of passwords, physical control measures, keys, locks, and more. A network may be vulnerable at many different points. (See Figure 15.15.) Valuable data may be stolen or copied from disks or tape by unauthorized individuals. They may

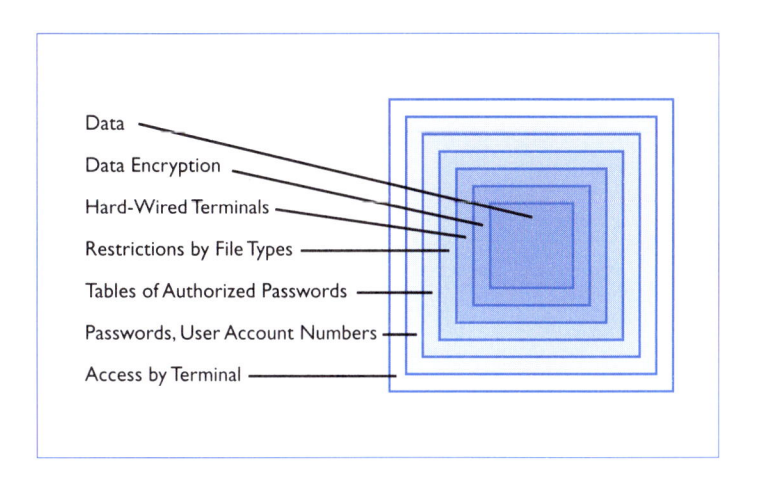

FIGURE 15.14 Layers of Security

- Data
- Data Encryption
- Hard-Wired Terminals
- Restrictions by File Types
- Tables of Authorized Passwords
- Passwords, User Account Numbers
- Access by Terminal

be lost or destroyed due to fire, earthquake, or other natural disasters. Computer hardware is subject to failures that can cause loss of valuable data or programs. Information moving between networks can also be lost or stolen.

Memory (Disks and Tapes)
- Tapes and disks can be stolen or copied.
- Users or maintenance personnel may intentionally or accidentally break security.
- Associates of users may learn information and reveal it.

Computer
- Failure of equipment may disable security system.
- Security codes for the computer may not always work.
- Radio-frequency radiation may be deciphered.
- Signals may be intercepted.
- Lines may be tapped.

Communications Link — Telephone, Microwave, Satellite
Lines can be tapped, signals intercepted; radio-frequency radiation can be deciphered.

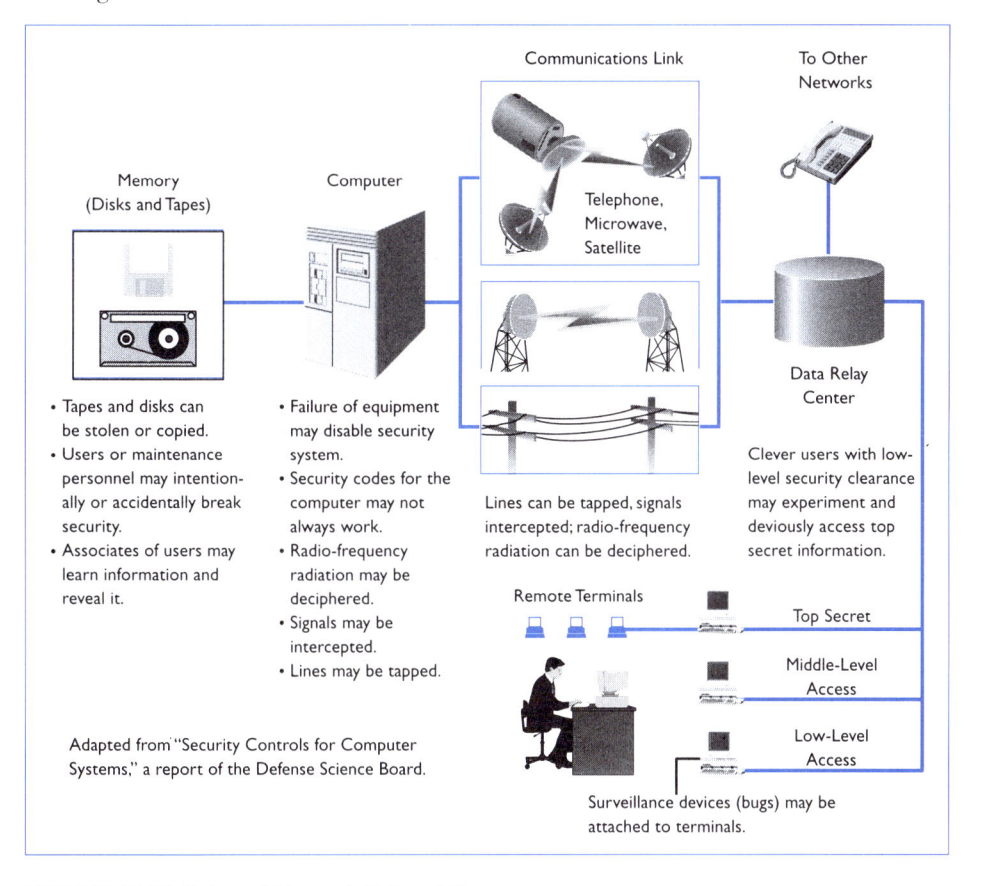

To Other Networks — Data Relay Center
Clever users with low-level security clearance may experiment and deviously access top secret information.

Remote Terminals
- Top Secret
- Middle-Level Access
- Low-Level Access

Surveillance devices (bugs) may be attached to terminals.

Adapted from "Security Controls for Computer Systems," a report of the Defense Science Board.

FIGURE 15.15 Points of Network Vulnerability

Communications links are the most vital parts of a communications system, and they too are vulnerable. Figure 15.16 shows the points where satellites, microwave circuits, land lines, or underground cables can be tapped by unauthorized users. Let us now look at some of the ways that physical plants are protected against unauthorized intrusions, destruction, or theft of data.

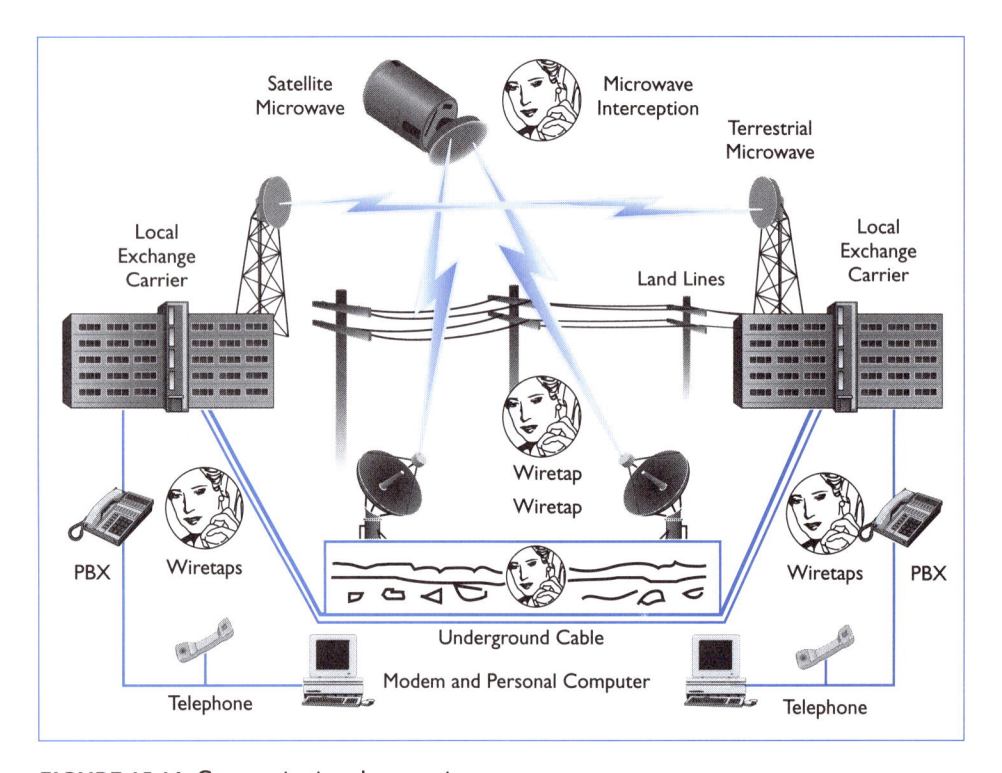

FIGURE 15.16 Communications Interception

Closed-circuit television is often used to scan an area and observe individuals who seek to enter computer rooms, terminal sites, or data transmission areas. (See Figure 15.17.) Unauthorized individuals are immediately identified and prevented from entering. In addition, X-ray surveillance, photographic surveillance, and time-lapse photography may be utilized to monitor doors, exits, or computer rooms. (See Figure 15.18.) Authorized users may be assigned identification cards, door keys, terminal keys, badges, or cards with bar codes, all of which are scrutinized before the individual is permitted access to secure areas.

Software Controls

A variety of software controls are used to protect data in a network. The physical security devices discussed above require keys or other objects possessed by the user,

FIGURE 15.17
Closed-Circuit TV Surveillance

FIGURE 15.18
Time-Lapse Photography Surveillance

whereas software controls depend on knowledge or information known only to authorized people.

A common means of controlling entry to a system is by restricting terminals so that they can access only certain kinds of data. For example, a terminal in a vice president's office may be authorized to access all data files, whereas those in the shipping room can access only a restricted number of files. **Passwords** and **user identification numbers** are required on most systems. Users cannot access data without current and correct user identification numbers, which are changed periodically to avoid use by unauthorized people.

Some systems automatically disconnect a user if more than three incorrect attempts at entry are made, thereby preventing a brute-force effort to enter numbers or passwords randomly until the correct one is found. By disconnecting the terminal after a limited number of tries, the computer makes it impractical to break the system this way because of the need to redial and log on after each disconnect.

Other software controls retain logs of unauthorized attempts to enter a system or maintain a record of those terminals or users seeking to access sensitive data. By auditing these logs, it is possible to detect efforts to compromise a system.

Port Protection Devices

Port protection devices (PPDs) are physically placed in a circuit to prevent unauthorized access. (See Figure 15.19.) The PPD is located in front of the host computer or the modem. These devices include microprocessors with program logic. They are able to scan input requests and check passwords, user identification numbers, or other codes before allowing a terminal to access the host computer.

FIGURE 15.19
Port Protection Device

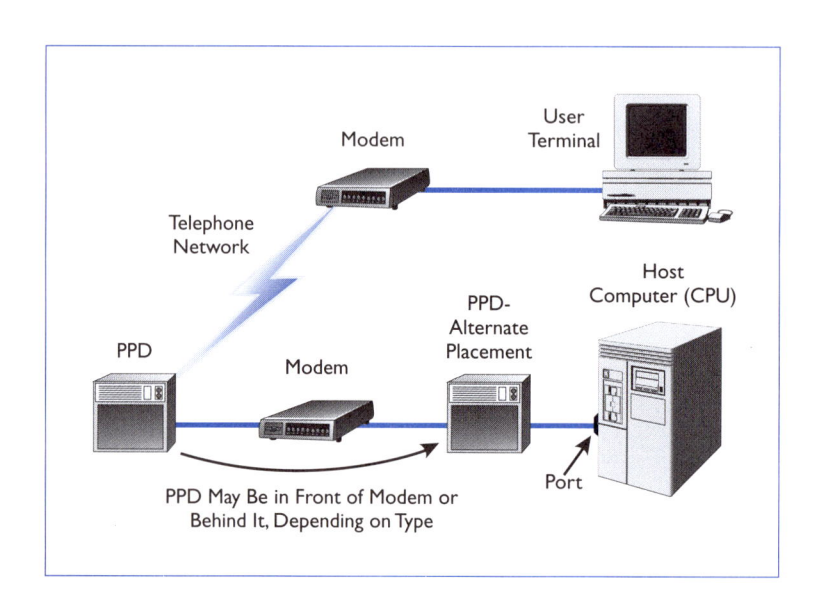

Encrypting Data

Once a user has successfully logged on to a system, **data encrypting** techniques prevent breaches of security. In the security system shown in Figure 15.20, keystrokes or messages from the originating terminal are converted into encrypted messages and sent over the line in place of standard ASCII or EBCDIC codes. Someone intercepting these messages would have trouble deciphering them without a **decrypting key**. The key allows the message to be converted back into ordinary English. Encrypting keys that perform this function may be programs or physical hardware.

A variety of **camouflage techniques** are used to disguise information at a terminal and to prevent unauthorized access. For example, the terminal may print out a line of Xs, strikeouts, or other obliterating characters before a user is asked to key in a password. When the password is keyed in over the strikeout line, the correct key-

```
CONFIDENTIAL MEMORANDUM                    dfjfjd/djdi63fayw

SUBJECT: RELEASE OF NEW                    epjsgsy980#,do@kd0opposmwoo
         PASSWORDS                         klsgtdz*2tas

John B. Elrod                              foc;./=klijd/she/jdu
Information Systems Manager                ero    efwe6

Department Managers:                       oit/drehjb(24.1jdrtqwpq,cxc=iwep[
The Information Systems Manager            udagdk,aekul we/---=1/()jtweiojn
will assign a new system of user           shys y eruefynwe/23957 x ewuehp.0
numbers and passwords. These               curhncd nuf8re/2673b heis sd/
numbers and words will be in effect        fg    q=7 54 /doi43 3/epv
for the next 90-day period.                hjccgdw86qwoim @kgfkti
```

Plain text (left) and the encrypted version
(right) as produced by a security system.

FIGURE 15.20 Plain and Encrypted Text

strokes are sent to the computer, but they are unreadable to any observers at the terminal. This prevents individuals from looking over someone's shoulder and copying a password or from rummaging through a wastebasket or trash barrel to locate valid user numbers or passwords.

NETWORK DOCUMENTATION

The preparation of **systems documentation** is an ongoing process in network design. Systems documentation consists of implementation plans, timetables, lists of equipment to be acquired, and other items. It also includes procedures and policy manuals as well as descriptions of network security, access, and control routines. Armed with a complete set of documentation and design plans, the network manager is ready to move into the last phase of systems analysis. In Chapter 16 we will see how this information is used to acquire the hardware, software, communications circuits, and personnel needed for the new system.

SUMMARY

Systems design involves considering *alternatives* and drafting a plan. Selection of a specific alternative is based on consideration of the *benefits* versus *costs*. *Consultants* are frequently used in the systems design phase. Different designs and configurations may be tested using computer *modeling and simulation* techniques.

The *PERT* scheduling method is useful in preparing implementation timetables. Detailed hardware specifications, plus software and communications specifications, are prepared for the new system.

Systems costs involve both capital investment and operating expenses. A *benchmark* is a test against which time or cost performance is measured. *Data security* factors must be considered in designing a new system. A policy should be established specifying who may access a network.

Passwords and *identification numbers* are used to control network access. *PPDs* prevent unauthorized system access. Security breaches may be prevented through *data encryption*. *Camouflage techniques* are used to prevent unauthorized system use.

Systems *documentation*, including timetables, lists of equipment, policy manuals, and more, is prepared. Government regulatory constraints are considered in systems design.

LP is a computer technique that determines the *best mix* of resources. *Queuing theory* analyzes waiting lines to balance loads. *Quality control* standards are used to monitor error rates and other parameters. *Linear regression* is a *forecasting* technique used to make predictions of future events. *Simulation and modeling* is a technique that allows experimentation with a network without disturbing its normal activities.

EXERCISES

1. Define systems design.
2. What are some typical benefits of a new system?
3. Describe network modeling and simulation.
4. How is linear programming used in communications?
5. List some of the costs considered in assessing a new system.
6. What are benchmarks, and how are they used?
7. List some of the ways that physical plants are protected against unauthorized intrusions.
8. What is the function of a PPD?
9. What is the function of data encryption?
10. Discuss a camouflage technique used at a computer terminal.

HANDS-ON PROJECTS

- Discuss communications system design with the individual charged with that responsibility at your campus computer center. Prepare a short report on your findings.

- Interview a small business proprietor and discuss communications systems. Make a list of benefits from a new system.

- Obtain the operating manual or user instructions from a piece of modeling and simulation software. Make a list of its features and capabilities.

- Develop an improved communications system for a small business. Make a list of the steps taken in designing the system.

- Visit a business equipped with communications facilities. Discuss personnel security requirements and background checks.

CASE SOLUTION
METRO SECURITY

COMMUNICATIONS IN ACTION

The communications manager at Metro Security studied its data and communications needs carefully. Working with security specialists, the manager concluded that the company was at risk in both its hardware and software environments. A plan that provided a high level of protection for both areas was designed and implemented.

Only selected employees are now allowed within the immediate area of the computer and its communications lines. These individuals are carefully screened and are given special badges and keycards. Closed-circuit television has been installed to monitor the computer room. The computer has been programmed to allow access by only a limited number of individuals who have a specific need to know certain kinds of information.

Port protection devices, which scan input requests and check passwords, are now installed at the front end of the computer. (See Figure 15.21.) A data encrypting system is used on all data moving between the computer and customers who require a high degree of security.

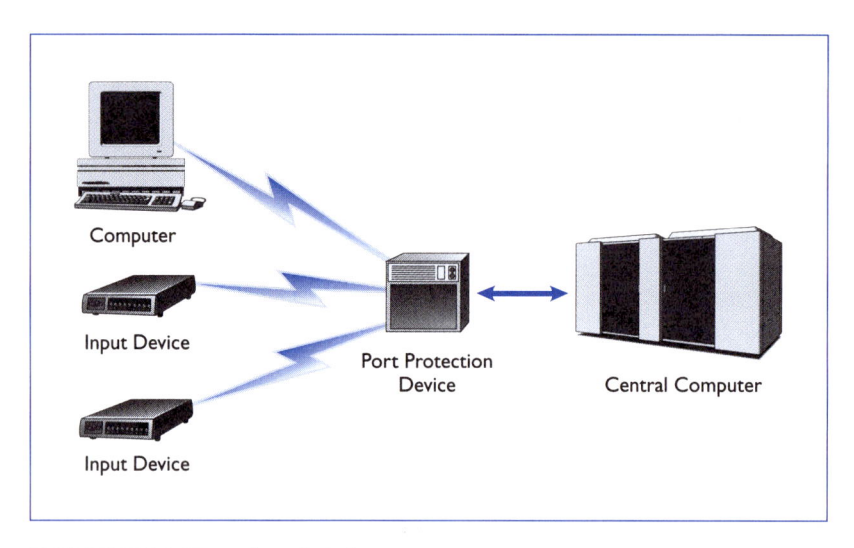

FIGURE 15.21 Metro Security's System

The computer maintains a log of all requests for service and any unauthorized attempts to access sensitive data. As a result of these procedures, Metro Security is able to maintain tight control over the movement of data, both within its central office and between the office and its clients. There has not been a security breach since the installation of the new system.

IMPLEMENTING COMMUNICATIONS NETWORKS

LEARNING OBJECTIVES

After reading this chapter, you should be able to:

- Discuss Electronic Data Interchange (EDI)
- Discuss major criteria in vendor selection
- Discuss the use of the prototype project
- Discuss the use of lead time schedules
- Contrast different system changeover plans
- Discuss systems optimization procedures

COMMUNICATIONS IN ACTION

CASE PROBLEM
OAKVIEW HOSPITAL

SYSTEM CHANGEOVER

Oakview Hospital provides medical services to a community of about 350,000 people. The hospital is fully staffed 24 hours a day, providing emergency care, in-patient and out-patient services, and a pharmacy. Many of Oakview's doctors and other staff members carry a beeper paging device, enabling the hospital to page personnel on short notice.

A number of doctors who practice at Oakview Hospital maintain private practices in a medical building several miles away but are always available for consultation. Neurologists, radiologists, and other specialists visit the hospital and interpret X-rays, Computerized Anatomic Tomography (CAT) scans, and other diagnostic media. However, it is often preferable for the hospital to transmit images of these films to the doctors' offices. This involves sending a dozen or more X-rays over a telephone line between locations since an immediate diagnosis is often necessary where patients are critically ill or injured.

The administration of Oakview Hospital has decided to install a new DBX and to upgrade the cellular telephone transmitter, which is located on a nearby hilltop. They also wish to make changes in the paging system. As part of the reworking of the communications system, new telephone lines will be installed to facilitate the transmission of X-rays and other diagnostic films.

What recommendations would you make to assist in this changeover? Refer to the end of this chapter to see how Oakview Hospital handled the conversion.

MOVING a network from the drawing board to a practical and financially feasible installation is a major undertaking that may take many months of effort and involve the outlay of hundreds of thousands of dollars. No matter how well conceived the system is, it will not perform properly unless it is built from reliable components and installed with the minimum disruption to the organization.

Previous chapters have described how networks are planned and designed. In this chapter we will study systems development and implementation. We will review the steps most organizations follow in actually building the network and testing it.

Because businesses differ in their major services, products, and goals, they require different kinds of communications systems and procedures. Communications networks must be tailored to meet the specific needs of each organization. Methods, procedures, and techniques should be selected to carry out organization goals in a regulated, orderly manner.

This chapter also explores Electronic Data Interchange (EDI) concepts and format standardization. EDI is becoming a standard by which organizations transfer forms and data in an agreed-upon format.

Firms that manufacture goods build their communications systems around the sales order or the job order. Banks and lending institutions structure their systems on the account or financial transaction. Insurance companies base their systems on the policy, while property listings are the focal point of real estate companies. Airlines, hotels, and motels use the reservation, and stockbrokers use buy and sell orders.

ELECTRONIC DATA INTERCHANGE

The introduction of high-speed data communications systems in business has brought about the need for standardization in forms design, content, and handling. Prior to the reliance on data communications, most businesses were free to generate printed forms of virtually any content and design. Many of these forms were handled internally, while some were mailed or faxed directly to other organizations. There were few constraints on forms organization and content; it didn't matter whether the customer's purchase order number came before or after the order date or the terms. As long as the information was present, it satisfied the user's needs.

To improve efficiency and reduce costs, many organizations have automated their forms-handling and processing systems. This automation has led to industry-wide standardization, known as **Electronic Data Interchange (EDI)**. EDI is the exchange of routine business information in a consistent format that can be processed by computer. EDI provides standards for many business transactions, including inquiries, planning, pricing, purchasing, scheduling, shipping, invoicing, and financial reporting.

In 1979 the American National Standards Institute (ANSI) established a group known as the Accredited Standards Committee (ASC) X12. Its goal was to develop uniform standards for the electronic interchange of business transactions. The ASC sought to facilitate order processing, shipping, handling, and similar transactions.

Using EDI Standards

An organization that seeks to implement EDI must first choose a standard and trading partners. **Trading partners** are other businesses or organizations that agree to exchange information according to the standard. Once this is done, documents are transmitted electronically between organizations, following the ASC standards. Physical documents are not mailed. Instead, the contents are sent electronically over a value-added network (VAN). The receiving organization accepts the electronic document and processes it, assuming that data items are presented in a predetermined sequence and format.

The system is efficient because the identifiers need not be mixed in with data. Consider the following data communication example:

    Customer: Smith Corporation
    Address: 900 Easy Street
    Telephone: (618)555-6765

In this example, much unnecessary data is being transmitted. The word "Customer" precedes the customer data field, the word "Address" precedes the address field, and so on. When an agreed-upon sequence is used, the communication can be shortened, saving time and cost. Once the sequence is established, only the customer, address, and telephone data fields must be transmitted, greatly reducing the amount of unnecessary information sent.

ASC X12 Standards

The basis for a document is a standard structure, shown in Figure 16.1. The structure defines a communications session, interchange envelope, and functional groups. Figure 16.2 illustrates a standard invoice form that is consistent with the **ASC X12** format. Figure 16.3 shows a detailed breakout of the sequence and format of data that will be transmitted for the form over the VAN.

EDI Benefits

Information transmitted electronically rather than physically, and conforming to EDI standards, has many benefits. Among them are the following:

1. Increased accuracy and better control over documents
2. More timely movement of information
3. Reduction in delays and in paperwork-handling tasks
4. Built-in security features that protect against unauthorized access
5. An audit trail to track the flow of messages
6. Reductions in cost and overhead

As more organizations shift to electronic communications, there is a greater reliance on EDI and less reliance on the movement of paper documents. AT&T and SprintNet, for example, market EDI network services, connecting vendors and suppliers worldwide.

Many systems still rely on paper documents rather than EDI. Regardless of the system in use, the reader should understand basic order processing, the inquiry system, word processing systems, and management information systems (MISs).

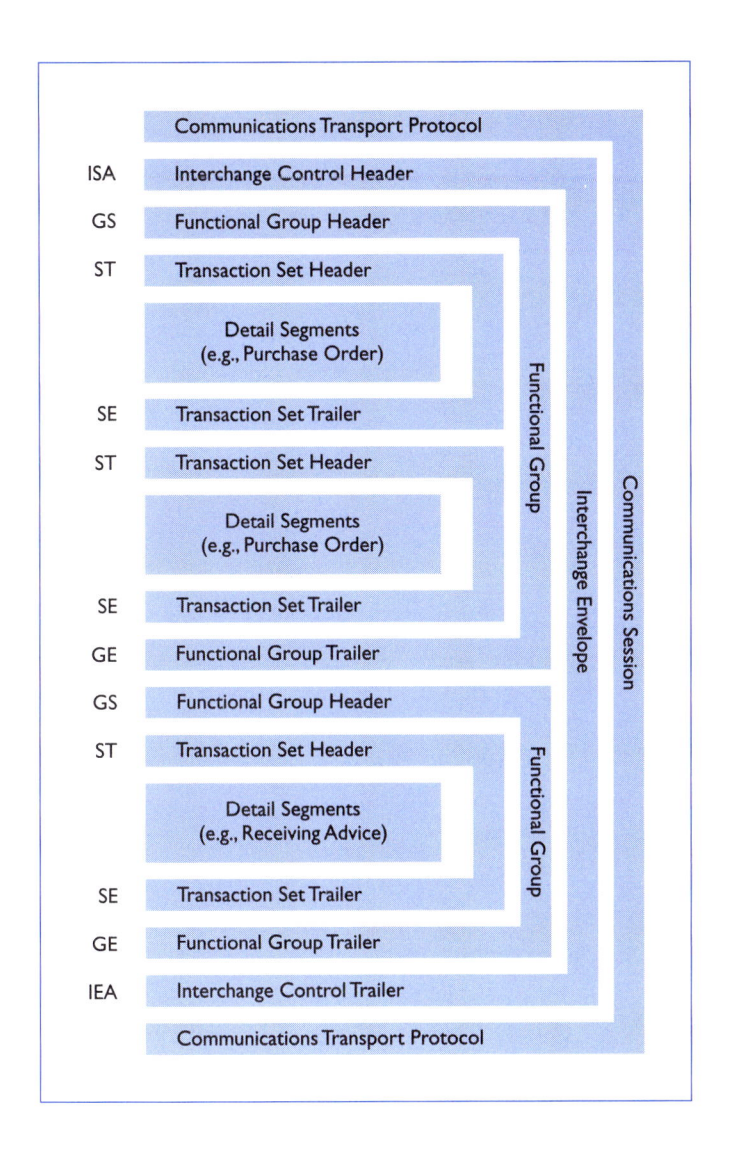

FIGURE 16.1
ASC X12 Structure of an EDI Transmission

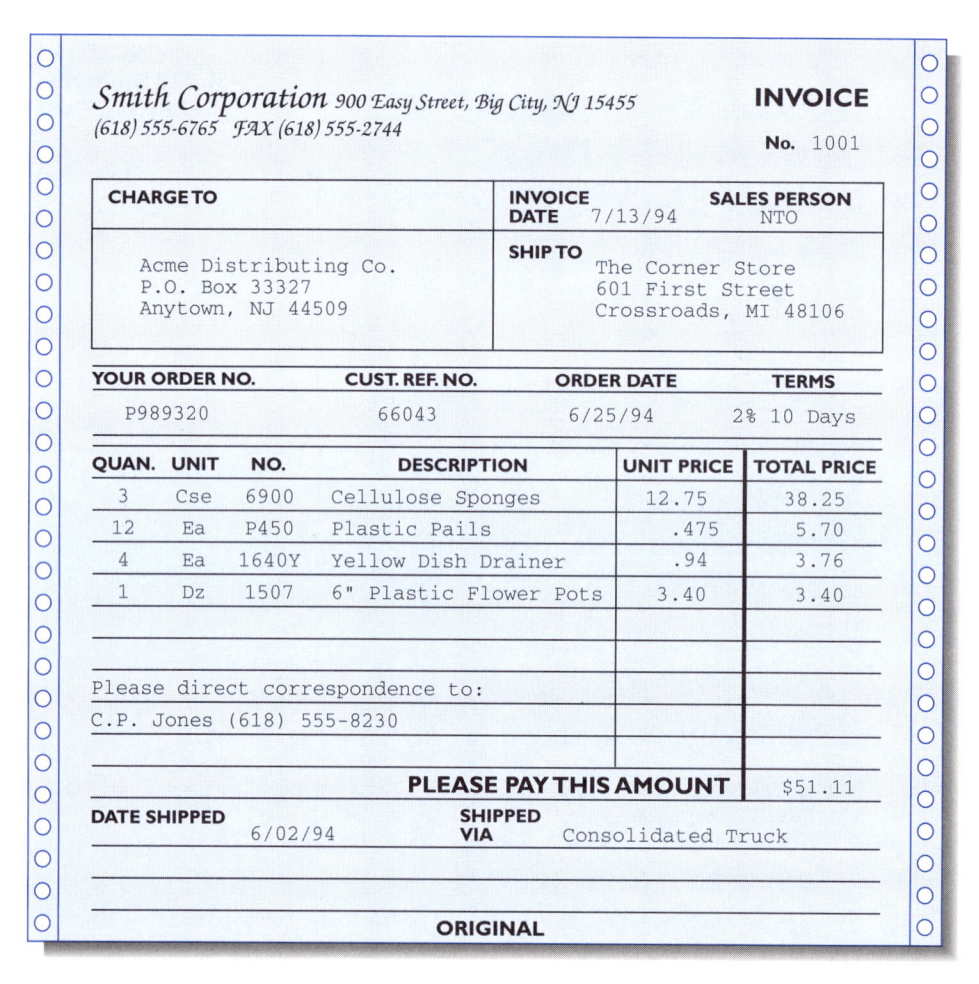

FIGURE 16.2 Standard Invoice Following ASC X12 Format

ORDER PROCESSING SYSTEMS

Order processing systems are one of the most widely used business information systems. Data generation, processing, and information flow are based on the **order** as it progresses through the system. The order processing system is used by companies that manufacture goods or products, wholesalers and retailers, printers, furniture manufacturers, and other types of businesses in which the main activity is the fabrication or manufacture of a good.

NOTES	ABC X12 FORMAT	SAMPLE INVOICE CONTENT	
Interchange Control Header, ISA Segment, see X12.5.	ISA*00*0000000000*01 PASSWORDME *01*123456789bbbbbb*987654321bbbbbb* 890714*2210*U*00204*000000008*0*P*:NL	Outside Envelope	
Functional Group Header, GS Segment, see X12.22.	GS*IN*012345678*087654321*900509 *2210*000001*X*00204N/L	Inside Envelope	
Transaction Set Header, ST Segment, see X12.22.	ST*810*0001N/L	Invoice	
	BIG*940713*1001*940625*P989320N/L	DATE 7/13/94 ORDER DATE 6/25/94 INVOICE # 1001 CUSTOMER ORDER # P989320	
	N1*BT*ACME DISTRIBUTING COMPANYN/L N3*P.O. BOX 33327N/L N4*ANYTOWN*NJ*44509N/L	CHARGE TO	Acme Distributing Company P.O. Box 33327 Anytown, NJ 44509
	N1*ST*THE CORNER STOREN/L N3*601* FIRST STREETN/L N4*CROSSROADS*MI*48106N/L	SHIP TO	The Corner Store 601 First Stret Crossroads, MI 48106
	N1*SE*SMITH CORPORATIONN/L N3*900 EASY STREETN/L N4*BIG CITY*NJ*15455N/L	REMIT TO (Selling Party)	Smith Corporation 900 Easy Street Big City, NJ 15455
	PER*AD*C.D.JONES*TE*6185558230N/L	CORRESPONDENCE TO	Accounting Dept. C.D. Jones (618) 555-8230
	ITD*01*3*2**10N/L	TERMS OF SALE	2% 10 days from invoice date

		QUANTITY	UNIT	SUPPLIER BRAND CODE	DESCRIPTION	UNIT PRICE
	ITI**3*CA*12.75**VC*6900N/L	3	Cse	6900	Cellulose Sponges	12.75
	ITI**12*EA*.475**VC*P450N/L	12	Ea	P450	Plastic Pails	.475
	ITI**4*EA*.94**VC*1640YN/L	4	Ea	1640Y	Yellow Dish Drainer	.94
	ITI**1*DZ*3.4**VC*1507N/L	1	Dz	1507	6" Plastic Flower Pots	3.40
	TDS*5111N/L	Invoice Total				
	CAD*M****CONSOLIDATED TRUCKN/L	Via Consolidated Truck				
Hash Totals	CTT*4*20N/L	(4 Line Items, Hash Total 20)				
Transaction Set Trailer	SE*21*00000 1N/L					
Function Group Trailer	GE*1*000001N/L					
Interchange Control Trailer	IEA*1*000000008N/L					

b = Space Character   * = Data Element Separator   N/L = Segment Terminator

FIGURE 16.3 ASC X12 Data Field Sequence

The steps in the order processing system, shown in Figure 16.4, are described below:

1. *Receipt of order.* The first step in order processing is receipt of the order by telephone, regular or electronic mail, or messenger service. The job specifications are entered on some medium, such as a job ticket, work order, sales order, or into a computer via a video display terminal (VDT).
2. *Acknowledgment of order.* After the order is received and entered, some form of **order acknowledgment** is usually communicated to the customer. This may consist of a telephone call acknowledging receipt of the order and giving the anticipated delivery date; mailing a copy of the order form; a written estimate showing plans, layouts, and cost quotations; or perhaps a confirmation sent from one computer to another.
3. *Filling order.* This step encompasses all the activities related to producing or acquiring the ordered goods. Materials are ordered from suppliers or manufacturers, or removed from stock, and manufacturing processes are performed. The filling of the order generates data regarding expenditure of funds for goods and services from outside sources, changes in inventory status, sales activities, and related labor costs. (See Figure 16.5.)
4. *Shipping order.* The ordered items have now been picked from stock, or manufactured, and are ready for shipment to the customer. **Bills of lading, shipping memos**, labels, and such are prepared to accompany the goods.
5. *Billing order.* After the order has been filled and the goods delivered, the charges are billed to the customer. This involves the preparation of an **invoice** showing the costs incurred during manufacture, removal from inventory, shipping, and other functions. In addition, a statement summarizing the charges on a group of invoices may be sent to the customer. Data from the invoice are transmitted to the accounting department for payment and collection.
6. *Receiving and posting payment.* The last step in the order system is the receipt and posting of the payment. Funds received must be deducted from the balance owed by the customer and posted on the company's accounting records. This step completes the order processing cycle.

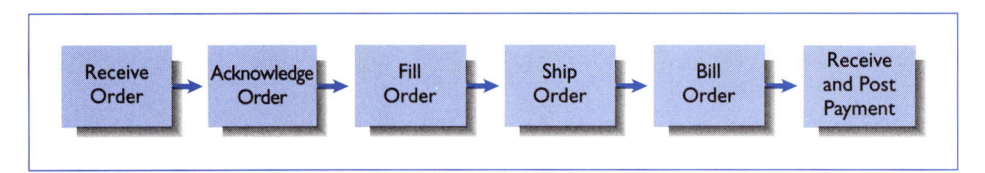

FIGURE 16.4 Order Processing System

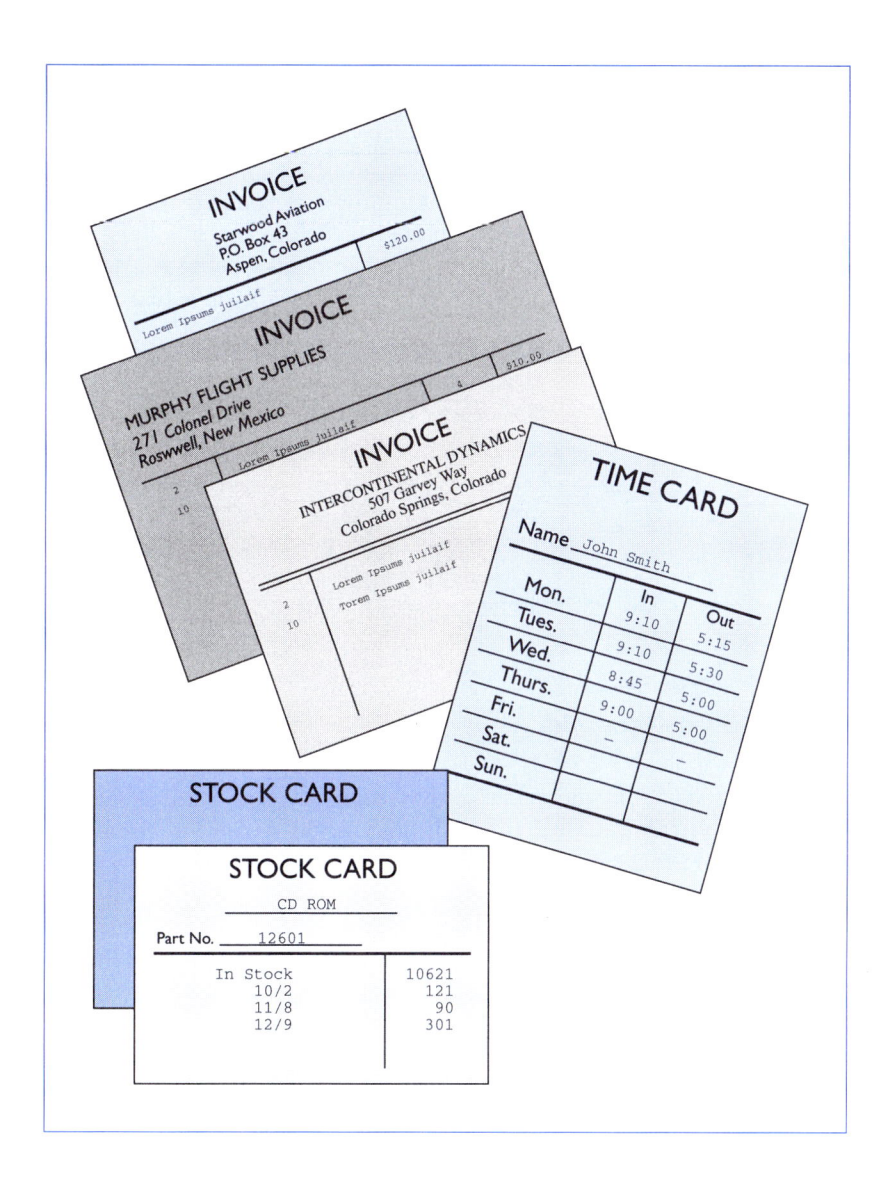

FIGURE 16.5
Data Generated When Filling an Order

INQUIRY SYSTEMS

Inquiry systems, a major type of information system, are used by hotels, airlines, banks, credit companies, insurance companies, and other organizations that maintain large databases on networks. Their focal points are inquiries and the information processing activities related to them.

An **inquiry system** consists of a database, a collection of logically related files, and a network of query terminals. (See Figure 16.6.) The database contains information on the remaining physical inventory or availability of goods and services. A database for a hotel chain or airline would contain information regarding such things as available reservations, connecting flights, time schedules, and prices. A company that stocks a large number of parts or goods would record information such as part numbers, selling prices, and quantities in stock. Banks and credit departments would record information on customer accounts, and insurance companies would maintain actuarial data and general policy information.

FIGURE 16.6
Inquiry System

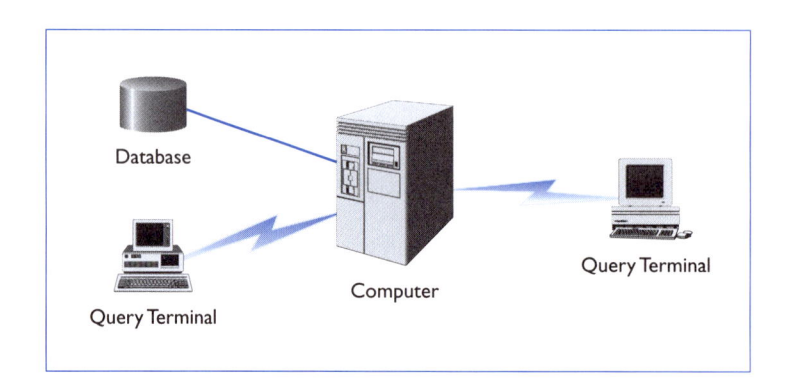

Users access the database from query stations or terminals. These stations may be located near the computer housing the database or at a remote location. Communications between the database and the query stations are provided by communications networks, telephone lines, messengers, or the mails.

The purpose of the inquiry system is to make a central body of information available to all users. These data must be current and reflect changes in the status of the database or inventory as they occur. For example, as parts are removed from stock, the quantity shown in the database must be altered to reflect the change. When a withdrawal is made from a bank, the balance on the customer's account must be adjusted. If additional flights are scheduled, data showing the time schedule, costs, and seating arrangements must be placed in the database for an airline.

Some database arrangements allow the system to be updated from remote terminals, others from a central location only. Some inquiries go directly to the database from a remote terminal, while others might be received at the database site by an operator who queries the files and relays the information back to the terminal.

Most inquiry systems involve the following steps, shown in Figure 16.7:

1. *Construct the database.* A database is set up listing the relevant information (parts available in stock, seats on a flight, room accommodations, credit limits, etc.). (See Figure 16.8.)
2. *Process queries.* **Queries** are received and processed through a network of terminals. For example, reservation clerks stationed at airports and branch offices

query the central database via computer terminals for the current information on available seats and schedules. Salespeople in department stores request approval via point-of-sale terminals. Employees in a manufacturing plant query the database by terminal to learn the number of units of a specific part in stock.

3. *Respond to query.* A response or reply is made to a query, providing the requested information. The database is searched and the required information located and communicated to the user. The data may be displayed on a video display terminal (VDT) or typed out on a printer. It may also be transmitted by telephone or mail.

4. *Perform file maintenance.* As changes occur in the status of the records in a database, the file is updated. When customers charge merchandise or write checks, these transactions are posted to their account balances stored in the database. As items are sold or taken from stock, the count in the inventory file is modified. As new units (parts, reservations, sizes, etc.) are made available, this information is added to the database.

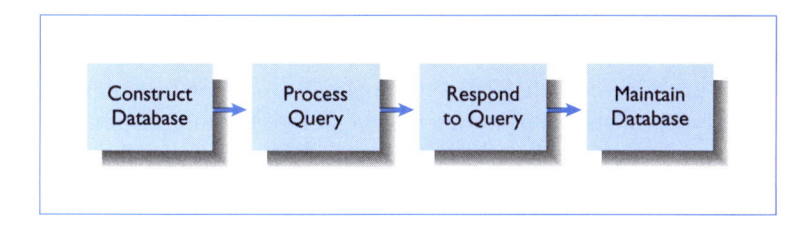

FIGURE 16.7 Steps for Setting Up an Inquiry System

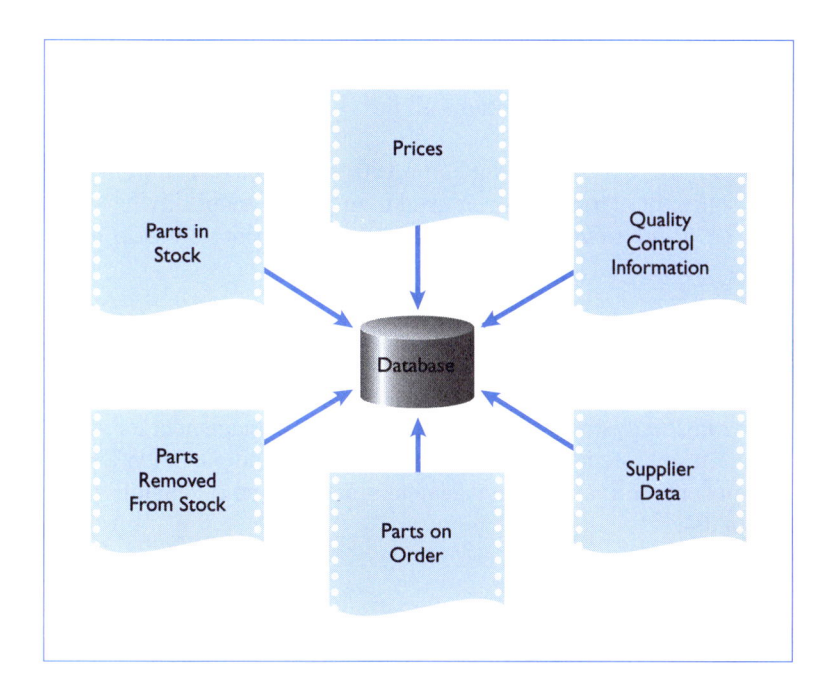

FIGURE 16.8 Types of Information in a Database for a Manufacturing Firm

WORD PROCESSING SYSTEMS

Word processing systems are designed to manipulate words, phrases, and textual matter, and to generate reports, manuals, documents, letters, correspondence, and the like. They differ from other systems in that they process strings of text rather than numerical data.

Word processing systems are used by firms that generate a great deal of written material. Law firms and insurance companies use word processing to prepare reports and documents related to clients. Advertising firms use it to produce brochures and letters, and manufacturers prepare training manuals and user guides.

Word processing consists basically of a cycle in which textual matter (words, sentences, and paragraphs) is entered, edited, revised, and printed out. The first draft may be spoken into a dictation machine for later transcription on a computer terminal or microcomputer. Editing and revising involve making corrections, changes, additions, or improvements in the text. The changes may be indicated manually on a copy, or they may be entered directly into the computer by the originator of the document. The final draft is output on a printer or other device.

The entire process of entering text and revising drafts is greatly facilitated by word processing software available on many small and large computers. Microsoft Word and WordPerfect are programs that allow the operator to enter text into the machine as a long, unformatted stream of words. Once entered, the information can be displayed, rearranged, or reformatted easily, using simple keyboard commands. On a network these activities can be done by different people. Some of these programs include automatic indexing, as well as grammar and spell checkers. These features allow the user to index a document automatically and check spelling against a standard or specialized dictionary entered by the user.

After all additions, revisions, and corrections have been entered into the draft, a finished copy is printed out. The final copy contains all the changes integrated into their proper places in the text stream.

The finished draft may be reformatted for improved appearance. Different line widths, spacing, type styles, or margins may be used to improve readability. The finished document may be printed out or routed over communications lines to other devices on a network.

MANAGEMENT INFORMATION SYSTEMS

A **management information system (MIS)** provides data to management for effective decision making. These systems vary in their scope, size, and capacity. Figure 16.9 illustrates a comprehensive financial management system, using a computer database and online terminals.

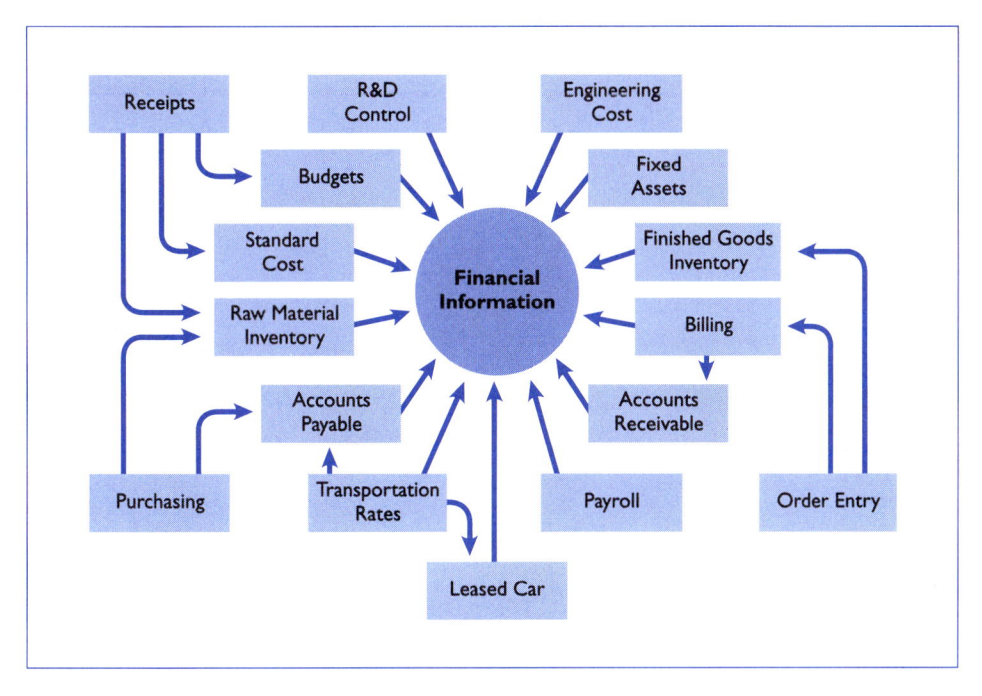

FIGURE 16.9 Management Information System

The database contains information on the firm's budgets, sales, engineering, billing, assets, payroll, transportation, and accounts receivable and payable. It is composed of several subsystems that handle order processing, inventory, payroll, and accounting functions. The order processing portion captures data on customer orders and includes information on routing, shipment, contract price, base price, credit, and raw materials and finished goods inventories. All of this information is extremely useful to the organization's managers. It improves the quality of decisions throughout the company and serves all levels of management in making key decisions.

Management information systems may be structured to provide important data for tasks like financial management, cost accounting, cost control, and personnel management. For example, reports can be generated for such matters as cash flow, trends in accounts payable and receivable, earning ratios, and turnover ratios.

The MIS gives managers data concerning distribution functions. These reports provide information on finished goods in stock or in transit, goods in production, or backlogged orders. An MIS prepares shipping schedules, routing data, and shipping cost tables. This type of information decreases late deliveries, misrouted goods, and over- or underproduction of goods.

Investment planning and management of capital assets can be included in an MIS. For example, managers can receive reports on capital outlays, returns on investment, cost centers, depreciation schedules, and equipment maintenance and installation costs. This facilitates planning the acquisition of new capital goods or the sale of outdated or unproductive equipment.

Cost accounting information can be processed by an MIS, which can be programmed to give reports on the cost of goods in manufacture. It can print out break-even points, points of diminishing returns, fixed and variable expense reports, and costs by product line, model, or individual unit produced.

Developing the database for an MIS usually follows the steps described below:

1. *Construct the database.* In this initial phase, a study is made of the elements to be included in the database. Types of information and records to be included are defined, and the manner in which the system will be accessed and maintained is planned. The type of output reports are described and designed.

    The layout of the records is one of the important elements to be considered when planning the database. The records must be consistently structured to allow maximum utility and access to the recorded data.

2. *Open access to users.* Users who will access the database for decision making must be provided with online terminals. This allows them to access files and records prior to making key decisions. Periodically, reports may be generated for management utilizing the information in the database. Some reports may compare corresponding data in different departments or time periods. Others may show sales versus costs or changes in the status of a specific variable. These reports may be output in several ways—some in hard copy on a line printer; others displayed on a video display terminal.

3. *Maintenance of the database.* As new information is gathered on business activities, the content of the database must be modified to reflect these changes. Outdated information is discarded; new data, facts, and figures are entered. Changes in the database are made either from a central location or from remote terminals.

HARDWARE AND SOFTWARE SELECTION

In the previous systems analysis phase, general characteristics of hardware and software have been identified. Performance specifications may have been written without reference to particular brands, products, or suppliers. It is now up to the network manager to convert these general specifications into pieces of hardware, programs, or services that are to be acquired. (See Figure 16.10.) **Vendor documentation** is carefully reviewed for specific features.

When selecting a particular piece of hardware or software, cost always plays a major factor. In addition, the manager must ask certain questions. For example, will the devices provide adequate speed, sufficient communications channels, and acceptable error rates? Does it physically fit into the space allocated? How reliable have previous products of the same brand been? Does the hardware meet required specifications?

FIGURE 16.10
Modem Feature Checklist

Asynchronous operation
Auto-answer
Auto-dial
Card module
Compatibility
  Bell 103
  Bell 212
  CCITT v.22 bisyn
Data rate:
  0 to 300 bps
  1,200 bps
  2,400 bps
  4,800 bps
  9,600 bps
Equalization
  Automatic adaptive
  Fixed compromise
FCC registered
Full-duplex operation
Line connection
  Fixed-loss loop
  Permissive
  Programmable
Loopback test modes
Manual originate
Stand alone unit
Synchronous operation
Telephone set connection
Two-wire leased line operation

Expandability is an important hardware consideration. Can the equipment be upgraded by simply inserting more circuit boards, or will an entire new device be required? Will cables have sufficient bandwidth to meet the organization's future needs? In making these decisions, cost-benefit studies, described in Chapter 15, may be undertaken. The goal is to purchase specific pieces of equipment with the greatest capacity and highest reliability at the lowest possible price.

VENDOR SELECTION

Often, similar pieces of communications equipment or software may be available from two or more vendors. These devices or programs may have similar characteristics, speed, and cost. The selection then will rest on factors other than the quality and price of the goods. The deciding factor sometimes is the reliability and capability of the vendor.

Long-haul communications circuits may be available from many different vendors. Some companies have provided long distance common-carrier facilities for many years, and others may be new to the marketplace. When charges are similar, the decision may be made based on billing and accounting procedures, markets served, or how credits are charged back.

Here are some of the criteria that managers review when selecting a vendor:

- Does the vendor have the experience and knowledge to install the equipment properly? (See Figure 16.11.)
- Are adequate service stations, maintenance staff, and backup devices available to minimize disruptions due to equipment failure? (See Figure 16.12.)
- Does the vendor offer training and instruction in the use of the hardware and software provided? (See Figure 16.13.)

- Are manuals, equipment documentation, service notes, and wiring diagrams available to the user? (See Figure 16.14.)
- Will the vendor assist in defining a user's needs and prepare a proposal for the equipment to be purchased?
- Does the vendor have a good reputation and history that indicates high-quality performance over a long period of time?
- Is the vendor financially stable?

FIGURE 16.11 Equipment Installer

FIGURE 16.12 Equipment Awaiting Shipment

FIGURE 16.13 Vendor-Provided Training Course

FIGURE 16.14 Equipment Documentation

Some organizations may be willing to pay more for a piece of equipment because the vendor has a good maintenance department and field support staff. Reliable and fast repair service may save the company more money in the long run. Others prefer to purchase "bare bones" equipment. Then they handle the installation, prepare their own documentation, and do all maintenance and training in-house. This independence allows organizations to tailor systems to their own needs.

LEASE VERSUS BUY DECISION

Another question that must be answered before actually acquiring new facilities is whether equipment should be leased or purchased. There are advantages to outright purchase of equipment. Multiplexers, communications lines, and switching equipment that are purchased outright fall under the full control of the organization. They can be moved about, modified, or sold without having to consult a third party. However, outright purchase requires an investment of capital. Another drawback is that facilities purchased outright may become technologically obsolete before they are paid for or physically worn out. Scrapping this equipment would be costly. Nevertheless, many organizations choose to buy their equipment rather than lease it.

Leasing of equipment and facilities also has advantages and disadvantages. A lease does not require an investment of capital. The lessee pays a monthly fee to the lessor for the use of the equipment. Usually the entire lease fee is tax deductible. Therefore, for some organizations, leasing may have tax advantages over outright purchase. Equipment purchased outright must be depreciated over its useful life, whereas the entire amount of the lease is tax deductible.

Technological obsolescence may be less of a problem when equipment is leased. If a new device or improved facilities become available, a lessee can return the equipment at the end of the lease, at which time more modern equipment can be leased in its place. Other factors in deciding whether to lease or buy are the availability of equipment, repair parts, insurance costs, maintenance fees, and installation charges. These factors must be carefully considered and are part of the systems development and implementation process.

THE PROTOTYPE INSTALLATION

Installing terminals, communications circuits, or data-handling procedures throughout an organization before they have been thoroughly tested could be costly. Even in the most carefully designed system, mistakes can be made. A **prototype installation** is sometimes used to test and debug a new system before it is fully implemented throughout an organization. A prototype installation is a carefully monitored facility designed to determine whether the equipment performs as specified under real-life working conditions.

For example, a large bank may wish to install new teller terminals, modems, multiplexers, and circuits in all its branches. It could use a pilot project to test the new network. (See Figure 16.15.) The engineers would convert only one branch to the new system and monitor how easily the tellers gain expertise in its use. They could also measure the system's reliability, repair record, and performance, giving themselves an opportunity to see if the vendor meets its commitments.

FIGURE 16.15
Prototype Installation. An installation such as this allows equipment to be tested in the field.

After the prototype project is working well, it is then implemented in the other branches of the bank. Pilot projects allow an organization to learn from its mistakes. Procedures can be worked out on a limited basis before going further. Manuals can be written and policies instituted based on experience and performance.

OVERSEEING THE INSTALLATION OF THE NEW SYSTEM

One of the network manager's major tasks is to oversee the actual installation of equipment and to ensure that the correct devices and software have been acquired and put in place properly. This function requires attention to lead time schedules, an orderly transition process, and orientation and training of personnel.

Lead Time Schedules

Lead time is the lapsed time between the ordering of a piece of equipment or service and its actual delivery. Lead time may be only a few days, or it may be weeks or many months. If a vendor has a completed and tested device on the shelf ready for immediate shipment, it may take only a few days from placing the order to delivery. On the other hand, if hundreds, or perhaps even thousands, of units are ordered, it may take a considerable length of time because most vendors do not keep such stock readily available.

Lead time must be considered, especially when ordering communications circuits. It may take many months for a common carrier to provide wideband circuits or adequate leased lines for a new facility. More than one network manager has experienced frustrating delays in getting a new installation up and running. Sometimes terminals are delivered and tested in a matter of weeks, but many months may elapse before leased lines are provided to connect the terminals to a remote computer. Thus, it is vital to see that all lead times are considered. A lead time schedule, such as the one in Figure 16.16, assists in this task. The schedule shows the date ordered, lead time, and expected delivery date.

ITEM	LEAD TIME IN DAYS	DATE ORDERED	EXPECTED DELIVERY
Multiplexer	60	1/01/94	3/01/94
T1 Communication Circuit	30	1/01/94	1/31/94
CPU with 640K Memory	20	1/01/94	1/21/94
Local Drop	10	1/01/94	1/11/94
Modem	10	1/01/94	1/11/94

FIGURE 16.16
Lead Time Schedule

System Changeover

One of the most important aspects of installing a new facility is the system changeover plan. New systems must be put in place with minimal disruption to the organization. Many business managers can tell stories about difficult transition periods. They report lost orders, customer complaints, employee dissatisfaction, and interference with the flow of work during the changeover period.

There are three basic approaches to implementing a new system. These include the phased-in conversion, the all-at-once conversion (sometimes called "plunge"), and the parallel systems conversion.

Phased-in Conversion. A **phased-in conversion** involves a step-by-step shift from an old system to a new one. Many organizations gradually change to a new system, rather than risk the shock and possible calamity of a sudden changeover. In this approach, one department, service, or task is converted at a time. (See Figure 16.17A) Only after that unit is running smoothly is another unit shifted to the new system. Following this approach, a bank, for example, might convert one branch after another to a new system of teller terminals. This approach allows time to adjust to the change and deal with problems that might occur. However, this method causes the various branches to be working under two different systems, which could create some confusion.

All-at-Once Conversion. A second approach is the **all-at-once conversion**. (See Figure 16.17B.) In this arrangement, a specific conversion date is established. On that date the operation of the old system is terminated and the traffic shifted to the new system. The changeover is accomplished quickly, and no parallel or backup system is in place during the conversion period. No backsliding is permitted because the old system is shut down; users must go to the new system. The advantage of the all-at-once transition is that all units in the organization are converted simultaneously.

In a bank, for example, a target date is set for conversion to the new terminals for the entire system. A weekend or holiday may be set aside for this task to minimize business disturbances. On the next business day, all transactions are handled on the new system. All-at-once conversions can be traumatic if the new system is not fully functional and debugged at the time of the changeover. Failure could mean lost sales, revenues, long delays, misrouted messages, or even bankruptcy.

FIGURE 16.17
Conversion Methods

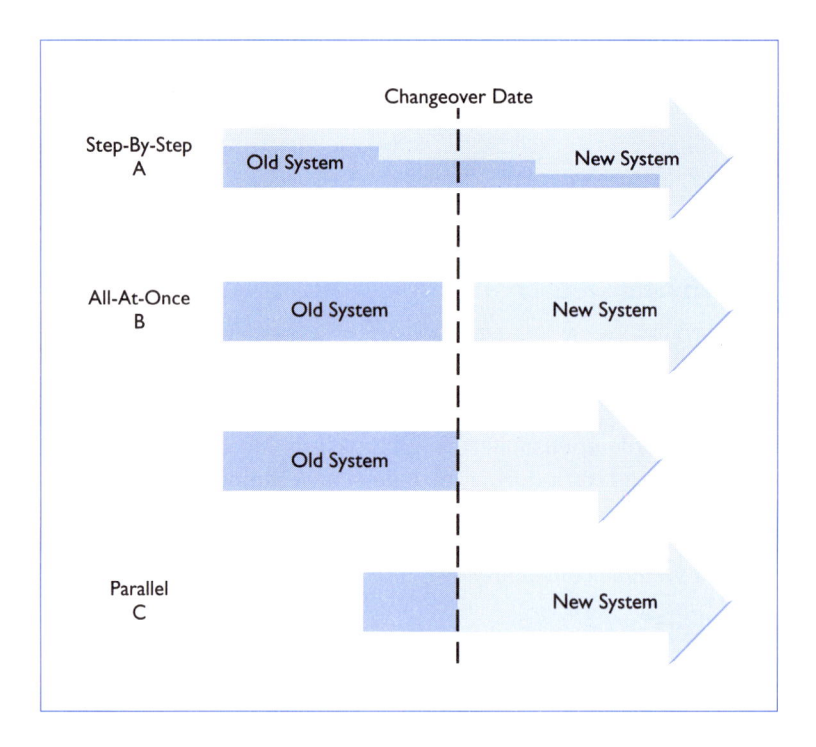

Parallel Conversion. Some organizations minimize the effects of a changeover by a **parallel conversion**. (See Figure 16.17C.) In this arrangement, the old system is kept in place while the new system is started up. Only after the new system has been debugged and is fully operational is the old system shut down.

In the bank example, new teller terminals are installed alongside the old terminals. Tellers are asked to use the new system, but if problems develop they may resort to the old system to process transactions. This arrangement has several advantages. It ensures that the organization will always have a reliable, functioning system in place. It also allows a period of time for users to adjust to the new system. The major disadvantage is cost. A parallel implementation requires keeping in place duplicate hardware, circuits, or personnel, all of which are expensive.

The choice of a particular mode of conversion depends on many factors. Data security, labor costs, reliability, availability of backup systems, and training costs all affect the choice. Sometimes a hybrid conversion plan is selected, allowing some departments of an organization to make an all-at-once changeover while others implement a parallel, or step-by-step, conversion.

Training and Orientation

A well-planned conversion effort allows adequate time for users to become familiar with the new system. The organization should provide users with orientation, training, and exposure to new hardware before they can be expected to become fully productive on it.

Instruction can be conducted in many different ways. Classes can be held to demonstrate the use of new terminals, switchboards, and telephones. Consultants may be hired to assist in training. Sometimes key personnel may be sent to manufacturers' facilities for instruction. Video tapes, film strips, slides, and training manuals may also be used in this effort.

EVALUATION AND FOLLOW-UP

The network manager cannot assume that all is well simply because a new system has been installed and is operating. One of the most critical tasks remaining is **systems evaluation and follow-up**. (See Figure 16.18.) This task consists of benchmark testing and systems optimizing. Both are required to maximize the performance of the new system.

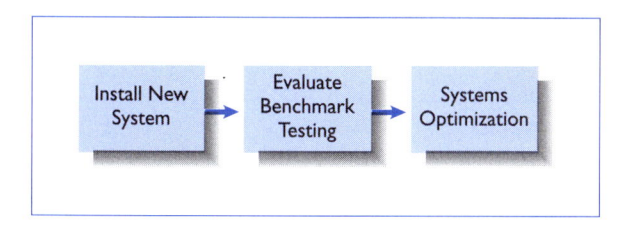

FIGURE 16.18
Systems Evaluation

Benchmark Testing

Benchmark testing consists of running a battery of tests and measurements against predetermined criteria. The object is to assure the analyst that the new facilities are performing up to expectations. A variety of techniques and tools are used in benchmark testing. (See Figure 16.19.)

If computers are involved, test programs are run to determine how long they take to execute programs and to ensure that all software is performing properly. For example, a computer program designed to route communications over selected common carriers must work properly. A benchmark test might systematically place calls over various circuits to make sure they are routed correctly.

FIGURE 16.19
Benchmark Testing

Other benchmark tests may be used to ensure that waiting time or queues are kept to a minimum or that certain throughput, error rates, or transmission speeds are being met. Final payment on the system is sometimes withheld from vendors until after benchmark tests are run and systems goals met. Benchmark tests may be developed throughout the systems analysis process; they always result in comparing performance against predetermined goals.

Systems Optimization

Some organizations expend a good deal of resources in planning and systems design, but fall short in the area of **systems optimization**. It is not always possible to predict precise traffic volumes or demands placed on terminals, multiplexers, or networks until they are actually installed. Good systems design requires fine-tuning of the system, making the necessary corrections and adjustments.

After analyzing results of benchmark tests, certain last-minute changes or final alterations may be called for. In systems optimization, changes and modifications are made in hardware, software, circuit selection, or personnel to obtain maximum performance from the system.

Systems optimization is particularly necessary in high-technology fields because new hardware, software, and facilities are constantly being developed and put on the market. These new resources might not have been available during the earlier phases of systems planning and design. Systems optimization enables new technology to be integrated in an organized way.

PREPARATION OF FINAL DOCUMENTATION

The last step of the process is the completion of final systems documentation. **Systems documentation**, usually begun early on and now completed, consists of preparing instruction manuals, policy and procedure guides, records of installations, wiring diagrams, service manuals, rate cards, and mileage and routing schemes. These documents are prepared to ensure the proper use and management of the new system.

Documentation is essential for several reasons. It assists new users in understanding the system and its components. It is also helpful in making system changes and modifications later, especially when the original systems planners and designers no longer work for the company. The presence of a complete set of documentation ensures systems continuity and consistency.

NETWORK MANAGEMENT AND CONTROL

Sometimes, after a new system has been installed and tested, it is turned over to others for operation. A well-designed and carefully implemented communications system may go awry, not because of design faults, but because it has been turned over to personnel who are unfamiliar with it.

Systems do not operate in a vacuum. They function in a fluid regulatory environment and in an atmosphere of changing technology and personnel. The managers of a network must be aware of this. They must monitor the organization's needs and the communications system's capability and continually modify or update the system to ensure that it meets the ongoing needs of the organization.

It is sometimes more cost-effective to turn over network management to a consultant or outside vendor. Sprint Communications, AT&T, and MCI all provide a range of network management services. They generate reports on system usage, error rates, unused capacity, line costs, and more.

In this chapter we have rounded out our discussion of communications systems by describing the final step of systems implementation. Chapter 17 discusses trends and issues. It looks toward the future of communications and provides insights into new technology and directions in the field.

SUMMARY

Electronic Data Interchange (EDI) is the exchange of routine business information in a format able to be processed by computer. It involves standards for many business transactions, including inquiries, planning, pricing, purchasing, scheduling, shipping, invoicing, and financial reporting.

Order processing systems track *orders* as they move through a process. *Inquiry systems* consist of a database and a network of query terminals. *Word processing systems* manipulate words, phrases, and textual matter. An *MIS* provides data to managers for effective decision making.

The *lease* versus *buy* option is frequently considered in systems development. *Systems development* involves the actual construction and testing of a system. Equipment leasing does not require an investment of *capital*. *Vendor documentation* consists of reports and printed data on facilities or equipment.

Equipment *expandability* is a major consideration in selecting facilities. *Vendors* are often judged on their experience, knowledge, and willingness to offer training. *Prototype installations* are used to test and debug new systems. *Lead time* is elapsed time between ordering a piece of equipment and its delivery.

System changeover involves the actual conversion from one system to another. *Phased-in conversions* involve step-by-step shifts to a new system. *All-at-once conversions* are usually made on a specific date. *Parallel conversions* involve two systems in place at one time. *Systems evaluation* and follow-up are important final tasks.

Systems optimization involves fine-tuning new facilities. High-technology fields often require systems optimization because of new innovations. *Systems documentation* is completed in the *implementation phase*. After a new network has been installed, it is sometimes turned over to others for operation.

Users must be given time to become familiar with the operation of a new system. Video tapes, film strips, slides, or demonstrations are used to orient new users to a system. *Field maintenance* and support are factors considered when selecting vendors.

EXERCISES

1. Define EDI.
2. Summarize the steps followed in a typical order processing system.
3. Describe the function of an inquiry system.
4. Describe the function of the word processing system.
5. Describe the functions of a management information system.
6. Contrast leased versus purchased equipment.
7. List some of the criteria assessed in selecting a vendor.

8. What are the advantages of a prototype installation?
9. List three different forms of system changeover.
10. What is systems optimization?

HANDS-ON PROJECTS

- Contact an organization that leases communications equipment. Make a list of the advantages of leasing.

- Interview a vendor of communications equipment. Discuss its capabilities. Prepare a short report on its services.

- Visit an organization that has recently installed new communications equipment. Prepare a short report on the conversion process.

- Discuss systems optimization with a communications manager. Prepare a short report on your findings and conclusions.

- Review the documentation for a communications system. What kinds of information are in the documentation file?

CASE SOLUTION
OAKVIEW HOSPITAL

COMMUNICATIONS IN ACTION

A careful timetable for conversion to the new DBX would have to be developed for the system changeover so that doctors and other hospital personnel would not be left without communications services. This factor ruled out any form of all-at-once conversion. A plunge into a new system, with no provisions for backup, could be a disaster, because of the myriad of start-up difficulties that could not be anticipated.

The administration also ruled out a parallel conversion because it would be too expensive. A parallel conversion would require dual transmitters, duplication of communications lines, and a doubling of staff during the changeover. After careful consideration, a step-by-step conversion was selected. (See Figure 16.20.) First, the new digital branch exchange was installed and tested. Then, groups of telephone lines were systematically switched over to the new DBX. Once the switchboard was tested and found to be functioning properly, the cellular telephone transmitter was installed. Both the paging system and regular telephone lines serve as backups.

FIGURE 16.20
Changeover Plan

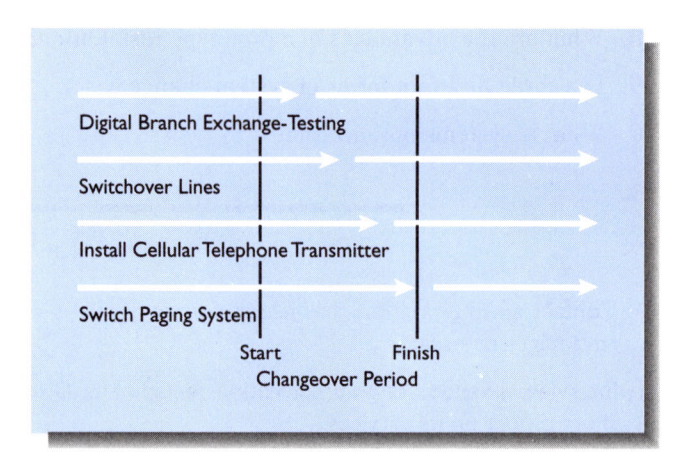

Digital Branch Exchange-Testing

Switchover Lines

Install Cellular Telephone Transmitter

Switch Paging System

Start   Finish
Changeover Period

Finally, the changes were made in the beeper paging system equipment. Several problems were encountered during this phase, but these did not endanger any patients because backup facilities were still in place. The careful planning of Oakview's staff enabled major changes to be phased into the communications system with virtually no interruption to service.

THE FUTURE OF COMMUNICATIONS

17

TRENDS AND ISSUES

LEARNING OBJECTIVES

After studing this chapter, you should be able to:

- Discuss communications and the changing workforce
- Describe how telecommuting will be used in the future
- Discuss connectivity and total systems integration
- Describe the automated office of the future
- Describe the growing fiber-optic network and digital communications
- Discuss the effect of deregulation on competition and vendor services

COMMUNICATIONS
IN ACTION

CASE PROBLEM
AMERICAN CREDIT

TELECOMMUTING SYSTEM

When Nate Duncan left his last job as a credit manager for a jewelry store, he decided to go into business for himself. He planned to set up a collection agency, using state-of-the-art communications. Duncan knew that with sound planning and the right facilities he could provide better service to customers at a lower cost than his competitors.

Nate Duncan's plan was to rent a large office in the central business district and open a credit and collection agency. This would involve setting up a suite with offices for every collection agent. Every office would be equipped with a desk, telephone lines, and a computer. Each employee would be assigned a group of accounts for collection. The agents' duties included calling debtors on the telephone, following up on previous calls, and sending form letters.

As Duncan investigated costs and other aspects of the new business venture, he ran into a few problems. The individual offices for collection agents would require renting a good deal of space, and rents in the downtown business district were very high. Also, parking was scarce and expensive. Insurance and utilities would add even more to the cost of the operation. Further, Duncan discovered during interviews with prospective collection agents that many of those he would like to have hired lived in the suburbs and were unhappy about making the long trip downtown.

How would you recommend that Nate Duncan use communications to acquire good employees, reduce his overhead, and still maintain service to his customers? Refer to the end of this chapter to see how Nate Duncan resolved his problem.

THE INDUSTRY will see continued expansion of innovations in communications technology as a new century approaches. Connectivity, LANs, and the linking of systems will be major directions taken in the next decade. There will be greater reliance on electronic mail, wireless message services, and global networks as more computers and communications equipment find their way into homes and offices. Because of time and cost savings, there will be greater dependence on teleconferencing as a substitute for personal or business travel. As more homes are added to the millions already on cable-access television systems, there will be dynamic growth in the teletext industry.

Improvements in communications will influence how and where we work. Many tasks now performed in offices will be done at home or in the field, rather than in centralized places of work. Telecommuting will become more prevalent. Undoubtedly, the way we work and play will be greatly affected by communications hardware, software, and systems that are swiftly moving from the drawing board to reality. In this chapter we will look at these and other visions of the future.

ISSUES TO WATCH

No one can tell for certain what lies ahead in the communications field, but some issues and industry trends are clear precursors of future directions. Let us review the significant trends and issues that will have great impact on communications in the decade ahead.

The Changing Workforce

Labor costs will continue to rise, which will cause employers to seek more cost-effective and efficient ways of doing business. Communications will play an important role in allowing businesses to serve more customers and accommodate a diverse workforce.

The percentages of blue-collar employees and those engaged in manufacturing occupations continue to decline, while the number of white-collar workers continues to increase. A larger proportion of the workforce will be engaged in office, clerical, communications, and computer-related activities. More and more products are being assembled from components manufactured in different locations around the globe, a trend that places greater emphasis on communications and global networking.

The workforce in the next decade will continue to include increasing numbers of women, non-white workers, and immigrants. A new employee and customer base continues to emerge. The customers served by business in the decade ahead require greater emphasis on multilingual communications and communications that address the needs of special groups, which include senior citizens, the disabled, and non-English-speaking people.

Changing Cities

As the populations of American cities continue to expand, transportation, road building, freeways, and other infrastructure elements have not kept pace. As a result, traffic and congestion have increased dramatically in many cities and on rural highways—and this situation will almost certainly continue to worsen. Traffic is increasing, and we are aiming to decrease our dependence on foreign oil. For these reasons, organizations are trying to find alternatives to the physical movement of people, records, and information.

The number of telecommuters will greatly increase. A **telecommuter** is an individual who performs productive work at home, linked to an office via communications facilities. Local, state, and federal governments are encouraging the growth of telecommuting to assist in solving their transportation problems. Businesses located in regions with high air pollution are also trying to find ways to solve commuting problems. Rather than having employees drive to a central work location, homes will be connected to offices via satellite, microwave, and ground communications links.

Worldwide System Integration

The decade ahead will see a continual shift toward greater connectivity and worldwide network integration. A trend that started in the late 1950s is growing into a worldwide phenomenon. Huge **worldwide networks** have evolved that link airlines, travel agents, hotels, and auto rental agencies. Originally, these services were available only to airlines and travel agents. Today, anyone with a computer and modem can access the network.

Many of these new networks will take the form of Global Virtual Private Networks (GVPN). (See Figure 17.1.) A GVPN provides advanced corporate communications facilities without the need for point-to-point transmission circuits. It relies on public telephone network switches and transmission facilities. There has been an explosive growth of GVPNs as multinational business organizations expand their worldwide coverage.

FIGURE 17.1 Global Virtual Private Network (GVPN)

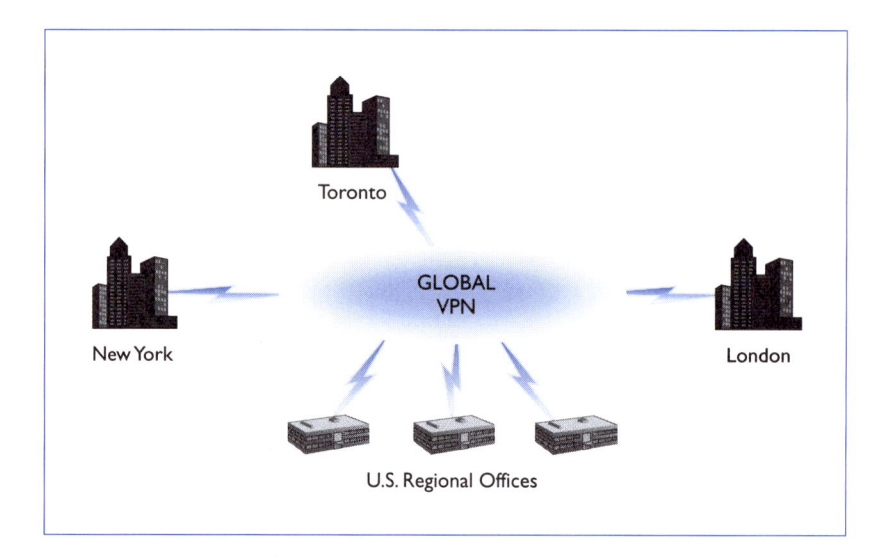

Many complicated problems must be faced in developing GVPNs because of the diversity in regulatory controls in different countries. Figure 17.2 illustrates a list of countries and common carriers, together with some of the features available on a GVPN.

Country	Carrier	Multilateral On-Net Dialing	Call-by-Call Selection	Switched Data	Calling Line ID	Network Name Display	Network Ring Again	Call Forward with Reason
U.S.	Sprint	✔	✔	✔	✔	✔	✔	✔
U.K.	Mercury Communications	✔	✔	✔	✔	✔	✔	✔
Hong Kong	Hong Kong Telecom	✔	✔	✔	✔	✔	✔	✔
Netherlands	PTT Telecom Netherlands	✔	✔	✔	✔			
Canada	Unitel	✔	✔	✔	✔	✔	✔	✔
Canada	Teleglobe	✔	✔	✔	✔	✔	✔	✔

FIGURE 17.2 Global Virtual Private Network Features

Standards are being developed that will allow facsimile, voice, video, and data communications to be handled on worldwide networks. It will be the rare business that will not be connected to a global network. Late-breaking news, stock quotations, reservations, and dozens of other services will all be available to users on an integrated network.

The Automated Office

Some of the most significant strides in communications have been made in office automation. **Office automation** is the integration of computers, copiers, fax machines, and other devices into a system for improving the orderly flow of information throughout a business. Only a few decades ago the major tools in the office were the dictation pad, mimeograph machine, manual typewriter, and rotary dial telephone. Communications were handled through the mail or by long distance calls assisted by human operators. In only a few generations, offices have changed radically.

The desktop computer is omnipresent. Its keyboard serves as the input device for worldwide networks. The facsimile machine is prevalent in many offices, and its use continues to expand. The linking of telephones, fax equipment, copy machines, duplicating equipment, paging systems, and cellular telephones is dramatically changing the way business is conducted.

Wireless Messaging. Today, many office systems include local area networks with many personal computers that are linked to E-mail systems and wireless message services. These services route messages via satellite to paging networks, which in turn route messages to pocket-sized digital pagers, paging receivers that fit in the palm of one's hand, or even to packet radio networks. (See Figure 17.3.) These services allow two-way digital communications and messages to move between mobile units in the field and computers located great distances away.

FIGURE 17.3
HP 95LX Palm-Top Computer. The palm-top computer includes Motorola's NewsStream receiver.

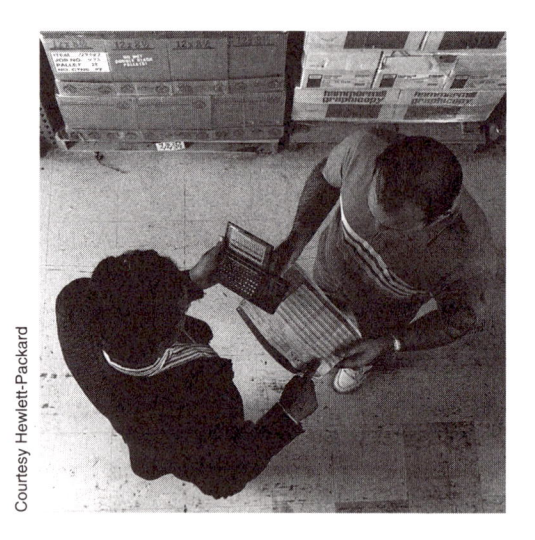

Courtesy Hewlett-Packard

For example, a report may be prepared by an employee at a remote location, using a laptop computer. The text is sent by wireless communications link to the office, where it is routed through a LAN to key personnel. After editing and revision, the report is duplicated in the office for distribution or transmitted over fax systems or digital networks to distant points. Although paper will not disappear from the office, the integrated electronic office system is well on the way to becoming the dominant means of doing business.

Connectivity Between the Macintosh and IBM Worlds. Only a few years ago two separate and distinct microcomputer worlds existed—the Macintosh world and the IBM Personal Computer world. Neither could communicate with the other. Barriers between these two systems are breaking down. The next decade will see greater connectivity in which Macintosh and IBM systems will be able to share software and data files easily.

It is data communications that will serve as the vehicle by which these two great domains will talk to one another. New hardware and programs will facilitate these connections. Figure 17.4 illustrates a group of Macintosh computers linked through a gateway to an IBM control unit and then to an IBM mainframe computer. Only a few years ago direct connections such as these were not possible because of the great divergence in their operating systems and network design.

Integration of Voice and Data

The integration of voice and data will continue to grow through the next decade. More and more offices will shift to integrated communications systems. PBXs will be replaced by DBXs, thus allowing voice communications to share the same hardware as video and data communications.

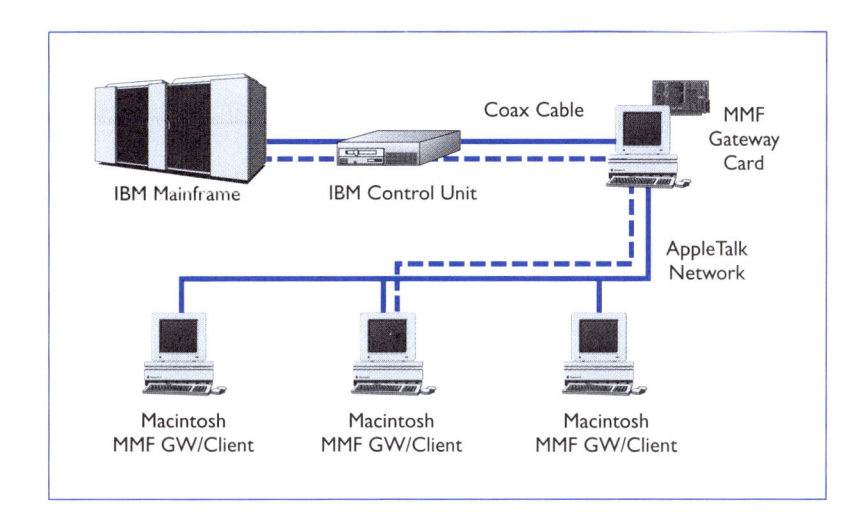

FIGURE 17.4
Macintosh-to-IBM Gateway

A telecommunications survey indicates that among Fortune 1000 companies the volume of voice traffic on networks will drop substantially. Today, data traffic on networks accounts for well over 30 percent of the traffic. There will also be an increase in the amount of facsimile transmissions. Only a few years ago, fax transmissions accounted for less than 4 percent of the network traffic. Today, it exceeds 6 percent and continues to grow substantially.

Developers are responding to the demands of office automation by constructing smart buildings. A **smart building** is prewired with coaxial or fiber-optic cable to all work areas. These buildings are also equipped with central computer facilities and digital switches. They enable workers to access communications networks, electronic law libraries, or information services.

Prewiring a building saves money and avoids the need for building alterations. Because coaxial cables are already in place, offices can be moved about easily. Even domestic users are wiring new homes with coaxial cable. This allows a network and server in a home office to support another computer in a den or kitchen.

Growth of LANs

The availability of reasonably priced and dependable LAN hardware and software means the increased use of LANs in the future. Small and large businesses are using LANs because they provide connectivity to their resources. More and more small businesses are sharing laser printers, plotters, or high-capacity storage devices with many terminals, using a LAN.

Medium- and large-size businesses are finding economies in LANs because they speed up the preparation of documents, allow sharing of resources, and give managers better control and security over records that are handled in the organization.

Growth of Information Services

Many companies have invested millions of dollars in huge databases of information; their reliance on information systems will continue to grow. The movement and management of information will take on increasing significance as government and private institutions make their databases available to users. The City of Santa Monica, for instance, currently allows residents to access the city's database. People can query the system for dates, times, and locations of meetings, services available to the public, and other information.

In the decade ahead, there will be increased reliance on joint efforts to make databases available to the public. The joint effort between IBM and Sears that created the Prodigy system is one example of a growing trend. For a minimal fee, users can access huge databases of information and can reserve hotel, airline, and theater tickets without using an agent.

Growth of Information Exchange Gateways

We have already discussed the trend toward the standardization of electronic documents. You will recall that the ASC X12 established standards for electronic documents, specifying the order and content of fields. The next trend in this direction will no doubt be information exchange gateways.

An **information exchange gateway** will take the form of a group of functions and services that allow organizations to exchange information, following the EDI standards. Messages will be handled interactively and data will flow between business partners and other agencies. Figure 17.5 illustrates an information exchange gateway that includes computer facilities, a data repository, and translation software. These electronic bridges will link businesses and allow purchase orders, invoices, and payments to be moved between organizations without requiring the mails or physical movement of documents.

FIGURE 17.5
Information Exchange Gateway

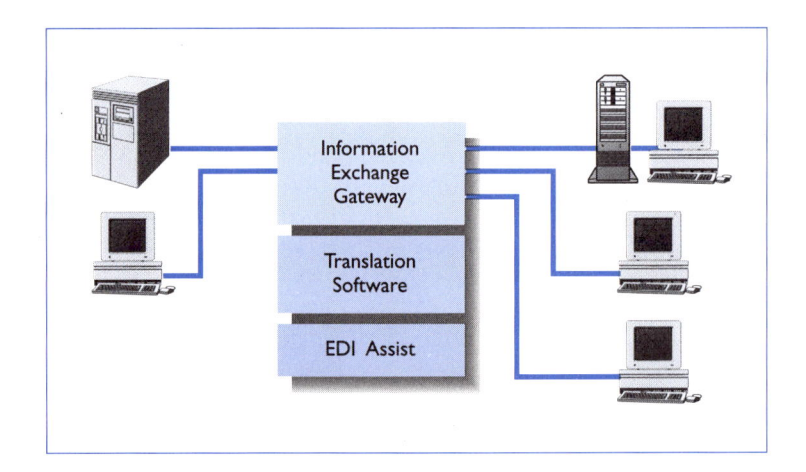

Growth in Microcomputer Usage

The decade ahead will see enormous increases in microcomputer usage and applications. This trend will include connecting personal computers, laptop, and palm-size machines into networks. Much of the stimulus behind this growth will spring from improvements in technology. Desktop computers will operate 20 to 30 times faster than today's machines. They will be able to store hundreds of millions of characters and information displayed on the screen will equal print quality.

Lightweight laptop computers, which have enormous power, speed, and capability, are in use today; even more powerful features are under development. They have built-in modems and are able to communicate over conventional telephone lines or the ISDN. Newer models will have transmitters that allow them to access databases via repeaters while they are being carried about or in moving vehicles. The declining cost and prevalence of personal computers are fostering the explosive growth in networks.

Fiber-Optic and Digital Transmissions

In the next ten years there will be a huge increase in the fiber-optic and digital transmission networks. The greater bandwidth of fiber-optic cables will mean more audio and video signals can be transmitted digitally.

Much of this growth will be focused on the **Fiber Distributed Data Interface (FDDI)** standards. This rapidly developing technology will allow transmission of 100 Mbps over FDDI circuits. IBM and other vendors are embracing this new technology. It will form the backbone of many LANs and connect both Ethernet and token-ring systems.

The ISDN continues to expand. As fully digital networks become the standard, reliance on modems will shrink. Research shows that the greatest gains will be made in the ISDN-Centrex, which will grow by 150 percent annually. There will be a major expanded market for voice/data terminals and data entry terminals that will use the ISDN.

A trend toward digitizing almost all telephone signals will develop. This will mean lower long distance rates because signals will be routed through digital packet-switching networks. The lower prices will be accompanied by higher quality transmission signals and less noise and static.

Frame Relay Switching

In Chapter 12, we discussed packet switching and frame relay switching. You will recall that standards have been established that enclose a message in electronic envelopes that include routing and error control information. The next decade will no doubt see greater reliance on frame relay communications.

Still faster and more efficient systems are under development. The **fast packet-switching** technology shows much promise over frame relay switching. Fast packet switching eliminates much of the message header and overhead information. It will allow intelligent LANs to be linked more efficiently than with frame relay or ISDN circuits. Fast packet-switching technology will show much growth in the decade ahead.

Industry Deregulation

The deregulation of the telephone industry, which started several decades ago, will continue. Many more vendors will enter and compete in the years ahead, resulting in an increase in the number of long distance carriers and the kinds and types of services offered. For instance, many more companies will market transmission circuits and local telephone service, as well as perform telephone installation and repairs. Lighter weight, computerized telephones and switchboards will continue to enter the marketplace, offering many features not now available.

AT&T, formerly limited by government regulations in the kinds of services it offered, will branch out in the next decade. For instance, AT&T will continue to pioneer a computerized phone switch system, using fiber optics. It recently acquired NCR Corporation, a leading computer manufacturer. This union will make AT&T a major force in worldwide telecommunications-based computing. Thus, AT&T is making the transition from simply being in the telephone business to being in the business of moving and managing information and computers. Other vendors, including MCI and Sprint Communications, will expand their share of this market and become even stronger competitors to AT&T.

Speech Recognition

Systems that will be able to recognize and decode human speech are under development. Computer **speech recognition** systems are able to understand ordinary speech uttered at conversational rates. It will someday be possible to build typewriters that take dictation and print out neatly formatted reports. Voice response devices will also be able to translate reports, letters, and memos into foreign languages. Human-assisted translation services now offered by common carriers will be replaced by fully automated technology, available to virtually all telephone users.

In the not-too-distant future we will likely see a telephone capable of automated translation. A person will speak into the mouthpiece in one language and his voice will emerge as a well-articulated translated message at the other end. While such systems will require computers with enormous processing speed, these machines are likely to be on the market by the end of the next decade.

Bypass

Today, most telephone calls originate over a pair of wires connecting an end user to a central office. The circuit is usually owned by a local operating company. Once the call reaches the central office, it may then be routed over non-Bell equipment.

Many companies are turning to **bypass**, a system of routing calls directly to switching centers that completely bypasses local operating company facilities. With bypass fully implemented, companies are able to route telephone calls and digital messages from one location to another without using the local switched network. With the installation of fiber-optic cables or microwave circuits, many companies are seeking to bypass the regulations and controls exercised by common carriers.

Few industries are expected to undergo the technological changes that the communications industry will face in the next decade. The influx of new technology, ideas, computers, and communications systems will shrink the world to a greater degree than ever before.

SUMMARY

The next decade will bring much change to the communications industry. Labor costs will rise and so will dependence on global communications. Cities will continue to expand, forcing many businesses to rely on *telecommuting* as a means of employing personnel. The trend toward an integrated worldwide communications system will continue. International standards and networks are being developed that will allow voice, video, and data communications to be handled on *worldwide networks*.

The office will change in the decade ahead. More emphasis will be placed on computers and communications. Integration will involve linking telephones, fax equipment, copy machines, cellular telephones, and other devices, and will result in a further expansion of the *automated office*. Users will rely on *Information Exchange Gateways* to process messages that conform to *Electronic Data Interchange (EDI)* standards.

Users will also rely increasingly on LANs to link computers and terminals and enable them to share resources. Organizations will continue to invest in building databases of information that will be shared by many users. A shift toward digital communications and the use of fiber optics and FDDI networks will continue. This will mean lower cost communications rates and higher quality signals. Greater use will be made of *frame relay* and *fast packet-switching* networks. There will also be greater reliance on *Global Virtual Private Networks (GVPN)*.

Developers will continue to invest in constructing *smart buildings*. The trend toward deregulation will continue, with many companies entering the industry. Firms will compete to provide long distance service, telephone installation and repair, and other services.

Speech recognition will mean voice-actuated typewriters and telephones that can translate from one language to another. Some companies are starting to rely on *bypass* as a means of circumventing local telephone offices. The changes in the decade ahead promise to further shrink the world in terms of both time and distance.

EXERCISES

1. Describe the ways the workforce has changed and how these changes affect the communications industry.
2. Prepare a short statement discussing how telecommuting will help resolve traffic congestion.
3. List some features of an integrated worldwide communications system.
4. Prepare a list of features that describe the automated office.
5. Write a short statement describing the impact of industry deregulation.
6. Write a short statement describing the kinds of changes expected in microcomputer systems.
7. Make a list of applications that are suitable for speech recognition devices.
8. Contrast the advantages and disadvantages of bypass and how it will affect communications users.
9. Write a short statement discussing the impact of a shift from analog to digital communications.
10. Contrast the advantages and disadvantages of telecommuting.

HANDS-ON PROJECTS

- Visit a local computer store and prepare a list of features indicating which computers are on the leading edge of technology.

- Visit a local business office and discuss the automated office with the manager. What steps will be taken in the future to further automate operations?

- Visit a local telephone sales office. Discuss equipment features. Prepare a list of new telephone features now being introduced.

- Log on to a system such as CompuServe. Make a list of the major information services available to you on the system.

- Log on to an information system such as CompuServe and monitor one of the forums dealing with communications. What kinds of issues and information are discussed?

CASE SOLUTION
AMERICAN CREDIT

COMMUNICATIONS IN ACTION

Nate Duncan decided to maximize productivity through telecommuting. He rented an office to serve as his headquarters and then decentralized the rest of his operations. He hired a secretary and an office manager to work in the main office. Duncan then hired a group of collection agents who would carry out their responsibilities, using a portion of their homes as offices.

Each collection agent's home was equipped with a desktop computer and voice-grade telephone line. (See Figure 17.6.) Employees needed to come into the central office only once a week for a two-hour staff meeting. The balance of their workweek involved making telephone calls, preparing letters, and handling follow-up queries from home. Employees would not need to commute to a downtown office on a regular basis, nor would permanent parking spaces be needed near the office.

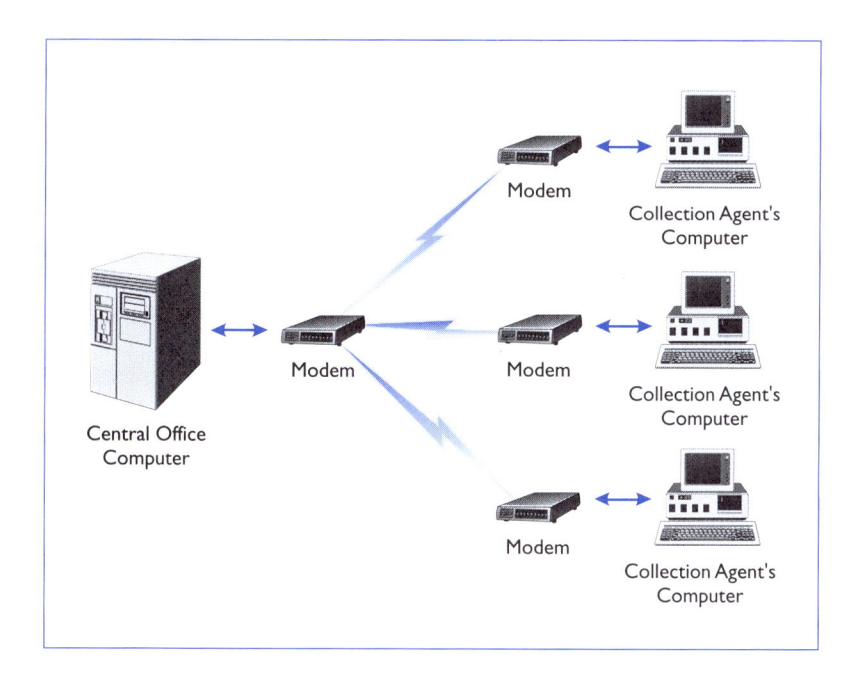

FIGURE 17.6
American Credit's Telecommuting System

Each morning agents call in to the office for their assignments. They download files consisting of account names, balances, and credit history. As they work, the agents update the files on their computers at home, and the summary information is transmitted over ordinary telephone lines to a central computer at the office. This enables the office manager to know the status of all accounts at all times.

The new system is working well. Most of the employees are happy with telecommuting. They avoid long commutes, can write off a portion of household expenses on their taxes, and have a great deal of freedom and flexibility in managing their time. For Nate Duncan the system means less overhead and no limitations on the number of agents he can employ. An unexpected benefit is that American Credit's operations can continue even in the most inclement weather. In the past, bad weather meant employees could not get to the office. Now, weather is not a factor in productivity.

APPLIED CASE PROBLEM: FAIRWAY DEPARTMENT STORES

LEARNING OBJECTIVES

After reading this chapter, you should be able to:

- Apply a systematic problem-solving approach to communications problems
- Analyze and make recommendations regarding local area networks
- Analyze and make recommendations regarding wide area networks
- Analyze and make recommendations regarding telephone systems with voice-grade lines
- Analyze and make recommendations regarding teleconferencing systems
- Discuss practical problems involved in communications systems changeover

THIS CHAPTER integrates the principles, methods, hardware, and communications facilities discussed throughout this book. A broad case problem that encompasses a wide range of communications facilities, including local area networks, microcomputers, mainframe computers, terminals, modems, and voice-grade equipment, is presented. The study begins with a description of Fairway Department Stores. Fairway will serve as a laboratory in which we will study a multifaceted communications problem in the context of a functioning organization.

The chapter opens with an Annual Report, introducing the student to Fairway Department Stores. An organization chart depicts the firm's structure. A photo gallery showing the firm's many departments and operations is then presented, followed by a discussion of the operation of various divisions of the company to provide background information.

A group of Communications in Action problems follows. First, a department and its functions are described; then students are asked to construct an element of a communications system and make recommendations regarding circuits, switchboards, terminals, etc., that will serve Fairway's needs. This process allows the student to apply the knowledge gained from this text in a practical manner.

By studying a communications system in a problem and solution context, students can develop an analytical approach to problem solving. The facts and scenarios presented in this case problem are based on real-life retailing organizations.

Students who work through the cases will soon discover that there is no one perfect solution to each problem. Recommendations should be constructed based on the company's need for a communications system that provides economy, reliability, flexibility, and expandability. These solutions must be implemented with the least amount of inconvenience to the organization and its customers.

FAIRWAY
DEPARTMENT STORES

Annual Report

Serving American Families Since 1903

FAIRWAY
DEPARTMENT STORES

H. Armstrong Roberts

This year marks our ninth decade of service, providing American families with high-quality home furnishings, hard goods, clothing, and apparel. Fairway promises to continue its policy of searching worldwide for the best merchandise at the lowest cost. At Fairway we never lose sight of quality and service for our patrons. Our success over the past years is attributable to you, our customers.

In the coming year, we plan to implement several improvements in our operations that will make shopping at Fairway an even more pleasant experience. Our "Shop by Phone" service will be expanded. We will improve our credit office services, providing complete and up-to-date information on your account.

Our buyers, using a new communications system, will scour the world in search of the best values in goods and services. We will institute a toll-free 800 service that will allow you to call us regarding the use or installation of any good or service we sell.

As Fairway nears the completion of its first century of service, we want to maintain your trust and remain your favorite place to shop.

William Masters

William Masters
Director of Marketing

Fairway's Organization

Fairway Department Stores is composed of four major regions: eastern, western, northern, and southern. Each region is headed by a corporate vice president. Within each region are five major divisions, each headed by a general manager. These include marketing, finance, distribution, human resources, and administrative services. Fairway operates 190 retail stores, most of which include catalog sales and pickup, as well as a full line of retail merchandise. This chart depicts the organization of the western region, which is representative of our other regions.

The marketing division includes four major departments. The purchasing department comprises both international and national purchasing sections. The catalog sales department includes customer pickup and customer delivery sections. The finance division is responsible for accounts payable and receivable. Administrative services provides support functions: data processing, credit authorization, and management of the communications networks. The human resources division handles employee wage administration, health and other benefits, and other tasks. The distribution division is responsible for warehousing goods and distribution to local retail outlets.

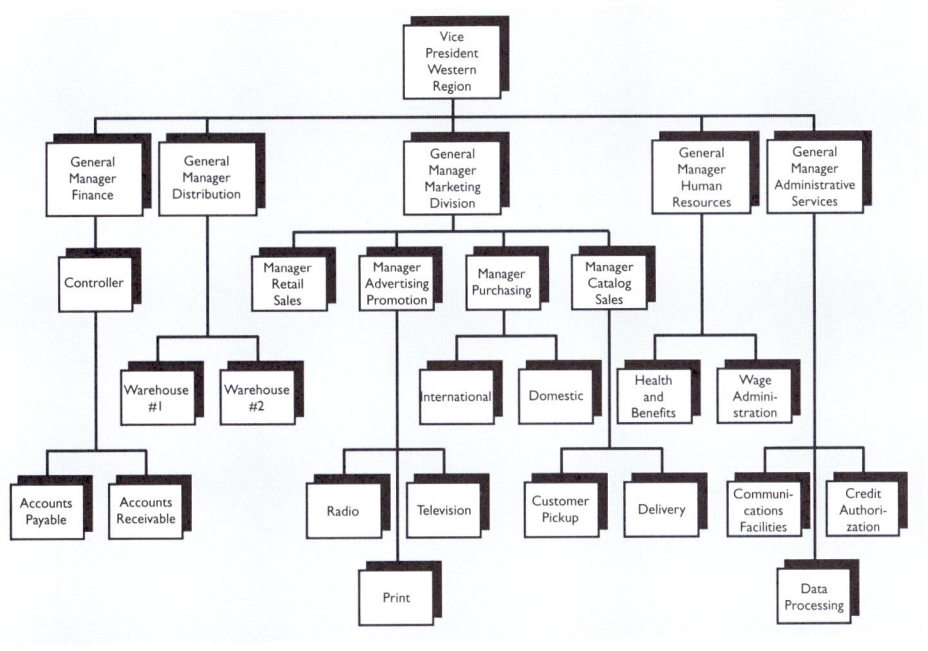

Each of the four regions is under the control of a corporate vice president, while the divisions are overseen by general managers. Major departments are directed by managers; below them are supervisors and line employees. The entire organization is administered by the company president. Fairway's customers are offered a wide variety of high-quality merchandise.

Fine Merchandise Sold By Fairway

- Apparel
- Appliances and housewares
- Sporting goods and bicycles
- Health and beauty aids, candy, notions
- Garden Supplies
- Hardware and tools
- Linens and bedding
- Outdoor and camping equipment
- Footware
- Home entertainment and electronics

GALLERY

We are proud to present the picture gallery, which provides you with a look at Fairway's day-to-day operations. These pictures reflect the dedication and commitment to high standards exhibited by our employees. Although it is difficult to show all the departments and functions that help make Fairway a leader in the retail industry, these photos represent the people that make up our family of employees at Fairway.

G.B Steinmetz/Ewing Galloway

Scott Wanner/Picture Perfect USA

Jon Feingersh

David Dempster/Offshoot

FAIRWAY
DEPARTMENT STORES

Financial Statement
Fiscal Year Ending December 31, 1993

	1993
Sales (in millions)	$5,000
Net income (in millions)	$200
Return on common shareholders' equity	10.5%
Stock price range	$26 – $44
Employees	70,000
Number of retail stores	190

Fairway's Corporate Divisions

Marketing

The marketing division is headed by a general manager who is in charge of purchasing, retail store management, catalog sales, and the advertising and promotion of goods. The purchasing department is responsible for acquiring goods from within the United States and around the globe. Each retail store manager is responsible for the retail sales within his or her store. Catalog sales provide both customer pickup and delivery services. The advertising department handles all promotion and media contact, including radio, television, and print.

Finance

The finance division is headed by a general manager who is responsible for accounts receivable and payable. The division provides the working capital and funds for the operation of all activities within the region.

Distribution

The principal activity conducted by the distribution division is the operation of numerous warehouses that handle goods between the manufacturer and the customer. Its functions include transportation, stockkeeping, inventory control, and maintenance of safe stock levels for all goods sold in the region. The distribution division is also responsible for the shipment of goods from warehouse to retail store, and between retail store and customers.

Human Resources

The human resources division is responsible for maintaining employee records, administering the wage and salary program, and providing employee health and benefits.

Administrative Services

The administrative services division provides a support function for all divisions in the region. It is responsible for all communications facilities and networks. The division operates the data processing center and the credit authorization departments. Together, these two departments maintain all the retail terminals located throughout Fairway's chain of stores.

FAIRWAY'S CORPORATE COMMUNICATIONS NEEDS

The case studies that follow illustrate the communications needs present in each corporate division of Fairway Department Stores. Study each problem carefully and propose a solution to the problem presented in each section.

COMMUNICATIONS IN ACTION

PROBLEM 1
FAIRWAY DEPARTMENT STORES

CATALOG SALES DESK

Approximately 50 clerks are assigned to the catalog sales desk, which takes telephone orders for catalog merchandise. Once orders have been received and confirmed they are sent to the distribution division so that stock can be picked from the warehouse and shipped either to the store for pickup or directly to the customer. Calls received by the catalog sales desk come from customers within a radius of approximately 50 miles of the store.

COMMUNICATIONS PROBLEM

Analyze the needs of the catalog sales desk and propose a communications system that will service telephone orders and requests. The system should also provide a mechanism for periodically communicating orders to the distribution division.

COMMUNICATIONS IN ACTION

PROBLEM 2
FAIRWAY DEPARTMENT STORES

PURCHASING DEPARTMENT

The purchasing department, part of the marketing division, is responsible for the acquisition of all goods and services for Fairway Department Stores. Approximately 25 full-time purchasing agents, who are in contact with suppliers and manufacturers throughout the United States and abroad, are employed in the department. These agents approve purchase orders and spend much of their time on the telephone discussing product specifications with suppliers. After an order is placed, a copy of the purchase order is sent to the distribution division in anticipation of the receipt of the goods.

COMMUNICATIONS PROBLEM

Analyze the needs of the department and design a communications system that serves its requirements. The system should contain both voice and digital transmission elements and allow agents to communicate worldwide at the lowest possible cost. The system should also provide for the transmission of purchase orders to the distribution division warehouses.

PROBLEM 3
FAIRWAY DEPARTMENT STORES

COMMUNICATIONS IN ACTION

GIFT REGISTRY DEPARTMENT

A gift registry department is located in each store. This department is most commonly used by customers who wish to select gifts for special occasions, such as weddings, engagement parties, showers, and other types of celebrations. A couple about to be married can choose a china pattern, silverware, linens, and household or other items and register their choices with the department. When customers come in to purchase a gift, they consult a clerk who provides a real-time display on a video terminal or generates a printout of the recipient's choices. As items on the computerized list are purchased, it is updated to avoid duplicate gifts. The department also offers gift wrapping and shipping.

COMMUNICATIONS PROBLEM

Fairway Department Stores requires a network that will connect terminals in the gift registry department. These terminals should have access to the gift registry database and be updated in real time to avoid purchases of duplicate gifts. Provisions must also be made to generate hard-copy printouts of items on gift lists.

PROBLEM 4
FAIRWAY DEPARTMENT STORES

COMMUNICATIONS IN ACTION

RETAIL SALES DEPARTMENTS

Cash registers with credit authorization capability are located on the sales floor and retail sales departments throughout Fairway's stores. A typical store has about 30 sales terminals, which are used to ring up sales, authorize charge purchases, handle merchandise returns, and complete other functions. Information from the terminals should be sent to a computer located in each store. Throughout the business day, sales and credit information is transmitted to various regional stores, where it is reviewed by marketing managers.

COMMUNICATIONS PROBLEM

Study Fairway's operations and design a network of retail sales terminals. These terminals should function as cash registers, provide credit authorization, and handle merchandise exchanges and returns. The data from each terminal should be transmitted to a central computer in each store on a real-time basis. Periodically, summary data should be transmitted to regional sales managers. In designing the system, include backup facilities so that interruptions in communications circuits will not disrupt sales on the floor.

COMMUNICATIONS
IN ACTION

PROBLEM 5
FAIRWAY DEPARTMENT STORES

COMPLAINT AND INFORMATION DESK

Fairway operates a centralized customer complaint and information service. Customers from anywhere within the region may call a single telephone number and be connected with a service operator. Customers do not pay telephone charges for this service, regardless of how far away from the store they are located. The service provides customer assistance or instructions on how to use merchandise 24 hours a day.

COMMUNICATIONS PROBLEM

Design a system that will provide 800 service to Fairway's customers. This service should be staffed by operators working out of a centralized location in each region and should be available 24 hours a day. Make recommendations regarding telephone facilities and lines.

COMMUNICATIONS
IN ACTION

PROBLEM 6
FAIRWAY DEPARTMENT STORES

ADVERTISING AND PROMOTION DEPARTMENT

A staff of graphic designers, copy writers, and layout artists are employed in this department. They prepare the advertising copy for newspaper ads and radio and television commercials. Copy is usually submitted by retail sales managers, then structured into newspaper ads. The ad is set in type and proofs are routed back to retail sales managers. They are then given to the print media for publication.

COMMUNICATIONS PROBLEM

Develop a communications system that routes text and graphics between the department's production staff and sales managers. Facsimile facilities should be incorporated. Recommend a means of transmitting finished copy between the advertising department and various local newspapers and broadcasting stations.

PROBLEM 7
FAIRWAY DEPARTMENT STORES

COMMUNICATIONS IN ACTION

DATA PROCESSING DEPARTMENTS

The data processing departments must have a means of communicating large volumes of data between regions. Division managers frequently share lengthy reports, marketing information, and personnel data. Stores that may be thousands of miles apart must be connected. A large percentage of the communications are digital in nature. Provisions must also be made for handling lengthy telephone calls and voice transmissions between regional offices.

COMMUNICATIONS PROBLEM

Plan a system involving a packet-switching network that will allow a large volume of voice and digital data to be routed between divisions. Because of the distances involved, microwave or satellite communications links should be included.

PROBLEM 8
FAIRWAY DEPARTMENT STORES

COMMUNICATIONS IN ACTION

CORPORATE MANAGEMENT

Corporate vice presidents and general managers are involved in long- and short-range planning. These individuals have budget responsibilities that allocate personnel, financial, and other resources. As a rule, top-level management meetings involve face-to-face communications. Top management frequently shares charts and graphs and commentary regarding the future direction of Fairway Department Stores. Individuals who are unable to attend high-level corporate meetings are often asked to review the proceedings of key meetings. Fairway's growth depends on general managers and vice presidents located at widely distant points working together effectively.

COMMUNICATIONS PROBLEM

Plan a system that will provide a teleconferencing hookup between each of Fairway's regional corporate offices. The system should include video, slow-scan TV, and digital transmission facilities. It should enable participants to see and hear one another. It should allow some means for presentation of slides and other graphics and should preserve a record of these for those who may miss the conference.

COMMUNICATIONS IN ACTION

PROBLEM 9
FAIRWAY DEPARTMENT STORES

DISTRIBUTION DIVISION

The distribution division is responsible for dispensing merchandise to customers. Dispatchers make up route lists the day before deliveries are to be made. Goods are then loaded onto trucks for delivery the next day. Once en route, trucks are sometimes routed to different locations, meaning that delivery vehicles must be in communication with the transportation dispatcher at all times.

COMMUNICATIONS PROBLEM

After reviewing Fairway's operations, design a cellular mobile telephone system for the trucks in the fleet. The system should enable drivers to contact the home base while en route to customers. It should provide reliable and consistent communications at a minimal expense.

COMMUNICATIONS IN ACTION

PROBLEM 10
FAIRWAY DEPARTMENT STORES

MAINTENANCE DEPARTMENT

Each Fairway Department Store employs a staff of maintenance and security personnel. These individuals are available 24 hours a day to assist with routine, as well as emergency, maintenance procedures or security problems. These individuals are dispatched when any emergency arises, such as broken pipes, broken glass, or liquid spills. It is important that they cordon off areas promptly, minimize damage, and place the retail unit back in operation as soon as possible.

COMMUNICATIONS PROBLEM

Design a paging system that will enable store managers to summon maintenance or security personnel quickly. It should include portable pagers that alert staff to the presence of an emergency. The system should operate both within the store and while maintenance or security personnel are off the premises.

Now that we have explored several communications problems, can you further expand on the system for Fairway Department Stores? Review Fairway's operations, corporate structure, and activities and make a list of communications needs that have not yet been addressed in your work. Refer to previous chapters on such topics as LANs, WANs, software packages, and communications media for ideas and suggestions on how to provide solutions and further expand the network.

GLOSSARY

10BASE-T. An Ethernet LAN cabling system using a pair of unshielded twisted wires.

10BASE2. A ThinNet Ethernet LAN cabling system using shielded coaxial cable.

10BASE5. A standard Ethernet LAN cabling system using shielded coaxial cable.

Acoustic Connection. The coupling of a telephone instrument and a modem by sound waves rather than direct physical wire connection.

American National Standards Institute (ANSI). An organization that publishes standards related to communications and data processing.

American Standard Code for Information Interchange (ASCII). A 7-bit transmission code, with an additional eighth parity bit, that can transmit up to 128 different characters.

Amplitude. The intensity or strength of a signal or sine wave.

Amplitude Modulation (AM). A technique that impresses information on a carrier by changing the strength of the carrier.

Analog Signal. A form of transmission in which information is represented as a waveform consisting of rising and falling wavelike patterns.

Answer Modem. A device that receives a transmission, using specially assigned frequencies.

Architecture. See *Topology*.

ASC X12 Data Field Sequence. A specification that defines the sequence and format of data that will be transmitted over EDI.

ASC X12 Standard. A document that defines a communications session, interchange envelope, and functional groups for EDI.

Asynchronous Transmission. A method of transmitting data in a serial fashion without concern for the clock.

Attention (AT) Codes. Codes sent to a smart modem that set up its operational characteristics.

Attenuate. To reduce the strength of certain frequencies of a transmitted signal.

Auto-Answer Device. Equipment that can detect a ring and answer a telephone unattended.

Auto-Dialer. A device that automatically dials a telephone number.

B-Channel. One of the channels of the basic rate interface which carries voice or data at 64 Kbps.

Bandwidth. The range of frequencies that can be transmitted on a circuit.

Baseband Circuit. A system that transmits digital data in the form of low voltages and low frequencies.

Basic Rate Interface (BRI). An interface consisting of two B-channels and one D-channel. Also known as 2B+D.

Basic Telecommunications Access Method (BTAM). A large mainframe communications package developed by IBM Corporation.

Baud. A measure of transmission speed based on the number of times a signal changes its state.

Baudot Code. An early 5-bit data transmission code, developed by Jean-Maurice-Emile Baudot.

Benchmark Test. An established time or cost yardstick that is used to monitor a new system or to measure it against predetermined standards.

Binary Coded Decimal (BCD) Code. A 6-bit code, with an additional parity check bit, that can transmit 64 different characters.

Binary Digit. A two-state bit representing either a 1 or a 0.

Bisynchronous Control (BSC). A synchronous transmission protocol in which one or more synchronizing characters are sent at the beginning of each block.

Bit. See *Binary Digit*.

Bits per Second (bps). A measure of transmission speed based upon the number of bits transmitted in one second.

Bridge Interface. Electronic circuitry and protocol software that enables a local area network to communicate with another local area network with the same protocols.

Broadband Circuit. A system that transmits digital information in the form of a modulated carrier over a coaxial or fiber-optic cable or microwave circuit.

Buffer. A block of computer memory that stores data until it is needed later.

Bulletin Board Services (BBS). Privately owned information data banks maintained on small computers that can be accessed by the public.

Burstiness. A transmission phenomenon in which data appear in bursts followed by pauses.

Bus Topology. An architecture in which elements in a network are connected along a single line.

Byte. A collection of binary bits that represent a letter, number, or special character.

C Band. The frequency band from 4 GHz to 6 GHz used in satellite transmission.

Cabling System. The wires that connect terminals, computers, or other devices in a network.

Call Cost Accounting. A procedure that measures telephone usage and charges calls to specific individuals, accounts, or departments.

Carrier Sense Multiple Access/Collision Detection (CSMA/CD). A baseband local area network system that uses bus topology and carrier detection to avoid message collisions.

Carrier Wave. A transmitted signal that is capable of having information impressed on it.

Cathode Ray Tube (CRT). See *Monitor*.

Cellular Fax Machine. A device that transmits a fax over a cellular telephone circuit.

Cellular Radio. A mobile telephone service that breaks down large geographic areas into cells, allowing users simultaneous access to channels within the region.

Center Frequency. The middle frequency between the mark and space frequencies.

Central Office. The office that performs switching for the telephone system.

Central Processing Unit (CPU). That part of the computer system that performs primary memory, arithmetic and logic, and control functions.

Centralized Data Processing. An arrangement in which data are maintained and processed at a central point, but may be accessed from many locations.

Centrex. A decentralized calling system in which each instrument is assigned calls directly from a set of incoming trunks.

Channel. A pathway, not necessarily a pair of wires, over which information can be sent.

Circuit. A physical pathway or pair of wires over which information can be sent and received.

Coax. See *Coaxial Cable*.

Coaxial Cable. A cable made up of two wires in which the inside conductor is centered and enclosed in an outer solid or braided conductor.

Command-Driven Software. Software in which directions are entered by keying in commands that execute various choices or options available to the user.

Common Carrier. A communications organization that makes its circuits or facilities available to others for a fee.

Communications Link. A channel, circuit, or other pathway over which analog or digital information can be transmitted.

Communications Medium. See communications link.

Communications Satellite. A relay station placed in synchronous orbit around the globe that receives signals from earth, amplifies them, and redirects them back to earth.

Communications Server. A device that can couple equipment not initially designed to be compatible with the system to a local area network.

Communications Software Package. A collection of one or more programs designed to facilitate communications between computers and terminals.

Conditioned Circuit. A circuit in which capacitance or resistance has been added to change its characteristics.

Consultative Committee for International Telephone and Telegraph (CCITT). An international organization that publishes standards related to communications, telephones, and telegraphs.

Control Character. A special nonprinting character that indicates special control functions, such as end of transmission (EOT), form feed (FF), etc.

Controller. A hardware device that connects a terminal to a communications line.

Coupler. See *Modulator/Demodulator*.

Credit Authorization Terminal. A special-purpose device that reads credit cards or data from a keyboard and is used to check customer credit.

Critical Path Method (CPM). A project control technique that specifies the key dates and routes that must be adhered to in order to complete a task on time.

Crossbar Switching. An early method of switching and routing telephone calls using electromagnetic devices.

Customer Information Control System (CICS). A program residing in a host computer that provides high-level monitoring of the entire communications process.

Cyclic Redundancy Check (CRC). A checking system in which a block of data is transmitted together with additional checking bits.

D-Channel. One of the channels of the basic rate interface that carries control signals and is used for switching purposes.

Data Circuit-Terminating Equipment (DCE). A modem, data concentrator, multiplexer, or other device that may be connected to a computer or terminal.

Data Communications. The transmission of information between two points, using microwave, telephone, fiber-optic, or other circuits.

Data Compression. The reduction or concentration of the number of characters or data bits in order to reduce the number of bytes stored or transmitted.

Data Concentrator. A device that collects data and forwards them at predetermined intervals over a communications circuit.

Data Frame. A block of information that contains a header, the data to be transmitted, and a frame checking code.

Data Link. A channel, circuit, or other pathway reserved for the transmission of letters, numbers, or other digital information.

Data Packet. A group of information bits containing a header, user data field, and variable information.

Data Security. The protection of data against loss or interference during transmission, processing, or storage.

Data Set. See *Modulator/Demodulator*.

Data Terminal Equipment (DTE). A microcomputer, cathode ray tube terminal, teleprinter, or other device that may be connected to a modem or data concentrator.

Database. The information gathered by an organization and structured in a manner that facilitates the retrieval and processing of information.

Dataphone Digital Service (DDS). A wide area network (WAN) offered by AT&T to send high-speed digital communications, using special T1 communications circuits.

Decibel (dB). A unit for expressing the relative intensity of sounds on a scale from zero for the average least perceptible sound to about 130 for the average human pain level.

Decoding. The decryption, or conversion, of data from a circuit.

Decompression. The expansion of compressed data back into its original form.

Decrypting Key. A code, large number, or word that allows a message to be decoded.

Decryption. See decoding.

Dedicated Line. See leased line.

Demodulation. The removal of data from a signal by stripping it from its carrier.

Deregulation. The removal of governmental controls on an industry.

Dialing. The sending of pulses or signals that route messages through the switched telephone network.

Dial-Up Line. A telephone line that is able to access and route calls through the switched network.

Dibit. A 2-bit number that is represented by a phase shift.

Dibit Phase Shift Keying (DPSK). An arrangement that encodes data by representing them as phase shifts.

Digital Branch Exchange (DBX). An automatic telephone switchboard that contains a microcomputer to handle switching.

Digital Data. Discrete information in the form of digits such as letters, numbers, or special characters; not analog.

Digital Key Telephone System (DKTS). A computer-controlled telephone system in which calls are switched and routed digitally.

Direct Distance Dialing (DDD). The capability of the switched network that allows users to dial long distance calls directly.

Distributed Data Processing (DDP). A method of processing data in which files are stored at many different locations and in which processing takes place at different sites.

Documentation. Reports, bulletins, flowcharts, or other material that describes a system.

Downlink. The circuit that sends a signal from an orbiting satellite down to an earth station.

Download. The process in which a program or file is received from another computer and stored on disk or primary memory in a local computer.

Dual-Tone Multifrequency Dialing (DTMF). A dialing system that uses two tones of different frequencies to actuate automatic switching.

Dumb Terminal. A terminal not equipped with a microcomputer, which cannot reformat data or perform logical operations, but can communicate with a computer.

Echo Suppressor. A circuit that reduces echo signals on a communications line.

EIA-232-D Interface. A published standard related to interfacing data terminal equipment and data communications equipment.

Electromagnetic Waves. That part of the energy spectrum where waveforms behave according to the laws of magnetism.

Electronic Banking. Banking operations that rely on communications to move funds electronically, rather than by the physical movement of checks or documents.

Electronic Data Interchange (EDI). A protocol that facilitates the transfer of business information in a consistent electronic standard format.

Electronic Industries Association (EIA). An industry trade group that sets standards for electronic equipment.

Electronic Mail. The movement of communications by electronic means, which eliminates the need for physically mailing documents.

Electronic Shopping. A means of purchasing goods via cable television or computer network.

Electronic Signal Switching (ESS). The use of a computer and solid-state switches to route telephone signals through the network.

E-Mail. See *Electronic Mail*.

Emulator. A program or software that causes one device, such as a terminal, to behave as if it were a different make or model of device.

Encoding. The conversion of letters or numbers to a code.

Encryption. The conversion of voice or data to a secure form for transmission.

End Office. A telephone station located nearest to the subscriber.

End User. The individual or organization that makes use of data processing or data transmission facilities.

Error Rate. The rate or frequency at which errors occur in transmitting or moving data over a circuit.

Ethernet. A local area network configuration developed by Xerox Corporation.

Even Parity. A checking system in which each character sent contains an even number of 1-bits in a byte.

Extended Binary Coded Decimal Interchange Code (EBCDIC). An 8-bit transmission code, with an additional ninth parity bit, that can transmit up to 256 different characters.

Facsimile Machine (Fax). A device that scans a document, reduces it to electrical pulses, and sends it over a communications line to another facsimile machine, where a copy of the original document is reconstructed.

Fast Packet Switching. A network protocol that eliminates the delay and overhead involved in processing frame address and routing information.

Fax Card. A circuit board inserted into a computer that gives it fax capabilities.

Feasibility Study. A preliminary planning study conducted to assess the cost, practicality, and goals of a new system.

Federal Communications Commission (FCC). The federal agency charged with regulating the electromagnetic spectrum.

Fiber Distributed Data Interface (FDDI). A fiber-optic standard that enables transmission at the rate of 100 Mbps.

Fiber-Optic Circuit. A circuit that transmits data by sending light through thin filaments of glass.

FidoNet. An informal bulletin board network that moves messages using low-cost long distance night rates.

Field Selectable Switch. A switch that allows the end user to select various options.

File Server. A magnetic or optical storage device, usually disk, that provides high-volume storage for a local area network.

File Transfer Protocol. A standardized procedure or method that facilitates the transfer of files between computers over communications lines.

Formatting. Output or display of information in which the line width or depth of a page is controlled or altered.

Frame. See *Data Frame*.

Frame Relay. A communications system that uses special wideband circuits and high-speed switches to route messages that conform to a frame relay standard.

Frequency. The pitch of a signal, based on the spacing between crests of a sine wave.

Frequency Division Multiplexing (FDM). A technique that allows several devices to send data on one line by allocating different frequency bands to each device.

Frequency Modulation (FM). A technique that impresses information on a carrier by changing its frequency.

Frequency Shift Keying (FSK). A technique for sending data that modulates a carrier above and below a center frequency.

Frequency Spectrum. The table of frequencies ranging from sound waves through to cosmic ray particles.

Front-End Processor (FEP). A computer placed in front of a mainframe to handle communications, switching, data security, and access control functions.

Full-Duplex (FDX) Circuit. A circuit that allows data to be sent and received simultaneously.

Gateway. Electronic circuitry and protocol software that enables a local area network to communicate with a dissimilar network using long-haul communications facilities.

Geosynchronous Satellite. A satellite placed in a fixed orbit around the earth, used for relaying transmissions.

GHz. One billion hertz.

Global Virtual Private Network (GVPN). A private network using public facilities that do not use dedicated physical circuits.

Half-Duplex (HDX) Circuit. A circuit designed either to send or receive data but not in a simultaneous fashion.

Handshake Procedure. A protocol that establishes an orderly sequence for initiating or terminating a transmission.

Hard-Copy Output. A permanent or residual copy of a message or printout.

Hard-Wire Connection. A physical or direct metallic connection between a device and a communications line.

Hardware. The physical equipment, devices, or machines used to process data or move information through a system.

Hawthorne Effect. The phenomenon that those under observation do not behave as do those who think they are unobserved.

Hertz (Hz). A measure of frequency; cycles per second.

Host Computer. A mainframe computer that performs the primary data processing functions; often served by a smaller front-end computer.

Hybrid Transformer. A device that splits one two-wire circuit into two two-wire circuits, or vice versa.

Inbound Services. A specially priced long distance incoming call service.

Induction Coil. A wire winding in a telephone instrument that connects the device to the telephone line.

Information Exchange Gateway. A computer facility with data repository and translation software that links businesses electronically.

Information Frame. A group of bits that contains a start of frame flag, frame header, data packet, and an end of frame flag.

Input System. That part of a computer system designed to receive information from keyboards, magnetic tape, or other media.

Institute of Electrical and Electronic Engineers (IEEE). An organization that publishes standards related to electronic circuitry and design.

Integrated Services Digital Network (ISDN). A transmission system in which voice, video, and data are transported using digital signals rather than conventional analog signals.

Interconnect Ruling. An FCC decision that allows non-Bell or foreign devices to be connected to the AT&T switched network.

Interexchange Carrier (IXC). A common carrier that offers long distance network services, routing calls over microwave, fiber-optic, or satellite circuits.

Interface. A common boundary between two or more pieces of communications equipment, computers, or terminals.

Interface Card. A controller card that connects a device to a network cabling system.

International Standards Organization (ISO). A worldwide organization that publishes standards related to communications and data processing.

Intertoll Trunk. Circuits that connect toll offices and route long-distance telephone calls.

Investigative Study. A detailed analysis of the speed, cost, and capacity of a proposed communications system.

K Band. The frequency band from 20 GHz to 30 GHz used in satellite transmission.

KERMIT. A widely used error-checking system that facilitates transfer of data between microcomputers and mainframes.

kHz. One thousand hertz.

Ku Band. The frequency band from 12 GHz to 14 GHz used in satellite transmission.

Large-Scale Integrated (LSI) Circuit. A microelectronic technology that manufactures thousands of electrical components on a single silicon chip.

Laser Beam. A high-intensity, sharply focused beam of light that does not spread.

Lead Time. The lapsed time between the ordering of a piece of equipment or service and its actual delivery.

Learning Curve. A curved line that illustrates the relationship between the number of times a task is repeated and the error rate and time required to perform it.

Leased Line. A direct dedicated telephone line that bypasses the switched network when routing.

Line. The physical wire, metallic, or optical path that transmits a signal between two points.

Line Amplifier. A device placed in a communications line to boost the signal strength of a circuit.

Line Loss. The reduction in signal strength caused by transmitting signals over a long distance.

Linear Programming (LP). A computer technique that selects the best mix when a complex group of components or resources are involved.

Local Access Transport Area (LATA). A post-divestiture geographic area served by a local telephone company.

Local Area Network (LAN). An arrangement in which computers are integrated into networks, usually within a distance of five miles, where they are able to share a database and access the resources of other computers.

Local Exchange Carrier (LEC). A telephone company that provides local calling services within a LATA.

Longitudinal Parity. A parity system (sometimes called horizontal parity) that is recorded at the end of a length of tape or transmitted at the end of a block to check accuracy.

Mainframe. A large permanently installed computer system.

Mark. A one (1) or the presence of a signal.

Mean Time Between Failures (MTBF). The average length of time between equipment failures or malfunctions.

Megahubs. A major switching point in a digital system consisting of signal transfer points (STPs) and other circuitry to route digital traffic over a network.

Menu-Driven Software. Software in which the user selects specific functions from a group of choices or options presented in a menu.

Mesh Topology. An architecture in which elements on a network are connected in an interwoven grid, using point-to-point wiring.

Message Collision. A condition where two messages are placed on a line simultaneously, creating an error condition in which messages are garbled.

Metering. A communications application in which a public utility reads gas, water, or electric meters from a remote point.

MHz. One million hertz.

Microcom Network Protocol (MNP). A modem transfer protocol that includes error correcting, flow control, and data compression logic built into the hardware.

Microcomputer. A desktop computer system that may be equipped with magnetic disk storage devices and other peripherals.

Microsecond. One millionth of a second.

Microwave Radio Link. A communications technique that transmits data between points by relaying microwave signals from station to station.

Millisecond. One thousandth of a second.

Minicomputer. A small computer, larger than a microcomputer, often used for data communications or to control switching.

Modem. See *Modulator/Demodulator*.

Modulation. The technique that impresses information on a carrier by changing its amplitude, frequency, or phase.

Modulator/Demodulator (MODEM). A device that converts digital signals from a computer or terminal into analog form and vice versa so that the signals can be transmitted over telephone lines or other circuits.

Monitor. A visual display device resembling a television screen, used for computer output.

Monitoring. See *Metering*.

Morse Code. An early transmission code consisting of dots and dashes that sends characters over a line in serial fashion.

Multidrop Circuit. A configuration in which many devices are connected to a single communications link.

Multimedia. The integration of computers, video tape, video disk, and communications facilities into a system capable of delivering color pictures, slides, images, diagrams, or audio presentations.

Multiplexer (MUX). An electronic device that enables two or more devices to transmit data on one circuit.

Multipoint Circuit. See *Multidrop Circuit*.

Nanosecond. One billionth of a second.

Network. A group of stations wherein information can be moved about between points or nodes within the system.

Network Control Program (NCP). Software that resides in a front-end processor and handles message routing and switching between devices on a system.

Network Hub. A branching point in a network to which are connected servers, workstations, or other devices.

Node. An entry point in a network wherein information can be input and received from the network.

Odd Parity. A checking system in which each character sent contains an odd number of 1-bits in a byte.

Open Systems Interconnection (OSI) Model. A protocol that establishes formats and procedures at different levels for transmitting information in a communications system.

Originate Modem. A device that generates a transmission, using specially assigned frequencies.

Oscillator Circuit. An electronic circuit that emits pulses in the form of a repetitive wavelike pattern.

Outbound Services. A specially priced long distance outgoing call service.

Output System. That part of the computer system designed to convert electrical pulses into a useful medium such as printed reports or information displayed on a screen.

Packet. A small segment of a message that is routed through a network and then reconstructed to form an entire message.

Packet Switching. A technology that allows voice or data to be sent over circuits by reducing messages to small segments, called packets, that are routed through a network.

Parallel Transmission. A transmission arrangement in which several bits of data are simultaneously sent over several channels in parallel.

Parameter File. A file that contains a telephone number and other pertinent information related to a computer to be called.

Password. A special word, known only to the user, that allows an individual to gain access to a system or selected files.

Phase Modulation (PM). A technique that impresses information on a carrier by changing the phase or point where a complete cycle is begun.

Phase Shift. See *Phase Modulation*.

Point of Presence (POP). A transfer point in a LATA where long distance calls are routed out of a LATA to a common carrier network.

Point-of-Sale Terminal. A device that reads data from tickets, tags, bar codes, or keyboard input; it is generally located in a retail establishment.

Point-to-Point Topology. A network architecture in which two or more devices are connected with a single communications link.

Port Protection Device (PPD). Equipment placed ahead of a computer or a modem that prevents unauthorized access.

Primary Rate Interface (PRI). An interface consisting of 23 B-channels and one D-channel.

Print Server. A high-volume printer (sometimes a laser printer) that provides high-speed output for a local area network.

Private Automatic Branch Exchange (PABX). An automated telephone switchboard.

Private Branch Exchange (PBX). A manually operated telephone switchboard.

Program Evaluation and Review Technique (PERT). A project control technique useful in preparing timetables for implementing complex systems.

Protocol. A formally prescribed set of rules that govern and control the timing and switching of communications equipment.

Prototype Installation. A test installation of facilities used to refine or check out a new system.

Public Access Digital Network. A privately owned communications system that transmits digital data for a fee and is open to the public.

Public Domain Software. Programs and software that are available to the public free of charge and that do not bear copyright protection.

Queued Telecommunication Access Method (QTAM). A mainframe communications software package that handles switching and error checking, analyzes message headers, and routes communications to specific programs.

Real-Time Processing. Processing that takes place at the time a transaction occurs.

Receiver. The earpiece on a telephone handset.

Remote-Job-Entry (RJE) Terminal. A batch-processing terminal that can read magnetic tape, disks, or other media and perform input and output operations.

Response Time. The delay or interval between making a request and the receipt or answer.

Reverse Channel. A low-speed channel used to send control data in the opposite direction.

Ring Topology. An architecture in which elements in a network are connected together as nodes or points around the perimeter of a circle.

Rotary Dial Telephone. An instrument equipped with pulse contacts, transmitter, and receiver, capable of actuating automatic switching equipment.

Router. A device that reads a message header and routes the communication on to the next switching device.

RTTY. See *Teletype*.

Script File. A stored sequence of commands, including passwords, security, and file protection commands, that can be passed back and forth between computers.

Secondary Storage. That part of the computer system that stores information optically or on tape or disk.

Semi-Automatic Business Research Environment (SABRE). A communications network used by airlines and travel agencies to book flights and make other reservations.

Serial Port. A circuit available on a computer that allows for the serial transmission of data.

Serial Transmission. A transmission arrangement in which bits of data are sent one at a time over a circuit.

Shielded Twisted Pair (STP). A twisted pair of metallic wires, covered with a shield, used in a LAN cabling system.

Simplex Circuit. A circuit capable of sending information in one direction only.

Sine Wave. A wave shape in which crests appear in an even rising and falling fashion.

Smart Modem. A modem with a built-in microprocessor that can reformat data, dial telephone numbers, or interact with a program.

Smart Terminal. A terminal that is equipped with a microcomputer and memory and that can reformat data and perform logical operations.

Software. The programs, protocols, or sets of instructions used to process data or move information through a system.

Sound Pressure Levels (SPLs). Varying intensity of pressures that convey sounds to the human ear.

Space. A zero, or the absence of a signal.

Squeezer. A software routine that condenses or compacts a file so that it will occupy less space in memory when stored or transmitted.

Star Topology. An architecture in which elements in a network are connected together much like spokes on a wheel.

Statistical Time Division Multiplexer (STDM). A multiplexer that allocates communication line time to a group of devices, based on the activity of the devices.

Subcarrier Channel. A secondary channel used to transmit multiplexed data.

Subscriber. An individual connected to a telephone network.

Subscriber Loop. The circuit connecting a subscriber to an end office.

Switched Network. The basic telephone system that is able to route calls from one point to another, using pulse dialing or DTMF signals.

Synchronous Optical Network (SONET). A fiber-optic communications network designed to transport high-volume synchronous signals.

Synchronous Transmission. A method of transmitting data in which characters or blocks of data are sent synchronized to a clock.

System. A group of components or elements that interact in a regulated manner and where a change in one element affects one or more parts of the system.

System Changeover. The process of converting from an existing system to a new system.

System Network Architecture (SNA). A set of standards and protocols for data transmission systems, developed by IBM Corporation.

Systems Analysis. The collection of pertinent data that describes an existing system, providing a foundation for changing, modifying, or creating a new or improved system.

Systems Design. The methodical consideration of alternatives and the selection of specific hardware, software, communications circuits, and personnel.

Systems Development. The implementation of a system in which equipment or services are purchased or acquired.

Systems Evaluation. The assessment of a new system, using benchmark tests or other procedures to determine whether it meets its design goals.

Systems Implementation. The phase of systems analysis in which equipment is physically installed, checked, and tested.

Systems Optimization. The making of final changes, modifications, or improvements in a system to obtain maximum performance.

T1 Circuit. A digital transmission circuit with a capacity to transmit 24 separate 64 kbps channels on one circuit.

Telecommunications. The broad field of communications involving the transmission of data, voice, or video information.

Teleconferencing. A method by which individuals communicate with one another, using closed-circuit television or audio hookup rather than physically traveling to a conference.

Telegraph. An early communications arrangement in which information was transmitted by using a sending key and a sounder.

Teleprinter. A machine that is equipped with a keyboard and a printer and that can send and receive messages; also known as a Teletype machine.

Teletext. The system by which news, weather reports, and shopping information are broadcast over television channels to homes and offices.

Teletype. An electromechanical device that sends and receives messages using either the Baudot or ASCII coding system.

Telex. A transmission system using Teletype terminals and the 5-bit Baudot code to send and receive data; also known as Telex I.

Telex I. See *Telex*.

Telex II. See *TWX*.

Teller Terminal. A transaction terminal designed for the banking industry and used to process debits, credits, deposits, withdrawals, and other entries.

Terminal. A device capable of receiving or transmitting information between one point and another or between a computer and a point.

Throughput. A measure of the amount of information moved through a system in a given period of time.

Time Division Multiplexing (TDM). A technique that allocates a small fraction of time to several channels so that they can share one circuit.

Token Passing. A method used to resolve contentions for a circuit where a baton or token is electronically passed from one device to another.

Toll Office. A switching office that routes calls over intertoll trunks.

Topology. The layout, design, and structure of a network.

Trading Partners. Businesses or organizations that agree to exchange information according to the EDI standard.

Traffic Analysis. A study that assesses a communications system and describes the kinds, types, and volume of messages handled.

Transaction Terminal. Terminals located in retail establishments and designed to process customer transactions.

Transmission Control Protocol/Internet Protocol (TCP/IP). A WAN data transmission protocol used on UNIX systems.

Transmission Frame. A block of data that begins with a flag and includes an address and control information.

Transmission Rate of Information Bits (TRIB). A measure of the volume of information sent over a line in a specified period of time, based on transmission speed, control characters sent, and other factors.

Transmitter. The mouthpiece on a telephone handset.

Transponder. Circuitry on a communications satellite that amplifies a signal and retransmits it.

Tree Topology. An architecture in which elements on a network are connected together much like a tree with branches.

Turnpike Effect. A phenomenon whereby users on a new system behave much like drivers on a newly opened turnpike where unexpected problems occur because of new patterns of usage.

Twisted Pair. A telephone circuit in which twisted metallic conductors transmit the signal.

TWX. A transmission system using Teletype terminals and the 8-bit ASCII code to send and receive data; also known as Telex II.

Unified Network Management Architecture (UNMA). A network management service offered by AT&T that provides for the orderly growth of a communications system.

Universal Asynchronous Receiver Transmitter (UART). A device that converts parallel bits into a serial stream of bits or vice versa.

Unloaded Line. A communications circuit from which line amplifiers and other resistive components have been removed.

Unshielded Twisted Pair (UTP). A twisted pair of metallic wires, without a shield, used in a LAN cabling system.

Unsqueezer. A software routine that expands a file that has been squeezed.

Uplink. The circuit that sends a signal from an earth station up to a satellite.

Upload. The process in which a program or file is sent over communications lines from a local computer to another system.

User Identification Number. A special code number, known only to the user, that allows an individual to gain access to a system or selected files.

User-Supported Software. Programs that are distributed without charge so that they can be tested and sampled by users, who are then asked to send in a contribution for the use of the software.

Value-Added Network (VAN). A communications system that is capable of routing messages through switching equipment, providing computer services and access to proprietary databases.

Vendor. An individual or organization that provides software, hardware, supplies, or communications equipment for a fee.

Video Display Terminal (VDT). See *Monitor*.

Videotex. The system in which weather reports, news, or shopping information is transmitted over telephone lines or coaxial cables to homes or office.

Virtual Telecommunication Access Method (VTAM). Communications software that resides in a mainframe computer and interfaces applications programs and the front-end processor.

Virus. An unwanted and difficult-to-detect program that erases or destroys valuable data.

Voice Digitizing. A technique in which analog signals, representing speech, are reduced to digital pulses for transmission through a digital network.

Voice-Grade Circuit. An ordinary telephone-grade circuit capable of carrying voice communications.

Voice Mail. An electronic store-and-forward technology that moves messages.

Voice Messaging Service. See *Voice Mail*.

VT Emulator Software. Software that makes a microcomputer appear like a standard VT terminal.

VT Series Terminals. A group of DEC terminals connected to a DEC mainframe.

Wide Area Network (WAN). A communications system that is capable of sending and receiving information and routing it over communications circuits without any significant enhancement or change in the character of the data handled.

Wide Area Telephone Service (WATS). The capability of the switched network that allows users special rates on calls made to distant points.

Wideband Circuit. A specially conditioned circuit that can carry a high volume of data, far exceeding a voice-grade circuit.

Windows Terminal Software. A program within Windows, a graphical user interface, that performs communications functions.

Wireless LAN. A LAN that connects devices on a network, using broadcast radio frequencies rather than cables.

Word Processing. The manipulation of words, phrases, or textual matter to generate documents, letters, or reports.

Workstation. An independent unit containing a microcomputer, keyboard, CRT, and other devices that may be interfaced to a network.

X.25 Standard. The CCITT standard that specifies the interface between data terminals operating in the packet-switching mode.

X.400 E-Mail Protocol. An electronic mail protocol that facilitates the movement of communications over a WAN.

XMODEM Protocol. A binary file transfer protocol that transmits data in 128-byte blocks.

XMODEM-1K Protocol. A binary file transfer protocol that transmits data in 1024-byte blocks.

X-ON/X-OFF Protocol. A flow control protocol used on early Teletype equipment, now largely replaced by other schemes.

YMODEM Protocol. A binary file transfer protocol based on the XMODEM protocol, used for transferring large files.

ZMODEM Protocol. A transfer protocol finding applications in moving files over packet-switched networks, and containing advanced error-checking features.

INDEX

A

Aaronson Distributors case, 138–139, 162–163
Abbreviations, 85
ACCUNET DDS Service, 172, 173, 181, 182, 309, 333
ACCUNET Packet Service, 309
ACCUNET Reserved 1.5 Service, 308
ACCUNET Spectrum of Digital Services (ASDS), 173–174
ACCUNET Switched 56 Service, 175, 309, 333
ACCUNET switched digital services, 174–175, 181
ACCUNET T1.5 Service, 174, 308, 333
Acknowledgement (ACK) signal, 201
Acoustic connections, 128, 450
Administrative terminals, 64
Advanced Research Projects Agency (ARPA) (DOD), 313
Air Resources Company case, 190–191, 210–211
All-at-once conversion, 414
ALOHANET, 147
AM radio, 146–147
American Credit case, 424, 435–436
American National Standards Institute (ANSI)
    communications standards developed by, 192, 397
    explanation of, 450
American Satellite, 22
American Standard Code for Information Interchange (ASCII)
    description of, 194–195
    explanation of, 450
    used on EIA-232-D circuit, 206
American Telephone & Telegraph Company (AT&T), 18
    900 service offered by (MultiQuest), 171, 172
    antitrust violations of, 21
    categories of services provided by, 167, 168
    consumer communications services provided by, 184
    costs of accessing ISDN through, 47
    deregulation of, 3, 20–22, 37, 322
    digital services offered by, 172–175, 308–309, 321, 333
    electronic mail system of, 307–308
    Global Business Video Services provided by, 178
    inbound services provided by, 170, 171
    interest in fiber optics of, 158, 159
    international communications services provided by, 180–182
    network management services offered by, 373
    outbound services provided by, 168, 169
    present directions of, 140
    teleconferencing services provided by, 178, 179
    UNMA service provided by, 175
    voice messaging services provided by, 182, 183
Amplitude, 30–31, 450
Amplitude modulation (AM)
    explanation of, 95, 450
    use of, 96
    weaknesses of, 97–98
Analog signals, 13, 30–32, 450
ANSI Windows, 196, 197
Answer modem, 118, 450
AppleTalk, 223
Architecture. *See* Topology.
ARCnet (Datapoint), 288
Arithmetic and logic unit (ALU), 73
ARPANET, 313
ASCII code
    description of, 194–196, 450
    extended, 195–197
    uploading by use of, 226
    used on EIA-232-D circuit, 206
ASCX12 data field sequence, 401, 450
ASCX12 standards, 397–400, 450
Aspect, 228
Asynchronous transmission
    explanation of, 92, 450
    use of, 253–254
AT&T. *See* American Telephone & Telegraph Company (AT&T)
Attention (AT) codes
    explanation of, 115, 450
    list of, 121
    modems using, 120
    smart modems directed by, 117
Attenuation, 88, 450
Attenuation distortion, 143
Audits, 358
Auto-answer device, 119, 450
Auto-dialer, 119, 450
Automated offices, 427
Automated teller machines (ATMs), 8, 68, 69
Automatic route selection (ARS), 379
Autonet, 333

B

B-channel, 47, 450
Baird, J. L., 17
Bancroft Merchandising case, 110, 134–135
Bandwidth
    explanation of, 86–87, 450
    of fiber optics, 158
    used in LANs, 279
    of voice-grade dial-up lines, 112
Bank of America Network, 314
Bank teller terminals, 67–68
Baseband circuit, 248, 450
Baseband LANs, 248, 279
BASIC, 73
Basic rate interface (BRI)
    explanation of, 47, 168, 450
    use of, 47
Basic telecommunications access method (BTAM), 215–216, 450
Baud, 36, 87, 450
Baudot code
    description of, 192–193
    explanation of, 451
    problems with, 193
    used on EIA-232-D circuit, 206
Bell, Alexander Graham, 13
Bell Laboratories, 21, 115, 116
Bell-type 103 modems, 127, 131
Bell-type 201 modems, 127–128
Bell-type 202 modems, 128
Bell-type 208 modems, 128
Bell-type 209 modems, 128
Bell-type 212A modems, 128
Benchmark tests
    explanation of, 375–376, 451
    use of, 416
Bills of lading, 402
Binary coded decimal (BCD) code
    description of, 194
    explanation of, 451
    used on EIA-232-D circuit, 206
Binary codes, 33, 452
Binary digits, 34, 451
Binary representation, 33
Binary signals, 33, 34
Bisynchronous control (BSC), 253, 255, 451
Bits, 34, 451
Bits per second (bps), 36, 87, 451
BNC connector, 278
Boeing Network Architecture (BNA), 313–314
Bridge interface, 289, 451
British Telecommunications PLC, 158, 330
Broadband circuit, 248, 450
Broadband LANs, 248, 279
Buffer, 103, 451
Bulletin board services (BBS), 232–233, 451. *See also* Electronic bulletin boards
Burstiness, 256, 451
Bus topology, 251, 287, 451
Business communications
    consumer communications as aspect of, 183–184
    digital services for, 172–175

465

inbound services for, 170, 171
information services for, 171, 172
Integrated Services Digital Network for, 168. *See also* Integrated Services Digital Network (ISDN)
international services for, 180–181
outbound services for, 168–169
overview of, 167
satellite services for, 175–178. *See also* Communications satellites; Satellite transmissions
teleconferencing services for, 178–180
Unified Network Management Architecture for, 175
video services for, 178
voice messaging for, 182–183
Business Communications Services Guide (AT&T), 167
Business International Long Distance Service (AT&T), 181
Bypass, 432–433
Byte, 34, 451

C
C, 73
C band, 155, 451
Cable-access television (CATV), 10, 11, 144
Cabling system, 275–278, 451
Call cost accounting, 46, 451
Camouflage techniques, 390–391
Carrier sense multiple access/collision detection (CSMA/CD), 286, 287, 289, 451
Carrier wave, 95–96, 111, 451
Carter, Thomas F., 21
Carterfone Company, 20, 21
Cases
 Aaronson Distributors, 138–139, 162–163
 Air Resources Company, 190–191, 210–211
 American Credit, 424, 435–436
 Bancroft Merchandising, 110, 134–135
 Fairway Department Stores, 438–449
 Farnsworth Petroleum, 348, 367–368
 Fidelity Bank, 82, 106–107
 Greene and Singer Consultants, 28, 49–50
 Larson Advertising Agency, 54, 78–79
 Law Offices of Parker and Parker, 266, 292–294
 Logan Electronics, 296, 317–318
 Metro Security, 370, 393–394
 Micros 'N Stuff, 214, 238–239
 Oakview Hospital, 396, 419–420
 Pizza Heaven Restaurants, 244, 263–264
 Shelby Investment Services, 2, 25–26
 World Sports Today, 166, 186, 187
 Worldcom, 320, 343–344
Cathode Ray Tube (CRT). *See Monitor*.
CCITT standards, 116, 122, 123–127
CCITT V.17 fax modems, 127
CCITT V.21 – 300 bps modems, 116, 123
CCITT V.22 – 1,200 bps modems, 123–124
CCITT V.22 – 2,400 bps modems, 124
CCITT V.23 – 1,200 bps modems, 124–126
CCITT V.26 – 2,400 bps modems, 125
CCITT V.27 – 4,800 bps modems, 126
CCITT V.29 – 9,600 bps modems, 126
CCITT V.32 – 9,600 bps modems, 116, 126
CCITT V.42 standards, 119

CD-ROMs, 11
Cellular radio
 developments in, 22–23, 150
 explanation of, 451
Cellular radio telephones, 150–152
Center frequency, 451
Central office (CO), 38, 451
Central processing unit (CPU), 72, 73, 451
Centralized data processing, 245, 451
Centrex, 61, 451
Channel, 36, 451
Charge-back systems, 375
Christensen, Ward, 200
Circuits
 conditioning of, 88
 explanation of, 36, 451
 range of frequencies in, 86, 87. *See also* Bandwidth
 specifications for, 374
 telephone, 111–113
Coax. *See* Coaxial cables
Coaxial cables
 construction of, 144
 explanation of, 452
 use of, 144–145, 248
 used for LANs, 277–278
COBOL, 73
Command-driven software, 231, 452
Common carriers, 3, 452
Communication channels
 data concentrators and, 104
 data encoding and, 93–94
 evaluation of, 86–88
 explanation of, 36–37
 hybrid circuits and, 88–90
 modulation and, 95–99
 multiplexing principles and, 99–103
 serial and parallel data transmission and, 90–92
 transmission modes in, 92–93
Communication software packages
 communications control, 220
 Crosstalk XVI, 223, 231
 front-end, 218, 219
 for front-end processors, 216–218
 mainframe, 215–216
 microcomputer, 222–232. *See also* Microcomputer communications packages
 microcomputer-to-host, 220–222
 Procomm Plus, 223, 226–228
 public domain, 235, 236
 Smartcom III, 223, 229–230
 system network, 219–220
 viruses in, 236
 Windows Terminal, 224–226
Communication technology, 8–12
Communications
 business services for international, 180–182
 costs of, 7
 evolution of, 12
 explanation of, 4, 5
 increasing use of, 3
 international, 180–182
 need for, 7
 pre-electronic methods of, 2–3
Communications industry

changes in, 248–249
changing workforce in, 425
growth in, 3
growth of telecommuting in, 425–426
Communications links
 companies providing, 140
 explanation of, 5, 139, 452
Communications managers, 353
Communications medium
 explanation of, 30, 452
 fiber-optic transmissions, 157–159
 hard-wire circuits, 141–145
 laser beams, 159–160
 microwave relay systems, 153–154
 radio circuits, 145–152
 satellite transmissions, 154–157
 types of, 29
Communications satellites
 for business communications, 175–176
 construction of, 155, 156
 cost of, 157
 explanation of, 154–155, 452
 SKYNET Digital Service of, 176–177
Communications server, 274, 452
Communications software packages, 214, 452. *See also* Software
CompuServe, 323
 commands for, 339–340
 explanation of, 333, 335
 logging on to, 338–339
 service rates of, 335
 subject index of, 338
Computer-aided manufacturing, 271
Computer viruses, 236
Conditioned circuits, 88, 142, 452
Connectivity
 crucial nature of, 297
 explanation of, 7
 between Macintosh and IBM, 428
Consultants
 for network design, 373
 for systems analysis, 354
Consultative Committee for International Telephone and Telegraph (CCITT), 71
 communications standards of, 44, 192, 203, 206, 253, 304
 explanation of, 452
 modem designations by, 101, 116
Consumer communications services, 183–184
Contention, 285, 286
Continuous wave (CW), 146
Control characters, 198–199, 452
Control Data Corporation, 332
Controller card, 218
Controllers, 217, 452
Cooke, Sir William, 13
Corporate Calling Card (AT&T), 168, 181
Cosmic rays, 85
Cost analysis
 as element of systems design, 375, 376
 used in systems analysis, 358–359
Credit authorization terminals, 66–67, 452
Critical path method (CPM), 385, 452
Crossbar switches, 39, 452
Crosstalk XVI, 223, 231
Customer information control system (CICS), 220, 452

INDEX 467

Cyclic redundancy check (CRC), 203, 452
Cylix, 333

D
D-channel, 47, 452
Data circuit-terminating equipment (DCE)
    explanation of, 204, 452
    handshake procedure used by, 208
    use of, 113
Data collection terminals, 65–66
Data communications, 4, 5, 452
Data compression, 204, 452
Data concentrators, 104, 452
Data decoding, 93, 94
Data encoding, 93, 94
Data encrypting techniques, 390–391
Data frame, 119, 453
Data link controls (DLCs), 253
Data links, 139, 453
Data packet, 259, 453
Data processing, 4
Data security
    access vs., 386, 388
    explanation of, 453
    as factor in system design, 386
    for LANs, 282, 284–285
    port protection devices for, 390–391
    through software controls, 388–390
    in transport layer, 260–261
Data terminal equipment (DTE), 61, 113, 204, 453
Data transmission, 92–93
Data transmission codes
    error-detection provisions for, 199–203
    types of, 192–199
Data transmission equipment
    special-purpose terminals, 64–68
    terminals, 62–64
    types of, 61
Databases
    access to remote, 323
    explanation of, 453
    need for access to, 22
Datagram mode, 260
Dataphone Digital Services (DDS)
    access to, 173–174
    explanation of, 172, 333, 453
    use of, 173, 309
Datastorm Technologies, Inc., 223, 226
dBASE, 282
Decibel (dB), 88, 453
DECnet, 301–302
Decoding, 93, 94, 453
Decompression, 204, 453
Decrypting key, 390, 453
Decryption, 94, 453
Dedicated earth stations, 176
Dedicated lines
    common carriers providing, 140
    explanation of, 112, 453
Definitions, 5, 6
DeForest, Lee, 17
Delphi, 340
Demodulation, 96, 97, 111, 453
Department of Commerce, 16
Department of Defense, 313

Deregulation. *See* Industry deregulation
Dial-up telephone lines, 111–112, 453
Dialing, 119, 453
Dialog information service, 340
Dibit phase shift keying (DPSK), 123, 124, 453
Dibits, 36, 453
Digital branch exchanges (DBXs)
    automatic route selection by, 379
    case example discussing, 28, 49–50
    explanation of, 42–43, 60–61, 453
    use of, 305
Digital central offices (DCOs), 44
Digital Centrex, 61
Digital Communications Associates, Inc., 223
Digital data, 4, 453
Digital data local channel (DDLC), 174
Digital Equipment Corporation (DEC), 221, 234, 301, 302
Digital key telephone systems (DKTSs), 58, 59, 453
Digital Network Architecture (DNA), 301–302
Digital signals, 30, 33–34
Direct distance dialing (DDD), 141, 256, 453
Dishes, 155
Disk farm, 302
Distance terms, 85
Distributed data processing (DDP)
    cases discussing, 244, 263–264, 296, 317–318
    description of, 245–247
    explanation of, 453
Distributed System Service (DSS), 302
Documentation
    analysis of systems, 357–358
    explanation of, 453
    preparation of systems, 391
Dow Jones News/Retrieval, 323, 332, 340–341
Downlink, 155, 176, 453
Download, 226, 453
DSI circuits, 113, 173
Dual-tone multifrequency (DTMF) dialing
    explanation of, 57–58, 454
    smart modems using, 117
Dumb terminals, 62, 454

E
E-mail, 10. *See* Electronic mail
EAASY SABRE Personal Travel Service, 341
Earth stations, 155, 156, 176. *See also* Communications satellites; Satellite transmissions
EasyLink Services, 307–308
Echo suppression, 88, 454
Edison, Thomas, 13
EIA-232-D interface
    25-pin connector, 206, 207
    explanation of, 205, 454
    function of, 206, 253
    standards for, 130
800 service, 170, 181
Electromagnetic waves, 16, 84, 454
Electronic banking, 8. *See also* Electronic funds transfer system (EFTS)
    case discussing, 82, 106–108
    explanation of, 454

Electronic bulletin boards
    case discussing, 214, 238–239
    development of, 232–233
    networks of, 233–234
    types of, 233
    use of, 234–235
Electronic data interchange (EDI)
    benefits of, 398
    explanation of, 454
    use of, 397–398
Electronic funds transfer system (EFTS), 8, 297
Electronic Industries Association (EIA)
    communications standards published by, 192
    explanation of, 454
    standard interface connection published by, 205
Electronic mail
    case discussing, 110, 134–135
    explanation of, 10, 454
    various systems of, 307–308, 327–329, 331–332
    X.400, 304
Electronic publishing, 9
Electronic shopping, 10, 11, 454
Electronic signal switching (ESS), 39, 454
Electronics
    advances in, 2
    historical overview of, 12–15
Emulators
    explanation of, 69, 454
    Smartcomm III and, 230
    types of, 69, 221, 222
Encoding, 93, 94, 454
Encryption, 94, 390, 391, 454
End of transmission (EOT) signal, 201
End office, 38, 454
End user, 454
Error-control mechanisms, 259
Error-detection provisions
    for data transmission codes, 199–203
    integrated with data compression, 204
Error rate, 363, 454
Ethernet, 281, 285, 287, 454
Ethernet clamp, 278
Even parity, 454
Even-parity system, 199
Expandability, 409
Extended ASCII code, 195–197
Extended binary coded decimal interchange code (EBCDIC)
    description of, 197–198
    explanation of, 454
    used on EIA-232-D circuit, 206

F
Facsimile machines (FAXs)
    case example discussing, 54, 78–79
    cellular, 152, 451
    explanation of, 70, 454
    types of, 71
Fairway Department Stores case, 438–449
Farnsworth Petroleum case, 348, 367–368
Fast packet switching, 311–312, 431, 454
Fax cards, 71, 454
Fax machines. *See* Facsimile machines (FAXs)

468 INDEX

Feasibility studies
  elements of, 353–354
  explanation of, 454
  stages of, 354–355
Federal Communications Commission (FCC)
  explanation of, 454
  function of, 17
  policy regarding 800 numbers, 170
  role in deregulation, 20, 21
Feedback, 29
Fiber distributed data interface (FDDI), 278, 431, 455
Fiber optics
  advantages of, 158–159
  explanation of, 157, 455
  growth in usage of, 431
  international standards for information transfer via, 158
Fiber-optics cables, 278, 282
Fidelity Bank case, 82, 106–107
FidoNet, 234, 455
Field selectable switches, 118, 455
File server, 272, 455
File transfer protocol, 455
Find America Directory Service, 184
Flag, 255
FM radio, 147–148
Forecasting, 383, 384
Formatting, 261, 455
Frame relay, 310, 455
Frame relay networks, 309–311
Frame relay switching, 431–432
Frames, 253, 455
Franklin, Benjamin, 13
Frequency
  explanation of, 31, 83, 455
  terms that describe, 85
Frequency division multiplexing (FDM)
  broadband LANs and, 279
  explanation of, 100–102, 455
  purpose of, 131–132
  time division vs., 103
  use of, 101–102
Frequency modulation (FM), 97–98, 455
Frequency shift keying (FSK), 98, 455. *See also* Frequency modulation
Frequency spectrum
  explanation of, 83, 455
  parts of, 84–86
Front-end processors (FEPs)
  explanation of, 74–75, 455
  function of, 75, 216–217
Front-end software, 218
Full-duplex (FDX) circuits, 88, 455
Full-duplex (FDX) modems, 116
FYI Reports, 306

G
Gamma rays, 85
Gateways, 288–289, 455
General Electric Network for Information Exchange (GEnie), 341
General Telephone and Electric (GTE), 325
GEnie service (General Electric Network for Information Exchange), 341
Geosynchronous satellites, 154, 455

GHz, 455
Global Business Video Services (GBVS), 178
Global virtual private network (GVPN)
  case discussing, 348, 367–368
  explanation of, 315, 426, 455
  features of, 426–427
Greene and Singer Consultants case, 28, 49–50
Guard Band, 101

H
H & R Bloch, 333
Half-duplex (HDX) circuits, 88, 455
Half-duplex (HDX) modems, 116
Handshake procedure, 131, 207–208, 455
Hard-copy output, 455
Hard-wire circuits, 141–142, 455
Hardware
  explanation of, 455
  inventory of, 363
  selection of, 408–409
  specifications for, 374
Hawthorne effect, 364, 455
Hayes Microcomputer Products, Inc., 115, 117, 120, 203, 223
Henry, Joseph, 16
Hertz, Heinrich, 16
Hertz (Hz), 84, 456
High-frequency radio, 147
Host computers, 215, 456
Hughes Aircraft Company, 19
Human voice, 85–86
Hush-a-Phone Co., 20
Hybrid circuits, 88
Hybrid networks, 326, 327
Hybrid transformers, 89, 456

I
I/O devices, 73
IBM 3270 emulators, 69, 220, 221
IBM Corporation. *See* International Business Machines (IBM)
Iconoscope tube, 18
IEEE 802.3, 285–287
IEEE 802.5, 285–288
Inbound services, 170, 171, 456
Induction coil, 37, 456
Industry deregulation
  availability of alternative networks due to, 322
  trends in, 20–22, 432
Industry regulation
  affecting network design, 373
  early developments in, 16–18
InfoPlex Word Processing System, 333, 334
Information exchange gateways, 430, 456
Information frame, 259, 456
Information services
  CompuServe, 323, 333, 335, 338–340
  Delphi, 340
  description of, 335
  Dialog, 340
  Dow Jones News/Retrieval, 340–341
  GEnie, 341
  growth of, 171, 430
  Official Airline Guide/Electronic Edition, 306, 341

Infrared waves, 84
Input systems, 73, 456
Inquiry systems
  explanation of, 403–404
  steps involved in, 404–405
Institute of Electrical and Electronic Engineers (IEEE)
  communications standards published by, 192, 285, 286
  explanation of, 456
Integrated Network Management Services (INMS), 373
Integrated services digital network (ISDN)
  advantages of, 46, 111
  basic rate interface in, 47
  case discussing, 166, 186, 187
  expanded market for, 431
  explanation of, 44, 168, 349, 456
  price structure of, 47–48
  primary rate interface in, 47
  services offered by, 168
  system design of, 46–47
  system features of, 44–46
Integrated voice and data network, 190–191, 210–211, 428–429
Intelligent terminals, 62, 63
Intelsat satellite, 19, 20
Interconnect ruling, 20–21, 456
Interexchange carrier (IXC), 42, 456
Interface, 204, 456
Interface cards, 273–275, 456
Interface devices. *See* Modems
Interface standards
  25-Pin connector, 206
  EIA-232-D, 130, 205–207
  explanation of, 204–205
  RS-449, 206
  used by modems, 130–132
International Banking System (IBS), 314
International Business Machines (IBM)
  introduction of personal computers by, 76
  mainframe software developed by, 215–216
  System Network Architecture developed by, 219
International communications, 180–182
International Facsimile Service (AT&T), 181
International Standards Organization (ISO)
  communications standards published by, 192
  development of OSI model by, 251–252
  function of, 456
Intertoll trunks, 40, 41, 456
Interviews, 356–357
Investigative study, 354, 456
ISDN. *See* Integrated services digital network (ISDN)
ITT, 21

J
Jacks, 129
Jenkins, C. F., 17
Jennings, Tom, 234

K
K Band, 155, 456
Kelvin, Lord William, 355

KERMIT, 203, 226, 456
kHz, 456
Kinescope, 18
Ku Band, 155, 456

L
LAN BIOS, 282
Language Line Services (AT&T), 184
LANs. *See* Local area networks (LANs)
Large-scale integrated (LSI) circuit, 22, 456
Larson Advertising Agency case, 54, 78–79
Laser beams, 159, 160, 456
Law Offices of Parker and Parker case, 266, 292–294
Lead time, 412–413, 456
Learning curve, 364, 456
Leased lines
    common carriers providing, 140, 141
    explanation of, 456
    operation of, 112–113
Leasing of equipment, 411
Leg, 180
Line, 36, 457
Line amplifiers, 142, 457
Line loss, 457
Linear programming (LP), 377–379, 457
Linear regression analysis, 383
Liquid crystal terminals (LCTs), 62, 63
Local access transport area (LATA), 41–42, 457
Local area networks (LANs)
    access protocols for, 285–286
    acquisition of, 289–290
    advantages for, 268
    baseband, 248, 279
    bridges used to connect, 289
    broadband, 248, 279
    broadband coaxial, 248
    business applications of, 270
    cabling system used in, 276–278
    carrier sense multiple access/collision detection and, 287
    case discussing, 266, 292–294
    components of, 272–275
    configurations of, 281–283
    design applications of, 270–271
    educational applications of, 270
    environment for, 267–268
    example of application of, 269
    explanation of, 248, 457
    gateway interface used to connect, 288–289
    growth of, 429
    network standards for, 285
    software and security for, 282, 284–285
    token-passing access and, 287–288
    use of, 56, 246–247, 266
    used in computer-aided manufacturing, 271
    wireless, 279–280
Local area system (LAS), 301
Local exchange carriers (LECs), 41–42, 457
Local loop, 39
Logan Electronics case, 296, 317–318
Longitudinal parity, 199, 457
Longitudinal redundancy check (LRC), 199, 200
Lotus 1-2-3, 282

M
Macintosh-to-IBM host connection, 221, 428

Mainframe computers
    elements of, 73–74
    explanation of, 19, 72, 457
    software for, 215–216
Management information system (MIS), 406–408
Marconi, Guglielmo, 16
Mark, 123, 457
Mayo, Elton, 364
MCI Communications Corporation
    business services provided by, 168, 170, 172, 175, 178, 180
    electronic mail system of, 307
    fiber optics interests of, 158, 159
    network management services offered by, 373
MCI Mail, 307
Mean time between failures (MTBF), 363, 457
Measurement list, 85
Medium-frequency AM radio, 146–147
MEGACOM WATS, 181
Megahubs, 457
Menu-driven software, 229, 231, 457
Meridian Digital Centrex, 61
Mesh topology, 251, 457
Message collision, 285–286, 457
Message service, 183
Message Transfer Agent software, 304
Message transmission, 29–30
Metering, 12, 457
Metro Security case, 370, 393–394
MHz, 85, 457
Microcom Network Protocol (MNP), 115, 119–120, 457
Microcom Systems, Inc., 115
Microcomputer communications packages
    Crosstalk XVI, 223, 231
    overview of, 222–223
    PC-Talk, 223, 232
    Procomm Plus, 223, 226–228
    QMODEM, 223, 232
    Smartcom III, 223, 229–230
    Windows Terminal, 224–226
Microcomputer-to-host software, 220–222
Microcomputers
    explanation of, 75–76, 457
    growth in usage of, 431
    networks of, 304–305
Microprocessors, 22, 116–117
Micros 'N Stuff case, 214, 238–239
Microseconds, 7, 457
Microsoft Corp., 223
Microsoft Word, 195
Microwave Communication, Inc. (MCI), 21, 22. *See also* MCI Communications Corporation
Microwave transmission links, 18, 153–154, 457
Microwaves, 153
Millisecond, 85, 457
Minicomputers
    explanation of, 74, 457
    growth in market for, 22
    integrated into communications systems, 74–75
Modems
    attention command set and, 120, 121
    Bell-type, 127–128
    CCITT standards for, 123–127

    connections for, 128–129
    dialing features of, 119
    explanation of, 97, 457
    hardware used for, 120, 122
    interface standards for, 130–132
    manufacture and marketing of, 115–116
    Microcom Network Protocol and, 119–120
    microprocessor-controlled, 116–117
    modes of, 118–119
    overview of, 110
    standard designations for, 115–116
    telephone circuits and types of, 111–113
    transmission speeds and formats of, 118
    universal asynchronous receiver/transmitter and, 113–115
Modular plugs, 129
Modulation, 95, 96, 111, 457
Modulators/demodulators. *See* Modems
Monitoring. *See* Metering
Monitors, 358, 458
Morse, Samuel, 13
Morse code, 95, 192, 458
Multidrop circuit, 249, 298, 458
Multimedia, 11–12, 458
Multiplexed radio, 150
Multiplexers (MUXs)
    development of, 100
    explanation of, 458
    frequency, 101–102, 455
    statistical time division, 103, 460
    time division, 100, 103, 461
Multipoint circuit. *See* Multidrop circuit
Multiprocessor networks, 298–299
Mustang Software, 232

N
Nanoseconds, 7, 458
Negative acknowledgment (NAK) signal, 201
NetWare, 284
Network addressable units (NAUs), 219
Network Control Program (NCP), 218, 458
Network hub, 275, 458
Network Layers, 300
Network Planning and Analysis Tools (NPAT), 372
Networks. *See also* Integrated services digital network
    basic concepts of, 245
    benefits of open systems interconnection model and, 261
    distributed data processing, 244–247, 263–264
    explanation of, 5, 458
    global virtual private network, 455
    integrated voice and data, 190–191, 210–211
    layers of open systems interconnection model and, 252–261
    local area. *See* Local area networks (LANs)
    open systems interconnection model and, 251–252
    packet radio, 147
    switched, 112–113, 140, 321, 322, 460
    synchronous optical, 158, 460
    topology of, 250–251
    value-added. *See* Value-added networks

INDEX

wide area, 249, 463
worldwide, 426–427
900 service, 171, 192
Nodes
    explanation of, 5, 219, 458
    in Tymnet system, 330–331
    workstation as, 272, 273
Novell NetWare, 284

O

Oakview Hospital case, 396, 419–420
Odd parity, 199, 458
Office automation, 427
Official Airline Guide/Electronic Edition (OAG), 306, 341
Ongoing committee, 353
Open systems interconnection (OSI) model
    benefits of, 261
    development of, 251–252
    explanation of, 458
    layers of, 252–261
Order acknowledgment, 402
Order processing systems, 400, 402, 403
Originate modem, 118, 458
OS/2 LAN Manager, 284
Oscillator circuit, 458
Outbound services, 168–169, 458
Output system, 73, 458

P

Packet, 256, 458
Packet radio networks, 147
Packet switching
    explanation of, 256–259, 458
    X.25 standard and, 259–260
PageMaker, 195
Paging systems, 147
Parabolic microwave antenna, 153
Parallel conversion, 414–415
Parallel stream, 115
Parallel transmission
    cost of, 92
    costs involved in, 90
    explanation of, 91, 458
Parameter files, 229–230, 458
Passwords, 389, 458
PC modem card, 122
PC-Talk, 223, 232
PC-to-DEC host connection, 221
PC-to-IBM host connection, 221
Peer-to-peer networks, 272
Personal computers (PCs), 22. *See also* Minicomputers with communications systems, 2, 25–26
    connections to host, 220–222
    introduction of, 76
Personnel requirements, 363, 374
Phase modulation (PM), 98, 99, 458
Phase shift, 35, 124, 458
Phased-in conversion, 413–414
Pizza Heaven Restaurants case, 244, 263–264
Plain old telephone service (POTS), 140
Point of presence (POP), 22, 42, 458
Point-of-sale terminal, 67, 459
Point-to-point topology, 249, 297, 298, 459

Pony Express, 13
Port protection devices (PPDs), 390–391, 459
Ports, 297
Primary rate interface (PRI), 47, 168, 459
Print servers, 274, 459
Private automatic branch exchange (PABX), 20, 42, 43, 60, 459
Private branch exchange (PBX), 42, 43, 60, 459
Private networks, 312–313
Procomm Plus 2.0, 223, 226–228
Prodigy, 336–337
Program evaluation and review technique (PERT), 385–386, 459
Project managers, 353
Protocols, 207, 459
Prototype installation, 411–412, 459
Public domain software, 235–236, 459
Pull-down menu, 226
Pulse dialing, 117
Pulse train, 94–95

Q

Q.922 frame format standard, 310
QMODEM, 223, 232
Quality control techniques
    forecasting as, 383, 384
    program evaluation and review as, 385–386
    simulation and modeling as, 384–385
    types of, 382–385
Queing, 379, 381, 382
Questionnaires, 358
Queued telecommunication access method (QTAM), 218, 459

R

Radio teletype, 147. *See also* Teletype
Radio transmissions
    cellular fax machines, 152
    cellular radio telephones, 150–152
    development of, 16
    FM radio, 147–148
    high-frequency radio, 147
    medium-frequency AM radio, 146–147
    multiplexed radio, 150
    overview of, 145–146
    videotex and teletext, 152
    wireless message centers, 148–150
Radio waves, 84
RCA Corporation, 21, 333
Real time, 7
Real-time processing, 7, 459
Receivers, 29, 37, 459
Regulation. *See* Industry regulation
Remote-job-entry (RJE) terminals, 66, 245, 459
Repeaters
    in cellular radio, 150
    explanation of, 88, 89
    series of, 90
Resource sharing, 270
Response time, 359–361, 459
Reverse channel, 459
Ring topology, 250, 459
Rotary dial telephones, 55–56, 459
Router, 459
RS-232-C standard, 206, 253

RS-449 standard, 206
RTTY, 147. *See also* Teletype

S

Satellite transmissions, 154–157. *See also* Communications satellites; Earth stations; SKYNET Digital Service
Scientific method, 356
Script file, 228, 459
Secondary storage, 74, 459
Security. *See* Data security
Semi-automatic business research environment (SABRE)
    access to, 341
    development of, 313
    explanation of, 19, 459
Semi-automatic ground environment (SAGE) air defense system, 18–19
Senders, 29
Serial ports, 114, 460
Serial stream, 115
Serial transmission
    costs involved in, 90
    explanation of, 91, 460
    use of, 91
Shared earth stations, 176
Shareware, 232
Shelby Investment Services case, 2, 25–26
Shielded twisted pair (STP), 276, 460
Shipping memos, 402
Side tone coil, 37. *See also* Induction coil
Simplex circuit, 87, 460
Simulation, 384–385
Sine waves, 30, 31, 460
SKYNET Digital Service, 176–177
SKYNET International Service, 180, 181
SKYNET Satellite Service, 309
Smart building, 429
Smart modems, 117, 460
Smart terminal, 62, 460
Smartcom III, 223, 229–230
Software. *See also* Communications software packages
    command-driven, 231, 452
    explanation of, 460
    front-end, 218
    menu-driven, 229, 457
    microcomputer-to-host, 220–222
    network, 275
    network design, 372
    for operation of LAN, 275, 282, 284–285
    to protect data, 388–390
    public domain, 235–236, 459
    selection of, 408–409
    specifications for, 374
    user-supported, 223, 462
    VT emulator, 221, 462
Solid-state switching, 39
Sound pressure levels (SPLs), 31–33, 84, 460
Sound waves, 30
Space, 123, 460
Speech recognition, 432
Sprint Communications Co., 21
    business services provided by, 168, 170, 172, 175, 178, 180
    electronic mail system of, 307
    fiber optics interests of, 158, 159

U

Ultraviolet (uV) waves, 85
Unconditioned voice-grade line, 142
Unified network management architecture (UNMA), 175, 462
Uninet, 332–334
United Press International (UPI), 306, 330
United States Radio Act (1912), 16
United Telecommunications, 332–333
Universal asynchronous receiver/transmitter (UART), 114–115, 462
UNIX, 234, 302–303
Unloaded lines, 142, 462
Unshielded twisted pair (UTP) systems, 276, 462
Unsqueezers, 204, 235, 462
Uplink, 155, 176, 462
Upload, 226, 462
U.S. Sprint Fast Packet Switching, 311
User Agent software, 304
User identification numbers, 389, 462
User-supported software, 223, 232, 462

V

V. modems, 116
V.24 standards, 253
V.28 standards, 253
Value-added networks (VANs)
    case discussing, 320, 343–344
    description of, 323–324
    environment leading up to development of, 321–322
    explanation of, 321, 323, 462
    information services as, 335–341
    miscellaneous, 333
    SprintNet, 323, 325–330
    Tymnet, 330–332
    Uninet, 332–334
    wide area networks vs., 323
VANs. *See* Value-added networks (VANs)
Variable resistor, 37
VAX cluster, 302
Vendor documentation, 408, 462
Vendor selection, 409–411
Ventura Publisher, 195
Vertical redundancy checks (VRCs), 199
Video communications services, 178

Video display terminals (VTDs), 62–64. *See also* Monitors
Video information, 4
Videophone, 21
Videotex, 152, 462
Virtual mode, 260
Virtual telecommunication access method (VTAM), 218, 219, 462
Viruses, 236, 462
Visible light frequencies, 84
Voice, human, 85–86
Voice communications, 4
Voice digitizing, 462
Voice-grade private line (VGPL), 174
Voice-grade telephone circuits, 112, 113, 462
Voice mail, 182, 183, 462
Voice messaging services, 182–183, 462
Voice transmission equipment
    digital key telephone systems, 58, 59
    for local switching, 59–61
    telephone instruments, 55–58
VT emulator software, 221, 462
VT series terminals, 221, 463
VT52 emulators, 221
VT100 emulators, 69, 221

W

Waiting line theory, 379, 381, 382
WANs. *See* Wide area networks (WANs)
Waveguides, 153
Wavelengths, 83, 84
Westar, 19
Western Electric Company, 21, 101
Western Union Telegraph Company, 13, 19, 140, 306, 380
Wide Area Network Design Laboratory, 372
Wide area networks (WANs)
    architecture of, 299–304
    Bank of America, 314
    developed by AT&T, 308–309
    explanation of, 249, 463
    fast packet-switching, 311–312
    frame relay, 309–311
    global virtual private, 315
    of microcomputers, 304–305
    private, 312–313

    public, 306–308
    SABRE, 313–314
    types of, 297–299
    value-added networks vs., 323
Wide area telephone service (WATS), 141, 169, 463
Wideband circuit, 463
Windows Terminal software
    explanation of, 223, 463
    operation of, 224–225
    popularity of, 226
Wire photo machine, 17
Wireless LANs, 279–280, 463
Wireless message centers
    explanation of, 148
    illustration of, 149
    use of, 150, 427
Wireless receivers, 148, 149
Word processing, 8–9, 406, 463
WordPerfect, 195, 282
Workstations, 272–273, 463
World Sports Today case, 166, 186, 187
Worldcom case, 320, 343–344

X

X-ON/X-OFF protocol, 200, 463
X-rays, 85
X.25 standard
    access to value-added networks through, 330–333
    explanation of, 203, 463
    packet switching and, 259–260
X.400 E-mail protocol, 304, 463
XMODEM, 226, 231
XMODEM error-checking system, 200–202
XMODEM-IK protocol, 202, 463
X.PC protocol, 332

Y

YMODEM protocol, 202, 226, 463

Z

ZMODEM protocol, 203, 463
Zworykin, Vladimir, 17, 18

SprintMail, 307, 327–329
SprintMail Fax, 328
SprintMail Newsclips, 330
SprintNet
  description of, 323, 325–328
  rate structure used by, 327
  security issues for, 386
Squeezers, 204, 235, 460
Stand-alone modem, 122
Standard Ethernet, 278
Star topology, 250, 460
Statistical time division multiplexing (STDM), 103, 460
Step-by-step (stepper) switches, 15, 39
Strowger step-by-step (stepper) switch, 15
Subcarrier channel, 101, 460
Subchannel, 36, 150
Subscriber loop, 39, 40, 112, 460
Switched digital services, 174–175, 181
Switched networks
  AT&T, 321, 322
  explanation of, 460
  leased lines and, 112–113
  packet switching and, 256, 257
  provision of alternatives to, 140
Switching
  explanation of, 38–39
  postdivestiture, 41–42
  predivestiture, 39–41
Switching equipment, 59–61
Synchronous data link control (SDLC), 253, 255, 299
Synchronous optical network (SONET), 158, 460
Synchronous transmission, 92–93, 254–255, 460
Syncom satellite, 19
System access control, 370, 393–394
System changeover
  approaches to, 413–415
  case discussing, 396, 419–420
  explanation of, 460
System network architecture (SNA)
  drawbacks of, 301
  explanation of, 21, 218, 299, 460
  function of, 219–220, 300–301
System operator (sysop), 234
Systems
  assessment of costs of, 375
  documentation for, 417
  evaluation and follow-up for, 415–417
  explanation of, 5, 460
  installation of new, 412–415
  management and control of, 417
Systems analysis
  assessment of personnel requirements as element of, 363
  audits used for, 358
  cost analysis used in, 358–359
  distortions in, 363–365
  elements of, 355–356
  equipment and hardware inventory as element of, 363
  explanation of, 460
  interviews as element of, 356–357
  overview of, 351–352
  questionnaires used in, 358
  scientific method used in, 356

systems documentation analysis as element of, 357–358
  traffic analysis used for, 359–363
Systems analysts, 352
Systems design
  data security and systems integrity as issues in, 386–391
  documentation as aspect of, 391
  examples of alternatives in, 371–372
  explanation of, 352, 370, 460
  quality control and, 382–386
  resource allocation as aspect of, 376–382
  software to facilitate, 372
  steps in, 373–376
Systems development, 352, 460
Systems evaluation, 352, 415, 460
Systems implementation, 352, 460
Systems optimization, 416–417, 460
Systems planning
  elements of, 352–353
  explanation of, 351–352
  role of feasibility studies in, 353–355

T
T45 access with M28 and M24 multiplexing, 174
Task force, 354
Telecommunications
  domains of, 4
  explanation of, 4, 461
  growth in, 18–20, 191
  organization of, 350, 351
Telecommuting
  case discussion of, 424, 435–436
  growth in, 425–426
Teleconferencing
  case example discussing, 138–139, 162–163
  explanation of, 11, 461
  services provided for, 178–180
Telegraph systems, 191, 461
Telenet, 322, 325
Telephone circuits, 111–113
Telephone systems
  development of, 13–15
  fundamentals of, 29–30, 37–38
  operation of switching in, 38–39
  postdivestiture switching in, 41–42
  predivestiture switching in, 39–41
Telephones
  digital, 44
  dual-one multifrequency, 57–58
  rotary dial, 55–56
Telephony, 37
Telephotography, 16, 17
Teleprinters, 62, 461
Teletext, 10–11, 152, 461
Teletype, 17, 62, 461
Teletype machines, 142, 147
Television
  analog signals generated by, 32, 33
  development of, 17–19
Telex
  explanation of, 17, 141, 461
  list of Western Union rates, 380
  merger of TWX and, 21
Telex I, 306, 461
Telex II, 306, 461

Teller terminal, 67, 461
Telstar, 19, 155
Telstar satellite, 19
10Base-T, 276, 450
10Base2, 278, 450
10Base5, 278, 450
Terminal software (Windows), 223–226, 463
Terminals
  administrative, 64
  bank teller, 67–68
  credit authorization, 66–67, 452
  data collection, 65–66
  dumb, 62, 454
  explanation of, 5, 19, 62, 461
  intelligent, 62, 63
  liquid crystal, 62, 63
  remote-job-entry, 66, 245, 459
  special purpose, 64–68
  transaction, 67–68, 461
  video display, 62–64. See also Monitors
  VT series, 221, 463
ThinNet Ethernet, 278
3COM Corporation, 284
3+Open network operating system, 284
3002 circuits, 113
Throughput, 360–362, 461
TI circuits, 113, 372, 461
Time, terms that describe, 85
Time division multiplexing (TDM)
  broadband LANs and, 279
  explanation of, 100, 103, 461
  frequency division vs., 103
Time-sharing market, 323, 324
Token passing, 286–289, 461
Token-Ring network (IBM), 288, 304, 305
Toll offices, 40, 461
Topology, 250, 461
Touch-Tone. See Dual-tone multifrequency (DTMF) dialing
Trading partners, 397, 461
Traffic analysis
  explanation of, 359, 461
  response time as element of, 359–361
  throughput as element of, 360–362
Transaction terminals, 67–68, 461
Transmission Control Protocol/Internet Protocol (TCP/IP), 302–303, 461
Transmission frame, 461
Transmission rate, 36
Transmission rate of information bits (TRIB), 360, 375, 462
Transmitters, 37, 462
Transponders, 177, 462
Transportable earth stations, 176
Tree topology, 251, 462
Tribits, 36
Triode electron tube, 17
Turnpike effect, 365, 462
25-pin connectors, 131, 206
20-milliampere current loop, 142
Twisted pairs, 141, 276, 462
TWX circuits, 17, 21, 141, 462
Tym electronic mail, 331–332
TymGram service, 332
Tymnet, 330–332
Tymsats, 330
Tymshare, Incorporated, 330